Week by Week

Plans for Documenting Children's Development

Week by Week

Plans for Documenting Children's Development

Barbara Ann Nilsen

Sixth Edition

WADSWORTH
CENGAGE Learning·

Australia · Brazil · Japan · Korea · Mexico · Singapore · Spain · United Kingdom · United States

Week By Week: Plans for Documenting Children's Development, **Sixth Edition**
Barbara Ann Nilsen

Editor in Chief: Linda Ganster

Executive Editor: Mark Kerr

Developmental Editor: Genevieve Allen

Editorial Assistant: Greta Lindquist

Associate Media Editor: Elizabeth Momb

Senior Market Development Manager:
   Kara Kindstrom

Executive Brand Manager: Melissa Larmon

Art and Cover Direction, Design,
   Production Management, and Composition:
   PreMediaGlobal

Manufacturing Planner: Doug Bertke

Rights Acquisitions Specialist: Roberta Broyer

Cover Image: © Cengage Learning

For product information and technology assistance, contact us at **Cengage Learning Customer & Sales Support, 1-800-354-9706.**
For permission to use material from this text or product, submit all requests online at **www.cengage.com/permissions.**
Further permissions questions can be e-mailed to **permissionrequest@cengage.com.**

Library of Congress Control Number: 2012940276

Student Edition:

ISBN-13: 978-1-133-60557-7

ISBN-10: 1-133-60557-5

Loose-leaf Edition:

ISBN-13: 978-1-133-94130-9

ISBN-10: 1-133-94130-3

Wadsworth
20 Davis Drive
Belmont, CA 94002-3098
USA

Cengage Learning is a leading provider of customized learning solutions with office locations around the globe, including Singapore, the United Kingdom, Australia, Mexico, Brazil, and Japan. Locate your local office at **www.cengage.com/global.**

Cengage Learning products are represented in Canada by Nelson Education, Ltd.

To learn more about Wadsworth, visit **www.cengage.com/wadsworth**

Purchase any of our products at your local college store or at our preferred online store **www.cengagebrain.com**

Printed in China
3 4 5 6 7 17 16 15 14

Contents

Preface   xi
Acknowledgments   xv
About the Author   xvii

INTRODUCTION: GETTING STARTED **1**

The 10 W's of Week by Week   1
How to Use This Book   14
Education CourseMate Website   19
Topics in Observation: Ethics of Documentation   23
Key Terms   25
Plans   25
Resources   26

CHAPTER 1   USING THE CLASS LIST LOG TO LOOK AT SEPARATION AND SCHOOL ADJUSTMENT **27**

Using the Class List Log   27
Using the Reflective Journal   32
Topics in Observation: Why Not Use Daily Logs or Daily Journals
    for Recording Children's Behavior?   35
Looking at Separation and School Adjustment   37
Observing Separation and Adjustment of Infants and Toddlers   49
Helping All Children with Separation and School Adjustment   49
Helping Professionals for Separation and School Adjustment Concerns   50
Other Methods   51
Key Terms   51
Plans   51
Resources   51

CHAPTER 2   USING ANECDOTAL RECORDINGS TO LOOK AT SELF-CARE **52**

Using the Anecdotal Recording   52
Looking at Self-Care Skills   61
Topics in Observation: Using All of Our Senses   63
Observing and Recording Infants and Toddlers in Routines   75
Helping All Children with Self-Care Skills   75
Helping Professionals for Self-Care Skills   75
Other Methods   76
Key Terms   76
Plans   76
Resources   76

CHAPTER ③ USING CHECKLISTS TO LOOK AT PHYSICAL DEVELOPMENT 77

Using the Checklist   77
Topics in Observation: Your Frame of Reference   86
Looking at Physical Growth and Development   88
Observing the Physical Development of Infants and Toddlers   103
Helping All Children with Physical Development   104
Helping Professionals for Physical Development Concerns   105
Other Methods   106
Key Terms   106
Plans   106
Resources   106

CHAPTER ④ USING RUNNING RECORDS TO LOOK AT SOCIAL DEVELOPMENT 107

Using Running Records   107
Topics in Observation: "The Stew"   113
Looking at Social Development   113
Observing Infants and Toddlers in Social Play   127
Helping all Children with Social Development   127
Helping Professionals for Social Development Concerns   129
Other Methods   129
Key Terms   129
Plans   130
Resources   130

CHAPTER ⑤ USING FREQUENCY COUNTS TO LOOK AT EMOTIONAL DEVELOPMENT 131

Using Frequency Counts   131
Looking at Emotional Development   136
Topics in Observation: Assessment and Curriculum Braid   152
Observing Emotional Development in Infants and Toddlers   153
Helping all Children with Emotional Development   154
Helping Professionals for Emotional Concerns   155
Other Methods   156
Key Terms   156
Plans   156
Resources   156

CHAPTER ⑥ USING CONVERSATIONS TO LISTEN TO LANGUAGE AND SPEECH. 157

Using Listening as an Observation Method   157
Listening to Speech and Language   166
Observing the Developing Language of Infants and Toddlers   176
Helping all Children with Language Development   176
Helping Professionals for Speech and Language Concerns   178

Topics in Observation: Diversity 179
Other Methods 181
Key Terms 181
Plans 181
Resources 181

CHAPTER 7 USING TIME SAMPLES TO LOOK AT ATTENTION SPAN **182**

Using Time Samples 182
Looking at Approaches to Learning 189
Piaget's Stages of Cognitive Development 192
Observing Attention Span in Infants and Toddlers 203
Helping all Children with Attention Span 203
Topics in Observation: Attention Span and Autism 204
Helping Professionals for Attention Concerns 205
Other Methods 205
Key Terms 206
Plans 206
Resources 206

CHAPTER 8 USING STANDARDIZED MEASUREMENTS TO LOOK AT COGNITIVE DEVELOPMENT **207**

Using Tests 207
Looking at Play and Cognitive Development 218
Assessing Other Developmental Areas While Observing Math and Science Activities 232
Topics in Observation: "Real" Curriculum 234
Helping Professionals for Cognitive Concerns 236
Other Methods 237
Key Terms 237
Plans 237
Resources 237

CHAPTER 9 USING RATING SCALES TO LOOK AT LITERACY **238**

Using the Rating Scale 238
Looking at Literacy 244
Learning to Read and Write 247
Topics in Observation: Books in the Sandbox 248
Helping All Children with Literacy 263
Helping Professionals for Literacy Concerns 266
Other Methods 266
Key Terms 267
Plans 267
Resources 267

CHAPTER 10 USING WORK SAMPLES TO LOOK AT CREATIVITY **268**

Using Work Samples to Observe a Child's Development 268
Looking at Children's Creative Development 275
Observing Creativity in Infants and Toddlers 281
Topics in Observation: Process Versus Product 288
Helping all Children with Creativity 294

Helping Professionals for Creative Art   295
Other Methods   295
Key Terms   295
Plans   295
Resources   296

**CHAPTER 11 USING TECHNOLOGY FOR
DOCUMENTATION OF DRAMATIC PLAY** **297**

Using Technology for Documentation   297
Topics in Observation: Protecting the Rights of the Child   305
Looking at Dramatic Play   306
Helping All Children with Dramatic Play   317
Helping Professionals for Play Concerns   318
Other Methods   318
Key Terms   318
Plans   318
Resources   319

**CHAPTER 12 USING DOCUMENTATION FOR CHILD ABUSE
SUSPICIONS AND LOOKING AT SELF-CONCEPT** **320**

Using Documentation for Child Abuse Suspicions   320
Diversity and Child Abuse   329
Looking at Self-Concept and Self-Esteem   331
Topics in Observation: Dealing with Families Suspected of Child Maltreatment   332
Helping All Children with Self-Esteem   343
Helping Professionals for Child Abuse and Self-Esteem Concerns   345
Other Methods   345
Key Terms   346
Plans   346
Resources   346

**CHAPTER 13 USING PROGRAM ASSESSMENTS
TO LOOK AT CHILDREN IN GROUPS** **347**

Assessing Early Childhood Programs   347
Topics in Observation: Assessing the Environment—Pointing Back at You   357
Looking at the Adjustment of the Child to the Program   359
Observing How Infants and Toddlers Adjust to Group Settings   373
Helping All Children in Group Settings   373
Helping Professionals for Program Evaluation and Support   375
Other Methods   375
Key Terms   375
Plans   375
Resources   375

**CHAPTER 14 USING THE PORTFOLIO FOR COMMUNICATIONS
WITH FAMILIES AND LOOKING AT THE
CHILD'S INTERACTIONS WITH ADULTS** **376**

Communications with Families   376
Using Portfolios for Progress Reports and Child Studies   385
Looking at the Child's Interactions with Adults   397

Observing Infants and Toddlers   400
Topics in Observation: *Does the* Week by Week *Plan Meet NAEYC
    Guidelines for Assessment?*   401
Helping All Children through Home and School Communications   402
Helping Professionals for Home and School Communications   403
Other Methods   403
Key Terms   403
Plans   403
Resources   403

CHAPTER 15   USING THE YEARLY PLAN TO OBSERVE AND RECORD CHILDREN'S DEVELOPMENT 404

Students   404
Practitioners   407

Glossary   409
References   414
Index   429

Preface

Week by Week is a documentation system guidebook for students and practitioners in early childhood education who work with infants through second-grade children. Each chapter has two main parts: the documentation method and the child development overview. The third part, the forms and weekly plans that integrate the method to document children's development, is found in the Education CourseMate website, accessed through CengageBrain.com. The purpose is to organize and plan intentionally, week by week, to build a Portfolio for each child, filling it with various pieces of evidence that document the child's development and behavior. *Week by Week* presents a manageable plan that will help gather documentation on *all* the children in the class or group, in *all* the developmental areas.

The first five editions of *Week by Week* have been used in a number of ways. Students in early childhood teacher preparation programs use the text for a course in techniques of documentation. Students in subsequent semesters in both associate degree and bachelor degree programs use the text for child development study and in field experiences. The text has been used in master's teaching preparation programs. Classroom teachers have used the text as a tool to help them organize their observations into meaningful Portfolios that document their children's development. It has also been used in Head Start, Even Start, child-care, and nursery-school settings. In this sixth edition, the Cengage website provides users with electronic copies of all the forms, as well as the week-by-week calendar, which can be adapted to the semester for students or the program year for classroom teachers. By "going digital," we move toward electronic Portfolios, which have several advantages:

- *Usability*—Forms can be personalized and used over and over.
- *Confidentiality*—In a computer file, children's information is kept more secure.
- *Professional presentation*—Printed documents can be spell-checked and formatted into a document suitable to share with families and other professionals.

How This Book Came to be Written

My original idea for the book was to share my system of child observations with practitioners like myself. The title, *Week by Week,* describes a year-long systematic plan for teachers to document each child's development by forming an extensive Portfolio that shows each child's progress in all areas of development. As my teaching venue changed from the preschool classroom to the college classroom, the book became a textbook. As a college textbook, it introduces students to methods—in the context of child development—that can be used and practiced during periodic visits into a classroom. It may be used for the sole purpose of observing, or as students participate in a field experience. It has been well received by students, and it is my hope that they will keep the book and renew their acquaintance with it when they have a classroom of their own. Then the full *Week by Week* plan will take on new meaning. There have been times when I've rediscovered books from my college days; and it is like meeting an old friend—we take up where we left off.

Week by Week for the Student. As a college textbook this book will be used for 13, 15, or 16 weeks. Each week you will be introduced to a different method and given one assignment to practice the method. If you are in a field placement for the whole semester, you can incorporate the *Week by Week* plan as you participate in the classroom activities. If you are taking a course in observation methods, you can make weekly visits just for observation, or you may be able to plan three or four longer visits and do several of the practice assignments during each visit. In either of these two plans, you will miss the day-to-day interactions. This is just for practice—a simulation of what you will be doing when you have a classroom of your own. CAUTION: Seeing children intermittently makes it impossible to draw decisive conclusions about their development. Also, it is important *not to talk specifically* about a child, teacher, or program by name when you are in your college classroom, dorm, or out with friends. **Confidentiality** is a part of the ethical responsibility of professionals.

You will practice this recording method by following the assignment on the Education CourseMate website. You or your instructor may need to modify this depending on your field placement situation.

Week by Week *for the Practitioner.* Maybe you used this book in your college class and now have your own classroom. Or perhaps you found this book and decided to make a commitment to better organize your contributions to each child's Portfolio. The Education CourseMate website provides information on how to schedule a manageable number of observations each week over the school year, returning to each developmental area several times. You will find a calendar on the Education CourseMate website that will help. Some additional forms are also included for your use in organizing the Portfolio and using it to individualize the curriculum. After all, that's what observing is all about. You observe, you assess, you plan, you implement, you observe, you assess, you plan. Remember that when you are totally responsible for the classroom, you will have to steal moments to write things down. That is the biggest hurdle to observing and recording. For help with this, note especially the "How to Find the Time" sections in each chapter. To achieve the goal of gathering a fairly equal amount of documentation on each child, use various methods, and revisit developmental areas three times over a school year. An organizational system can be used to ensure that you are gathering an approximately equal distribution of Portfolio documentation on all children.

The teacher using the *Week by Week* system will gain skill in using various methods of recording observations, and will be reviewing child development and good teaching practices. Knowledge of child development, observation methods, and curriculum are not separate from each other, but interdependent. One must know what to look for to be a good observer, and mindful teachers make decisions based on what they see. The *Week by Week* system will enable the teacher to document important information about each child, information that is usable for measurement and reporting, as well as accurate and objective.

Chapter Organization

Each chapter has two major sections, with the third in the Education CourseMate website, accessed through CengageBrain.com. See the inside back cover for a listing of the book elements.

Using the. . . First, we introduce a **recording** method and acquaint you with its uses. Observing and recording has been a challenge for early childhood teachers. Gathering meaningful data that can be used for several purposes is a skill that can be learned, but just as with any other artisan, there are different tools for different tasks. Each chapter presents a documentation tool, a description and illustration of its use, the advantages and disadvantages of the tool, pitfalls to avoid when using it, hints for incorporating technology that can make the job easier, and suggestions on how to find the time to accurately record events while in a busy classroom. This book, however, is more than just a manual to teach observation methods—there are many of those out there. It is designed to be a system, organizing observation methods and child development into a manageable schedule, equitable to each child.

Looking at . . . Each chapter then reviews an area of development that can be assessed using this particular method of recording. People have asked why there is so much emphasis on child development in this text instead of on observation methods. You never can know too much about child development, and we need to know what to look for in order to see it. It is always a danger to divide child development into pieces, so this comes with the reminder that every area or domain is interdependent and affects every other, but that there still has to be some way to divide it into segments and make it manageable. That philosophy fits in well with the *Week by Week* objective: to take the huge task of gathering meaningful developmental data in a natural setting, over time, to build a Portfolio that depicts what the child knows and can do. That is the purpose of this book, this system.

The Education CourseMate Website. On the Education CourseMate website, accessed through CengageBrain.com, you will find a systematic plan for each week. Each week's plan is divided into parts (Part A, Part B, etc.). The website contains the weekly observation plans, along with forms and a way to divide the group into small segments to assure that every child is observed in every developmental area at least three times during the school year. Each of the plans has instructions for both students and practitioners, making this book a *keeper* for students to use later. Each of the week's plans includes instructions on "What to Do with It." This suggests where to file the documentation, how to use it in conversations with the child and the family, and actions. Actions are suggestions for adding to the curriculum in this particular area, including Read a Book, a listing of related children's books with books available also in Spanish; In the Environment; In the

Curriculum; and In the Newsletter. All of these are resources to use the documentation not just for recording progress but also for individualizing learning. A part of the weekly plan also includes a Reflective Journal, which poses open-ended questions to guide the teacher to look inward. These are for the writer's consideration of the events of the week, personal attitudes, self-analysis, and promises for the future. These are private journal entries, not a part of the child's records. The CourseMate icon appears within each chapter to prompt you to take advantage of the many features provided.

Instructor and Student Supplements

The Instructor's Manual with Test Bank. An Instructor's Manual with Test Bank is available for download on the instructor website. The online Instructor's Manual contains information to assist the instructor in designing the course, including learning objectives, chapter outlines and summaries, teaching and learning activities, and additional print and online resources. For assessment support, the Test Bank includes true/false, multiple-choice, matching, short-answer, and essay questions for each chapter.

Online ExamView. Available for download from the instructor website, ExamView® testing software includes all the test items from the Test Bank in electronic format, enabling you to create customized tests in print or online.

Online PowerPoint Slides. Ready-to-use Microsoft® PowerPoint® lecture slides cover content for each chapter of the book.

Education CourseMate Website. Cengage Learning's Education CourseMate brings course concepts to life with interactive learning, study, and exam preparation tools that support the printed textbook. CourseMate includes an integrated eBook, quizzes, flashcards, downloadable forms, videos, and Engagement Tracker—a first-of-its-kind tool that monitors student engagement in the course. The accompanying instructor website offers access to password-protected resources, such as electronic versions of the instructor's manual, test bank, and PowerPoint® slides.

New in This Edition

There are always new studies, new editions of old favorites, and issues that I didn't know about just a few years ago. This new edition makes the text current and hopefully more relevant and useful for the reader with updated information throughout. All references have been updated to ensure that the most current information is included. These References are in a separate section at the back of the book.

Home Visitor. While many who use this textbook are or will be classroom teachers, the field of home visiting for the purpose of supporting, involving, and educating family members has grown nationwide. Some of you may find employment in this gratifying aspect of early childhood education; so where it is applicable, I have inserted sections from that viewpoint, assisted by friend and colleague Mary Haust, an expert in this field.

Early Elementary. Sometimes just a chance comment just hits home. A colleague at a conference mentioned that some of the early childhood faculty in her state thought this book was too focused on the preschool-age child. Indeed, early childhood does reach into the early elementary grades, and we certainly want teachers who understand child development, authentic assessment, and developmentally appropriate curriculum to teach in those grades. I took that to heart, and have updated charts, text and photos to reflect the full spectrum of early childhood.

Video Cases. A new feature with the sixth edition is the link to short video segments to illustrate concepts discussed in the chapter, along with questions to consider while viewing the videos. All video cases can be accessed through the Education CourseMate website at CengageBrain.com.

Emphasis on Using Technology for Observation. Almost everyone has a cell phone that takes photos, creates and stores text documents, and even accesses the Internet. With each new advance in technology come never-dreamed-of applications. Using cell phones and hand-held computers in the classroom seems problematic, but their use, not abuse, can be one more tool for teachers.

Acknowledgments

My thanks and love to my family, who are my biggest supporters, my friends Carol and Marsha, who love me like a sister, Mary Haust who contributed to the home educator/visiting segements of this edition, my colleagues near and far who dedicate themselves to the care and education of America's children, and to the students who teach us something new every day.

Sincere appreciation to Mark Kerr and Kara Kindstrom, who believe in my work; Genevieve Allen; and the staff at Cengage for their assistance, patience, and creativity in putting my ideas into reality. A special "thank you" to the reviewers who provided valuable feedback and helped to shape the final work: Melody Deprez, Georgetown College; Colleen Fawcett, Palm Beach State College; Patricia Hofbauer, Northwest State Community College; Amanda Barche Lindberg, Ivy Tech Community College; Lisha Linder, McHenry County College; Maureen O'Neil, Tallahassee Community College; Les Potter, Daytona State College; Jeanne Williams, Pulaski Technical College.

About the Author

Barbara Ann Nilsen retired in 2006 as professor and chair of the Teacher Education and Early Childhood Department at Broome Community College, Binghamton, New York, where she taught in the classroom and online. She continues her online teaching and community, state, and national involvement in early childhood education, and working with community colleges for program improvement. She was also the grant director of NYSECEONLINE and the Early Learning Opportunities collaborative project for Building Brighter Futures for Broome. The author received her EdD in Early and Middle Childhood from Nova University. She has been active in local, state, and national early childhood professional development initiatives such as New York State Career Pathways, New York State Children's Program Administrator Infant/Toddler, Family Child Care Credentials, and NAEYC'S Early Childhood Associate Degree Program Accreditation project. She is the co-author, with Virginia Albertalli, of *An Introduction to Learning and Teaching: Infants through Sixth Grade*, and the author of the *Observation and Assessment Professional Enhancement* text.

This text is dedicated to the busy hands, open minds, and caring hearts of all who work with young children. You bear the worthy name: Teacher. I welcome your communication by email at nilsenba@sunybroome.edu.

Introduction: Getting Started

IN THIS INTRODUCTION

▶ Why Observe?
▶ Why Write It Down?
▶ What Are the Roles of the Observer?
▶ Why Use Different Methods?
▶ What Is a Portfolio and What's In It?
▶ What Is Not in the Portfolio?
▶ Who Can Read the Portfolio?
▶ Why Use Portfolio Assessment Rather Than Testing?
▶ When to Observe?
▶ What Is the Week by Week Plan?

HOW TO USE THIS BOOK
▶ Using the . . . Observation and Recording Method
▶ Looking at . . . Child Development
▶ Chapter Features

OBSERVATION THOUGHT

"We aren't observing to back up what we think but to think about what we're observing."

NAEYC Standards naeyc

The following NAEYC Standards for Early Childhood Professional Preparation are addressed in this chapter:

Standard 3: *Observing, Documenting, and Assessing to Support Young Children and Families*

Standard 6: *Becoming a Professional*

The 10 W's of Week by Week

EXERCISE **Observe (or imagine):**
▶ a clock
▶ the inside of a refrigerator
▶ a traffic light

Exactly what do you see? What are your observations telling you? What will you do as a result of what you see? Write down what decisions you might make based on those observations.

The word *observe* brings to mind the action of looking, seeing, and not participating, but viewing the action as an outsider. In any context, observing is just the first step in determining action. The first stage, taking in information, occurs simultaneously with evaluation and selection of a course of action. The clock is observed, usually not to admire the design but to determine the time. Looking inside a refrigerator may indicate that a trip to the store is needed or that the source of a foul odor should be investigated. The traffic light is a lovely shade of green, but its meaning is more important. That observation produces action: Go!

Everything we see is not just observed but also immediately interpreted for meaning. A decision is made either to do nothing or to act. The observation may be so insignificant that it is sensed but not acted on. Later it might prove to be important, like that traffic light that was green, but the car in the cross street came through the intersection anyway. When filling out the accident report, those details are important.

Why Observe?

When a teacher observes a child, information is collected and could be measured against a whole body of knowledge about child development in general and that child in particular (Figure I–1). Information is then used to make decisions about the next actions. Someone has estimated that a teacher makes thousands of decisions in a day. Each decision is based on observations evaluated for meaning and the most appropriate responses. This *observe-decide-act* sequence is repeated over and over again throughout the day.

Let's observe a child painting at the easel and see what we can see in Figure I–2.

© Cengage Learning 2014

Figure I–1 Why observe?

© Cengage Learning 2014

Figure I–2 Common activities yield knowledge of the child.

Safety. The most important reason for watching children is to keep them safe. Seeing a potentially dangerous situation and rushing to prevent an injury is the most basic example of observe-decide-act. A child waiting to paint may be observed trying to wrestle the brush away from the painter. With angry looks and harsh words, she is trying to gain control of the painting area. The teacher rushes over and intervenes before the painter is knocked aside or a brush is poked into someone's eye.

Physical Health. Recognizing the signs of sickness or disease is another reason to observe, decide, and act. This also can protect the physical health of others. The teacher may notice a few small red spots behind the painter's ear. She casually pats the child's arm and feels bumps beneath the skin. These observations, along with the knowledge that the child's brother had chicken pox two weeks ago, prompt the teacher's decision to isolate the child and call the child's family to take the child home. For chicken pox, of course, it's already too late. Everyone's been exposed!

Figure I–3 Observing a child's work, as well as the child as she works, gives valuable information.

© Cengage Learning 2014

Figure I–3 shows artwork that the child painted on her return to school after having chicken pox.

Assistance. Observation may indicate that help is needed. A child is observed preparing to paint at the easel. The teacher sees that the paper supply is gone. He gets more from the cupboard and shows the child how to attach the sheets with the big clips and where to hang the painting to dry.

Discover Interests. The adult observes the child choose a play area and talks with the child about the play. This observing, remembering, and affirming is a friendly thing to do. It also is another way of building bridges from interests to planning, from home to school, and a way of making the curriculum relevant. The theme of animals (in the beginning stages of drawing recognizable objects!) emerges in the painting. The observer remembers the home visit where this child showed a menagerie of pets who might be potential classroom visitors!

Learning Styles and Teaching Strategies. Watching a child reveals personality and learning styles and could give clues to teaching strategies. By observing the painter, learning styles are indicated that will work better for her—maybe verbal directions, being shown, or trial and error. Reflective

observation of the student's learning process leads the teacher to adapt teaching strategies to the child's styles and needs.

Curriculum Planning. Teaching is building bridges, making connections between new information and old based on topics that are relevant and of interest to the group. The teacher plans related experiences and learning opportunities (the methods of learning, pedagogy) to help children explore and construct meaning of the content, subject matter, or skill. A knowledge of child development research with indicators of normal development for a certain age helps the teacher intentionally plan curriculum for the group as well as for the individual child based on assessments. The group has enjoyed and mastered easel painting so the teacher plans that next week he will introduce watercolors, demonstrating the technique of washing the brush between colors, knowing that children of this age have gained enough small muscle control to accomplish this task.

Extend Children's Learning. Through observations, teachers can see that teachable moment, that budding interest, and that blossoming skill. Providing materials, activities, and opportunities to build on that observed development will capitalize on it. From observing the painting filled with alphabet letters, the teacher decides this is a good time to bring out the alphabet magnets and invite the painter to play with them.

Communication with the Child. Teachers talk with every child, and what better subject to discuss with them than the child's activities? Every child deserves the individual attention of the teacher. By discussing what the teacher observes with the child, the child can give the reason or explanation in a way that makes sense only if the teacher asks the child. That is the basis for Piaget's cognitive questioning method (Piaget & Inhelder, 1969), to delve more deeply into children's "wrong" answers. In that way, thinking processes are explored. Results or answers are not simply considered incorrect, but teachers reflect on possible reasons for the answers to explain how the answer was derived. This may involve more conversation with the child, or the family, to get a better understanding of the background knowledge leading to the answer. The teacher says to the painter, "You worked hard on that painting. You used red, blue, and yellow, and you made straight lines and curved lines. Would you like to tell me how you did it? What did you do first?"

Guidance. Prevention is always better than remedy. Redirection is better than discipline or punishment. From observations, potential problems can be averted. The painter's brush is approaching the wall.

The teacher reminds the child, "Paint on paper," guiding the brush back to the paper on the easel.

Measure Progress. Children change so quickly. Based on knowledge of child development, certain changes are expected and anticipated. Comparisons over time can measure that development. The teacher observes that the painter moved from experimentation with line and color to painting recognizable objects. She proclaims that the smiling face with dots is a picture of her brother who is just getting over the chicken pox. The teacher can see her control of small muscles and the frustration when the paint does not flow in the way the painter thinks it should. The child's social world is portrayed in the pictures she paints. Many areas of development can be observed in this one activity and in changes from paintings done a few weeks ago.

Assessment. Teachers watch children to gather information. That is **assessment**, the process of documenting a child's knowledge, skills, and attitudes in measurable terms. Assessment may take many forms, but the premise here is that observation is the best method. Naturalistic inquiry, studying children in their natural habitats, results in seeing the child "exhibiting the highest levels of competence," unlike in contrived situations where children are put into strange, anxiety-producing situations (Pellegrini 1998). Information is gathered to measure the child's development against accepted stages or a set of developmental norms. Assessment measures where the child is at this point in time. It may alert the observer to unusually delayed or accelerated development.

Evaluation. **Evaluation** is the decision-making step of assessment; probably the most precarious because it is the step that considers the information gathered through assessment upon which judgments are drawn and decisions made about future directions. Evaluation is based on prior knowledge and comparing observations with that prior knowledge. Knowing typical child development stages that include social, emotional, and cognitive domains gives the observer a lens through which to view the child.

The observer of the painter has collected paintings over several weeks and judges that this child is in the stage when children are beginning to represent thought, not just experimenting with the materials. A sticky note as to the importance of this example may be placed on the back of the painting, noting, "She has moved from making circles and controlled straight lines to painting faces, and was smiling and singing while painting." The teacher may decide to bring out a plastic skeleton for the science area or

read a story about sick children to give the painter ideas about anatomy. A copy of this drawing is filed in the child's Portfolio for later comparisons.

For all of these good reasons, teachers observe children. That informed observation, measuring what is seen against what is known, is assessment and evaluation of the child's development and behavior.

Referral. Sometimes questions or even red flags arise when a teacher observes a child. Certain behaviors, actions, and skills—or lack of them—will send an alert calling for a closer look at a developmental area.

From the child's paintings, the teacher observes some alarming messages. The teacher may ask a probing question such as, "Would you like to tell me about your painting?" and the child's answers may lead only to more questions. It is important not to rush to conclusions (especially based on a child's art products).

Further reflection and closer observation of behavior over time may warrant discussing a concern first with the family or other professionals within the agency, and then perhaps suggesting a referral to the family. The **referral** may be for further evaluation in a specific area, such as hearing, speech, physical, or cognitive development. Family involvement and decision making in the referral process are the pivotal factors. Families are recognized and deferred to as the authority on the child.

There may be situations where it is necessary to report suspicions of neglect or abuse. Knowledge, careful judgment, empathy, and consideration are important skills for the teacher in all of these circumstances, for both referrals and reporting.

Communication with the Family. Talking with the **family** about the child's daily activities communicates the following to them:

> ▶ Their child is under a watchful eye.
> ▶ This teacher observes and relates important developments in their child's actions, rather than giving the family a test score they might not understand how to evaluate.
> ▶ The family is included in the world that the teacher and their child share.

Unfortunately, many children and families have come to expect to receive only bad reports, phone calls, and notes from school, which bring a sense of dread. Too often, the only communications they receive about their child relate misbehaviors, failure to perform to expectations, or commands for the child or family to take remedial action. In contrast, discussing observations from the day's observed activities or documentation from the Portfolio with the child's family gives positive, substantive information about the child's progress, compared only to her previous work, not anyone else's. Observation gives descriptive accounts of the child's behavior and skills from the point of view of achievement rather than deficit; what she can or has done, rather than cannot or will not. Observations are shared with families in formal and informal ways.

The paintings in the child's Portfolio previously were scribbles, and then become pages filled with lines and deliberate designs. The teacher and child show her family the collection in the Portfolio. The family realizes that the teacher *knows and observes* their child's work from a different point of view.

Self-Reflection of Teaching Methods. Observing is not just looking at a child but also thinking about our influence on the child and the child's effect on us. The teacher notices that no one is painting anymore and wonders what the cause could be. By observing and recording, questions can be answered and the teacher's own effectiveness can be measured. The interest a child has in the planned activities will indicate to the teacher if the activities are appropriate. Activities that are not challenging or too difficult will be avoided or abandoned by the child. By closely watching what keeps a child involved, the observer can learn what skills the child is working on and modify activities to meet those needs.

This type of observation is active research, constantly accumulating data to analyze for its meaning. Yetta Goodman (2002) says "kid watching" involves "teachers who interact with students and who monitor class activities in order to understand more about teaching and learning, mostly learning (p. 13)."

Accountability. Data drives decisions, from the star ratings of movies, to the walk/don't walk signals at a crosswalk. Collecting high-quality data through reliable child assessments is a way to view the child and the program objectively. Preschool programs are often funded through special governmental funding at the state and federal level, with private funds through foundations and organizations, and by the families of the children themselves. Initiatives that are expected to prepare children for school by enhancing social, language, and cognitive skills—especially for children from economically disadvantaged homes and for children of special needs—are under scrutiny to demonstrate their effectiveness. Is the teacher, curriculum, program, or school doing what it says it will do? Proof is needed to show that children are learning and meeting the standards and expected outcomes. This area of child assessment is the focus of close examination to prove the worth of early childhood programs.

Accountability takes on many forms. The program or school is accountable to the funding or sponsoring agency. Assessment for funders calls for statistical data gathered by research-based methods and showing demonstrable outcomes of groups of children. Policymakers also use this kind of assessment to measure the benefits of one type of program or initiative over another. The purpose is to maximize the investment for the greatest gain.

The type of accountability that is mostly addressed in this text, however, is that of the teacher to the child and family. By systematically using observation, along with other types of assessment tools, the classroom teacher and caregiver can gather information to show each child's progress, raise an awareness of potential difficulties, and intentionally plan curriculum that will help the child develop and learn. A teacher might observe the following:

"This child's painting shows increases in small muscle control, attention span, interest in alphabet, and is increasingly detailed." The teacher's notes on the back of the painting relate the significance of this work in light of developmental progress. It shows the child is learning. Documentation of all types can:

- provide evidence of children's learning in all domains.
- provide insight into learning experiences.
- provide a framework for recording each child's interests and developmental progress.
- emphasize learning as an interactive process.
- show advantages of concrete activities and materials as opposed to group testing situations.
- enable teachers to assess knowledge and abilities in order to increase the challenge to match the child's level. (Helm, Beneke, & Steinheimer, 2007)

Why Write It Down?

EXERCISE **Using a separate sheet of paper, list the kinds of writing you do in a day. Jot down the reason for each.**

"I'll remember this and write it down later." Everyone has said this and then not written it down. It is lost with all the other details of life that intercede and blur the image, blotting out specifics and erasing the exact words. **Recording** is used here to refer to a written account or notation of what has been observed. What are the reasons for writing down what has been seen? (See Figure I–4.)

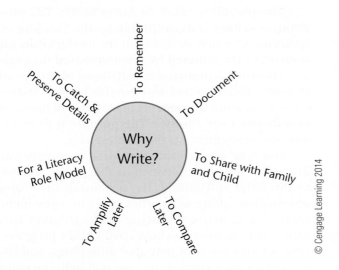

Figure I–4 Why Write?

© Cengage Learning 2014

Grocery List

eggs	vegetable soup
milk	toothpicks
chocolate chips	paper towels

banking

dry cleaning

birthday card for Louise

© Cengage Learning 2014

Figure I–5 Write to Remember.

To Remember. The grocery list (Figure I–5), even if it is left at home on the refrigerator door, sticks in the memory longer because it was written down. Many students copy their notes over or condense them as a study technique. There is a connection between writing and memory. The written words form a visual and kinetic or physical connection in the brain, assisting memory and recall even when the visual cues are not present.

To Compare. A child's height is measured with a line on the wall, and it is surprising a few months later how much she has grown without anyone realizing it. If that mark had not been made, the change would not have been noticed. Children are expected to change, so a mark of comparison is needed. Relying on a memory of the child one, three, or six months ago is inaccurate and unreliable. By writing observations down, teachers have tangible comparison points. Portfolios, collections of the child's work, and written observations are becoming an accepted method of documenting a child's progress. Written observations that are thorough, objective, regular, and done during daily routines and child-initiated play are accurate measures of the child's progress.

To Amplify Later. Sometimes there is no time to write the whole incident, so a few strategic notes written and dated at the time can be just enough to jog the memory for a longer, more complete narrative written later.

The teacher shows a new song chart and has just said, "Look up here, all eyes on the chart." Andrew asks, "What's 16 plus 16?" A puzzled look comes over the teacher's face, followed immediately by one of irritation for the interruption. Andrew repeats his

question louder. "Thirty-two, now let's look at this new song chart." Andrew replies, "Oh, you want all thirty-two eyes looking at the chart." This tells us about Andrew's thinking, his beginning understanding of math concepts, and causes the teacher to vow to listen more closely to children's questions. This is a wonderful incident to relate to Andrew's family to demonstrate his thinking and his humor. The teacher just had time to write "eyes, 16, 32" with the ever-present pad and pen. That was enough to enable the teacher to fully write about the incident later.

To Catch and Preserve Details. Details are quickly forgotten. Insurance companies want auto accident reports written at the scene because of the frailty of human memory. Fine details that seem so clear or so unimportant now can best be preserved by writing them down. These details can give clues to trends or correlations that are not seen at the time. On closer examination and comparison later, they gain significance. For example, keeping some data on which areas of the classroom the child spends their free time in and how long they stay there gives much information about the child. Without some method of tracking, there is no way to recall details like this that can yield important information.

To Serve as a Literacy Role Model. Children need to see adults writing. Literacy is an important concept to teach young children. The importance

Figure I–6 Busy teachers jot short notes to amplify later.

Dramatic Play Area—paper and pencil next to the play phone, sheets cut for grocery lists attached to a pad on the play refrigerator, calendars on which children can write important events to remember

Block Area—paper, markers, tape for signs on buildings

Large Motor—paper, markers, tape for signs signifying what the climber is today (a rocket ship, a house on fire, Jenny's house)

Sand/Water—paper and pencil nearby to write down a mark to indicate what sinks or floats, draw pictures of what has been found hidden in the sand; paper to list who is waiting for a turn

Cubbies—paper and pencil to list what children say they want to do outside today, to decide which toys to load in the wagon

Group Area—chart paper, markers to take surveys of favorite things, lists of things to remember contributed by the group, safety rules

Figure I–7 A Literacy-Rich Environment.

of the written word is emphasized when children see its usefulness and practical application by their role models, the adults in their lives. When an adult writes something down, a child often asks, "What are you doing?" A reply such as "I'm writing this down so I won't forget" lays literacy foundations for the child (Figure I–6). It shows that writing is a way to help memory, that what is written is constant, and it stirs the child's desire to want to write himself. A literacy-rich environment is one with accessible writing materials to encourage him to do just that (Figure I–7).

To Document. Reliable research demands hard data. It is necessary to preserve in writing—to **document**—what has been observed to substantiate it. Recording methods that include facts rather than inferences along with the date and time of the recording are essential to meaningful documentation. The details must be preserved to see progress, trends, and correlations.

It is especially critical if a child discloses an incident of abuse. The reports must be accurate and show that the child was not led or influenced in order for the disclosure to be supportable evidence. One would like never to deal with this, but for the protection of the child it is important not to jeopardize the testimony by failing to document or keeping inaccurate records. You will read more about this in Chapter 12.

What Are the Roles of the Observer?

You may have various roles or reasons or situations for observing:

Participant observer. If you are a teacher, then you observe children all the time, but *Week by Week* will guide you to use a different lens while you go

about the various activities in leading and caring for the children in your group. You might be a student teacher who is learning about children by being in a classroom, assisting where you are needed, and perhaps fulfilling assignments at the same time. Either way, you will need to have paper and pen handy at all times to be sure you jot down important notes (remember, writing aids the memory). If you are planning to observe a specific child or all the children with a specific type of recording tool, have the time and place planned so that you are prepared. Each chapter in *Week by Week* will give you some tips on "How to Find the Time".

Non-Participant Observer. You may have the luxury of having no responsibility in a classroom other than observing and recording. You may be a teacher visiting someone else's classroom to learn, or you may be a student completing an observation assignment. Your place in the classroom should be out of the way, but in a place where you can see and hear what is happening. The classroom teacher can assist you in finding the right spot. Try to avoid letting any child "feel" watched by gazing around the room rather than staring. Avoid eye contact or conversations with the children, but appear friendly and nonthreatening. Answer the children's questions about what you are doing directly by saying you are writing down what is happening in the classroom and go back to your work.

Some schools (especially lab schools) have an observation booth where students, family members, or other professionals can observe children without being seen. This nonintrusive vantage point does not influence the children's behavior. Sometimes vision or clear sound may be hampered by the placement and technology available. Video recordings of classroom activity are another way of observing. This will be explored in Chapter 11.

Why Use Different Methods?

EXERCISE **How many ways can you cook a chicken? Make a list. Here's a start:**

- fry
- broil
- stew
- microwave

Why are there so many ways to cook a chicken? Because there are different end results from each method. The cook may be looking for a certain consistency, lowering calories, tenderizing, or cooking it within a short period of time. Similarly, there are many different methods of recording observations because the end result from each method is different. Yes, they are all based on observing the child and measuring the observation against standards in order to make decisions about immediate and future actions, but they differ in technique, content, and approach. *Week by Week* presents many different methods, along with a review of a developmental area, but the method is not limited to recording only that particular area. In the cooking example above, once the technique of frying or stewing or microwaving is mastered it can be applied to other foods and modified for a variety of desired results. Just like cooking, once the recording technique is mastered, it can be applied to other developmental areas and modified to fit the recorder's style and selected outcome. While the recording methods in *Week by Week* are paired with a specific area of child development, most of the methods can be used for assessment of any area of development. The recording methods can be classified using the web design (Figure I–8).

Each method is a technique to focus on a behavior, skill, or action of an individual child or the whole group. The **narrative** recordings, such as Anecdotal Recordings, Running Records, and Interviews, tell

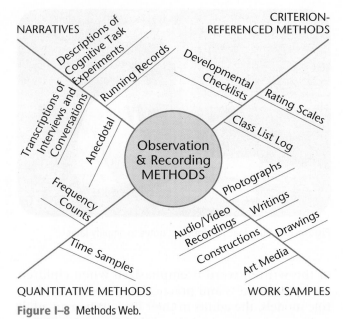

Figure I–8 Methods Web.

© Cengage Learning 2014

a story. They bring the reader along by providing the actual details of actions, words, and results. The **criterion-referenced** recordings, such as Class List Logs, Checklists, and Rating Scales, provide a predetermined skill or standard to look for and measure against. The **quantitative** recordings, such as Time Samples and Frequency Counts, provide a numerical count of individual or group actions that then can be interpreted in various ways. These methods lose most of the raw data, the actual details that narratives preserve, but are useful for certain purposes.

The **Work Samples**, such as drawings, writings, constructions, sculptures, and media-preserved work (audio or video recordings or photographs), give a visual account of the child's activities from which assessments are made. Each category and method within the category is distinctive and useful, with its own specific technique, advantages and disadvantages, and best applications. These methods will be presented, practiced, and recommended for specific purposes throughout this book.

What Is a Portfolio and What's In it?

The systematic gathering of information about the child is **Portfolio** assessment. Portfolios are more than a scrapbook or folder full of unrelated pieces of paper. Gronlund (2003) states, "Simply collecting samples of students' work and putting it in a file does not constitute a Portfolio. Much greater care is required in the development of a Portfolio so that it will be useful in instruction and assessment" (p. 159). Portfolios provide information on each child as an individual, on child development in general, and on the diversity of children. Portfolios give the opportunity for family involvement through communication centered on the child's work, and they help the family become involved in the curriculum. From building Portfolios, teachers learn to assess and plan a curriculum for each child individually, see progress over time, and reflect on teaching practices (Shores & Grace, 2005).

Danielson and Abrutyn (1997) describe three types of Portfolios. *Display* Portfolios are scrapbooks of photographs of children's activities and learning experiences in the classroom without teacher comments or showing progress over time. *Showcase* Portfolios are the best pieces of the child's work, either self- or teacher-selected, and without evaluation or information about progress or affecting the curriculum. *Working* Portfolios include selected but typical Work Samples along with teacher documentation to show the child's progress as well as the teacher's observations. It is on these Portfolios that curriculum is based and future actions planned for the child, with input from the child, the family, and other professionals if needed. *Week by Week* guides the teacher in the collection of documents for this last type, the **Working Portfolio**.

Portfolios draw from multiple information sources and are gathered in the child's natural surroundings by persons familiar with the child and the environment. They are collected over time, so they clearly show the child's progress.

A Portfolio is an individual folder for each child in the class, gathering information from multiple sources (Figure I–9). Eventually the Portfolio may hold many pieces of the child's work, teachers' observations, photos, and video or audio recordings, so it should be expandable. All Portfolios should be stored in a locked file cabinet or file box to assure that they are accessible only to authorized people, including the staff working with the children and the director. The Portfolio is available to the family upon request and to the child.

Child. The child contributes Work Samples such as drawings, artwork, and samples of writing and language. Media, such as audio and video recordings and photographs, also can be included. The Portfolio is a book about the child, so from a very early age, the child has a voice in the included works.

Families. Families—the true authorities on the child, since they know the child better than anyone—submit information to the Portfolio on forms and with written comments.

Teachers. Teachers who see the child regularly submit formal observations using a variety of methods

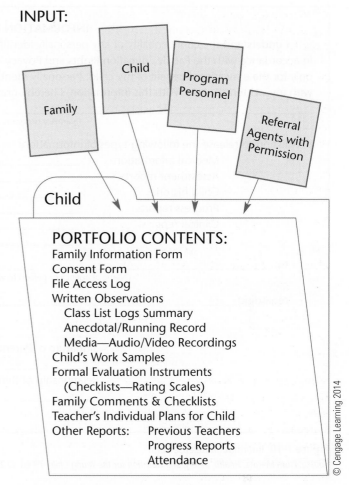

INPUT:

Child

PORTFOLIO CONTENTS:
Family Information Form
Consent Form
File Access Log
Written Observations
　　Class List Logs Summary
　　Anecdotal/Running Record
　　Media—Audio/Video Recordings
Child's Work Samples
Formal Evaluation Instruments
　　(Checklists—Rating Scales)
Family Comments & Checklists
Teacher's Individual Plans for Child
Other Reports:　Previous Teachers
　　　　　　　　　Progress Reports
　　　　　　　　　Attendance

© Cengage Learning 2014

Figure I–9 Portfolios contain information from multiple sources.

to best record different kinds of data in the most objective styles. Informal observations are included as important events worthy of remembering for a variety of reasons. Copies of periodic progress reports prepared for the family are also included.

Staff. Staff in the program who have contact with the child may write a submission for the Portfolio. The cook, the bus driver, and the nurse all see the child from a different perspective in different settings and have information to contribute that may be filed in the Portfolio.

Previous Teachers. Previous teachers' records may be passed on in the Portfolio or may remain in the Administrator's file, depending on the program or school policy.

Referral Agents. With consent forms, the program and referral agencies can exchange information. A release form must be used before information is shared. See Figure I–10. Referral agencies may include reports or suggestions for working with the child in the Portfolio.

INFORMATION RELEASE FORM

I understand the confidentiality of any personally identifiable information concerning my child shall be maintained in accordance with the Family Education Rights and Privacy Act (P.L.93-380), federal and state regulations, and used only for the educational benefit of my child. Personally identifiable information about my child will be released only with my written consent. With this information, I hereby grant the

_____

(Name of program, agency, or person)

permission to release the following types of information:

Medical information	_____
Assessment reports	_____
Child histories	_____
Progress reports	_____
Clinical reports	_____
(Other)	_____

to: _____

(Name of agency or person to whom information is to be sent)

regarding _____

Child's Name   Birthdate   Gender

_____

Signature of Parent or Guardian

_____

Relationship of Representative

_____

Date

© Cengage Learning 2014

Figure I–10 Information Release Form.
Source: From Marotz, *Health, Safety, and Nutrition for the Young Child*, 7th ed. © 2009 Cengage Learning.

What Is Not in the Portfolio?

There is another file accessible to the parents or legal guardians, the teachers, and licensing authority on request. Those files are kept in an administrative filing cabinet, separate from the child's Working Portfolio that is accumulated by week-by-week records. The contents of the administrative file include extensive medical information and any other confidential information that is not appropriate for the child's Working Portfolio. If there are any suspected, but as yet unsubstantiated, concerns about possible child abuse, those records should be kept in a separate confidential file, separate from the child's health records and Working Portfolio. Any Anecdotal Recordings that document a possible disclosure of child abuse should be placed in this confidential file. A copy of the filed Child Abuse Reporting Form and notations tracking the action should also be retained there. The teacher's Reflective Journal is the writer's private property, not to be kept with children's records (preferably kept at home).

Who Can Read the Portfolio?

The Portfolio includes documentation of all developmental areas for helping, measuring, and reporting the child's progress. Documentation is arranged chronologically and by developmental areas, logged in on an Portfolio Evidence Sheet so that contents are noted. Because of the completeness and intimacy of a Portfolio, its contents must be protected from unauthorized viewers. The National Association for the Education of Young Children's *Code of Ethical Conduct* (NAEYC, 2005) under the section on Ethical Responsibilities to Families reads:

P-2.7—We shall inform families about the nature and purpose of the program's child assessments and how data about their child will be used.

P-2.8—We shall treat child assessment information confidentially and share this information only when there is a legitimate need for it.

Families. Families can read the portfolio contents to receive feedback about their child, to learn about the curriculum and approaches the teachers are using, and to provide them with glimpses into the child's day to share and discuss with the child. Custodial parents or legal guardians have the right to see and control school records under the Family Educational Rights and Privacy Act (Buckley Amendment) passed by Congress in 1974. In the basic belief that early childhood programs are in partnership with families, the records are subject to their inspection. The systematic plan of gathering information has nothing to hide, for it seeks to provide objective, descriptive documentation.

As a part of the enrollment process or on the necessity to make a referral, the family should complete an Information Release Form (see Figure I–10). Permission must be obtained before releasing certain information to outside agencies. The family has the right to know and give permission. This form is kept on file with the child's medical history and records in the administrative office.

Program handbooks should inform families that their child's Portfolio is open to them any time. At the end of the year, the family usually determines whether it will go to the next teacher, next center, the public school, or home. The school will obtain written permission before releasing any Portfolio document to others. The exceptions are school officials with a legitimate educational interest and officials for use in audit or accreditation associations (with names deleted from these documents). In emergencies, the information is used to protect the health of the individual (Berger, 2012.)

Practitioners. Other teachers and program personnel who interact with the child may look at the Portfolio contents to get to know the child, and to collaborate and share ideas about how to plan curriculum that will fit the child's expanding development.

These discussions are a form of professional development as teachers reflect and interpret documented observations.

Community Agencies. Occasionally, people who have a need or a right to know may see the contents of the Portfolio. Those people may include a program evaluator who is gathering developmental level data, not on individual children but on an aggregate of all the children, or an accreditation validator looking at how the program records developmental information or seeking proof of a systematic authentic assessment plan. An ethical way to inform the families and the program of who has seen the contents of the file is to include a **file access log** (Figure I–11) in each file. Each person who views the file, other than the teacher(s), signs the log, providing the date, identity, agency represented, and reason for looking at the file.

The Child. Children above the toddler age can be involved in seeing, contributing to, and talking about the contents of the Portfolio. They can participate in self-assessment and feel satisfaction in their work samples and the written observations they see collected in the Portfolio. *Week by Week* will address this in each chapter in the "What to Do with It" section.

Why Use Portfolio Assessment Rather Than Testing?

Chapter 8 will discuss standardized testing and its use and misuse; this book will guide you in using Portfolios as an authentic, reliable way to assess children's development. Much has been written to promote Portfolio assessments (Martin, 2009; NAEYC, 2003; Cohen & Wiener , 2003). A review of the benefits of Portfolio assessment includes its ongoing purposeful

The record of _____ was reviewed by the following:
(child's name)

DATE	NAME/TITLE	AGENCY	REASON	SIGNATURE

© Cengage Learning 2014

Figure I–11 File Access Log.

Go to the Education CourseMate website to download a copy of this form.

assessment done during authentic activities (play) in a naturalistic setting without diverting children from natural learning processes.

Portfolios can be a valid, reliable replacement or augmentation for standardized testing. Organizations such as the NAEYC and National Association of Early Childhood Specialists in State Departments of Education (NAECS/SDE) take this position on assessment: "To assess young children's strengths, progress and needs, use assessment methods that are developmentally appropriate, culturally and linguistically responsive, tied to children's daily activities, supported by professional development, inclusive of families and connected to specific, beneficial purposes" (NAEYC, 2003, p. 2). They call for more authentic assessment methods that provide documentation gathered from multiple sources over a period of time in the child's natural environment (Figure I–12).

Here are eight principles for guiding the decision on how to assess children (Neisworth & Bagnato, 2004, pp. 204–208):

▶ *Utility*—Can the assessment be used to guide the individualized curriculum?
▶ *Acceptability*—Is the assessment socially and culturally relevant?

Figure I–12 Close observation of routine events helps the teacher evaluate and make decisions.

© Cengage Learning 2014

▶ *Authenticity*—Does it yield information about the child's typical behavior in natural settings?
▶ *Equity*—Does the assessment collect and interpret findings fairly?
▶ *Sensitivity*—Does the assessment provide for the measurement of a full range of abilities?
▶ *Convergence*—Does the assessment look at all the domains of development?
▶ *Collaboration*—Does the assessment gather information from several sources with the family as the authority on the child?
▶ *Congruence*—Does the assessment make allowances for differing abilities, evidence based?

The *Week by Week* systematic plan for Portfolio building will enable the user to gather data to meet the needs of authentic assessment as outlined in the eight principles above in a manageable way. It meets the guidelines for appropriate assessment for planning instruction and communicating with families, identifying children with special needs, and for program evaluation and accountability. See the Education CourseMate, accessed through CengageBrain.com for the full NAEYC position statement. Many kinds of scientists—sociologists, anthropologists, archeologists, biologists—gather field data of their subjects, carefully describing and cataloguing to make meaning of their specimens later. Teachers are just such scientists, taking the **ecological view** by studying children in their naturalistic settings, not a controlled laboratory, but in an environment that is just a part of the child's world that centers around the family and the community.

When to Observe?

From what you have read so far, you see that seeing children in the natural setting of the classroom, while they are actively participating, gives us the best indicators of their capabilities. This means that while children are engaged in play they gain knowledge, organize their world, and develop their bodies, minds, emotions, social skills, and language. In play, children can be themselves with their behavior speaking the language of who they are and what they think and feel. While observing play, every domain of development can be assessed by documenting behavior and analyzing it for indicators of development. In the chapters that follow, documentation methods are presented along with a review of child development so that the observer will look at children's play as an opportunity to measure attainment, support forward progress, and plan the environment and curriculum to help achieve it. *Week by Week* is a play-based assessment system.

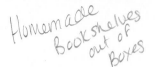
Homemade Bookshelves out of Boxes

What Is the Week by Week Plan?

EXERCISE **How long do these big projects take? What steps lead to completion of the projects?**

▶ Conception to birth
▶ Earn a college degree
▶ Lose 25 pounds
▶ Crochet a bedspread

Some of those projects take months, some take years, some take a lifetime. Each one begins with a plan that has small steps along the way leading to the completion of the project. None can happen overnight. Some may even seem impossible, but when broken down into manageable steps, planned and worked on over a period of time, each can be accomplished. Eventually the desired goal will be reached.

Teachers of young children *know* they should be keeping written records on each child's behavior for many good reasons, but there is one seemingly insurmountable obstacle: *time*. This book begins with the premise that writing down observations of children's activities is the preferred method of assessing and documenting children's development.

"But I don't have time!" Every busy adult working with children has said it. The teacher's priority is to applaud the climb to the top of the ladder, redirect that arm ready to throw a block, or give a thoughtful response to a family member as she hurriedly says on her way out, "He's running a little fever and had a touch of diarrhea this morning, but he says he feels fine." The role of the teacher is to provide physical and psychological safety and intellectual challenge to each child. The teacher also strives to maximize the teachable moment and expand on the child's interests and conversations.

Those two responsibilities, accurate record keeping and responsiveness to the needs of each child, seem incompatible. Time and attention for record keeping is minimal. Teachers who know they should be making written records are caught in a bind. They recognize the importance of keeping accurate records on which to base evaluations or plan individualized curricula. The difficulty, and for some the impossibility, is doing this while interacting with children.

Major accomplishments require time and planning. A meaningful Portfolio of a child's development and work is not gathered in a few days. Authentic assessment is achieved when each child's development is observed and documented objectively and periodically. The results are strategies to facilitate the child's progress to the next developmental level by individualizing the curriculum. When the teacher knows that one or more children in the class have reached a certain level of development, plans can be specified for them to advance. There is a pattern of observe, assess, plan, implement, evaluate, and record. This is repeated in each developmental area for each child, but only when an authentic performance-based assessment system is in place that allows this to happen efficiently.

To accomplish this desirable goal, the task must be broken down into manageable segments, planned, and executed in a systematic manner. "A responsive play-based curriculum has always required educarers to be systematic and careful observers of individual children's ability to develop skills, integrate experiences, and construct knowledge" (Bergen, Reid, & Torelli, 2001, p. 5). Programs need a system for gathering and using developmental information through observations and note taking. The teacher can place materials for recording observations in strategic places around the room, thus preplanning and organizing to successfully record observations. Skills, tools, materials, help, and dedication to the plan are needed to systematically build a Portfolio demonstrating a child's development.

I was teaching a college course in observation techniques, but struggling to apply the methods in my own classroom. There were mounds of checklists—one for each child—index cards and notepads all over the room. When I tried to write a daily journal or mark a checklist, I could not remember children like Johnny who floated all over the room, never doing anything "noteworthy." This plagued me until I realized *I had to have a plan*. Several books on observation methods advocated a systematic plan but none of them outlined one, so I developed my own. After calculating the weeks in the school year, what I wanted to know, and the appropriate method to record it, I had a systematic plan. That plan, refined through many years of teaching and research, is presented in this book.

In *Week by Week*, when the word *teacher* is used, it refers to the recorder who is documenting the child's behavior. It may be the early childhood student in a practicum experience, a teacher in a child care setting, or a teacher in a classroom setting. And in the sixth edition, it may mean the home visitor. The recorder may have the minimum required hours of in-service training, a CDA (Child Development Associate), associate degree to advanced degrees, or teacher certification. Whatever the qualifications on paper, the children call this person "teacher" because she is in the teacher role, and she will be called by that worthy name in this text.

How to Use This Book

Every chapter has two main parts: instruction on a method or tool to use in observing and recording young children's development, and a section on an area (domain) of child development. This does not mean that the method is the *only* way to gather information on the child but is an effective, efficient tool. In addition to the textbook, there is the Education CourseMate website, accessed through CengageBrain.com. In each of the next 14 chapters, a recording method is presented and practiced.

Using the . . . Observation and Recording Method

Each chapter presents a different method of writing down or documenting what the observer sees and hears in the classroom or on the playground, during the regular activities and routines of the day as they are happening.

Throughout the book are Exercises, interactive sections inviting the reader to answer a question or formulate a list. Readers should write their "answers" in pencil, to be erased for privacy, or on a separate sheet of paper. These exercises are designed to introduce a concept that is applied in the following portion of the text. These are called exercises because they serve to strengthen the reader's understanding.

EXERCISE **A house builder uses many tools. Next to each of the following, write its purpose:**

_____ Hammer:
_____ Screwdriver:
_____ Saw:
_____ Tape measurer:
_____ Sandpaper:

Just as a builder has many tools, each with a distinctive purpose, so the teacher should have many recording tools and observation methods to use for specific purposes. There are several different kinds for different occasions or situations. Some tools are better than others at capturing certain kinds of behaviors, skills, and activities. If we were observing and recording physical development, a developmental checklist would be more efficient than a narrative describing every action of the child's movements. Speech and language are best captured on an audio recording, but can also be recorded efficiently on a checklist; but then we lose the exact words, inflections, and context of the situation. Each chapter will present a method

or technique along with a description and examples of that method linked to one of the developmental areas in which it can be used. That is not the *only* method for that development area, nor is that method only to be used in that developmental area.

Advantages and Disadvantages. A hammer is not adequate to turn a screw; likewise, a screwdriver does not efficiently drive in a nail (although some of us have attempted to use it for that purpose). We present an observation tool or method in each chapter, described and illustrated with examples. Some are methods that will be familiar, some will be new. Some will be simple to grasp and use, while others will take more practice. Some are used often, whereas others are used periodically or only in special circumstances.

Pitfalls to Avoid. With every one of the builder's tools, incorrect use may result in a dangerous situation or an outcome that is less than desirable. Using a stiff paintbrush leaves unwanted streaks in the paint or varnish, for example. The description of the observation method will also include some cautions about the method or its use. These are not necessarily disadvantages, but they are presented to raise awareness of misuse or common mistakes and are included to maximize the usefulness of the method.

Using Technology. New products and electronic devices can be used to more efficiently manage documenting children's development. This section in each chapter will suggest some products or applications that could be used to collect, organize, store, and report the documentation. Some are inexpensive and handy, while others may require financial investment and a change in practice. Teachers are change agents, seeking to facilitate change in others, so we, of all people, should be open to change ourselves.

How to Find the Time. In this section, there will be some suggestions on how to find the few minutes that it takes to accomplish the documenting of children's behavior while managing the classroom at the same time. It can be done!

Time? When is there time to write? A developmentally appropriate classroom for young children dedicates blocks of time to children's choice of activities. These are self-initiated, with materials and equipment available on shelves the children can reach themselves. Whole group activities are limited to very short periods, if at all. That leaves the teacher with time, once the environment is prepared, to observe, make notes, and even closely follow and document a child's play. If there is no time for this, the teacher should look at the environment, the schedule, the ratio of children to adults, the curriculum, and the teaching practices. Program and school administrators who support time given to observation value it with resources that empower the teacher. Perhaps there is work to be done in those areas before observation techniques can be implemented.

If you are a student using the recording method to complete an assignment, you have the advantage of time. You may be able to concentrate on children's movements and listen and write down their exact words without interruption. Now imagine yourself as the teacher trying to capture the same information using the same method while supervising the whole room for safety, reading a book, wiping a nose, washing your hands, and keeping track of the time to transition to the next part of the daily routine. It is tough, but it can be done. However, it takes time-management skills, flexibility, concentration, classroom organization, and cooperation from the other adults in the classroom (Figure I–13).

Review Box. At the end of each recording method section is a short definition of the method and other areas of development or behavior on which it can be used now that you have a working knowledge of the method's procedure, advantages, and disadvantages.

At the end of each child development section, other recording methods are suggested for documenting the progress in that area. This demonstrates that the methods and areas of development are linked in *Week by Week* and not exclusive of each other. Using some kind of reliable, regular documentation system is the goal.

Figure I–13 Planning to observe is the secret to meaningful, useful, and authentic assessment.

Looking at . . . Child Development

The other half of each chapter is a discussion of one domain or area of child development, so you need to know what to look for when you are observing. That is what you are recording: each child's development, When the radiologist shows the X-ray of a broken bone to the parents of the crying child, they look at it but may not *see it as she does*. Without her specialized knowledge, they look at the same visual image but understand it at a different level. The teacher needs the specialized knowledge base of child development in order to understand the recorded events.

Child Development. Without a foundational knowledge of child development, behavior is observed, seen, but not recognized for its importance. For that reason, each chapter includes an overview of a developmental area discussing influences, milestones, terminology, and key theories. There is an emphasis on the child's observable skills and behaviors that demonstrate progress. This is not a comprehensive child development text, but it does present and review each developmental domain as it relates to that chapter. Knowledge of child development helps you to understand what typical children of this age know and can do. Your observations will help you know what this particular child knows and can do. When you put those two together, you have evaluated the child and now can individualize the curriculum so it is not so hard that it is frustrating, nor so easy that it is boring. Like Goldilocks, it will then be "Just right."

The word *development* is an important one to understand. It is more than just change. Some important developmental principles include the following:

1. Development in one area influences and is influenced by what takes place in other developmental areas.
2. Development is sequential with later abilities, skills, and knowledge building on those already acquired.
3. Development occurs at varying rates from child to child, and at uneven rates across different areas in the same child.
4. Development results from biological maturation and experiences.
5. Early experiences, positive or negative, have later effects, and there are optimal periods for certain types of development to occur.
6. Development progresses from simple to complex.
7. Development occurs best when children have secure relationships with responsive adults and peers.
8. Development is influenced by social, emotional, and cultural contexts.

9. Children learn in multiple ways, seeking meaning of the world around them, so a range of teaching strategies is effective in supporting learning.

10. Play is an important vehicle for all areas of development.

11. Development advances when children are challenged with opportunities to practice new skills just beyond their level of mastery.

12. Child's experiences shape their motivation and approaches to learning.
(adapted from Copple & Bredekamp, 2009)

The triangle, illustrating the expanding nature of development, is used throughout the book to represent the expansion of skills and knowledge that begins in a limited, crude way, but broadens and builds upon prior experiences, moving wider and deeper (Figure I–14).

Observing Infants and Toddlers. Observing infants and toddlers takes patience and perseverance. The changes in infants are very subtle so that a trained eye must be an alert observer as well as knowledgeable in developmental milestones that occur with frequency during the first two years. Young infants have long periods of seeming inaction while they sleep, gaze around the room when awake, or perform repeated motions such as opening and closing their mouth as their hand comes into view. Some kinds of recording methods just are not helpful in capturing young infant behavior. As the infant develops into an active mover, it is more challenging for the recorder to write rapidly enough to describe the actions. An even bigger challenge is to step back and process what is observed and recorded into meaningful, significant developmental events.

Each chapter will include insight about infant and toddler development and suggest efficient ways that careful observing and meaningful recording can be accomplished. Usually the best times for recording infant and toddler behavior is during routines such as arrivals and departures, eating, toileting, napping, and interaction with children and adults, including language exchanges (beginning with sounds and responses). Baby-watching is fascinating, but even more important is applying what we know about development to make meaning of those movements and sounds (Figure I–15).

Helping all Children. An important part of each chapter's discussion of child development is a section that discusses the differences that may be observed in a child's behavior and development because of other factors such as special needs or diverse cultures.

Children with Exceptionalities. You will encounter children who exhibit behavior outside of the range of typical development. Whether a child has been diagnosed with developmental delays or learning difficulties, or has an exceptionally broad knowledge or ability, often the early childhood teacher is one of the first people outside the home to interact with the child and begin to notice differences beyond the range

© Cengage Learning 2012

Figure I–15 Observing infants and toddlers requires flexibility but discipline.

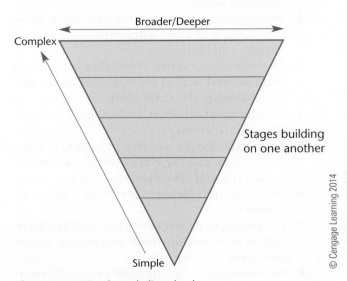

© Cengage Learning 2014

Figure I–14 Triangle symbolizes development.

of normal expectations. This section of each chapter will discuss that particular developmental domain, such as physical or language, how those exceptionalities may manifest themselves, and what the teacher could do to help the child and the family. Children with special needs are included in most early childhood groupings, and it is the teacher's responsibility to meet the differing needs as effectively as possible.

Diverse Cultures. The word *culture* may have many meanings, but we are using this one: "Culture is a shared system of meaning, which includes values, beliefs, and assumptions expressed in daily interactions of individuals within a group through a definite pattern of language, behavior, customs, attitudes and practices" (Maschinot, 2008, p. 6). This expands the traditional list of physical appearance and personality traits, foods, dress, and language to ways of understanding an individual's attitudes, intentions, and motivations that guide their behavior. The goal is to better understand one another's culture so that the child we are sharing is not placed in an environment that is in conflict.

One of the biggest differences between individualistic and interdependent cultures is the view of the individual. Considering these basic values can guide an awareness of other cultures toward a better understanding of "where they are coming from." In individualistic cultures, such as mainstream America, children's autonomy, independence, and ability to make choices and problem solve is valued. This undergirds the practices of promoting early self-help skills, applauding assertiveness, and leadership. In interdependent cultures, the values are of obedience, "fitting in," and sacrificing personal goals for the good of the group. Each chapter will include a section to guide your thinking on how cultural differences may affect behavior and development, and what the teacher can do to understand and negotiate on behalf of the child.

Helping Professionals. When working with children and families, teachers are often the resource or intermediary between people who need specialized advice and services and the professionals and agencies. This section is included in each chapter to acquaint the reader with the types of specialists to whom the teacher may refer the family. Each program should have a list of specific referral agencies and professionals from which the family can choose, with guidance from the people they trust.

Seeking help is also affected by culture. African Americans may prefer to turn to clergy or a senior member of their extended families. Latinos turn to a godparent or grandparent, clergy, or directly to God. White Anglo-Saxon Protestants may be reluctant to turn to anyone outside the family. Jewish parents say their families would turn to a doctor or psychotherapist. Irish parents might turn to a priest. Cambodian parents turn to a monk or community elder. When seeking intervention referrals with families, cultural backgrounds should be considered.

Other Methods. The recording methods and developmental areas are linked in this book to familiarize you with both. However, once you have learned about the methods, you will see that development may be assessed using several different methods. At the conclusion of each chapter, there is a feature that suggests which other methods would be suitable for documenting the developmental area featured in the chapter.

Home Visitor. For those students and practitioners working in the home, your program has likely already defined what record keeping is required and what, in addition, is useful. A Portfolio, as described in the introduction, is an informative tool to record a child's development. The contents suggested for the classroom Portfolio align well with the information home visitors generally collect and maintain about each child visited.

Finding the time to accurately document what was observed at each home visit can be especially challenging to home educators who usually are in transit between visits, reflecting on what just happened, and preparing mentally for the next visit. Experienced educators have found that, if families are comfortable, videotaping the visit as it happens, tape recording and/or writing on sticky notes the key observations after the visit, or writing short observations during the visit are all helpful tools when completing the visit narrative. It is also important that normed, valid, reliable, and culturally sensitive child development measures be utilized and maintained as part of the Portfolio. Home visitors should routinely compare how their written observations align with those measures of development.

Standards. Almost every profession has established standards for itself and its constituents to describe the guiding principles and practices. *Week by Week* seeks to assist in meeting these standards, whether for accreditation, preparation program improvement, or for more qualified early childhood professionals. Child performance standards guide early childhood program administrators, teachers, and curriculum planners in areas such as physical, social, emotional, language, literacy, and creativity. These standards are often available on the Internet and in publications from the organizations. There is a cross reference of standards that are related to chapters in *Week by Week* in the inside cover.

Chapter Features

Exercises. You have already seen the Exercise feature that occurs periodically within the book, designed to personalize the concepts, involve the reader, and focus attention on what follows. The reader is invited to think and write the answers to these exercises to build connections with the content.

It Happened to Me. Vignettes of my classroom experiences are scattered throughout the book. These anecdotes illustrate points about child development from children I have known and mistakes I have made that taught me what not to do. Some are observations my college students have written. Others are humorous stories related to me. All are stories, incredible, yet true. There are millions that *got away* because I never wrote them down! Many of these are remembered because after reflection on the real meaning of the incident, they taught me a lesson. They are not all positive ones, but are included because we often learn best from our mistakes. Many events became more important than I thought they were at the time. I hope you will begin to collect your own stories that have taught you lessons about teaching and life.

Topics in Observation. Within each chapter there is a separate section that gives insight into a topic related to child development or observation. This is to stimulate the reader's thinking about an issue or a concept to deepen knowledge. The one in

---

Professional Preparation Standards In professional preparation, whether in the initial licensure of early childhood teachers or in associate degree programs, observation and assessment of children's development is an integral part. We are guided by the National Association for the Education of Young Children's *Preparing Early Childhood Professionals: Standards for Initial Licensure, Advanced, and Associate Degree Programs 2010 NAEYC Standards for Initial and Advanced Early Childhood Professional Preparation Programs (NAEYC 2010).*

Key elements of Standard 3

3a.—Understanding the goals and benefits, and uses of assessment—including its use in development of appropriate goals, curriculum, and teaching strategies for young children.

Week by Week—explains the reasons why observation of all developmental domains is important in assessing and planning for the young child.

3b.—Knowing about assessment partnerships with families and with professional colleagues to build effective learning environments.

Week by Week—includes sharing observations and Portfolio contents with families and Helping Profesionals for each developmental domain.

3c.—Knowing about and using observation, documentation and other appropriate assessment tools and approaches, including the use of technology in documentation, assessment, and data collection.

Week by Week—introduces and leads practice of several methods of documenting observations, pointing out the benefits and disadvantages of each. It presents information on standardized assessments and their proper use as well as how technology can collect and manage documentation.

3d.—Understanding and practicing responsible assessment to promote positive outcomes for each child, including the use of assistive technology for children with disabilities.

Week by Week—stresses the **ethics** of equitable, factual, and confidential documentation.

3d.—Knowing about assessment partnerships with families and other professional colleagues to build effective learning environments.

Week by Week—provides guidance in sharing documentation with the child, the family, and specific helping professionals in each weekly plan. (See inside cover for correlation chart of *Week by Week* chapters and these standards.)

It Happened to Me

Why Doesn't Johnny Paint?

Early in my preschool teaching career, a mother asked me after class, "Why doesn't my Johnny ever paint? He never has any paintings to bring home." I thought, "Of course he paints! Everyone paints at the easel. There are always children on both sides for more than an hour every day. We use gallons of paint and reams of paper every year. Of course, he paints!" I started watching Johnny closely. Sure enough, he never chose easel painting. Even more revealing from my closer observation was how little I knew about what Johnny ever did. He was one of those children who did not draw attention to himself by negative behavior. He played and followed the rules of the classroom. At the end of the day, I had no idea what Johnny, and many others like him, had done. This is why we need to plan observations to include all children, not just those who demand our attention.

this chapter is to guide the reader in the Ethics of Documentation.

Key Terms. Every profession has terms that are common to people who work in that field. Throughout the chapter, important words appear in bold type to draw your attention. They are listed at the end of each chapter; you can use this list as a self-check to be sure you understand their meaning. Each term is listed and defined in the Glossary at the end of the book.

References. At the back of the book is a complete alphabetical bibliography of all the references used to substantiate the content of the book and give credit to ideas and concepts. Every effort has been made to include the most current research and to cite references accurately so you can seek them out for further information.

Resources. Resources listing helpful books and articles on selected topics are included at the end of the chapters. These are books or websites that may be useful in further exploration of a chapter's topics.

Education CourseMate Website

Week by Week Plans. In the Preface, and earlier in this chapter, I explained the dual purpose of this book. It is primarily a textbook to introduce early childhood students to the importance of documenting children's development and building individual child Portfolios for authentic assessment and curriculum planning, all within the context of child development milestones. On the Education CourseMate website, accessed through CengageBrain.com is a student assignment to complete during that week of field experience. Alternatively, several chapter assignments could be combined and completed in three or four lengthy visits over a semester.

For the Student. You will practice this recording method by following the assignment in the Education CourseMate website, accessed through CengageBrain.com. You or your instructor may need to modify this depending on your field placement situation.

For the Practitioner. To achieve the goal of gathering a fairly equal amount of documentation on each child, use various methods and revisit developmental areas three times over a school year. An organizational system can be used to ensure that you are gathering an approximately equal distribution of Portfolio documentation on all children.

The monumental task of documenting every child in the class will become a series of small weekly plans, using the methods learned in each chapter to observe the developmental area that has been reviewed. *Week by Week* is a systematic plan to gather documentation on each child, in every developmental area, over a period of time, using a variety of recording methods. Some methods record small specific bits of information on all the children in the class. Other methods focus on one child, gathering detailed information. The *Week by Week* plan usually gathers both kinds of information each week, rotating developmental areas and individual children. The children are arbitrarily divided evenly into four observation groups (A, B, C, D) so that selection of children for individual focus is by predesigned plan (Figure I–16). This gives every child a fair representation rather than depending on attention-getting behavior as the documentation cue, resulting in large folders on some children and thin ones on others.

WEEK	METHOD	AREA	ON WHOM
1	Class List Log	Separation and Adjustment	All
	Work Samples	Art	All
	Reflective Journal		Self
2	Anecdotal Record	Self-Care	Group A
	Class List Log	Self-Care	All
	Reflective Journal		Self
3	Checklist	Physical Development	All
	Anecdotal Record	Physical Development	Group B
	Reflective Journal		Self
4	Running Record	Social Development	Group C
	Class List Log	Social Play Stage	All
	Reflective Journal		Self
5	Frequency Count	Emotional Development	All
	Anecdotal Record	Emotional Development	Group D
	Reflective Journal		Self
6	Interview and Checklist	Speech and Language	Group A
	Class List Log	Speech and Language	All
	Reflective Journal		Self
7	Time Sample	Attention Span	All
	Interview and Checklist	Speech and Language	Group B
	Reflective Journal		Self
8	Developmental Checklist	Cognitive	Choice
	Checklist	Math and Science	All
	Interview and Checklist	Speech Language	Group C
	Reflective Journal		Self
9	Rating Scale	Literacy	All
	Interview and Checklist	Speech and Language	Group D
	Reflective Journal		Self
10	Work Samples	Creative	All
	Anecdotal Record	Creative Process	Group A
	Progress Reports*		Group A
	Reflective Journal		Self

(Continued)

© Cengage Learning 2014

Figure I–16 *Week by Week* Plan.

WEEK	METHOD	AREA	ON WHOM
11	Media	Dramatic Play and Blocks	All
	Running Record	Dramatic Play	Group B
	Progress Reports*		Group B
	Reflective Journal		Self
12	Class List Log	Self-Esteem	All
	Anecdotal Record	Self-Identity	Group C
	Progress Reports*		Group C
	Reflective Journal		Self
13	Setting Observation	Environment	Visit
	Class List Log	Group Interactions	All
	Anecdotal Record	Group Interactions	Group D
	Progress Reports*		Group D
	Reflective Journal		Self
14	Class List Log	Interactions with Adults	All
	Checklist	Physical Development	All
	Progress Reports		Group D
	Reflective Journal		Self
	*See Week 14, Assignment C		

* Progress Reports are not an observation method but a suggested plan for periodic updates of the child's development.

© Cengage Learning 2014

Figure I–16

 Go to the Education CourseMate website to download a copy of this form.

You will notice that new methods are introduced each week and preceding ones are used again, perhaps in a different developmental area and on a different group of children. This shows the versatility of various methods, while assuring that all children are recorded equally and in all developmental areas. The Education CourseMate website includes an extended chart so that the teacher can continue to plan past the first 14 weeks, following the plans to build a meaningful progressive Portfolio on which to base curriculum decisions and chart achievement.

What to Do with It. This phrase will become familiar to the reader. At the end of each chapter presenting a recording method, a filing place is suggested along with a Portfolio Evidence Sheet (Figure I–17) on which to note its presence, similar to a table of contents. These recordings are the teacher's contributions to the Portfolio being built on each child. The child, the family,

and other program personnel also may contribute meaningful data to the Portfolio. Again, the goal is not just a collection of papers but a working, growing body of knowledge about the child for the purposes of

- documenting progress
- documenting typical and atypical behavior for intervention
- planning curriculum and classroom environment changes

Much has been written in the last 10 years concerning Portfolio building. The lack of a systematic plan for gathering that information, using a variety of methods, has led to this book. The purpose of the methods, rationale, instruction, and child development is to come to *know the whole child*. By knowing and reflecting on this knowing, the teacher can truly plan and assess learning and progress.

PORTFOLIO EVIDENCE OF CHILD'S DEVELOPMENT

NAME _____ PROGRAM _____

List the pieces of documentation in this portfolio that include information about each developmental domain. Make notes for further reference, curriculum planning, or questions for further research.

Evidence Type	Date	Recorder	Notes
PHYSICAL – the child's large and small muscle development, abilities in self-care routines			
SOCIAL/EMOTIONAL – the child's social and emotional development, self-concept			
SPEECH/LANGUAGE – the child's speech and language development			
LITERACY – the child's interest and interaction with reading and writing including work samples			
CREATIVITY – the child's creativity and sociodramatic play, including work samples			
COGNITIVE – the child's cognitive development including science, math, technology, attention span			
ADJUSTMENT TO GROUP – the child's separation and adjustment to the program and interacting in groups as well as interactions with adults.			

©Nilsen, B. (2013). *Week by Week: Plans for Documenting Children's Development.* Belmont, CA: Wadsworth Cengage Learning.

Figure I–17 Portfolio Evidence Sheet.

Go to the Education CourseMate website to download a copy of this form.

TOPICS in OBSERVATION

Ethics of Documentation

Ethics should guide documentation in the following ways.

Accuracy

With every method of observation, there is a responsibility to record the raw data (facts) as accurately as possible. This is done by making notes as completely and promptly after observing as possible because memory and details slip as time passes.

The best recording is done *as the behavior is observed*. Some methods you will learn about are strictly factual, while others do have elements of judgment inherent in them. Carefully choose those methods and use them wisely.

Objectivity

Methods that preserve the raw data (just record the facts) are more objective (without bias or opinion) than others. That does not mean that one method is better than another or that biases and opinions can't enter into any recording. It is the responsibility of the recorder to capture what is seen and heard without interpretation. Again, the methods will contribute to the recording of data or interpretation. Be aware of that possibility. Objectivity also includes the practice of regularly gathering data on each child in the group because each child deserves an equal representation in observing practices. The *Week by Week* plan seeks to make that selection of subjects more arbitrary, thus equalizing the number and topic of the documentation added to each child's Portfolio.

Labeling

We all sort and categorize the information we take in. That is how we attempt to make sense of the world. It is important not to draw premature conclusions or diagnoses about a child based on limited information or to label a child or behavior. Our observation methods are designed to document the facts and to try to avoid categorizing a child as "bold," "hyperactive," or "shy."

Intended Purposes

Students are writing about children for the purpose of observing and interpreting milestones in child development, seeing theories in action, and practicing recording methods. The college policy will dictate the final distribution of the child's work gathered by the student so that no unintentional breaches of confidentiality or inferential and biased statements could be made by the practicing student.

Practitioners' purpose in recording is to document a child's behavior, assess, and plan for that child accordingly. Documenting should not be used to build a case against a child for any reason or to threaten or humiliate a child or family.

Sharing with the Family and the Child

For students, sharing with the family is only done under the direction of and with the approval of the teacher. For practitioners, observations should be related to parents using tact and much deliberation about how they will be received.

(Continued)

TOPICS in OBSERVATION   *(Continued)*

Talking to the child in front of the family should also be done considerately. Sometimes children want privacy and a sense of being a person apart from the family. The teacher could ask the child, "May I tell your family about how long you painted today when we show them the painting?" Sometimes the child needs to hear his accomplishments related to the family. Discussing misdeeds or concerns, however, should be done in private, away from the child and other families.

CONFIDENTIALITY

Students will mask the identity of the children they observe by using only initials or some other neutral identifier. No last names should ever appear on any student's recording. Permission from a family member may be required by the school or program. It is the student's responsibility to inquire about the policy and abide by it. The file must keep the documentation private from anyone other than the instructor, the child, the child's family, and those who have a legal "right to know."

Writing enhances memory. This point has been strongly emphasized as the reason for writing observations. Discussions outside the classroom with friends, or one's own family, require discretion. Sometimes stories are related for illustration, but they should never include children's names or details that could identify the child or their family. Complaining, satirizing, or criticizing children or families is unprofessional.

Professional behavior is guided by wisdom, kindness, and most of all, respect for an individual's privacy. Let's make a commitment to uphold NAEYC'S *Code of Ethical Conduct* (NAEYC, 2005).

Sharing with the Child and the Family. At the end of the day or session, what the teacher observes can be related to the child. What a wonderful send-off when the teacher says, "You painted a long time at the easel today" or "Today was a good day of sharing toys for you." The teacher shows by specific positive reference that the child's activities of the day were noticed and important. This is not the time for reminders of misdeeds or warnings about tomorrow. This is also an opportune time to share that same kind of positive information with the family member picking the child up. If the routine does not provide that face-to-face contact, a note (even in the form of a quick email message, perhaps with a digital photo attached) or a phone call (even to an answering machine) communicates to the family that the teacher has been carefully watching their child and saw something important. It builds relationships between child, family, and school, and the self-esteem of all. Examples of this type of communication are included in each of the weekly observation plans.

As a student, most likely it will not be your role to communicate with the family, although it depends on your field experience situation. Examples are included for those who do have this responsibility and as a model for those who will someday have direct communication with families. Communication with the child and family members about what we observe is an important part of our job, yet one for which teachers receive little preparation. Reading this section will help you begin to formulate your own family communication attitudes and practices.

By now you have probably noticed the shift in language from *parent* to *family* as explained in the Preface. This term includes the parents and close family members who provide primary care for the child. Chapter 14 contains a further discussion of this rationale when it addresses sharing the Portfolio in family conferences (formerly Parent Conferences).

Actions. Because observations are meant to stimulate a decision, a section called *Actions* is included with *Read a Book* suggestions of a few books to read with children about the area of development. The *In the Environment* section suggests small changes or additions to the environment to help stimulate this area of development. *In the Curriculum* gives a few ideas about curriculum projects based on children's interests. Read *Engaging Children's Minds: The Project Approach* (Katz & Chard, 2000) for a full description of this topic. This section also includes ways to individualize the curriculum. The section *In the Newsletter* suggests topics for newsletter articles or ways of sharing anecdotes or children's work.

The Reflective Journal. For each week, a group of open-ended questions are provided to guide the teacher in looking inward. These are for the writer's own consideration of the events of the week, personal attitudes, self-analysis, and promises for the future. These are private journal entries, not a part of the child's records. These will be discussed again in Chapter 1. These are found on the Education CourseMate website, usually in Part C of each week's plan. Please keep them in a safe place because they should be your honest self-reflection and a log that you keep week by week.

The Week by Week Plan

The *Week by Week* plan guides the student so that all developmental areas are observed at least once. In real life, the areas must be revisited repeatedly to accomplish the objective of seeing change over time, so the plans are extended to 40 weeks in the total plan. Care has been taken to observe each child equally in all developmental areas using a variety of methods. (See the Education CourseMate website for an overview of that plan.) The weekly plans for the rest of the year are included on the Education CourseMate website, so it can be a manual for use in an early childhood program throughout the year. Adaptations for class size and situations are explained.

That is how this book is arranged. It is meant to be a weekly plan for recording observations of each child's development and used as a basis for planning curriculum. The outcome of the plan is a meaningful, comprehensive Portfolio.

You will need a new file folder for each child in your class, plus a few extras for new children through the year. Write names on tabs, last name first, and place the folders in alphabetical order.

Place in the file any information supplied by the parents.

A Portfolio Evidence Sheet is a summary of all the recordings in the Portfolio so that the reader can see at a glance what is contained there, a type of table of contents. You will duplicate the one supplied at the end of Chapter 1 to place in each Portfolio.

This introduction sets the stage, gives you the background, and acquaints you with the format of the book. The next steps are yours. Complete the exercises and adapt the plans for your particular group of children. At the end of 14 weeks, you will have accumulated sizable Portfolios on each child, with documentation in each developmental area. If you continue the plans throughout the year (see Education CourseMate website), you will see the progress the children make and you will become a better observer, recorder, and teacher.

Key Terms

assessment	narrative
confidentiality	objective
criterion-referenced	Portfolio
document	quantitative
ecological view	recording
ethics	referral
evaluation	Work Samples
family	Working
file access log	Portfolio

Plans

Go to the Education CourseMate website, accessed through CengageBrain.com for the following:

The week's plan (Parts A and B) for observing and recording individual children and the whole group on a specific developmental domain. This includes the forms you will need. You can print them off or fill them out on the computer or handheld device.

What to Do with It—where to file the week's documentation.

Sharing with the Child and Family—suggestions on the way to discuss your observations.

Actions—curriculum suggestions for reading specific titles of children's books to enhance that developmental area, changes or additions to the learning environment, curriculum activities, and suggestions for your newsletter for family activities to reinforce the learning.

Reflective Journal—guiding questions for you to fill in and keep private.

Resources

Copple, C., & Bredekamp, S. (eds.) (2009). *Developmentally appropriate practice in early childhood programs*. Washington, DC: National Association for the Education of Young Children.

Helm, J. H., Beneke, S., & Steinheimer, K. (2007). *Windows on learning: Documenting young children's work* (2nd ed.). New York: Teachers College Press.

Snow, C. E., & VanHemel, S. B (eds.). (2008). *Early childhood assessment: Why, what, and how.* Washington, DC: National Academies Press.

CHAPTER 1

Using the Class List Log to Look at Separation and School Adjustment

OBSERVATION THOUGHT
"Every child deserves to be observed and recorded objectively, individually and on a regular basis."

NAEYC Standards **naeyc**

The following NAEYC Standards for Early Childhood Professional Preparation are addressed in this chapter:

Standard 3: Observing, Documenting, and Assessing to Support Young Children and Families

Standard 6: Becoming a Professional

IN THIS CHAPTER

- Using the Class List Log
- Using the Reflective Journal
- Topics in Observation: Why Not Use Daily Logs or Daily Journals for Recording Children's Behavior?
- Looking at Separation and School Adjustment
- Observing Separation and Adjustment of Infants and Toddlers
- Helping All Children with Separation and School Adjustment
- Helping Professionals for Separation and School Adjustment Concerns

Using the Class List Log

EXERCISE **Make a list of all the people you have had contact with today. Note what color shirt each person was wearing.**

Some assumptions can be made about the list in the preceding exercise. It may be difficult to list every person one is with, but easy to remember more significant people. It also may be difficult to remember the color of the shirt each person wore, especially for casual contacts. It would have been easier if one knew at the beginning of the day what the assignment was and noted it as it occurred. At the end of the day, or after the fact, recall is more accurate concerning some people and some facts than others. Memory might fail regarding people who demanded no attention and received none.

The teacher's clearest recollection at the end of the day is usually of those children who did memorable things. The memory might be a child splashing paint across the room or one singing every song from the latest Disney movie. Children who cause no trouble or draw no attention to themselves might not be remembered at the end of the day.

A method is needed to guide the teacher to record information about every child in the class. The same category of information should be recorded for every child in the group on the same day: It is more equitable to standardize the criteria and collect data on all the children in the group.

Memory cannot be trusted for accuracy or remembering each child.

The **Class List Log** is a method or format to record one or more short, specific pieces of information about each child present on that day. It is designed to be quick and easy—something every teacher is looking for—and it provides information on every child in the group. It records facts that may be interpreted later or incorporated into another type of developmental comparison over time. The Class List Log criterion is determined in advance and is the same for each child (Figure 1–1).

Prepare forms by alphabetically arranging the first names of the children on a vertical half sheet of paper. This arrangement allows for the quickest way to find the space to jot a note. There is a line at the top for the date. Using a date stamp is a good routine to follow;

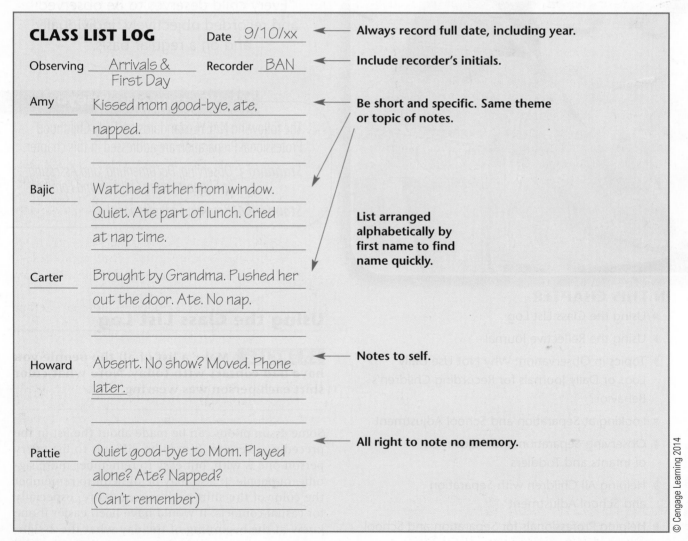

Figure 1–1 Class List Log Example.

 Go to the Education CourseMate website to download a copy of this form.

this assures the date is on every recording, including the year. Leave as much space between names as possible. Two forms may be made vertically on one page and kept on hand for various purposes. Bits of information can then be copied over or cut apart and stapled into each child's file. (Blank Class List Logs are provided on the Education CourseMate website at CengageBrain.com, along with directions on how to easily alphabetize the names. A Class List Log is ideal to place on a hand-held computer.) The availability of the Class List Log form is essential to its usefulness.

While the children are engaged in play, the recorder uses the Class List Log to record information on one preselected skill or behavior and record a small bit of description of this information for each child in the group. Select important information that can form a baseline for working on a skill or recording a specific type of behavior. This provides a natural information-gathering process that can be used for individualized curriculum planning and repeated later in the year for comparison. For example, cutting could be observed by placing children's scissors on a table with interesting papers to cut, such as gift wrap, wallpaper samples, or comics. The observer sits nearby with a Class List Log and makes notes as each child works in that area. As another example, large motor skills could be observed easily as children go through a maze or play on the playground that includes climbing, balancing, throwing, jumping, and crawling skills. It is important to date every observation, including the year.

EXERCISE   **Mark the following Yes or No for suitability of Class List Log criteria.**

_____ 1. has toileting accidents
_____ 2. is able to cut
_____ 3. listens to story
_____ 4. pours own juice, usually without spilling
_____ 5. sleeps at rest time
_____ 6. writes name in cursive
_____ 7. is considerate of others' feelings
_____ 8. can pedal a tricycle
_____ 9. understands concepts of front/back, up/down, loud/soft
_____ 10. uses words to resolve conflicts
_____ 11. follows classroom rules

Answers:

Items 2, 3, 4, 6, 8 can be checked by direct observation of the tasks. The remainder are things you have observed in the past and from your knowledge of the child **summative observation**. You can select items for the Class List Log that are appropriate for the age of the children in your group.

Remember that the Class List Log is best for recording on-the-spot observations or memorable frequent events, so "toileting accidents" would be useful in the toddler class, but hopefully not in older groups. "Can pedal a tricycle" could be recorded on a Class List Log if most of the children have the opportunity to ride that day while the teacher observes and records. "Writes name in cursive" is a primary-age skill, but if a child is still printing it can be noted on a Class List Log. "Understands concepts of front/back, up/down, loud/soft" probably is not best recorded by a Class List Log. It would take several observations or a specific planned activity to observe and record each of these concepts on all the children. "Follows classroom rules" could be recorded on a Class List Log from memory, but it would be untrustworthy (as memories are) and possibly biased, so other recording methods would be better for this behavior.

Uses

The Class List Log might be used to take attendance or to make notes on one specific behavior for a specific purpose. For example

▶ separation from family
▶ large muscle: specific skills such as climbing, standing on one leg for five seconds, walking the length of the balance beam, alternating feet coming down stairs, hopping, dribbling a ball
▶ small muscle: cutting with scissors, printing first name, rolling a ball, folding a napkin or paper in half, putting together a puzzle, handwriting
▶ language: reciting nursery rhymes; responding to vocabulary such as over/under, small, bigger, biggest; relating a story in sequence
▶ literacy: looking at a book from front to "reading" pictures, reading level
▶ math: rote counting, using one-to spondence, computation ability
▶ science: placing items in s items by color or size, foll a lab experiment (prim
▶ art: painting lines alphabet letters (to tally each ti week), leve'
▶ blocks and role in drama made, intricacies

Advantages

The Class List Log is an efficient recording method because it

- is quick and easy.
- records specific information on every child in the group.
- gives specific, dated, brief, factual information.
- can be transferred to other forms of recording as base information.
- can be used later for comparison.

Disadvantages

The Class List Log may not be desirable because

- the form becomes outdated as children enter or leave the group.
- rewriting is time consuming.
- limited information or data is recorded.
- it must be repeated to be valuable for comparison.

Pitfalls to Avoid

The recorder should remember to

- always date each entry (a date stamp is great).
- include the time of day and setting, if pertinent.
- select an observable criterion.
- write short, factual notes.

Using Technology

Technology refers to tools that make a task easier. While we may think the term refers only to electronic equipment, it also includes any object or supply that helps make a job easier or more efficient. Here are some tools that will help you manage information you gather with a Class List Log.

Clipboards. Sometimes we neglect to think of the most obvious. A clipboard holding paper, with pencil or pen attached, or several brightly colored ones placed strategically around the room will make it convenient to jot down details as they happen.

Index Cards and Sticky Notes. Who can be without these? Tuck them in your pocket, along with pen or pencil, and be ready to jot down notes to be filed or added to a more amplified documentation later on.

Mailing Labels. These can be used to efficiently transfer information gathered in a Class List Log format. By preparing sheets of labels with children's first names in alphabetical order, either by hand or on the computer, the important developmental information gathered from observations can then be transferred to a sheet of paper in each child's Portfolio.

Date Stamp. Small stamp-pad tools with moveable dates are invaluable to help with one of the most important and basic pieces of information we gather. How many of us have photos from past years without dates on the back, making it difficult to remember when they were taken? The date stamp can be used on each of the mailing labels, on Portfolio entries, and on children's work as it is added to the Portfolio. Date stamps are inexpensive and can be placed in many areas of the classroom. Children can be taught to date their own paintings and artwork.

Hand-held Computer. A hand-held computer or cell phone that can hold text documents can be useful for the Class List Log. Use a documents app for recording quick notes. Later, the information can be sorted and stored in individual children's electronic files in a matter of minutes. You won't have to copy notes over, cut up lists and tape them into file folders, or even use address labels. The Portfolio Evidence (available on the Education CourseMate website at CengageBrain.com) can then be used as the outline for storing each piece of documentation according to developmental area. This week's recording on separations or adjustments (discussed later in the chapter) would be electronically pasted under that heading with the date; others later in the year will be added there for a cumulative record.

If your cell phone has email capabilities, you can send yourself an email with notes from your Class List Log or Reflective Journal. Some people are so adept at text messaging that it may be quicker than handwriting notes.

Of course, making notes in any format, handwriting or using technology, always takes second place in the priority of supervising and interacting with children.

How to Find the Time

Having the forms already made and available around the room (on those clipboards mentioned earlier) makes Class List Logs easy to use. Because they are designed to record one small piece of data—the same one on each child—they are not time consuming. By carefully selecting the observable, important developmental task or behavior that you are recording, information can be gathered on every child in the group in a relatively short period of time.

❓ What to Do with This Information

On the Portfolio Evidence (the index of all pieces of data you have on this child), note the type of documentation that provides information for this developmental area (e.g., Class List Log by entering "CLL"). If it is a recording on the individual child, it is filed in the child's folder. If it is a recording method that includes the whole class or a group of children, it is filed in the Class File. The individual's information may either be copied into the child's file, appear as a summary in the child's file, or be referred to directly from the Class File. The recorder's name and date are noted (Figure 1–2). If bits of data are on mailing labels, these are attached to a page in each child's Portfolio with the date. Class List Log sheets can be cut apart and each child's portion stapled, taped, or pasted on a sheet in the Portfolio. Later, observations in this category will be added to this page.

If the program uses a developmental checklist or criteria from the state's standards, the bits of information can be transferred to the checklist category in the child's Portfolio with the date and specifics. For example, Class List Log information gathered on cutting may be transferred to a developmental checklist on small muscle development.

Information gathered with the Class List Log could be shared with the family verbally at the end of the day. "Today, Aillio used the scissors to cut up the funny papers. He worked hard at cutting along the lines." A written note (Figure 1–3) could be sent home informing families, "Today, Aillio worked hard at cutting." The note is "good news" you can share with the family, not just about milestones but about attempts, and efforts. This shows you know and value their child.

Figure 1–3 Happy notes are a method of communicating with families.

If a skill below the expected level of development at this age or stage is observed, a curriculum plan is implemented for that child to address this area. This gives the child the opportunity to practice and advance the skill.

The Class List Log is an effective method to use in the first week of school to record observations. This method recognizes that the teacher's first priority is establishing relationships with the child and family. The observations of separations and first impressions are important ones to record, providing an outward manifestations of each child's attachment and separation. The Class List Log provides a quick, easy format on which to record first observations without consuming much of the recorder's time.

Remember that the Class List Log should record important information, skills or behaviors, that is objective (observed, without bias or summarized), rather than subjective (judgmental).

EXERCISE   **Mark these phrases *S* for subjective or *O* for objective.**

_____ jumped from 18 inches
_____ very smart
_____ nice boy
_____ grabbed toy and said, "Mine!"
_____ doing fine
_____ she's a challenge
_____ polite
_____ counted to 8
_____ recognized name
_____ called someone a bad name
_____ clapped to "Bingo" song
_____ enjoyed music time

Check yourself: OSSOSSSOOSOS

PORTFOLIO EVIDENCE OF CHILD'S DEVELOPMENT

Evidence Type	Date	Recorder	Notes
ADJUSTMENT TO GROUP – the child's separation and adjustment to the program and interacting in groups as well as interactions with adults.			
CL	9/12/	BAN	Waved bye, involved in play

Figure 1–2 Portfolio Evidence Sheet.

Using the Reflective Journal

Which of the following things would you rather discover yourself than have someone else tell you?

_____ You have bad breath.
_____ You are unzipped or unbuttoned.
_____ You have food stuck between your teeth.
_____ You are prejudiced against something.
_____ You are acting unprofessionally.

The **Reflective Journal** is a teacher's place for recording personal thoughts. It is like a **diary** in that it is private, with the word reflective bringing the image of deliberating, wondering, pondering, thinking, and rethinking (Figure 1–4). Its purpose is not to provide documentation of children on which to assess their development; rather, it is a place to think about yourself in your daily interactions with children. Teachers also need to be learners, and that learning begins within, inquiring about one's own motivations, influences, molding experiences, culture and cultural biases, values, and beliefs (Balaban, 2006).

Seeing children in their natural setting, including the observer as a participant and a partner in the research, takes time and effort, sometimes suspending adult agendas to consider events of deeper significance (Curtis & Carter, 2008). Thinking and wondering about the child, the teacher's role, the classroom

9/10	The First Day! It's a large class with many more boys than girls. They're going to give me a run for my money! They seem to have adjusted well for the first day 😊 and are eager to learn the routines, especially to explore the classroom. Carter was already in the Teacher's Cupboard. Said "What else ya got in here? Can I have that?" He's so cute. I'm especially interested in who makes friends . Today Jeff, Pia, Maurice, Jan & Chanique played together. I think this clearly will help me be a better observer. I'm so tired!
9/20	Day 2: I found out today that I need to find ways to separate Scott & Jeff -- together they're dynamite! They had me so busy doing damage control. I can't remember what the other children did. Oh yes, Casper left to visit another class for 45 min before I realized he was gone!
12/3	Wow has it been that long since I last wrote. I have parent conferences in two weeks. I better start better record keeping!

© Cengage Learning 2014

Figure 1–4 This diary example was written at the end of the day. It was difficult to remember details about every child.

environment, and the policies of the child care center all help the teacher to evaluate and transform what needs to be changed or modified. Teachers need opportunities to inquire into their own experiences and tell their own stories as a method of action research, collecting and analyzing data, and coming to conclusions. These **reflections** may be private or shared with a mentor and discussed for further reflections. The following are some resources discussing such inquiries

- *Learning from Young Children in the Classroom: The Art and Science of Teacher Research* (Meier & Henderson, 2007) contends that teacher's reflections on the classroom experiences are research, an inquiry for deeper understanding based on gathering data.
- *Learning Together with Young Children: A Curriculum Framework for Reflective Teachers* (Curtis & Carter, 2008) contains natural classroom episodes that demonstrate how observation is used to plan curriculum and give deeper insight into the child and the teacher.
- *Next Steps Toward Teaching the Reggio Way: Accepting the Challenge to Change* (Hendrick, 2004) features stories of how teachers implemented the philosophies of the Reggio Emilia schools in the United States.
- *Learning from the Children: Reflecting on Teaching* (Villareale, 2009) is a collection of a teacher's Anecdotal Recordings and her reflections on them and the lessons she learned.

The Reflective Journal Mirror

The Reflective Journal is like looking into a mirror (Figure 1–5)

- *External view*—When looking into a mirror, the viewpoint is from the outside, as others see the person. The Reflective Journal is an opportunity to explore the view that others see and compare it to the inner, deeper meaning. It helps the observer see as others see.
- *Quick check*—Often the mirror is used for a quick, overall glance to see that clothes and hair are satisfactory. A Reflective Journal can be a place for a cursory overview of performance, feelings, or events of the day without getting into deep analysis.
- *See changes*—Changes in appearance are identified by looking in the mirror. Gray hairs (or disappearing ones) or extra pounds are noticed visually when reflected in the mirror. The Reflective Journal can help the writer notice changes about thinking and attitudes.
- *Close examination*—The mirror can be used for a concentrated examination of a certain area.

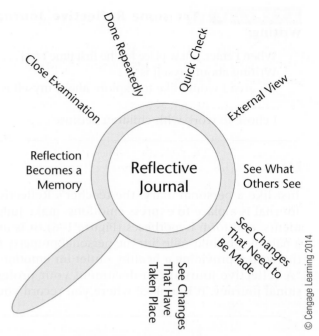

Figure 1–5 The Reflective Journal is like a mirror.

© Cengage Learning 2014

It may be a changing spot on the skin, clothing alignment, or a new wrinkle that has appeared overnight. The Reflective Journal can be a private place to self-examine a troublesome area. It may be premature or too private to discuss with someone else. An attitude toward a child or coworker, a creeping doubt about one's ability, or a prejudice that has come into one's consciousness can be closely examined in a journal.

- *Make changes*—When a look in the mirror shows something is askew, missing, or undone, the resultant action is an adjustment to correct the problem. Reacting to visions in the mirror is one of the purposes of looking. Writing in a Reflective Journal raises issues that call for change and presents the opportunity to resolve to take action. The Reflective Journal becomes an agent of change.
- *Done repeatedly*—Glances in the mirror are done many times a day, sometimes using substitutes such as windows in storefronts to re-examine certain areas. The Reflective Journal brings the teacher to an inward examination again and again, whether in writing or in thinking.
- *Reflection becomes a memory*—The vision in the mirror is remembered. Looking internally through a Reflective Journal to examine values, beliefs, and feelings also forms memories. Those become as real as physical experiences. Reflection is more than daydreaming. It can be a life-changing experience.

Try some Reflective Journal writing:

When I enter a new place for the first time I feel . . .
Writing about myself is . . .
An area I would like to explore about myself is my . . .
I chose to work with children because . . .

Uses

Just like a personal diary, the teacher's Reflective Journal is a place to express emotions, make judgments, and form hypotheses (Figure 1–6). It is not a part of the child's file but the personal property of the writer, providing a healthy outlet for emotions. "A reflective journal can document your professional journey. It is a place where you record your thinking about complex issues. . . . Writing may generate ideas and emotions about changing yourself and the organization you work in" (Forrest & McCrea, 2002). This type of recording must be kept separate from the assessments of the development of the child. *For privacy, it must be kept at home, away from the work site.*

The Reflective Journal is useful

- to express emotions or questions; to let off "steam"; to express anger, frustration, or elation; or to express worry concerning a child or the child's family, a coworker, supervisor, or self.
- for self-examination of attitudes, biases, or prejudices.
- to pose theories about a child's behavior that are from intuition.
- to explore remedies, strategies, advantages, and disadvantages of possible solutions.

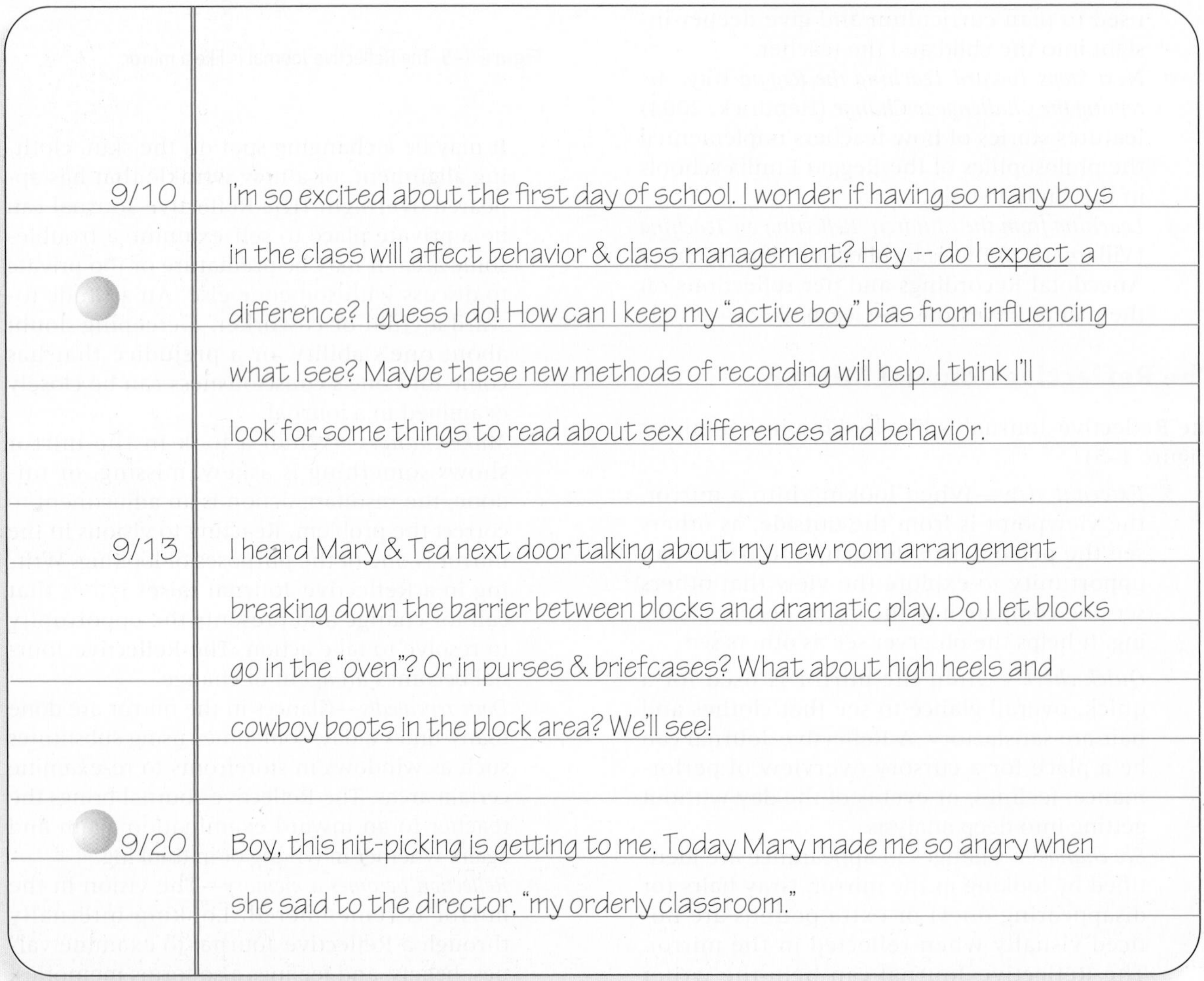

9/10	I'm so excited about the first day of school. I wonder if having so many boys in the class will affect behavior & class management? Hey -- do I expect a difference? I guess I do! How can I keep my "active boy" bias from influencing what I see? Maybe these new methods of recording will help. I think I'll look for some things to read about sex differences and behavior.
9/13	I heard Mary & Ted next door talking about my new room arrangement breaking down the barrier between blocks and dramatic play. Do I let blocks go in the "oven"? Or in purses & briefcases? What about high heels and cowboy boots in the block area? We'll see!
9/20	Boy, this nit-picking is getting to me. Today Mary made me so angry when she said to the director, "my orderly classroom."

Figure 1–6 Reflective Journal Example.

© Cengage Learning 2014

TOPICS in OBSERVATION

Why Not Use Daily Logs or Daily Journals for Recording Children's Behavior?

EXERCISE   On a separate piece of paper (for your eyes only), describe what you did yesterday—all the people you met, and what you did and said.

Many people working with children know they should write about the children. Many even have written diligently in a notebook or in each child's file every day. The difficulty comes when the days get busy, some children's behavior is more memorable than others, and objective assessment-type information is needed. An entry in a daily log or journal written at the end of the day is likely to omit details in sequence (Figure 1–6). Exact conversations and movements, which give so much important information to the assessment of children's development, are forgotten. At the end of the day, the strongest memories are those frustrations and difficulties. When it comes to remembering what each child did, the few who were the most difficult are most vividly recalled. Some are remembered at the end of the day because of an unexpectedly advanced skill or a novel, cute incident. The problem occurs when trying to remember the children in the middle. Those are the children who cause no trouble, who quietly abide by the rules, float through the day, doing nothing out of the ordinary to attract attention. Informal diary writing leaves those children out day after day after day.

This same difficulty occurs when writing in each child's page in a notebook. At the end of the day, try as one might, some children are not memorable. How can a teacher say to the family member, "I don't know what your child did today. I can't remember a thing." Instead, general comments are made, not based on hard data. The child is cheated out of being the focus of the observer's attention. It is not out of malice but because of the unsystematic way this type of recording is done. There is no hard data. Observations are written from memory, after the event.

The other shortcoming of the daily log or journal as an observational method is its subjectivity. People have used diaries traditionally for writing their innermost thoughts and feelings. Subjective recordings are those that are influenced by state of mind, point of view, or inferences into the meaning of events. The opposite are objective recordings, which are detached, impersonal, and unprejudiced, recording facts rather than feelings and generalities. For the purpose of fair assessment and documentation of each child's development in all areas, objective methods should be used. The goal is an objective measurement system for each child. Daily log entries do not help the teacher meet that goal.

Analyze your entry written in the preceding exercise. Can you separate the objective and subjective parts?

Reflective Journal for a Home Visitor

For practitioners and students working in a home setting, the value of a reflective journal cannot be understated. The nature of the work requires considerable independent thought and action; there are no colleagues immediately available to share ideas and observations, as in a classroom setting. Home educators, as a rule, need to have a method for thinking about their daily practice both for personal analysis and growth and to better prepare for supervisory sessions. Reflecting in a journal at the end of each day gives the home educator a practical method of "replaying the day" and validating the work accomplished, while identifying topics that might be explored with a supervisor, mentor, or colleague.

Advantages

The Reflective Journal is useful as

 ▶ an outlet for emotions.
 ▶ a vehicle to work through theories and to clarify and expand thinking.
 ▶ a record of professional development.

 Disadvantages

The Reflective Journal is not useful for assessing children's development because it is

 ▶ written after the event when facts are lost.
 ▶ highly inferential and emotionally based.
 ▶ not comprehensive in recording information remembered on each and every child, only those who stand out.

 Pitfalls to Avoid

The Reflective Journal is personal. It is important to maintain trust that what is written there will not be read by anyone. Keep it at home. Get in the habit of writing in it every week. Go beyond the guided questions and use it to vent your feelings, questions, ideas, and theories. Keep it safe.

 Using Technology

Many people now are in the habit of reading their email or texting several times a day. Getting in the habit of entering a Reflective Journal entry is a convenient way to record thoughts, preserving them in a computer document, and printing them out periodically to review them. If you find that you can think and write better at the computer, you can open a new document window, note the date, and let your thoughts flow. Save it in a folder or copy it to a disk where only you can access it. Blogs (web logs) are online reflections (some deep and some superficial), posted online that can be kept private or opened to selected or general public. A private blog is an electronic form of a journal and can be used in the same way as the Reflective Journal. It is inappropriate to make your blog public when it contains information about the children you teach as is publishing your own Reflective Journal. A Reflective Journal entry is only for you.

 How to Find the Time

The Reflective Journal, because it is personal and not used for direct assessment, takes personal time. This

It Happened to Me

Picky Mother

Was she ever a picky mother! I had strict instructions on how the child's socks needed to be pulled up over the snowsuit legs before the boots were put on. The mittens were to be on before the snowsuit so the cuffs were pulled down over the mittens. The hat had to be snugly down over the ears before the hood was pulled up. And be careful not to knot the scarf on top of the snowsuit too tightly and to move the knot and the ends to the back of the hood. Can you believe it! And we had 15 other children to get ready as well. It helps just to write about recalling the irritation I felt (still, after 20 years!). That's the value in writing a Reflective Journal, the place where your feelings can be expressed and dissipated, somewhat.

is done after the work day has ended or at home. For many people, writing is a chore; for those people, this task may be difficult. For others, writing is therapeutic and this task may be enjoyable. In either case, setting aside the time will result in time well spent.

 What to Do with the Reflective Journal

Because of the confidential, subjective nature of the Reflective Journal, it must be

 ▶ kept secure and private, away from the workplace.
 ▶ used as an emotional release that may not be possible in any other form.
 ▶ used to take a measurement of your personal and professional development in working with children and their families and with coworkers.
 ▶ used to explore questions, develop theories, and examine biases.
 ▶ reviewed at intervals to examine changes in thinking and attitudes and measure professional development.

REVIEW

CLASS LIST LOG

Alphabetical first name list to record small, specific pieces of information on each child in the class.

Types of Information to Record

single elements of adjustment to routines
single elements of self-care
single elements of physical development
social development stage
clear articulation of speech
single elements of understanding math, science concepts
single elements of literacy development
frequency of choices of learning centers (one Class List Log in each center for logging choice, such as painting easel, dramatic play area, computer blocks)

REFLECTIVE JOURNAL

Personal diary kept separate and private from children's recording.

Types of Information to Record

thoughts
expressions of emotion
questions
self-evaluation
reminders

Looking at Separation and School Adjustment

A smooth transition from home to school at the beginning of the year or as a child enters a program provides for the child's immediate comfort and contributes to later success.

Attachment's Relationship to Separation

EXERCISE **Using a separate sheet of paper, make a list of objects that are important to you. How did they become so valued? How would you feel if they were destroyed in a fire, lost, or stolen?**

People form an **attachment** to objects and other people for a variety of reasons. An object might be something attained after hard work and much preparation. It may be a gift received as an expression of love. Sometimes the longer an item is in one's possession, the more valuable it becomes. Strong attachment or value makes it hard to part with that object or person. Familiarity provides comfort. Separation brings a feeling of loss. The infant is on a journey that begins with total dependence, but with nurturing and attachment the child moves toward independence, a journey that will take many years.

The infant's relationship with adults begins at birth as needs are met through "a warm, intimate and continuous relationship" that gives "satisfaction and enjoyment to both the mother and child (Bowlby, 1969, p. 13) This attachment to the family emerges from built-in survival techniques and responses. In the early weeks, the provider of those needs is irrelevant to the infant as long as the needs are met. The infant begins to focus on the face, voice, and smells of those close to him, and he begins to form mental images of those who hold him. Bowlby (1969), Yarrow (1964), and Ainsworth, et al. (1978) have all done important studies on this process of attachment. These studies are the basis for guiding expectations and practices. The professional caregiver's role is to build the child's bond to the family as the primary adults and to the teacher as a trustworthy substitute.

In the first few weeks of life, the infant responds to and attends to any nearby caregiver (Figure 1–7). This is the survival instinct: Without adult provision of needs, the infant could not live. Attachment formed in the first months of life by holding a crying infant teaches lessons about the world such as

- children learn that their caregiver will be available in times of need
- children learn that they deserve the loving attention they receive
- children learn what to expect from social relationships
- children learn how to interact appropriately with others (Riley et al., 2008, p. 20)

Between eight weeks and six months, the infant begins to discriminate between familiar people, such as the family, and unfamiliar people. The child is more responsive, and smiles and vocalizes more to familiar people than to unfamiliar people, exhibiting distress at separation. There are implications for infants entering child care prior to six months old. As the infant is beginning to differentiate between self and significant others, the primary caregivers should be consistent people who are responsive to the infant's needs. Infants may exhibit **stranger anxiety** as they

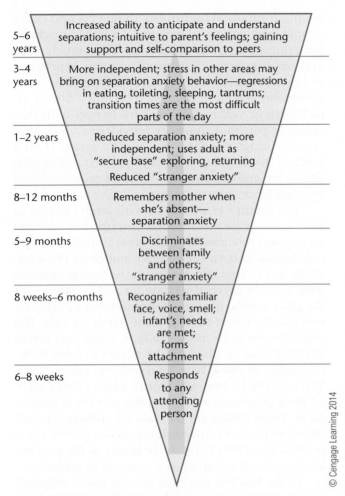

5–6 years	Increased ability to anticipate and understand separations; intuitive to parent's feelings; gaining support and self-comparison to peers
3–4 years	More independent; stress in other areas may bring on separation anxiety behavior—regressions in eating, toileting, sleeping, tantrums; transition times are the most difficult parts of the day
1–2 years	Reduced separation anxiety; more independent; uses adult as "secure base" exploring, returning Reduced "stranger anxiety"
8–12 months	Remembers mother when she's absent— separation anxiety
5–9 months	Discriminates between family and others; "stranger anxiety"
8 weeks–6 months	Recognizes familiar face, voice, smell; infant's needs are met; forms attachment
6–8 weeks	Responds to any attending person

© Cengage Learning 2014

Figure 1–7 Development of Independence—Separation and Adjustment to Out-of-Home Experiences.

are increasingly aware of the difference between close family and other people. However, Schaffer and Emerson (1964) found that most infants are capable of forming a number of attachments at the same time. The role of the teacher is to support the infant's attachment to the family. This can be done by providing reminders of the family. Images (photographs), voices (tapes), and smells (belongings) surrounding the child during the day at the center will help to maintain that attachment during the family's absence. This gives assurance to the family and the child that their bond is the primary one. The caregiver maintains that bond during their hours away from each other.

Infants and toddlers maintain contact or stay near the attached person throughout the day in child care by creeping, walking, and following those important people. The child uses vocal signals— cooing, crying, and eventually words—to maintain contact. Older infants and toddlers begin to

anticipate the coming separation at the end of the day. This may happen when they see their coat and diaper bag being readied by the caregiver or when they see the family member arrive. This is what is called **separation anxiety**. This is a normal part of development but distressing to all involved. The family member may see it as a sign of rejection, but should be assured that it indicates the child can have a secure attachment to more than one person, and that the transition from one to another is sometimes difficult. The intensity of this stage is dependent on many factors: attachment to the family, temperament of the child, and experiences with consistent responsive caregivers. It can be minimized by establishing those **good-bye rituals** that Balaban speaks about in a very helpful book on this subject, *Everyday Goodbyes* (2006). She advises families to establish a good-bye routine such as a high-five, rubbing noses, or three quick hugs, a ritual that is consistent every time they part (Figure 1–8). It serves as a dependable signal that leads the child to trust that

© Cengage Learning 2012

Figure 1–8 Good-bye rituals help the child and the family with the transition and separation.

▶❚❚ TEACHSOURCE VIDEO ACTIVITY

Go to the Education CourseMate website to watch the video entitled 0-2 Years: Attachment in Infants and Toddlers.

What did the adults in each of these scenarios do to form attachments with the child?

- are more curious, flexible, and persistent.
- have better impulse control. (pp. 321–323)

With important outcomes associated with attachment, giving attention and developing strategies to assist in this important developmental area are critical.

Preparation for Entering Programs or School

EXERCISE Using a separate sheet of paper, list important "first" events in a lifetime (such as birth, first step, first tooth, first date).

Beginnings are memorable events. They are celebrated with much thought, preparation, and anticipation. Photographs, videos, and certificates are concrete remembrances of the occasion. Memories are recited in detailed stories of the process. Lengthy discussions relate what went well and reflect on what did not and how it could have been done differently.

Anew school year, entrance to a new child care center or school, or even the beginning of every day are important events. These beginnings are worthy of careful preparations, thoughtful processes, and detailed recording. Making smooth transitions into the program, whether for the first time ever or the first time that day, begins long before the adult and child come through the door.

Important Information Gathering Prior to the First Day. Every program has its own information-gathering form for facts about the child from the family. The type of program, the objectives, and state regulations prescribe the type of information gathered on this form. A copy is placed in the child's Portfolio for the teacher's reference. The original is kept in the program office.

EXERCISE On a separate sheet of paper, make a list of information you think should be included on a family information form.

Refer to the Family Information Form (Figure 1–9) and see how many pieces of information you thought of and which ones you feel are of the highest priority.

The family is the most important source of information for assessing the child's development. By requesting developmental information, the program is recognizing the family unit as the child's first teachers, the ones who know the child best. By asking nonintrusive but open-ended questions about the child on intake and in

the family member will return, even though parting may be full of tears and anger. For younger children, a three-step process—Observe, Ask and Respond (OAR)—during arrival and departure times can help ease transitions. Observe and record what you see, ask questions of yourself and others, and respond respectfully and sensitively to each child during transition by slowing it down to the child's pace or changing the environment to be more welcoming (Miller & Britt, 2008).

As the child has experiences outside of the security of home and family, the basic need to feel a sense of belonging and comfort is challenged. Life in group care is different from life at home. Adjusting to discontinuity between home and the center may be stressful. The child may use separation anxiety as a tool to receive special attention and special promises that may result in a relaxation of standards of behavior. The family member may feel guilt or ambivalence for leaving. The teacher's responsibility is to provide the child with a sense of security, build a sense of school family as well as home family, and empower the family member to leave without guilt or losing a battle. Good-bye routines, once established, work well at helping to ease tension.

Why all the attention to this area? Research has indicated some serious long-term consequences from separations of families and children. Bjorklund and Bjorklund (1992) summarized the attachment research of Bowlby (1969), Ainsworth et al. (1978), and others to suggest that securely attached children

- are more independent (than unattached children).
- have a more positive self-image.
- engage in positive social interactions with peers.
- have fewer behavioral problems.
- are able to negotiate in conflicts.
- score higher in IQ and standardized tests.
- are more socially competent, self-directed, and attentive at age 35.

THE B.C. CENTER
FAMILY, HEALTH, AND DEVELOPMENT FORM

Child's Name: _____ Date of Birth: _____

HEALTH HISTORY
Type of Birth: _____ Was the child preterm? _____
Does your child have a history of the following:
Frequent Colds: _____ Frequent Diarrhea: _____ Asthma: _____ Nosebleeds: _____
Ear Infections: _____ Stomach Aches: _____ Seizures: _____ Headaches: _____
Urinary Infections: _____ Please indicate what brings on the above conditions if you know: _____
_____

What illness(es) has your child had? At what age?
Chicken Pox: _____ Scarlet Fever: _____ Hepatitis: _____ Diabetes: _____ Mumps: _____
Measles: _____ Other: _____
Does your child vomit easily? _____ Does your child run high fevers often? _____
Has your child had any serious accidents? If so, please explain: _____
_____

Does your child have allergies? If so, how are they manifested?_____
Asthma: _____ Hay Fever: _____ Hives: _____ Other: _____
What causes the allergy?_____
Does your child have any **food allergies?** _____
Does your child receive any medication regularly? _____
Do you have any concerns in these areas: Speech: _____ Physical: _____ Hearing: _____

DEVELOPMENTAL HISTORY
Please answer to the best of your memory!

At what age child: crept: _____ sat alone: _____ walked alone: _____ dressed self: _____
named simple objects: _____ spoke in sentences: _____ slept through the night: _____
began toilet training: _____
Words your child uses for urination/bowel movement:_____
Are there any eating problems?_____
Any dietary restrictions (vegetarian, etc.)?_____
How would you describe your child's personality?_____
Are there other childcare arrangements during hours when the child does not attend this center?
_____

How does your child respond to other children?_____
Has your child had any other group play experiences?_____
How does your child cope with separation?_____
Have there been any recent family changes that we should be aware of?_____
What do you find best comforts your child?_____
Does your child have any fears that you are aware of?_____
How does your child show stress and what relieves it?_____
Do you have any special concerns about your child's development?
_____
_____

Is there any other information you wish to share with us regarding your child? _____
_____
_____

Figure 1–9 Family Information Form. (Courtesy of and reproduced with permission, BC Center, Broome Community College, Binghamton, NY.)

preparation for parent conferences (more about that in Chapter 14), families are guided in

▶ being more observant of their child's behavior.
▶ understanding early childhood development.
▶ sharing and comparing assessments with the school.
▶ developing realistic expectations for their child.

Many questionnaires have been developed for families to assess their own child's development and are used as screening devices to identify those children who may have developmental delays. *The Ages and Stages Questionnaires System* 3rd ed. *ASQ-3* (Squires & Bricker, 2009) is an especially easy tool to use. It has a few selected questions in developmental areas at 11 intervals between four months and four years of age.

Families should be consulted concerning their goals for the child and expectations of the program. This can be done in an informal conversation, a more formal interview, or in a questionnaire. McAfee and Leong (2002) recommend these procedures for eliciting information from families

▶ Be respectful of family and community culture, customs, and language.
▶ Advise families about what information will be helpful.
▶ Use existing communication opportunities.
▶ Be able to get needed information related to a problem or concern.
▶ Have parents do some assessment and documentation. (pp. 62–63)

Personal Meetings. Building a relationship with the child and the families begins before the first day at school. This can be done in a variety of ways, depending on the program, the timing, and the age of the child.

EXERCISE   **Check the ways you get acquainted with someone:**

_____ phone conversations
_____ reading a questionnaire they have answered
_____ visiting one another's home
_____ introductions
_____ work on a task together
_____ have a common interest

Home Visits. One of the best ways to get to know the child in the family context is to make a home visit. This is a scheduled visit by the classroom teacher to the child's home. It is different from the formal home visiting program that will be discussed later. The teacher home visit can be used to fill out the

necessary paperwork and begin to establish a bond with the child in the child's surroundings. A home visit is not to inspect or to judge but to better understand the family situation. It is usually done in pairs by the people who will be directly interacting with the child. It often helps to bring an activity or some piece of the school's equipment along, such as a toy or a book. Families and children would be interested in an album of photographs of school activities and people. It is important to provide time for the family and child to ask questions and tell stories of their family. The visitors will not only talk, but also listen.

This is a friendly, short visit to get acquainted. It can determine the families' needs of assistance from the program or school. Families can ask questions or express concerns they may have. And they can explore ways in which they can be involved in the life of the program. A home visit can be an excellent opportunity to explain the typical arrival and departure procedures, to inform the family and the child of the daily schedule, and to suggest to the family what they should provide (Figure 1–10).

The visitor talks and begins to make friends with the child by smiling and making gestures of friendship without overpowering or demanding the child's participation. The family watches the developing relationship. Reactions may vary depending on their knowledge and trust of the program and their feelings about the impending separation. Some visitors take a photograph of the family that will greet the child on the first day. Giving the child a photograph of the teachers will begin the acquaintance on a visual level also. Having the child draw and then posting the drawing in the classroom for the child to look for on the first day is also a good strategy. Of course, notes about the visit are written and placed in the

Figure 1–10 A home visit is a way to establish a relationship between the teacher, the child, and the family. (Courtesy of B. Nilsen)

It Happened to Me

Stuck in the Ditch

After a home visit I was backing out of a long driveway covered with snow. I went off the edge into a ditch and got stuck. I had to go back inside and call for help, which took a long time in coming. In the meantime, the family and I continued visiting over coffee. In the year after that visit, it seemed like I had a closer relationship with that mom. Later that year when her husband died suddenly of a heart attack, I was able to support her and her children in a way that I don't think would have happened if we had not had those inopportune hours together.

Class File or program's file and are confidential, open only to those directly responsible for the child, including the parents.

🏠 Home Visitation Programs

There are many well-known home visitation programs that deliver parenting education and seek to reduce child abuse.

Home Instruction for Parents of Preschool Youngsters (HIPPY) is a parent involvement, school readiness program that helps parents prepare their three-, four-, and five-year-old children for success in school and beyond. The parent is provided with a set of carefully developed curricula, books, and materials designed to strengthen their children's cognitive skills, early literacy skills, and social/emotional and physical development. www.hippyusa.org

Parents as Teachers Born to Learn incorporates home visiting as a component that has demonstrated results promoting child development, positive parent–child relationships, and early identification of delays or health issues. www.parentsasteachers.org

Early Head Start, available in many communities, seeks to engage families with their child in home visits, helping families to become teachers of their children. www.ehsnrc.org

Home visits for public school teachers have been found to be effective in school adjustment, family involvement in the child's learning, and changes in teacher attitudes. After home visits, teachers often are able to relate better with the child with greater understanding of the context in which the child lives, as well as building rapport with the family. Unfortunately, the percentage of parent involvement declines throughout the school years K–12 (Trends, 2003). It does not need to be so and should not for research shows that school and family partnerships are essential to school success. A less recognized outcome of No Child Left Behind is the requirement for schools to involve and communicate with parents about the students' achievements. This partnership is recognized for positive outcomes of student achievement, attendance, behavior, health, and other indicators of success (Epstein & Sheldon, 2006).

Early childhood programs have long valued the positive relationships with families and set home/school partnership as an expectation. Some programs have instituted some effective strategies.

As a home visitor there is a unique opportunity to observe and promote healthy attachment so that children can separate from a primary caregiver when moving to a group setting. Being in the home allows the educator to observe relationships and responsiveness in the everyday context of family life, and to provide support and activities that promote healthy attachment between the parent and child; and then between the child and other caregivers, including the educator.

Visit to the Program or School. Child care centers invite the family to bring the child to visit the center by appointment, so they receive individual attention. After-hours seems to work best. A typical day's routine is reviewed, from arrival through departure. The family can take a tour of the center to see the rooms and areas the child will be using. The child can play and become familiar with the room and equipment. This is easier without the distraction of other children and the impending separation from the family. A nutritional snack time with the visitors sets a social atmosphere. An unhurried visit can help the child adjust to the environment.

Many primary schools have an orientation for Kindergarten children—or new children to that school—that includes a bus ride, eating in the cafeteria, meeting the teacher, and touring the school. This helps the child anticipate what will be happening when the school year begins to make the transition easier.

Through visits the child forms a visual image of the program and begins to build positive images of himself or herself there. This also builds the relationship of trust with the family. The family sees this is a good place for the child and experiences the program's willingness to be a part of the support system to their family.

Formal Family Orientation. Many programs (schools and centers) have a "family only" orientation where staff is introduced, policies are reviewed, and relationships between the family and the program are established. Food, adult chairs, and friendly greetings set the tone of partnership and cooperation. Providing child care during this orientation will not only assist more families to attend, but will also be one of the first signs that this is a family-friendly place.

A tour of the setting and a short video or slide presentation showing the "action" of the program help establish a positive atmosphere. Families' questions and concerns are anticipated in a short, reassuring presentation. The staff communicates the recognition of the needs of families and the dedication of the program to cooperate and accommodate as much as possible. Humor, understanding, and active listening are characteristics that will make this step in the transition smoother. Individual relationship-building between family and staff at this orientation helps alleviate anxiety for the family, the child, and the staff. This is useful on the first day and throughout the year, as situations develop that no one can presently foresee. An opportunity for individual questions or even anonymous questions will help to provide an open forum.

Transitions for Infants. One might think that little babies, wrapped up and sleeping, won't even notice who is taking care of them. Wrong! Stress of infants in child care has been measured by their cortisol level (cortisol is a hormone released when the body is under stress). It has been found, however, that if the mothers spent more days adapting their children to child care, attachments remained secure without spikes in the cortisol level (Ahnert et al., 2004). That tells us that child care programs enrolling infants should encourage, if at all possible, the mother to spend several hours for several days at the center with her infant before leaving the infant with the teacher. This can be time spent acquainting the child with the teacher, but it also gives the mother assurance that the child will be well cared for. Children sense the parent's ambivalence about leaving, so this reduces that transference of anxiety from adult to child.

Working with Families for Arrivals and Departures

EXERCISE **Think about the necessary foundations or building blocks of family–teacher relationships. Write the characteristics in the blocks in Figure 1–11.**

Qualities such as trust, open communication, respect, a friendly face, approachability, kindness, and understanding might appear in the blocks exercise.

Enrolling in a new program, and even beginning every day requires policies and practices that help

It Happened to Me

Which One Is the "Teacher"?

A professor was visiting a student teacher in the infant room of a child care center, arriving before the student (oh, no!). While she was waiting for the student to arrive, she observed three women sitting, holding babies, warmly talking with them, jostling them, feeding them. Later in the visit, she learned that one of the three was the mother of an infant who was transitioning the baby to the center. What a compliment to the caregivers that the care they were giving was like "mother-care." That's the way it should be. As for the student—well, that's another story.

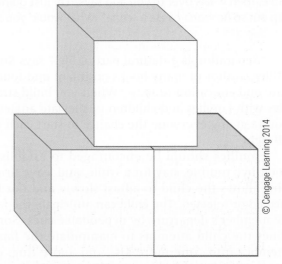

© Cengage Learning 2014

Figure 1–11 Building Blocks of Family–Teacher Relationships. Fill in the skills, qualities, and activities that will build strong relationships.

the child adjust to a new environment; they are necessities in growth and development.

The partnership of families and teachers gives the child the confidence that needs will be met by trustworthy adults. When there are barriers such as jealousy, fear, or differences in value systems that are not addressed, it is more difficult for the child to adjust to and develop in that environment. Open communication between family and program personnel is an important process.

If it is the beginning of the school year and all children are entering for the first time, a staggered first day, or first week, may be possible: Half, or a portion, of the children attend one day or one morning, with the other portion coming on a second day or in the afternoon. The rationale is that children are learning the routine and adjusting to the setting in small groups. This allows the staff to closely observe and interact with fewer children, forming friendships with them. Staff also can anticipate if there may be a separation stage to work through and begin to consult with families about strategies.

Every child should be greeted upon arrival. The greeter or door person sets the mood for the day, letting the child know he or she is important. The smile communicates acceptance and friendship. Greeting the child by name, and commenting on an event in the day that the child will particularly enjoy helps prepare for a good day ahead. This cannot be stated emphatically enough. Every child should be greeted and made to feel welcome!

Think About It . . .

A family member brings his child to your program for the first time. He gets the child interested in the water table, then walks over to you and says, "I'm just going to slip out so he won't cause a scene." What would you say?

"Separation is a natural part of life," says Susan Miller, author of many books on infant and toddler care and education (2002). "When you build strategies with families and children to alleviate anxieties, you're giving everyone the chance to start each day off right."

Families should be encouraged to establish a good-bye routine, stay for a while, and leave firmly. This allows the child to adjust slowly and not feel rushed or rejected. The child can anticipate the family member's departure by dependable cues. Sometimes the child attempts to manipulate the family member into "one more kiss, one more hug, one more. . . ." Sneaking out is discouraged no matter how much the family member sees it as an easier

way. The disappearing parent undermines a child's sense of security. This mistrust leads to a fear that every time he gets involved in play or turns his back, the loved one will leave. Families should trust the staff's concern for the child and be assured that the needed comfort is given. The staff assists the family in involving the child in the routines and activities of the classroom and, if necessary, helps the family say good-bye with conviction. A phone call to the family later to say the child is no longer crying will alleviate the anxiety.

Alice Honig (2002) reminds families and caregivers to arrange for comfort spaces and to make the transition into the day gradual and relaxed. She says to look for the sparkle in the child's eyes as a sign that the child is ready to be engaged in play and exploration. Szamreta (2003) relates her experiences using and expanding peek-a-boo games and materials to help toddlers practice going-away/coming-back behavior as a motivation for engagement with materials, and to transition from home to school (p. 88). Pantley suggests many strategies including the Magic Bracelet as *The No-cry Separation Anxiety Solution* (2010).

Planning for the end of the day is an important part of curriculum as well. It helps to have the child's belongings all in one place, such as a cubby or mailbox system, so there is no last-minute hunt for paintings or library books. When dismissal time is the same for everyone, some programs use closing circles, a hand squeeze, or recall and review of the day as a way to signal the transition from the program to home.

If children leave at different but predictable times, it is up to the teacher to give the child a cue that the departure time is approaching so the child can bring closure to the activity and mentally prepare for the change. When the family picks up unpredictably, the teacher can help the child cope with the change by assisting in the closing of the activity and engaging the family member in conversation so the child can work independently to prepare to leave. Unfortunately in the long days of child care, the arrival and departure may be handled by different people. Koplow (2007) says, "Arrival and departures, snack, lunch, rest and toileting . . . often find those essential routines in the hands of less familiar and less qualified adults assigned by administrators who consider 'noninstruction' time unworthy of the teacher's attention (pg. x)." Only through communication and policies that recognize the importance of routines can the child's adjustment to school, and back to home, be as comfortable as possible.

Primary School Arrivals and Departures

In primary school, children arrive and leave by walking, bus, or other transportation without the teacher and family interacting on a daily basis. Arrivals are busy times with clothing, backpacks, and record-keeping of attendance and lunches, keeping everyone occupied. But this too is an important time to make notes of the child's appearance (in case the child is unwell), and the child's temperament or behavior. Often they have been awakened before they were ready, eaten breakfast (or not) in a hurry, and sent off from their familiar environment. It is the teacher's job to set the tone for the day, have transition activities and routines to get the children involved, and to welcome each child.

The reverse is true at the end of the day, bringing the day's activities to a close in a relaxed way, gathering belongings, and sending each one off with good feelings about their day and their learning. Communication with the family is done most often through notes, phone calls, or email. With technology, communication with families is easier than ever.

Separation Anxiety and Difficulties

EXERCISE Describe an incident of separation difficulty you have witnessed.

_____

As families consider leaving their child in someone else's care, there are psychological issues for all concerned: the family, the child, and the teacher. It is important to know about how a child develops attachments, as well as about the possible effects of separation on those attachments. There are strategies for helping the child and the family cope with the trauma of separation that reinforce the primary family–child relationship.

Think About It . . .

Describe what feelings each of these people might have on the first day of school or care in a new program: the family, the child, and the teacher or caregiver.

Separation Anxiety Behavior. A child in the midst of a "separation anxiety attack" may display out-of-control behavior. It is embarrassing for the family member, who is fearful that the teacher will judge the child or the family in a negative way. And it is difficult for the teacher to address the emotional needs of an unfamiliar child. The family, and many other children and families as well, may be looking on. It is equally difficult for the child who is

distressed and out of control, needing someone to help. These extreme moments call for calm reassurance that the family will return at the end of the day. An established good-bye routine, such as "kiss, hug, nose rub, bye-bye," and a prompt departure helps the child anticipate the family member's departure and come to rely on the family member's return.

The distressed child, of course, should receive holding and comforting as long as necessary to help overcome the feeling of abandonment. Often the child rejects any physical contact or comforting from this new adult. The teacher respects this, but shows reliability of care and interest in the child's difficult moment. The teacher offers choices of activities that may be of interest to the child. The child may be kicking and screaming. This should be ignored if it is hurting no one or gently restrained if it is aimed at the teacher, other children, or furniture. Removal of the child from the curious stares of other children prevents embarrassment and copycat behavior from others.

Verbal and body language convey understanding for the feelings of loneliness and anger. The child is reassured that the family member will return. The teacher communicates the desire to help the child gain control and have a safe, happy time while she is here. Reading a book, singing a song, rocking, or stroking the child's back sometimes helps soothe those feelings. Continued violent reactions call for patience, tolerance, and endurance. The child is mourning and grieving for the absence of familiar people. To try to distract is to deny the child's feelings. They will eventually subside. Sometimes the most effective teacher action is just quiet acceptance of the strong emotions without overtures to distract the child. Each child has individual behavior patterns to be learned. The teacher seeks the most effective relaxation techniques for each child. The child builds trust in the family member's return and learns **coping mechanisms.**

EXERCISE What would you say to this child? See Figure 1–12.

_____

Separation Anxiety Warning Signs. Difficulties with separation may not always appear at the beginning of the year, the beginning of the day, or in a violent emotional outburst. Sometimes partway through the day or the year, a child who appeared adjusted to school begins to display some difficulties: Crying at the family member's leaving or the inability to eat, sleep, or play all can happen at any time. What is

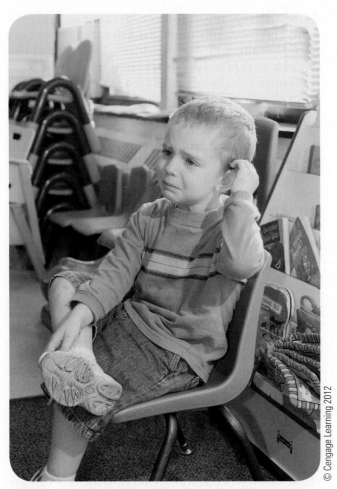

© Cengage Learning 2012

Figure 1–12 What would you say to this child?

going on? It may be the maturing process. As the child develops, thinking changes. She may be passing into a new stage. That happy baby who held out her arms wide to the teacher is now burying her head in her dad's coat. She may be the toddler who takes one look at the caregiver, looks at her mom, and kicks and shrieks as her coat is removed. The child grabs it back, latches onto her mom's pocketbook strap like it is a life preserver, and will not let go. It may be the child who came happily each day with a smile and a picture she drew for the teacher now says, "I don't like it here. I wanna go home." It is just as important for the teacher to respond promptly to more subtle separation behavior. Such behavior can take many forms: difficulties in eating, sleeping, toileting, learning, or social difficulties.

Eating. For the infant, refusal to take nourishment is an immediate danger signal. Teachers can try various positions of holding during feeding and even blocking the infant's view of the family member.

Communication with the family member about feeding routines ahead of time, and even a phone call to verify and seek advice, may be helpful. A joint effort of family member and teacher should make this difficulty short-lived. Continued difficulty may need the involvement of the pediatrician and other support personnel.

For toddlers and preschoolers, eating away from home may be distressing, perceived as a betrayal of that personal time with close family members. A relaxed environment without pressure from teachers, along with familiar foods and utensils, will help ease this time. It usually is just a matter of days until children adjust and join in the sociability of mealtime and look forward to it with enthusiasm. If a child is crying at mealtime, refusing food day after day, or indicating by behaviors that this is a stressful time, the situation demands attention. Family member–teacher communication, sometimes with a referral agent such as the director or the pediatrician, can usually work this through.

For primary children, eating in a noisy cafeteria can be a stressful time. The school should do what it can to make school mealtimes positive social experiences and conducive to good eating habits.

Sleeping. Environmental changes can affect sleep, so children in new places may have difficulty resting. Other children's schedules and sleep patterns may keep the child from sleeping. The new environment, governed by licensing regulations, may add to the child's difficulty in adjusting to sleeping away from home. The teacher gathers information from the family on the child's sleep patterns. On each day's arrival, family members give information about last night's sleep. Everything possible is done to make the environment conducive to the child's relaxation. Music, favorite toys, books, or a blanket help with sleep routines and should be individual choices for children. Children having adjustment problems to center care may have continued sleep disturbances.

Again, the close observation and responsiveness of the teacher to the individual child's needs will help. Communication with the family for understanding and accommodating the child's needs to the center's practices also helps (Figure 1–13). Sleep deprivation might result in the child's irritable behavior and increased anxiety for the adults.

Making notes on the child's sleepy times of day, indicators of sleep needs, techniques that relax the child, positions of sleep, and toys or physical items normally taken to bed are important pieces of information for the child's file. Sharing and exchanging information such as this with the family will help the child's adjustment to sleeping

© Cengage Learning 2012

Figure 1–13 Family members and teachers need to communicate about children's routines.

It Happened to Me

Wrapped in Love

I was visiting in an infant room and saw a baby about six months old wrapped in a large red shawl while the teacher fed him. She later explained he was having difficulty adjusting and would not eat or sleep at the center. Through trial and error, she and his mother came up with the idea of bringing in something of the mother's from home. Wrapped in his mother's shawl, he was wrapped in the essence of her love and security. Now he could eat and sleep.

away from home. It also assists substitute teachers in meeting the child's needs when the regular teacher is absent.

Toileting. For two-year-olds, managing toilet needs on their own is a big accomplishment, but it is not without relapses for a variety of reasons. Adjustment to a new place may upset that delicate balance. The child is curious and may frequently use the child-sized toilet as a novelty. The new stimulating environment full of active play areas and new playmates may result in forgetfulness or inattention to toileting cues, leading to accidents. A matter-of-fact attitude by teachers, along with a change into familiar clothing after a toileting accident, usually is all that is necessary to help the child cope with these events.

Some children, however, have a delicate emotional response to new places, making it difficult to eliminate

in this new surrounding. A child may hold the genitals, lay over a chair until the urge passes, or even cry from a severe stomachache. It is up to the teacher to be a detective, interpreting these subtle clues. Once the cause is determined, appropriate action can be taken. Again, communication with the family about the child's patterns, times, and physical cues is an important part of making the child comfortable. Family members taking the child into the bathroom and talking about using it should be part of the first visit or first day at the center. Continued disruption in toileting may cause bladder infections or constipation and other disorders. A daily, unobtrusive observation of the child's toileting behavior is also a part of the record-keeping procedure. Any extraordinary behavior should be noted factually and shared at the end of the day with the family member, away from the presence of the child.

Participation. The child who is experiencing separation difficulties may not be able to attend to the learning activities that are planned. He may have difficulty making choices or staying with a task. Transitions from one area to another or interacting positively with other children may precipitate crying or tantrums. After a normal adjustment period, if this behavior is observed, it should be recorded. Reference to it later will indicate the stages the child has gone through in the separation process.

Social Interactions. When a child is in emotional turmoil, it may affect the child's outward behavior toward others. The child may cling to one teacher, transferring attachment to another adult. That is a healthy coping mechanism in an infant and toddler and, temporarily, for the preschooler. A branching out of friendships and social contacts is expected after a time. Some interventions may be necessary if that is not observed.

Children who are experiencing separation difficulties may be socially withdrawn. The group situation may be overwhelming. The child just needs some time to watch and see how other children are handling it. A sensitive teacher will allow the child this luxury of watching, along with an occasional commentary on what the other children are doing. The child is invited to join the play. The teacher will also be familiar with the stages of play and have realistic expectations for the child's positive social interactions. Communicating with the family to know the child's social history will also help to better understand the child's reactions. It would be helpful to know the positive or negative experiences the child has had with siblings and other children who are the same age.

Acting Out as a Symptom of Separation Anxiety. Separation anxiety, feeling alienated from environments and familiar people, can occur at any age. For some children, the new environment is so stimulating that their self-control is not strong enough to govern their behavior. The child may be unaccustomed to so many playmates and play areas. Inappropriate and unsafe actions may erupt, which might result in rejection by other children. The teacher redirects or restricts behavior. The staggered first day can help to ease this transition. For the child entering the program once it has already begun, it may be overwhelming. Other children are already established in routines and have formed friendships. The teacher coaches the new child through routines and introduces expectations in various areas to help the child adjust.

The child comes into a new situation not knowing the rules and the people; she feels rejected and abandoned by the family. When the teacher places herself in those little sneakers, it helps ease the child through these difficult times.

When the child is sending a signal of distress or going through a new phase, the best defense is that close communication and understanding between family member and teacher. "Partnering in children's separations" is a phrase that conveys the reciprocal relationship that everyone involved is responsible for addressing the cause, negotiating a solution, and working to implement its success (Jervis & Polland, 2007). There are mixed feelings of balancing family, work, and school for everyone. It is helpful to have a talk, outside of the child's hearing, about the change. This may reveal some events at home that upsetting to the child manifested in classroom behaviors of insecurity and separation anxiety. Together, some ideas can be generated about how to help everyone cope with changes or troubled times.

It Happened to Me

Mid-September Reflection

We had gotten through those first days and weeks. All those plans for smooth transitions seemed to have paid off. Each child came ready to play and said good-bye to the family willingly. They had fallen into the routine of the day. Today during free play, I could move from area to area, observe their play, comment on their actions, add a prop here and there, and enjoy their absorption with the activities of their choice.

Then I heard a noise, a long sucking in of air with a quiet sort of high-pitched wail.

Where did it come from? I looked around the room. Children were climbing and sliding and going in and out the door on the climber, which was their spaceship today. A boy was sitting at the table in the dramatic play area with a police hat on. He was packing a lunch pail with dishes and silverware, talking to another boy who was stirring "soup." Several children were in the block area piling blocks, laying out carpet squares, and standing up farm animals. Sandbox players were pouring, shoveling, and digging for shells they found hidden there. Two children at the easel, a boy on one side and a girl on the other, were busily making lines and circles. There it was again! I looked around again. Same scene as before, but now I could locate the source of the sound. It seemed to be coming from the boy at the easel. As I looked closer, he stared at his paper as his hands moved methodically up and down. He watched the paint as it dripped from the brush; then I heard the sound again and saw his face muscles tense into a frozen stare.

I walked over and placed my hand on his shoulder. The dam broke. He let out all those sobs he had been trying to hold in! He was missing his mom and had tried to hide it for an hour but just could not hold it in any longer. Were there signs I could have seen before it got to this point? Were there others who were feeling this internal sadness, holding it in check but inwardly hurting? Was I being smug and self-congratulating without really addressing the issue of separation with those who were least capable of coping with it—the children? I vowed to be a more empathetic observer and to use more touch as a message to each child that I am here to support and comfort if they need me. Tomorrow I'll read *The Kissing Hand* by Penn (2008) to stimulate some discussion about separation and the ever-returning parent.

Permanent Departures and Good-byes

Just as beginnings are important, so are endings.

EXERCISE **Using a separate sheet of paper, make a list of ending celebrations, rituals, or customs.**

Bringing closure to a letter, a day, or a life has emotional importance. It closes the circle.

A good-bye party for a child who is moving or leaving the program helps recognize the child for the contribution she made to the class. Classmates can present physical reminders of her friends there. Though it is a sad occasion, it can be a part of learning to say good-bye. By attempting to remain in contact, a sense of the larger community is felt with her as a link to the next city, state, or country. This helps both the child leaving and those remaining.

At the end of the year, a child-centered farewell celebration (as opposed to cap-and-gown commencement for preschoolers) can be planned. This is also a time for remembering (part of the cognitive process); expressing positive feelings for one another (social and emotional development); and drawing, dictating, or writing remembrances (literacy and art activities).

Planning for departures as well as arrivals is an important part of the teacher's responsibilities and also offers opportunities to observe. How does the child organize for the end of the day? What is the child's response to the cue of the approaching end to an activity? How does the child greet the family member at the end of the day? These are possible Class List Log criteria.

Observing Separation and Adjustment of Infants and Toddlers

Throughout this chapter, the issues of attachment, separation, and adjustment have been discussed. During the first few years of life, attachments are formed with the primary adults in the child's life. In observing and recording infants and toddlers, a child's approaches are interpreted through behavioral clues, helping the staff gain a better understanding of the child's relationships with others and how the separation and reunion plays out. The Class List Log on arrivals, departures, and routines will yield information

to track how the child is faring in making adjustments to the out-of-home program. Feelings of the child and the family member can be observed and recorded

▶ Eye contact between child and family member
▶ Following the family member to the door or reaching toward the door
▶ Sound or verbal protest on leaving
▶ Reactions to the receiving caregiver
▶ If distressed, how does the child find comfort? (Cohen et al., 2008)

Communication with the family about the transition from home to school is an important tool to better understand the child's cues and the way the family deals with transitions in other situations. Keeping notes of the needs of each child can help everyone remember—one baby may need to be wrapped in the blanket from home, another may need to be held by the same teacher until the family member leaves, while another does best if placed near other children.

Departures are equally as important as arrivals. The teacher notes the time that the family will pick up the child in order to help prepare the child by gathering belongings, telling the child that it is almost time to leave, and then watching for what makes for the smoothest transition once the family member arrives to receive the child.

It may also be helpful to note what the family member needs on leaving or arriving. Seeing what each child needs and planning accordingly is a part of being a responsive, respectful caregiver. Sharing information at the beginning and end of the day in the form of written notes can help everyone remain "in the loop" for the child.

Helping All Children with Separation and School Adjustment

Children with special needs, from a variety of cultures, or those who may not speak English are entering programs nationwide. The teacher has the responsibility to be prepared to help these children make the transition into the program as stress-free as possible. Prior knowledge of the child, no matter what the situation, helps this process. Specific knowledge of these special populations is imperative. Family and professionals providing information, research, and extra observation and patience will all be required.

Children with Special Needs

The Americans with Disabilities Act of 1990 (P.L. 101-336) protects against discrimination based on a person's disability. Children with disabilities must be admitted into settings that have been adapted to accommodate them. When children with special needs are integrated into a group, it is important to have knowledge and information concerning the exceptionality and this child's situation, in particular before the first day they come to school. This can be obtained from the family information form, a home visit, or the child's report from helping professionals if the parents have given permission for its release.

The family of a child with a disability may be more anxious about leaving the child in a school setting. That anxiety may be transferred to the child—making separation more difficult for all. Child and family alike need the reassurance that the child will be well cared for and accepted. In fact, inclusive settings often help to foster children's ideas about helping others, the understanding of emotions, and acceptance of individuals with disabilities (Diamond, 2001).

For children with visual impairments, audio recordings about the routines and what to expect from a typical day would be helpful. If the child is hearing-impaired, this could be done through a picture album. The teachers should become familiar with the language the child will be using to communicate. Knowledge of a child's physical impairments will help modify the setting to be more accessible. Of course, the building already meets the guidelines for accessibility under the Americans with Disabilities Act (P.L. 101-336). Modifications may need to be made within the classroom arrangement and in the thinking and approach of the staff. Any modifications for the child preferably will be made before the child enters the program. Emotional or behavioral disabilities should be understood thoroughly through conferences with the family and helping professionals so that the teachers are prepared and react in an appropriate and consistent way.

Diverse Cultures

The attachment between family and child varies in each culture. For some, the infant never is physically apart from an adult, being held, carried, or touched almost constantly. For these children, physical and emotional separation needs special attention. In other cultures, children are expected to become independent very quickly, so any expectation of separation anxiety is not understood or tolerated. An awareness of cultural parenting styles and attachment and separation practices will help the teacher adjust expectations and actions.

For the child who is non-English-speaking, it is most helpful if the teacher learns a few of the most important words such as greetings, routines such as "Eat," "Toilet," "Clean up," "Mother/father returning soon," and "I can help you." This can be accomplished by asking the family, working through an interpreter, or researching translations at the library. The child will need time and an environment that is child-centered. When the environment is restricted by a teacher's directions and highly emphasizes following directions, the non–English-speaking child will have difficulty adjusting. Play is a universal language, and once the child feels comfortable, the lure of play will help her feel more comfortable.

Meeting the needs of each child as an individual necessitates preparation, understanding, and careful observation skills.

Helping Professionals for Separation and School Adjustment Concerns

If a child is having separation or classroom adjustment problems beyond his ability to cope, it may be necessary to consult helping professionals. After consultations with families and the director or program personnel, outside professionals who may help include the following:

pediatrician—physician specifically trained to care for the health and wellbeing of children

child psychologist—conducts screenings for diagnosis and treatment of children with emotional, behavioral, or developmental problems

child psychiatrist—provides counseling or consultative services to individuals or families who may be experiencing problems

play therapist—child psychologist who uses play to diagnose and treat children who may be withdrawn, nonverbal, or traumatized

school guidance counselor—trained personnel in emotional development who can support the child and work with the family in areas of school adjustment or other school-related difficulties

Other Methods

Other Methods to Record Separation and Adjustment:

Anecdotal and Running Records
Checklists/Rating Scales
Conversations and Interviews
Work Samples
Media

Key Terms

attachment	reflections
Class List Log	Reflective Journal
coping mechanisms	separation anxiety
daily log or journal	stranger anxiety
diary	subjective
good-bye rituals	summative observation

Plans

Go to the Education CourseMate website at CengageBrain.com to find the following:

Class List Log form (although no form is really needed. You can create your own alphabetical list on filler paper or mailing labels.)

Plan Week 1 Part A, Directions for a Class List Log on Separation and School Adjustment, including What to Do with It, Portfolio Evidence Example, Sharing with Child and Family, Actions—Read a Book, In the Environment, In the Curriculum, In the Newsletter

Plan Week 1 Part B, Directions for Work Samples for All

Plan Week 1 Part C, Reflective Journal

Resources

American Academy of Pediatrics. (2011). *Caring for our children: National health and safety performance standards: Guidelines for out-of-home child care* (3rd ed.). Elk Grove Village, IL: American Academy of Pediatrics. http://nrckids.org.

Balaban, N. (2006). *Everyday goodbyes: Starting school and early care: A guide to the separation process.* New York: Teachers College Press.

Goldman-Frazier, J., Fernandez, M., & Marvo, K. (2005). Separation and continuity in the lives of infants and toddlers. *Zero to Three,* 25(6), 1–72.

Jervis, K., Polland, B. K. (2007). *Separation: Supporting children in their preschool transitions.* Washington, DC: National Association for the Education of Young Children.

Meier, D. R., & Henderson, B. (2007). *Learning from young children in the classroom: The art and science of teacher research.* New York: Teachers College Press.

Pantley, E. (2010). *The No-cry separation anxiety solution: Gentle ways to make good-bye easy from six Months to six years.* New York: McGraw-Hill.

Villareale, C. (2009). *Learning from the children: Reflecting on Teaching.* St. Paul, MN: Redleaf Press.

CHAPTER 2

Using Anecdotal Recordings to Look at Self-Care

> ## OBSERVATION THOUGHT
> "Observing and recording does no good if it does not change the teacher's practices or individualize the approach the teacher uses with each child."

NAEYC Standards **naeyc**

The following NAEYC Standards for Early Childhood Professional Preparation are addressed in this chapter:

Standard 3: Observing, Documenting, and Assessing to Support Young Children and Families

Standard 6: Becoming a Professional

IN THIS CHAPTER

- Using the Anecdotal Recording
- Looking at Self-Care Skills
- Topics in Observation: Using All of Our Senses
- Observing and Recording Infants and Toddlers in Routines
- Helping All Children with Self-Care Skills
- Helping Professionals for Self-Care Skills

Using the Anecdotal Recording

Maralyce went into the bathroom in the three-year-old classroom. After considerable time, she could be heard screaming and crying. The teacher rushed to the door to find Maralyce standing by the toilet, pants around ankles, trying to adjust streams of toilet paper to cover the seat. Every time she put one strip on, another would slide off. The teacher asked "What's wrong, Maralyce? Why are you crying?" Maralyce sobbed, "Mommy said I can't go potty 'til I cover the seat, and it won't stay on." The teacher went and quickly got tape and gave it to Maralyce. She taped the paper on the seat, sat down quickly, and let out a "Wooo!" The teacher saw the still-developing coordination of a three-year-old in conflict with a parental expectation. She was inclined to say, "You don't need that paper. The seat is clean." However, she wanted Maralyce to have a way to do it herself and did not want to contradict the family's authority and instructions.

There are incidents that need to be remembered exactly as they happened. They tell a story that lets the reader see, hear, and feel as if he were there. The story contains a factual account of an incident that may be typical or out of the ordinary. The incident, however, is best remembered in its entirety. The most factual recording method is **Anecdotal Recording**. It can be used to

> portray an incident that indicates a child's development in a specific area.
> record a humorous incident to share with families.
> preserve the details of a curious incident for later reflection.
> record the exact details of a child's disclosure of an incidence of abuse.
> exemplify a child's typical behavior.
> record the details of an incident that is totally foreign to the child's typical behavior.

The Anecdotal Recording is a **narrative** account of an incident anywhere from a few seconds to several minutes in length. The Anecdotal Recording recounts the event, telling the reader when, where, who, and what. It does not answer the question "why" in the body of the recording. That conclusion or **inference** is separated from the recording. An inference is an informed judgment or conclusion based on observation. When we see a child crying, our inference is that the child is sad or hurt. We may or may not be correct.

Every newspaper reporter, police officer, and insurance claims adjuster knows that facts written on the scene or very shortly thereafter are the most accurate. When an event occurs that is important to remember, a few notes are jotted down to refer to later. If an interesting conversation is happening, it is recorded word for word. It is written, as much as possible, as it is happening (Figure 2–1). By the end of the day, the notes are amplified and rewritten into a full account while the details are still fresh. It can be written on regular lined paper. It helps to fold the paper in half vertically and write on the left side so that the explanatory comments can be written in the right-hand column. In this way, comments of the recorder are placed separately from the recording. The reader then knows the difference between the actual recounting of the incident and the writer's

inferences. It is also possible to fold the paper so the comments are not visible. Another reader can then draw independent conclusions about the incident.

This is an **open method**, a narrative that preserves the details so that different interpretations can be made, determined by the reader's focus. The reader receives a mental picture of that event by reading the words.

An Anecdotal Recording is a written replay of an incident. In Figure 2–1, note the following characteristics of an Anecdotal Recording

> It sets the stage for the reader: "In cubbies dressing for outdoor play."
> It identifies the characters, the target child by name—Sherita—and the other child by initial for anonymity—D (this may even need to be blotted out later): "Sherita and D and Teacher." Abbreviations are used for speed in the writing.
> The account describes the action in detail: "Sherita bends over with eyes close to D's coat zipper."
> It describes the interaction between the characters. "T bends down and says …"
> It records exact quotes, including pronunciation as it is heard. "I tan't dit it!"
> It concludes with a result or reaction between characters. "You're my buddy, right?" Sherita: "Right, D."

Separate from that account in the right-hand column, the teacher writes comments, inferences, judgments, questions, and reminders

> comments on development: "Helper attitude"
> actions: "Talk to speech therapist for an update"
> reminders: "Place Sherita and D together at lunch"
> curriculum plans: "Bring in dress-up clothing with separating zippers"

On a separate note, the teacher reminds herself to copy the anecdote for the other child's file, and then she will make appropriate notes in the right-hand column relating to that child's part in the incident, blocking out Sherita's name for anonymity.

With the inferences in the right-hand column separate from the actual recording of the incident, it is easily folded back for a fresh viewpoint. Other readers may interpret the incident differently. Inferences or evaluations may differ, depending on the role of the observer. Child D's family might infer she is not getting proper attention from the teacher. Another child's family might wonder why this helpless child is in such an advanced class, demanding time

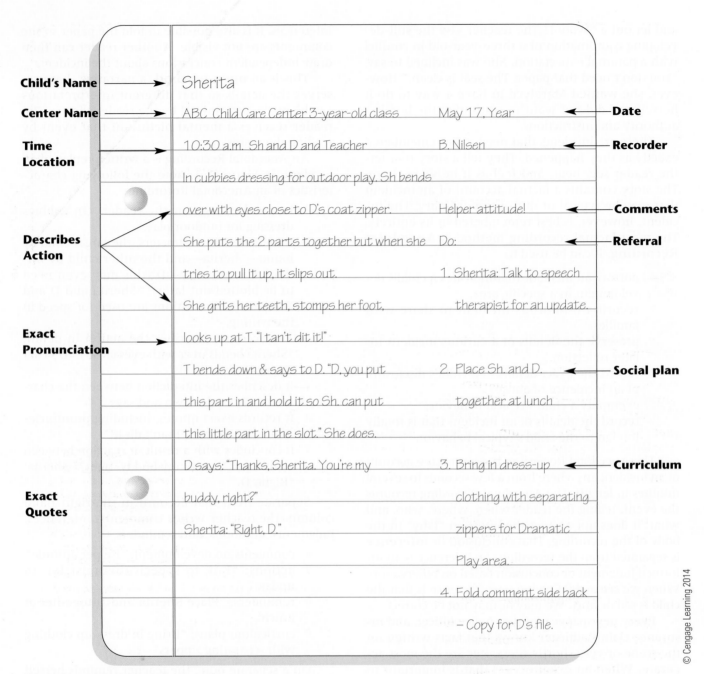

Child's Name ——→ Sherita

Center Name ——→ ABC Child Care Center 3-year-old class   May 17, Year   ←—— Date

Time
Location ——→ 10:30 a.m. Sh and D and Teacher   B. Nilsen   ←—— Recorder

In cubbies dressing for outdoor play. Sh bends

over with eyes close to D's coat zipper.   Helper attitude!   ←—— Comments

Describes
Action ——→ She puts the 2 parts together but when she   Do: ←—— Referral

tries to pull it up, it slips out.   1. Sherita: Talk to speech

She grits her teeth, stomps her foot,   therapist for an update.

Exact
Pronunciation ——→ looks up at T. "I tan't dit it!"

T bends down & says to D. "D, you put   2. Place Sh. and D.   ←—— Social plan

this part in and hold it so Sh. can put   together at lunch

this little part in the slot." She does.

D says: "Thanks, Sherita. You're my   3. Bring in dress-up   ←—— Curriculum

Exact
Quotes ——→ buddy, right?"   clothing with separating

Sherita: "Right, D."   zippers for Dramatic

Play area.

4. Fold comment side back

– Copy for D's file.

Figure 2–1 Anecdotal Recording Example.

from the teacher. Another teacher might deduce that this child needs some instruction in self-care skills. The speech pathologist might be overjoyed to hear Sherita express herself in nearly recognizable words. The teacher might write a comment to the side, "Sherita is the youngest in her family so seldom has a chance to be the helper. D has often excluded Sherita from play, so this may be the beginning of a friendship." All people read the same account, but their inferences are different because of their perspectives.

Sociologists and anthropologists use "ethno-graphic eyes" to write field notes when describing a society. It is the difference between note taking and note making. Note taking is the descriptive field notes that give the reader a re-creation of the sensory information (seeing, hearing, feeling, and smelling). Note making is the interpretation of what is being observed. In Figure 2–1, the description of zipping the coat and the exact quotes are examples of note taking. "Helper attitude!" is the interpretation—it is note making.

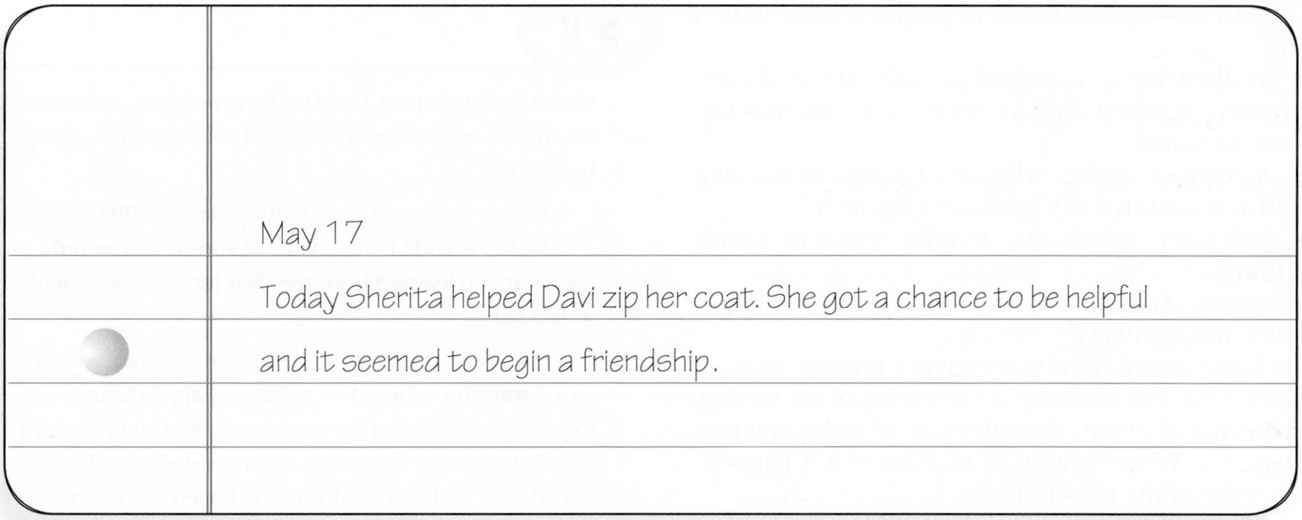

Figure 2–2 Diary Example.

Many people use the term Anecdotal Recording when what actually has been written is a diary account (Figure 2–2). This type of recording is true, but it is not factual. It summarizes actions, draws conclusions, and leaves out information that could be useful. Compare Figure 2–2 to Figure 2–1. See that the Anecdotal Recording in Figure 2–1 gives enough detail so that the reader has the feeling of being there. The Anecdotal Recording relates the following:

body positions—"bent over, eyes closed"
actions—"puts two parts together," "slips out"
reactions—"grits teeth," "stomps foot," "looks up"
exact words—"Davi, you hold this," "Thanks Sherita"
inflection and pronunciation—"I tan't dit it"

The reader "sees" the incident. She "hears" the conversation along with emphasis as it was spoken. Then, more accurate and individual judgments based on the reader's perspective are made.

EXERCISE **Mark the following sentences Yes if they fit the criteria for Anecdotal Recording or No if they are inferences, explanations, or not exact quotes.**

_____ a. Tara ran over to the cubby area.
_____ b. She had on a short shirt and wanted to get her jacket.
_____ c. Stacey asked her, "Why do you want your jacket on?"
_____ d. She said her stomach was cold.
_____ e. Tara shrugged her shoulders.
_____ f. Stacey went over and zipped the jacket for Tara.
_____ g. Tara thanked her.

Answers:

a. Yes. It tells where she went and how she went there.
b. No. How does the reader know what she wanted? Just describe what is visible: "She had on a short shirt. She got her jacket from the hook."
c. Yes. These were the exact words.
d. No. This is not a direct quote. Instead, write, "Tara said, 'My belly is cold.'"
e. Yes. Body motion is described.
f. Yes. Action is described.
g. No. This is not a direct quote. Instead, Tara said, "Thank you, my dear."

The Language of Observation

When writing narratives (descriptive observations), there are thousands, perhaps millions, of words from which to choose to convey to the reader exactly what we see. We use various parts of speech, so here's a review of the kinds of words you can use:

Read the following parts of speech and the words listed there and picture how different they are from one another:

Verbs—words that describe actions
walk, march, strut, stroll, tiptoe, clomp
Said—screamed, whispered, demanded, murmured, shouted

Adverbs—an additional descriptive word with a verb

walked softly, marched proudly, strutted confidently, strolled rhythmically, tiptoed quietly, clomped heavily

screamed loudly, whispered softly, demanded gruffly, murmured shyly, shouted joyously

Adjectives—words that describe nouns or names of things

toothy grin, tear-stained face, vigorous head-shake, mournful cry

Tense—word form that conveys present, past, or future time. For accuracy in the timing of the writing to the actual event, the selection of tense makes a difference. When writing an account as it is happening, write in the present tense:

"She runs over to the other child and gives her a big hug."

When writing from recall or briefly jotted notes, write in the past tense:

"She ran over to the other child and gave her a big hug."

Sequence—narratives tell stories and are usually told from beginning to end. Some cultural groups, by tradition, tell stories in other ways. When writing directly from observation, the narrative is told in the order in which it occurs

Observer Bias—interpretation is conveyed by the choice of words. While narrative recording allows less room for bias, the selection of words can subtly suggest the reader's less-than-objective description. Selecting just the right words conveys so much more meaning, but bias can creep in:

"zipped D.'s jacket," not "helped D. zip her jacket"

"jumped and fell," not "was clumsy"

"gave a piece of clay" not "shared the clay"

"eyes widened, mouth open" not "looked surprised"

This may seem like a lot to remember as you are writing down events, but practice and discussion with colleagues for advice will improve your narratives so they are more objective eye-witness accounts of what you saw and heard, conveying the sense of "being there" to the reader.

Learning Stories

Learning stories, another name for Anecdotal Recording adopted from New Zealand early childhood practices, concentrates especially on the children's disposition toward learning (Reisman, 2011). It captures the action and communication, and then adds the observer's comments to make meaning

▶ ❚❚ TEACHSOURCE VIDEO ACTIVITY

Visit the Education CourseMate website, accessed through CengageBrain.com and select an age group to observe.

Watch each segment, writing down OBJECTIVELY and DESCRIPTIVELY the child's actions. Use the principles that you learned from the chapter in the segments noted below.

0–2 Years—Observation Module. When you get to 12 minutes where the toddler is approaching going down stairs, actually write an *Anecdotal Record* of what you are observing. Draw some conclusions about this child's development based on what you observe.

2–5 Years—Observation Module. When you get to the eight minute segment where the girl is crying, write an *Anecdotal Record* of what you are observing. Make some conclusions or ask questions for more information based on what you observe.

School-Age: Cognitive Development. Write an Anecdotal Record of what occurs in this bartering activity trying to capture as much of the direct activity and dialogue as you can. Draw some conclusions about each child's development.

from what is observed and what can come next. The learning story recreates the opportunity for other readers, including the child's family, to reflect on the situation and its meaning. The child himself, when he hears his play episode read back to him, can also give explanations of the processes that took place. What a rich experience in learning this provides for all.

The verbal snapshot of an episode you observe and record can turn into what are called learning stories. People forever have used the oral tradition of telling stories to illustrate a point, teach a lesson, or ponder a truth. Your observations can do those things too. The story is initiated by something that a child or group of children does. It describes what is happening. Then you talk about it with colleagues or the child's family. It can include the application of child development principles to explain the deeper meaning of a common activity, show how an objective or standard is met or a benchmark reached. It can then be a springboard for a discussion of what could come next: additional materials so the child can explore further; a more challenging activity so

Figure 2–3 Examine this photograph and write an imaginary Anecdotal Record.

the child can stretch the learning; or a dialogue with the child about what you saw and what it meant to the child. These activities take a very short observation and turn it into a learning opportunity for all involved.

EXERCISE Look at Figure 2–3. Write an imaginary Anecdotal Recording as if you were there. Remember the technique: description and quotes. Have someone else read your Anecdotal Recording and ask if they can picture exactly what happened from your writing.

What to Write About

It can be as easy as A-B-C. Start with the Antecedent— what was the setting and what took place before the event; the Behavior itself described in detail, not summarized; and the Consequences of the behavior—what was the effect on the child or those around her (Baker and Brightman, 2004). Those new to anecdotal writing may wonder what kinds of incidents or episodes should be captured in an Anecdotal Record (or learning story). The observations should be primarily from the positive, recording "can do" episodes; not from the deficit but from the credit side of the child's behavior. Carr (2001) gives some suggestions (and examples) of structured observation opportunities to look for:

> Finding an interest:
> Things of interest (toys, books, activities)
> Topics of interest (frequent conversations centering around a specific topic)

Cues about individual differences (preference for non-messy activities)
Activity (preferences, length of time in various activities)
Being involved:
Constraints to involvement (reluctant to try new things)
Special rituals that signify safety (props or objects that help involvement such as a toy or special sweater)
Characteristics of activities where children appeared to be involved (with a friend, small group not whole group)
Challenges that keep children going (successful, safe activities such as hand tracing)
Special people (reassurance of adult nearby)
Persisting with difficulty:
Characteristics of uncertainty or difficulty (will try if…)
Ways to assist with challenge (asks for adult help)
Ways to insert challenge or difficulty (next step after mastery of an easier one)
Expressing an idea or a point of view:
The "hundred languages" adapted from Reggio Emilia (various ways children express their ideas in addition to language)
Sequences of difficulty (advances within "language")
Stories that revealed creative approaches (new, creative ways of expression)
Taking responsibility:
Adult–child collaboration on joint tasks (adult and child work together on puzzles)
Peer collaboration on joint tasks (push each other on swing, build a block tower together)
Children taking responsibility for other children's wellbeing (comforting a child in distress)
Children taking responsibility for the program (picking up blocks without coercion)
(Adapted from Carr, 2001, pp. 109–114)

The Ounce Scale (Meisels et al. 2003) is an observational assessment for infants and toddlers from birth to three and a half that reviews developmental background and then provides questions for the observer to answer in six major areas of development. Anecdotal records substantiate checklist items. It is another way that various methods can be combined to give a richer understanding of the child.

EXERCISE Watch a person performing a routine task such as walking to and turning on a light, getting something from a purse, or coming into a room and finding a seat. Write an

Anecdotal Recording so the reader can mentally visualize the exact motions of that person. Have someone else read your recording to determine if it is descriptive and not inferential.

Home Visiting and Anecdotal Recordings

There is no question that home educators spend much fewer hours with children, but the time they do have is focused on a child or a parent-child dyad for at least 30 to 60 minutes per encounter. Having that time to focus on a single child gives ample opportunity to identify actions worthy of recording. Anecdotal Recordings can serve as "stepping stones" for discussion and reflection with parents, helping parents to make associations between the child's point in development and behaviors or actions noted. Anecdotal Recordings could be made into a "booklet" to share with family when they exit the program.

Uses

Anecdotal Recordings can be

- used for preserving details about any developmental skill, behavior, or incident for later judgments and reflection.
- given to other people for their independent evaluations.
- used as an accurate, detailed recording method in suspicion or disclosure of child abuse.

Think About It . . .
What advantages and disadvantages do you see in using an Anecdotal Recording?
Read those that follow and see if you agree.

Advantages

Anecdotal Recordings

- need no special forms.
- are preserved facts and details from which any reader may draw conclusions.
- give a short, contextual account of an incident.
- give the reader a "sense of being there."
- separate judgments or inferences from the details of the incident.
- are useful for recording all areas of development.

- are necessary for capturing exact details for specific purposes such as speech/language development and child abuse disclosure.

Disadvantages

Some of the shortcomings of Anecdotal Recordings include the following:

- Choosing which incidents to record gives the writer selectivity that may influence positive or negative collections.
- Intense writing is necessary to capture all the details, quotes, and body movements.
- Focusing on writing diverts attention from interactions with children.
- The Anecdotal Recording can only focus on a few minutes of action.
- The Anecdotal Recording can only focus on one or two children at a time.

Pitfalls to Avoid

Random selection of children to write about in an anecdotal format presents the same problem as diary entries. There is usually some child performing attention-getting behavior. Other children would never have a focused anecdotal record in their file because they are placid, follow the rules, and rarely draw attention to themselves.

This is overcome by the Week by Week Portfolio plan. It specifies a few children a week as the focus of in-depth recordings. These children are not selected randomly but from a planned numbering system from the alphabetical Class List Log. In addition, the developmental area to be observed is suggested so that the selection of what to write about and when is more objective, and documentation is collected in all developmental areas. With the Week by Week plan, information is gathered on all the children every week in a different developmental area. In addition to that, a more focused observation and recording is done on a specified group of children. Over the course of a year, using the Week by Week plan, each developmental area is revisited at least three times for each child. Also, each child is the focus of at least three Anecdotal Recordings. Visit the Education CourseMate website, accessed through CengageBrain.com, to download the full Week by Week plan. Section D illustrates how the Week by Week plan documents the developmental areas for each child in the class.

You may have difficulty: if you are unable to write fast enough or read your handwriting later;

selecting the descriptive, objective language; or if English is your second language. You may be able to use a small tape recorder (if your voice cannot be heard by anyone else), make extensive notes with your own form of shorthand, or write in your own first language and then rewrite your narrative as soon as possible after the observation (Martin, 2007).

Using Technology

There are various electronic recording devices that may be used to capture events as they are happening that may be faster and more accurate than writing about the incident while it is happening (or shortly thereafter). Cell phones and hand-held computers can record audio and video, as well as text.

Audio Recording. Audio recorders can be useful for capturing the details that will help you write an Anecdotal Recording later. Tape-recorded notes can be transcribed quickly by a fast typist into a computer file. The transcription can be noted on the corresponding developmental area of the electronic Portfolio Evidence Sheet. Printing out the Anecdotal Recording stored in this way also makes it easier for the family or other staff to read.

Video Recording. This is the best way to capture all the details of an incident. Unfortunately, the very advantage—capturing everything—is a disadvantage in that it takes too much time to sift through the material to determine what is mundane and what is important developmental information. It is also difficult to focus the camera on one specific child without the child becoming self-conscious and changing behavior from natural to unnatural. Filtering out background noise and action is also difficult for all but the most experienced videographers. Video recordings can, however, be useful for practicing Anecdotal Recording skills.

Voice Recognition Software. There are inexpensive or even free computer programs that allow your speech to be transferred into electronic text. This makes Anecdotal Recording easier to do and easier to read than handwriting.

Text on a Smart phone. Some people can type text faster than they can write. This may be a very efficient way to preserve anecdotal data and later move it to an electronic Portfolio.

How to Find the Time

Using the recording devices (as discussed above) can save time. Using a voice recognition program (mentioned previously) can also speed the transfer of notes into a detailed account. When you are writing about self-help skills, keep a pad and pen nearby at mealtime, in the cubby area, and in the bathroom; this will enable you to capture those details when they happen.

What to Do with This Information

An Anecdotal Recording preserves specific information that can be used in many ways. It contributes to the overall assessment and evaluation of the child when combined with other information-gathering resources. It is stored in the child's Portfolio (Figure 2–4).

Child's Portfolio. If the incident captured in an Anecdotal Recording involves more than one child, it can be copied and the names of other children blocked out to place in more than one file. Block out names other than the child of this Portfolio. The previous incident could be placed in Sherita's file with Davi's name blocked out. It could be copied for Davi's file with Sherita's name blocked out. In this particular incident, blocking the name may not be necessary, but it does establish a practice of confidentiality. Sometimes it is unpredictable what judgments the reader will make

PORTFOLIO EVIDENCE OF CHILD'S DEVELOPMENT			
Evidence Type	Date	Recorder	Notes
PHYSICAL – the child's large and small muscle development, abilities in self-care routines			
CL	9/14/	BAN	Needs help handwashing
AR	9/19/	MLS	Sings handwashing song

Figure 2–4 Portfolio Evidence Sheet Example.

about the other children involved. The teacher's copy in the Class File preserves all names for reference.

In the Portfolio, this Anecdotal Recording will serve as documentation for judgments made about the child: "Sherita is using words in conversations now (language development) and even helping other children (social development)."

This recording can be compared to earlier incidents: "Compare anecdotal record of 2/13 to those of 9/27, 10/14, and 12/20 to see the progress Sherita has made."

Curriculum Planning. Class activity ideas come from close observations: "I think I'll bring in some clothes with separating zippers for the dramatic play area to give all the children some practice. That sequined vest I got at a garage sale will be a hit."

It can be the basis for making an individual plan: "Sherita is beginning to play near other children. Strategies: Model play and sharing behaviors, connect Sherita with Davi in a cooperative activity, read a book to small group including Sherita, and initiate playmate discussion."

The recorder may decide to further investigate or question a concern: "Listen more closely to Sherita's language and ask the speech pathologist if this is age-appropriate."

Other Teachers on the Team. The recording may be read by others on the team to gather their opinions on the meaning of the incident: "Does this incident seem like unusual behavior for Davi from what you've been seeing?" Seeking the advice of colleagues not responsible for the child is also a way to gain the perspective of an uninvolved professional. Of course, the names would all be blocked out. Without written parental permission, records are not shown to anyone outside the team.

Sharing with Families. If you are a student using this textbook, you should not be sharing information directly with the family. That is the teacher's job. However, students may share their written observations with families if they have been cleared by the teacher in charge of the classroom and perhaps the instructor of the course.

When sharing information with the family, the teacher should always be aware of the program's or school's protocol, especially when suggesting there may be a developmental problem and recommending a referral. Remember, "the child is an extension of the family" and this is a very sensitive area. Suggesting that there might be a problem should not be undertaken without first conferring with a supervisor or thinking through exactly how it should be worded.

Giving the family a copy of the incident provides them with a glimpse into the child's day: "Here's a little incident I wrote down today about Davi getting some help getting ready for outside play. I know you've been working on her manners. She spontaneously said, 'Thank you' and invited the other child to be her friend."

Actions or behavior are recorded descriptively as a way to explain development to the family: "Sherita initiated helping another child today for the first time. I thought you'd like to read about it. We'll be working on helping her develop more ways to play cooperatively."

Factual examples illustrate the teacher's assessment or concern to the family: "Sherita's language seems to be at a younger stage. Here are some examples I tape-recorded. Maybe you'd like to take these to talk with the speech pathologist and see if a full evaluation is recommended."

Conferring with Helping Professionals. With permission from the family, Anecdotal Recordings can be read by helping professionals. This allows people such as the speech and language pathologist, child psychologist, art teacher, and social worker to draw their own conclusions. They evaluate the

REVIEW

ANECDOTAL RECORDING
Detailed incident on one child (others may interact in the incident), including the setting, action/reaction, exact quotes, and result. It should be detailed enough for the reader to "be there."

Types of Information to Record Using Anecdotal Recording
This method is useful for recording any incident, usual or unusual. It can give information on the following:

separation and adjustment
self-care skills
physical development
social development
emotional development
language and speech
attention span and interests
cognitive development
literacy
creativity
sociodramatic play
child abuse observation or disclosure
self-esteem

incident based on their specialized knowledge and area of expertise: "The strategies you've been working on with Sherita in therapy seem to be working. Here's an incident in which she helped another child. What do you think we should do next?"

Talking with the Child. The child can give insight into an incident and also should be aware of the recorder's interest and writing about her actions: "Davi, I wrote down about how Sherita helped you with your jacket today. Then you invited her to be your buddy." The child may respond with an explanation or further conversation.

Evidence to Child Protective Services. An Anecdotal Recording is an acceptable evidence to document a child abuse disclosure. When a child reveals information that may indicate abuse, it is important to accurately write down how the disclosure came about. The record must contain the exact questions and comments of the adult and the child. Behavioral or visual indicators may raise suspicions of abuse. The Anecdotal Recording preserves details and factual descriptions without conclusions or judgments. Read more about this in Chapter 13.

Go to the Education CourseMate website, accessed through CengageBrain.com for copies of the form and plans in this chapter, and more information about Anecdotal Recording.

Looking at Self-Care Skills

EXERCISE **On a separate sheet of paper, list the things you do for yourself that give you pride; for example, changing a tire, programming the DVD recorder, cruising the Internet.**

"I can do it myself!" Those words spoken, sometimes defiantly, stand as a declaration of independence or a statement proclaiming a milestone accomplishment. Why are a child's **self-care** (sometimes called self-help) skills important, other than to free the adult from tasks previously done for the child? The accomplishment of taking care of one's own needs is a progression throughout childhood. Maria Montessori said, "Little children, from the moment they are weaned, are making their way toward independence (Montessori, Holmes, 1912)." It can be viewed as **development**, moving from simple to complex tasks in an orderly, predictable sequence, but at an individual rate for each person. The sequences of self-care skills incorporate many other components of developmental areas and contribute to self-worth and competency. The observer can assess, facilitate, and celebrate those accomplishments (Figure 2–5).

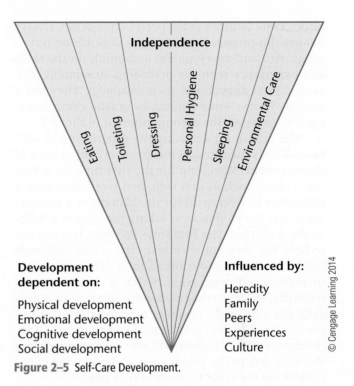

Figure 2–5 Self-Care Development.

The self-care skills are closely allied to the self-care activities that are affected by separation anxiety such as eating, sleeping, personal hygiene, and toileting. This is probably because they are the tasks a parent does for a child. These are the most tenuous when the parent is no longer present. For the youngest child, they are the basis of survival and comfort. They become common elements in different environments for the older child. They are actions that are expected responsibilities of the caregiver, routines that can be sources of observation and development assessment, and the basis for curricula planning.

It is important to note here, and later in the chapter, that self-help skills and the quest for independence may bring cultural dissonance. The practices of eating, toileting, and sleeping are steeped in cultural and even family differences that may bring families of young children in conflict with teachers, caregivers, and a program's policies and practices. Conflicts can be reduced by knowledge, sensitivity, and communication regarding these practices, especially upon enrollment, but also in the everyday interactions between program staff and families.

Development of Self-Care Skills

Each self-care skill follows a sequential path of development, beginning in a limited, crude way, but broadening and building upon prior experiences. Babies suck before they chew, eat with their fingers before they use a spoon, spoon before fork, fork before knife, knife before potato peeler. This series always follows this progression because it depends on physical growth and development and builds on the skills and experience with the preceding attainment. The skills do not appear and then disappear. They last a lifetime unless some trauma or drastic event interrupts or prevents the accomplishment of the task.

The reason for knowing the progression of self-care skills is the same as it is for every other area of development. Watching for the first time an action takes place, such as first step, first word, first time a child goes to sleep without the blankie, is a reassurance that development is taking place. It is a milestone, a marker. The first time the baby reaches out to hold her own bottle or takes the spoon and feeds herself is a momentous occasion. It demonstrates an increasing self-responsibility that is an indicator of maturity. Besides recognizing the mastery of a new skill, the adult then provides practice and more opportunities for the child to perform that task independently. The caregiver will also be looking toward the next task in the progression and providing experiences for the child to attempt that task.

Once the child has mastered the spoon, the family introduces a little fork and demonstrates the stabbing motion that differentiates a fork from a spoon. This is planning curriculum based on developmental level. The teacher sees that one child is ready for this at 10 months. Another is still working on the spoon at 12 months. This is individualizing the curriculum, developmental education. Families and teachers do it all the time without realizing it.

Self-Care and Autonomy

EXERCISE **At what point did you feel independent of your family? List the milestones toward that accomplishment.**

Autonomy, the process of governing oneself and providing for one's own needs is the goal of childhood. For twenty-first-century children, that seems to be a very long process. The human infant is born totally helpless, but by one-and-a-half years, he is mobile and wanting to do more things for himself. Teachers still need to be protective and restrictive while allowing the child opportunities to begin to be more independent. Erikson (1963) describes this conflict as Autonomy versus Shame and Doubt. To develop autonomy, children need both ability and opportunity. Ability is readiness. A child who has not yet developed small-muscle skills cannot be expected to manage buttons and zippers on clothing. While they want

It Happened to Me

Children Need Help Sometimes

I was observing in a progressive early childhood program where independence was a founding principle. Children served themselves snacks and meals when they were hungry, played inside or outside by choice, napped when they felt tired, and generally went through the day without routines or schedules. I was walking around amazed at how children were spending long periods of time at activities of their choice when I heard a sound from the bathroom. I walked by and saw a little one about 18 months old trying to change messy pants. Unfortunately, the job called for extensive clean-up of clothing, body, and eventually the floor and sink. When I called attention of the teacher to the situation, she indicated that the child should be allowed to do it independently. It didn't seem to me that the child had the physical skills to do so, nor was the inadequate clean-up hygienic for the rest of the children. This is where their ideology and mine collided.

to dress themselves, or more likely undress themselves, their lack of physical coordination may prevent them from doing so. The other aspect of autonomy is opportunity. When a child is never allowed to feed herself because she makes a mess, or to wash his own hands because he doesn't do it thoroughly, the child will be dependent longer.

Autonomy is related to **individualists** whose cultural value is independence. Developing self-help skills at an early age is promoted as an expectation.

Gonzalez-Mena (2008) raises some important questions about the cultural contrasts of individualists and collectivists. **Collectivists** have come from a tradition or political system where the individual is devalued and the focus is on the group and interdependence. This sees self-help skills as less important than helping others. Collectivists value modesty over self-esteem and humbleness over achievement. In many cultures, feeding, dressing, and bathing the child long after the child is physically capable of doing it herself is seen as a demonstration of love, caring, and good parenting. In the routines of the early childhood classroom, these two perspectives contrast with each other. The role of the teacher and the program is to be aware and sensitive to cultural perspectives in the

TOPICS in OBSERVATION

Using All of Our Senses

EXERCISE Using a separate piece of paper, make a list of what you can observe about a child from senses other than seeing:

hearing   touching

smelling   tasting

The word observe is understood to use sight as the primary source of taking in information; however, all senses are receptors of information on which to base decisions.

Seeing

Visually, information is gathered on the child's physical appearance, actions, and reactions. From all those visual cues, inferences are made regarding the child. See Figure 2–6 for some examples.

body appearance—physical growth and development, health, delays, physical limitations, racial or ethnic group

clothing, hairstyle, hygiene—socioeconomic level, family style and care

activity level and body movements—emotional state, aggressiveness, health

approach to play, work, other people—self-esteem, learning style, cognitive level and style, role models

Hearing

The adult attunes to the message being communicated, from the first "coos" to intricate stories recounted with sound effects and voice. Many areas of development can be assessed from listening.

emotional state—laughter, crying, whining, teasing, anger, silence

cognitive development—vocabulary, content, grammar, problem-solving strategies, humor, storybook characters

physical development—formation of teeth, tongue, and jaw

health—nasal or bronchial congestion, wheezing, possible hearing difficulties affecting speech, digestive sounds

family—home language, activities, siblings, other family members, other significant people in the child's life, television and video usage

sociability—play stage, themes, playmates, leadership

Visual Cues	Inferences
Height, weight, body proportions, coordination, glasses, brace on leg, hearing aid	Physical growth and development, health, developmental delays, physical limitations
Skin color, hair color, eye shape	Racial or ethnic group, health, cosmetic use
Clothing, hairstyle, hygiene	Socioeconomic level, family style and care
Activity level	Emotional state, health factors
Facial expressions and body language	Emotional states, attention, interest
Playmates, interactions	Social stage, personality, sexual preference of playmates, aggressiveness
Approach to play, work, other people	Self-esteem, learning style, cognitive level and style
Mannerisms	Role models—family, TV characters, other children
Evidence of injury	Accident, surgery, abuse

Figure 2–6 Visual cues may lead one to make inferences about children.

© Cengage Learning 2014

(Continued)

TOPICS in OBSERVATION   *(Continued)*

Touching

Some information may not be apparent to sight or sound. The reaction to an adult's soft touch might seem unusual, giving rise to conjecture about the origin of that response.

muscle tone—firm muscle tissue, eating disorders, and some diseases

illness—fever, rashes, cold, clammy skin

stress—tension in the body, trembling, goose bumps

injury—swelling, reaction to touch indicating a tenderness

response to touch—cuddle, withdrawal, rigid

Smelling

Smelling gives the keen observer clues about

hygiene—cleanliness, tooth decay, bed wetting

illness—respiratory infections, chronic allergies or sinus conditions, diseases such as diabetes that may give off a sweet odor

home odors—smoking, seasonings, animals, perfume

safety—ingestion of a poisonous substance

Tasting

Taste probably would not be used to gather information on the child.

The "Sixth Sense"

The observer should pay attention to instinctual, or "gut" feelings. Sometimes there is something about a child sensed not by eyes, ears, nose, or touch, but by a feeling. Professionals must rely on substantive information; often this heightened awareness is not to be used as a measurement, but as an indicator that hard evidence needs to be gathered. The keen observer uses all senses to gather information. The knowledge of child development is applied, using multiple methods of documentation of the observations. All of this information gathering is used to benefit the child and the program.

It Happened to Me

Smelly Clues

A colleague relates that she worked with a student in remedial reading instruction who also had a history of learning difficulties and classroom disruptions. He smelled of nasal congestion. The family was assisted in getting a medical evaluation for him. Tubes in his ears remedied the problem, and he was transformed as a student. All because of a smelling observation!

self-help skills area, and to act and plan in such a way to support the values of each child's home culture.

Older preschoolers and school-age children in what Erikson (1963) calls the Initiative and Industry stages want to take on adult-like activities and are competent and confident in mastering skills and acting independently.

When to Help and When Not To

There is always a fine line between giving assistance and being manipulated. "Never help a child with a task at which he feels he can succeed" is good advice. When a child has the small muscle skill to perform self-help skills, she should be encouraged and allowed to do it. When she is in a hurry, not feeling well, or is getting increasingly frustrated, a helping hand is needed. However, some children who can, won't. There may be many reasons for what is sometimes called **learned helplessness.** This may be due to family interactions with the child, including older siblings, treating the child as a baby, or making her feel incompetent. On the other extreme, impossibly high standards that the child feels unable to reach may cause her to give up in futility. Some teachers fall into the trap of over-caring for the dependent child so that it becomes a habit. Sometimes children themselves will overdo for another child whom they perceive as needy or younger. This sometimes happens when a child with a special need is in the classroom. While we want to encourage caring for one another, both adults and children should help each individual feel competent and confident.

Children who have had no experience of success in becoming independent have a fundamental lack of confidence in their own self-worth. In Miseducation: Preschoolers at Risk (2000), David Elkind gives the following practical advice: "Children are just learning these skills, so it is important not to force them. . . . The important thing, as I have tried to suggest, is to find a healthy middle ground between doing everything for children and doing nothing for them and expecting them to cope with the adult-sized world" (p. 111).

Self-Care Skills in the Curriculum

By observing with the developmental progression in mind, observations become assessments and tools for planning curriculum. The area of self-care is not always recognized as a curriculum. It is taken for granted, probably because it develops so naturally. Early childhood environments can support competent self-care skills through

> appropriate expectations for the task, age, and individual child's abilities.
> appropriate sizes of furnishings.
> clear expressions of expectations to the child.

Occupational therapists often work with young children on these tasks. Upon consideration, taking care of one's own body functions involves many areas of development and contributes not only to physical but also emotional wellbeing. Both muscle strength and coordination are necessary for these tasks. A great many thinking processes are involved in each skill, beginning with body awareness of the cues of hunger, tiredness, need to eliminate, and feeling cold or hot. The

connections between past experiences build and form new thinking patterns.

Certainly, self-care skills are necessary for social acceptance. It is part of that whole realm of manners and out-in-public actions. These are learned by observing and imitating role models and from direct instruction. The learning depends on the child's desire to be accepted and liked. There is a feeling of accomplishment and increased self-esteem when one can do something independently, without assistance. Following surgery or an illness, people report how good it feels just to be able to brush their own teeth or go up a few steps. Those actions become so natural, done without thinking or appreciating their complexity. In childhood, they are skills to learn, moving from basic to complex levels.

Individual differences are significant in self-care skills. Predictability of body rhythmicity is seen dramatically in the Thomas and Chess (1977, 1980) longitudinal studies. The studies indicated that feeding, elimination, and sleeping patterns at 2 months were consistent or at least similar at 10 years old. In addition to physical differences, social, racial, and cultural influences, as well as birth order may affect self-care development. Lynch and Hanson (2011) warn, "Expectations for children concerning feeding, sleeping socializing, and speaking, as well as the use of discipline, to mention only a few may vary widely across cultural groups" (p. 11). The book reviews many different cultural beliefs important for teachers to know. Information on the child's self-care skills can be gathered from families and observed in the natural routines of the day in the group setting. These are part of the developmental process, so the observer realizes that each child attains these milestones on an individual timetable (Figure 2–7).

Observing Self-Care Skills

Self-care skills are points of observing and recording used to recognize milestones, plot and share progress, and plan curriculum. The normal progression of the self-help skills of dressing, feeding, toileting and washing, and general is illustrated in Figure 2–7.

Eating. In infancy, the adult is the source of nourishment to the child, whether by breast or by bottle. The infant depends on the adult to provide the acceptable food at regular times and as the infant gives signals of hunger. Reflex actions of rooting (turning toward the cheek that is touched) and sucking once the nipple is

	Dressing	Feeding	Toileting and Washing	General
1 to 2 years	Removes socks Tries to put on shoes Raises arms to put on shirt or coat	Lifts cup to mouth Feeds self with fingers then spoon Hands empty dish to adult	Wipes face with napkin or towel Rinses hands under water and dries Gives indicators of elimination in diaper	Remembers where things are kept in house Use pail or container to carry things Climbs to reach things
2 to 3 years	Can make clothes off to put on other articles of clothing but tries easily and gives up. Generally cooperative when helped.	Can use a fork, but still prefers spoon or fingers. Will feed self preferred food. Drinks from glass.	Verbalizes toilet needs in advance. Retention span for urination lengthening—can "hold" longer.	Can open some doors with easy or low knobs
3 to 4 years	Undresses self. Can put on most articles of clothing and can manipulate buttons and zippers, depending upon their size and place. Can put clothes away in drawers or hang them up given right height hooks.	Usually eats with fork. Can pour from pitcher into glass with few mishaps. Enjoys eating with family but dawdle.	May insist on washing self in tub but does it imperfectly. Very few toilet accidents. Often wakes up at night and asks to be taken to toilet.	Can tell own age, sex, and first and last name. Can follow two- and three-step directions. Able to stay at preschool without parent.
4 to 5 years	Laces shoes: some children learning to tie. Dresses and undresses with little or no assistance, especially if clothes are laid out. May dawdle excessively over dressing. Can tell front from back but still have trouble getting some garments on properly.	Uses fork and spoon appropriately often needs help to eat "tough" meat. Likes to "make" own breakfast and lunches (dry cereal, peanut butter sandwiches)	Can handle and dry self, at least partially. Can perform toileting hand washing and drying, May forget sometimes.	Plays with peers with less supervision. Can put toys away but usually needs reminding. Can help with many household chores set table, empty trash, feed pets. May "forget" some steps.
5 to 6 years	Ties own shoes. Can manage almost any article of clothing. Can assist younger brother or sister in getting dressed.	Can use all eating utensils but is sometimes messy. Aware of appropriate table manners but tends to forget them.	Bathes and dries self with minimal supervision. Usually does not wash own hair but may help. Totally self-sufficient in toilet routine.	Can make own bed. Put soiled clothes in hamper. Learning to distinguish left from right.
7 to 8 years	Taking more interest in clothing selection and appearance.	Interested in foods and cooking, Uses table manners in public.	Complete bowel and bladder control but stress may interfere. Bathing & washing are tolerated but not thorough.	Can take personal responsibility for room and pets but may be intermittent.

Figure 2–7 Examples of self-help skills for various age groups.

Source: Adapted from Allen/Cowdery. *The Exceptional Child*, 6th ed. © 2009 Wadsworth, a part of Cengage Learning, Inc. Reproduced by permission.

felt on the lips are built-in muscle responses. They enable the infant to receive nourishment. By three or four months, the baby will begin to recognize the breast or bottle, reach for it, and hold it firmly. In another month, the baby begins to push it away when full. By six months, the pincer grasp of thumb and forefinger enables the baby to indiscriminately pick up small food items (and fuzz balls) and get them into the mouth. This means the teacher must give extra caution to the cleanliness of the environment. The teacher must be vigilant regarding small ingestible and indigestible items. Soon the teacher will begin to give the baby the opportunity to eat small bits of appropriate food items while the child is securely strapped in a high chair or infant seat.

By one year, she begins to display likes and dislikes of foods by their appearance or a single taste. As language explodes in the second year, she can recognize and name many foods. The sorting skills of the three- and four-year-old transfer into food groups, beginning with likes and dislikes. Eventually, she can classify meat, vegetables, fruits, drinks, and breads. She is learning the names for the individual items based on visual and aromatic cues.

In the second year, the child begins to assert independence by grabbing the spoon, the bottle, or the cracker. He now has the small motor skills to get them to his mouth fairly accurately, and he has teeth to chew. Three- and four-year-olds gain skill at using utensils: spoon first, then the fork, then the knife. They should be given the opportunity to practice under supervision (Figure 2–8). Gentle reminders and pointers for using the silverware effectively are given. These children can pour efficiently if the pitcher is lightweight and clear, and also they can see the liquid approaching the spout. It helps if the glass or paper cup has a fill line for a visual cue to stop pouring. It helps to place the glass on a tray to catch "over pours" until control is gained.

By late four and early five years, children have the physical mobility and manual dexterity to help themselves to food as it is passed. They love to assist in the preparation of peeling foods with proper utensils and supervision. They can set the table, fold napkins, clear the table, and be quite helpful in the whole mealtime routine. By the time children are in school, they have mastered eating skills, if not manners. Eating in a large, noisy cafeteria can be disturbing to children and may take some adjustment. Teachers should do what they can to promote a social, stress-free atmosphere. Good nutrition is important to learning, so many schools have a breakfast program and some even have weekend meal programs. Teaching healthy eating is a part of the health curriculum and has become a part of the national agenda to address childhood obesity.

Learning and language connected with eating begins with the recognition of food sources, such as the breast or bottle. Accompanying vocabulary is built as the teacher says, "Here comes the baba, baby hungry?" The creeper finds tidbits on the floor, but her ability to discriminate between food and nonfood items is not developed, possibly placing her in danger.

Culture and eating—Every culture has its wonderful food traditions, but the feeding of infants and young children may have differences beyond the taste and preparation of foods. The family and teachers are role models for development of eating behaviors such as acceptance of new foods which sometimes takes 10 to 15 years (Savage 2007). Food choices, restrictions, mealtime conversations, pressures to eat or not eat, and foods served as a reward all are a part of the culture of

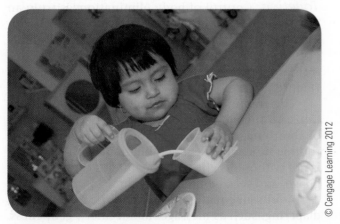

© Cengage Learning 2012

Figure 2–8 Pouring takes physical skills, concentration, and patience.

It Happened to Me

Impatience with Pancakes

We were making pancakes in the preschool room, and our foster grandparent was helping the children pour the batter and flip the pancakes. Each child struggled as they carefully slid the spatula under the pancake and at the crucial moment flipped it over, hopefully in approximately the same place it had been on the pan. It was a tedious process, sometimes requiring several tries before each pancake was flipped successfully. Grandma's patience was at its limit. As the umpteenth child tried to flip the pancake, she grabbed the spatula and said, "Oh @$#$, just let me do it!"

eating (Eliassen, 2011). Self-feeding, food exploration, food consumption, and uses of food as art materials are highly charged issues. The program's feeding practices should try to coordinate the family's and the program's goals through discussions and flexibility.

We often feel that way; we can do it faster and more efficiently, but children need to try in order to succeed. No place is that seen so dramatically as in self-help skills. Sitting at a table that fits them, serving and passing foods, and interacting with peers and adults in pleasant conversation teaches many social lessons. Children develop their taste for new foods in the first six years, so providing a variety of nutritious foods from which to choose influences their attitudes toward nutrition.

Think About It . . .

What table rules did you learn as a child? How did you learn them?

The social-emotional aspects of eating are lessons that are learned early. The aura of mealtime lasts a lifetime. It may be a relaxed, social gathering or a tense, emotion-laden time of restrictions and prohibitions. Adults are responsible for the physical environment of cleanliness, safety, appropriateness of menu, cognitive connections, and language and vocabulary expansion. They are modeling table

It Happened to Me

Bad Example

I was observing in a child-care center at morning snack time. Some of the children had been doing puzzles and playing with clay at the table, while others had been painting, stacking with blocks, shoveling sand, and looking at books. The teacher rattled a box of sweet cereal puffs, and the children came running to sit at the table. She stood behind each child, scooped up a handful of cereal from the box and placed it on the bare table in front of each one. She poured juice from a can into paper cups and set them in front of each child. She said, "OK, eat, and no spilling." She stepped away from the table and ate a candy bar from her pocket.

manners and providing an emotional atmosphere where psychological safety and individualism are recognized.

When children participate to their ability in the preparation of the meal or a particular dish, it builds the feeling of competency. Children learn a lot from measuring, stirring, cutting, and spreading, which enhance small muscle skills. Of course it takes more time and patience, but its importance is in the learning process that is taking place.

Children learn they are trusted when they are given autonomy over choices among healthy foods. By participating in food preparation, serving, and self-feeding, they feel competent. When they interact with others during mealtime, they learn skills that they will be using around the table the rest of their lives. Because eating disorders are beginning as early as ages three and four, close attention should be given to mealtimes and the emotions involved.

In the standards pertaining to nutrition and food service described in *Caring for Our Children: National Health and Safety Performance Standards: Guidelines for Out-of-Home Child Care* (American Academy of Pediatrics, 2011) Standard 4.3, toddlers are encouraged in self-feeding; mealtimes are conducted in a relaxed atmosphere with furnishings, utensils, and servings all aimed at promoting independence and social skills. School breakfast and lunch programs provide basic nutrition, but many lack adult conversation, modeling, or direct instruction in table manners or social behavior.

Think About It . . .

"It Happened to Me: Bad Example" is a true Anecdotal Recording, unfortunately! What was wrong with the teacher's practices?

Toileting. Control of body eliminations is truly an illustration of development: from no control with only reflex actions, through the steps dependent on physical growth, to a complex set of controls and releases dependent on many other factors (Figure 2–9).

The infant has no control over body eliminations, so the adult performs all the necessary tasks of absorbing, catching, cleaning, and diapering. This routine function, like any other done with an infant, is not without its effect on the infant's cognitive, language, and social-emotional realm.

Adults give many messages to the infant during diapering, such as messages about safety, gentleness,

Remembers to flush and wash hands

Uses toilet unassisted

Uses toilet with reminding

Verbalizes toilet need fairly consistently

Dry at night if taken up

Indicates need for bowel movement on toilet

Indicates soiled diaper

Usually dry after nap

Fusses to be changed

© Cengage Learning 2014

Figure 2–9 Toileting Development.

hygiene, acceptance of body elimination, and sexual attitudes. When a teacher expresses unpleasantness at the task by a facial expression of disgust, or verbally such as saying "Yucky," the infant confuses the message. He does not know it is the task, and not him, that is the cause of the unpleasant facial expressions and expressive language.

EXERCISE Ask a parent to recount a toilet-training story (everyone has at least one), and write it down as it is told. Use the criteria for an Anecdotal Recording.

Usually children are well into their second year before they begin to recognize the body signals of an impending bowel movement and, even later, the need to urinate. The physical growth of muscles is occurring, along with the mental attention to body signals. Unfortunately, it is at a time when there is a strong desire to gain more control of the world. In this battle to control the body, the child and the adult are often at opposite poles, making toilet training a chore many adults dread. The struggle can be eased by recognizing the turmoil going on inside the child. She is given control, since the adult cannot control it anyway. Kinnell's practical book *Good Going!* (2004) gives this advice: "It is annoying to have to clean up the child and wash all the clothes, but it is a part of the learning process for the child. Fighting the inevitable accidents or punishing the child for them will certainly slow the process" (p. 13). Curriculum for this area is in environment preparation, positive role models, and sometimes, direct instruction. Even school-age children have occasional accidents that can cause them embarrassment. These should be handled sensitively. Frequent toileting accidents in a school-age child may be indicators of health or emotional difficulties, and the child should be referred to the school nurse.

Environment. The adult's role is to provide an environment that encourages the desired action: potty chair, steps to the toilet, child-sized toilet seat, books, pictures, pleasant room decor. The bathroom often is overlooked as a place where learning occurs. Interesting pictures at the side and back of the toilet give "goers" thought-provoking visual aids. Of course, visual reminders of hand washing will link toileting with personal hygiene.

EXERCISE Toileting is an emotionally charged subject for child and adult. Finish these reflective statements:

The most uncomfortable part for me about working with children surrounding toileting is . . .
I think it is because . . .
Maybe it would be better if I . . .

It Happened to Me

Am I Clean?

This happened to a friend of mine: In a four-year-old class, a child had gone to the bathroom while they were having snack. She waddled back from the bathroom with her pants around her ankles, turned around, bent over, and looking through her legs yelled, "Am I clean?" "Yes, you're clean. Good job wiping," said the teacher matter-of-factly. The girl returned to the bathroom, dressed, washed her hands, and returned to snack. This is an example of an anecdotal record that uses objective, descriptive language. The reader can "see" it.

Role Models. Toileting is sometimes aided by the social aspect in group care because of the child's natural imitative nature. When one child uses the toilet, others will want to do it also. When a child is praised for potty use, it is likely to occur again and again and eventually become a routine.

Direct Instruction. Some children may need to be taught proper use of the toilet and toilet paper. This is best accomplished on an anatomically correct doll. Teachers should avoid performing this task on a child in an enclosed bathroom stall. For children still needing assistance, stalls are without doors or the task is performed with the door propped open. This is a precaution against possible child abuse allegations.

As the child is expanding her vocabulary, a consideration of which words to use for body elimination functions should be explored so that families and teachers attain consistency. This also gives a positive rather than negative connotation to the function. The struggle over toilet training is an emotionally and culturally sensitive topic that is enhanced by the teacher's partnership with the family and the child. Lynch and Hanson (2011) give the reminder that "in the United States, toilet training between the child's second and third birthday is a common practice and is highly valued by many families. However, this practice may be viewed by many other cultural groups as unnecessary and too early" (p. 11).

Culture and Toilet Training. Here is another issue that has cultural differences and is emotionally charged. Cultures have different ways of toilet training. Even within the American culture there are differences, with some families stressing getting babies out of diapers at a very early age and others tending to wait until the child displays signs of "readiness." In many cultures, as described by Small (2005), babies are allowed to be bare-bottomed and to eliminate at will. Probably that is not a practice that could be followed in child-care settings, but the interaction between the adult and the child in regard to potty training can be an area of conflict, not only because of ethnic cultures, but also because of family cultures and practices. Time allotted to toilet training is a factor when children are cared for in groups. A negotiation between the caregiver, the family, and the child is necessary to address the needs of all. Education, communication, and trust can assist in a mutual solution.

Think About It . . .

What does "It Happened to Me: Am I Clean?" tell you about the child's stage of development? Home influence? The teacher?

Dressing. It is always easier to knock down a building than to build it, delete a page of type than write it, and criticize than praise. So it is with dressing—the first step in self-care is taking clothing off. Parents have all experienced, at least once, the shock of a stark-naked child appearing when they were just fully clothed a few minutes before. Dressing is a developmental progression of skills (Figure 2–10).

Children can be given the power to take off the articles of clothing they can manage. By the time they are two or three years old, they can take off their shoes at naptime, their hat after coming in from outside play, and all their clothes at bath time. They should do what they can do. By selecting clothing that children can manage themselves, such as boxer pants, the child finds the task much easier—easier than a one-piece jumpsuit or buttons up the back of a dress.

EXERCISE **Make a list of clothing fasteners that are difficult even for adults. How could they have been designed differently?**

Teachers can add play items with buttons, snaps, zippers, and ties to the curriculum to encourage practice of those skills. It is always amazing how a child can squeeze into a leotard and tutu over a pair of jeans and a sweatshirt and sneakers. If they want

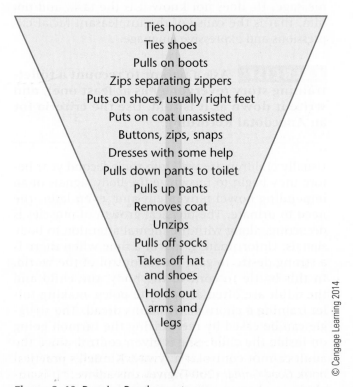

Ties hood
Ties shoes
Pulls on boots
Zips separating zippers
Puts on shoes, usually right feet
Puts on coat unassisted
Buttons, zips, snaps
Dresses with some help
Pulls down pants to toilet
Pulls up pants
Removes coat
Unzips
Pulls off socks
Takes off hat and shoes
Holds out arms and legs

Figure 2–10 Dressing Development.

Figure 2–11 Dress-up clothes give practice in buttoning, zipping, and tying.

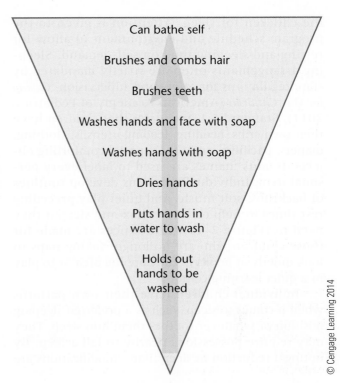

Can bathe self

Brushes and combs hair

Brushes teeth

Washes hands and face with soap

Washes hands with soap

Dries hands

Puts hands in water to wash

Holds out hands to be washed

Figure 2–12 Personal Hygiene Skill Development.

it on, they will find a way. Inviting dress-up props stimulate interest and practice skills (Figure 2–11).

When helping a child after toileting or getting ready to go outside, the child should be assisted with what they cannot do and encouraged to do what they can. The adult can pull up the pants and let the child pull up the suspenders. The teacher can start the separating zipper and let her finish it or finish tying the bow after she has crossed the ties. Remember: Never do for children what they can do for themselves. School-age children take more of an interest in selecting their own clothes but are often careless about hanging up jackets and keeping track of belongings.

Personal Hygiene. Body cleanliness and care of the infant is, of course, the sole responsibility of the adult (Figure 2–12). It is a physical function that is building associations in the infant between certain events. "They change my diaper and wash my body and hands." "They set me in the high chair, wash my hands, and then give me food." "They take me away from the table and wash my face and hands." In the first year, these associations are being made. In the second year, when the child gains mobility and small muscle control, he can go to the sink, which is adapted so she can reach it, and wash her hands. He is taught to do this after going to the toilet or wiping her nose, or before eating. He can manage to turn on the water, wash, dry, and go on with play. In the fourth and fifth years, small muscle control is more developed. The child can now efficiently handle combing hair, brushing teeth, and bathing in the tub with supervision.

Recognition of the need for washing is a difficult lesson for young children to learn because of the "invisibility" of germs. They are concrete thinkers. When they look at their hands and see no dirt, they find it incomprehensible that they should wash, especially if they did it once that day already. Social acceptance and cognitive bridging reinforce personal hygiene habits until the child is into the elementary school years when microscopic particles are understood.

By the time children are school age, they are competent, if not thorough, in personal hygiene. They may need reminders about hand washing after toileting and before eating and step-by-step instruction on procedures to wash away soil and germs. Lessons on cleanliness and care of their appearance are a part of a social studies and health curriculum.

Sleeping. Sleep needs and patterns are individual, but follow a developmental pattern. Individual differences are seen in the amount of sleep children need, how they get to sleep, how soundly they sleep, and their usual waking-up routines.

Children in group care tend to be overstimulated because of many available playmates and play things. This is lessened by stress reduction throughout the day and by planning for smooth transitions, as well as by alternating active and quiet activity choices. Prior to nap time, consistent routines such as mealtime, teeth brushing, and listening to music or a story help prepare the children for sleep. Attention is given to the program schedule and environment to allow for resting and sleeping time on self-demand. Sleeping arrangements often are strictly mandated by state regulations for safety and supervision. *Caring for Our Children* (American Academy of Pediatrics, 2011), Standard 5.1, mandates that children have their own cribs, bedding, feeding utensils, clothing, diapers, pacifiers, and other special comforting objects. Infants' names are used to label every personal item. Individual programs develop routines of backrubs, soft music, and quiet play preceding rest times to help children relax and sleep if they need to (Figure 2–13). Allowances are made for those children who are no longer taking naps to look quietly at books in the napping area or to play in a quiet learning center.

Individual children have their own patterns when it comes to sleep, such as a preferred sleeping position or whatever soothes them into sleep. They may require possessions nearby to fall asleep. By noting a reduction in sleep times, modifications are made for the child who no longer requires a nap. Communication of daily sleep patterns between home and school assists both the family and the center in meeting the needs of the child.

Family and staff daily reports are used in most centers to convey this type of information at arrival and departure times. Sharing "what works" benefits the child at home and at the center.

School-age children's sleep habits can directly affect their ability to pay attention and participate in learning. Discussions about general health and the part that rest and sleep play in wellbeing are a part of the health and science curriculum.

Care for the Classroom

Caring for the classroom environment is another area of development.

EXERCISE **Observe the room you are in. What are the items in the room (or the arrangement of items) that encourage self-care? (Examples: "Wastebasket available" or "Paper towels at child-level.")**

Some observable signs of a child's participation in classroom care are
- selects toys for play
- puts a toy back in its place
- plays actively without adult leadership
- follows classroom routines
- cleans up spills
- helps prepare for activity
- can carry breakable objects
- performs "job chart" tasks
- demonstrates safety awareness
- assists another child to do a task

While an occasional newspaper story may highlight a young child's extraordinary competence in an emergency, there have been just as many horror stories of children left alone at a very young age, most with dire results. Some of these children are caring for even younger siblings, and often there are tragedies. The concept of self-care is not meant to hurry the child along to independence before he is ready, but rather to allow him the freedom and responsibility for self-care. This is done in small, manageable steps that build confidence and competency. Children eventually develop the ability to make safe self-care decisions. The age varies for the individual child when she can be allowed to play unattended in a room at home, go down the street alone, and eventually stay at home alone for a short time. It also is affected by the home setting, the

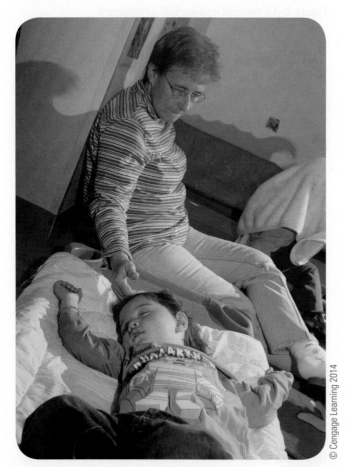

© Cengage Learning 2014

Figure 2–13 Allowances should be made for children's individual sleeping patterns.

neighborhood, and prior experiences. There should be a history of smaller, successful instances of self-care. Parents are in the business of working themselves out of a job and building into the child the competencies for self-care. It is done one day at a time.

Many classrooms and home environments use job charts for daily responsibilities. This is an organized way to ensure care of the environment. It also teaches that each person must do a part for the good of the group (Figure 2–14).

In the classroom as well, children become competent in self-care as they learn the routines. They can meet realistic expectations for cleaning up after themselves and should be given responsibilities for themselves and others. There are children who are so averse to cleaning up that they are reluctant to play with anything, so they do not have to put anything

away. Clean-up time is easier with the aid of effective transitions. These begin with a warning that playtime is almost over, which helps prepare children to end play and begin to pick up. Little ritual songs or signals, such as music or a bell, work better than an adult yelling, "Pick-up time!" See Figure 2–15. There are many resources for the teacher to assist in smoother transitions. (See Resources, Smith & Smith, 2006.)

Adults can make pick-up time fun by using child-sized brooms, small vacuum cleaners, and toy trucks to transport toys back to their clearly labeled places. Adults can also give children appropriate choices: "Are you going to pick up the blocks or the dolls?" Even when the children played with neither of these choices, this reinforces group participation in taking care of the classroom and initiates the concept of environmental responsibility.

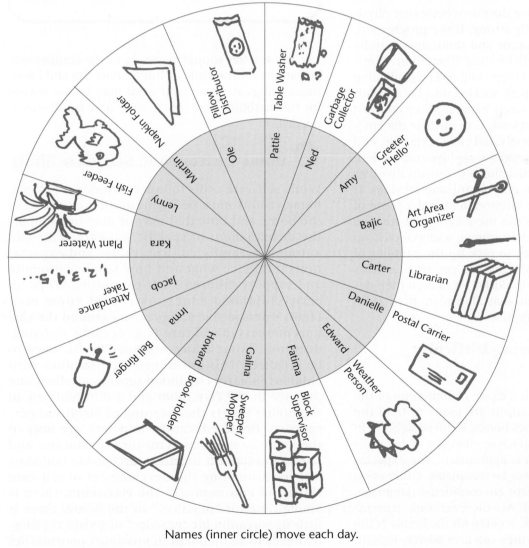

Names (inner circle) move each day.

Figure 2–14 Job Chart. (Reprinted with permission from Carol Fuller, Conklin Presbyterian Preschool, Conklin, NY.)

© Cengage Learning 2014

Pick up, pick up.
Everybody do your share.
Pick up, pick up.
Pick up everywhere.
To the traditional "Today Is Monday" tune:
It's time to pick up.
It's time to pick up.
Mary's picking up blocks.
Jack's sweeping sand.
Tania's finishing her painting.
Soon it will be snack.

Figure 2–15 Pick-up songs help make an orderly environment everyone's responsibility.

The Importance of Self-Care

Children who can care for their own bodies are physically and psychologically strong. It is a progression, though relapses may occur and reminders may be needed. There will likely be some frustration. Families sometimes wonder if their child will be graduating from high school in diapers, sucking on a bottle, with zippers unzipped. That rarely happens; they do learn along the way. The adult's role is to mediate the environment to be child friendly and child accessible, and to provide realistic expectations, positive role models, and direct, specific instructions. Clean-up involves classification, seriation, and organizational skills. It builds a respect for the environment and a sense of responsibility. Teachers can use a variety of creative clean-up strategies, such as singing a special pick-up song, games, challenges to pick up the number of blocks to equal the child's age ("Oh, you are four years old, you can pick up four blocks"). Children then develop these self-care skills that allow them to be independent and socially accepted.

If the Child Is Having Difficulty with Self-Care

The teacher begins with a closer examination of the environment. Modifications are made to help the child, such as low clothes hooks, reduced lighting in the nap area, or steps up to the changing table or toilet. If the environment is appropriate, the expectations for the child may not be reasonable. Other areas of the child's development are considered (language, cognitive, small muscle). Are these self-care expectations realistic? After this, a talk with the family is the next step to find out if they can give advice, insight, or assistance.

It Happened to Me

"Women's Work"

In my classroom, we had daily jobs that rotated. One was to wash off the work/snack tables (before the teacher did it with disinfectant). In my young days as a teacher, one day a boy's father arrived when the boy was washing off the table. The father took the sponge from his son and told me, "That's women's work." The family had emigrated from the Middle East, and I had no idea that the task was offensive to them. That was my rude awakening to the home/school conflict of cultural practices. What would you have said or done?

The teacher should be aware of the families' expectations for the child at home, how the child does these things at home, and what may be the reason for this inability here. More time may be all that is needed.

Home Visitors and Self-Care Skills

While self-care skills follow a sequential pattern, home visitors must be cognizant of the context of the home and how that may or may not support the development of specific self-care skills and autonomy. Family culture, values and expectations influence what and how families promote and support children's self-care skills. While all early childhood educators should know each family's perspective and practices around the various markers of self care (e.g., feeding, toileting, dressing), home educators, specifically, need to be sensitive. It is not unusual for families with children in early childhood settings to allow one practice in the classroom and a different one in the home; that is the meaning of bicultural perspective. Home educators, however, are only in the home so it is important for the educator and family to establish together "acceptable boundaries" for promoting the development of self-care skills and autonomy. In the classroom, there is ample time for "practice." In the home, there is little opportunity for "practice" in a visit; the family needs to be on board to promote opportunities for "practice."

Observing and Recording Infants and Toddlers in Routines

The physical care routines that make up most of the infant/toddler day are ideal times to observe the child's physical, social, emotional, and intellectual development. See Chapter 13 for daily routine record sheets for infants and toddlers.

Feeding and eating. This usually occurs at regular times throughout the day so use note-taking, not just of the times and amounts the child consumes but other things as well. At various ages and stages, the development of responsiveness to the feeder and the food, the child's interest and ability in self-feeding, and coordination of eyes, hands, and mouth give developmental information. The give and take between child and adult feeding is a training ground for the later give and take of conversation.

Diapering/Toileting. In addition to the record-keeping required for noting diaper changes and toilet-training, these are times of one-on-one exchanges between the child and caregiver. Observations can be made on the child's awareness of his body and the diapering or toileting activity, his willingness to be physically moved during the process, and again the adult-child interaction through eye contact and language.

Napping. Notations of the child's daily sleeping routines are regular information-gathering routines for caregivers. Beyond the times spent in sleep, napping also provides clues about the child's individuality. Does the child willingly go to sleep or need a certain routine to find comfort and relaxation in order to sleep? Does the quality of sleep seem deep and restful or restless? How does the child awaken and respond to the activity going on around her?

Anecdotal records can capture the details of the child's feeding and eating, diapering and toileting, and napping, preserving the details while providing a place to comment, interpret, question, and plan. The records are excellent documents to share with the family, showing the rapt attention that the caregiver is giving to the child beyond the necessary routines.

Helping All Children with Self-Care Skills

It has already been mentioned that cultural differences are seen most in the area of self-care skills. The teacher needs to be sensitive to different attitudes and practices. The family role of providing cultural socialization must be accommodated in the program through the cultural competence of the teachers, clarifying their own values and assumptions (Lynch and Hanson, 2011). This can be done through home visits, research, family questionnaires, and gaining information from watching the child and family together. Adjustment of routines for these differences is the appropriate action rather than forcing the child to conform. Communication and coordination between school and home must occur for the benefit of the child.

Children with special needs, as previously mentioned, should be allowed to do all they can for themselves with assistance when necessary, providing instructions in different formats such as photos, modeling, or gestures, and allowing extra time to complete the task. A checklist of self-help skills as an assessment can be used as a baseline to plan for the intervention and development of skills within the child's capability. Self-care routines are **adaptive skills** that children must learn to act independently according to their culture's expectations. The day's routines are common to all children, and involve identified sequences. They do not interfere with regular programming and do not require additional staff or special training. These routines also need to be coordinated with family life, so collaboration between program and family is necessary for continuity of practice. Reviewing of the routines of the day and setting specific goals for the child in each routine can be implemented and serve as communication between all team members, family, and the child. Self-care skills, sometimes called **functional skills**, are frequently a part of the Individualized Family Service Plan (**IFSP**) for younger children or Individualized Education Program (**IEP**) for children older than three. Implementation may require that some modifications are made to the environment and expectations. All children have the need to feel competent and responsible.

Helping Professionals for Self-Care Skills

Other professionals may be consulted depending on the area of difficulty.

pediatrician—for a thorough physical checkup to rule out any possible physical reasons for difficulties

social worker—for advice on family and center or school practices and expectations

occupational therapist—to examine more closely fine muscle skills involved in self-care

child psychologist—to explore the child's attitudes and reasons for refusing to care for herself

Other Methods

Other Methods to Record Self-Care:

Class List Log
Checklists/Rating Scales
Running Records
Frequency Counts
Conversations and Interviews
Work Samples
Media

Key Terms

adaptive skills	IFSP
Anecdotal Recording	individualists
autonomy	inference
collectivists	learned helplessness
development	narrative
functional skills	open method
IEP	self-care

Plans

Go to the Education CourseMate website, accessed through CengageBrain.com for the following:

Note for Adjusting Week by Week Plan to Your Class
Anecdotal Recording form
Plan Week 2 Part A, Directions for Anecdotal Recording on Self-Care for Group A, including What to Do with It, Portfolio Evidence Sheet Overview Example, Sharing with Child and Family, Actions—Read a Book,
In the Environment, In the Curriculum, In the Newsletter
Plan Week 2 Part B, Class List Log on Self-Care and What to Do with It
Plan Week 2 Part C, Reflective Journal

Resources

Marotz, L. R. & Allen, K. E. (2013). *Developmental profiles: Pre-birth through twelve* 7e. Belmont, CA: Wadsworth, Cengage Learning.

American Academy of Pediatrics. (2011). *Caring for our children: National health and safety performance standards: Guidelines for out-of-home child care programs* (3rd ed.). Elk Grove Village, IL: American Academy of Pediatrics. Available online at http://nrckids.org.

Diffily, D., & Sassman, C. (2004). *Teaching effective classroom routines: Establish structure in the classroom to foster children's learning.* New York: Scholastic.

Gonzalez-Mena, J., Eyer, D.W. (2007). *Infants toddlers and caregivers: A curriculum of respectful, responsive care and education* (7th ed.). Boston: McGraw-Hill.

Gonzalez-Mena, J. (2008). *Diversity in early care and education: Honoring differences.* New York: McGraw Hill.

Kinnell, G. (2004). *Good going!* St. Paul, MN: Redleaf Press.

Lynch, E. W., & Hanson, M. J. (2011). *Developing cross-cultural competence: A guide for working with children and their families* (4th ed.). Baltimore, MD: Brookes.

Safe Kids USA. www.safekids.org. Nationwide network to prevent unintentional childhood injury.

CHAPTER 3

Using Checklists to Look at Physical Development

© Cengage Learning 2012

IN THIS CHAPTER

- Using the Checklist
- Topics in Observation: Your Frame of Reference
- Looking at Physical Growth and Development
- Observing the Physical Development of Infants and Toddlers
- Helping All Children with Physical Development
- Helping Professionals for Physical Development Concerns

OBSERVATION THOUGHT

"Because some children have reached a certain developmental level does not mean that others should be there too. They have other strengths."

NAEYC Standards **naeyc**

The following NAEYC Standards for Early Childhood Professional Preparation are addressed in this chapter:

Standard 1: Promoting Child Development and Learning

Standard 3: Observing, Documenting, and Assessing to Support Young Children and Families

Standard 6: Becoming a Professional

Using the Checklist

EXERCISE **Complete the following Checklist.**

_____ I read Chapters 1 and 2.

_____ I completed each exercise in Chapters 1 and 2.

_____ I enjoyed writing in my Reflective Journal.

_____ I underlined key passages.

_____ I know the definition of _development_.

A **Checklist** is a predetermined list of criteria against which the recorder answers yes or no. In Checklist ratings, the recorder reads the criterion, decides on an answer, and makes a checkmark as an indication of an affirmative answer. Some of the preceding criteria are observable, whereas others are judgmental or inferential. Mark those with a J. The third and fifth items are not observable.

Checklists are described as a **closed method** because no raw data or evidence is recorded, just the judgment (inference) of the recorder about the criterion. Checklists are highly selective, only giving the recorder the opportunity to record a decision concerning the criterion. That does not mean it is not useful or accurate, but the reader has no raw data or details to check the recorder's decision. This is a characteristic of Checklist recording.

A valid child development Checklist records the attainment of accepted developmental milestones of knowledge, behavior, and skills. For a Checklist to be an effective tool, the observer must be very familiar with the criteria and able to assess the criteria accurately. Therefore, the criteria should be clearly observable, leaving little room for subjective judgments. If not, two raters may see the same child performing a skill, but rate the skill differently. Checklists' criteria should be appropriate to the population they are assessing and the developmental sequence of the criteria. Many programs and teachers design their own Checklists to fit the goals and objectives of the program and the population the program serves, but these may be less accurate than Checklists designed by child development experts.

When the criterion is arranged in the order in which normal development occurs, a Checklist can be a forecaster or predictor of the skills or behaviors that will appear next. In this way, a Checklist helps the teacher to individualize the curriculum by suggesting what experiences to provide in the next stage. For example, it is easy to see the following criteria in developmental sequence:

_____ X _____ Child sits unassisted 2/12.
_____ X _____ Child creeps 6/26.
_____ Child pulls to a standing position.
_____ Child walks holding onto furniture.
_____ Child walks alone.

When the criteria are arranged in developmental sequence and the observer has checked that the child sits unassisted and creeps, the next stage is pulling to a standing position. The teacher can then provide an environment that stimulates pulling up to a standing position, such as stable furniture and interesting things to look at above the creeping level. The teacher may plan activities in which the child is lifted to a standing position and supported for short periods of time.

Each criterion should measure the presence or absence of the knowledge, behavior, or skill. Checklists sometimes contain criteria that ask the recorder to judge or summarize groups of actions. For example, a Checklist item on small muscle skills may list the following:

_____ Coordinated eye/hand movements

The teacher observed the child putting puzzle pieces into the correct holes. The meaning or summary of that skill could be inferred as "coordinated eye/hand movements." This type of criterion leaves much room for interpretation and the greater chance that it is subjective rather than factual, objective recording. Valid Checklists list specific knowledge, behaviors, and skills, in developmental sequence, that describe exactly a movement, skill, or behavior. This leaves the recorder only to answer the basic question, "Is the child doing that or not?"

EXERCISE Mark the following Checklist items O for observed or I for interpreted.

_____ 1. can sit unassisted for two minutes
_____ 2. uses pincer grasp to pick up small objects
_____ 3. enjoys pulling self up on furniture
_____ 4. able to do most small muscle skills
_____ 5. can walk six feet on a four-inch balance beam
_____ 6. can cut
_____ 7. moves gracefully
_____ 8. increasing strength and dexterity
_____ 9. gives little attention to small muscle activities
_____ 10. balances on one foot for five seconds

Answers:

Check yourself:
1. O—The position is observable, and time is measured.
2. O—How the child picks up the object is observed.
3. I—Whether the child enjoys it or not is interpreted by observing behavior and forming a conclusion. If the criteria were "Pulls self up on furniture," it would be O.
4. I—What are most small muscle tasks? It is not clear what they are and if they are observed or not.

The following list (items 5–10) appears printed upside-down at the top of the left column:

 5. O—The length and width of board is a precise measurement, and action is observable.
 6. I—The criterion is too broad. More accurate criteria would be "Can cut a straight line" or "Can cut a curved line."
 7. I—The observer has much latitude in deciding if the movement is "graceful." An observable criterion is "Moves without bumping into objects in the room" or "Moves to rhythm of music."
 8. I—Increasing from what? This is not measurable. An observable criterion is "Can suspend body weight on bars for 10 seconds." or "Can catch an 8-inch ball from 10 feet."
 9. I—Judgment of the observer is recorded rather than observed behavior. An observable criterion is "Spends minutes on small muscle activity."
10. O—Position and time measurement is specific. This is an objective criterion.

If Checklists were used for every increment, in every skill or behavior, in every developmental area, the Checklist would be unwieldy. Well-constructed Checklists are specific and limited to observable milestones. They are used with other methods of recording to document the specifics of observations. Repeatedly you will read that exclusively using one observation method will not present the whole picture of the child.

The Checklist is reused periodically to measure progress along the developmental continuum. Each notation on the Checklist should be dated or coded to a date such as using a different colored pen for first, second, third, and fourth observations along with the date corresponding to the color. Using a different number, coded to a date, is another way to indicate when the criterion was attained.

If progress is not indicated by observing criteria farther along the scale, the teacher takes a closer look to be sure the data are correct. The Checklist may indicate significant lags that need to be addressed. A discussion is held with the family, possibly referring them to helping professionals for a full evaluation. The decision may be made just to wait and watch for another period to see if the skills develop. Child assessment is more than a list of discrete skills to be attained. These are but small indicators that change is taking place within the child, changes that are complex and intertwined with each other. Checklists lose the action and activity of growing and learning in a particular context. Reading a Checklist gives little indication of what the child is really like. However, it can be an important part of an overall assessment plan.

A Checklist is an effective tool to share with the family. It shows expected developmental progression and the level attained within those expectations. It indicates the dates of the observations and how much progress has taken place over that time. It may reveal accelerated or delayed development in specific areas, showing the child's strengths or areas yet to be developed. The Checklist becomes a permanent part of the child's Portfolio or file.

Checklists, and their content or format, can be varied to meet the needs of the recorder or program (see Figures 3–1 and 3–2). Some recorders recommend using different colored pens for each rating period. Many observers and Checklists are entering the technological age with computer scanning and analysis.

Limitations to Checklists

1. Checklists do not preserve the details of a conversation where vocabulary, tone of voice, and exact words give the essence of the exchange.
2. The observer sees behaviors and skills and makes a decision as to the presence or absence of the criteria. Once the checkmark or indication is made, there is no further notation about the event. You will notice that most of the items in the Checklists in Figures 3–1 and 3–2 (adapted from Marotz & Allen, 2013) are directly observable. The date is noted when the behavior or skill is observed instead of just including a checkmark in the box. The second row for dates is for the mastery of that skill. Beaty, in *Observing Development of the Young Child* (2010), inserts a column next to each criterion to use for note taking in order to make the Checklist more of an open method. Beaty refers to these notes as "evidence" because they retain details of why the observer made that judgment. Of course, it will be necessary to return to the lists periodically to record the child's progress.
3. Checklists are not as useful for anticipating emerging development or in planning curriculum to help the child reach the next milestone. They provide a snapshot in time, but there may be many intervening factors as to why on that particular date, the behavior or skill is not observed.

PHYSICAL DEVELOPMENTAL MILESTONES		
BIRTH THROUGH TWO YEARS OLD	**Date observed**	**Date observed**
Birth to 1 month		
Engages in primarily reflexive motor activity		
Maintains "fetal" position especially when sleeping		
Holds hands in a fist: does not reach for objects		
Turns head from side to side when placed in a prone position		
1 – 4 months		
Rooting and sucking reflexes are well developed		
Grasps with entire hand; strength insufficient to hold items		
Movements tend to be large and jerky		
Turns head side to side when lying in face up position		
Raises head and upper body on arms when placed on stomach		
Begins rolling from front to back by turning head to one side and allowing trunk to follow		
Can be pulled to a sitting position with considerable head lag (at beginning of period)		
Can sit with support, holding head steady, on lap or infant seat		
4 – 8 months		
Uses finger and thumb (pincer grip) to prick objects		
Reaches for objects with both arms simultaneously, later reaches with one hand or the other		
Transfers objects from one hand to the other, grasps object using entire hand (palmar grasp)		
Handles, shakes and pounds objects, puts everything in mouth		
Holds own bottle		
Sits alone without support, holding head erect, back straight and arms propped forward for support		
Pulls self to crawling position by raising up on arms and drawing knees up beneath the body		
Lifts head when placed on back		
Rolls over from front to back and back to front		
Begins scooting backward, sometimes accidentally, when placed on stomach; soon will learn to crawl forward		
Enjoys being placed in standing position, on someone's lap, jumping in place		
8 – 12 months		
Reaches with one hand leading to grasp an offered object or toy		
Manipulates objects, transferring them from one hand to the other		
Explores new objects by poking with one finger		
Uses deliberate pincer grip to pick small objects, toys and finger foods		
Stacks objects; also places objects inside one another		

Figure 3–1 Physical Development Checklist, Birth Through Two Years Old. (*Continued*)
Source: Adapted from Marotz & Allen, *Developmental Profiles: Pre Birth Through Adolescence*, 6th ed. © 2010 Cengage Learning. Reproduced by permission.
http://www.cengage.com/permissions.

PHYSICAL DEVELOPMENTAL MILESTONES		
BIRTH THROUGH TWO YEARS OLD	Date observed	Date observed
8 – 12 months		
Releases objects by dropping or throwing; cannot intentionally put an object down		
Begins pulling self to a standing position; begins to stand alone, hanging on furniture for support, moving around obstacles		
Creeps on hands and knees; crawls up and down stairs		
Walks with adult support		
May begin to walk alone		
1 year olds		
Crawls skillfully and quickly; gets to feet unaided		
Stands alone with feet spread apart, legs stiffened and arms extended for support		
Walks unassisted (write age in months here)		
Uses furniture to lower self to floor, collapses backward into a sitting position or falls forward on hands then sits		
Releases an object voluntarily		
Pushes/pulls toys while walking		
2 year olds		
Walks with a more erect, heel-to-toe pattern; can maneuver around obstacles in pathway		
Runs		
Squats for long periods while playing		
Climbs stairs unassisted (one step at a time)		
Balances on one foot momentarily, jumps up and down, but may fall		
Begins to achieve toilet training (depending on physical and neurological development) although inconsistent		
Throws large ball underhand		
Holds cup or glass in one hand		
Unbuttons large buttons, unzips large zippers		
Opens doors by turning doorknobs		
Grasps large crayon with fist; scribbles on large paper		
Climbs up on chair, turns around, and sits down		
Stacks four to six objects on top of one another		
Uses feet to propel wheeled riding toys		

Figure 3–1

PHYSICAL DEVELOPMENTAL MILESTONES		
THREE THROUGH EIGHT YEARS OLD	**Date Observed**	**Date Observed**
3 year olds		
Walks up and down stairs unassisted. Alternating feet going up but one step at a time coming down		
Balances on one foot for a few seconds		
Kicks a large ball, catches a large bounced ball with both arms extended		
Feeds self; needs minimal assistance		
Jumps in place		
Pedals a small tricycle or other wheeled toy		
With crayon, uses vertical, horizontal and circular strokes		
Holds crayon or marker between first two fingers thumb		
Turns pages of a book one at a time		
Builds a tower of eight or more blocks		
Begins to show hand dominance		
Carries a container of liquid, such as a cup of milk, without much spilling, pours from pitcher into another container		
Manipulates large buttons and zippers on clothing		
Washes and dries hands, brushes own teeth but not thoroughly		
Achieves bladder control. Write age here _____		
4 year olds		
Walks a straight line (tape or chalk line on the floor)		
Hops on one foot		
Pedals and steers a wheeled toy, avoiding obstacles		
Climbs ladders, trees playground equipment		
Jumps over objects 5 or 6 inches high, lands with both feet together		
Runs, starts, stops and moves around obstacles with ease		
Throws a ball overhand		
Builds a tower with ten or more blocks		
Forms shapes out of clay – cookies, snakes		
Draws some shapes and letters		
Holds crayon or marker between two fingers (not fist hold)		
Prints name and other words		
Paints and draws with a purpose – names drawings but most are unrecognizable		
Threads small wooden beads on a string		
5 year olds		
Walks backward, heel to toe		
Walks unassisted up and down stairs, alternating feet		
Can turn somersaults		
Touches toes without flexing knees		

Figure 3–2 Physical Development Checklist, Three Through Eight Years Old. (*Continued*)

Source: Adapted from Marotz & Allen, *Developmental Profiles: Pre Birth Through Adolescence*, 6th ed. © 2010 Cengage Learning. Reproduced by permission. http://www.cengage.com/permissions.

PHYSICAL DEVELOPMENTAL MILESTONES		
THREE THROUGH EIGHT YEARS OLD	Date Observed	Date Observed
6 year olds		
Can ride a bicycle without training wheels		
Body movements more precise but still some uncoordination		
Writes numbers and letters with varying degrees of precision and interest		
Folds and cuts paper into simple shapes		
7 year olds		
Balances on either foot		
Bats balls, manipulates computer mouse, knits, paints with accuracy		
Practices new motor skills until mastered		
Holds pencil in tight grasp near tip		
8 year olds		
Can play social games like team sports, dancing		
Improved agility, balance, speed, strength		
Copies words and numbers from blackboard with accuracy		

Figure 3–2

4. The observer's decision may be influenced by personal biases. The Checklist provides no way for the reader to form an independent opinion. The reader has to trust the recorder's judgment. This shortcoming of Checklists can be overcome by having various individuals recording with the Checklist. This gives more than one person's opinion regarding the criteria.

5. Because of its lack of detail, the Checklist is not a method that is reliable for documentation of suspected child abuse.

Home Visiting and Checklists

The examples of Checklists for monitoring development are also appropriate to use in the home setting. Many home visiting programs have chosen Ages and Stages because of its "user friendly and parent involvement" format. Because of the limited time in the home, relying on parent reporting is most helpful with one caveat. Parents may not differentiate between an emerging and accomplished skill. For example, a toddler may accidently kick a ball while trying to chase after it; the parent may interpret that as child is "able to kick a ball." It is important that home educators plan activities that allow the educator (and parent) the opportunity to observe both emerging and accomplished milestones found on chosen protocol.

Uses

The Checklist method of recording
- records the presence or absence of predetermined criteria.
- shows the sequence of developmental progress.
- measures progress.
- can be used as a screening for developmental lags.
- can be used as a curriculum planning tool for individualizing the curriculum.

Advantages

The Checklist is
- time- and labor-efficient.
- comprehensive. (It may cover many developmental areas in one Checklist.)
- a documentation of development.
- an individual documentation on each child.
- a clear illustration of the developmental continuum.

Disadvantages

The Checklist
- loses the details of events.
- may be biased by the recorder.

- depends on the criteria to be clearly observable.
- may have many items to check, making it time consuming.

Pitfalls to Avoid

Checklists seem like they can be done from memory, but memories are inaccurate and can be biased. The recordings should be from direct observation.

Checklists can be unwieldy if the recorder is trying to do too much at one time. To actually observe and record on a Checklist, it helps to either select one child to observe over a period of a day in all developmental areas, or select one developmental area and observe all children in that area.

Be sure that the Checklist is broad enough to include skills and behavioral milestones at prior levels as well as future ones. Children's development is uneven, and a child may be functioning at a young level in one area and an advanced level in another. The unchecked criteria give guidance about curriculum planning.

Many Checklists are covered by copyright. Either purchase the rating sheets or receive permission to copy them. It's the honest thing to do.

Using Technology

A Checklist can easily be loaded onto a hand-held computer and some Smart phones or a netbook. In the classroom, all you have to do is open the document, check what the child has attained, and save the document with the child's name. It can later be downloaded into the child's electronic Portfolio.

How to Find the Time

Checklists are not time consuming if you select only a portion of the Checklist and observe all the children for the chosen developmental area. On another day, select a different developmental area. This procedure will help you to focus your attention on one type of behavior, and you can observe each child in that particular way. The Week by Week plan provides a system for recording every developmental domain, for each child, several times through a school year.

What to Do with It

Programs usually purchase a commercially developed Checklist or devise a Checklist to match program goals and the age range of the children in the program or class. An individual Checklist is kept in each child's Portfolio or file and noted on the Portfolio Evidence Sheet (Figure 3–3). Periodically, the recorder re-examines each developmental area. It is objective only as long as the Checklist closely describes exact observable behavior rather than vague generalizations that may be interpreted many ways.

Families have access to this Portfolio and the Checklist. It is a good tool to show families the developmental sequence and the documentation of their child's accomplishments. Focusing on the accomplishments rather than the areas yet to be attained is a positive way of evaluating a child's development.

Some Examples of Checklists

Teachers Safety Checklist: Indoor Spaces, Outdoor Spaces (Marotz, 2012). A checklist to periodically assess the health and safety of the physical environment in an early childhood facility. Some of the items may be superseded by local or state regulations. (Figure 3–4, and Figure 3–12).

PORTFOLIO EVIDENCE OF CHILD'S DEVELOPMENT			
Evidence Type	Date	Recorder	Notes
PHYSICAL – the child's large and small muscle development, abilities in self-care routines			
CL	9/14/	BAN	Needs help handwashing
AR	9/19/	MLS	Learning handwashing song
CK	9/23/	BAN	Physical devel. – small muscle, plan special activities
AR	10/15/	MLS	Episode in blocks, piles small blocks 5 high
CK	12/17/	MLS	Improved small muscle devel.

Figure 3–3 Portfolio Evidence Sheet.

1. A minimum of 35 square feet of usable space is available per child.

2. Room temperature is between 68°–85°F (20°–29.4°C).

3. Rooms have good ventilation:

   a. windows and doors have screens.

   b. mechanical ventilation systems are in working order.

4. There are two exits in all rooms occupied by children.

5. Carpets and draperies are fire-retardant.

6. Rooms are well lighted.

7. Glass doors and low windows are constructed of safety glass.

8. Walls and floors of classrooms, bathrooms, and kitchen appear clean; floors are swept daily, bathroom fixtures are scrubbed at least every other day.

9. Tables and chairs are child-sized and sturdy.

10. Electrical outlets are covered with safety caps.

11. Smoke detectors are located in appropriate places and in working order.

12. Furniture, activities, and equipment are set up so that doorways and pathways are kept clear.

13. Play equipment and materials are stored in designated areas; they are inspected frequently and are safe for children's use.

14. Large pieces of equipment, e.g., lockers, piano, and bookshelves, are firmly anchored to the floor or wall.

15. Cleaners, chemicals, and other poisonous substances are locked up.

16. If stairways are used:

    a. Handrail is placed at children's height.

    b. Stairs are free of toys and clutter.

    c. Stairs are well-lighted.

    d. Stairs are covered with a nonslip surface.

17. Bathroom areas:

    a. Toilets and washbasins are in working order.

    b. One toilet and washbasin are available for every 10–12 children; potty chairs are provided for children in toilet training.

    c. Water temperature is no higher than 120°F (48.8°C).

    d. Powdered or liquid soap is used for hand-washing.

    e. Individual or paper towels are used for each child.

    f. Diapering tables or mats are cleaned after each use.

18. At least one fire extinguisher is available and located in a convenient place; extinguisher is checked annually by fire-testing specialists.

19. Premises are free from rodents and/or undesirable insects.

20. Food preparation areas are maintained according to strict sanitary standards.

21. At least one individual on the premises is trained in emergency first aid and CPR; first aid supplies are readily available.

22. All medications are stored in a locked cabinet or box.

23. Fire and storm/disaster drills are conducted on a monthly basis.

24. Security measures (plans, vigilant staff, key pads, locked doors, video cameras) are in place to protect children from unauthorized visitors.

Figure 3–4   Teachers' Safety Checklist: Indoor and Outdoor Spaces.

Source: From Marotz, *Health, Safety and Nutrition for Young Children*, 8th ed. ©2012 Cengage Learning.

TOPICS in OBSERVATION

Your Frame of Reference

Everyone looks at the world through a unique **frame of reference**. That frame of reference can be compared to a picture frame to help understand the concept (Figure 3–5).

A frame is the boundary or outer limits around a picture. Each person's understanding or "vision" is limited by boundaries different from every other person's, formed from past experience but influential in viewing the present and the future. The teacher must consider this when observing children because it determines how the child is viewed. Some experiences that form the frame of reference follow:

Childhood. Each person's childhood is unique, even for children born in the same family, even for twins. When observing a child, adults subconsciously reflect on their own childhoods. These factors may influence how the adult sees the child. Values adopted from our families and society influenced by socioeconomic level, race, religion, ethnicity, and gender enter into the observational framework.

Education and Training. The educational level and philosophies learned affect the teacher's perceptions and judgments of the child being viewed. Philosophies of the training curriculum influence what meaning you attach to what you see.

Past Experiences with Children. Many people working with children have had experiences as parents, grandparents or may have started out their career caring for younger siblings, babysitting as a teenager, and now caring for extended family members. Those new to the profession, with little experience, are going to see behaviors and incidents differently from those with much experience.

Own Learning Styles. With the advent of more knowledge of individual learning styles, it becomes clearer that a teacher's learning style is as important as the student's. Depending on the acute sensory reception, the observer will absorb information in different ways:

auditory learner—from language and sounds the child makes

visual learner—from actions, scenes, and pictures of the child's behavior

tactile learner—from touching the child

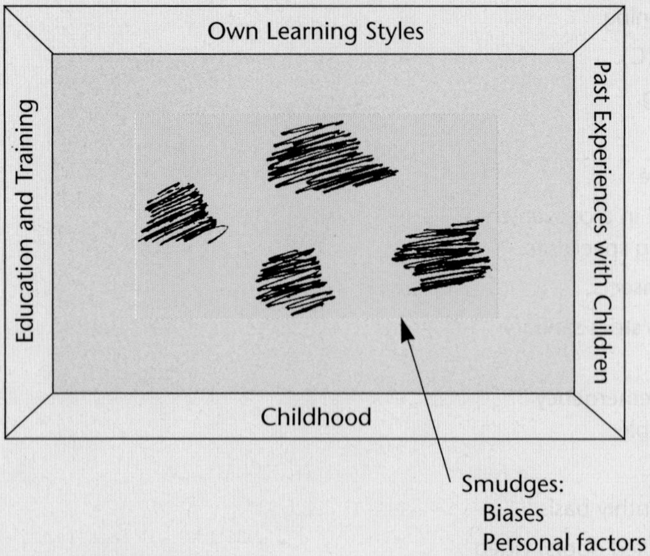

SMUDGES ON THE GLASS

The frame of reference is the perimeter, but the viewing is done through the glass. There may be smudges on the glass that are biases that keep the observer from seeing the child objectively.

Biases for or Against the Child. Individual **bias** and prejudice are human factors that

Own Learning Styles

Education and Training

Past Experiences with Children

Childhood

Smudges:
Biases
Personal factors

Figure 3–5 Frame of Reference.

(Continued)

TOPICS in OBSERVATION   *(Continued)*

may interfere with a clear view of the child. Those biases may even be positive ones, such as the child's attractive appearance or charming personality, causing the child's needs to be overlooked because of personal feelings that get in the way. Strengths of the child may be overlooked because of a prejudice or bias that will negatively affect objective observation. Some might be the following:

sex—may prefer boys or girls

hair color—may love or hate redheads

racial or ethnic—stereotypic beliefs

economic or social status—rich or poor may interfere with how the child is perceived

personality clashes—may love or hate children who are whiny, mischievous, active, sassy, bold, shy

prior contact with the family—older child was in the class

physical attributes—beauty, handicaps, weight

hearsay—prior teachers influence opinion

Personal Factors That Affect Observation. Adults may have their own situations that have nothing to do with the child but may affect the observer enough to interfere with objective recording:

health—headache, awaiting test results, impending surgery, pregnancy, or premenstrual syndrome

stress—financial, personal, or workplace tension

outside pressure—gathering evidence to document a decision or a referral

The observer's consciousness is raised on these issues through reflection. By selecting objective observation methods, communicating and sharing observations and conferences with coworkers and parents, these biases can be minimized.

Some days might not be good ones to gather information and make decisions. The professional acts ethically.

It Happened to Me

"BMW vs. Harley"

One year I had two little girls in my preschool class. One, whose mother brought her in her BMW, parked at the end of the sidewalk in the No Parking Zone, and the mother swooped in on her high heels and full-length fur coat. In the same class was another little girl whose mother drove her to school on the back of her Harley. This mother clanked in wearing full leathers, a chain link necklace, tattoos, and feather earrings. Now, looking at those two children without the smudges on my frame of reference because of these facts was very difficult. I had to be honest with myself and trust objective recording methods to filter out those biases.

The *Brigance Diagnostic Inventory of Early Development* II (Brigance, 2010) is a comprehensive Checklist to assess development and diagnose developmental delay.

The *Child Observation Record (COR)* (High/Scope Press, 2006) is an ascending Checklist for cognitive, movement, and social-emotional development dependent on Anecdotal

Records (Key Experience Notes) prior to completing the Checklist.

Developmental Profiles: Pre-Birth Through Adolescence, 7th ed., (Marotz &Allen, 2013), provides one-page-for-one-year developmental Checklists that give the milestones for that year. The text provides more specific information, learning activities, and developmental alerts.

Early Learning Observation & Rating Scale, (Coleman, West & Gillis, 2010), is an observation Checklist across seven developmental domains to determine learning progress and possible early signs of learning disabilities.

Observing Development of the Young Child, 7th ed., (Beaty, 2010), is a Checklist with an evidence column for three- to six-year-olds with ascending criteria in all developmental areas–child development and curriculum planning resources.

Ages and Stages Questionnaire, 3rd ed. *(ASQ-3)* (Bricker & Squires, 2009) is an age-related series of developmental screening questions answered by parents or primary caregivers and is designed to identify the few infants and young children who require more extensive evaluation.

The Work Sampling System 4th ed., (Meisels et al., 2003) has Checklist components in personal and social development, language and literacy, mathematical and scientific thinking, social studies, the arts, and physical development. It assesses children's skills, knowledge, behavior, and accomplishments.

REVIEW

CHECKLIST
Listing of related criteria against which skills, knowledge, or behavior are measured indicating yes or no, present or not present. Can indicate milestones attained and areas yet to be developed.

Types of Information to Record Using Checklists
- self-care skills
- physical development—large muscle/small muscle skills
- stages of social development
- stages of emotional development
- stages of language development
- stages of cognitive development—specific criteria such as "knows colors, shapes, recognizes numbers"
- stages of literacy development
- stages of creative development
- stages of sociodramatic play
- aspects of self-concept

Go to the Education CourseMate website, accessed through CengageBrain.com for checklist forms, plans, and resources.

Looking at Physical Growth and Development

EXERCISE **Using a separate sheet of paper, list five phrases to describe your body.**

Read the chapter, then return to your descriptions and mark them G for growth areas and D for development areas.

Bodies change. They grow and develop. What is the difference? **Growth** refers to changes in size, quantitative change, and those changes that can be measured in increasing numbers such as height, weight, head circumference, and teeth:

▶ Most infants range in length from 18 to 21 inches at birth and are expected to grow longer and taller.

▶ By 36 months, the toddler has molars and a total of 20 "baby" teeth, and is expected to grow more.

▶ The average five-year-old weighs 38 to 45 pounds and is expected to increase in weight as she grows older.

▶ Between the ages of six and eight, the body takes on a lanky appearance as arms and legs grow longer, with permanent teeth replacing baby teeth, and developing more adult-like features.

There are norms, or averages, established by statistical analysis of large groups of people. These are the established ranges for average growth of weight and stature at specific ages (Figure 3–6). Tables like these can alert observers to significant variations that warrant further investigation for the cause.

Other changes can be measured in numbers that are not physical. Vocabulary also "grows" because it can be measured in numbers. The toddler has a vocabulary of 50 to 300 words. The attention span is growing too. It can be measured in seconds but sometimes minutes and even hours if the child is interested in the activity. Attention span is expected to increase as the child matures.

Development is also change, but qualitative change, increasingly better, more complex, and more coordinated. Development, like growth, occurs in sequential, predictable stages, yet is different for every individual based on several factors. Physical development, involving both large and small muscle coordination, begins with **reflex** actions and progresses to

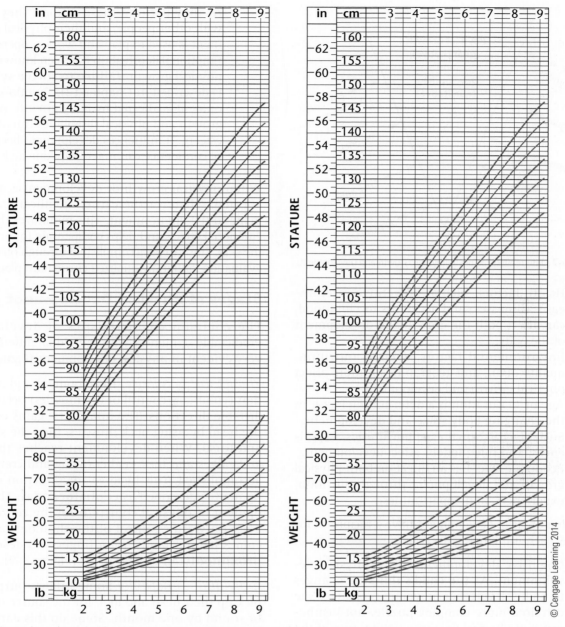

Figure 3–6 Height and Weight Charts. Kuczmarski, et al 2000, National Center for Health Statistics.

© Cengage Learning 2014

rudimentary, then fundamental movement quality during the preschool years. It forms the basis for refinements that are used in all active sports.

As you can see from Figure 3–6, in the first eight years, boys and girls weigh and measure very much the same. As puberty approaches and occurs there is a widening gap between weight and height between girls and boys.

EXERCISE **List all the factors you can think of that affect physical development.**

Now read on and see how many factors correlate to your list.

Many factors affect growth and development (Figure 3–7):

▶ Genetics determines thousands of characteristics of growth and development, such as body size, sex, and coloring.
▶ Prenatal care, including the mother's nutrition and physical condition, and even age contribute to prebirth growth and development.

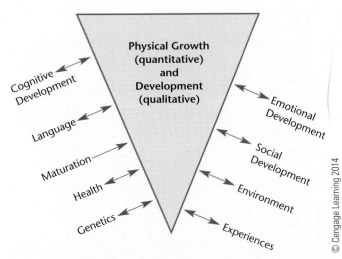

Figure 3–7 Interrelated Factors in Physical Growth and Development.

© Cengage Learning 2014

- Health factors, such as preventive care, diseases, illnesses, and accidents in childhood, can affect both the growth and development of the body.
- Environmental factors, such as nutrition, quality of air, and geographic location, affect physical growth and development.
- Age or maturation is a determining factor in the changing body's size and development.
- Social factors, such as opportunities, experiences, and role models, affect development.
- Economic level has an effect on both physical growth and development through nutrition, experiences, and opportunities.

Other areas of development have a reciprocal influence, each influencing the other:

- Cognitive development affects physical development. As the child's thinking changes to higher levels, her movements change. She can do a more complex puzzle, not just because of physical dexterity but because of the ability to visualize pieces of the whole. It is also through physically manipulating materials that the child's cognitive structures build, experiencing soft and hard, hot and cold.
- Language and physical development are interdependent. As the child physically develops, he also learns new vocabulary for movements (jump, skip, pirouette). By following verbal directions, processing language, he learns how to perform physical tasks. "Hold the bat up straighter, away from your body."
- Social interactions with other people encourage physical development. By imitating the actions of others, children learn to perform tasks such as painting, swinging, and riding a bike.

As they perform these actions, they interact with other people, and their physical development is used to play and work cooperatively.
- Emotional deprivation has been known to stunt physical growth (**failure to thrive syndrome** is described in Chapter 12). Emotional development is affected by body growth. Abnormal growth and physical disabilities can affect self-esteem. It influences development because lack of confidence can make someone awkward.

When physical growth or development is adversely affected, whatever the cause, modifications can be made to the environment. This minimizes the social-emotional effects and helps compensate for or improve the skill. This can be accomplished through observation, evaluation, and individualized curriculum planning.

Stages of Physical Development

The common characteristics of development: Predictable sequences with individual differences are very evident in physical development (Figure 3–8).

Predictable Sequence. Development and coordination (voluntary control of the muscles) occur in predictable directions. The infant first gains control of the head by using neck muscles, then the shoulders and torso. When development reaches the thighs and calves and toes, real crawling and creeping are accomplished. This head-to-toe direction of development is described as **cephalocaudal.** The development of physical control from the center of the body outward—control of the shoulders and arms comes before hands, then fingers—is described as **proximodistal,** or near to far (Figure 3–9).

Individual Timetable. Some infants purposefully pick up their head and look for the source of a voice or sound by one month. Some do this earlier than others. Some children are walking by 10 months, and others not until 16 months. A baby will not walk until she can. An adult cannot make a baby walk before the muscles are strong and coordinated enough to accomplish the task.

Readiness. Physical development vividly illustrates the predictable, sequential, individual aspects of development. In other areas of development, such as emotional and cognitive development, the stages are not as easily observed. This visual reminder is an important concept to apply to curriculum planning in all areas. The child's body and mind must be ready before she can accomplish the skill. All the other steps have come before it to lead the way, serving as a benchmark of readiness for the next step.

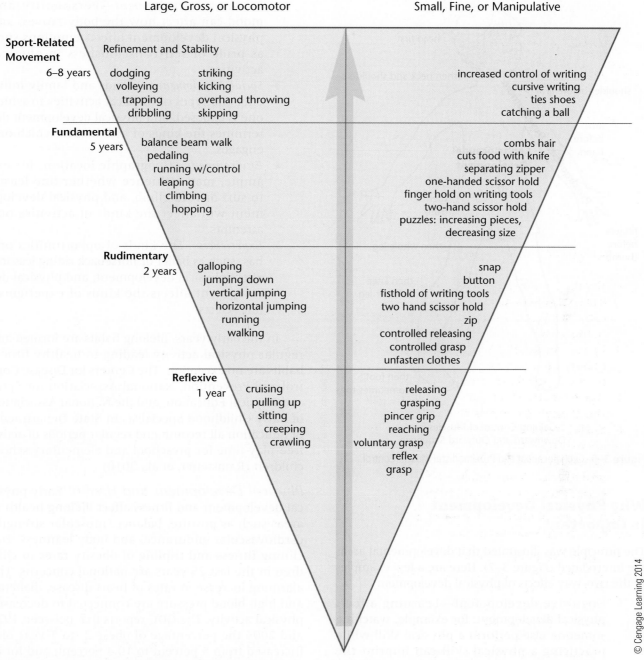

Figure 3–8 Muscle Control and Skill Development. Adapted from Gallahue & Cleland-Donnelly (2007) *Developmental physical education for all children.* Champaign, IL: Human Kinetics.

By the age of one and a half, a child has accomplished the basic physical skills of mobility (**large muscle** or gross motor) and manipulation (**small muscle** or fine motor). The next 48 months will see vast increases in coordination and integration of all body structures. By the time children are five, they have acquired body control. The skills of walking, running, climbing, balancing, pushing, pulling, lifting, carrying, throwing, catching, and striking prepare them for life functions and all the sports and recreation skills.

EXERCISE Turn the sound off on a television show. Observe just the facial and body movements of the people you are viewing. What does that tell you about that person?

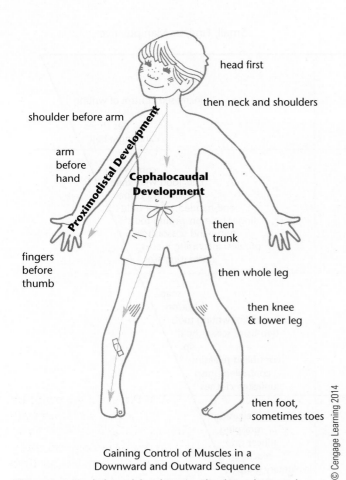

head first

then neck and shoulders

shoulder before arm

Proximodistal Development

arm
before
hand

**Cephalocaudal
Development**

fingers
before
thumb

then
trunk

then whole leg

then knee
& lower leg

then foot,
sometimes toes

© Cengage Learning 2014

Gaining Control of Muscles in a
Downward and Outward Sequence

Figure 3–9 Cephalocaudal and Proximodistal Muscle Control.

Why Physical Development Is Important

The principle was illustrated that developmental areas are interrelated (Figure 3–7). Here are a few examples of the two-way effects of physical development:

- Cognitive development—Learning affects physical development; for example, watching someone else perform a physical skill while practicing a physical skill can imprint the brain to perform that skill.
- *Language*—Verbal directions can tell the body to move in a certain way, and new vocabulary describe body movements.
- *Maturation*—As one ages, body movements are perfected; and as the body develops, more complex activities can be performed.
- *Health*—Good health habits can affect development, while diseases and illnesses can affect health.
- *Genetics*—Inherited diseases or disorders can affect physical development; but development probably does not affect genetics.

- *Emotional development*—Personality and mood can affect how the body moves, and physical development affects emotions such as pride or self-consciousness in physical activities.
- *Social development*—Friends and family influence the types of physical activities to which one is exposed, and physical development determines the kinds of activities in which one engages.
- *Environment*—Geographic location, for example, may influence whether one learns to surf or rock climb, and physical development will affect the kinds of activities one attempts.
- *Experiences*—The kinds of opportunities one has, such as ballet or horseback riding lessons, affect physical development; and physical development affects the kinds of experiences one selects.

In the early years, lifelong habits are formed and regular physical activity leading to healthy fitness habits are no exception. The Centers for Disease Control and Prevention, National Association for Sport and Physical Education, and the National Association of Early Childhood Specialists in State Departments of Education all recommend regular periods of active free-play time for preschool and elementary school children (Ramstetter, et al., 2010).

Physical Development and Health. Early physical development and fitness affect lifelong health in areas such as posture, balance, muscular strength, cardiovascular endurance, and body leanness. Declining fitness and tripling of obesity rates in children in the last 25 years are national concerns. The alarming increase in rates of heart disease, diabetes, and high blood pressure are connected to decreased physical activity. The CDC reports that between 1976 and 2006 the percentage of obese 2- to 5-year-olds increased from 5 percent to 10.4 percent; and for 6- to 11-year-olds the percentage went from 6.5 percent to 19.6 percent (Figure 3–10). There is a significant racial disparity with Mexican-American adolescent boys and non-Hispanic black girls having the largest increase in obesity (Ogden & Carroll, 2010). In 2010, the United States Department of Health and Human Services launched Healthy People 2020, a continuing campaign to advocate and plan for a more active population. Early and middle childhood objectives are new to this continuing effort to improve the physical, cognitive, and social-emotional foundation for lifelong health, learning, and wellbeing (www. healthypeople.gov/2020).

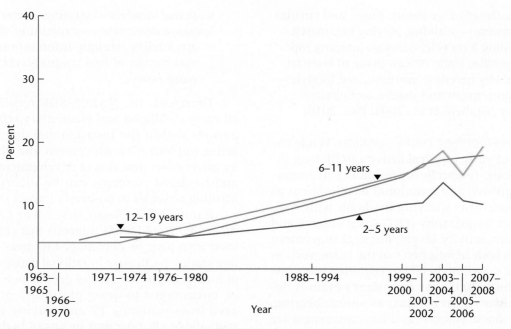

Figure 3–10 Trends in Obesity. (Ogden & Carroll, 2010, NCHS Health E-Stat)

There are many potential factors leading to this physical decline: a reduction in physical education classes, increased availability of sodas and snacks in public schools, growth in fast-food outlets across the country, "super-sizing" food portions in restaurants, increased numbers of high-fat grocery products, plus the explosion of media targeted at children with advertising campaigns that promote foods such as candy, soda, and snacks. The typical child sees about 40,000 of these advertisements a year (Kaiser, 2004). Children spend less time in outside play and sports than the children of 20 years ago (Juster et al., 2004). Formal physical education programs and even free-time recess periods find children less active. The reduction of recess time (unstructured, freeplay) to give more time to academic work and for punitive reasons impacts its positive effects of a child's physical, creative, social, and emotional development (Ramstetter, 2011).

Little research is available on children under the age of two, but there is increasing concern regarding this link between electronic media (television and videos) and decreasing physical activity. A large study found that in a typical day, in children under six, screen media use equaled reading or being read to (Rideout et al., 2006). The American Academy of Pediatrics issued a policy statement (2011) discouraging any viewing for children under age two and limiting viewing to two hours a day for preschoolers. In 2011, the Academy made recommendations to pediatricians to ask parents and patients about media use, encouraged them to discuss

food advertising as they monitored TV viewing, to limit non-educational screen time to less than two hours a day, and none before the age of two years. It called on pediatricians to be advocates in their own communities as well as to Congress regarding the harmful effects of media for obesity and its related diseases, social and emotional disturbances, and to be proponents of program and community efforts to instill a lifestyle of regular exercise (AAP, 2011).

Changes in family structures, with both parents working outside the home and turning child-rearing over to others or to the children themselves, has been blamed for children not playing actively. Violence in the neighborhood has also kept some children from playgrounds or from playing outside in the street or yard (Burdette, 2005). Schools have been reducing their emphasis on physical education as mandates for improved academic performance and budgetary woes increase.

Health-related physical fitness involves four components that can easily be incorporated into the early childhood curriculum:

muscular strength and endurance (the force both large and small muscles can produce developed from exercising longer)—climbing, jumping, pumping on a swing

flexibility (range of motion in a joint developed by slow stretching and movements)—pretend movements such as climbing, reaching, not bouncing while stretching *cardiovascular efficiency* (heart, lungs, and circulatory system)—walking, playing tag, marching, riding a tricycle, dancing, jumping rope

body composition (ratio of lean tissue to body fat affected by heredity, nutrition, and lifestyle)—nutritious meals and snacks, and physical activity (Graham et al., 2004; Pica, 2010)

Physical Development and Cognition. While the importance of early physical activity to lifelong fitness is obvious, researchers are finding its importance to cognitive and emotional development as well. Neuroscientists studying the brain with Positron Emission Tomography (PET) scans observe and measure brain activity levels. Physical movement that involves both hemispheres of the brain, such as creeping and crawling, heighten cognitive functioning (Hannaford, 2005). As the infant's brain is developing, sensory systems such as vision, hearing, taste, smell, touch, balance, and body awareness are functioning at their most primary stage. The body's central nervous system is beginning to integrate these systems. As the infant continues to grow and develop, this integration comes under the control of the infant, and responses to senses become automatic and unconscious. This **sensory integration** allows the brain then to process more complex information. When this integration is interrupted for some reason, it may result in the child acting disorganized, confused, and frustrated, and may ultimately interfere with learning (Isbell, 2007). Early perceptual sensory motor experiences can increase brain functioning and lead to cognitive gains. There is no doubt that exercise and good nutrition are necessary for learning and growing. As children become more mobile, cruising, creeping, toddling, it should not be surprising that their vocabulary is rapidly increasing as they add more nouns in answer to their constant, "Whaddat?" This demonstrates the interplay of physical, cognitive, and language development domains.

Even though physical play is in the social domain, Pica (2010) reminds us that the mechanisms involved expand the realm of cognitive benefits as well. In the position statement on young children and recess, the National Association of Early Childhood Specialists in State Departments of Education (NAECS-SDE 2002) lists content areas that can be explored on the playground:

natural elements—experiencing wind, dirt, water, seasons

physics—using a see-saw, merry-go-round, swings

architecture and design—building with natural materials

math and numbers—counting, keeping score

language development—explaining, describing, articulating, seeking information, and making use of oral language/vocabulary/word power

Therefore, the NAECS-SDE recommends that all early childhood and elementary schools include periods within the instructional day for free and active outdoor play. Movement and physical activity affect other domains of development, and movement-related concepts can be incorporated into learning activities to positively impact learning.

Hannaford, in *Smart Moves: Why Learning Is Not All in Your Head* (2005), suggests that children: create their own toys; be encouraged to make up imaginative stories; participate in rational dialogue by the age of four years; honor care of people, pets, and objects; be encouraged to delay gratification; be discouraged from watching TV and playing video games; and, above all, take part in lots of body movement opportunities for full limbic system development. It is vital to brain development. The interplay of mind and body is not surprising but is a re-emphasis of the importance of physical activity to overall success in learning and living.

Physical Development and Social-Emotional Development. Researchers also point out that large muscle skills have social and emotional effects on children's views of themselves and their perceptions of how others feel about them (Coakley, 2004; Gallahue, 2003; West, 2000). Success-oriented physical education meets not only the child's need for motor skill development but also the social-emotional development qualities of competence, belonging, and self-worth.

Cortisol, the hormone released during stress, undermines neurological development and can affect cognitive, motor, and social development. Pica (2010) makes the case for the importance of physical development beyond fitness, emphasizing the relationship to social-emotional, creative, and cognitive development. She relates movement to all curriculum areas.

Childhood obesity has become a national concern with the trends rising for school-age children, especially among non-Hispanic black and Mexican-American children. The interrelated factors of physical development may not affect health, but can cause children (especially girls) to be ridiculed and rejected, which may cause low self-esteem and lead to unhealthy dieting and food-related problems such as bulimia and anorexia.

Physical Development and Play. As infants become more social, they interact with objects and other people in play. At first, play is a sensory manipulation. The infant reaches out and takes hold of a rattle or a toy, or grabs his father's nose. As the child's muscles eventually become coordinated through experience, he will discover that he can cause the toy to make a sound or can make someone smile. In an ever-increasing spiral of complex actions and reactions, the child's play repertoire expands. The child learns that play is pleasurable, self-motivating, not expected to produce a specific outcome, and requires the integration of several different skills to continue. This play is inborn in animals and humans. Playing appears to be linked to social adjustment and improved physical condition (Power, 2000).

As children mature, their physical ability to run, throw, catch, climb, and kick is often channeled into more formal kinds of play such as sports games with rules. Success in sports depends not only on physical ability but also on emotional stability, self-control, and social competence. Games for young children, however, should be those in which all children can find success, so there should be no competition. Traditional games such as Duck, Duck, Goose, where only one or two children are moving and the rest are observing, can be embarrassing and discouraging and should be eliminated from organized play. Cooperative games, not those with one winner and the rest losers, can help young children develop team spirit and encourage them to seek out game-playing for its intrinsic rewards. In addition, losing produces negative feelings that can affect emotional development (low self-esteem) and social development (promoting self over others).

Young children should be given every possible opportunity to build their physical skills. It is a misconception that children are just normally engaged in vigorous activity. When children three to five years old were observed in various preschool settings, they engaged in 4 to 10 minutes of moderate-to-vigorous physical activity per hour (Pate, 2004), falling far short of the recommended 120 minutes of physical activity a day, half of which should consist of structured activities. For older children even in structured competitive games—those who need the most practice get the least amount of time to play. Children cannot develop their physical skills if they are on the sidelines. In *Active Start: A Statement of Physical Guidelines for Children Birth to Five Years,* 2e (NASPE, 2009), specific guidelines address the physical activity needs of children during the first five years. The book begins with the following position statement: "All children birth to age five should engage in daily physical activity that promotes movement skillfulness and foundations of heath-related fitness." The NASPE guidelines recommend school-age children accumulate at least 60 minutes and up to several hours of physical activity per day, while avoiding prolonged periods of inactivity and 159 minutes of instructional physical education per week throughout the school year. The guidelines from this association are outlined in Figure 3–11.

Observing Physical Development

The teacher closely observes children's physical activity for many purposes.

For Safety Maintenance. It is the adult's responsibility to prepare a safe environment for children.

EXERCISE **Using a separate sheet of paper, list five safety features you would plan if you were designing a room for young children.**

Accidents occur frequently in the early years because of increased mobility, lack of coordination, inability to anticipate and avoid dangerous actions, or lack of supervision. The newly mobile infant requires crawling surfaces that are sanitary and free of ingestible objects. Beds and changing tables must have high sides, safety straps, and adult supervision. For the infant and toddler, surrounding equipment must have a stable base as the standing infant pulls himself up. He uses furniture for handles and stabilizers as he begins to walk around. Children are built to run and climb, motivated by curiosity and newfound physical skills. When running and climbing are seen as a form of active learning, physical coordination, and a source of self-esteem, modifications to the environment are made to provide for safe moving. Climbing on objects not meant to be climbed can be dangerous, so furniture must be secured. Other climbing experiences should be provided, within a manageable range of the child's climbing ability. A soft mat is placed underneath to cushion inevitable falls. Places should be provided for running or jumping in the classroom. Look at where children are running and climbing, and make it as safe as you can, altering the environment to eliminate the unsafe conditions. All stairways and doorways must be blocked from the little cruiser.

Position: All children birth to age five should engage in daily physical activity that promotes health-related fitness and movement skills.

	INFANTS	TODDLERS	PRESCHOOLERS	EARLY SCHOOL AGE
1.	Daily activities dedicated to explore movement and environment	At least 30 minutes of structured physical activity daily	At least 60 minutes of structured physical activity daily	At least 60 minutes of age-appropriate physical activity daily
2.	Settings encourage and stimulate moment experiences and active play for short periods several times a day	At least 60 minutes unstructured physical activity daily and not more than 60 minutes sedentary activity at a time except sleeping	At least 60 minutes unstructured physical activity daily and not more than 60 minutes sedentary activity at a time except sleeping	Moderate physical activity with most of the time being spent in activity that is intermittent in nature
3.	Physical activity to promote skill development and movement	Opportunities to develop movement skills	Encouraged to develop competence in fundamental motor skills	Participate in several bouts of physical activity lasting 15 minutes or more
4.	Environment meets or exceeds recommended safety standards for large-muscle activities	Indoor and outdoor areas that meet or exceed recommended safety standards for large-muscle activities	Indoor and outdoor areas that meet or exceed recommended safety standards for large-muscle activities	Participate each day in a variety of physical activities designed to achieve optimal health, wellness, fitness and performance benefit
5.	Responsible individuals understand and provide structured and unstructured physical activity	Responsible individuals understand and provide structured and unstructured physical activity and movement experiences	Responsible individuals understand and provide structured and unstructured physical activity and movement experiences	Extended periods (2 hours or more) of inactivity are discouraged for children, especially during the daytime hours

Figure 3–11 ACTIVE START: A Statement of Physical Activity Guidelines for Children Birth to Five and Physical Activity for Children: A Statement of Guidelines for Children 5–12, 2nd ed (2004).

Source: Reprinted from Active Start: *A Statement of Physical Activity Guidelines for Children Birth to Five Years* [2002], with permission from the National Association for Sport and Physical Education [NASPE], 1900 Association Drive, Reston, VA 20191, USA.

An Outdoor Area Checklist (Marotz, 2012) features criteria on surfaces, equipment, natural aspects, security, storage, safety, and educational usefulness (Figure 3–12).

EXERCISE Use the Outdoor Areas Checklist to practice Checklist recording, and review the criteria for safe environments.

Mobility and coordination increase the risk of accidents. As independence grows from the onset of crawling onward, children have the urge to get things for themselves. Leaving an area, climbing into a cupboard or onto shelves, or attempting tasks beyond their capability and judgment present dangers. Toddlers and preschoolers need an environment with interesting things to do, opportunities to help themselves in learning centers, and adequate supervision for safety and to facilitate play. Then the potential for accidents can be reduced. The emphasis on safety should not be construed as a reason to eliminate challenging physical activities. It is through experiencing the thrill of reaching the top rung on a ladder, scaling to the top of a rock wall, or standing atop a large boulder that children gain confidence, both physically and psychologically.

For Assessment. Watching children move gives the observer information, leading knowledge, and theories about the contributing factors for the following aspects of physical development:

height—parents' height
weight—nutrition, metabolism, television habits, family's physical fitness

OUTDOOR AREAS

1. Play areas are located away from traffic, loud noises, and sources of chemical contamination.
2. Play areas are located adjacent to the premises or within safe walking distance.
3. Play areas are well drained; if rubber tires are used for play equipment, holes have been drilled to prevent standing water.
4. Bathroom facilities and a drinking fountain are easily accessible.
5. A variety of play surfaces, e.g., grass, concrete, sand are available; shade is provided.
6. Play equipment is in good condition, e.g., no broken or rusty parts, missing pieces, splinters, sharp edges (no open "S" hooks or protruding bolts), frayed rope.
7. Selection of play equipment is appropriate for children's ages.
8. Soft ground covers approximately 12 inches in depth, are present under large climbing equipment; area free of sharp debris (glass, sticks).
9. Large pieces of equipment are stable and anchored securely in the ground; finishes are non-toxic and intact.
10. Equipment is placed sufficiently far apart to allow a smooth flow of traffic and adequate supervision; an appropriate safety zone is provided around equipment.
11. Play areas are enclosed by a fence at least four feet high, with a gate and workable lock for children's security and safety.
12. There are no poisonous plants, shrubs, or trees in the area.
13. Chemicals, insecticides, paints, and gasoline products are stored in a locked cabinet.
14. Grounds are maintained on a regular basis and are free of debris; grass is mowed; broken equipment is removed.
15. Wading or swimming pools are always supervised; water is drained when not in use.

Figure 3–12 OUTDOOR AREAS CHECKLIST.

Source: From MAROTZ, *Health, Safety, and Nutrition for the Young Child*, 7th ed. © 2009 Cengage Learning. Reproduced by permission. http://www.cengage.com/permissions.

movement—age, experiences, inherited capabilities, self-esteem, physical energy level, possible disabilities

Written observations provide documentation for comparisons over time to show progress. From observations, assessments may be made on the child's growth and development. Further evaluations may be recommended if assessments indicate results fall below the normal range.

In the Environment. It is the teacher's role and responsibility to provide a safe environment to meet the developmental needs of the children. Usually the classroom space is predetermined, so the teacher makes decisions on furnishings and room arrangement based on teaching philosophies and priorities for space.

Indoor Play. Lack of space is the reason many teachers give for not designating classroom space for a large muscle area. A climber and space to jump, tumble, and run require open, nonfurnished areas. A clear floor space of 50 square feet per child is the minimum needed for toddlers and preschoolers. Less usable space reduces gross motor activity and

group play, and may increase aggression (American Academy of Pediatrics, 2011, Olds, 2001).

A designer of innovative developmental environmental facilities for children, Ania Rui Olds (2001) bases designs on four basic environmental needs:

1. to encourage movement
2. to support comfort
3. to foster competence
4. to encourage a sense of control (pp. 8–11)

In the physical environment, the adult assures safety, provides opportunities, and gives support. The developing skill determines the environment and curriculum (Figure 3–13), which includes all the skill opportunities that have already been attained so they can be refined and practiced. New experiences are added to the old.

Home Visitors and Physical Development

A home educator, as a visitor in the home, does not have the ability to change the home environment in the same way that a classroom teacher does. However,

SKILL	ENVIRONMENT
Infants	
Rhythmic movement	Rocking chair, music
Crawling	Clean, cushioned surfaces to crawl on, under, through
Pulling up/standing	Stable furniture to hold
Walking, holding on (cruising)	Furnishings placed close together
Walking alone	Smooth, nonslip carpeted surface
Climbing	Low, padded platforms with padded surface beneath
Pushing, pulling, and lifting	Movable materials, tubs, wheeled toys
Toddlers: Above, plus	
Climbing	More challenging apparatus, three or four stairs with railing
Scooting	Wheeled toys
Running	Clear, carpeted area for running
Jumping	Sturdy, low platforms
Pushing, pulling, and lifting	Heavier, movable equipment
Throwing	Large, lightweight balls
Preschoolers: Above, plus	
Balancing	Climbing and balance apparatus
Pedaling	Tricycles, scooters
Hopping	Floor games and patterns
Throwing and catching	Balls and beanbags, targets
Striking	Bats, rackets, foam balls, wiffle balls suspended from ceiling
School-agers: Above, plus	
Dribbling and shooting	Basketballs, baskets, and court
Running races	Team games
Gymnastics	Padded surface, horse, and parallel bars
Dancing	Rhythmic group dancing

© Cengage Learning 2014

Figure 3–13 Developing skills determine the environment and curriculum.

It Happened to Me

"Pants"

I was observing my preschool children climbing on the climber in the classroom. One boy, taller and heavier than all the rest, had difficulty climbing the ladder. He would try and try. I thought perhaps it was that he just didn't know how, so I tried to talk him through it without lifting him up (I probably couldn't). He still couldn't do it. Then I looked closer. For one thing, his torso was long and his legs were short, making him out of proportion. Also, because he was heavy, in order to purchase pants to fit his waist, his parents had to buy a size so large that the crotch was long, almost to his knees. Have you ever tried to climb a ladder with your knees tied together? It must be what it felt like. I had a little private conversation with his mother, and we thought about possible solutions: shorts, pants with stretch. It wasn't just the pants but his weight, body proportion, and lack of arm strength, but he wanted to climb so badly that he eventually could once the clothing barrier was solved. Again, it pays to watch closely, not just check off "No" to "Able to climb a ladder."

home educators need to consider what kinds of learning environments and opportunities the child has both in the home and outside of the home, and to be comfortable, when necessary, discussing options for strengthening the learning environment. Just as in a center, a child needs a safe space and materials to explore, experience, and develop within the home setting and adequate time "playing and exploring" outside of the home. Educators in home settings should be well versed on what resources can be accessed to expand opportunities for children and families, should the need arise.

EXERCISE If you were designing a playground for infants, toddlers, preschoolers, or school-age children, what kinds of equipment and surfaces would it have?

Outdoor Play. Traffic, school, and work schedules, less play space, and even neighborhood dangers contribute to what Rivkin (1995) calls "vanishing habitats for play." The benefits of outdoor play to physical development—as well as to sensory learning, appreciation for nature, and expending energy—are obvious, but families and teachers seem to give it less and less attention. The outdoor environment should also be considered to maximize development in all areas.

Crawlers and walkers need materials that are safe and soft for first crawling and walking efforts indoors and out. Carriage and stroller paths past interesting things to look at begin the infant's outdoor experience. Paths later can be used for toddling, walking, and wheeled toys. Gentle inclines provide climbing and rolling down fun. A variety of natural materials such as grass, sand, wood, and smooth rocks provide sensory experiences in texture. Wind chimes, birdfeeders, and portable tape players provide hearing experiences. The area is enriched with a variety of toys for manipulation, pretend play, and construction. Even infants need outdoor play (Figure 3–14).

Preschoolers need the same type of equipment and surfaces as the younger children but more challenging and separate. They need climbing apparatus and balancing equipment. They need steep hills to climb and roll down, and movable construction materials. Riding toys, swings, and sports equipment such as balls, bats, nets, and ropes also facilitate physical development.

Environments for early school-age children should provide opportunities to develop noncompetitive activities such as dancing, tumbling, skating, swimming, and the supportive skills for sports such as running, throwing, and catching. In elementary school, recess is usually the one free-play time of the day when children can make choices. As children's opportunities for outdoor play are reduced by busy lives, neighborhood risks, and the culture of inactivity, the need for recess is greater. However, in the climate of pressure for academic performance, recess is sometimes sacrificed for remedial work or disciplinary measures. It is often the time when children are supervised by aides rather than their teachers. If teachers were on the playground, a great deal could be learned about children's physical and social behavior (O'Brien, 2003).

Physically challenged children can use the paths for wheelchairs and raised water and sand play areas for accessibility. Children with visual impairments are provided tactile and auditory stimulation

© Cengage Learning 2012

Figure 3–14 Even the littlest ones need an enriched outdoor environment full of sights, sounds, and a variety of textures.

materials. A real garden provides gross motor exercise as it is dug, raked, and weeded; it also encourages science, language, and sensory pleasure.

Play in Nature. In thinking of outdoor play, there is a movement to provide children with experiences in nature beyond a planned playground, out where there are trees to climb, plants and insects to examine, and a connection with nature with an outcome of appreciation and ecology of natural resources (Figure 3–15). Louv, author of *Last Child in the Woods* (2005), coined the phrase **nature deficit disorder**, attributing physical and behavioral problems to the lack of outdoor free play in natural surroundings. Children have three types of experiences with nature. Direct experiences involve actual physical contact with natural settings and nonhuman species. These are unplanned, spontaneous play in a backyard, a nearby forest, meadow, creek, or abandoned lot where plants and animals and their habitats can be explored. Indirect experiences are

Figure 3–15 Children need experiences with nature.

© Cengage Learning 2012

activities that are more programmed or planned such as botanical gardens, zoos, aquariums, museums, and nature centers. Caring for pets or domesticated animals are also indirect experiences. Vicarious or symbolic experiences occur when nature is encountered in books, television, and films. Urban, suburban, and even rural children's experiences usually move from vicarious, to indirect, to planned as they get older. A study of children diagnosed with Attention Deficit Hyperactivity Disorder (ADHD) showed that children who regularly play in outdoor, natural settings were found to have milder symptoms than those who played indoors or in traditional outdoor playgrounds (Taylor, Kuo, 2011).

Erickson and Ernst (2011) reviewed the research of the benefits of daily nature play:

▶ *Health*—Increased levels of physical activity leading to better motor skills and increasing distance vision.

▶ *Smarter*—Variety and options in nature stimulate creative thinking, lengthen attention span, reduce stress, higher cognitive function.

▶ *Feel better*—Increased feeling of wellbeing, lower levels of anxiety, strengthens social bonds.

▶ *Good for the earth*—Early experiences lead them to care about the natural world.

The Dimensions Educational Research Foundation is conducting research on the skills children develop through their regular interactions with the natural world showing the value of comprehensive nature education for young children. Many schools, parks, and nature centers are creating Nature Explore Classrooms, where children and adults can explore nature as a part of children's daily learning. Nature Explore® is a collaborative of the Arbor Day Foundation and Dimensions Foundation. Nature classroom

designs include outdoor spaces for building, music and movement, climbing, gardening, messy materials, gathering, and nature art. They use natural materials in construction and for storage (Figure 3–16).

Curriculum Planning. Through physical development and achievement, children's self-esteem and confidence are enhanced. Go back and take a look at Figure 3–7. Note the arrows go both ways. Physical development is influenced by those factors as well as those developmental areas being influenced by physical development. Cognitive and emotional development can have an effect on physical development. Kindergarten and primary age children are more attentive after recess; they stay on task longer and can resist fidgeting (Pellegrini & Holmes, 2006).

Besides helping children be more engaged learners after physical activity, educational concepts can be introduced through physical activity, mathematics (counting in games), science (movement activities that teach about the body), the arts (movement, drama, dancing), and literature (acting out stories). Almost any educational objective can be enhanced by getting children actively and physically engaged.

Planned activities can be documented using different methods to indicate the child's reaction to the experiences and development of skills. Over time, this record becomes valuable evidence of the efforts and celebrations of accomplishments. The developmental Checklists show skills for practicing and improvement and list the next skill that is to be introduced and encouraged. Vygotsky (1978) calls this the zone of proximal development, the

© Cengage Learning 2014

Figure 3–16 Nature classrooms where children and adults explore.

"distance between the actual developmental level. . . and the level of potential development. . . under adult guidance or in collaboration with more capable peers" (p. 86). With the help of an adult or another child, the developing child can approximate the skill before he really can accomplish it on his own. This brings promise, the feeling of success, and builds rapport with those who support the attempt. Wilson (2011) recommends providing observation and recording tools for children for outside play such as hand lens and clipboards, using natural materials for art projects, and involving children in growing plants and caring for animals.

The curriculum is individualized by referring to assessments to determine the level of motor development each child has attained. Daily plans for the whole group would include a variety of large muscle activities. They address the key experiences previously discussed. Individual children benefit from specifically focused activities to help them achieve the next level of development. They must, however, have many opportunities for success at their present level without feeling pressured or required to try something they are not sure they will attain. The skillful teacher addresses needs by combining planned activities with the child's interests; like the song line says, "A little bit of sugar helps the medicine go down."

Share with Children and Families. Relating observations to families not only informs them of the child's activity that day, but is an opportunity to teach child development principles and raise the child's self-esteem.

EXERCISE **How do you think a child would feel about the following comments?**

> "Now you can stand up all by yourself!"
> "Look at how you are sitting up! You're so strong."
> "You worked so hard at that balance beam today."
> "You climbed to the top of the climber today. How did it feel up there?"
> "You were able to dribble and make a basket!"

Accomplishments, as well as attempts, should be relayed to the child and the family. Telling the family good news in front of the child is a self-esteem booster for everyone. When the formal observation documentation such as Checklists or Anecdotal Records is shown or given to families, they see the progress and become involved in setting goals and strategies for the next skill or level. If the assessment indicates a significant developmental lag or regression, the family is consulted in private. This is to determine if it coincides with what they have observed. Then a follow-up action can be decided—maybe just to wait a while for the skill to develop or to seek further advice depending on the situation and the family's decision.

Differences between the Physical Play of Girls and Boys

EXERCISE **How are boys and girls different, other than anatomically?**

It is generally believed that physiologically, men are stronger than women, but women have greater endurance. There are other differences seen very early in life. Male one-year-olds already spend more time in gross motor activities, while girls of that age spend more time in fine motor activities.

The social treatment of girls and boys, regarding toys and movement, begins very early. It is virtually impossible to control for that factor. This makes it difficult to determine what indeed is genetic and what is learned. Many studies have shown gender differences in toy selection, adult interactions with girls and boys, fantasy play themes, and types of play (Figure 3–17). Boys were found to be more aggressive and more than three times more frequently labeled as having ADHD (attention deficit hyperactivity disorder, Bloom, 2007) and girls more domestic; boys more physical and girls

© Cengage Learning 2012

Figure 3–17 Boys are more likely to engage in rough-and-tumble play.

more verbal. The exact cause of those differences is still under debate.

Think About It . . .
How does Figure 3–17 make you feel? What would you do if you were the adult in charge?

Knowing what we know about boys' greater need for physical activity, the curriculum pushdown has reduced the time children are spending in play-based learning. Barbarin (2010) points to this as a risk factor, especially for African-American boys. Another factor may be that because early childhood care and education is a field with predominantly female personnel, their own genetic and social predispositions guide play expectations for girls and boys. That subtle bias can be seen in the low priority for large muscle equipment and curriculum in early childhood environments outside and especially inside, often relegated to a certain time usually in a gym or open area. Often, female personnel give quick responses and attempt to discourage rough-and-tumble play in the classroom because they fear injury, that the play will escalate into real fighting, and that it will overstimulate and encourage the continuation of rowdy play (Carlson, 2011). The biases are not so subtle in comments such as "Boys don't cry" or "Young ladies don't do that." Rough-and-tumble play or play wrestling is more often not allowed, not addressed in policies, and yet is tolerated in moderation in classrooms because it is a frequently occurring behavior (Tannock, 2007).

Longitudinal studies have been done on rough-and-tumble play, defined as active physical running and wrestling accompanied by laughter rather than frowning and hitting (Pellegrini, 2006). Rough-and-tumble play is not about territories or possessions. Participants take turns as victim and victimizer. Pellegrini's studies found that rough-and-tumble play was engaged in typically by boys who had high social skills. The studies contend that observation of rough-and-tumble play can be a social competence indicator. It leads to games with rules, role taking, and problem solving. Rough-and-tumble play is not only a physical release but "may facilitate friendships and promote cooperative pro-social behaviors and attitudes" (Scott & Panksepp, 2003). A well-planned preschool classroom includes space, equipment, and floor covering so that large muscle, whole-body experiences can be managed

safely. Some policies and rules for rough-and-tumble play may include:

No kicking
Tags with open hands only
No choking
Keep hands away from hair and head
Smiles stop — Play stops (Carlson, F 2011)

Small Muscle Development

The coordinated functions of arm, hand, and fingers are often taken for granted.

EXERCISE **Pick up each of the following items: chair, book, dime, hair. Perform each of the following tasks: zip a zipper, tie a shoe, write your name. Now perform the above tasks with your non-dominant hand. Notice the different movements and functions of your small muscles.**

For the first few months of life, the small muscles of hands and feet are moved by reflex, rather than by purposeful movements controlled by thought. Apply pressure to the palms of the infant, and her mouth opens and her head flexes forward (Babkin reflex). Stroke her palm, and her hand closes into a grip around the object so strong it can hold her weight. Stroke the sole of her foot, and her toes extend. Over the course of the first year, the infant develops control over these small muscles, first by reaching, corralling, and grasping with the entire hand. By age one, the infant can use the thumb and forefinger in a pincer grasp. Letting go, or releasing, comes later than grasping. This explains why an infant holding onto an earring or a lock of hair has a hard time letting go of it.

▶❚❚ TEACHSOURCE VIDEO ACTIVITY

Watch these three segments on Gross Motor Development on Education CourseMate website, accessed through CengageBrain.com. Which principles from the chapter do you see illustrated? Did you notice a common theme regarding individual development?

0–2: Gross Motor Development of Infants and Toddlers

2–5: Gross Motor Development for Early Childhood

5–11: Gross Motor Development for Middle Childhood

These small muscle skills are connected to eye and hand coordination, the cephalocaudal and proximodistal development of the whole body, and thought processes. They will continue to develop into the more specific motions needed to twist, squeeze, pinch, button, snap, zip, pour, pick up small objects, insert, and cut. All of these skills are leading to the achievement of readiness to write. Other developmental skills also signal that the child is ready for writing:

> balance without using the hands
> grasp and release objects voluntarily
> handedness predominates, with one hand leading and the other following
> eye-hand coordination
> construction experiences—putting things together, parts and whole concept
> increased attention span

The developmental sequence is

> scribbling, holding tool in a hammer hold
> scribbling, with finger hold
> control of tool to close a circle shape
> making straight lines
> drawing with the characteristics of writing
> beginning of alphabet letters
> ability to make a square
> printing name—in uppercase letters
> printing name—in uppercase and lowercase
> left-to-right progression of letters and words

Observing Small Muscle Development. The physical environment includes materials and opportunities for the child to practice small muscle skills. The baby touches and grasps any objects within its reach, appropriate or not: Grandpa's glasses, a hot coffee cup, or a dust mote floating through the air. The toddler grabs, carries, dumps, fills, manipulates whatever is movable: toilet paper, stones in the driveway, knickknacks on the coffee table, or items on the supermarket shelf. The preschooler practices writing with whatever tools are available: a stick in the dust, Mommy's lipstick, or a paintbrush in tar. It is important for the observer to watch what the child is touching, then evaluate its potential for harm. If necessary, the adult intervenes before damage is done to the child, the object, or the environment.

The observer in an educational setting sees the movements as indicators of development and documents what the child can do on this date so that periodically the record is updated to check if progress is being made. Knowledge of the child's abilities at this stage influences the kinds of equipment, materials, and activities the teacher provides. An infant is given items

that are easy to grasp and offer some immediate signal, such as a rattle or a toy with a bell or squeak. The toddler is given items to stack, fill and dump, pound, squeeze, and manipulate, such as clay dough and puzzles with simple, large pieces. The preschooler is provided with smaller manipulatives such as building bricks, puzzles with smaller pieces, lacing cards, scissors, and a wide array of writing tools and papers. Activities to help develop the whole arm, whole hand, and pincer grip all contribute to the preschooler's increased small muscle development used in writing (Huffman & Fortenberry, 2011).

The small muscle task of the early school grades is handwriting. How children should learn handwriting has evolved from the Montessori method of tracing letter forms, pages of practice, copying words, to emergent literacy believing that when the child finds it important to convey a message in writing, they will produce a resemblance of the letters. Children commonly grasp writing tools tightly and press down hard enough sometimes to tear the paper. There are various forms of printing, printscript is the common letter forming and D'Nealian print that has more slanted lines that appear between printscript and cursive writing. Distinguishing between some letters is difficult, such as b and d, E and F, n and m. Experiences with print, the child's own motivation, and the classroom environment as well as small muscle development all influence the child's handwriting ability. Sometimes having a list of children's names to copy, using children's names on a waiting list for a certain activity, and planning a daily journal-writing time are activities that stimulate handwriting.

Documentation of small muscle development can be made with Checklists, Anecdotal Records, and samples of the child's work on paper. The first scribbles, the first alphabet letters, the first name writing, and the first "I love you" note are precious and graphic illustrations of the small muscle development as it leads to literacy. These are important evidence to be added to the Portfolio and shared with families to illustrate the child's small muscle development. Stages of small muscle development also are integrally involved in both art and literacy and are discussed again in later chapters.

Observing the Physical Development of Infants and Toddlers

Developmental assessments of infants and toddlers occur routinely in health-care settings. Well child visits give the health-care provider information on changes in height, weight, responses, and attainment of normal milestones of development. These assessments are considered screenings looking for indications outside the wide range of normal that warrant further evaluations. Some standard assessments are vision, hearing, and exposure to lead. These early assessments are not accurate as predictors of later performance, but are monitors of the child's wellbeing.

In an early childhood setting, babies' awake hours are filled with play, exploration, movement, and expressing feelings (precursors to language development). Observations can be made while the infant is moving freely in the environment such as the crib, on the floor, or in someone's arms. Once the infant has coordinated her small muscle skills, observe and record how she handles toys, food, and art materials as they are introduced and used. Use recording methods that preserve the details of what the child is playing with and, more importantly, how she is moving her body and hands. The Checklist records milestones in physical development while other methods are more useful in describing the creeping, crawling, walking, grasping, clutching, letting go, and rolling, stacking, throwing.

For infants, body awareness, learning the names of parts of the body, and naming parts as they are washed and moved are the beginnings of the large muscle curriculum. Using the Developmental Assessment Checklist, the adult can see what the child has accomplished

It Happened to Me

He Sure Can Cut!

We had been working with Andy's small muscle skills, finding ways to interest him in trying some cutting instead of always playing with blocks and on the climber. We found some construction machinery catalogs and invited him to cut and paste to make a book to take home. He worked for several days at it, and we saw those cutting skills improve so dramatically we sent home a "Happy Note" about the news. Mom came in a few days later and said, "You know those cutting skills you've been working on with Andy? He's been working on them at home too. He got the scissors and cut up all the chains in my jewelry box into little pieces!" Gulp! Teaching should come with disclaimers, "We cannot be responsible for the application of newly learned skills in a unsupervised environment."

and continue to give her practice to refine that skill. If she can roll over, then she is frequently placed on the floor and coaxed, called, lured by a toy, or gently rocked to practice the rolling. She will be sitting up soon, so she can be propped in a sitting position several times a day for short periods to give her a new view. Moving to a beat is an important curriculum goal, so music, rhythm instruments, singing, and dancing are planned daily.

Older infants and toddlers begin the quest to explore beyond their body. Toys and activities to manipulate and move are a necessary part of the curriculum. Activities are planned for interaction with adults and materials chosen to keep interest. The adult models and introduces new ways of playing.

Locomotor movement, such as creeping and crawling, transfers weight from one side of the body to the other. This is a necessary skill for walking because all the more complex skills build on it. To stimulate creeping and crawling, interesting objects and pictures are placed at floor level, not too far away to be frustrating but alluring enough to produce forward motion. Crawlers want interesting things to crawl on, such as unbreakable mirrors or pictures under sheets of Plexiglas on the floor. Texture mazes on the floor and up the first two feet of the wall are stimulating environments planned for infant and toddler motor development. Feeling the steady beat, Weikart (2000) believes, is a primary ability to basic motor skill development, so those games of "Patty Cake" and baby rumbas are planned curriculum activities. Reading poetry, repeating fingerplays, and reading stories with repetitive lines provide verbal experiences with rhythm.

To encourage children's physical activity, Pica (2010) suggests the following:

- arranging the environment to allow for movement
- buying equipment and props with movement in mind
- demonstrating enthusiasm for physical activity
- helping children understand why movement is important

Helping All Children with Physical Development

Culture and Play

The rising concern over childhood obesity has lead researchers to investigate how biological, environmental, and socio-cultural factors relate to play. One aspect of study is how culture affects young children's physical activity especially by looking at children in the home setting. *The Observational System for Recording Physical Activity in Children—Preschool* (OSRAC-P) by McIver and colleagues (2009), still in its development phase, indicated that children were less active during indoor play interactions with family members. Other studies by Goodway and Smith (2005) looked at African-American and Latino families, where obesity rates are higher, and found these families had low levels of physical activities with their children and primarily sedentary lifestyles. Socio-cultural and physical environments (rural/urban) may also contribute to the differences. From Emma and Jarrett's (2010) analysis of the research, parent education, teacher education, and cultural beliefs related to physical activity will be the determining factors in improving young children's physical activity and health.

Children with Disabilities

When a screening indicates that further assessments should be conducted, the child is referred to a specialist who will do a more complete evaluation dictated by the screening outcome. Appropriate remediation and further recommendations are often to be included in a program with other children of the same age, but with some modifications. Adapting the environment and planning for exceptional children will build on the abilities they do have. The curriculum is adapted so they have the closest match to what the rest of the class is doing. This is what is known as the **least restrictive environment**. If the class is marching, the child in the wheelchair can push along in the parade or beat the drum. The child with a hearing impairment can watch the beat being tapped out and feel the vibration of the drum. The child who does not speak can lead the band. The child who is visually impaired can play an instrument in one location. The child who speaks no English can move and play with everyone else.

Just as with any other child, the basis for planning the curriculum begins with the assessment of where the child is in that developmental area. More information is usually present about the area of disability, from family information and the child's file with reports from helping professionals. The observer needs to attune to the areas other than the one affected. Sometimes there is a bias or unconscious attitude that other developmental areas are similarly affected. That is not true. Other areas could be right at the age or stage level with other children. They could just as easily be advanced. Objective observation and recording, without bias concerning the disability, is important.

The concept of **Universal Design for Learning (UDL)** is that the environment (physical, social, and curriculum) is planned to give ALL students access. It includes modifications to the physical environment, both indoors and outdoors, and strategies for multiple ways to experience and learn. The suggestions for classroom modifications for children with special needs listed below are just as applicable to all children.

For children with physical impairments, make modifications to the environment to match the disability:

Visual: Encourage the use of hearing and touch to explore the environment

Keep the pathways of the room wide and free of obstructions

Describe your actions as you do them

Use large labels or Braille, depending on range of visual disability

Provide many sensory and tactile materials in the room

Encourage sighted children to help if necessary, identify themselves when nearby, and explain what they are doing and how

Orthopedic impairments:

Keep the pathways of the room wide and free of obstructions

Include nonlocomotor activities in games and learning activities

Modify the classroom tools with large knobs or grips

Encourage other children to help when asked. Adapted from Gerecke and Weatherby (2001)

Physical development is maturational based on genetics. All children develop under those influences that are also affected by nutrition and opportunity. Non–English-speaking children and children of diverse cultures are not different physically from others in the group. It may be in the communication of expectations with both groups that any difficulties arise. Modeling and acceptance will help all children feel the freedom to try physical activities.

Helping Professionals for Physical Development Concerns

If observation and assessment reveal a developmental lag, the family is consulted, following confirmation by others on the team. The family will be referred to their medical provider, such as the pediatrician, or a specialist for an evaluation of the child's physical skills. Others who may become involved in evaluations of physical developmental lags follow:

occupational therapist—a specialist who evaluates activities of daily living (feeding or dressing themselves) and provides therapy for assisting in the mastery of these activities

neurologist—a physician who specializes in the diagnosis and treatment of disorders of the nervous system, treating symptoms of pain and motor impairments

physical therapist—a specialist who evaluates capabilities for standing, sitting, and ambulation and provides therapy for people who have problems with these functions

Other Methods

Other Methods to Record Physical Development:

Class Log List
Anecdotal/Running Record
Media such as photographs or video recording

Key Terms

bias	least restrictive
cephalocaudal	environment
Checklist	nature deficit disorder
closed method	proximodistal
failure to thrive	reflex
syndrome	sensory integration
frame of reference	small muscle
growth	Universal Design for
large muscle	Learning (UDL)

Plans

Go to the Education CourseMate website, accessed through CengageBrain.com for the following:

Check List forms on Physical Development for All

Plan Week 3 Part A, Directions for a Checklist on Physical Development, including What

to Do with It, Portfolio Evidence Sheet Example, Sharing with Child and Family, Actions—Read a Book, In the Environment, In the Curriculum, In the Newsletter

Plan Week 3 Part B, Directions for Anecdotal Recording of Physical Development for Group B, including What to Do with It and Sharing with the Child and the Family

Plan Week 3 Part C, Reflective Journal

Resources

American Academy of Pediatrics. (2011). *Caring for our children: National health and safety performance standards: Guidelines for out-of-home child care* (3rd ed.). Elk Grove Village, IL: American Academy of Pediatrics.

Carlson, F. M. (2011). *Big Body Play: Why boisterous, vigorous and very physical play is essential to children's development and learning.* Washington, DC: National Association for the Education of Young Children.

Cuppens, V., Rosenow, N., & Wike, J. (2007). *Learning with nature idea book: Creating nurturing outdoor spaces for children.* Lincoln, NE: The National Arbor Day Foundation.

Isbell, C., Isbell, R. (2007). *Sensory Integration: A guide for preschool teachers.* Beltsville, MD: Gryphon House.

Kalich, K., Bauer, D., & McPartlin, D. (2009). *Early sprouts: Cultivating healthy food choices in young children.* St. Paul, MN: Redleaf Press.

Keeler, Rusty (2008). *Natural Playscapes: Creating Outdoor Play Environments for the Soul.* Redmond, Wash: Exchange Press.

Louv, R. (2005). *Last child in the woods: Saving our children from nature-deficit disorder.* New York: Workman.

Lyman, P., Feierabend, J., & McNamara, D.M. (2008). *Move it 2!* DVD. Chicago, IL: GIA Publications.

Olds, A. R. (2001). *Child care design guide.* New York: McGraw-Hill.

Pica, R. (2010). *Experiences in movement and Music: Birth to Age 8* (4th ed.) Belmont, CA: Wadsworth/Cengage Learning

Sanders, S. W. (2002). *Active for life: Developmentally appropriate movement programs for young children.* Washington, DC: National Association for the Education of Young Children.

CHAPTER 4

Using Running Records to Look at Social Development

OBSERVATION THOUGHT

"When we look at what the child cannot do, we fail to see all the child can do."

NAEYC Standards naeyc

The following NAEYC Standards for Early Childhood Professional Preparation are addressed in this chapter:

Standard 1: Promoting Child Development and Learning

Standard 3: Observing, Documenting, and Assessing to Support Young Children and Families

Standard 6: Becoming a Professional

IN THIS CHAPTER

- Using Running Records
- Topics in Observation: "The Stew"
- Looking at Social Development
- Observing Infants and Toddlers in Social Play
- Helping All Children with Social Development
- Helping Professionals for Social Development Concerns

Using Running Records

EXERCISE Read the Running Record that focuses on Larry (Figure 4–1). Cover the right-hand column with a sheet of paper; make comments or inferences about Larry as indicated from this incident.

From the exercise, you see that a **Running Record** uses the same technique as the Anecdotal Recording. It is a factual, detailed, account written over a span of time. Actions are described and quotes are recorded as precisely as possible. Commentary or

Time Recording Began   Recorder

Nov. 14   10:15 a.m.   BAN recorder   *Use initials after first mention of name for time saving.*

LARRY   4 Yrs., 2 mo.

Larry is in the play kitchen with Susan, Allison, and Marie. M: <u>put the eggs in the refrigerator.</u> L. takes 2 dishes and 2 forks and sets the dishes on the table. Hands forks to Andrea, sitting at the table. L. gets another plate and fork and sets it at another chair. Andrea goes by on a big truck and L. gets on the back. A: yells, <u>Get off!</u> L. gets off then stands watching her as she goes on. L. stands watching. Still watching, L. walks into other room where A. went with truck. To Mike: <u>These robbers stole our truck,</u> pointing to A. M. has the gas tank. He just looks up. L: <u>She needs some gas,</u> points to A. A: <u>No, they didn't tell ya.</u> M. holds gas tank to chest. A. rolls towards them. L. puts two hands out to stop the truck. She drives by and he just watches. L. walks back into other room and gets into rocker boat. A. and S. come by on two trucks. A to L: <u>Can you show us the cemetery?</u> L. doesn't answer. H. rocks fast with Lucy and S. gets on. L. rocks fast. They hand him dolls. He holds them. Kevin gets in and rocks. S: <u>You need to get off this boat.</u> Lucy to L: <u>You're our neighbor.</u> L: <u>I can stay on here.</u> Sets dolls down. Picks them up. Lucy purposely falls out of boat. She laughs, gets back in and rocks fast. Lucy: <u>You're making me fall off.</u> L. stops rocking. Steven comes over to get in. L: <u>You're too heavy.</u> K. comes with blocks. L. drops them into trucks parked nearby. L: <u>We need some money.</u> Jumps out. Climbs up climber, runs down slide, back to boat. Chews on fingernail. Other boys dropping blocks into boat. L. laughs loudly. Stands up in boat, smiling. <u>No more money</u> he says loudly. He takes the doll and throws it out, throws out some blocks. L. gets out and throws some blocks back in. 1: <u>More money, more money.</u> Gets back in the boat. Girls in boat tip over backwards on purpose, laughing. He pulls blocks out and takes 2 over to the shelf and drops them nearby. Screws up face, arms out. <u>Too much money. Why are you doing this?</u> Gets into boat and starts stacking the blocks in it. Kevin gets in. They rock and sing, <u>Do, do, do, ya need some gas?</u>

10:26

Action

Exact Quotes

Follow target child

Comments: Play entry tactic

Comments: Where did this come from?

Asserts himself

Uncertain?

Accepted into the game

Beginning cleanup!

A new friend!

Time ended   Teacher's questions ⓘ   *Should blocks be allowed in this area? Ask Betty.*

Note:
Bare record could be copied for other children's files if no negative events took place or block other names

Figure 4–1 Running Record Example.

© Cengage Learning 2014

interpretation about the recording is written separately from the actual account. The recorder decides to observe and write for a period of time, focusing on one child or one play area. A nonselective narrative documents a specimen of that child's or that area's action.

The Running Record is written as the events are happening, while the Anecdotal Recording usually is written shortly after a significant event. The Anecdotal Recording is a little story with a beginning, the action, and an ending. Running Records are indiscriminate, giving a more objective glimpse into a normal (or what may turn out to be an abnormal) segment of time. That is not known, however, before the recorder begins to write. Everything that happens in that time segment is recorded: the mundane, the boring, the unexplained. At the end of a time period, the recording stops. This may not necessarily be at the end of the event. A Running Record is like turning on a video camera and just letting it run for a certain amount of time, recording whatever occurs. A Running Record is most useful in giving a naturalistic view of a short time in the life of a child.

When a learning center or area of the classroom is the focus of a Running Record, the Record can help evaluate the usefulness of the area and if the area needs any modifications. Particular learning centers or classroom areas are more suitable for viewing specific skills. A Running Record in the large muscle area obviously gives information on children's climbing, running, or jumping skills, but also can yield valuable information on social, emotional, and verbal development. Imaginative play, social interactions, and self-concept are illustrated vividly in the dramatic play area as well as in the block area. Small muscle skills, literacy development, and social and verbal skills are observed easily in the art area or during play at the sand or water table. Running Records of 10 minutes at any one of these areas can be extremely informative.

The Running Record requires intense concentration and focused attention. Other staff are needed in the room to be sure all children are supervised adequately; any recording in progress is secondary to a child in need. Any time recording must be interrupted, a line is drawn and the ending and return times are noted. Recording may be resumed once the situation is under control.

EXERCISE On a separate sheet of paper, describe how you might feel if someone were watching you carefully for 10 minutes and writing notes.

Uses

The Running Record

- records detailed segments of behavior occurring in a certain time block.
- focuses on an individual child to show a naturalistic view of a part of the day.
- can be analyzed for evaluation of many developmental areas: physical, social, emotional, language, self-concept, attention span, problem solving, memory, learning style.
- documents evaluation of developmental areas for child study.
- can focus on a particular learning center or classroom area to see what typically occurs there.

⊕ Advantages

The Running Record is helpful because it

- is written at the time the behavior occurs, so it is less likely to be affected by bias and more likely to include lots of detail.
- can be used for a variety of purposes—developmental assessment, deeper understanding of the child, information for other professionals for further analysis.
- details a normal segment of time in the day, giving a more natural view.

Figure 4–2 Observation may change behavior, so the observer attempts to be unobtrusive.

© Cengage Learning 2014

One caution in using the Running Record, or any other recording technique, is the possible effect it may have on the child's behavior (Figure 4–2). It may make the child feel uncomfortable or act in an artificial way. The recorder must be sensitive to that self-consciousness. When such behavior is observed, the writing would then stop and efforts made to be less obvious in the future. In a classroom where observation and recording go on all the time as a natural part of everyday life, children often cease to notice. If they are shown the notes, even if they are not yet able to read, they feel more comfortable about the writing. Talking with the children about what was observed helps them understand the purpose behind the writing. When they hear the teacher talk with their family about the episodes from the notes, they realize that their actions are important and meaningful. Warning: Any negative occurrences or difficulties observed should not be discussed with the family in the presence of the child.

It Happened to Me

Artist's Model?

I was sightseeing on a bus, my first time in a foreign country, feeling very special and looking all around at the scenery, when I felt someone watching me. A young man toward the rear of the bus was sketching on a pad. "Oh," I thought, "he's an artist. This country's full of artists. He must be sketching me." So I turned my best side toward him, sat up straighter in the seat, and sat still with a facial expression I wanted captured on his pad. As he was leaving the bus I craned my neck to see the pad. It was a forest scene he was working on, apparently from memory. Because I thought he was watching me, I changed my behavior.

▶ reveals many areas of development in one recording.

▶ can evaluate the effectiveness of a learning center or area.

⊖ Disadvantages

The Running Record may

▶ make the subject feel watched, become uncomfortable, and change behavior, destroying the nature of the recording.

▶ not show normally occurring behavior in the time segment.

▶ make the adult unavailable to facilitate or observe what is happening in the rest of the room because attention is focused on the recording.

▶ tire and drain the recorder because of its intensity.

EXERCISE Figure 4–3 contains a Running Record on which to practice. Find the recorder's mistakes, then return to this point and check yourself.

Answers:

(printed upside down)

The term *plays* is too generic.

Ann is standing at the sand table, filling tiny containers with a scoop, tongue between teeth. Q and T are also filling cups.

"Talks" is not recording exact quotes.

To Q: "I can get these all fuller than you."

"As usual" can be in the right column as a note by the recorder to indicate knowledge about Ann's play partner preference

This was an example of good action description. The reader can "see" the action.

Oops. Not the exact quote.

"Snow."

How does the observer know what Ann thinks? Exact quotes were not written down.

A grabs the shovel away from Q

It is helpful to know what other children joined the group.

B, K, and S come over.

This is a summary.

A watches them fill empty containers. To B, K, S: These are mine and they're filled with snow. What's in yours?

But where did she go?

A skips over to the Dramatic Play area where C and D are putting on dress-up clothes.

Recorder wrote the quote with the pronunciation as it was heard. Good.

ABC Center	Ann Wade
4 yr. old class	BAN recorder
Sep. 28	

9:30	Ann plays with other children at the sand table. She talks with Q most of the time.
	She picks up a shovel and scoops sand into a sifter, watching it sprinkle and calling it snow.
	When Q picks up the shovel, Ann thinks she should have it back so she grabs it away. Q gets another one. As children come over, Ann gives them attention and asks them questions.
	After a while, Ann skips over to another group of children she wants to play with. She says, "Hey, watcha doin?"

Figure 4–3 Find the record's errors in this Running Record.

[The following text appears upside-down at the top of the left column:]

9:39
Recorder did not include the end time.
go to the dance!" She twirls away.
then wraps herself in a shawl. "There, now I'm ready to
A puts on a skirt, gloves (works to get every finger in), and
Not much detail here

EXERCISE Practice writing a Running Record. Take a separate sheet of paper right now, fold it in half, select a person to watch, and write down everything that person does and says for 10 minutes.

Rate your Running Record:

> Did you mention the setting so the reader knows where it took place?

> Did you write the date and time you started?

> Did you write your name on it as the recorder?

Look over the words you used and make sure they described actions, not summarized them or gave reasons for them. The words should form mental pictures:

> If you used any of the following words, perhaps you fell in the trap of summarizing: *because, wanted to, tried, saw, played, looked (emotion), noticed, pretended.*

> If more than one person was involved, did you write down the conversation word for word?

> Now go back and in the right column write what judgments you would make about this person's physical, cognitive, social, and emotional development.

> What did this segment of action show about that person? What questions did it raise about why the person acted that way?

Running and Anecdotal Records are like written movie scripts, exactly describing actions, facial expressions, and exact words of the players.

Home Visiting and Running Records

Running Records, as described for the classroom setting, are difficult to do in the context of a home visit without the addition of an engaged third person (another visitor or the parent) and/or an environmental setting that draws the child into playing without adult interaction. Viable options for the home setting are videotaping the visit or parts of the visit and using the tape as a base for writing Running Record, or bringing a colleague or supervisor to record the visit. Either way, the educator is then able to work with the child, children, or parent and child and to collect and use Running Records for the purposes suggested.

Pitfalls to Avoid

Running Records are time- and energy-intensive, so the recorder must be sure that the children are safely involved and under the supervision of at least one other adult for interaction; only then should a Running Record be started. Because of the objective technique, it probably is not a method that a volunteer could be asked to do, but the supervision could be assigned. Attention to safety and the interactive needs of children always takes precedence over recording.

Another pitfall is that close observation tends to make the target child feel observed, which can alter behavior. The recorder must be careful to observe from far enough away so as to not interfere with the child's actions, but close enough to hear conversations. Sometimes, the location of a chair on the other side of a piece of equipment, behind the child's line of vision but within hearing distance, can be effective.

Often other children enter into the Running Record in interactions with the target child. Because this will be filed in one child's Portfolio, other children's names should be blotted from this particular recording for anonymity.

A Running Record can yield a great deal of insight into a child's usual activities, but it can be so mundane as to seem unimportant. It is not. As a true measure of a child's development and behavior, naturalistic observation like a Running Record is invaluable.

Using Technology

A video camera is a wonderful tool for capturing live action. There is no way a written Anecdotal or Running Record can compare, but using a video camera does take time, patience, and the knack for being in the right place at the right time. Using a video camera can also be intrusive. (See a discussion of this in Chapter 11.) Whenever anyone but the most experienced model sees a camera aimed their way, they change their behavior. It is difficult to capture spontaneous, meaningful video footage.

Hand-held computers and smart phones can be helpful because many people can type or text faster than they can write. Using a keyboard also makes it easier to add the Running Record to an electronic file on each child. Electronic files, mentioned in Chapter 3, are easy to manipulate, do not take up classroom storage space, are easier to keep confidential, and can also store artwork and photographs.

How to Find the Time

Running Records are one of the most time-intensive recording methods. To concentrate fully on one child and write accurately and descriptively about the child's every action and conversation takes undivided attention. That means that this recording method—in its purest sense, done as the action is taking place—is not practical for the person who is also responsible for the classroom. A modification can be to jot notes and amplify them later; however, time dulls the accuracy of the memory, so it is never as rich as what really happened. We are therefore faced with the dilemma of how to make time to complete Running Records.

The student teacher or student visitor may have the luxury of doing Running Records without having any other classroom responsibility. This is a wonderful learning experience and one that should be practiced. Not only can it be a great help to the teacher, but it can be a learning experience for the student by sharing the Running Record with the teacher and then discussing the interpretation. Another option is for the program administrator to arrange for coverage of the teacher's classroom for a brief period each day so the teacher can sit and watch children's play. Or a classroom volunteer could be trained in this method under the direction of the teacher. However it is arranged, Running Records are valuable pieces of documentation, and a 10-minute observation in every developmental area usually provides enough detail or depth to enable the observer and the reader to draw some conclusions about the child's level.

❓ What to Do with It

Following the actual recording, the teacher can make notes in the right-hand column in the same categories as the Anecdotal Record:

- explanations
- comments about development
- questions for further investigation
- plans for the child based on the observation

REVIEW

RUNNING RECORD
Detailed account of a segment of the child's day, written as observed. Includes settings, descriptions of actions and interactions, and exact quotes.

Types of Information to Record Using Running Records
Any segment of the child's day, usual or unusual. It can yield information on the following:

- separation and adjustment
- self-care skills
- physical development
- social development
- emotional development
- language and speech
- attention span and interests
- cognitive development
- literacy
- creativity
- socio-dramatic play
- self-esteem

The Running Record is filed in the target child's Portfolio after noting its presence on the Portfolio Evidence Sheet (Figure 4–4). It may be read to the child at a later date to form the basis of a conversation about the child's activities. The teacher can ask questions such as, "When you were piling the blocks up and ran out of blocks, you stopped building. Is there something

PORTFOLIO EVIDENCE OF CHILD'S DEVELOPMENT			
Evidence Type	**Date**	**Recorder**	**Notes**
SOCIAL/ EMOTIONAL – the child's social and emotional development, self-concept			
RR	10/1/	BAN	Freeplay – blocks, painting books
CL	10/3/	MLS	Solitary

Figure 4–4 Portfolio Evidence Sheet.

© Cengage Learning 2014

TOPICS in OBSERVATION

"The Stew"

Once upon a time, a chef set out to make a stew by preparing the ingredients and placing them on the stove to cook. After a period of time, the chef took a deep ladle and sampled a bit of each of the ingredients to judge the progress of the stew. Some needed more time to cook, so the chef extended the cooking time. The broth was lacking in flavor, so the chef added some spices. It was too salty, so the chef added a potato to take away some saltiness. The chef still was unsatisfied with the taste, so a master chef, a stew expert, was called in to give an opinion. More modifications were made to the stew.

The stew was then served to the first diner, the chef's mother, who declared the stew "Marvelous!" The Board of Health inspector closely examined each part of the stew, looking for irregularities, without actually caring about the whole stew. The vegetarian, repulsed by the meat in the stew, stopped eating, vowing to make comments to the cook. One diner thought it needed more salt, while another thought it was too salty. The unserved portions of the stew were refrigerated and reheated the next day making the flavors mellower and texture softer. The smart chef wrote down the recipe so that future stews could be as flavorful, but the chef knew it all depended on the ingredients available. But alas, some of the diners had moved on to other restaurants, so they never got the full, aged taste of the stew. Ah, if they could only taste the stew now.

Meaning

The stew is the child made up of many areas of development. The family brings the child to the teacher with knowledge, skills, and abilities. The teacher works with those to bring them to a certain expected level. A sample of the child's development is made to determine progress in development and further actions. In some areas, nothing is needed but time. In other areas, additions are made in the curriculum to assist in development. Sometimes, behaviors that are getting in the way of learning are modified. Expert advice is sometimes needed, so the family and teachers seek the referral and advice of helping professionals.

Hopefully, the family is pleased with the progress of the child, overlooking some areas still developing. Some observers look at specific areas while not seeing the whole child, such as a speech pathologist, dentist, or physical therapist. The child's progress may not be acceptable to some who have special interests or biases. Over time, the child grows, develops, and changes, but past teachers and resource people do not have the opportunity to observe the progress. The family and teachers who have a record of the changes know what worked for that child. Each child is unique, however, and the teacher realizes the necessity for adapting the environment and curriculum for each child and group. It is sad that not everyone gets the opportunity to appreciate the transformation.

else you could have used to continue playing there?" or "When you were at the Writing Center, I heard you say something about writing a letter and an elephant but I couldn't hear what you said. Do you remember?"

The Running Record that includes other children who interacted with the target child can be copied, with the teacher then making notations in the right-hand column about the second child. When the record is filed in a child's Portfolio, the names of the other children should be blotted out.

Go to the Education CourseMate website, accessed through CengageBrain.com to download Running Record forms, plans, and resources.

Looking at Social Development

Two children are pulling on the same toy. "It's mine!" "No, I want it!" An adult comes over, takes it away from one and gives it to the other. "You've got to share! Don't be so selfish."

That is not sharing. That is robbery. That is rein-forcing the concept that bigger people can take things away from smaller people. True sharing is the willing relinquishing of one's rightful possession to another person. Social competence is the ability to get along with others. It is the ability to express, understand, and control emotions, and display social problem-solving skills. "OK, Jasmine, you can have it as soon as I finish playing with it and I'm almost done." But how do chil-dren learn not to be selfish? How do they develop an awareness that other people have wants and needs? How are they able to express their own needs in a nonaggressive yet assertive way and control their own emotions? Social competence, just like all other devel-opmental domains, is affected by three realms: biology (temperament and genetic influences), relationships (responsive adults), and environment (exposures to threats such as extreme poverty, violence, substance abuse, abuse, and neglect).

During the early years, children learn how to es-tablish and maintain relationships with others, enter into groups and get along, and adapt their own wants and needs to meet society's expectations. Through this process, children are integrated into their society. They enter this learning process with their own particular dispositions and relationship history. When children are in child care, the quality of the relationship with caregivers and peer groups as well as the social and emotional climate all have a reciprocal effect on the socialization process (Howes & James, 2002). Observa-tion of a child's play gives indicators of social behavior, cognitive, language, and motor skills. A careful record-ing and assessment of social play can give specific in-formation about the level of the child's functioning in each domain.

The Importance of Play to Social Development

▶ Individual and team sports?
▶ Arts?
▶ Computer games?
▶ Hobbies?

Some early childhood programs are criticized for emphasizing or even allowing play. "They're not learning anything there. All they ever do is just play." The word *play* is used repeatedly in dis-cussing social development and many other areas as well. An understanding of play and its impor-tance is necessary to child observers because it is a vehicle for learning. In fact, play equals learn-ing, learning *to* play and learning *from* play (Singer, 2007). The tendency to play is natural and emerges sequentially in most children. It can be negatively impacted by brain disorders such as autism, social neglect, and trauma. For play to thrive, motivate, and enhance all areas of development, it requires the scaffolding support of an adult, not to dictate or restrict the play, but to set the stage and supply the necessary ingredients of time, materials, approval, and modeling.

The phrase "Play is the child's work," or varia-tions of it, has been the theme or motto for defend-ing play and advocating for play. The Concept Map in Figure 4–5 illustrates the developmental areas in-volved in play, the kinds of play, its connection with language arts, and the necessary provisions for play. The opposite word from *play* is *work*. The constructiv-ist theory (DeVries & Kohlberg, 1987) contends it is through play and interaction with the environment that children construct mental images and processes. This is *work* in the sense that it has purpose and a def-inite goal. When an attempt is made to differentiate play from work, the dividing line becomes blurred. Play has been described and researched by many people.

Rubin, Fein, and Vandenberg (1983) formed this description of play:

▶ Play is intrinsically motivated.
▶ Play is relatively free of externally imposed rules.
▶ Play is carried out as if the activity were real.
▶ Play focuses on the process rather than any product.
▶ Play is dominated by the players.
▶ Play requires the active involvement of the players.

The International Association for the Child's Right to Play (IPA, 1992) declares that play, along with the basic needs of nutrition, health, shelter, and education, is vital to developing the potential of all children. Play is instinctive, voluntary, and spontaneous. Play helps children develop physically, mentally, emotionally, and socially. Play is a means of learning to live, not merely a way to pass time. Docia Zavitkovsky, a lifelong ad-vocate of play said, "Discovering and questioning the world in rich play environments gives children the tools to become creative, knowledgeable, integrated human beings. This is true for adults too. Play matters, at all ages and stages" (Docia Zavitkovsky, Play Matters).

It is obvious that play can take place without other people, so solitary play is not just a stage but a type of play. Play with other people involved is democratic, without rules. Each player has some authority over the play. By observing, it is evident that not every player has equal power or as much power as they may want. Conflict in play erupts

when the social development of the players is un-even. All the other developmental areas—cognitive, language, physical, and emotional—contribute to play's success.

Social Competence and School Readiness. Successful interaction with age-mates is a crucial predictor of not only academic success, but also mental health and wellbeing. Social-emotional skills that support

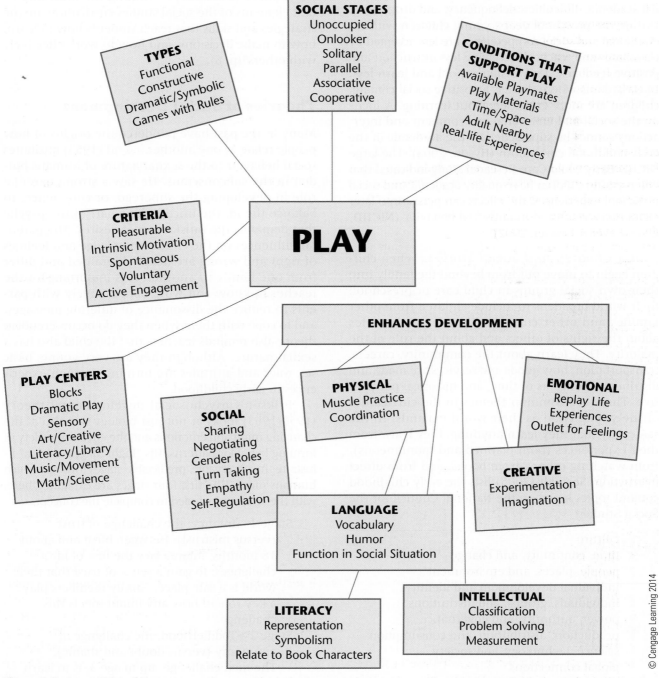

Figure 4–5 Concept Map of Play.

© Cengage Learning 2014

school readiness enable children to learn. They include confidence, curiosity, intentionality, self-control, relatedness, capacity to communicate, and cooperativeness (Willis & Sciller, 2011). Children who scored higher on prosocial competence were later in the year assessed to be more "cognitively ready" for school (Bierman et al., 2009), and children who were more helpful in first grade had greater literacy skills in third grade (Miles & Stipek, 2006). Barriers to the development of these skills place the child at risk of difficulty adjusting to school routines and later problems such as potential academic difficulties, delinquency, and drug abuse. During the preschool years, young children without emotional and social competencies are less accepted by classmates and teachers, receiving less instruction and positive feedback. They dislike school and learn less. In classrooms where there is a positive social climate, children are more enthused about learning. A focus on the social and emotional environment and interactions cannot be superseded by the academic in the early childhood curriculum (Hyson, 2008). The large NICHD Early Child Care Research study indicated that when young children have quality academic and social preschool experiences, the effects can persist into later elementary years and in antisocial behavior (NICHD, 2002; Raver & Knitzer, 2002).

Young Children and Social Studies. When children begin to move out from beyond the family into their own social groups in child care or preschool, their world broadens to include children from other families and other cultures. They learn the rules about the rights of others and about the rule of the majority. They learn about the community, careers, transportation, how goods and services are made and distributed, concepts of time, and historical perspective. These are common themes in the curriculum of the young child as their world expands. In the same way that they learn anything, they learn from their experiences (both planned and spontaneous), from watching others, from books, and from direct instruction. Seefeldt (2005) lists the early childhood content topics based on the National Council for the Social Studies:

- culture
- time, continuity, and change
- people, places, and environment
- individual development and identity
- individuals, groups, and institutions
- power, authority, and governance
- production, distribution, and consumption
- science, technology, and society
- global connections
- civic ideals and practices

Think About It . . .

Look at the list and think about how many of these topics are appropriate curricula for young children. It is not the academic subjects of geography, history, or economics, but how people are the same and different and how they can bridge the differences to all get along, that develops social competence.

Wallace (2006) says, "Among the most important elements of the social studies curriculum are the strategies and skills that teach students how to learn, how to make decisions, and how to work effectively with others"(p. 8).

Theories of Social Development

Many in the past have pondered the origins of how people relate to one another. Freud (1953) attributes social behavior to the sexual nature of humans hidden in the subconscious. He saw a strong parental role in developing the superego, or conscience, to balance the id, the unconscious part of the psyche that demands the satisfaction of desires. The parental influences on the child's knowledge and feelings of right and wrong are deeply ingrained and differ from one family to another. It is important for the teacher to know and work cooperatively with parents to reduce the dissonance of differing messages, and to cope with them when they do occur. Freudian theory also reminds teachers that the child also has a sexual nature. Although they are very young, basic sex roles and attitudes are forming through experiences in early childhood.

Erikson's psychosocial developmental theory (1950/1963) looks at not just biology but also at the changing mind and emotions and the effects of society in forming behavior patterns. His "Eight Stages of Man" illustrate the observable, predictable stages through which humans move. The first four stages are explained here, with the last four included to complete the concept.

Stage 1—Infancy: the challenge of trust (versus mistrust). Between birth and about 18 months, infants face the first of life's challenges: to gain a sense of trust that their world is a safe place. Family members play a key role in how any infant meets this challenge.
Stage 2—Toddlerhood: the challenge of autonomy (versus doubt and shame). The next challenge, up to age 3, is to learn skills to cope with the world in a confident

way. Failure to gain self-control leads children to doubt their abilities.

Stage 3—Preschool: the challenge of initiative (versus guilt). Four- and five-year-olds must learn to engage their surroundings—including people outside the family—or experience guilt at having failed to meet the expectations of parents and others.

Stage 4—Preadolescence: the challenge of industriousness (versus inferiority). Between ages 6 and 13, children enter school, make friends, and strike out on their own more and more. They feel proud of their accomplishments or, at times, fear that they do not measure up.

Stage 5—Adolescence: the challenge of gaining identity (versus confusion).

Stage 6—Young adulthood: the challenge of intimacy (versus isolation).

Stage 7—Middle adulthood: the challenge of making a difference (versus self-absorption).

Stage 8—Old age: the challenge of integrity (versus despair).

These stages include the developing social role in each stage. Unlike Freud, who looked into the past to find reasons for pathological behavior, Erikson looked to the future, not giving up hope that the past can be overcome. Erikson's theory also stresses the importance of adults in understanding and meeting children's needs in each stage. This affects how the child feels about himself and interacts with others.

It Happened to Me

"Bad Dolly"

As I observed children in dramatic play episodes, I frequently saw the child, who I knew had never been spanked, viciously spanking dolls for "bad" deeds. While we had a "no guns" rule, children were very creative in forming LEGOs, TinkerToys, and even artistically chewed pieces of bread into guns. We later gave up on that rule after reading *The War Play Dilemma* (Carlsson-Paige & Levin, 1987). But what was the motivating factor for violent dramatic play? Power!

Piaget's work in cognitive theory (Flavell, 1977) has significance for children's social development. Children's thinking governs their actions. As the child takes in new information, the child interprets it differently at different stages. Before infants reach **object permanence**, that is, until they acquire the awareness that objects continue to exist outside their sight, infants will not "miss" their mother. Once infants have cognitively reached that stage, other people's faces are compared to the mental image of the mother, and that mismatch results in separation anxiety. The young child is described in Piaget's theory as **egocentric**, only able to see things from his own point of view. The child thinks, "I want this ball so I should have it," and takes the ball from another child. When the adult says, "How would you like it if he did that to you?" it has no meaning. The child cannot mentally picture himself with the ball in his hands with another child taking the ball away. This is just too much abstract cognitive processing for his ability at this stage. This is the underlying factor of social actions in the preschool years: the conflict between what one child wants (and thinks he should have) and the desires of another. Recognizing this, adults take many actions to account for this, such as having enough duplicate toys so that the need for possession is met. Once the child becomes verbal, the adult repeats phrases children can use. Phrases such as "You could say, 'I want to play with that ball when you're done'" or "Tell her 'I don't like it when you take that away from me'" help the child function socially.

Behaviorists' social learning theory (Skinner, 1953; Watson, 1950) describes how learning takes place when it is reinforced either negatively or positively. This behaviorism is the reason that spanking or punishment works (for a while), and why praise or reward encourages behavior to occur again. This is external reinforcement of behavior. Parents and teachers, however, want the child to be *intrinsically motivated,* that is to do the right thing even when no one is there to say, "Good job," or "No." When appropriate recognition for *right* and *wrong* deeds is given, the child sees the results from those actions and forms a thinking process for making choices about right and wrong for next time. Hopefully, the adult does not have to be present for reinforcement for the child to make the *right choice.*

Maslow's work (1970) investigating the causes of behavior also was based on met or unmet needs. His "Hierarchy of Human Needs" chart is familiar to students of psychology (Figure 4–6). It has the most basic survival needs at the bottom of the pyramid, moving up to social needs, and eventually to

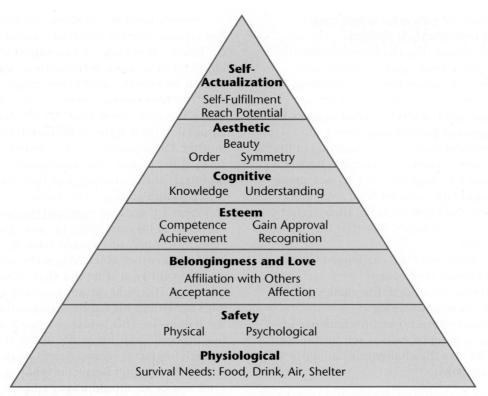

Figure 4–6 Maslow's Hierarchy of Needs.
Source: Adapted from Maslow, A. H., 1970, *Motivation and Personality*, 2nd ed. New York: Harper & Row.

self-actualization. This is where satisfaction comes from—from serving others rather than self.

From Maslow's work, it is clear that physical and psychological safety are necessary for children to develop. Schools have learned that a hungry child cannot learn, so national programs provide nutritious breakfasts and lunches. Similarly, the physical and aesthetic environment influences behavior, so millions of dollars are spent in homes, schools, restaurants, arcades, and businesses on color, furnishings, lighting, and aesthetics to influence human behavior. The classroom environment is an important factor in learning, since it attends to both the physical and psychological needs of the children and adults. The affective needs of acceptance, recognition, affection, belonging, and love are the work of the curriculum of the social development area. From names on the cubbies to hugs at the end of the day, children thrive socially in the environment that meets their emotional needs.

Vygotsky (1978) heavily emphasized the role that culture and play have on children's development, providing the foundation of skills in preparation for later learning and functioning. He saw play pretending ("Let's pretend we're driving to the store") as representations in practice for literacy. In

pretend play ("I'll be the baby") children explore social roles. Through language, the child explains his mental context ("I'm the husband"). Social play, especially with an older child or adult, stretches the child's play to a level beyond the present, providing a **scaffold** (Bodrova & Leong, 2006). This word is appropriate: Think of a scaffold making the painter tall enough to reach, when in reality she cannot reach the highest spot. It is the assistance that provides success. This **zone of proximal development (ZPD)** is the level where a child can function through a support system of more mature thinkers. Think of it as a child riding a two-wheeled bicycle yelling "I'm riding the bike!" as her dad runs alongside holding onto the seat. She feels what successful riding is like though she has not yet attained that level.

Kohlberg (1981) studied and expanded Piaget's ideas about moral development into stages that are the basis for moral behavior, the ethics of interacting with one another. He used situational stories to learn how respondents justified their selection of solutions. In the Pre-Conventional level, morality of an action is judged by its consequences. He proposed that In Stage 0, judgments of right and wrong were based solely on what the individual liked or did not like. In Stage 1, Obedience and Punishment,

It Happened to Me

The Beginning of Conscience

I was talking with the mother of a two-year-old when the mother looked down. Her little girl had a fistful of little pieces of paper. She admonished her, "Don't throw those pieces on the floor." The little girl looked up at her mom, closed her eyes, and opened her hand. This was a great example of a beginning conscience. She only believed something was wrong if someone is watching. She demonstrated her egocentric thinking: If she did not see it, neither did her mother. She was in the morality stage of the right or wrong of behavior judged only by others, and if they didn't see? Oh well, it must be alright.

an action is wrong if it results in punishment, and the worse the punishment, the more serious the action must be. There is no recognition of the other person's point of view, corresponding with Piaget's egocentrism. In Stage 2, the moral action is determined by what is best for the individual with limited interest in others; only as far as it is good for himself. By using Kohlberg's theories, it is obvious that the young child's behavior is dictated by what is best for her, not for anyone else. Some see that as a selfish view, others as the development of the self in the context of society.

Think About It ...

How did you learn to share? Who taught you how to behave in "public?" When did you realize that other people had rights too?

The process of learning those things is **socialization**, how each family, culture, or group teaches the young by example and by direct instruction the way to interact with others. The social skills of sharing, treating people fairly, manners, neatness, and empathy are transferred from one generation to another. These are the skills that make society safe and relatively fair for everyone.

Implications of Social Learning Theory on Early Childhood Practices. In recent years there has been an increased interest in identifying social factors such as the ability to have friends, maintain interactions,

and cultivate **social competence**. Children who are able to control their physiological, emotional, and behavioral responses are socially competent, which enables them to function in a social atmosphere as well as in a learning environment. It is during the preschool years that this regulatory control system is formed. Five major clusters of social skill behaviors, with the acronym CARES, have been identified (Elliott, McKevitt, & DiPerna, 2002, p. 1042):

1. *cooperation*—behaviors such as helping others, sharing materials with a peer, and complying with rules
2. *assertion*—initiating behaviors such as asking others for information, and behaviors that are responses to others' actions, such as responding to peer pressure
3. *responsibility*—behaviors that demonstrate the ability to communicate with adults and show concern about one's property
4. *empathy*—behaviors that reflect concern for peers' or significant adults' feelings
5. *self-control*—behaviors that often emerge in conflict situations, such as responding appropriately to teasing or to corrective feedback from an adult

Stages of Social Development. The word *development* indicates that the change that takes place in the way a child interacts with other people is qualitative. It is a change that can be measured not in numbers but in refinement. It moves from simple to more complex in a predictable sequence, but at different rates for individual people **Stages of Play**. Parten's Stages of Social Play have long been referred to when classifying the development of social play (Figure 4–7). Although we will speak of them as stages, they have been found not to be stages with an ascending level of involvement, but more like forms of social play seen at all ages at varying times. Parten's stages have been modified (Hampton & Fantuzzo, 2003):

Negative play or nonplay (unoccupied play): The child does not focus on any toy or activity: He follows the adult but does not engage in any sustained way.

Onlooker play: The child watches other children play but does not get involved. This is used frequently by children in new situations. They scope out the territory. It is also the style of children who are shy, emotionally depressed, or just not feeling like getting involved. The teacher attends to both behaviors, assesses possible causes, and decides if action is indicated. The adult may decide to issue an invitation to

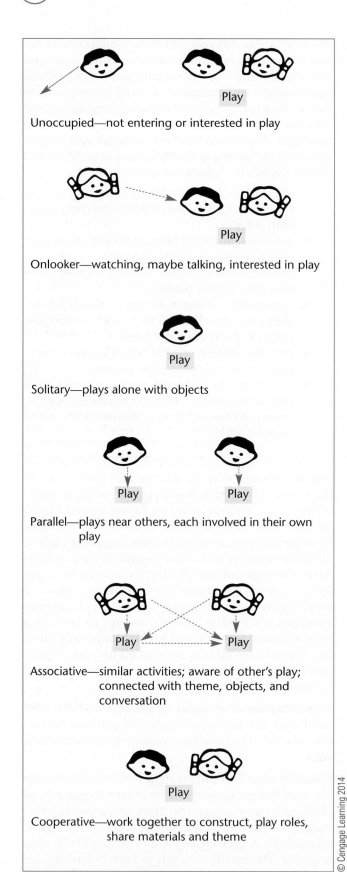

Figure 4–7 The Stages of Social Play.

© Cengage Learning 2014

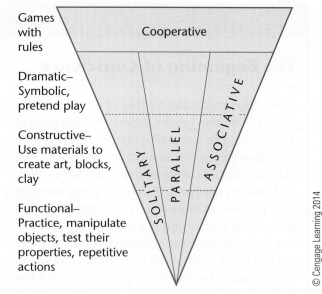

Figure 4–8 Types of Play.

© Cengage Learning 2014

play. In this way, she can role-model how to join in the play. The decision may be to allow the child to have control over joining or not.

Solitary play: The child plays independently, totally focused on his own play without looking or talking to other children. This type of play is often used for manipulation and practice, stress release, or by choice. It is a way of gaining familiarity with a new toy, game, or sports equipment. It is the repetitive motion that makes a skill become natural. Many find this relaxing and rewarding.

Social attention play (parallel play): The child plays independently but is aware of other children. There is minimal social contact. It is not solitary play, but it is not involved either. It entails companionship but not cooperation, affiliation but not association.

Associate play (associative play): The child talks to others, smiles, and exchanges toys but does not adjust her behavior to match or complement the other child's.

Collaborative play (cooperative play): The child engages in mutual, reciprocal roles, and adjusts his behavior to the actions of the other child.

Types of Play. Besides the stages of play, another dynamic enters play. Children's play can be also observed and coded using Rubin's play matrix (Rubin, 2001). It is the "how" of play. Four categories of play are seen in the social stages of play (Figure 4–8).

Functional play: Actions are repeated for practice and exploration. A child paints all over the paper, his hands, and the legs of the easel. Clay is squeezed, patted, rolled, poked, and cut. Blocks are piled and knocked down; containers filled with them, then dumped. No end product is in mind; it is manipulation of materials. People do this all the time in sporting goods stores as they take practice swings with golf clubs or baseball bats.

Constructive play: This play produces a product. The manipulation of the paintbrush turns into a recognizable flower. Clay balls are piled on one another and named a "snowman." Blocks are piled, and the builder calls it "The Umpire *[sic]* State Building."

Dramatic play: This play takes the player into the world of pretend. The paintbrush becomes a bee buzzing toward the flower, gathering nectar. The snowman is moved along the table, talking to other clay creations and wondering what will happen when the sun comes out. The builder takes a monkey from the jungle set and has King Kong climbing up the building. Participation, with or without props, in the world of fantasy is classified as this type of play. It is in **dramatic play** in that children exercise power, power over a world that they now can control, over objects and over others (including dolls and action figures). In pretend play with others, the child must keep track of her own role as well as those of the other players and adapt when the story evolves. This requires a high level of cognitive and social flexibility, more often seen in school-age children (Diamond, 2006).

Games with rules become part of the play repertoire as children move toward their fifth and sixth years. This coincides with mathematical reasoning and the social-emotional stage of industry, of putting things in order. By this age, children are bringing themselves into control, passing the egocentric stage, so now they can see from another's point of view. This stage also appears at a time when children's language skills are more developed, and they are able to play in a more cooperative way. Remember that the stage of cooperative play does not refer to the absence of quarrels. In fact, in this stage school-age children tend to enforce the rules for others, while overlooking them for themselves.

Observers of social development should be able to recognize and label social play using Parten's stages (forms) of play (unoccupied, onlooker, solitary, parallel, associative, cooperative) and Smilansky's and Piaget's play categories (functional, constructive, dramatic, games with rules).

EXERCISE **Using Parten and Hampton's, Smilansky's, and Piaget's terms, classify the following players.**

1. Jake and Donald are sitting across from each other, building with separate LEGO sets. Jake and Donald are in the ___ stage, demonstrating the ___ type of play.
2. Heather, Greg, and Lisa are putting on a puppet play in a cardboard stage. Louise has been watching for several minutes. Louise is in the ___ stage, while Heather, Greg, and Lisa are in the ___ stage, demonstrating ___ type of play.
3. Piku is at the art table making balls of clay and poking them with a pencil. He is in the ___ stage of play, demonstrating ___ type of play.
4. Barry is laying parallel rows of blocks and Birdie is riding a truck back and forth between them. Barry and Birdie are in the ___ stage of play, Barry demonstrating ___ type of play. Birdie is demonstrating ___. She says, "I'm delivering bread to the store." Now her play is ___.

Answers:

In checking your understanding of the play stages and types, you should have recognized the following: (1) parallel, constructive; (2) onlooker, cooperative, dramatic; (3) solitary, functional; (4) associative, constructive, functional, dramatic.

Observing Social Development Stages in the Home

As you think about the stages of social development, home visitors need especially to consider what defines the "social world" of each child receiving services in the home and how that might impact social development. For home educators the opportunity to observe the quality of interactions that a child has with other family members is a benefit not afforded educators in the classroom to the same degree. On the other hand, home educators generally do not have the opportunity to observe the child in play in a non-home environment where other children beyond their own

▶ ❚❚ TEACHSOURCE VIDEO ACTIVITY

Go to the Education CourseMate website, accessed through CengageBrain.com, to view Young Children's Stages of Play: An Illustrated Guide.

As you watch these video illustrations of Stages of Play, make a list of the other different developmental areas that you observe the children are using as well as those pointed out by the narrator.

siblings are present. Given that, educators should consider how to routinely provide play and exploratory experiences beyond the home where stages of social development can be observed and monitored.

The Need for a Selfless Society

Moving from selfish to selfless takes more than changing a few alphabet letters. It is a total transformation from self-centered, immediate gratification to other-centered, altruistic generosity. The goal of maturity in a moral society is to become less concerned with one's own needs and desires by giving priority to those of others. A person, group, or society that only lives for itself is constantly in conflict. Often, more than one person wants a particular object or for their own opinion to prevail, and everyone cannot be satisfied. From that conflict came the rules of the tribe, then laws. Now laws are so numerous and complex that entire buildings are needed to hold the books that list and interpret them all. People devote their lives to interpreting, enforcing, changing, and even breaking them. There are also some people in a society who cannot fill their own needs, so others are needed to help generously if they are to survive. The task of raising the young to be selfless is necessary for the survival of the society. What a responsibility! This is a long struggle that begins with small steps.

Think About It ...

Think about how the following laws or rules restrict your freedom for the good of society.

- Only licensed physicians can practice medicine.
- Drive on the right side of the road.
- Items in a store must be exchanged for payment.
- Use utensils, not hands, for serving items from the salad bar.
- Buckle up your seatbelt in the car.

In caring for, teaching, or working with young children, the development of the social domain is a high priority. It does not develop separately from physical, cognitive, or emotional areas, but simultaneously moves forward, influenced by many of the same factors of genetics, environment, culture, and society. Helping a child learn the rules of the tribe will help him function in that group. It is a necessary skill for both physical and psychological wellbeing (Figure 4–9).

The infant is only concerned with fulfillment of needs, totally dependent on reflexes and signals calling for responses to those signals. The hungry baby

Figure 4–9 Attaining social development is not without its struggles.

never considers the mother's dinner getting cold. The baby crying in the middle of the night pays no heed to parents' early work schedules. The crawler pulls the cat's tail, or the toddler takes a truck from another. The needs and wants of the other person are not deliberated or weighed or even considered at all. Years and much growing and developing must take place before the child sees the point of view of the other person. It takes even longer before she can place the other person's needs ahead of her own with generosity and empathy. She has much growing up to do before living up to society's expectations and taking on the responsibility for others. Along that path there are observable stages—developmental milestones—which are aided in their arrival by interactions with adults.

Self. The newborn infant (neonate) is governed by reflexes:

rooting reflex—when stroked on the cheek, the neonate turns toward that side. (It is not to see his mother better.)

babkin reflex—when the palms are stimulated, the neonate's fingers curl around it and grasp it. (It is not to play with daddy's finger.)

walking and stepping reflex—when held so that feet or toes touch the floor, the neonate makes a walking, stepping motion. (It is not to dance with her sister.)

moro reflex—when a loud noise, bright light, or loss of support is experienced, the neonate startles and flings out his arms. (It is not reaching out to be held because he was scared.)

But what is the neonate doing socially? The infant can see very well close up, looking at close faces and registering information about what is seen and heard. The baby's kinesthetic sense (body movement and position) is present so the baby senses she is held, rocked, or touched. Babies are usually soothed by motion, crying less when rocked. The baby imitates and matches facial expressions. As early as one month, infants are aware of what is going on around them, and by four months, they try to change their parent's facial expressions to be happier. Some babies right from the start are more gregarious, responsive to others, and open to friendly overtures (Figure 4–10). Others are much more serious and reserved, limiting social contacts to just a few people. This personality type affects social interactions, and it may be evident throughout the child's life. All areas of development—physical, cognitive, and emotional—are being affected by and are affecting social development.

The implications for social development seem clear. The adult role is to meet the baby's needs, first of all in physical care but also in the social and emotional realm. The infant who has attention and is prompted to respond to coos and words is being prepared for verbal conversations. The environment stimulates cognitive development. Psychological needs are met by being close and handling the baby gently and responsively. Interactions are initiated and provide an interesting environment that responds to what the baby indicates she likes. These met needs give the infant a secure base from which to emerge into the social realm with the abilities to function in it.

Self-Gratification. During the first year, the infant is focused on receiving what he needs to survive and be happy, whatever that takes. This is the stage of his attachment to his parents, as well as the beginning of his independence from them. During the first months of life, the baby increases imitative behavior with smiles and laughs as the adult feeds, dresses, and cares for him. In the second half of the first year, the baby shows separation anxiety, trying to recapture the presence of the ones who meet his needs. He also begins some social exchanges by reaching out his hands and arms to be held, kicking or making noises to gain attention. He is becoming mobile, so now he can crawl to his mother and pull on her leg. He is beginning to learn that he is no longer allowed to cry, sleep, play, eat, or act strictly by his own desires. He may be put down for a nap when he is not "ready" or be told "No" when he reaches for his grandpa's glasses. He cries and uses whatever social skills he has learned to get what he wants. He also is beginning to exert social control by turning away from the spoon, withdrawing a plaything, or withdrawing from a smiling auntie, pulling back his social self.

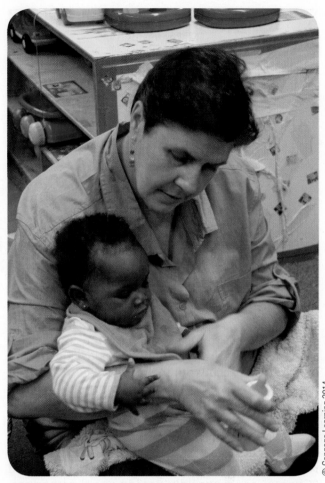

© Cengage Learning 2014

Figure 4–10 Social development begins with the infant's needs being met.

The play that infants engage in during the first year is mainly manipulation. They experience the object in every way possible: touching, squeezing, biting, smelling, shaking to listen, and throwing to see the reaction. A favorite game is peekaboo, which builds the cognitive structure of what goes away is not gone forever but returns. This game prepares the infant for separation. Another favorite game is to throw the toy away and have someone return it. It is a social give-and-take, action and response. It also reinforces not only object permanence, but also that power over other people to get them to do what he wants them to do. It is the precursor for taking turns, sharing, and playing baseball (Figure 4–11).

This process over the first two years is moving from being solely focused on the self to the consideration of others. It is dependent on the infant's capabilities and the supportive adult behaviors. Figure 4–12 graphically portrays the stages involved, the roles of child and adult, as well as the desired outcomes (Kostelnik et al., 2009).

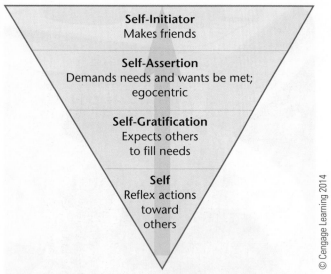

Figure 4–11 Stages of Social Development.

Self-Assertion. In the second year, the child generalizes all other social relationships. She expects that everyone, especially other children, will treat her in the same way as her parents: accepting, acquiescent, providing what she needs and wants. When this does not happen, she cannot understand it.

Language is developing at this time also, so vocabulary and verbal expression come into the social realm. Words and phrases such as "No!" "Mine!" and "Gimme" are repeatedly used in social gatherings. "Please" is expected to yield miraculous results, with objects or toys being the lure of toddler friendships.

Self-Initiator. Three-, four-, and five-year-olds are blossoming social beings. At this age, they have the verbal, physical, and cognitive skills to begin to interact more with each other. They engage in **associative play**—doing a similar type of activity, involving the same play theme or with similar types of toys—but in this stage they still are "doing their own thing." They are not working together toward a common goal; they just happen to be near each other, talking about what each of them is doing.

Some children begin collaborative or cooperative play as four-year-olds, producing a common product such as a block building, a road in the sand connecting areas, or dinner in the dramatic area. All players are working out a common plan. They are still in the Preoperational Stage, still egocentric, but they are beginning to engage in this kind of play. The teacher prepares an environment that will enhance social development by providing enough materials so that solitary and parallel play are not thwarted by the child's having to "steal" from others. Cooperation and sharing

are planned into the routines and curriculum by such things as helper charts, joint projects, songs, stories, and puppet plays. Competition during this period is not understood, so it is not an appropriate method of group interaction. Games with winners and losers—who can be the best, the fastest, or the neatest—reinforce selfish attitudes. Cooperation and concern for others are the major social tasks of this age. Children who have had experiences in rule-making for the classroom and in their enforcement in an acceptable way get along better. They know and understand the reasons for rules. They are careful observers of others who are breaking the rules. This is the beginning of moral development, recognizing right from wrong.

Difficulties between children are best handled not by the teacher as the judge. The teacher's role is as a facilitator for negotiation, helping those involved to tell each other their point of view. The children decide in a democratic manner. This kind of facilitation assists children in cognitive development (problem solving) and moral development (beginning to see someone else's point of view). Because bullying—victimizing another child by exclusion, teasing, or even physical aggression—is seen in three- and four-year-old children, the teacher's role is more active than that of a facilitator alone; the teacher must first of all be a protector, then an active encourager of friendship formation through curriculum and intervention (Dunn, 2004).

Excluded children, those who have difficulty being accepted by peers, have some common characteristics. Disliked children often ignore other children's overtures to play, misunderstand peers' emotions, and are aggressive (Kemple, 2004). A strategy to help excluded or disliked children is to pair them with a younger child with whom they can feel more socially confident. Likewise, they may be paired with those who are socially competent as a model. Alternatives to aggressiveness through role plays, books, and puppet plays may give such children problem-solving ideas to be remembered when conflicts arise. Asking provocative questions when children are engaged in good guy/bad guy play is a strategy to divert possible antisocial activities: "How does Spiderman weave the web?" (Jones & Cooper, 2006).

Observing Social Development in Play

The observation of children interacting with each other—or "kidwatching," as Goodman (2002) calls it—can be extremely amusing. They reveal so much of themselves and all areas of development as they play. Information on physical, cognitive, language, emotional, and social development can be gathered as children interact with the environment and other people.

© Cengage Learning 2014

PHASE	AGE OF ONSET IN MONTHS	INFANT CAPABILITIES	SOCIAL OUTCOME	ROLE IN INDIVIDUATION PROCESS	ADULT BEHAVIORS THAT SUPPORT INDIVIDUATION
I	0–1	Sucking; visual tracking; grasping; cuddling; vocalizes; social attunement	Reflexes; shared gazing; orienting toward caregiver	Proximity to caregiver	Observation of states; prompt basic care
II	1–2	More time quietly alert; sensory learning about people and objects; molding to caregiver's body; continues interesting activities; coos and goos	Beginning social responsiveness; mutual cueing	Begins differentiation between self and objects; more ways of maintaining proximity	Provide objects; engage in turn-taking play; give prompt basic care; respond sensitively to different states
III	4–8	Sits, grasps; creeps; increased interest in objects; sensory learning: mouthing, manipulating, examining, banging; laughs, yells, and squeals; babbling	Recognizes familiar people; shows clear preferences among people; intentionality limited to previously learned actions; playful; social smile; laughter	Beginnings of social expectations; stranger fear; maintains proximity by following, checking back on caregiver after short excursions	Provide a safe environment for floor exploration; establish limits for child; respond predictably
IV	9–14	Walking, climbing, running; joyful exploration; curious; excited; beginning use of language and gesture; person and object permanence becoming clearer; trial-and-error problem solving; intentions conveyed by language, gesture, and action; makes requests; comprehends words; complex babbling	Strong desire for approval, inclined to comply; self-willed; increased self-control; social variety of emotions; social play with adults; interest in events	Maintains proximity by following and calling caregiver; strong preferences for particular people; protests separation; uses caregiver as a "base of operations" and moves outward; recognizes that others act; beginning to cooperate	Protect from hazards (child has mobility without judgment); respond promptly to communicative acts; set and maintain routines and limits; provide opportunity for independence; use language to comfort; explain leaving child with familiar adults; have patience
V	15–24	Increase of all motor tasks; skillful exploration; rapid increase in language and nonverbal communication skills; offers objects to preferred adults; self-recognition and person permanence; pointing, says words, then word combinations	Is likely to cling, then run away; plays "mother chase me!"; self-willed: "No" before compliance; considerable amount of self-control; self-comforting; may show sudden fear after departure from caregiver; may cry from relief at caregiver's return	Realizes caregiver's goals are not own goals; may be ambivalent about dependence/independence; can play happily in absence of preferred person; uses "gifts" of toys in seeking proximity, more language	Verbalize about departures, reassure; tolerate rapid changes in approach and withdrawal; use language to discuss events, relationships, objects, etc.; allow child to control some holding on, letting go; make social expectations clear over and over; have patience
VI	24–30	Good understanding of ordinary language; intentionality well developed; mental problem solving; ability to ask for help based on need; goal-directed behavior; self-definition of gender and age	Increasing interest in other children; peer play and communication stronger; mutually regulated social interactions; pretend play	Realistic sense of self and others; uses a wide array of techniques to maintain proximity (helping, conversation, play stories); can cope well with separations	Continue to reassure, support, and provide affection; praise efforts at self-control and independent behavior; provide experience with another toddler

Figure 4–12 The Individuation Process and Appropriate Adult Responses.

Source: From Kostelnik/Phipps-Whiren/Soderman/Gregory. Guiding Children's Social Development and Learning, 6th ed. © 2009 Cengage Learning.

It Happened to Me

"The Overheard Parent Conference"

I was in a conference with the parent of probably the brightest child I ever had in my preschool class. We were talking about his development when he appeared at the door, obviously listening. We invited him in and discussed his progress in the various areas of development. In talking about social development, I remarked that I had not seen him playing with any other children. Indeed, he could make elaborate block structures, read books on his own, draw and paint recognizable objects, but he had no friends. He was just a shadow player. He asked, "Am I supposed to play with other children?" His mother explained that he could do all these other things at home, which he did, but at school he had other children to play with and that is why he was here. "Oh, OK." And from that day forward, he moved into play groups, talked with other children, interacted, and became a welcome play partner. It was his intellectual ability that helped him be a friend. It taught me that it helps if children know adults' expectations of them (and to be sure that conferences are private, although this one was all positive and turned out successfully).

Anecdotal and Running Records. Social play observations are caught vividly with Anecdotal and Running Recordings that capture both the actions and the words. Such a narrative gives a lasting memory of an event that can be fraught with meaning to every reader. One of the foremost kidwatchers is Vivian Paley. Her books of Anecdotal Recordings, many about boys and girls in dramatic play, are not only entertaining but also full of meaning. In *Boys and Girls: Superheroes in the Doll Corner* (1984), Paley relates a discussion with the children about where the real work of school is happening in the classroom.

Paley is skillful in asking open-ended questions such as, "How can you tell if you're working or playing?" She accurately records children's conversations as well as her questions that explore their thinking. Reeny, an African-American child in *The Girl with the Brown Crayon* (Paley, 1997), joins her classmates in a study of

the books of Leo Lionni and leads them to learn about self-identity. These books are wonderful examples of Anecdotal Recording and thoughtful teaching.

Children with Challenging Behavior. One of the biggest challenges in group settings is disruptive behavior. An alarming Yale study found that preschoolers in state-funded programs were being expelled for behavior at more than three times the rate of children K–12, with a higher rate for African-American boys (Gilliam, 2005). When young children are together, conflicts are inevitable and they often challenge teachers, families, and administrators. Through behavior, the child is communicating what he may not be able to put into words. Sometimes, children's behavior is a normal part of a developmental stage, but misunderstanding or lack of understanding on the part of adults misinterprets the behavior as defiance, "naughty," or obstinate. All behavior should be viewed within the context of biology, interactions, and environment. There is a tremendous cost when a child has extreme, challenging behavior. The child suffers peer rejection, mostly punitive contacts with teachers, unpleasant family interactions, and even faces potential school failure (Center for Evidence-Based Practice, 2003). Programs that focus on social skills such as getting along with others, following directions, identifying and regulating one's behavior, and engaging in social conversation and cooperative play have been shown to improve outcomes in school (Zins et al., 2004). Documentation of children's behavior through Anecdotal and Running Records can show what happens right before, and exactly describe the behavior and what happens after each outburst. This can give clues to the teacher and consultants for supportive suggestions to help meet the child's needs.

Checklists. Most developmental Checklists have a section for social play, usually using the stages and types previously mentioned. Checklists provide descriptions of typically occurring behavior and may be used to uncover children who may not have reached the indicators for their chronological age on many items on the list. Those children may have personality and temperament differences that are completely normal for them. Children from diverse cultural and family backgrounds may not *usually* do many of these things. When this Checklist shows children are having social difficulties, the teacher assesses the cause and plans for a classroom that is supportive and accepting.

The Penn Interactive Peer Play Scale (Hampton & Fantuzzi, 2003) lists social behaviors such as play disruption (physical and verbal aggression, grabbing, demanding, destroying, tattling, whining), play disconnection (ignored, withdraws, unable to enter or sustain play), and play interaction (helps, makes up play activities, problem-solves, invites others to join).

The Play Skills Checklist in Baker (2004) is designed for families to assess basic play skills—skills for playing alone and with others—of a child with special needs. Assessments of this type are used to build on the child's strengths and serve as a guide to set goals for areas of development.

The Play Observation Scale (Rubin, 2001) reviews the stages and types of play and provides a coding sheet to record observations on a Time Sample. This measure focuses on an individual child for one hour looking for solitary, parallel, and group behaviors, and peer conversations.

Observing Infants and Toddlers in Social Play

The infant is not developmentally able to sustain a higher level of play because of limited language and still-developing cognitive, social, and emotional skills. That does not keep the child from seeking out those social contacts. Signs of empathy and caring are often observed in one- to two-year-olds, crying upon seeing another child cry, spontaneously helping someone who is unhappy or retrieving something that has been dropped.

In the second year, walking widens the social world considerably. Now the child can walk over to other children and initiate interactions. Because of social immaturity, however, often those overtures to play may be in the form of grabbing a toy, biting, or screaming. The responses may be less than friendly.

By the end of the second year, children have begun to make friends. They recognize other children with whom they have frequent contact. They imitate and initiate overtures of affection such as hugging, kissing, and giving objects to others. Occasionally, they make eye contact, engaging in little conversation. Mostly they are involved in their own play and play objects. Still possessing immature cognitive, social, and emotional structures, sharing and turn-taking are limited, if present at all. Some very young children have been observed in friendships. In *The Friendship Factor* (2002), Rubin discusses some factors that contributed to these early friendships:

- secure relationships with their mothers
- relationships with older siblings or children
- their mothers were friends
- the children were at similar developmental levels, and had similar temperaments and behavioral styles

It Happened to Me

I saw a 12-month-old child, upon seeing his mother crying, take the pacifier from his own mouth and offer it to his Mommy. He knew if it made him feel better when he was sad, it should work the same way for her. That's evidence that even very young infants can empathize with others.

Helping all Children with Social Development

A concept that is being used successfully is the **Response to Intervention Model (RTI)**, a multi-tiered framework that meets the needs of all students. It uses the graphic of the pyramid that mirrors the Universal Design for Learning (Chapter 3) for all, with more intensive intervention as the needs increase in severity. This same model of universal treatment to increasing intervention is used by the Center on Social and Emotional Foundations for Early Learning (See Figure 5–14).

Disabilities and the Social Environment

Children with disabilities can function quite well in classrooms where the staff understands their capabilities as well as their disabilities and modifies the environment so that each child can succeed to the highest level possible. Free play in smaller spaces for close proximity play, with teachers providing low structure with minimal rules but a wide variety of toys, provides the best environment for social interactions for children with or without disabilities. While meeting the learning needs of children with disabilities, inclusive settings have been shown to contribute to emotional understanding and acceptance in typically developing children (Diamond, 2001). There seems to be little difference between the number or quality of friendships for children with disabilities and typically developing children in inclusive settings (Goldman & Buysse, 2007). This environment promotes imitation of peers by younger children and those with developmental delays. Some modifications to the environment are made specific to the child's needs.

Social interactions depend heavily on communication. For the child with a hearing loss, this is a barrier. Early involvement with hearing children as social role models and alternative communication techniques are helpful in promoting social development. For the teacher, this also means learning some way to communicate with the child to facilitate social interactions with the child's peers and to interpret the classroom environment.

Vision impairment does not necessarily cause social problems, but more likely it is society's reaction to the impairment that has a negative effect. Curiously, the more severe the impairment, the less negative the reaction, possibly because of the sympathy effect. Children with thick corrective lenses may be rejected as a playmate by other children just from appearances. The teacher can inform children of the nature of the child's vision and how it may affect the child in the classroom, inviting other children's assistance and acceptance. The teacher as a role model provides an environment that is safe, but allows all the freedoms and challenges that other children receive.

Children with physical limitations are now included in regular classrooms, advertisements, and television shows. Familiarity with prostheses, walkers, and wheelchairs is helping to bring about more social peer acceptance in group settings. Children have a desire to be helpful, yet the danger exists for them to do too much, reinforcing learned helplessness. It is important for every child to be included in every classroom activity to the fullest of her ability. This will go a long way toward facilitating peer acceptance as well.

Children with Autism

More and more children have been diagnosed with **autism**, a pervasive developmental disorder that affects verbal and nonverbal communication and social interaction. Autism's onset and recognition of symptoms occur between 18 months and 4 years of age. It is a spectrum disorder that ranges from mild to severe, and sometimes is displayed in repetitive motions such as hand flapping or word repetitions, rocking, sniffing, resistance to change in routines, and unusual responses to sensory experiences. About 40 percent of children in autism are nonverbal, so sign language, computer tools, and picture boards are often helpful. Because the early childhood classroom is a highly stimulating place, with many social learners, as well as sensory experiences, children with autism have difficulties that may be seen as behavior problems, sometimes before diagnosis. The classroom staff need to be aware of the child's diagnosis

It Happened to Me

Sammy 25 years later

Recently when I was grocery shopping I saw the mother of a child I had in my preschool class. I said hello to Sammy's mom and went on with my shopping. A few aisles later she searched me out to tell me "the rest of the story" on Sammy. He graduated with two degrees from a world-famous university but was unemployed, living at home, and not functioning well. He has had many job interviews because of his academic background, but his weak social skills seemed to be the blockade to getting hired. He was finally diagnosed as autistic. As I recall Sammy as a preschooler, he was a solitary player, a strange conversationalist, a social loner even at four years old. At the time I attributed it to growing up in a household with adults who treated him like an adult in family pursuits and conversations, parents who themselves may have been outside the norm socially. Sammy was just different too. Now we know so much more about children like Sammy. Could his outcome have been different if there were a diagnosis and early intervention? I hope children like Sammy today have the opportunity for better futures. And I hope Sammy finds his way.

and particular behavioral characteristics in order to help the child adjust to the group environment and to make modifications for the transition. A screening tool recommended for children aged 6 to 24 months by the American Academy of Pediatrics and widely used is the CSBS-DP (Wetherby & Prizant, 2003). It asks families to answer 24 multiple-choice items on emotion and eye gaze, communication, gestures, sounds, words, understanding, and object use. The results determine whether a full evaluation is needed.

When there is a child with autism in the classroom, the adult's reactions and interactions will be models for the group. Dr. Stanley Greenspan, well known for his floortime techniques, has many suggestions on how to help children with autism to relate, communicate, and think (Greenspan, 2006).

Culture and Social Interactions

Different cultures have different social styles, such as eye contact and facial expressions, the amount of social distance with which people are comfortable, the amount, type, and parts of the body for social physical contact (Lynch, 2011). The teacher familiarizes himself with the cultures of the children in the group and transfers that awareness to assist the child to feel comfortable socially in the classroom. If a child does not speak English, the teacher, even though he may not speak the child's language, can act as a body language translator and an advocate for the child with the other children. The family, through an interpreter, can supply the teacher with a list of common words and their meanings.

Some cultures hold a belief in collectivism, the view that the good of the group is more important than that of the individual (Bornstein & Cote, 2001; Tyler et al., 2005). This can impact the child's social relationships to others such as sharing, giving up toys to younger children, the right to privacy, and being unique and distinct from each other; these are concepts that are learned from family attitudes very early in life (Gonzalez-Mena, 2008). Sensitivity to these attitudes may explain children's and families' reactions to emphasis placed on the importance of the individual.

The social climate of acceptance for all children will be extended to any child with differences. Having a friend is one of the most important motivators in learning and feeling successful and happy. The teacher must do all in his power to make that happen.

Helping Professionals for Social Development Concerns

If all the efforts of the staff and observations documented by Anecdotal and Running Records or social Checklists indicate a child is having a problem in social development, some action must be taken. In a talk with the family, the teacher can discuss her concerns. This is a sensitive area since no family wants to hear that their child is rejected and friendless. Family dynamics and values are closely woven with social development, so the utmost care should be taken. The family probably already has clues that the child is having difficulty. The child may be reluctant to come to school, with crying and tantrums every morning. The child may be getting into fights, hurting and being hurt. Together, some of the possible causes are explored and some plans agreed on.

If the problem is prolonged or appears so severe that it is determined inadvisable to delay advising the family and seeking professional help,

then helping professionals may be consulted. After the medical personnel have ruled out any possible physical cause, then the psychological causes could be examined. Some of those professionals might include one or more of the following:

social worker—counsels individuals and families, serves as advocate or consultant to agencies or schools

family therapist—psychologist specializing in working with families in the treatment of an individual or family group

play therapist—psychologist or psychiatrist using play for diagnosis, dialogue, and treatment of childhood social-emotional disorders

child psychologist—evaluates, diagnoses, and treats children for emotional, social, cognitive, and behavioral disorders

Other Methods

Other Methods to Record Social Development:

Class List Log—who plays with whom notation of level of social play stage

Checklists—Social development portions of comprehensive Checklists

Anecdotal Recording Checklists and Rating Scales

Frequency Counts—How many play encounters occur with another child during one day? How frequently does a child lead/follow another child during one day?

Interviews or discussions about friends

Time Samples—who the child is with during free choice time

Work Samples—child's friends depicted in artwork, collaborative work such as murals, joint buildings

Photographs, audio, or video recordings capturing child's interactions with others

Key Terms

associative play	functional play
autism	games with rules
constructive play	object permanence
cooperative play	onlooker play
dramatic play	parallel play
egocentric	Running Record

Response to
    Intervention
    Model (RTI)
scaffold
social competence
socialization

solitary play
unoccupied
    play
zone of proximal
    development
    (ZPD)

Plans

Go to the Education CourseMate website, accessed through CengageBrain.com for the following:

Anecdotal/Running Record form

Plan Week 4, Part A, Directions for Running Records of Social Development for Group C, including What to Do with It, Portfolio Evidence Sheet Example, Sharing with Child and Family, Actions—Read a Book, In the Environment, In the Curriculum, and In the Newsletter

Plan Week 4, Part B, Class List Log of Social Development for All, including What to Do with It and Sharing with Child and Family

Plan Week 4, Part C, Reflective Journal

Resources

Association for Childhood Education International. (2006). *Global guidelines for the education and care of young children in the 21st century.* http://www. acei.org.

Greenspan, S., & Wieder, S. (2006). *Engaging autism: Using the floortime approach to help children relate, communicate and think.* Cambridge, MA: DaCapo Lifelong Books.

Kostelnik, M. J., Gregory, K., Soderman, A. K., & Whiren, A. P. (2012). *Guiding children's social development and learning* (7th ed.) Belmont, CA: Wadsworth: Cengage Learning.

Levin, D. E. (2003). *Teaching young children in violent times: Building a peaceable classroom.* Cambridge, MA: Educators for Social Responsibility.

Miller, K. (2000). Caring for the little ones: Friendships in the baby room. *Child Care Information Exchange* (133, 62), May/June 2000.

Palmer, D., & Neugebauer, B. (2006). *Connecting: Friendships in the lives of young children and their teachers.* Redmond, WA: Exchange Press.

Riley, D., San Juan, R., Klinkner, J., Ramminger, A. (2008). *Social & emotional development: Connecting science and practice in early childhood settings.* Washington, DC: National Association for the Education of Young Children.

CHAPTER 5

Using Frequency Counts to Look at Emotional Development

OBSERVATION THOUGHT

"Useful observations cannot be gathered the week before progress reports or family conferences are due."

NAEYC Standards **naeyc**

The following NAEYC Standards for Early Childhood Professional Preparation are addressed in this chapter:

Standard 1: Promoting Child Development and Learning

Standard 3: Observing, Documenting, and Assessing to Support Young Children and Families

Standard 6: Becoming a Professional

IN THIS CHAPTER

▶ Using Frequency Counts

▶ Looking at Emotional Development

▶ Topics in Observation: Assessment and Curriculum Braid

▶ Observing Emotional Development in Infants and Toddlers

▶ Helping All Children with Emotional Development

▶ Helping Professionals for Emotional Concerns

Using Frequency Counts

EXERCISE How often did you do each of the following today?

> eat
> go to the bathroom
> talk on the phone
> say your pet phrase ("Oh well," "Basically," or "Whatever")

Much behavior is habitual, done without thinking. Occasionally, those habitual actions become really important. More attention is given to how often and what food is eaten when someone is on a diet. Measuring or counting is a part of decision making. If a person is experiencing an illness, the number of times one goes to the bathroom may be an important symptom. Legislators tally the number of pro and con calls received on an issue. Weight before beginning a diet, the number of phone calls, or an unusual change in body functions are indicators that provide information for comparison. In behavior modification, a measurement is made, action taken, and then a new measurement is taken to see the significance of the change.

In the classroom, a **Frequency Count** can measure repeated actions of a child, the whole group, or the teacher. It is a method to quickly tally targeted behavior. It is sometimes helpful to count specific actions that occur often in one day or session, such as hitting, children running, or the teacher saying, "Don't." Strategies can then be implemented to reduce negative actions or behavior, or to increase desirable ones.

EXERCISE Frequently occurring actions that may occur in a group of preschool children follow. What is your estimate of how many times a day each action happens? In the following list, place a + next to the ones you would like to increase and a – next to ones you would like to decrease.

_____ **1.** spills
_____ **2.** biting
_____ **3.** punching
_____ **4.** "Thank you."
_____ **5.** vomiting
_____ **6.** using the book area
_____ **7.** sharing
_____ **8.** "Don't ..."
_____ **9.** "OK, guys."
_____ **10.** "Teacher, Teacher ..."

Answers:

Candidates for a reduction are numbers 1, 2, 3, 8, 9, and 10. Numbers 4, 6, and 7 could be increased. Number 5 is an infrequent event and would not be a measurable criterion for a Frequency Count or a reduction plan. It is necessary to note such an incident, however, on a health form or a short Anecdotal Recording. In an infant room, this may be a more frequent event. Number 2 is more likely to occur in a toddler room, because it is an expected behavior. If it were a frequent behavior in a kindergarten room, with an individual child, or many children, the teacher would begin to search for answers—after she applied first aid, of course. Biting, of course, is not expected behavior for kindergarten students.

Frequency Counts are a way of seeing just how often an event happens. The purpose is to try to change undesirable behavior. If the action is negative and excessive for the age or stage expectations, then a plan is implemented to try to reduce it. If an expected behavior is not present or not happening often enough, then a plan is made to try to increase it. After a period of time, another Frequency Count is taken to measure the success. The process is documented by a Frequency Count to "prove" if the remedy or theory works.

This is not recommending a program of behavior modification where positive behavior is rewarded so it will increase, and negative behavior is punished so it will decrease. It is more a measurement of the teacher or learning process, like a pretest and a posttest. It assumes a change will take place. The agents of that change may be time, direct instruction, modeling, planned experiences, or self-regulation. Bandura's social learning theory (1977) recognized that the change, called learning, results from an interaction between thinking, acting, and the environment.

Figure 5–1 is an example of a Frequency Count. Spills seem to be happening many times a day in this classroom, and the staff is concerned—beyond being simply irritated—about the messes. They complain

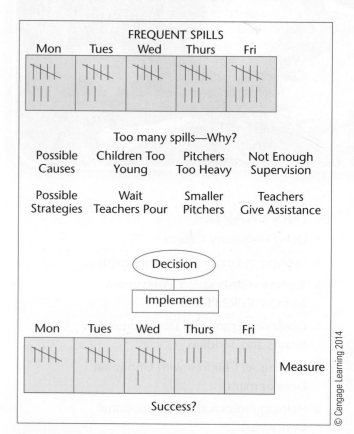

Figure 5–1 Frequency Counts to Measure Reduction of Undesirable Behavior.

and then talk about some possible reasons. The children may be too young to initiate pouring, or the pitchers available are opaque, too heavy, and have no lids so the liquid comes out unexpectedly for novice pourers. Perhaps the adults are not sitting at the table with the children but using that time to prepare for the next activity. Each of the possible reasons suggests possible strategies. A decision is reached, and the strategy is implemented. A later Frequency Count measures whether the strategy is successful or not.

Using the Frequency Count to Document Frequently Occurring Behaviors

Other classroom situations and possible strategies for Frequency Count measurement follow:

- *decrease aggressive acts*—prosocial or emotional curriculum
- *decrease the need for teacher intervention*—more self-help shelves for materials and supplies
- *decrease inappropriate use of materials*—helper chart to encourage responsibility
- *document individual child with transition difficulties*—individual Frequency Count and implementation of special warning before it is time to change activities
- *decrease use of punitive guidance techniques*—training in positive guidance
- *decrease domination of adult voices in the classroom*—tape recorder to monitor and make teachers aware of voice level
- *increase cooperative play*—buddy time when each child and a friend choose an activity to do together
- *increase interactions with families*—weekly happy notes
- *increase eye-level talking with children*—small chairs in each learning center for teacher to sit on while observing play and talking to children
- *increase scanning supervision of whole room*—posters for teachers on every wall that remind them to "SCAN"
- *increase use of learning area*—place an adult there to interact with the children
- *increase self-care*—equip room with cleaning equipment, low shelves, paint smocks with Velcro, dress-up clothes with elastic and Velcro

Using Frequency Counts to Measure Prosocial and Antisocial Behavior

Groups of young children are emotionally and socially immature, resulting in disagreements and a lack of empathy for one another. The goals of adults who

It Happened to Me

The Spilling Song

In a center I visited recently, a spill occurred. Immediately, a teacher jumped up and turned on a record player with a little song about spilling. She later remarked, "That same child deliberately spills every day." I asked about the song. "Oh, they love it." Do you think the teacher's response to spilling increased or decreased spilling at snack time?

work with children are to decrease antisocial behavior and increase prosocial behavior. Frequency Counts can measure the effectiveness of a chosen strategy or intervention, or the progress that children make just from maturation and experience in a group setting.

A Frequency Count tallies each time a specified behavior occurs. The Frequency Count example in Figure 5–2 shows a group of 11 children on a certain day. Huy made no social contacts. What does that mean? We cannot tell from this recording. That means that it is a closed method. All the details except for the name of the child involved and the fact that it occurred are lost. The reader does not know the nature of the action, what precipitated it, any conversation from the incident, or the result. The purpose is solely to count.

EXERCISE Interpret what the information in Figure 5–2 could mean.

What kind of a player is Carol? Solitary, parallel, cooperative (not the traditional meaning, but play stage meaning)?
What do you think Edward did?
What about Huy? Why do you think he has no tallies?

Probably Carol is in the advanced cooperative stage of play but immature emotionally. She had a lot of social contacts, but she may not have her emotions under control.

After reading the rest of the chapter, particularly regarding the difference between girls and boys, come back and think about Edward here. Huy probably is not making many social contacts because of his language barrier. Isolated children are neither prosocial nor antisocial. The common definition of an introverted, withdrawn, quiet person is, "He's antisocial." In this

FREQUENCY COUNT

Date <u>March 01 Year</u> Recorder <u>BAN</u>

Make a tally mark in the column next to the child's name each time you observe a behavior that you would classify as prosocial or antisocial.

CHILD'S NAME	PROSOCIAL Helping, sharing, hugging, calling another child by a kind name	ANTISOCIAL Hurting, hoarding, bad name calling, rejecting another child
Amy	✓✓	
Bajic	✓✓✓	✓✓✓✓
Carol	✓✓✓✓✓✓	✓✓✓✓✓✓
Danielle	✓	✓✓
Edward		✓✓✓✓✓✓✓
Fatima	✓	
Galina	✓✓✓	
Huy		
Irma	✓✓	✓
Jacob	✓✓	✓✓
Kara	✓✓✓✓	
Totals	24	22

© Cengage Learning 2014

Figure 5–2 Frequency Count Example.

 Go to the Education CourseMate website to download a copy of this form.

case, it probably is not deliberate or willful, just lack of confidence: "When in doubt, do nothing" syndrome.

Prosocial and antisocial Frequency Counts give indicators of the emotional tone of the classroom. Prosocial behavior is the outward manifestation of empathy, caring for another person through an action. In encouraging caring communities, Frequency Counts help the teacher clearly see patterns of individuals who are displaying these behaviors.

Frequency Counts can be used in selected circumstances, not as a part of the weekly system of classroom information gathering. Effective measuring before and after a strategy or over a period of time gives important documentation of the degree of change during the interval. The Frequency Count can be used to gather information on a frequently occurring behavior of a specific child. Perhaps a child

is having out-of-control anger outbursts throughout the day. Frequency Counts can be used in interventions with a child with exceptionalities, intellectual, emotional, or behavioral, to measure a specific behavior. Doing a Frequency Count and amplifying it with notes of times, circumstances, and short descriptions may give clues about the triggers, intensity, and duration of each event. Patterns may appear from this kind of behavior recording so that appropriate planning and strategies can be implemented. Some call this event sampling (Bentzen, 2009; Martin, 2007).

A Frequency Count is a part of the Observation Toolkit for Mental Health Consultants (Artman, 2011 p. 29), recording classroom behavior at various times of the day: arrival, group, centers, snack, small group, outside, rest, departure.

Home Visiting and Frequency Counts

The structure of home visits does not lend itself to doing Frequency Counts as described in the text because the time allotted to a home visit does not allow enough time to do meaningful counts. However, an educator in the home who wants to explore the frequency of a specific behavior, action, or concern should consider engaging the parent or primary caregiver to record the information over a defined period of time. Home visitors need to be specific about what is to be observed and recorded and how the information should be gathered and written down.

Advantages

Frequency Counts are

- a quantitative measurement on which to base strategies for change.
- quick to record, with no details, just tallies to write.
- useful for quantitatively and objectively measuring frequently occurring behaviors.

Disadvantages

Frequency Counts can

- lose the raw data, with no details recorded.
- only measure one kind of behavior, making the results highly selective.
- allow the recorder's bias to enter the recording.

Pitfalls to Avoid

Frequency Counts

- can select behaviors to measure that do not occur often (we hope), such as accidents requiring stitches, incidents of child abuse, and guinea pig escapes.
- infer from one sample that this is normal behavior. (It may have been an unusual day, so results are not indicative of a normal day.)
- allow much interpretation from one recorder to another. (For example, "Was that sharing when Aiko handed Katerina the Play Doh because Katerina demanded it?")
- are an intense recording method that requires the adult to be free from child-interaction responsibilities, which is not always possible.

Using Technology

If you are counting the frequency of one child's target behavior or actions, you can attach a counter to your belt. If counting a specific behavior of a group of children, the tallies on each child should be separate, so a pencil-and-paper tally sheet is the most efficient tool.

How to Find the Time

This method takes very little time. It may be one of the least time-consuming methods not capturing details, quotes, and situations; only recording the occurrence of the target behavior.

What to Do with It

The information gathered from a Frequency Count is more than food for an inquiring mind, although it may indicate that no change is needed. It is a tool to measure a baseline, the commonplace, the usual. It is the basis for judgments about the need for change. A strategy is implemented to attempt the change; then more Frequency Counts are taken to measure progress and

REVIEW

FREQUENCY COUNT

A recording of predetermined frequently occurring behaviors to quantify their frequency, and for comparison later after a strategy is implemented.

Types of Information to Record Using Frequency Counts

- frequently occurring separation difficulties of individual children
- frequent requests for assistance or reminders of self-care behaviors
- frequent observances of social play stages
- frequent prosocial and antisocial incidents in a period of time
- frequency of language used in a certain function such as to enter play area or solve social difficulty
- frequency of use of book area during free play time
- frequency of choice of creative area—visual arts, blocks, sociodramatic

PORTFOLIO EVIDENCE OF CHILD'S DEVELOPMENT			
Evidence Type	**Date**	**Recorder**	**Notes**
SOCIAL/ EMOTIONAL – the child's social and emotional development, self-concept			
RR	10/1/	BAN	Freeplay – blocks, painting books
CL	10/3/	MLS	Solitary
FC	10/11/	MLS	Mostly positive interactions
AR	10/13/	BAN	Waiting turns

Figure 5–3 Portfolio Evidence Sheet Example.

success. The process is a kind of mini-research, an experiment in a behavior-modification format. The completed Frequency Count is filed in the Class File because it contains information on all children. Noteworthy information is entered in an individual child's portfolio on the Portfolio Evidence Sheet (Figure 5–3). Depending on the topic and subject of the research, it can be shared as a victory in progress with families, other teachers, and the administration. It can be used as a needs assessment for equipment, materials, or teacher training. The post-intervention Frequency Count can be used in reporting to funders or the administration the difference new equipment or training has made. Periodically returning to the Frequency Count method will measure how long-lasting the effects of the project have been.

Go to the Education CourseMate website, accessed through CengageBrain.com for Frequency Count forms, plans, and resources.

Looking at Emotional Development

Stages of Emotional Development

EXERCISE What emotions would these events stir in you? How would you express them?

You won the $3 million lottery.
You are asked by your best friend to cosign a $20,000 loan.
You are told the plane has lost power; prepare for a crash landing.
You have lost an heirloom ring that has been in your family for five generations.
You just got a phone call from the lottery office that they made a mistake. You did not win the money after all.

Emotions are the complex processes that we use to measure our environment, assess its safety or danger, and adjust our behavior based on that assessment. The ability to make that assessment changes over time, from infancy to adulthood, with the ability to interpret the environment and react in appropriate ways. The development of emotional behavior occurs in predictable stages, but in individual ways in their expression and control. As the human matures, the capacity for distinguishing between various emotions intensifies, and along with it the ability to recognize those same emotions in others. Finding acceptable expressions and control of those emotions is a lifelong struggle for the ability to control the intensity at both ends of the emotional balance.

Studies of emotions have found that there are emotions common to all humans (Figure 5–4). These **core emotions**—fear, rage, and love—were researched in the work of J. B. Watson (1914). These core emotions form the basis for all other emotions, which are just more finite distinctions of fear, rage, and love. Core emotions are, at first, pure responses to stimuli. Within the first year, however, their appearance becomes more deliberate and recognizable (Figure 5–5). As the child develops cognitively, socially, emotionally, and verbally, core emotions are experienced along a spectrum from mild to intense and even mixed emotions. Adults can help children with the range of emotions by observations and naming the more finite label for the emotion, expanding the vocabulary and understanding of feelings.

A technique of co-creating scripts with young children combines writing down what the child says has happened and her feeling and child's drawing if she wishes. It shows the adult cares, coaches words to say, and provides a literacy role model showing that we write down important events (Murray, 2008).

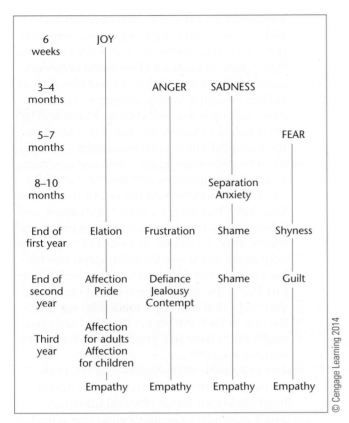

Figure 5–4 Emergence of children's emotions during the first three years of life.

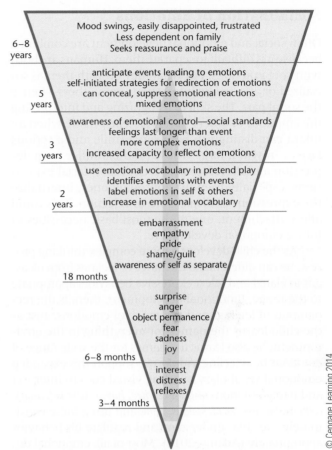

Figure 5–5 Emotional Development.

In the infant, these emotions are expressed first by reflexes, varying in intensity. They are usually governed not so much by the situation as by **temperament**. One baby expressing joy or contentment may lie passively, while others may move about actively. Babies differ in the intensity of their crying, which depends more on their particular style than the range of their discontent. These temperaments are genetic, but over time other influences will affect change in emotional responses. Parental influence on temperament has been studied by many researchers. Thomas and Chess (1977) have done research on the long-term effects of mother-child interactions on personality and emotional development. They identified nine temperamental traits that can be observed not only in the infant, but continuing throughout life:

1. *activity level*—physical motion
2. *rhythmicity*—regularity of biological functions
3. *approach or withdrawal*—initial reaction to new stimulation
4. *adaptability*—flexibility after initial reaction
5. *intensity of reaction*—energy level of responses
6. *threshold of responsiveness*—intensity of stimulation needed to produce a response
7. *quality of mood*—general behavior

8. *distractibility*—outside stimulation changing ongoing behavior
9. *attention span and persistence*—length of time activities are maintained

EXERCISE Think of yourself and one other person you know well and jot down, on a separate sheet of paper, descriptors in the nine categories of temperament.

	SELF	FRIEND
1.		
2.		
3.		
4.		
5.		
6.		
7.		
8.		
9.		

Examine the differences. Why are you different from your friend? Genetics? Family influences? Experiences with peers?

Socialization of Emotions

Often social and emotional development are combined because it is difficult to separate them. Humans are born with core emotions, but what they do with them is socialized or affected by interactions with others—hence the social part. The skill of recognizing and interpreting the emotions of others starts very early in life when an infant can distinguish between a smile and a serious face or frown. Infants whose mothers suffer from depression and therefore may lack certain facial expressions, especially friendly, approving ones, internalize the expressions as displeasure or rejection. This could affect attachment, one of the most basic necessities in future emotional development.

As the child develops a more complex thinking process, he can differentiate the range of feelings from pleasant to elated and select expressive behaviors appropriate to the range. Emotional development, then, is the recognition of feelings and the range of emotions. Just as the child learns the names for everything in the environment, he also learns the names for the wide range of emotions he is feeling. Adults can support this expanded emotional vocabulary by using visual cues to interpret and name emotions such as *excited, happy, worried, angry, comfortable, interested, jealous, calm,* and using these words to help the child understand and regulate his behavior appropriately (Adams, 2011). Most of all, emotional development is learning to control and express emotions in socially acceptable ways. Humans spend the rest of their lives trying to interpret the feelings of others, which in turn has implications for the development of self. Goleman (2006) describes this ability as **emotional intelligence**: recognizing the emotions of others and having the self-awareness and impulse control to manage one's own emotions. School readiness, early school success, and, later, accomplishments in the workplace are dependent on this emotional intelligence or competence (Galinsky, 2010). Intervention programs have been successful in teaching children how to do this, making them better able to function in relationships in school, home, and ultimately, the workplace.

Infants are born with basic emotional responses that will become more defined in how they are expressed as other areas of development become more mature. As thinking levels develop, the causes of the feelings and more choices of expression are understood.

Emotional regulation or **executive function** is the ability to monitor and manage one's thinking, attention, feelings, and behavior through the development of cognitive and neural skills (Thompson, 2009). Control and appropriate expression of emotions are learned, just as other skills are, through

modeling—seeing how others, react and express emotions. Whenever an adult shows emotion, intentionally or not, the child observes and adds it to his own storehouse of reactions to replay in later situations. He learns the emotional significance of events and common behaviors associated with expression of emotions such as yelling, swearing, crying, silence, increased activity, talking it out, and coping. Example: The car is stalled in traffic, and the driver leans on the horn and utters some profanities.

direct instruction—naming emotions and describing actions, consequences, and alternatives. Talking about emotions is an important function of language. Discussing feelings, their causes, and subsequent actions is a way to teach emotional competence. Example: "It looked like you were very angry when you thought Aaron was taking your toy but then you saw that he had one just like yours and got them mixed up. When you said, 'That's mine,' it made him see that the one in his hand wasn't his. Next time you might say, 'I have one just like that. Is that one mine or yours?'"

positive or negative reinforcement—smiles, nods, verbal praise or scowls, stern looks, no-no head shakes, or harsh physical touching. Adult reactions to a child's emotions reflect to the child the seriousness of the event, the adult's concern over it, and a comforting knowledge that the adult understands and will help. Example: The child stumbles and hits her head. The adult looks over, assesses the situation, and continues talking or rushes over and says, "Ouch, that must have hurt. Let me see if you need a bandage." Using body language can give the child indications of appropriate or inappropriate actions.

Inhibited children repress their emotions, resulting not only in added stress but also in the inability to learn how to practice social competencies; inhibited children will not learn how to express anger, fear, and frustration appropriately. Children without social skills and language to express emotions resort to socially unacceptable words and actions that cause them to be rejected by peers and labeled by adults as acting out.

Emotions are socialized or influenced in their recognition and expression by adults in the child's world. Americans show more intense expression of emotions than Chinese and Japanese people. This may cause children from Eastern cultures to be ill at ease in a setting where discussion and free expression of emotions are encouraged.

It is sometimes difficult to interpret the inner cause for the outward expression of emotions. This is a learned skill. The observer infers the cause based on prior knowledge of development and behavioral cues. Each individual is different, and before language appears, it is impossible to be certain of the emotions observed in a child. Between two and three years old, children use the words *happy, angry,* and *sad* (in that order)—and later *scared, surprised,* and *disgusted*—to describe their own and others' emotions. Notice the correlation to the core emotions. By five years old, children can match and label a broader range of emotions from pictures (Widen & Russell, 2003).

Joy, Love, and Happiness

EXERCISE　What does happiness look like? What might be some causes of happiness?

The most recognizable characteristic that suggests joy or happiness is smiling (Figure 5–6). Those first smiles are reputed to be reflex responses to

© Cengage Learning 2014

Figure 5–6 Joy is easy to recognize!

It Happened to Me

When Are You Going to Control Your Temper?

My two sons and I were sitting at the dining room table doing homework when they started arguing over a pencil, the way seven- and nine-year-olds will. The argument got more and more heated until the furious nine-year-old flung the pencil at his brother. The pencil seemed to spin in slow motion as it narrowly missed his brother's eye. I was relieved that it missed, but outraged that he would do such a dangerous thing. I got right in his face, and yelled, "When are you going to learn to control your temper?" At that moment I realized I was out of control and he was wise not to say, "When you do, Mother."

digestion rather than an emotional state. Smiles in response to human voices are seen at three weeks, and to familiar faces by three and a half months. Laughter, in response to physical stimulation such as tickling, then to more social situations, begins at four months. The reciprocal sharing of smiles, coos, and laughter is part of the attachment process needed for the coming separation, cognitively and physically. Emotional development is closely aligned with social interactions and cognitive development. When the infant can differentiate between self and others and realizes the primary caregiver is not with her, anger and fear combine to form separation anxiety. The emotional task of infancy is the formation of trust (Erikson, 1965), the confidence that needs will be met, mother will return, and all is well. That is the foundation for mental health.

Joy is manifested after the age of one from situations that have favorable results. To young children, that means satisfying their own desires. As they work on autonomy, the accomplishment of tasks brings joy in the form of pride. As they near four and five years old, happiness is meeting adults' expectations. Children at that age are working toward empathy. They can now find joy for what is happening to others rather than self. That is a goal of social development for the benefit of the whole community.

The Absence of Joy. Factors that influence this emotion begin, as always, with what is inborn. Some infants just have a generally happy behavior. Others are more irritable and harder to find in a state of satisfaction and calm. That inborn temperament may be the beginning point. Interactions with the mother, primary caregivers, and others are extremely important. In cases studied in which infants were deprived of social interactions, physical, mental, and emotional disorders were seen contributing to the **failure to thrive**. In situations of neglect, conditions of poverty, or physical illness, emotional damage can be seen as well.

Think About It...
How do you deal with difficult situations?

Children exhibit different behavior to deal with the absence of joy in their life. First, children may be in denial. They may use fantasy or refuse to recognize the difficult situation by acting as if it were not so. Children use this technique to come through abuse, removing themselves emotionally from the situation until it becomes unreal, a sealed-off part of their life. Children may regress to an earlier stage of behavior to escape the reality of the difficulty. By recording a child's progress, an observation of regression can be a warning that something may be bothering the child. Withdrawal might be used as protection from facing the absence of joy. By not interacting socially, there is less risk of pain. Negative emotional experiences activate the same pain centers in the brain as physical distress (Eisenberger et al., 2003). Emotional distress may be exhibited in physical ailments such as stomach aches or headaches that have no physiological basis. Sadness, withdrawal, low interest level, and physical pain may be symptoms of childhood depression, an increasingly prevalent phenomenon in children aged 2 to 12 (Papalia & Olds, 2008).

By evaluating children's social behaviors against the typical stages, clues may suggest a possible emotional trauma. When children act out, there may be many causes. It may be a realistic behavior for this age or stage, an expression of emotional need, or a disregard for others because of the emotional pain the child is experiencing. Observing the indicators of defense mechanisms should be noted and studied further.

When a child appears to show sadness, the teacher has some steps to take (Figure 5–7). The

Figure 5–7 A child with an absence of joy is a concern.

© Cengage Learning 2014

first one is to recognize the emotion and not show disapproval or denial even if the emotion is not justified. So often adults say, "Smile for me," or "You shouldn't feel that way." The emotion is real to the person feeling it and should not be denied by an outsider. Second, trying to get the child to forget about the feeling is a short-term solution. Pretending happiness does not help when the child is experiencing loneliness from missing the family member who left him at day care. Acting silly to get the child to smile or involving him in an activity only temporarily relieves the difficulty.

Koplow (2007) entitles a chapter "If You're Sad and You Know It" reminding readers that many children are not living out the carefree joyful time of childhood but may be experiencing sadness, anger, fear, and worry. Denial of these emotions deprives children of developing constructive ways of expressing their feelings and receiving empathetic responses from adults with dialogue that helps to name, affirm, and mediate the negative feelings.

Children under Stress. Stress causes the rise of the stress hormones adrenaline and cortisol which aid in immediate actions when in danger. Prolonged periods of the rise in these levels can cause emotional, behavioral, and learning problems in children. Their inability to find ways to understand the cause of the stress and to aleviate it sometimes results in extreme behaviors such as hitting, tantrums, or withdrawal. Stress is most often seen in physical reactions of crying, withdrawal, aggressive outbursts, and self-comforting behavior such as hair twirling, thumb sucking, and biting fingernails; but it can also manifest itself in a more internalized way, such as headaches or stomach aches. Young children are more likely either to distance themselves or communicate distress in some way other than verbally, whereas older children learn to try to problem-solve or verbalize the feelings and possible reasons (Jewett & Peterson, 2002).

There are three major sources of **stress** for children. The first is within the child, from a temperament that is slow to adjust to change and fearful of new people and experiences. As the child matures and builds confidence, the feeling of stress due to change may dissipate, or the child may develop coping mechanisms to alleviate the negative feelings. Stress may cause the child to become more withdrawn, less socially outgoing, and less prone to engage in risky behavior.

The family can be a source of stress for the child. An abusive or neglectful family is stressful and damaging to a child's developing social and emotional wellbeing. Family situations such as poverty, ill health, death, divorce, remarriage, new siblings, and moving are stressful as well. Even families with no pathology who only want the best for their child may involve the child in so many scheduled activities that she has no downtime, no time to relax or unwind naturally, which can be stressful.

The world itself is a stressful place. Instant and graphic images of dramatic, scary events such as war, accidents, disease, and famine play out in every living room, giving the child (and adults, too) a feeling of vulnerability, leaving all to question, "Am I safe anywhere? Will it happen to me? Can anybody take care of me and protect me?" It is not surprising that children feel stress. Natural disasters and tragic national and international events reach young ears, eyes, and minds. Teachers need to be prepared to support young children and assist their families through these traumas with peaceful classrooms, stress-reducing activities, and secure, reliable relationships and resources.

An interesting phenomenon that puzzles researchers, as well as anyone who wonders about cause and effect, is the coping mechanisms that some children develop. Some children appear to be **resilient** with "the ability to adapt well to adversity, trauma, tragedy, threats, or even significant sources of stress" (APA, 2011). Rutter (2006) found that resilience can result from (1) controlled exposure to risk rather than avoidance; (2) absence of other environmental factors such as poverty; (3) extensive coping mechanisms; (4) "turning point" experiences; or (5) biological or neural structures that constrain the effects of stress. Advances in brain science indicate that the human brain is designed to be resilient, to overcome risk, and to store information not as dry facts but as connected with emotional experiences (Brendtro & Longurst, 2005). Strong emotional attachments with nurturing adults can lessen the effects of stress on a child's mind and body (Center on the Developing Child, 2011). Children who are resilient exhibit empathy, detachment from the dysfunctional behaviors of others, a sense of humor, and personal power. This can be attributed to what Brendtro, Brokenleg, and Van Bockern (2002) call the Circle of Courage model, involving belonging, mastery, independence, and generosity. Despite the best intentions, families and teachers cannot always protect children from traumatic events in these uncertain times. Dr. Stanley Greenspan (2002) gives four basic principles in helping to develop a secure child:

- *spending time together as a family*—establishing warm, nurturing relationships
- *expressing feelings*—assisting children to recognize and give words to feelings with empathy, paraphrasing to extend the conversation and meaning
- *reassurance*—couched in reality that the child can understand at her level
- *contributions and helping others*—adults leading children to gain confidence and overcome helplessness

Teachers with a belief in the capacity for the spirit to overcome difficult situations can assist every child learning **coping skills**. The child's competency and empowerment will help bring joy and happiness out of deprivation. When children learn coping skills, they can generalize these skills to any situation that is unpleasant. In this way, they can address the difficulty in an emotionally healthy way.

Coping skills are learned in the same ways other skills are learned. The first step is the recognition of the cause of the problem. This will help the child, at her developmental level, understand why she has this feeling. The emotion is named, and the normalcy of these feelings will help the child move toward a solution. For example: "You're not happy today because you didn't want to say good-bye to your dad and see him leave you. Everyone feels sad sometimes when they want to be with someone and they can't. What are some things you could do until he comes back?"

Adults role-model coping mechanisms for children. "I think I'll put on this happy record. It always makes me feel like smiling when I hear this song." Some direct instruction can take place by using discussions following books or puppet scenarios in which characters have similar feelings of sadness or loneliness. Helping children to learn ways to deal with their feelings is a part of the social-emotional curriculum.

Anger and Aggression

EXERCISE **Using a separate sheet of paper, list 10 things that make you angry. What do you do when you are angry?**

Developmental Stages of Anger. Anger develops from the unmet needs of the self. When a baby rolls over and gets stuck next to the bars of the crib, that cry is an angry one. She wants to move, but something is preventing her from carrying out that urge to move. That same feeling will overcome her 20 years later when she is late for work but stuck in traffic. The response is usually different (sometimes not). Anger is energizing. It motivates the child to chase down the one who took his tricycle while he was off picking dandelions. It enables the adult to clean the whole house after an argument with a friend. Some of those actions may address the cause of the anger, while others act as a valve to let off steam. This **displacement** of anger's energy has been the subject of much research, with varying results (such as, "Does punching a pillow displace the anger or connect venting and violence?"). The major objection to

Figure 5–8 Tantrums are common in toddlers, displaying newly developed emotions without the inner controls to manage them.

displacement is that it does not solve the problem, just vents the energy and may in fact link anger and striking out as a pattern of behavior.

In the child's second year, she is seeking to be autonomous, to rule herself. She is angry when those attempts are resisted, even if it is for her own safety. Her lack of full language development makes it difficult for her to express her desires or her feelings about being thwarted or denied, so anger and frustration are increased (Figure 5–8). The egocentricism contributes to angry feelings. The child can only see her own point of view (egocentric). She cannot understand why she cannot have the tricycle back after leaving it for 10 minutes, just because she wants it. She wants it, so she believes she should have it. With the struggle for autonomy, it is not surprising that defiance, an angry stance against authority, begins in the second year. The battle of wills is beginning here, and depending on the child's temperament and the parenting style, it may be a long, difficult one or less severe.

Toward the end of the second year, a more complicated form of anger appears. It is usually caused when the child's will and actions are contrary to another's. The adult wants the child to do or not do something, or another child has possession of an object the child wants. Tantrums are often seen in the grocery store or at the mall, where there is so much visual stimulation. Attractive, desirable objects are all around, but so are restrictions the child cannot understand. They are told not to touch, but they see their mother is touching. They are told they cannot have it, but objects are placed at eye level and within their reach.

The temper tantrum can be seen in the classroom for the same reasons. With the teacher's time divided among several children, demands for time and attention are many and often delayed. Equipment and materials in the toddler room are well thought out to provide many duplicates to keep competition for toys to a minimum. Still, tantrums will occur, so the teacher should be prepared to understand their causes and deal with them in an understanding way. He gives attention to the causes and the safety of the child, not the behavior. That prevents it from becoming a battle of wills.

EXERCISE **Answer this question: At what age is aggression at its peak?**

> a) 18 months – 3 years
> b) 4 – 7-year-olds
> c) 8 – 12-year-olds
> d) 12 – 17-year-olds

Most people think that adolescents are the most aggressive group, but in reality, toddlers18 months to 3 years old are the most aggressive. In this period, children's thinking and behavior center on fulfilling their own wants and needs; they have limited language to express what they want or feel, and have not yet developed the self-control to delay the gratification of their desires (Tremblay, 2008).

Aggression. **Aggression** is the expression of anger that results in physical or emotional damage to people or property. Aggression has been the subject of much research. Jacquelyn Gentry of the American Psychological Association states, "Kids who see constructive ways to deal with anger, frustration, and disappointment are learning violence prevention" (quoted in Chamberlin, 2000, p. 54). Genetic or biological causes are being researched to learn if medications or genetic manipulation can reduce aggressiveness. Family influence on aggressive behavior is being studied to identify the cycle over the generations and try to intervene in its recurrence. Society's influence, especially violent television programming, has been the focus of a large segment of aggression research, with much of it pointing to high correlations. The predictability and treatment of childhood aggression as well as the influences of sex differences on aggression are other aspects of these studies. All of these underscore the problematic nature of childhood aggression and the complexity of its effects on behavior. These cannot be minimized or trivialized, but there are some basic understandings about children and aggression that every teacher should recognize.

EXERCISE **What does aggression in the classroom look like? Make a list. Scary, isn't it?**

Aggression is developmental. Children are aggressive at various predictable stages (Kostelnik, Whiren, Soderman, & Gregory, 2012). Two- and three-year-olds act aggressively mainly to attain or maintain possession of items or territories. They will use physical violence, hitting, kicking, and biting to keep or get what they want. Two-year-old aggressiveness is described as instrumental aggression. It works! Hit the person who has the toy and he lets go. Knock the person off the bicycle so now she can get on. As language skills increase, the child can speak rather than act, and eventually negotiate. However, some factors such as young mothers who smoke, younger siblings, and low income have been found to predict that a very young, aggressive child 17 to 42 months old has a higher risk of more serious antisocial behavior in adolescence (Tremblay et al., 2004). This study of 500 children concluded that interventions in learning less aggressive and more prosocial behaviors at this age would have more of an impact than similar efforts 5 to 10 years later.

In four- and five-year-olds, the frontal cortex of the brain controls reactions to strong emotions so they are better able to control themselves. Preschoolers are also beginning to use words to express their desires but may still be resorting to grabbing, stealing, or hiding items to keep them. Early school-age children use negotiation more often, but shift from physical to verbal aggression. Name-calling, mean talk, and threatening to withdraw friendships are the ways school-age children are aggressive. Physical aggression by the majority of children reduces as they progress from kindergarten through high school.

Types of Aggression. When closely examined, aggressive acts can be classified into four types (Figure 5–9).

Accidental. Young children are physically uncoordinated. Much of the hurtful actions take place because they are inaccurate walkers and touchers (Figure 5–10). Stepping on each others' fingers, exploratory touches that end up hurting, and manipulation of materials and equipment in ways that hurt someone else are common. While a child is digging vigorously in the sand, it flies into someone's eyes. While walking through the block area, she knocks down a pile of blocks. A child slides down the slide and knocks down

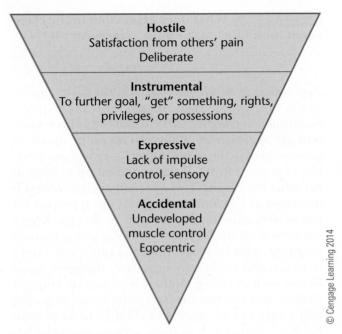

Figure 5–9 Types of Aggression.

© Cengage Learning 2014

the person standing at the bottom. All are incidents that can be classified as aggression but were unintentional. However, young children cannot understand intentionality. If they are hurt, they interpret it as aggression and feel vindicated in hitting back. When the adult says, "She didn't mean it," those words have little meaning for the young child. The observant adult can only reduce this type of aggression by creating a safe environment with constant supervision. Positive guidance techniques such as "Shovel the sand into the bucket," "Build inside these dividing lines," or "Wait to slide down until that person is out of the way" can help preschool children have a little more control over their behavior.

Expressive. Sometimes the pleasure of smashing something just to feel the jolt, not from anger or frustration, is the motivation for an aggressive act. There may be unintended consequences. Read "It Happened to Me: It just felt good!"

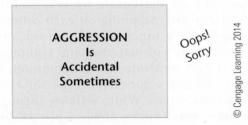

Figure 5–10 Accidental Aggression.

© Cengage Learning 2014

Instrumental. Territorial rights have been the cause of wars throughout history. The goal was not killing and maiming but to take or defend property, land, or ideals. Since young children are social learners and emotionally and linguistically

It Happened to Me

It just felt good!

At story time Ethan loved to sit behind Jolena and run his fingers through her long curly hair. Most of the time she ignored it, but occasionally he would hit a snarl and she would feel the hair pull. She yelled out "Stop it you!" and Ethan burst into tears. He had no idea why she was yelling at him. Expressive aggression; it just felt good—to him.

It Happened to Me

The Red Telephone Struggle

Two four-year-old girls wanted the red telephone in the dramatic play area. They each had a tight hold on an end of the receiver. This meant they were very close together, struggling in a pulling match. Gritting their teeth, looking eye to eye, they each grunted, "I want it," "I want it." I observed this but waited a few seconds to see what would happen. I could have gotten the other phone and talked to them about it, but I waited. It went on longer and longer. Their faces turned red, and neither showed signs of increasing violence nor of giving up. Minutes went by. I had to restrain myself from entering in, but I knew they could learn from the experience and I was curious as to how it would end. Finally, after many minutes of stalemate, one dropped her end, turned, and flounced away. The one left holding the phone (you guessed it) dropped it and flounced off herself.

immature, they take what they want without asking or thinking of the other person. Unfortunately, when the stronger child continually wins the struggle over possessions, she learns that aggressive behavior works. It becomes the instrument to get what she wants.

Physical aggression decreases in the early school years as children learn the rules of the classroom and school. As their verbal skills increase they become more capable of solving disputes and disagreements by negotiation and problem solving. With this increased language ability comes more verbal hostility in name-calling, hurtful insults, and the beginning of spreading rumors leading to rejection.

Hostile. When an action is deliberately planned to hurt either physically or emotionally, it is a hostile act. Young children usually are not planning to hurt someone, but because of accidental, expressive, or instrumental aggression, the child who feels pain attributes it to a deliberate act. We can see this thinking in the hair-pulling incident about Ethan and Jolena. "I didn't mean to pull your hair," Ethan said. "You pulled my hair on purpose!" Jolena cried as she retaliated with a slap. And so it goes.

Causes of Aggressiveness. When seeing aggressive acts through the lens of development in the types previously mentioned, hurtful actions are expected behavior in young children. Without sophisticated reasoning powers or language to express the emotions they are feeling, actions and reactions are a natural outcome of frustration and mistakenly placed motives.

Children are learners, so when they see that aggression is effective for others, they are more apt to participate in it themselves. Studies by Belsky and others have reported that children in center-based child care had increased levels of aggression (Belsky, 2007). There is a growing body of research that shows punitive adult behavior increases child aggression. It calls for families and teachers to develop more appropriate discipline strategies.

Children in child care may act out increased aggression. When children see the aggressor getting what she wants, getting attention, or other children copying the aggressive behavior, increased aggressive acts result (Goldstein et al., 2001). Poorly supervised, physically abused, harshly disciplined, and neglected children are at risk of antisocial behavior (Knutson et al., 2005; Pollack, 2008). And television viewing led the American Academy of Pediatrics to state, "Extensive research evidence indicates that media violence can contribute to aggressive behavior, desensitization to violence, nightmares, and fear of being harmed" (2001).

Aggression in Boys and Girls. For many years, research has looked at hostile aggression as a greater problem for boys than girls (Figure 5–11). More boys are reported by teachers and families as aggressive, peaking at three years of age. Garbarino (2006), who has studied boys who have been involved in violence, says that they suffer from "emotional illiteracy," a restricted range of emotional expression, and a restricted language to express emotions. Archer studied more than 40 other studies examining physical aggression in boys and girls, and analysis showed that boys were more physically aggressive, but that aggression declined rapidly after the preschool years (Archer, 2004). That physical aggression often takes the form of rough and tumble play or playfighting, where children test themselves against others and learn physical restraint so as to not use too much force. In his study *Why Gender Matters*, Leonard Sax says, "There are no differences in what girls and boys

It Happened to Me

"That'll teach you to hit!"

While shopping I saw two little boys scuffling, and then one was crying. The mother gave the older one a swat and said, "There, that'll teach you to hit!" Profound. That was exactly what she was doing.

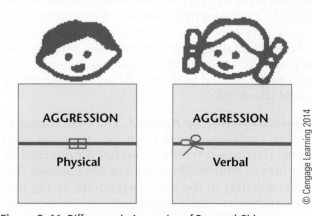

Figure 5–11 Differences in Aggression of Boys and Girls.

© Cengage Learning 2014

can learn, but there are big differences in the ways to teach them" (2005). It may be surprising that girls are actually more aggressive than boys but in relational aggression that is displayed by exclusion: "You can't play with us" (Crick, Ostrov, Appleyard, Jansen, & Casas, 2004). Other researchers suggest that while girls may be less physically aggressive in the school years, the more aggressive girls tended to show more physical aggression in their teens (Tremblay et al., 2004):

▶ Many became adolescent mothers.
▶ Many were raised by single parents.
▶ They experienced higher levels of psychiatric disorders.
▶ They had children who were more aggressive.

No matter what the cause, aggression is a problem in group settings of children, in the home and in society as a whole. A task of the early childhood field, then, is to attempt to reduce the aggression because intervention of aggressive behavior that increases after the age of six is much more difficult to accomplish (Loeber, Lacourse & Homish, 2005).

Aggression Can Be Changed to Assertion. The adult will not always be present to prevent scuffles over toys or disagreements over turns or rights. Physical aggression, typical in early childhood, becomes less frequent with development as executive function increases. Executive function (Seguin & Zelazo, 2005) is the ability to self-regulate thought, action, and emotion because of the development of cognitive and neural skills. Helping children become more assertive is another of those lessons that have many rewards (Figure 5–12). The child who can express what he wants or needs is more likely to receive it than the child who grabs. The child who can defend himself verbally from aggressors gains self-esteem and prevents himself from becoming a victim. Assertion skills will give the individual the autonomy to make their own needs known. When others must guess, they may do so incorrectly. Assertion, too, is developmental. It progresses from the two-year-old saying "Mine" to the three-year-old saying, "I had that first," and the four-year-old saying, "Maybe we could take turns."

Aggression Must Be Reduced. The first reason to reduce aggression is safety, in the classroom or at home (Figure 5–13). This is not just for the present, but for the future. Many studies have shown that aggressiveness in the early elementary grades predicts aggressiveness in early adulthood (Anderson & Huesman, 2003). This continuity is disturbing, yet

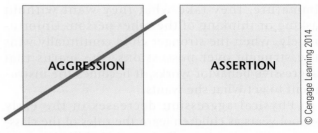

Figure 5–12 Aggression—No! Assertion—Yes!

holds the promise for early childhood education. The goal of emotional control is a critical one. Lowering aggression before the early elementary age can have long-lasting effects on society. Children can learn to exhibit prosocial behavior through a variety of strategies.

1. Label prosocial acts as they occur naturally.
2. Point out instances where unintentional lack of kindness was shown, and describe an alternate, prosocial approach.
3. Create opportunities for children to cooperate.
4. Use prosocial reasoning when talking with children.
5. Reward prosocial behavior.
6. Administer group rewards.
7. Demonstrate a variety of prosocial behaviors.
8. Demonstrate constructive ways of responding to other people's prosocial behavior.
9. Be positive when engaging in prosocial behavior.
10. Point out the prosocial behaviors modeled by yourself and others.
11. Use positive attribution to increase children's prosocial self-images. (Kostelnik et al., 2012, pp.406-407)

Challenging Behavior. Challenging behavior has been defined as "any repeated pattern of behavior or perception of behavior that interferes with or is at risk of interfering with optimal learning or

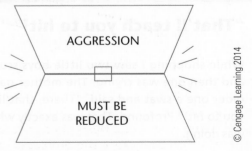

Figure 5–13 Aggression must be reduced!

engagement in pro-social interactions with peers or adults" (Smith & Fox, 2003). Young children are by nature impulsive. They are developing a whole repertoire of what is the right and wrong thing to do, but they have not yet got it altogether. They are developing the ability to regulate their behavior by inhibiting their actions. All of these strands of development influence behavior that conforms to the situation. Some children who are still learning these lessons of self-regulation have difficulty, especially in group settings. Emotions get out of control because of their lack of understanding and inability to control impulsive behavior.

Expulsion rates from preschools have been reported to be 3.2 times higher than for any grade K–12 (Gilliam, 2004). Because of its serious affects on social interaction, mental health, school success, and educational and life adjustment into adulthood, challenging behaviors exhibited by young children have been the focus of attention by educational and mental health professionals. With higher and higher estimates of the preschool population exhibiting disruptive, noncompliant, aggressive, defiant, or oppositional behavior, The Center for Evidence-based Practice: Young Children with Challenging Behavior (www.challengingbehavior.org) was created to research prevention and intervention efforts and to develop resources to assist families and caregivers. The center found that the long-term negative affects of challenging behaviors could be prevented by nurturing and positive parenting, high-quality early education environments, caregiver interactions, and early access to mental and physical care (Dunlap, 2006). Risk factors that contribute to prevention include lack of prenatal care, low birth weight, maternal depression, early temperament difficulties in infants, developmental disabilities, and early behavior and adjustment problems (Qi & Kaiser, 2003). The Center's Pyramid Model (Figure 5–14) promotes social and emotional development in high-quality out-of-home care with positive caregiver interactions and prosocial skills and positive peer interactions for all children. These programs are based on an effective workforce with systems and policies that promote and sustain the use of evidence-based practices.

Intervention begins with identification of a challenging behavior that distinguishes it from a developmentally typical behavior. Reliable screening and assessment, appropriate referrals, adequate access to services are barriers to behavior intervention. Fear of labeling or a bias against early identification lead to underuse of services. Delays in addressing behavior problems often cause the problems to escalate. Intervention for all and for targeted children begins

by teaching children skills that can replace the challenging behaviors, such as functional communication, self-management skills, and peer-related social skills. By identifying and changing the antecedents (those activities and practices that trigger challenging behavior), giving children acceptable choices, rearranging furniture and schedules, and altering instructions, one can increase the probability of appropriate behavior. This is where the practices in *Week by Week* can help. Document children's development using various methods such as developmental Checklists, Anecdotal and Running Records, and Frequency Counts to gather data. Interpret and reflect on the data to give the teacher information on which to base classroom practices and to make referrals if necessary. The main premise is that early identification and remediation of challenging behavior in a child's preschool career can prevent delinquency in adolescence, school dropout, gang membership, adult incarceration, and early death (Loeber, 2005).

Bullying. Young children are socially immature and are establishing themselves in a new setting with new people. Out of this quest to belong, some children resort to exercising control by verbally or physically overpowering another child. Preschool girls are more likely to threaten to withdraw friendship or exclude another child (Nelson, 2005). Teacher's responses need to be proactive and preventative first by setting an emotional climate of acceptance for all

Figure 5–14 Pyramid Model for Promoting Infants and Young Children's Social Emotional Development was developed by the Center on the Social and Emotional Foundations from Early Learning at Vanderbilt University (2008).

and by being aware of any indications of victimization by exclusion as well as physical aggression that occurs (Sprung, 2005). Through modeling, class meetings, role play, puppet dramatization, and appropriate children's literature that stimulates discussion, the teacher can give children the words to help them seek inclusion into a group: "I want a turn to play with that when you're done," as well as for the victim, "It makes me mad when you try to take my toy away from me." Punishing the bully only furthers the bully-victim syndrome (Gartrell, 2011), so the teacher works both to empower all children and help each one find identity within the group. When a child picks on another, excludes them from play or calls them a name, the adult should make it clear that it is unkind behavior and not acceptable. Bullying escalates when children as a group focus on a vulnerable child. Those in the group feel powerful and belonging, but the object of the bullying feels betrayed and powerless. Prevention in class meetings, story discussions, and activities that promote inclusiveness are needed. A more direct intervention may be called for when there is a pattern of bullying behavior or one child is the continual target of unkindness. Direct instruction on identifying the feelings of others, how respect is the mode of social interaction in this classroom, and self-assertion can help a target child defend against bullying. This is an increasingly observed behavior in all segments of society but, as always, early childhood is the window of opportunity to teach and model social competence.

What works? This question is the subject of many research studies, comparisons of curriculum, and debates over the effects of placing young children in groups. The conclusion is that if young children are cared for in a major portion of the day, it should be in a high-quality program where their social and emotional needs are considered in addition to the cognitive and academic focus. The curriculum should include intentional teaching of problem-solving strategies to all children, with more intensive interventions used with children who are at higher risk. This is an investment that has been shown to result in lower social problems far into the child's school and social life (McCabe & Frede, 2007).

Fear and Shyness

EXERCISE **What are you afraid of?**

Development and Fear. The first fear is of strangers. That only happens after the child has developed an awareness of separateness from others and has formed mental images of those familiar faces that are seen frequently. Sometimes even these may cause terrified screams. This change, at around six months, signals a changing cognitive development. The infant is constantly matching new pictures with the old. Any discrepancy—glasses/no glasses, hair up/hair down—that does not match the mental image triggers the fear response (Figure 5–15).

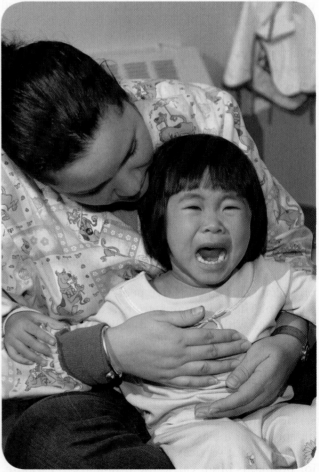

Figure 5–15 Children have many fears.

© Cengage Learning 2012

▶❚❚ TEACHSOURCE VIDEO ACTIVITY

Go to the Education CourseMate website, accessed through CengageBrain.com, and view: School Age: Emotional Development.

What strategies does the teacher present to children to counteract a bully? Do you think they would work? How about for preschoolers?

Other fears develop around two and a half years once a child's thinking is more advanced. Fears develop from the child's inability to make sense of the world. With limited understanding, everything is magic and anything is possible. There could be a grizzly bear under the bed. The house might blow away. The closet might be full of scary things that come out at night. These fears can be planted by tales the child hears from other people, adults included. Television or a fantasy book, read for fun and imagination, can produce fears. Fears of monsters, of nightmares, and of being hurt persist into the sixth and seventh year, when a firmer understanding of reality and fantasy is formed.

EXERCISE What does fear look like? Describe the physical changes that take place when you are afraid. How can others tell you are afraid? What helps quell the fear?

Fear is exhibited by wide-open eyes, screaming, crying, a rigid body, occasional uncontrollable trembling, retreat or withdrawal, or when seeking adult help. Some of the same strategies that help the child deal with anger can be used with fear. Talking about the fear by naming the emotion, not denying the feeling, and working together to help the child cope with the feeling are approaches that have been successful. The child can be encouraged to draw or act out the fear, write or dictate a story about it, or eventually face up to it little by little.

Shame, a Form of Fear. During the second year, when the child is struggling with autonomy, a stronger sense of guilt or shame is developed. This shows that the thinking processes have been categorizing actions as acceptable and not acceptable. This is a necessary step in moral development. When the child does something perceived as unacceptable, feelings of shame develop. These are extremely strong in children who have strong family authority without the opportunity to make decisions for themselves.

Four- and five-year-olds are in what Lickona (1983) calls Stage 1 of Moral Development, "You Should Do What You're Told." Children at this age, he says, believe that "what's right is doing what grown-ups tell you and the reason to do what you're told is you could get in trouble if you don't" (p. 114). Children who develop shame are

It Happened to Me

A Scary Dream

A four-year-old girl came into day care one morning, carrying her blanket and looking very serious. (No one spoke to her father as he dropped her off. No one greeted the little girl or noticed her facial or body expressions.) I was there observing a student teacher involved in an activity, who also did not notice the girl. She walked over to me, a perfect stranger, and laid her head on my shoulder.

"You look like you're still sleepy," I said.
"No, I had a bad dream last night," she said quietly.
"Do you remember what the dream was about?" I asked.
"It was scary. Dreams are what you think about when you're sleeping." That was profound, I thought.
"But dreams aren't real," I replied, thinking that might help.
"I know, but you still wake up scared." How true.

I needed a four-year-old to remind me that even unreal things can make us feel real feelings. We trust that someone will notice, care, give voice to our fears, and help us face them not feeling alone. Listen to the children.

those who are constantly reminded that they are not doing as they were told. It sometimes leads them to believe there is something inherently wrong with them. It may be that the adult's expectations were unrealistic for the child's ability to comply. The feelings of inadequacy and shame are all the child knows in this situation. As children become more aware of rules and expectations, then infractions bring a feeling of guilt and anxiety. This can become a life-long inhibition to do what is perceived as wrong behavior. It helps to develop inner controls to self-regulate behavior.

Shyness, a Form of Fear. Much research in the last 10 years has been focused on the general subject of **shyness** with more than 30 phrases to describe the behavior of social withdrawal (Rubin & Coplan, 2010). From the child development realm we know that there are periods when most children are afraid of strangers and new situations. Apart from that we also know that it is in the temperament of some people to be wary of new situations and slow to warm up in social situations. So, besides developmental and temperamental reasons, research shows two major motivations for social withdrawal. One is fear and anxiety, the feeling of lower self-esteem, lack of confidence in social situations, and even social phobia. The other is the non-fearful preference to solitude, object orientation rather than people orientation. Teachers, parents, and even children's story books consider shyness as a negative characteristic (Coplan, Hughes & Rowsell, 2010). Coplan, one of the major researchers in shyness, reminds us that "not all forms of social withdrawal are problematic" and that it is common in early childhood, but becomes increasingly maladaptive in later years (Coplan & Weeks, p. 67).

Shyness may be a type of fear that appears around eight months to new situations and people. The child at this age realizes separateness from parents. As a preschooler, the exposure to new social situations outside the home may be accompanied by feelings of discomfort. Children are self-conscious when they are the focus of attention, and are beginning to take the "other" perspective and consider what another is thinking about them, bringing feelings of inadequacy (Figure 5–16). Some children are most comfortable observing or withdrawing from the action until they are sure they can function. This should be accepted as a feeling not to be denied, changed, or negated. The adult helps the child find ways to understand and cope with the feeling.

As children enter school and encounter more children, as their cognitive functioning increases, they begin to compare themselves to others. Some may feel inadequate or a diminished self-worth. This is difficult for them to resolve and may result in social and emotional withdrawal. The teacher can help the child to mentally rehearse successful encounters and give coaching on how to enter and participate in a group. Empty praise is not helpful, nor is labeling, like "the shy one." Care should be taken to give opportunities without pushing.
The teacher should
- get to know each child as an individual.
- provide quiet and observation spaces in the classroom.

Figure 5–16 Children who are labeled "shy" often continue that behavior.

- make all children aware of the routine and changes.
- use transition techniques that allow for children to conclude previous activity before moving on.
- give choices in participation, allowing observing without embarrassment.
- work with family to determine the best approach for each child. (Swallow 2000)

The Emotionally Secure Environment

The role of the family and early childhood environment is to reduce the effects of negative emotions. They can help the child develop healthy attitudes, inner controls, and acceptable expressions. It begins with an atmosphere of mutual trust between the home and the program or school with adults that provide warm, positive

It Happened to Me

"He is mostly a solitary player"

I was reviewing a child's portfolio with his mother, speaking about each area of development. When discussing the social emotional area, I described the usual activities her son was involved in at school. Whenever I observed him he was either playing alone with classroom equipment or wandering around the classroom, watching other children play. His conversations were mainly with the adults and it seemed like he was invisible to the other children. He was comfortable with classroom routines, could accomplish the large and small muscle tasks of a four-year-old, and was cognitively engaged with math, science, and literacy activities. As his mother and I talked, now that I think about it, she sat curled into herself, hugging her purse in her lap, not making eye contact, and answering my questions with one word or short phrases in a soft voice I could hardly hear. So, where did his inhibited social behavior come from?

interest and involvement. There are predictable limits on unacceptable behavior, consistent non-punitive consequences to unacceptable behavior, and adults who act as positive role models. Room arrangements and routines are reassuring and stress-reducing. The rooms are physically comfortable, without too much sensory stimulation. The curriculum is appropriate for the age and stage of the child, reflecting an attitude of acceptance for mistakes and responsiveness to the individual. Learning activities promote internal satisfaction rather than emphasis on strict obedience or pleasing the adult. The schedule gives children freedom to move, make choices, and use creative play outlets. All these contribute to a stress-free environment, control of negative emotions, and encouragement of the positive ones of interest, curiosity, and enjoyment. This is accomplished by assessing the children's developmental levels and planning curricula from topics, themes, or projects that come from the children's world.

EXERCISE Using a separate sheet of paper, make a list of prosocial (caring and empathetic) actions you would like to see in your classroom. Now make a list of antisocial actions you probably witnessed but wished you had not. (These are typical behaviors of young children without emotional self-control.)

The physical environment is the first area to assess in providing for the emotional and prosocial development of children. An environment that is not safe or comfortable may contribute to stress and misbehavior. Identify possible environmental factors that can affect behavior—such as temperature, cleanliness, equipment, and interior design—including color, displays and textures, sound, and lighting.

The curriculum of the preschool can include special attention to the emotional life of the children. Songs such as "Where Oh Where Is [child's name]?", books such as *The Temper Tantrum Book* (E. Mitchell), group activities with puppets with faces showing various emotions, and free play time where large muscle, active, free play is encouraged are a few ways to accomplish this. For lesson plans see "Lessons Plans on Emotional Life," by Hut et al. (in Koplow 2007, p. 132–171).

This is the connection between emotional development and Frequency Counts on prosocial and antisocial actions. Frequency Counts are done occasionally to take the social-emotional temperature of the room. They give an objective, quantitative measurement of the environment. It may be the temperature is "normal" and nothing else needs to be done. It may reveal there are "hot zones"—certain children who are having difficulty controlling aggressive tendencies. These children could benefit from some intervention, since aggressive behavior affects social relationships, self-esteem, and, ultimately, success in school.

Help with Emotional Expression

Think About It...
How do you feel when someone says, "I know just how you feel"?

Do you want to scream, "No, you don't. How can you? Your experience was different from mine. You had different supports to lean on. You are different from me. You can't know how I really feel. I'm only letting you see a bit of what I really feel"?

How do you feel when someone says, "Don't feel that way"?

Will you stop feeling because they said that? Does it make the hurt or anger go away because they commanded it? You do feel that way. What you are trying to do is deal with it.

Emotions and their expression are very personal. As much as someone would like to alleviate another's pain, it is one of those times when a person only knows what he feels. The role of the family and teacher is to respect the child's emotions, not deny that they exist. "I can see that you are really sad over that." The adult models an acceptable way to express the emotion, "When I get sad or hurt, I sometimes cry and want to be alone." And everyone needs a friend who offers, "When you are ready to talk about it or need a hug, I'm here." In the case of angry and aggressive emotions, the same technique can be used. "I can see that you are really angry over that, but I can't let you hurt other people. When you are ready to tell your friend what made you so angry and try to work out the problem, I'll be here to help you. Until then you can paint at the easel or cut clay with scissors to get yourself under control."

Home Visiting and Emotional Development

Perhaps one of the greatest benefits of providing early education in the home is the potential to work with a child in the context of the family and be able to enhance and strengthen the parent-child relationship, the foundation for healthy emotional development. That does demand an extra layer of skills for the educator: knowing when and how to address in what ways the home environment and relationships within that environment can influence the child's emotional development.

TOPICS in OBSERVATION

Assessment and Curriculum Braid

EXERCISE Try making a French braid in a volunteer's hair by sectioning the top and separate into three parts, placing the left strand across the center, bringing the center strand to the left, switching their positions. Gather additional hair from the back of the right ear and add it to the strand that is now on the right. Keep taking additional hair and combining it with the main strands.

It's not so easy, is it?

The skillful teacher weaves many different strands together to plan the day's activities and measure whether the plan was effective for the group and for individual children (Figure 5–17). It begins with the strand of CHILD DEVELOPMENT, the teacher's knowledge of how children in general change over time in all the different domains or areas. That is not just one strand, but many made up of the teacher's formal learning about stages, theorists, and philosophies. Also in that are the strands of the

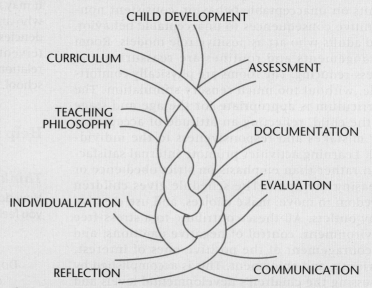

Figure 5–17 Development, assessment, and curriculum are three strands of the braid of appropriate programs for young children.

© Cengage Learning 2014

(Continued)

TOPICS in OBSERVATION   *(Continued)*

teacher's own experiences with children and how knowledge and experiences lead the planning and practices in the classroom.

Another major strand is ASSESSMENT. The teacher applies the general patterns of child development to each child in the group by getting to know them through observation as the children interact with their families, the other children and adults in the room, and the classroom environment. The observations are both informal throughout the day and formal in written documentation of what the teacher sees. Watching for clues is the basis for answering questions such as, Are they safe and healthy? Are they actively engaged? Are they growing, developing, learning? What do I know about each child to answer those questions?

CURRICULUM is the third major strand of the braid made up of the program's goals and objectives for all the children. It has strands of knowledge of planning activities that involve the various curriculum areas: physical activities, blocks, manipulatives, art, literacy, dramatic play. Curriculum planning is influenced by philosophy, geography, current events, and available resources. It is made more specific for the group because of what the teacher knows about that group; and even more specific for the individual children in the group.

The teacher adds to these main strands by EVALUATING the assessments. It is not enough just to measure, but the interpretation of those measurements leads to intentional decisions about each child. Is the curriculum meeting the child's needs? Is the child making forward progress in the domains of development: physical, cognitive, social/emotional, language, and literacy?

When assessments and evaluations are made, they area part of the COMMUNICATION to those who need to know. First, the teacher communicates to the child who wants to know that the details of her work are recognized. Someone is paying attention. The families want to know what is happening to the child during their absence. They want to know the accomplishments, the funny stories, the details—not just the bad news. They want most of all to know that the child is learning and changing in a way that will prepare him for the vision the family has for him in the future. Sometimes outsiders need to know about the group in general or a child specifically. The teacher's assessment and evaluation are important for accountability, for consultation about a concern, or reporting important information that will benefit the child.

This braid is really a loop of learning: observing, documenting, analyzing, planning, measuring, reporting, and starting over again. And so it goes, around and around, the strands are braided together and looped back into itself again—growing, changing, improving.

Observing Emotional Development in Infants and Toddlers

Much has already been said about the development of emotions from birth. First it is that attachment that the child feels toward the familiar caregivers. Infants and toddler learn from family and caregivers what is expected of them and what they can expect of others. (Day, Parlakian, 2004). It can be summarized by saying, "It's all about relationships." From relationships children receive comfort, safety, confidence, and encouragement. They are learning who they are by how they are treated. This is described as **responsive care** when adults adjust to the child's temperament. The adult's recognition and ability to adjust to the child's temperament is called the **goodness of fit** (Kristal, 2005). When programs caring for infants and toddlers move them once they walk, once they crawl, once they talk without recognizing their emotional needs for attachment, the child may exhibit emotional upset. Programs recognizing the child's need for a consistent caregiver practice continuity of care where the primary caregiver moves with the small group of children from infancy into the third year. This relationship-based philosophy benefits the child with a caregiver who knows the child, the family and minimizes the trauma of transitions. (Raikes & Edwards, 2009).

Sensory integration. The infant or toddler (as do we all) takes in information through the senses (vision, hearing, touch, movement, taste, and smell) and organizes or integrates this information with increasing body control over her actions and reactions. Depending on temperament, some people can handle many sensory experiences at once. For others, this puts them into sensory overload, and they have difficulty interpreting and acting appropriately on the information. They are frustrated, become agitated, and may shut down to block out the stimulation.

Self-regulation. The young child is gaining control of bodily functions, managing powerful emotions, working to maintain focus and attention (Florez, 2011; Epstein, 2009; Riley, 2008). This will be the foundation of functioning in all areas of development. Observing the infant as he interacts with environment, family members, and other adults and children will give indications of the child's temperament and ability to self-regulate. Williamson and Anzalone (2001) suggest four areas that are the core of behavioral regulation:

Arousal: the ability of the infant to maintain an alert state when awake and transition between sleep and awake periods—Marcus is a child who needs to lie awake in the crib before being picked up and brought into the action of the room.

Attention: the ability of the infant to focus and ignore other stimuli—Jose watches the ball roll around on his highchair tray and at the same time opens his mouth as the caregiver feeds him.

Affect: the response of the infant to sensory stimulus—Caroline stiffens when she is held lying down face up, but when she is held upright facing out into the room she relaxes and smiles.

Action: the ability to organize body movements to achieve a goal—Deirdre opens a small box that contains blocks, takes some out, closes the lid, then opens it again and takes out more blocks. She repeats this action over and over until the box is empty.

Helping all Children with Emotional Development

"Significant mental health problems can and do occur in young children. In some cases, these problems can have serious consequences for early learning, social competence, and lifelong health." This is how the National Scientific Council on the Developing Child (2008) opens a working paper on the issue of mental health problems in early childhood. Social and emotional problems can affect the child, the other children, the family, and the teachers, and can be predictors of later physical and emotional and academic problems. Young children are especially vulnerable to the stresses of child abuse or neglect, family turmoil, neighborhood violence, or extreme poverty (Gunner, 2007). African-American boys are particularly vulnerable and appear to fall behind very early in their life, as early as 9 to 24 months old (Aratani et al., 2011). These hardships early in life can damage the developing brain.

Young children are especially vulnerable because of the following:

▸ They are so strongly influenced by the relationships of those around them that interventions and treatments of only the child are ineffective.

▸ Children's responses to trauma are so different from adults, and often serious harm is not recognized because of their lack of language or understanding of the experience.

▸ Variability in behavior is a characteristic of the developing child and may mask emotional difficulties.

▸ Professionals working with young children often lack the knowledge, skills to identify, and the capacity of mental health services to treat emotional disorders in young children.

▸ Cultural beliefs and understanding may interfere with access to mental health services.

For these reasons, the early childhood practitioner's ability to observe and record children's behavior is paramount to helping identify potential long-term mental health difficulties.

Behaviors that Warrant Concern for Emotional Development

Infants and Toddlers (Birth to Age Three):

▸ Chronic feeding or sleeping difficulties
▸ Inconsolable "fussiness" or irritability

- Incessant crying with little ability to be consoled
- Extremely upset when left with another adult
- Inability to adapt to new situations
- Easily startled or alarmed by routine events
- Inability to establish relationships with other children or adults
- Excessive hitting, biting, and pushing of other children, or very withdrawn behavior
- Flat affect

Preschoolers (Ages Three to Five)

- Engage in compulsive activities (head banging)
- Throw wild, despairing tantrums
- Withdrawn: show little interest in social interaction
- Display repeated aggressive or impulsive behavior
- Difficulty playing with others
- Little or no communication; lack of language
- Loss of earlier developmental achievements. (Cohen et al., 2005)

Young School-agers (Ages Six to Eight)

- Extreme emotional outbursts
- Inability or unwillingness to make friends
- Easily frustrated
- Inability to attend to tasks
- Act out to gain attention
- Need constant reassurance or approval.

Emotional Development of Young English Language Learners

Emotional development can be seen in all children as we observe how the classroom environment affects them and how their emotional behaviors affect others. For children who are English language learners, both the culture and the lack of the ability to communicate feelings make it more difficult for the teacher to interpret and understand what the child is feeling. It may be manifested in extreme shyness, unwillingness to participate, crying, or temper tantrums. The teacher, working with the family, can assess the child's abilities in her first language and then individualize the instruction, accepting nonverbal behavior without pressure, providing for successful solitary play episodes, interacting with the child in a patient manner, and providing a safe way for the child to try out new vocabulary words and short expressions.

Emotional Development of Children with Disabilities

For children with developmental delays or disabilities, emotions are a large part of the child's successful adjustment. Children with autism and children with attention deficit disorders may have emotional difficulties adjusting to group settings. Consistent routines, clear communication, and family contact will help the teacher make the necessary adjustments to the classroom so that the learning environment can meet the needs of the child.

When children with physical disabilities are included in programs with other children, self-comparisons are made. The other children are also learners with still-developing social skills, understanding, and empathy. Fear, rejection, and curiosity may be the emotions expressed by the classmates, causing loneliness, doubt, and low self-esteem in the child with disability. The teacher prepares the other children in the group, just as the environment is prepared, to receive the child with a disability. By providing adaptive apparatus, such as wheelchairs, walkers, hearing aid cases, and eyeglass frames, the children can experiment how it feels to use these things. Many more books now include children with differing abilities, both in regular storylines and in nonfiction child-level explanations of disabilities.

Children with emotional disorders in the classroom will affect the emotions of both the staff and other children. Difficult behaviors, aggressiveness, withdrawal, and acting out are always challenges for the staff. For the child with chronic emotional disorders, it is an even greater challenge. Acceptance and knowledge of the disorder and approaches to use will be part of the preparation for this child. Information from families, records from other professionals working with the child and the family, and individual research will provide the teacher with a background and strategies to deal with the child. Other children can be informed and helped to understand the nature of this child's needs so that a caring atmosphere is created for all.

Helping Professionals for Emotional Concerns

Helping professionals, such as social workers, psychologists, or psychiatrists, may be involved in consultations, assisting in emotional development difficulties. The staff will use each other for re-sources to seek answers to emotional behavior problems. Discussions with parents in the initial interview and intake process, and in open commu-nication opportunities such as at open house, par-ent meetings, and social events, give the teacher insight about the child. When all other attempts are not working, a more formalized discussion with the parents may be necessary. The emotional realm is subjective and also personally connected with the families' and teacher's emotions. A con-ference should be approached sensitively, seeking a partnership of ways to help the child. Caution is taken not to lay blame, make diagnoses, or criticize. The teacher is prepared to suggest refer-rals for further evaluation. They may include the following:

medical personnel—pediatrician, neurologist (treatment of brain and central nervous system disorders)
mental health professionals—psychiatrists, psychologists, social workers, therapists
support groups—mentor families; family resource centers; cooperative extension agents; school, religious, or community agencies

Other Methods

Other Methods to Record Emotional Development:

Anecdotal/Running Records
Developmental Checklist or Rating Scale with emotional development component
Dialogues/Discussions with child about emotions
Media recordings depicting emotions

Key Terms

aggression	goodness of fit
coping skills	resilient
core emotions	responsive care
displacement	self-regulation
emotional	sensory integration
intelligence	shyness
executive function	stress
failure to thrive	temperament
Frequency Count	

Plans

Go to the Education CourseMate website, accessed through CengageBrain.com for the following:

Frequency Count form
Plan Week 5 Part A, Directions for Frequency Count of Social-Emotional Development, including What to Do with It, Portfolio Evidence Sheet Example, Sharing with Child and Family, Actions—Read a Book, In the Environment, In the Curriculum, In the Newsletter
Plan Week 5 Part B, Anecdotal Recording of Emotional Development for Group D, includ-ing What to Do With It.
Plan Week 5 Part C, Reflective Journal

Resources

Artman, K., et al. (2011). *Observation toolkit for Mental Health Consultants.* www.ecmhc.org/documents/CECMHC_Observation_Toolkit.pdf
Bos, B. (1990). *Together we're better.* Roseville, CA: Turn the Page Press.
Center on the Social and Emotional Foundations for Early Learning. http://www.vanderbilt.edu/csefel/.
Epstein, A. S. (2009). *Me, you, us: Social-emotional learning in preschool.* Ypsilanti, MI: High Scope Press
Gartrell, D. (2011). *A guidance approach for the encour-aging classroom,* 5e. Belmont, CA: Wadsworth Cengage Learning.
Greenspan, S. (2002). *The secure child: Helping chil-dren feel safe and confident in a changing world.* Cambridge, MA: Perseus Publishing.
Hyson, M. (2004). *The emotional development of young children* (2nd ed.). New York: Teachers College Press.
Jacobson, T. (2008). *"Don't get so upset!" Help young children manage their feelings by understanding your own.* St. Paul, MN: Redleaf Press.
Koplow, L. (2007). *Unsmiling faces: How preschools can heal* (2nd ed.). New York: Teachers College Press.
Raikes, H. H., Edwards, C. P. (2009). *Extending the dance in infant and toddler caregiving: Enhancing attachment and relationships.* Baltimore: Brooks Publishing Co.
Schiller, P. (2009). *Seven skills for school success: Activi-ties to develop social & emotional intelligence in young children.* Beltsville, MD: Gryphon House.
Teaching Tolerance, www.tolerance.org

CHAPTER 6

Using Conversations to Listen to Language and Speech

NAEYC Standards **naeyc**

The following NAEYC Standards for Early Childhood Professional Preparation are addressed in this chapter:

Standard 3: Observing, Documenting, and Assessing to Support Young Children and Families

Standard 6: Becoming a Professional

IN THIS CHAPTER

- Using Listening as an Observation Method
- Listening to Speech and Language
- Observing the Developing Language of Infants and Toddlers
- Helping All Children with Language Development
- Topics in Observation: Diversity
- Helping Professionals for Speech and Language Concerns

Using Listening as an Observation Method

EXERCISE **What might the following sentences tell you about the person speaking?**

"Howdy, y'all."
"I've just had a dialogue with my stock broker. . ."
"When I was in France. . ."
"I'm so stupid. . ."
"Thith ith fun!"
"I ain't got no job."
"Dey gonna come get you bein' bad."
"Wa wa."

"You raise sheep? How do e-w-e do it?" (spells
    out ewe)
"Na na, na na, na."
"You sister him?"

Observing by listening is done naturally all the time. The message received by the listener is not just the words and their meaning. Inferences are made about where the speaker is from, the speaker's self-esteem, educational background, social situation, ethnic group, and even mental age. Subtle, and sometimes not so subtle, clues are given about their interests, economics, and experiences. The listener notices teeth formation, facial expression, body language, eye contact, sense of humor, and vocabulary choice. All of these may give more information about the speaker than the actual words spoken. Listening during regular activities and in more formal interviews are excellent ways to assess language and other areas of development.

Informal Observations of Language

Social discourse or discussions and questioning methods were first called **action research** by Kurt Lewin in 1948. Asking questions to stimulate thinking is an age-old learning method that dates back to the Greek philosopher Socrates. It is a way for teachers to find out what they want to know and to seek answers about their own classroom. Talking with children and their self-reporting are accepted fact-finding methods. **Conversations** take several forms, depending on the age of the child, situation, and information to be gathered. **Informal conversations** happen all the time in the normal functioning of the child in the environment. As the adult talks with the child about her actions, he asks, "Wow! How did you get that to stand up on that little end like that?" or "Can you think of another way to use these old pieces of plastic someone gave us?" Arrival and departure times are important times for conversation. Planning how to introduce the day or to get the child involved in an activity on arrival will help ease the transition and set the tone for the day. Departures are times for rehearsing one or two of the meaningful events of the day so they are on the child's mind, perhaps long enough to talk about them at home. It is not the time to remember misguided behavior or give warnings like, "Tomorrow I hope you'll remember the rule about not hitting." Snack and mealtimes should include the adults sitting and eating with the children, acting as role models for social conversations.

Listening to Language Play. An excellent time to listen to conversations is when children are playing: listening to conversations they are having with their friends, hearing the give and take and problem-solving strategies. These opportunities allow the conversation to flow in a natural way so as to gather spontaneous samples of what the child is doing and thinking. When children are engaged in activities, words flow out. They play with language sounds from infancy with babbling and cooing and even reciprocating with an adult in what sounds very much like a conversation back and forth. Nursery rhymes and children's songs give opportunities for language play, repeating sounds, words, and phrases, which can sometimes turn into little humorous incidents and jokes. Toddlers are beginning to play with words to display the beginning of humor, using a banana like a telephone and laughing hilariously at the mistake. In the preschool years, children play with sounds by placing various sounds at the beginnings of familiar words, playing at rhyming. They may play with a word by trying it out with other consonants, "Ball, pall, mall, hey, I said mall. My mom shops at the mall." They begin the endless round of knock-knock jokes before they understand the way they work. They may test out forbidden words such as "poopy head" or worse.

Environments for Conversation. Interior designers plan conversational groupings of furnishings that are comfortable and close together, not meant for 10 or 15 people, but for 2 to 5 or 6. In an early childhood classroom, small tables, cozy areas with pillows to accommodate two to four or five children, areas where a few children can play with the sand table, block corner, or side-by-side painting easels promote talking between children or adults stationed nearby. Small cozy spaces with lower-level room noise ease stress that may inhibit conversations. When the hands are busy, with opportunity for sensory experiences with sand, water, clay, fingerpaint, and drawing materials, conversation flows more easily. Dramatic play props that are intriguing also bring out intriguing conversations. The temporal environment provides extended time for conversations to occur and extend. Allowing silences and wait time for answers to questions in conversations gives thinking time, resulting in richer responses. The emotional environment provides freedom of expression without fear of being told the answers are wrong or stupid or unacceptable.

🏠 Home Visiting and Conversations

"Having conversations" is a key element of the early childhood home visit. Educators not only have the opportunity to have focused conversations with the child throughout the visit but also to assess how the home environment supports the child's language development. There are a number of tools educators can use to monitor language development such as Ages and Stages (Bricker & Squires, 2009). Beyond using a reliable tool, educators want to identify who regularly "converses" with the child, consider what those language interactions typically look like (engaging or directive, richness of vocabulary, frequency of exposure to language, etc.), and how the educator can expand, when necessary, language experiences for the child beyond the home visit.

Child Interviews

EXERCISE **When you want to know something about the following subjects, whom do you ask?**

> What postage is due on this package I'm mailing?
> How many automobiles were shipped into the United States last year?
> How long do I cook a five-pound roast?
> What medicine can I take for this cold?
> Do I need a haircut?
> Where does it hurt?

It Happened to Me

"Frosting the Cake"

It was the last day of a student teacher's practicum, and the supervising teacher was planning to surprise her with a cake, involving the children in spreading the chocolate frosting. Two boys stood at the side just watching. One was a swaggering five-year-old, the role model of a four-year-old who had been following him around. The world-wise five-year-old stood at the side with arms folded over his chest and said, "It looks like sh** to me." The imitator then folded his arms and said hesitantly, "It looks like poopie to me too."

To receive a reliable answer to a question, it must be addressed to the person who most likely knows the answer. Scramble the answers to the questions in the preceding exercise to see how foolish it is to ask the wrong person or even guess the answer. It only makes sense, then, to gather information about the child from the child. Harste, Woodward, and Burke (1984) use the phrase "the child as the informant." By listening to the child, both what is said and how it is said, information is transferred upon which evaluations are made.

EXERCISE **Using a tape recorder, talk to five children of different ages between one and eight. This tape will be used repeatedly in this chapter to illustrate speech and language development.**

> Carry on a little conversation beginning with a greeting, "My name is _____. What's your name? How old are you? What are you doing? Where did you get that? What are you going to do with it?"
> What differences did you hear in the way children of various ages answered the questions?

Interviewing, or asking children questions to find out what they know or what they are thinking about, is an age-old technique. The early childhood field has a prestigious role model for interviewing children in Piaget (Evans, 1973), who used the "clinical" interview, writing meticulous notes on the questions and answers. He began with his own children, but extended his interviews to others to delve deeper into their thinking and understand their wrong answers to questions.

Talking with young children can be interesting and rewarding (Figure 6–1). It also can be frustrating because of their short attention span and egocentrism (only understanding things from their own point of view). Sometimes they do not speak clearly enough to be understood. Questioning children brings surprising results: Ask a child, "What color is a banana?" The child may say white, yellow, black, or purple. Each of those answers are "correct" in their own right depending on the child's experiences and mental image of the word "banana." Ask a child, "What color is an apple?" The answer may be white, red, yellow, green. Are those wrong answers? On a standardized test there would be only one right answer.

There are many formal tests of speech and language that use picture recognition, imitating letter sounds, comprehension, and sentence completion.

© Cengage Learning 2014

Figure 6–1 Talking with a child can be interesting and a source of developmental assessment.

These are used primarily by speech and language pathologists in determining a child's level of speech and language ability. The family and the teacher are concerned most of all with communicating with the child. Formal evaluation measures are used only when that communication seems to be hampered by speech or language delays or difficulties.

Structured Interviews. A **structured interview** gathers specific information about the child's understanding of certain concepts. The adult sets up items for the child to choose—big/little; short/long; over/under; red/blue—things that go together or things that do not belong. Selected pictures or books are often used to elicit conversation. During the interview, speech and language skills are assessed (Wortham, 2008). An interest questionnaire can give older children an opportunity to express their likes and dislikes and give us an insight into a child's happiness or self-esteem, with questions such as, "What would you like to know more about?" or "The most interesting thing I have done at our school during the past week is . . ." or "What is your favorite thing to do at school?" Responses may be written in a log by older children or dictated to the teacher. Dictation gives the child a role model for literacy, seeing spoken words translated into permanent print. It also gives the child an opportunity to think and reflect on the past. Through dictation, the child expresses feelings by elaborating on thoughts and feelings.

Efficient questioning techniques and skills make the most of the interviewing method. There is a hierarchy of questions (Bryen & Gallaher, 1983) that yield progressively more information while requiring more complex levels of comprehension.

> *Yes/no questions*—"Do you want a drink?"
> *What (object)*—"What's this?"
> *What (action)*—"What are you doing?"

> *Where (location)*—"Where's the dolly?"
> *What (attributes)*—"What color is this?"
> *Who (persons)*—"Who is picking you up today?"
> *Whose (possession)*—"Whose boots are these?"
> *Which (selection)*—"Which cookie cutter do you want?"
> *When (time)*—"When are you going to paint today?"
> *How (manner)*—"How did you make those dots?"
> *Why (cause-effect)*—"Why did that paper rip?"
>   (p. 103)

Each type of question requires more thought, understanding of the Wh- questions, and longer, more revealing answers. A **closed question** is one for which the asker already knows the answer and is testing the receiver. All but the last two of the preceding list are closed questions. They may give information about a child's specific knowledge, but not about the thinking processes or creativity. An **open question** such as "What's another way . . ." or "Can you tell me how . . .?" gives more insight and is a more natural conversation model. Asking children open-ended questions (those for which the person asking does not know the precise answer) is a technique to help the child think, imagine, and solve problems.

EXERCISE **Here are some typical questions. Put a checkmark by the open-ended questions.**

▶ *Observing*—"What do you notice here?"
▶ *Recall*—"What did you see at the zoo?"
▶ *Differences*—"How are they different?"
▶ *Similarities*—"How are these the same?"
▶ *Ordering*—"Can you order these colors from lightest to darkest?"
▶ *Grouping*—"Which of these go together?"
▶ *Labeling*—"What is the name of that group?"
▶ *Classifying*—"Which cubes here are red?"
▶ *Concept Testing*—"This cube is blue but does it belong?"
▶ *Causes*—"Why do you think that happened?"
▶ *Effects*—"What happens if . . .?"
▶ *Feelings*—"How do you think she feels?"
▶ *Generalizing*—"What usually happens to water in the freezer?"
▶ *Questioning*—"What could you ask her?"
▶ *Anticipating*—"What do you think will happen?"
▶ *Making choices*—"Which one would you like?"

(Adapted from Sigel's Questioning Model in Pelligrini [1991])

All but naming, labeling, classifying, and concept testing are open-ended questions.

Diagnostic Interviews. Besides listening to the message, the listener can also examine how the child is using language and the quality of the speech production. It then becomes a **diagnostic interview** as well. Interviewing can be a process to confirm a problem that may need remediation. Both casual conversations and structured interviews can be diagnostic. Interviewing with the purpose of assessing speech and language development or exploring the child's knowledge of concepts with young children can be done in small groups and makes them more relaxed in the company of their peers; the responses are richer because of their interactions. Opinions are stated; interpretations or reasons for an event can be explored. This style of interview is a little conversation with a purpose.

The style of the questioner is also a factor in interviewing. Some people are more comfortable engaging in a conversation that is spontaneous and flows from the exchange between the child and adult. Others may prefer a more structured format for uniformity and comparison as well as comfort with the method. Questions for discussion or interviews with preschool children will be provided for the interview assignments, but the observer or recorder is free to **record** more natural conversations if that is more comfortable.

Facilitated Conversations

There are times during the day when **facilitated conversations** can be planned to gain more insight into children's thinking. During a class meeting at the beginning of the day, the theme or project can be the subject, finding out how much children know about a subject and planning together how to learn more. Free play and other planned activities are excellent times for short, purposeful conversations individually or in small groups (Burman, 2009). In the High/Scope curriculum, children regularly plan their activities of the day in facilitated conversations with the teacher and small groups. Later they review their work-time experiences and represent them in drawings or written descriptions.

The Mosaic Approach: In the Reggio Emelia view of the child, children are experts in their own lives, skillful communicators, and active participants and are meaning makers, researchers, and explorers. Clark, a researcher in London, has been involved in developing methods to listen to young children. The Mosaic approach combines drawing together pieces to complete a picture of children's perspectives, concentrating on listening to the children as they work with adults to gather information and assess it, interpreting the meaning, and discussing the question, "What is going to change or remain the same as a result of

this process?" In this approach, children become researchers using observation and interviews to gather information, and then finding ways to represent both the process and what they have learned. Listening to children is the key in this process (Clark, 2007).

What Can You Learn About a Child By Listening?

EXERCISE In the following categories, list on a separate sheet of paper what you might learn about a child by listening to speech and language as well as content.

Family
Culture
Physical development
Health
Age or stage of development
Socioeconomic level
Cognitive development
Self-concept
Needs
Temperament
Activity level
Humor
Television viewing habits
Imagination
Problem-solving abilities
Social development

In each category, there are the obvious bits of knowledge that can be acquired by listening or asking the child questions.

family—manners, attitudes, as well as finding out inside information such as a new baby is on the way

culture—customs, holiday celebrations, common activities

physical development—abilities like riding a bike with no training wheels, interests such as dancing or karate, missing teeth, muscles, or structure of the mouth and jaw

health—nasal congestion, "I threw up before I came to school," "My arm hurts."

age or stage of development—grammatical construction, "Me do it."

socioeconomic level—"We're flying to Disney World" or "We slept in the car last night."

cognitive development—"If I want more cookie I can just break this one up and have lots," "Eight, nine, ten, eleventeen, twelveteen."

self-concept—"Nobody likes me."

needs—"Help me, I can't do it."

temperament—"I CAN'T DO IT!"

activity level—"I'm gonna swing on a swing, then I'm gonna ride a bike, then I'm gonna dig in the sand, then I'm gonna . . ."

humor—"Where does a sheep get a haircut? In the baabaa shop."

television viewing habits—"I'm gonna be a Power Ranger."

imagination—"I have this refrigerator and it follows me wherever I go so I can have a cold drink whenever I want it."

problem-solving abilities—"I tried it this way but it didn't work so I tried this and it worked!"

social development—"If you don't give me a turn I won't invite you to my birthday party."

Listen to children talk, sometimes prompted by a few open-ended questions such as:

"Do you want to tell me about . . .?"

"How'd you do that?"

"Then what happened?"

"What do you think will happen next?"

"Hmmmmm."

Listening as the Foundation for Language Development

Listening underlies speech and language development components (Figure 6–2). Articulation is dependent on the ability to listen and discern the differences in sound and then reproduce those different sounds clearly enough to produce meaningful language. Vocabulary is the range of words for objects, feelings, actions, and thoughts. The function of language is the communication of needs, and eventually thoughts and questions. Grammar is the part of language development that applies rules of the specific language. All these develop from simple to complex as the child matures if hearing, cognition, and body parts are working effectively. There could be another layer underneath the whole of speech and language development, and that is emotional development. All systems could be in working order, but emotional stress, trauma, or abuse could interfere with oral communication.

Jalongo (2007, p. 38) gives the following guidance for supporting children's oral language:

- Children must interact with more competent language users in order to master language.
- Acknowledge that every child's language or dialect is worthy of respect.

- Treat children as if they are conversationalists, even if they are not talking yet.
- Be sure to speak to all children, not just those capable of advanced speech.
- Listening can help us to identify with the child's feelings.
- Ask children to talk about things that truly matter to them.
- Design activities that encourage children to listen to one another carefully.

Documenting Children's Language

One of the main reasons to write down observations is to remember. How many cute stories of children's antics have been lost because they never were written down? Besides losing the stories, writing down what the child says, while he is saying it, gives permanence to the words. That is an underlying principle of literacy; words that are written down are preserved forever for anyone who can read them. An adult who writes and reads back to the child what he said becomes a role model of literacy, showing the child that words are permanent. Sometimes the opportunity to write is not convenient, and just a note with a few words is enough to bring recall of the whole conversation. Expanding those notes as soon as possible after writing will ensure their accuracy. Rereading the transcriptions of dialogues later may bring insights that were not present at the time of the writing. Sharing the quotes and their interpretations with the child and with the family can involve others in the meaning-making process (Burman, 2009).

Taping Children's Language Development. While technology is a separate section at the end of the discussion of each observation method, it receives more attention when it comes to language development. To carry on meaningful interviews and conversations with children, intense note-taking interferes with attention to the child, eye contact, and close listening. The audio or video preserves not just the words or sounds of speech, but the inflection of the voice, the pace of the responses, and the pitch that is unique to the child. In addition to language development, recording children's verbal interactions with peers gives information about the child's social development, literacy, self-concept, interactions with adults, and cognitive development, revealing what children know about their world.

Transcribing tapes into written notes is time-consuming, but short segments can yield so much information that the time is well-spent. It is also

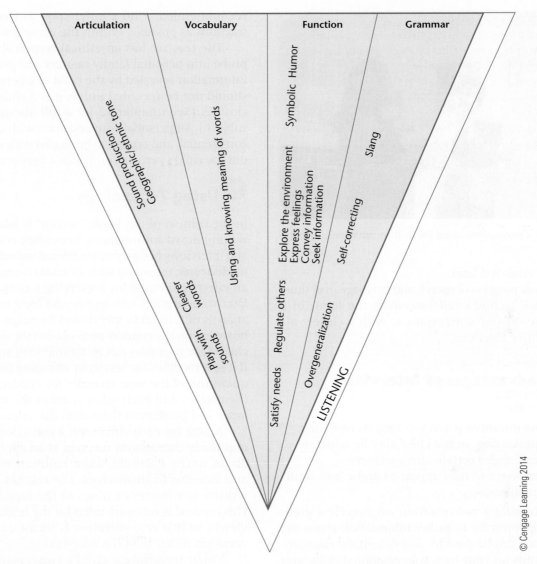

Figure 6–2 Speech and Language Development.

© Cengage Learning 2014

possible to keep a log and use the time feature on the recorder to note significant segments on the tape. This form of observation is especially valuable when it can be collected over a long period of time, such as when the infant is first beginning to make sounds and words, through the toddler stage when short sentences have so much meaning, and into the preschool and early school years when listening to the child's language is a window into his thinking.

Confidentiality Issue

Just a reminder to teachers: The child is the client. In that special relationship, what a child tells a teacher is privileged information, just as with a doctor or a lawyer. It is important not to use this information for a general topic of conversation, only to help the child (Figure 6–3). The exception, of course, is the child's disclosures of possible abuse. This is discussed in a later chapter.

Advantages of Conversations and Interviews

Interviews can

- reveal the child's prior knowledge about the world to help plan meaningful learning experiences.
- help the child organize her thinking, talking it through, externalizing the internal thinking.
- yield multitudes of information both in content and in language production from natural situations.

© Cengage Learning 2014

Figure 6–3 Conversations about the child are confidential among the staff.

- be analyzed later.
- show progress of speech and language over time.
- raise a child's self-esteem as the focus of a one-on-one conversation, with a closely attentive listener.

Disadvantages of Interviews

Interviews are

- time intensive when focusing on one child.
- intimidating, so the child may be reluctant to speak under certain circumstances.
- intrusive and may appear to probe into confidential areas.

Conducting a conversation or interview gives you the opportunity to gather information about the child, which can be used for assessment. Its effectiveness depends on your own conversational skills; you must listen actively and formulate questions based on the child's lead. A language sample can be gathered effectively in this way through a written record of the child's exact spoken words, taken in the context of the child's activity, usually in conversations with you or other children. A dated series of language samples over time can demonstrate the child's growth and progress

Pitfalls to Avoid

Children may be uncomfortable with interviews. When holding individual formal interviews with each child, it is important to emphasize that the special conversations will be held with each child and everyone will have a turn. If a child appears anxious during the interview and is reluctant to speak, the interviewer should stop and observe the child in a more natural setting.

A busy classroom may interfere with the interview, but isolation in another room is not recommended. Find a quiet spot, as free from distractions as possible, within the classroom.

The teacher has an ethical responsibility not to probe into personal family matters and practices. Any information revealed by the child of a personal nature should not be recorded unless it is a child abuse disclosure. (See Chapter 12 for a full discussion of this subject.) All personal conversations with children are confidential, and are not to be shared with others without the child's permission. This is a very sensitive area.

Using Technology

In the context of this book, "record" is taken to mean writing down information. Recording conversations and interviews has a more traditional meaning referring to electronic recording such as audio recording. This is an effective method for preserving a conversation for later transcription into words and for a more careful analysis of the child's speech and language. It depends, however, on the comfort zone of both the adult and the child. Tape recording can be intimidating and intrusive. If it is, it modifies the results by changing behavior. Frequent use of the tape recorder for children to record themselves and each other reduces the intimidation factor and familiarizes them with the tape recorder.

A tape for each child with a collection of recordings made throughout the year is an appropriate addition to the Portfolio. Most children enjoy taping and listening to themselves. The teacher also makes written summaries or notes of the tape recordings. This method is recommended for the beginning interviewer so that concentration is focused on the conversation rather than the note-taking.

Video recording a child's conversations yields even more information than an audio recording because you also see facial and body expressions. Any kind of overt preservation of a child's behavior—writing, audio, or video recording—has the possibility of altering the behavior, so care must be taken to obtain a natural sample so that it is objective and authentic.

How to Find the Time

The teacher talks with the children throughout the day—carrying out the routines and instructions necessary to achieve the goal of getting through the day. However, the amount of time left for one-on-one or even meaningful group conversations seems to be smaller. We know, of course, how important verbal exchanges are to knowing each child, learning what they know, and meeting their emotional, social, and cognitive needs. The teacher can look at every aspect of the day and see opportunities for individual conversations.

Arrival time offers an opportunity to have a brief conversation with each child, getting feedback on what has happened since they were last together, how the child is feeling, or telling what the teacher has in store for the group that day. A Class List Log near the entryway can help to quickly capture important points. When children work and play is an ideal time for the teacher to circulate and comment on the play, extending the conversation. Anecdotal notes, even abbreviated to be expanded on later, only take a few moments. Class meetings can be an opportune time to have wonderful conversations. The tape recorder or a second person writing notes can preserve these important times that provide developmental information. The ever-present notepad and pen can capture that "unforgettable" quote to be amplified later with who, what, when, where, why to build an anecdote that includes the quote.

❓ What to Do with It

The Structured Interview questions and answers are filed in the child's Portfolio and noted on the Portfolio Evidence Sheet (Figure 6–4). Anecdotal notes or jottings from conversations or Informal Interviews are also filed in the Portfolio. Significant parts can be highlighted with a marker to draw attention. The information yielded can be noted in respective categories on the overview sheet, such as cognitive, social, self-identity, or emotional.

Tape recordings are also filed in the Portfolio. A sheet is attached to the tape, listing the dates and subject (and counter number, if possible) of each recording. Full transcriptions are not necessary unless there is some reason to amplify documentation of a developmental area or to provide the raw data/exact wording for a referral.

REVIEW

CONVERSATIONS OR INTERVIEWS
Recording a child's verbal interactions either in writing or in audio recording.

Types of Information to Record Using Conversations or Interviews

- informal conversations that are spontaneous
- interviews that are structured for a specific purpose
- a child's viewpoint on school adjustment
- a child's self-responsibility views
- a child's self-evaluation of physical skills
- a child's self-evaluation of friendships and social interactions
- a child's self-evaluation of emotional difficulties
- to listen carefully to a child's speech and language
- to assess a child's attention span for conversations
- to assess a child's cognitive development:
  physical knowledge
  logico-mathematical knowledge
  social knowledge
- to assess a child's literacy development
- to discuss a child's creative work or play

PORTFOLIO EVIDENCE OF CHILD'S DEVELOPMENT			
Evidence Type	Date	Recorder	Notes
SPEECH/LANGUAGE – the child's speech and language development			
CL	10/16/	BAN	Difficult to understand
CK	10/19/	MLS	Many unchecked items. Referral?
Audio tape	11/20/	KBE	Conversation between Teacher and child for use in further evaluation

Figure 6–4 Portfolio Evidence Sheet Example.

The tape-recorded conversations or interviews make excellent resources for listening closely to a child's speech and language. The next section, on speech and language development, gives guidelines for listening and evaluating, both from live and tape-recorded conversations.

Go to the Education CourseMate website, accessed through CengageBrain.com for plans and resources for this week.

Listening to Speech and Language

Speech and language develop in a progression of five different areas:

Phonology—the sounds of language, otherwise known as speech
Vocabulary—the words of language, names of persons, places, things, actions, thoughts, and feelings
Grammar—how the words are put together to make phrases or sentences in the language

It Happened to Me

"A reem a ivd i a re"

The speech of a child in my preschool class was almost unintelligible. One day at class meeting, he had something to say to the group. It sounded like this:

"A HA A REM US ITE N A REEM A IVD I A RE"
The child's mother and grandmother assured me that his father had spoken just like this when he was four and that he grew out of it. I'm not a speech therapist, but I was concerned about how his speech might interfere with his ability to relate socially to other children. Amazingly, they were able to understand him easier than I could, and he got along well for quite a few months until one day when the mother was in the classroom and saw his frustration at not being understood. He was evaluated and started speech therapy.

Oh, you want to know what he was saying? "I had a dream last night and I dreamed I lived in a tree."

Discourse—how sentences are put together to tell stories, give explanations, express thoughts and feelings
Pragmatics—the rules about how to use language in social contexts such as greetings, mannerly requests and responses, eye and body contact, and distance while talking

All of these occur in a social context, learned as all things are learned by listening, observing, receiving direct instruction, experimenting, reinforcement, and refining. Humans are social beings and language is the primary vehicle of communication to function in the social world. The growing body of research linking language to literacy increases early childhood education attention on language. That, along with more and more dual language learners in early childhood classrooms, makes the understanding and promotion of language development of great importance.

Receptive Language

"Listen before you speak" is not just wise advice but actually the progression of language development.

Receptive Language. An important principle of language development is that the **receptive language**, the capacity to listen, hear, and understand, is almost always greater than the **expressive language**, which is the capacity to speak and convey messages (Figure 6–5). The one-year-old is told, "Go give Grandma a kiss." The infant crawls or walks to Grandma and gives her a kiss. He cannot say anything close to, "I want to kiss my grandma," but from his actions that is interpreted. He can understand the words of the request, act on them, but cannot say or express the words himself. When people are learning a second language, they always can understand far more than they are able to actually say themselves. This principle is also displayed when a person has a thought or idea but has difficulty explaining

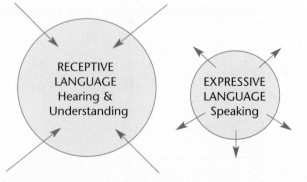

Figure 6–5 Receptive language is always greater than expressive language.

it to someone else. They say, "I know what I mean, but I just can't explain it." Receptive language, understanding verbal communication, is greater than the ability to express thoughts verbally except where there are other factors such as auditory processing problems or cognitive disorders.

Learning to Listen. Listening is a vital skill to react to danger signals and obtain information. Because listening is an ability present at birth in most children (unless they have a barrier such as hearing loss or cognitive processing) it is often overlooked as an area to be cultivated and developed. Every parent knows that teaching a child to "listen" is one of the most important lessons to be learned. In this context, listening becomes synonymous with obeying. We are talking here about the kind of listening that processes sounds to make meaning, learning to discriminate between different sounds, and building phonics skills necessary for speaking and reading.

Receptive language, greater than expressive language, also has some direct implications for anyone around young children. The phrase "Little pitchers have big ears" comes from this principle. Although children are physically small, unsophisticated, and unable to speak themselves, they are "taking in" what they hear. It will eventually be expressed. Not only is this a warning for adults to monitor their conversations in the presence of young children, but it is also a reminder that this is a fertile learning time. All that is said, read, and sung is received. It emphasizes the importance of adults talking to babies who cannot yet communicate back. The foundations for vocabulary and language not yet present are laid in these early months and years.

Language Acquisition. Exactly how language is acquired has been the focus of much study and controversy. As infants say their first words—ma, da, see, bye, hi, no—they get positive reinforcement to repeat those meaningful sounds when the adults around them smile and repeat the word back to the infant. Behaviorists and social learning theorists, such as Skinner (1957) and Bandura (1977), say this imitation and positive response is how language develops. Children who are deprived of hearing language can end up permanently incapable of learning and using language. Noam Chomsky's (1965, 2000) work broadened the view of how language is acquired with studies indicating that children from all cultures develop language skills in the same sequence at close to the same time, supporting a biological approach to language. His idea is that there is a Language Acquisition Device (LAD) present in all humans, but not animals. Proof of this are the choices in grammar that children make automatically. No one teaches a child to say "goed." It comes from

It Happened to Me

Lily Patio

I was observing in a classroom of two-year olds, always a delightful experience except when more than one of them is having a temper tantrum. The teacher laid out large pieces of green felt to resemble lily pads on the rug, and the children were singing the "Speckled Frog" song. As twos will do, one little girl was doing her own thing, jumping from one lily pad to another. She jumped with great gusto and proclaimed, "I'm on my lily patio." This reinforced for me again that language meaning is regulated by experience. She knew what a patio was, something you sit on, but she had no experience with lily pads so this must be a lily patio. "That silly teacher was saying it wrong." Makes sense to me!

the internalization of language. The process converts to a past tense using an untaught rule. It also causes the switch from "goed" to "went" a little later. Interactionist theorists, such as Bruner (1983), agree that there are behavioral and biological aspects, but they emphasize the role of an environment in which adults support language learning and use. Developmentalists such as Chomsky (1968) believe that intelligence precedes language acquisition, as illustrated by the parallel development of cognition and language; whereas Vygotsky (1962) disagrees and believes children are speaking internally to solve difficult problems.

Whatever theoretical base one takes, it is early experiences with language through nurturing relationships with family and other adults that directly influence a child's language development.

Three key findings from brain research relate to language development in the following ways:

- Biology (nature) blueprints the brain for language, but positive interaction with nurturing adults (nurture) is also necessary for effective communication.
- Early experiences and interactions stimulate brain circuitry and affect spoken and written language.
- Brain development is dependent on experiences at optimal times for acquiring different kinds of knowledge and skills.

By early experiences, positive interactions, and communication with others, a child learns language, the key to lifelong learning. Hart and Risley (2007) found some astounding results in a study that measured the language experiences of children of different socioeconomic classes in the first four years of life. Children between one and four years old in families that were on welfare heard 13 million words; children in working-class families heard 26 million words; and in professional homes children heard 45 million words (p. 198). There were also proportional differences in vocabulary used in naming and recalling people, places, and objects; words used to ask or demand; and responsiveness to the child during interactions. The differences that Hart and Risley found at three years of age were strongly linked to school performance at age nine. They concluded that a part-day preschool program at four years of age for children in language-deficient homes could not make up the difference. A conclusion from this study is that language intervention needs to be a priority of every infant/toddler out-of-home program as well as the focus of family education. The study also concludes that preschool may be too late to make an appreciable difference in a child's language development.

The adult role in language acquisition cannot be denied. When children are provided an environment where people are talking to them, singing, sharing stories and books, they talk sooner. When adults respond to babies' early sounds, those sounds occur more frequently. Reinforcement, encouragement, expectation, and rewards for language stimulate development. It is a combination of all of these factors working together, so the important principle for parents and teachers of young children is the recognition and response to each child's attempts to communicate.

EXERCISE **Read the following sentence aloud:**

"Eres el/la heredero de una herencia. Ve inmediatemente a Madrid y pregunta por el alcalde. Él te va a indicar lo que debes hacer."

Expressive Language. You have just spoken Spanish. You have the speech. You have the sounds because Spanish is a phonetic language, but you do not have the language unless you know the meaning. Have you communicated in Spanish? Only if the hearer or receiver knows the language. (The sentence says: "You are the heir of a fortune. Go at once to Madrid and ask for the mayor. He will direct

you.") It would be important to be able to receive that message!

Speech. As explained in Chapter 1, the words growth and development are often used interchangeably. However, they have different meanings. The words speech and language are so often used together that most people think they are the same also. Not so! **Speech** is the sound produced to make the words. The reason that the tip of the triangle—Beginning Sounds—in Figure 6–6 is outside the language circle is that the child makes sounds before they are language, experimenting, playing with tongue and voice. Once those sounds become "mama" with the expectation that Mama will respond, then those sounds become language. **Language** is the term for words and phrases that convey meaning. There can be speech without language (just making random sounds). There can be no audible language without speech. Nonverbal communication is body language or gestures, the way of conveying messages without speaking.

The smallest units making the sounds of the words are the phonemes, the sounds of speech. These are **phonemes**: /u/, /o/, /a/, /m/, /p/, /b/, /t/, /n/, /k/, /ng/, /y/, /g/, /f/, /v/, /sh/, /zh/, /l/, /rth/, /ch/. These are in the order in which they typically appear developmentally. Along with vowels to link them, words are formed. These are called **morphemes**, small units of sound that have meaning. It is interesting that /m/ is one of the first sounds an infant can make, and in most languages of the world, the word for the person who bore them begins with the /m/ sound: mother, mama, mamone (Ouseg, 1995).

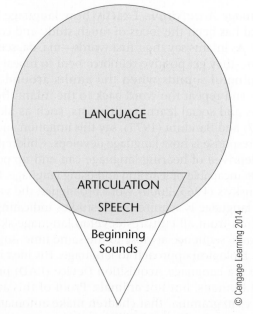

Figure 6–6 Speech as a part of language development.

The infant begins to make sounds at birth, crying, not purposefully but by reflex, just like reflex actions in other developmental areas. Within the first month, crying becomes more differentiated, so the teacher can begin to tell the difference between the hungry cry and the painful cry. During that first month, preverbal infants can even differentiate between the sounds of /ba/ and /pa/ (de Villiers & de Villiers, 1986).

During the second month, more purposeful and pleasant sounds emerge: cooing and squealing. Those can be written down because the sounds are phonemes that are recognizable as vowels. As the infant gains muscular control of the lips and tongue, the consonants appear in babbling and, later, in imitation of adult talking. "Ba ba, ma ma, da da, pa pa," understandable approximations of longer words, are usually frequent by the end of the first year.

Infants can make and hear all the sounds found in every language. The "click" sound in southern African languages or the sound made by blowing through his lips like a cross between a /p/ and an /f/ in the Japanese language are made but later lost by English-speaking children. These sounds are heard in babbles of all babies around the world, but disappear or are added by one year of age, depending on the language they are learning. Kuhl (2004) calls infants "citizens of the world" at this stage. This accounts for the difficulty adult learners have with certain sounds of the second language they are learning. The ability to make those sounds has disappeared from their repertoire. It also makes the case for exposing infants and toddlers to other languages to help preserve those sounds. Brain research also shows that music and language are intertwined, governed by rules and basic elements, phrases and repetitions. The natural melody of language is critical to a baby's language development, fostering communication, cognitive, and social skills (Deutsch, 2010).

The precise articulation or production of phonemes, the sounds of language, is a long developmental period. Some of the more difficult combinations of sounds may not be present until six or seven years old.

EXERCISE Listen to the tape you made in the tape-recording exercise again, listening closely and looking at the following articulation chart. This outlines the usual progression and expectation of acquiring certain sounds. Did the children you listened to produce these sounds clearly?

p, w, h, m, n (usually by three years)
b, k, g, d, y (usually by four years)
f, ng, t, r, l (usually by six years)
ch, sh, j, s, z, v, th, zh, br, tr (clear by seven to eight years)

By the time children are four years old, they have usually developed the vocabulary, language structure, and grammatical rules needed to communicate about their world. Because young children are learners, their speech and language will be imperfect. They still may have **articulation** (sound) errors, which will continue to develop into the seventh year, especially combinations such as wh (whether), rth, ch, and sz. Those imperfections can be categorized but are not necessarily cause for alarm. Some of the common mispronunciations in the preschool years are the following:

substitutions—"wabbit" for "rabbit"
omissions—"tar" for "star"
distortions—"caaa" for "car"
additions—"pisghetti" for "spaghetti"
lisps—"thith" for "this"

Speech and language screening in the preschool years is recommended, and especially indicated if the child is very difficult to understand. The role of the early childhood educator is one of facilitator, interpreter, and responder rather than remediator. Content and meaning are the most important aspects when talking with young children.

Stuttering. It is normal for all speakers to have difficulty selecting the right word, communicating a thought, or speaking so that the words flow naturally. This occurs frequently to young children as speaking learners. Stuttering or **dysfluent**, repetitive speech, interrupts the thought flow, repeating sounds or words with sentences like "I, I, I, I w-w-w-want it." It is for most children a temporary, often short-lived, disorder that disappears in 75 to 80 percent of cases without formal intervention (Yairi & Ambrose, 2005). If there is a history of dysfluent speech in the family, or if the stuttering persists and interferes with the child socially or emotionally, it may require further evaluation. In any case the adult listener should listen patiently without telling the child, "Now, just slow down" or "Don't talk so fast" or "Your ideas just get ahead of your tongue." Statements like these draw the child's attention to the stuttering and add to the stress. Teachers can:

Modify the rate of your own speech as a role model
Create a relaxed speaking environment, not forcing or hurrying the speaker
Listen attentively for the message without commenting on the speech pattern
Reduce the complexity of your own speech in repeating and responding (Panico, Daniels & Claflin, 2011).

If this does not pass in a few weeks, further investigation may be needed to look for stressors or other factors. A private conversation with the family should begin the inquiry, along with notes on when the stuttering began and the child's reaction to it.

Language Development. After a child's first birthday, vocabulary grows (because it can be measured in numbers) at a fantastic rate. Listen again to the taped conversations: Count the number of different words each child said. Did it increase with age?

While the word *the* is the most frequently used word in the English language, it is not among the first words the child says. Early words include:

Social expressions such as *hi* and *bye-bye*
Labels for familiar people – *Mama* or things
    (*doggie, ball, [ban]nana*)
Action words – *down* and *here*
Describing words such as *hot* and *big*
Negatives – no, all gone
Words for repetition such as *'gain* and *more*
Possessives such as *mine* (Lindfors, 1987)

Look at the explosive increase in vocabulary from the ages of 18 months through 6 years, shown in Figure 6–7.

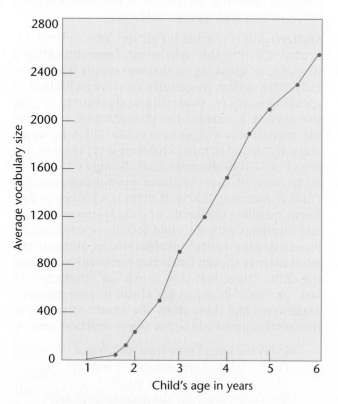

Figure 6–7 The Vocabulary Explosion!
Source: From Machado. *Early Childhood Experiences in Language Arts,* 9th ed.
© 2010 Cengage Learning.

Beginning Communication. The beginning talker starts with one word. It is quickly joined by others, all names for people or objects. They are spoken with various inflections and sometimes accompanied by gestures such as pointing or arm movements that convey a more sophisticated message than labeling. Single words between 12 and 18 months become requests or questions. These one-word utterances that have meaning are **holographic** phrases.

EXERCISE "Mama" is one of the first words a baby says. How many meanings can be interpreted by the way you say it?

These are soon followed by short two-word sentences called telegraphic phrases. Examples of the **telegraphic** phrases are "Doggie gone" and "Look baby." When telegraphic phrases occur, the child has acquired language. She is expressing herself using the sounds of speech.

EXERCISE Listen to the children on the tape. Did any of them use just one word to convey a whole thought?

Language is developing, changing from simple to complex in a predictable pattern, but at individual rates. The child is developing a sense of **syntax**, the order of words in a sentence that make it understandable to others: "Mama go," "Baby ba ba." His language is the combination of heredity, social interactions, and emotional environment. Cognitive or learning ability and physical development all combine to make this happen. The interdependence and simultaneous development of many areas are vividly illustrated in language development.

EXERCISE Describe how speech or language might be affected by the following:

Hearing
Muscle development
Geography
Abuse
Siblings
Heredity
Ethnicity

EXERCISE From the children you listened to, could you gather any of the preceding information?

It takes many years for the grammatical construction to move from one-word holographic sentences to the telegraphic but meaningful few-word sentences to complex sentences with prepositional phrases and correct tenses and plurals. Children seem to have an inner sense of picking up plurals and past tense from hearing adults speak. At first they say "mouses" instead of "mice" because they have heard "houses" meaning more than one house. They will say, "I goed to the store," though they have never heard anyone say that. They have heard others say, "I washed the dishes." This application of simple grammatical rules to all plurals and past tense words is **overgeneralization**. Children internalize the grammatical rule and apply it to all words in that category. Over time, this self-corrects, usually by five years of age.

The development of language follows this progression:

Birth–6 months: crying, cooing, vowel-like babbling

6–12 months: increased babbling, repeats sounds, kiss sounds, whines

12–24 months: speaks first word, vocabulary increasing, one- to two-word sentences with meaning

2–3 years old: uses two- to five-word sentences, verbs, prepositions, adds plurals, uses pronouns, uses articles, uses conjunctions, uses negatives, asks questions, sings songs, tells simple stories

3–4 years old: asks why, what, where how, loves word play, tells sex and age, full name, answers questions, names some colors and is counting

4–5 years old: uses five- to six- (or more) word sentences, uses words to shock, argues, acts out stories, life happenings, likes to dictate words to a story, uses etiquette words, knows many songs and nursery rhymes

6–8 years old: adult-like conversations using appropriate grammar, tells jokes, riddles, stories in sequence, elaborate descriptions (Adapted from Machado, 2013).

EXERCISE How complex were the sentences in the tape recording of conversations? Were there any examples of overgeneralization?

Language and Literacy Connection. The critical role that early education plays in language and literacy development was emphasized in the National Academy of Sciences report, "Preventing Reading Difficulties in Young Children" (Snow, Burns, & Griffin, 1998). In seeking solutions to ready children for school success, researcher David Dickinson points out that language is a literacy activity that provides the vocabulary, structure, and meaning verbally that will be found later in the printed word. In the Home-School Study, Dickinson and Tabors (2001) learned much about the linkage between language and literacy. The income level, vocabulary, the opportunity to hear books read and learn the concept of words and books, and child care quality all have correlations to later school success. This has implications for teachers of young children. Families and child care staff can maximize language use throughout the day.

To encourage children's language development:

▸ At snack and meals, sit with children and have family-style mealtime conversations.
▸ Encourage discussions about non-immediate events, remembering details from the past.
▸ Encourage children to use new vocabulary words learned during class lessons.

When reading to the group:

▸ Identify important words and concepts.
▸ Encourage children to talk about aspects of the story.
▸ Respond to children's questions.
▸ Link books to themes and other activities.
▸ Avoid long stretches of talk and stay on the subject.

During free play:

▸ Children need opportunities to talk with each other.
▸ Minimize interruptions—teacher involvement in dramatic play tends to disrupt and disengage the players.
▸ Engage individual children in conversations using a variety of words, especially novel words. (Dickinson & Tabors, 2001, pp. 252–254)

Functions of Language. Children develop in the more complex use of language. Their first single words convey recognition and description, "Ma ma," "Ba ba." Very quickly, they learn that their language can be used to influence others. Those same words can now call others to communicate a need: "Ma ma," "Ba ba." As they gain vocabulary and willfulness, communication takes the form of commands such as "Go" and "No bath." With mobility and experience in a wider environment, their language expands not only in vocabulary but in using it to describe what they see: "My ball." They convey information ("Ball all gone") as they watch the ball going down the toilet. They seek information in their second year with incessant "Where Daddy go?" "Where doggie go?"; and in the third and fourth years with the constant "Why?" questions. They begin to express feelings—"So sad" after a scolding, and the "So sorry" that softens a grandma's heart. By four and five years old, cognitive development is moving toward the symbolic stage, when reading and writing develop. The symbolic stage appears in language too: "I have an idea." Humor emerges in double meanings of words and puns. By five, the concept of rhyming appears.

The pragmatics of language involve three major communication skills that may vary across cultures:

- Using language for different purposes such as greeting, informing, demanding, promising, requesting
- Changing language according to the needs of the listener or the situation, such as talking differently to a baby than an adult, giving background information to an unfamiliar listener, and speaking differently in a classroom than on a playground
- Following roles for conversations and storytelling, such as taking turns, introducing topics of conversation, staying on topic, rephrasing when misunderstood, using verbal and nonverbal signals, and maintaining a distance apart when speaking (American Speech-Language-Hearing Association, 2011).

Social and Nonverbal Language. Nonverbal gestures such as signs or signals come before words. A baby with arms outstretched is making an understandable but silent plea. Asking a one- to two-year-old, "Where's your nose?" elicits a knowledgeable response months before the child can say the word "nose." *Sometimes biting is the nonverbal gesture for young children who may not have the language development to express feelings like frustration or even excitement and happiness.* By observing gestures, providing vocabulary for feelings, and also listening for words, the caregiver can learn about the child's needs, what he knows, and even what he is thinking. Kinnell (2002) warns teachers and parents alike: "Despite even the best efforts of the best teachers to prevent it, biting still (unfortunately) does happen. When it does occur, teachers must be prepared to respond appropriately and effectively" (p. 7).

Very young children without hearing impairments can learn to communicate using sign language even before they can speak. Daniels, in a fascinating study (2001), tells of infants learning to convey

It Happened to Me

The French Waiter

We had set up a restaurant in our classroom for dramatic play, complete with picture menus, order pads, aprons, and tableware. It was well-used, indicating the children had experience in ordering and eating in a restaurant. One child's experience went far beyond our expectations when he took on the role of the waiter with towel over his arm and carried on the whole dialogue with an affected French accent. What a surprise!

important messages such as "more," "yes," "no," "come" months before they could say the words. She also studied the effects of hearing children learning sign language, showing positive results on later reading scores. The connection between physical, cognitive, and language development domains has resulted in building vocabulary and earlier communication skills.

Children show social and cognitive skills in their language as well. Think about each of the children on your tape as they talked with you.

Did they demonstrate a "turn-taking" kind of conversation where they knew they were to speak, then you would have a turn, or was it more of a monologue?

Did they make eye contact?

What was the facial expression as they spoke?

What gestures did they use, if any?

What could you tell from the tone of voice that just writing down the words would not convey?

EXERCISE **Practice your ability to place bits of language in chronological order of their normal development. Number the following from the earliest to the latest in the progression of development:**

___ "Want milk"

___ "Waader"

___ "When I grow up, I'm gonna be a ballerina."

___ "No"

___ "mum mum mum mum mum"

___ "I goed to the store."

___ "Wha's dat?"

___ "ah-ah-ah"

Answers:

Answers are: 8, 5, 2, 4, 1, 7, 6, 3.

like but self-centered.

consonants and vowels), imperfect grammar, and adult-

speech, questions, refusals (this can come anytime after

nants and vowels, approximations of words, telegraphic

The sequence of normal development is vowels, conso-

Listening. The art of listening (receptive language) is one that is practiced from birth (and even before). It is a process that involves the physical construction and nerves to collect sound waves, cognitive functions of giving attention, discriminating between sounds, understanding and remembering. It affects social interactions and is tempered by emotions. Everyone has experienced conversations with people who "just don't listen." It is frustrating and disrespectful, resulting in miscommunication and misunderstanding. To facilitate language, the adult must listen to the child and also help the child develop listening skills, even speaking to infants as if they were conversationalists, describing the world around them and the routines of the day.

There are types of listening for which the teacher plans various activities based on the children's age and levels of understanding:

Appreciative listening—pleasure in music, poems, stories, passive.

Purposeful listening—following directions, giving responses

Discriminative listening—aware of changes in pitch and loudness

Creative listening—imagination and emotions stimulated

Critical listening—thinking through responses to open-ended questions and deciding on most logical solution (Machado, 2013).

Facilitating Language. Children learn language through interaction with adults who: show an interest in conversations, model verbal etiquette (such as saying please and thank you), use descriptive and interesting words, and use complete sentences and standard grammar (Willis & Schiller, 2011). The environment is quite enough so that conversations can be heard and there is an atmosphere of trust and willingness to listen carefully to what the child

is saying. Kratcoski and Katz (1998) suggest these strategies:

Expansion—respond, expanding holographic and telegraphic sentences
C: "Doggie eat." T: "Yes, the doggie is eating."

Extensions—response and addition of new information
C: "Doggie eat." T: "Yes, the doggie is eating. Doggie is hungry."

Repetition—repeats phrase
C: "Doggie eat." T: "Eat, doggie. Eat, doggie."

Parallel talk—describes child's action
C: "Doggie eat." T: "Yes, doggie is eating. You feed the doggie her food."

Self-talk—describes own action
C: "Doggie eat." T: "Yes, doggie is eating. I gave the doggie her food."

Vertical structuring—uses questions to facilitate longer sentences
C: "Doggie eat." T: "Yes, the doggie is eating. Does she want a drink?"

Fill-ins—conversation structured for child to provide word to complete the statement
T: "Doggie wants a drink. Let's get her some _____."
C: "Water!"

Play "conversational ball"—the conversation goes back and forth between the two parties. The child is a learner, so he may drop the ball. The adult always catches or picks it up and tosses it back. Speak, listen, respond, listen, speak, listen, respond; so goes the spiral of a conversation (Figure 6–8).

The Quiet Child. Some children are shy or reluctant, for a variety of possible reasons, to speak out in large groups, small groups, or even with the teacher. It is a concern, but this is just the child who needs careful observation and opportunity without pushing. First it is important to find out if the child can speak by talking with the family. If the child does not talk at home or if the home language is different from that at school, different strategies can be implemented. If it is the case that the child speaks freely at home but not at school, then there is a sigh of relief, but other questions then arise. Does the child appear comfortable in the classroom and actively participate in ways other than verbal? Is the child accepted by other children? Is the child given opportunities to speak with wait time without drawing attention to the nonverbal behavior? Begging and cajoling and even harassing the child to speak should be avoided; rather, the teacher should focus on the

© Cengage Learning 2014

Figure 6–8 The adult should always return the conversational ball.

child's strengths and abilities, being patient and inviting. When the child does speak (see it happened to me, "He Shared His Expertise"), it is important to minimize the surprise and excitement, accepting the child's new expressiveness without fanfare.

Show and Tell. Many programs have a time when a child can present an item and speak about it. This may be a contrived way to force speaking before the group that may cause more problems than benefits. The child may be reluctant to talk about the item, not want to have other children touch or play with it, or not have sufficient language to describe it, all of which are counterproductive and place stress on the child. A variation could be when the teacher presents an item to spark conversation such as an interesting shell, an unfamiliar tool, or even an item in a bag that is only felt and not seen.

Memories. Photographs of experiences are excellent conversation starters. After having a field trip or a special visitor, looking at photographs of the experience can elicit conversation. A class photo

It Happened to Me

He Shared His Expertise

Jason was a very quiet four-year-old when he started preschool. Several weeks went by while he just watched other children, without interacting or speaking in the classroom. Some children just need more time to adjust to a situation. We spoke to him about the day, what he was doing, greeted him at the door without pressuring him to speak or commenting on his silence. In private talks with his mother, she said that was his way of coping with new situations. She assured us he was very verbal at home. This continued for weeks and into months, with his mother assuring us this was his little game. He did begin to play with objects in the classroom, first the sand and blocks. He eventually began to interact with other children, but still without speaking. We still tried not to draw attention to it, but spoke to him as we did to all the other children in conversation as they played.

One day in February, when the project theme was dinosaurs, he brought in a book from home. At the door he held it open to me and said, "This is a stegosaurus." I was shocked; and the children even commented, saying, "He talked!" I said, "Jason, that's the first thing you've ever said to me. I wonder why you chose today to talk." He said matter-of-factly, "I wanted to share my expertise about dinosaurs with you." (Exact words, I swear.) From that day on, he talked occasionally with peers and teachers as he played. I often marvel at the strength of will he had all those weeks. His willpower held us all hostage to his little game.

album with photos of each child, his or her family, and classroom events throughout the year will become a favorite, with each child talking about his or her own thoughts and feelings about the pictures.

"Teacher, be quiet." One of the marks of quality early childhood programs is that children's engaged, happy voices are predominant. While there are a few times during the day when the adult's voice gives reminders to the whole group, adult voices should not be heard above the children's. In fact, the quieter the adult speaks, the quieter the room becomes in an effort to hear. In the exercise that follows, listen not only to your actual language, but how much your voice is heard above the children's. Leave pauses in dialogue so children can respond; and with infants, recognize every sign of attention and sound as a part of the conversational ball game, back and forth.

Language Role Models. Adults are language role models for children. Teachers of young children fall into some habits that are not helpful to children. Some are reviewed here to alert the reader to consider the impact on the child. We would not use some of these teacher-ese phrases with other adults (Figure 6–9).

EXERCISE Observe your own language by setting up a tape recorder in the classroom or wear a small portable one in your pocket. Tape a 30- to 60-minute sample of yourself "for your ears only." Analyze it for your common language habits, and see if any changes need to be made in the language role model you are presenting to children.

Figure 6–9 Poor examples of language role models.

The Tester. "What color are your peas?" asking questions that are like quizzes. Instead, "Do you like peas or the corn we had yesterday better?" An adult would not ask a bystander, "What color is your shirt?" or a friend, "How many bracelets are you wearing today?"

The Helper. "Can Mrs. Nilsen help you with that?" Some adults fall into the trap of speaking of themselves by name in sentences spoken to young children, like the much criticized "we" of the health profession. Instead, "Would you like me to help you with that?" A neighbor would think it odd if a person spoke of herself when saying in a sing-song voice, "Mrs. Nilsen heard your dog barking all night."

"Use Your Words." If the child had the words, she would use them. Give the child a phrase she can use like, "Tell her, 'It hurts when you do that to me.'" Imagine a car is stopped at a red light and the driver behind it sounds his horn. The first driver leans out and says sweetly, "Use your words."

"How Would You Like It if She Did That to You?" The egocentric, preoperational child is unable to see a situation from another's perspective; unable to put herself on the receiving end of the action or word. A more understandable phrase might be, "Remember when you got sand in your eyes from someone flipping the shovel? That's what you just did to Lois. It hurt your eyes and now her eyes are hurting in the same way. How else could you use the shovel?"

Incorrect Grammar, Slang, and Lazy Articulation. Using "We was" rather than "We were"; calling children "Kids" or "Guys"; dropping the /g/ at the end of -ing words are common language habits. Some other common phrases to consider deleting from a teacher's script:

"We don't do that here." Well, she just did. "You need to put that away now." He really NEEDS to play with it longer. It is the schedule or the teacher who needs him to put it away.

"Use your indoor voice." What does that really mean? "Use your walking feet." What other feet does she have?

Parents often ask at pick-up time, "Are you ready to go home?" Yikes, as the teacher you are READY for him to go home, it's time to clock out. This should not be a choice, so do not ask as if it were.

These types of language habits are not helpful to language learners and are disrespectful of children without the speaker even realizing it. As language role models and empathetic humans, adults should speak to children in the same manner they speak to peers. By listening to a tape of themselves, teachers can become aware of those habits and try to correct 'em (them). Teachers with an awareness of the potential for misunderstanding or imitation become better language role models for young children.

Tone and Volume. Each person's voice is unique and used in various ways by habit and necessity.

EXERCISE **Say this sentence in many different tones and loudness:**

"Please pick that up."
List the various meanings you have conveyed.

It could be a polite request, a stern command, an impatient order, or a descriptive sentence focusing attention on a particular toy. Verbal tone and volume can add to the aggressiveness of the classroom atmosphere by conveying anger, displeasure, and even dislike. If the goal is to reduce aggression in the classroom, it begins by treating and talking to children with respect, modeling not just the words and meaning but also the tone we want children to use.

Observing the Developing Language of Infants and Toddlers

Since language development is an indicator of many other domains of development—social, perceptual, and cognitive—close observation of infants and toddlers as they begin to communicate is important. While development varies among individuals, certain milestones can give clues that typical development is progressing. The first clues are in receptive language, long before a child speaks. In the first four to six months, infants display an understanding of what is spoken to them by turning when their name is called. By ten months, the infant can follow simple directions complying with requests like, "Come here." By one year, single words are spoken, usually to name significant people in their world, Mama, Dada, doggie. By age two children have a vocabulary of about 50 words. By the age of three vocabulary has exploded to about 1,000 words. Concerns arise when there are significant delays in reaching the speech and language milestones. (Figure 6–10). If a child is not producing these skills, a full evaluation should be recommended.

Helping all Children with Language Development

Society is increasingly culturally and linguistically diverse, as well as aware of differing abilities. It is advisable for teachers to be bilingual, whether in a second cultural language or sign language.

English Language Learners

Schools and teachers must be ready to receive a child speaking a language other than English (Figure 6–11). The following statistics from the National Clearinghouse for English Language Acquisition (http://www.ncela.gwu.edu/) may be surprising, but they underscore the reality of the United States—it is becoming more and more diverse, and teachers need to prepare for non-English speakers in classrooms. This increasing diversity has important ramifications for our teaching.

- Seventy-nine percent of English as a second language learners (ESL) in the United States speak Spanish as their first language.
- In 2008–2009 there were more than five million English language learners in grades PreK through 12.
- The states with the highest increase in residents speaking English as a second language in the last decade are surprising: Indiana, Kentucky, Tennessee, Arkansas, North Carolina, South Carolina, Virginia, Georgia, Alabama, and Colorado.
- The states with the highest number of ESL students enrolled in school were California, Texas, Florida, New York, Illinois, North Carolina, and Arizona.

Bilingualism is a great advantage for teachers; however, there are so many different languages spoken in many classrooms it would be impossible for teachers to be fluent in all of them. Therefore, sensitivity to the child's needs is called for when the child does not speak the language of the classroom or the teacher. It may be that the child speaks a dialect such as African American/Black English (AAE/BE), a sociocultural variation of English shown to have its own structure and eligible for language remediation. Many group settings include children whose home language is not English. ESL students frequently come into the group knowing no English at all. Many schools have labeled these children Limited English Proficient (LEP), seeing their lack of English as a deficit rather than recognizing their proficiency in the

LEVEL	AGE RANGE	ASSOCIATED SKILLS
Prespeech	Birth to 10 months	Development of sound (perception and production) Development of gestures Concomitant changes in nonlinguistic development Rapid development of sound perception; infant a few weeks old can distinguish phonological contrasts in human speech; speech production rooted in infant's crying and vegetative noises; play with speech sounds including reciprocal speech sounds with others begins after three months; between 6 to 10 months consonant and consonant-vowel imitations are evident in babbling
First Words: Emergence of naming	10 to 13 months	Single-word comprehension Single-word production Individual differences in single-word use Gestures that function as words Attention can be directed with object names ("see the dog," "Amy, dog"); by 13 monhts receptive vocabulary from 17 to 97 words; as speech production increases, gestures decrease
Word combinations	18 to 24 months Transition between production of single words with complex meanings to multiword phrases	Nature of word combinations and individual differences Parallel developments in other developmental domains Use of word combinations initiates shift into sentence use; size of spoken vocabulary undergoing rapid acceleration and expansion of types of words, especially verbs; parallel development includes gestural imitation, classification of objects, and multigesture strings in play indicating the need for accompanying cognitive development to allow language development
Grammaticization	20 to 30 months (fundamentals of grammar) 36 months (competent speaker)	Acquisition of rules of morphology and syntax Speed of morphemic acquisition Nature and sequence of grammatical development Uniqueness of language development for this age Application of rules Mastery of irregular patterns and rules Aquires a baseline of cognitive and language development

Figure 6–10 Four Levels of Language Development.
Source: From Benner, *Assessment of Children with Special Needs*, 1st ed. © 2003 Cengage Learning.

language they have already learned. In the past, assessments given in English indicated major delays and mistakenly prescribed remediation for many of these children. English Language Learners (ELL) are overrepresented among low-achieving students at all socioeconomic levels and the gap in reading and math continues throughout the grades (Garcia & Frede, 2010). Since English language proficiency is the foundation for later school success, early childhood programs (such as Head Start) offer the best opportunity to help develop language and literacy in both English and the home language. The goal then becomes dual language learners (DLLs), giving children the time to be listeners before they start speaking the second

Figure 6–11 Teachers must be ready to receive families of diverse cultures.

language (Tabors, 2006). Preschool programs with full English immersion have been found to be less effective than bilingual and dual lingual programs in English language development (August & Shananhan, 2006).

Espinosa (2008) has challenged some common myths concerning English language acquisition, pointing to the importance of establishing a child's home language first, supported by dual language, high-quality early childhood programs. Espinosa says that learning two languages after age three is beneficial to all, and will not result in academic delays when social and cultural strengths are also recognized. Others hold the view that even very young children can and will learn two or more languages at the same time without detriment to either (Genesee, 2004).

More tolerant approaches have been developed to help the child become bilingual, not pushing to be monolingual, nor attempting to extinguish the first language. This approach is described as additive, supporting the first language while adding a second. Nemeth (2009) makes these suggestions:

> Repeat and emphasize important words in English.
> Use body language, gestures and facial expressions to augment communication
> Make adaptations around the classroom to include models of each child's home language and culture.
> Use authentic props and real items to help develop language to talk about these things
> Use the talents of bilingual staff, volunteers, family members, and children (p. 21, 22)

A basic educational principle is the acceptance of each child. Acceptance provides an environment, experiences, and support to help the child progress to the next level. Children learning a second language will progress through the same language development stages as an infant and toddler, beginning with single important words, then to telegraphic stages. They proceed through them with the same stage predictability of any other child learning language. The same techniques of teaching and observation are used regardless of the language the child speaks. See more about assessment and culture in this chapter's "Topics in Observation."

Federal legislation under civil rights and education provide for ELL and children with Limited English Proficiency (LEM) to receive educational supports to assist them in learning English either within the classroom or in a parent-approved

► ❚❚ TEACHSOURCE VIDEO ACTIVITY

Go to the Education CourseMate website, accessed through CengageBrain.com and view English Language Learner: Partnering with Parents to Promote Oral Language and Literacy

How did the teacher support the parent and child's language development?

placement. Parents must receive notice of the plan for and progress of their child in a language they understand. It's the law.

Children with Differing Abilities in Regular Classrooms

Children with differing abilities in speech, language, or hearing may be placed in regular classrooms. Other children become their role models, and communication skills become more functional in this responsive environment. The same strategies that are recommended for effective therapy carried on in the classroom are applicable to any early childhood teacher. The choice between sign language, or manual communication, and speech reading (commonly called lip reading) is decided between experts and families of the hearing impaired. The family makes the decision about their child. The early childhood program or school responds to that decision just as it would to any other family decisions, with sensitivity and willingness to adapt to meet the needs of the child.

Helping Professionals for Speech and Language Concerns

Speech and language disorders are often first diagnosed in early childhood programs. As children develop, families expect their verbal skills to be emerging but often are not aware of, or choose to ignore, what may be a problem in this area. It is not life-threatening; it often is compensated by the parents and other children in the family; and it can be cute and entertaining.

A speech and language screening is routinely administered to preschool children to detect possible difficulties. Informal interviews may act as that screening.

TOPICS in OBSERVATION

Diversity

EXERCISE In a crowded place—at the supermarket, at the fair, on a bus—just take a look around. Do you see any two people who are alike? Look at noses. Just noses. Are any exactly the same shape or size? People-watching is a fascinating pastime.

Every person is different and yet the same. Genetics, age, environment, or trauma result in variations. Generalities help make sense of the whole. Averages have been calculated based on large numbers of people, but even then many will not fit within the range of average. Assessments and professional practice are based on averages that may not represent valid measurements for some children. Diversity is a fact of life, but thinking and attitudes sometimes are so narrow that the truth is overlooked. Adults are supposed to be past the egocentric stage, so they should understand statements such as, "How would you like it if . . .

▶ no one learned how to pronounce your name?"
▶ there were never any pictures of people who looked like you in your classroom?"
▶ the food never had familiar flavors and spices?"
▶ no one would hold your hand in a circle?"
▶ the teacher planned activities that were always too difficult for you to do?"
▶ you had to have money for school tomorrow for a field trip and your family didn't have it?"
▶ letters always went home addressed to parents and you didn't have two parents (or any)?"
▶ everyone else was thin and you were fat?"

Different notes in a song, colors in a rainbow, or flowers in a field are valued. Why not individual differences? They are often rebuffed, ignored, and rejected, causing disharmony and hurt feelings. While working with children, observing and evaluating their development, comparisons to norms must be made very cautiously. The environment should represent and reflect everyone's individuality, and an attitude of acceptance must prevail. Here are some practical ways of accomplishing this.

Individual Differences
No child will be at the same developmental level as another. Even within each child, the level of development may be different in different areas. Differences deserve to be observed, evaluated, and acted on if necessary, but they should not be labeled unusual or strange.

Special Needs
Some children might not have developed within the normal range of expected levels. A strengths model looks at the abilities of the child as decision points for the placement. The role of the program is to keep the areas of special need from interfering with other normally developing skills. Authentic assessment, for every child, looks at the individual areas of development to note the highest level of achievement rather than what the child cannot yet do.

Cultural/Ethnic Diversity
When families enroll their children in early childhood programs, they may have very different attitudes towards language development. Some desire to preserve their home language in the next generation, so may enroll their children in programs that reinforce the home language or are designated as bilingual programs. Others may reinforce the home language by enrolling their children in outside-of-school classes

(Continued)

TOPICS in OBSERVATION *(Continued)*

or religious or cultural organizations to learn and maintain the home language. Those who want their children to fit into the mainstream culture may see the role of the school and teacher to be teaching the child in English to assimilate into the culture, not to accept bilingualism. They may use the child as the bridge to better understand English themselves.

In the first three years, dual language learners (children from homes speaking two languages, or where one language is primary and the environment and school speaks English) may combine elements of both languages or switch back and forth, but the vocabulary may be smaller in both languages than if monolingual. In the later preschool age, children are better at differentiating the language to use in different social settings, such as home and school. By the early school years, they can form more complex sentences in both languages and begin to self-correct pronunciation and grammatical construction. The stages of language acquisition are fairly recognizable from receptive (listening and understanding but not speaking), telegraphic (using one word sentences), to short sentences without articles or with misplaced subject/verb sequences.

Developmental and behavioral norms and professional practice are based on the majority culture and may be diametrically opposed to those of a minority culture. Familiarity and sensitivity to the cultural and ethnic differences of the population of the classroom is essential. Epstein (2009, p. 148–9) urges an awareness in interactions with children, families, and our colleagues from different backgrounds regarding personal space, smiling, eye contact, touch, silence, time concepts, gender roles, autonomy, and adult authority.

By displaying a willingness to learn and a desire not to offend, families and teachers will build a partnership for the child.

What's in a Name?

A deliberate effort has been made in this book to use the most popular names from many different cultures. It is extremely important to learn the correct pronunciation of the first and last names of all the children and families in the class, not giving them American nicknames unless the family especially requests it. It is a learning experience for the teacher and the other children to learn to pronounce ethnic names and can be a point of teaching tolerance, understanding, and cultural awareness. It must begin with the teacher's attitude.

When to Seek Help for Speech and Language

The family is consulted if the child is nearing three years old without much language. Documented observations over a time showing little progress when compared to a chart of norms can help explain the concern. The teacher presents options for referrals to professionals who will conduct preliminary screenings or full evaluations. That referral should begin with the medical personnel or the pediatrician. Chronic ear infections often go unnoticed and can cause hearing loss that may affect language development. There are many other possible causes. Early detection for diagnosis and possible intervention is recommended. This dialogue takes place with empathy for the family's feelings and also with knowledge of community resources. If potential problems are indicated, a full evaluation usually is recommended either by the child's pediatrician or by the program team. Teachers and early childhood programs should have referral lists from which the family can choose an agency or professional to perform this evaluation. Some of the following helping professionals may become involved:

audiologist—conducts screenings and evaluations and diagnoses hearing problems; assesses hearing aids and teaches clients to conserve hearing and to use residual hearing *speech and language pathologist*—conducts screenings, evaluation, diagnosis, and treatment of children with communication disorders

otolaryngologist—a physician who specializes in diagnosis and treatment of ear, nose, and throat disorders, sometimes known as an ENT (ear, nose, and throat) physician

American Sign Language interpreters—translate spoken language into sign language and vice versa for people with hearing impairments

Other Methods

Other Methods to Record Speech and Language Development:

Class List Log—a screening device for specific aspects of speech such as clarity, or language such as "talks freely with peers"

Anecdotal/Running Records—exact quotes are included (as they should be), obtaining a sample of the child's speech and language

Checklists/Rating Scales—formal evaluation instruments can evaluate progress in development

Key Terms

action research	language
articulation	morphemes
closed question	open question
conversations	overgeneralization
diagnostic	phonemes
interview	receptive
diversity	language
dysfluent	record
expressive language	speech
facilitated	structured
conversations	interview
holographic	syntax
informal	telegraphic
conversations	speech

Plans

Go to the Education CourseMate website, accessed through CengageBrain.com for the following:

Plan Week 6 Part A, Directions for annotating informal conversations, including What to Do with It, Portfolio Evidence Sheet Example, Sharing with Child and Family, Actions—Read a Book, In the Environment, In the Curriculum, In the Newsletter

Plan Week 6 Part B, Directions Class List Log of Speech and Language on All (Checklist included)

Plan Week 6 Part C, Reflective Journal

Resources

Burman, L. (2009). *Are you listening? Fostering covnersations that help young children learn.* St. Paul, MN: Redleaf Press.

Derman-Sparks, L., Edwards, J. O. (2010). *Anti-bias education for young children and ourselves.* Washington, DC: National Association for the Education of Young Children.

Hildebrand, V., Phenice, L. A., Gray, M. M., & Hines, R. P. (2008). *Knowing and serving diverse families.* Upper Saddle River, NJ: Pearson Education.

Jalongo, M. R. (2008). *Learning to listen, listening to learn.* Washington, DC: National Association for the Education of Young Children.

Kinnell, G. (2002). *No biting: Policy and practice for toddler programs.* St. Paul, MN: Redleaf Press.

Lynch, E. W., & Hanson, M. J. (2011). *Developing cross-cultural competence: A guide for working with children and their families* (4th ed.). Baltimore, MD: Brookes Publishing Co.

Nemeth, K. N. (2009). *Many languages, one classroom: Teaching dual and English language learners.* Silver Springs, MD: Gryphon House.

Tabors, P. O. (2008). *One child, two language,* (2nd ed.). Baltimore, MD: Paul H. Brookes Publishing.

Stuttering Foundation of America, www.stutteringhelp.org.

National Stuttering Association, www.nsastutter.org.

CHAPTER 7

Using Time Samples to Look at Attention Span

OBSERVATION THOUGHT

"Teaching is not about transferring knowledge. It is about learning, and the one who learns the most is the teacher."

NAEYC Standards **naeyc**

The following NAEYC Standards for Early Childhood Professional Preparation are addressed in this chapter:

Standard 3: *Observing, Documenting, and Assessing to Support Young Children and Families*

Standard 6: *Becoming a Professional*

IN THIS CHAPTER

- Using Time Samples
- Looking at Approaches to Learning
- Piaget's Stages of Cognitive Development
- Infants and Toddlers and Brain Development
- Observing Attention Span in Infants and Toddlers
- Helping All Children with Attention Span
- Topics in Observation: Attention Span and Autism
- Helping Professionals for Attention Concerns

Using Time Samples

Think About It . . .

How much time did you spend in the last week sewing? reading? gaming? shopping?
When is your attention span the longest?

Think about the choices you make. Your choice of activities is governed by some assumptions:

- You are more likely to do what you like to do rather than what you have to do.

© Cengage Learning 2012

- You do what you have the opportunity to do. Your sewing machine may be broken. You have no new novel to read. You have no money for shopping. You would if you could.
- If your first choice, your favorite pastime, is not available, you may choose a related activity. Your sewing machine is broken, so maybe you do some hand sewing. You have no new book to read, so you reread an old one. Instead of gaming or shopping, you read about it in magazines or the newspaper.
- If you have finished all the sewing projects, read all the books, played that game, or shopped that mall already, you may be bored with those choices.
- If you have a new pattern you want to try, a bestseller waiting, or a new game or mall just opened, you cannot wait to try it and will avoid all other choices, people, or tasks.
- You are more likely to do it if you feel you will be successful or challenged but not frustrated. You know you can sew a dress, so perhaps you decide to try a jacket. You will work on it until you get to a difficult part. Depending on your personality, you may work at it, rip it apart, and start over, or abandon the project altogether. If you are a slow, deliberate reader, then probably reading is not a favorite pastime. If you feel inept on the computer, then gaming may not be your forte. A person planning to lose weight before the next season might be frustrated with shopping and leave the store after trying on only one bathing suit.
- You may choose your activity because your friends are doing it too. They call and say, "Let's meet online to play or go shopping." You had not planned to, but you want to be with them and so you join them.
- While you are at a task of your choosing, time passes quickly. You look up at the clock and cannot believe you have spent four hours working on that garment, reading that book, playing that game, or shopping at that mall. The total absorption in the activity also resents intrusions and any attempt to draw you away. The phone rings; you let the answering machine get it. It is time for lunch, so you grab a sandwich and eat it while you are reading. You hurry through the game or back from shopping and pick up a pizza for dinner. If someone comes and tells you it is time to stop and to come do something else, it makes you angry. You may ignore the first call, the second, and the third.

Factors Influencing Children's Attention Span

What does **attention span** have to do with observing young children? When they have their choice, where, what, and with whom do they choose to spend their time? By observing children's choices of activities a spectrum of information is gathered. The same principles lead children's activity choices.

The design and arrangement of work areas affect attention span. Children's distractibility or inability to focus attention may be more about the environment than about the child. Quiet activities such as reading, puzzles, and small manipulatives that are too close to noisy areas such as blocks or large muscle activities are interrupted and attention is disturbed. Traffic patterns that cut across areas such as block building or dramatic play intrude on concentration and methodical thought. Materials that are not presented in an organized way break attentiveness if additional materials need to be sought out rather than being close at hand. Before interpreting a child's behavior as due to a short attention span, a close examination of the environment is the first step.

The child's choices reveal interests. Avoidance or cursory completion of assigned or chosen tasks may suggest lack of competence. Bessie just loves painting at the easel, so she rushes to get there first, puts on her smock, and gets ready. Miss Jones says, "Bessie, before you start painting I want you to come and paint this hand plaque for your mother." Bessie reluctantly goes to the table, quickly paints the plaque, and returns to the easel, where she paints for the next 15 minutes. Miss Jones wonders to herself, and maybe even writes on her Class List Log, "Short attention span, painted part of plaque and left." Was Bessie interested in painting and does she have a long or short attention span? What made the difference?

The child may select related activities when the first choice is not available. William headed straight for the water table after he hung up his jacket. It was closed. He moved to the climber, but it was taken down, replaced by a writing center. He went into the bathroom, ran water in the sink, wadded up paper towels, and blew them around in the water. Someone had to use the bathroom, so he came out. He climbed up on the shelf and jumped off three times before the teacher came over and tried to get him to come to the new writing center. He refused. She wondered, "Why is he doing these things today?" Children will find a way to do what they want and need to do. William found water play soothing, and climbing helped him work off extra energy. Those were two activities his

© Cengage Learning 2014

Figure 7–1 New activities attract attention.

body, temperament, and development needed, but the activities were denied by the environment, so he manufactured them himself.

Novel, new activities attract children's interest (Figure 7–1). The next day when William came to the classroom, he saw that there was a computer in the writing center. He ran right over and started touching the keys. Marvella showed him how to turn it on and asked him if he wanted to use the dinosaur program to write a story with her. "Sure." Miss Jones wondered, "I couldn't get William over here yesterday. I wonder what made the difference."

Children will choose and give attention to activities where they find success. Bessie may have rejected the teacher's painting project, preferring her own. Maybe she never painted a plaque before and was afraid to try. She had trouble controlling the small brushes the teacher provided, but she knew how to use the big brushes and many colors at the easel. She knew easel painting would be successful. William was not lured by the teacher's invitation to the writing center. He had tried to write his name

when his mother made him practice, and he could not do it to please her. If he went to the writing center, he probably would have to write. "No way! Stay away! I'll just stick with water play and climbing and jumping. I know I'm good at those."

Children are sometimes influenced by their friends' choices of activities. Bessie looked over at the art table. "Oh, my friends are all at the art table with shells and twigs and leaves and stones and bottles of glue. They're calling me over. I've never used glue before. My mom says it's too messy." She joins them and watches for a few minutes. "Now I know how to do it!" She works as long as they are there. When they leave, she may decide to finish her collage or leave it and follow them to the next activity they choose. She may choose an activity because that is where the adult is. She likes to be near Mr. Jim. If he had invited her to do the plaque, she would have stayed there longer.

Children involved in an activity may be reluctant to bring it to a close. Timmy's block building is growing taller and wider. He gets more blocks and makes a road up to the building's door. He gets out the little animals and builds a pen for them. Then he gets a tub of cars and drives it up the road to deliver new animals. The teacher says, "Time for everyone to come to circle time." Timmy keeps building. She says, "Timmy, put the blocks away and come to circle time. You have played there a whole hour." There are too many blocks and animals and cars to put away and the building does not yet have a roof or a barn for the animals. It is not finished, and he realizes he did not even have time to play in the water table yet, and he always plays in the water table before circle time. He has been in the block area the whole free-choice time.

A child with sensory integration difficulties may have difficulty processing all the various sights, sounds, smells, and textures, which are received all at one time. It either causes the child to become immobilized, unsure of which sensory message to follow, or results in the child frantically attempting to respond to each perception. The measurement of attention span for this child may be misinterpreted.

Measuring Attention Span with Time Samples

One of the characteristics commonly used to describe young children is "short attention span." Families will often report that children who cannot sit still one minute at the dinner table will sit for two hours watching a video and never move. (Is it any wonder that families do not fully cooperate with "Television

Turn-Off Day"?) From the preceding adult and children's examples, there are many variables that determine the length of attention span. By watching children as they choose and participate in activities, a wide spectrum of development and behavior can be assessed and evaluated.

The **Time Sample** is an efficient recording method that tracks children's choices, their playmates, and the time they spend in one area. It is a method suitable for children three years old and older in group settings. It may be a mixed-age group or homogeneous-age group. Obviously, if it is recording the children's choices, it is only used in a program and at a time when children have choices. That assumption is based on developmentally appropriate practice for young children from birth through eight years old (Copple & Bredekamp, 2009).

> *Infants*—Observing the infant's cues, the adult is able to judge when the baby would like to be held, carried to a new place, or shifted to a new position. (p. 77)
> *Toddlers*—Adults adapt schedules and activities to meet individual children's needs within the group setting. (p.100)
> *Three- through five-year-olds*—Teachers allocate extended periods of time in learning centers (at least 60 minutes) for children to engage in activities at a complex level. (p.153)
> *Six- through eight-year-olds*—Children have ample time and opportunity to investigate what sparks their interest. (p. 222)

Figure 7–2 is an example of a Time Sample. A segment of the free-choice time is selected. One half hour works well, begun after the children have all arrived and are actively engaged. The learning centers or choices are listed down the left margin. Five-minute intervals are filled in across the top from the time the recording begins. The recorder looks at each area and writes down the names of the children who are in that area at that moment. After a quick glance, a circle can be drawn around the names of the children who are playing cooperatively. That does not refer to the absence of arguments, but to the social stage of working together for a common goal, as described in Chapter 4. The recorder notes also if an adult is in that area, then looks on to the next area to be observed. The areas are all scanned, and names of players are written down. A category at the bottom designates the names of children not in any area at the time, perhaps in transition, perhaps wandering around not involved in play.

When the next five-minute period begins, the process is repeated. If the recorder knows a child remained in the area for the last five minutes, a straight line is drawn, saving a few seconds. If the child left and returned, the name is rewritten. Children do move quickly. Every five minutes the process is repeated.

EXERCISE From the Time Sample example, choose one child and follow the child for a one-half-hour segment. Draw some conclusions about the following:

- the child's interests
- where the child feels competent (probably is most developed)
- where the child may not feel competent (may be the least developed area)
- the stage of play
- the length of attention span
- if the child is teacher-dependent or avoids the adults
- what questions it still leaves in your mind about this child

Of course, a total evaluation of a child's development is not drawn from one recording, just as it should not be drawn from one test score. Time Samples should be done periodically to see trends and to amplify other documentation methods.

Analysis of the Time Sample Example

1. *Who do you think is the oldest child in the class?*
2. *Who is probably the youngest?*
3. *Whose family member was most likely the volunteer (see FV for family volunteer)?*
4. *Who likes to be with the teacher assistant (TA)?*
5. *What are the most popular areas of the classroom?*
6. *What is the least popular area?*
7. *What strategy did the TA use?*
8. *Where was the teacher (T)?*
9. *Which child is missing halfway through the Time Sample?*
10. *Who is the child who needed the teacher's attention?*
11. *What finally worked?*
12. *What well-used area did not sustain long periods of play?*
13. *What might be the reason?*
14. *How long would you expect four-year-olds to stay at a task?*

TIME SAMPLE

Red Class
Class a.m. (fours) Date 2/26/XX Recorder B. Smith

TIMES (at 5-minute intervals)

	9:20	9:25	9:30	9:35	9:40	9:45
Puzzles new floor puzzle	Amy Carter Howard ⟨Jenny⟩	Amy → →	→ → TA	Martin Kara	Jacob	Bajic
		TA Ole	TA			
Art/ Collage	Ole Irma Patty T A	Jacob	Amy → (Jenny)	Carter → Ned → FV Bajic →	→ → FV	→ → FV
Easel	Kara	Irma Patty	Irma	Howard		Galina/Jacob
Lg. Muscle - Climber	(Edward Fatima)	Galina	Jacob	Irma (Jenny)	Galina Kara Ole TA	(Irma Patty)
Blocks	Galina Martin	(Edward Fatima) → →	◯ Galina →	◯ →	(Irma Patty)	Kara Martin
Sand Table	Jacob	⟨Kara Jenny⟩ Martin	Ole → TA	Ole Fatima Patty TA	Amy → (Edward) →	→ Ole TA
Dramatic Play (shoe store)		Amy		Jacob	Martin	
Book Area	Danielle → Ned → FV →	Bajic →	Patty → → →		Jenny TA	Irma → TA
Watching	Bajic					

◯ denotes cooperative play   → denotes continued play   ✶ denotes play difficulty

FV family volunteer   TA teacher assistant

Figure 7–2 Time Sample Example.

Go to the Education CourseMate website to download a copy of this form.

© Cengage Learning 2014

A Time Sample is a closed method because the recorder writes down where children are at that moment (raw data) but does not include details of what they are doing, how they are doing it, or what they are saying. The symbols indicate inferences the observer makes as notes are recorded, such as: circles for cooperative play, arrows for uninterrupted play, and a jagged circle for aggressive play. A Time Sample is a very revealing method of gathering and recording information that can be interpreted for many purposes. It even reveals where the adults spend their time and the most and least used areas of the room. Evaluation of children, adults, and curriculum choices all can be made from the Time Sample.

Infants and Young Toddlers and Time Samples

Time Samples are not appropriate recording methods for infants and young toddlers. Because infants and young toddlers (under two years of age) are still in the Sensorimotor Stage of cognitive development, their attention is dictated by sensory stimuli—such as sight, sounds, and movement—and is not self-controlled. They may show interest in an object or person for a period of time because it is novel, but that attention quickly moves to other things. A more appropriate method of recording learning approaches would be using an Anecdotal or Running Record, describing the child's actions and using that documentation for indications of what Williamson and Anzalone (2001) call the four A's introduced in Chapter 5: arousal, attention, affect, and action for sensory integration.

Arousal is the ability of an infant to maintain an alert state and to make the transition between sleep and wakefulness. When the child is fully awake and alert is the best time to introduce new experiences.

Attention is the ability of an infant to focus on a desired task or even to ignore.

Affect is the emotional response to sensations.

Action is the infant's ability to engage in goal-directed behavior.

Some aspects of temperament, those inborn characteristics of behavior, also can give indicators of approaches to learning:

Activity level—how much time a child will attend to an activity (attention span)

Approach and withdrawal—reaction to new experiences

Adaptability—responses to change in routines, new people, or environments

Physical sensitivity—awareness and reactions to sensory stimulation

Persistence—amount of time given to a task relative to its difficulty

Resistance or distractibility—return to an activity after distraction (Thomas et al., 1968)

These observable behaviors are documented by Time Samples in older children, but the actions of younger children require closer and more individual observation.

Time Samples in the Home Visit

While Time Samples as described are meant for a classroom setting, the information gleaned from samples is important. Educators in home settings need to consider how they might observe and monitor the same kinds of information (interest, temperament, strengths, stage of play, reliance on adult, etc.) and also how learning is encouraged and supported beyond the visit. Curiosity, persistence, creativity and confidence are all markers that begin in infancy and become increasingly observable as the toddler matures, provided there is a home environment where learning is encouraged and supported. Helping parents/primary caregivers to recognize, promote, and celebrate children's learning becomes an important additional task for the home educator.

Advantages of the Time Sample Method

The Time Sample is helpful because it

- gathers information on all the children in the class at one time.
- gives quantitative (numerical) information about attention span. (Cindy spent _____ minutes at the easel.)

- indicates the child's play and interest preferences.
- gives clues as to children's strongest areas, inferred by choices.
- gives clues about the child's less-developed areas, inferred by avoidance.
- can indicate the stage of play the child is in.
- can show preferred playmates.
- can track adult positions in the room.
- shows which areas of the classroom are most used.
- shows which areas of the classroom are underutilized.

The recorder can develop abbreviations and adapt the form and method to meet the individual program.

 Disadvantages of the Time Sample Method

The Time Sample

- records no details about the nature of the play.
- may not capture children moving while the recorder is writing.
- makes inferences that may not be accurate.
- is time intensive for the recorder.
- is effective only where a long period of free-choice play is offered.
- is not as effective for toddlers because most play is solitary or parallel, and movement from area to area is more frequent due to these children's shorter attention spans.
- must be done periodically, or it is too judgmental.

 Pitfalls to Avoid

Time Samples should be repeated every few weeks to avoid placing too much credence on one isolated Time Sample (as in the exercise interpreting this Time Sample).

The Time Sample is time-consuming, but it is a method that a family member or a volunteer—a nonparticipant observer—could be assigned.

Children must have free choice of activity areas for the Time Sample to be effective. If there is a teacher-led activity during that free-choice time, it can be indicated.

Use alternate methods of assessment of infants' and young toddlers' approaches to learning.

 Using Technology

A timer is a useful tool to remind the recorder to scan the room again and note where each child is working. Hand-held computers with timers can be used as well. The Time Sample form can be loaded on a hand-held computer using the Documents to Go program or on a laptop and can then be used electronically to record the names of the children. Later, when the completed form is downloaded, summary results of each child's activities can be stored in an electronic Portfolio for each child.

 How to Find the Time

The Time Sample can be time-consuming, but on a day when free play or free-choice time is going smoothly, the teacher, assistant, or volunteer is only briefly occupied and can perform other tasks between the recording periods. By carefully planning self-directed projects and curriculum, adult intervention is minimized, leaving time for this kind of record keeping.

 What to Do with It

Once a Time Sample is completed, it is stored in the teacher's Class File. Since it has information on all of the children present on that day, it is not copied for individual children's Portfolios. Notation of the Time Sample is recorded on the Portfolio Evidence Sheet (See example in Figure 7–3) with information summarizes on each child placed in that child's Portfolio.

Example: From the Time Sample in Figure 7–2.

Amy—At the beginning of the day Amy moved around the room frequently, stopping at puzzles and dramatic play. She painted and worked at the sand table for longer periods of time. Her play was solitary. 2/26/12

Edward—Edward and a friend moved together from the climber to an involved block-building project that occupied them for more than 10 minutes. They then moved to the sand table, where they played cooperatively. 2/26/12

These summaries give information on play choices, movements, and level of social play. Subsequent Time Samples will be used for comparison to see if the child is in a consistent pattern of play or moving among the choices in the classroom. These comparisons can be used to measure progress in development as well as to make individual plans for a child who may need some encouragement to extend or experience other choices offered.

Go to the Education CourseMate website, accessed through CengageBrain.com for Time Sample forms, plans, and resources.

PORTFOLIO EVIDENCE OF CHILD'S DEVELOPMENT			
Evidence Type	Date	Recorder	Notes
LITERACY – the child's interest and interaction with reading and writing including work samples			
TS	10/24/	BAN	No literacy choices
CL	10/30/	BAN	Recognizes name on helper chart

Figure 7–3 Portfolio Evidence Sheet Example.

REVIEW

TIME SAMPLE

Documentation of the duration of a child's chosen activity. Can be compiled on an individual child or an entire class by noting each child's location in the room at regular intervals of time.

Types of Information to Record Using Time Samples

Location of child at regular intervals. It can also yield information on the following:

 interests

 areas of strength

 patterns of behavior

 areas that may not be developed by noting
  activities the child never selects

 playmates

 social play stage

 child's selection or avoidance of adults in the
  classroom

 length of time a child stays in one area

Looking at Approaches to Learning

EXERCISE **Try the exercise to determine your learning style.**

You've purchased a new appliance or a piece of equipment. Do you

- read the directions before starting to put it together?
- lay out all the parts and fit them together and refer to the directions if you get stuck?
- have someone to help you, reading you the directions while you put it together?
- leave it for later if it doesn't go together on the first try?

These represent visual, auditory, and tactile attention span and learning styles.

One of the fundamental requirements for learning is a focused attention span. People with brain dysfunctions that prevent them from focusing and filtering all the stimuli that come into the brain at once have difficulty learning. Cognitive development begins with attention span and is the topic of this chapter and continues into the next.

Learning is not just a matter of memorizing information. It is highly complex and differs from individual to individual. Some people learn best by hearing, reading, and memorizing, whereas others learn best by touching, moving, and interacting either with materials or with people. The art of teaching does not begin with knowing the pupil, but with knowing oneself. Recognizing that others learn in ways different from us profoundly affects understanding and teaching. Teaching then becomes the orchestration of experiences for all modalities or ways of learning. The traditional method of "recite, memorize, and test" has been unsuccessful for many people. Learning comes from internally constructing new skills and concepts for themselves. The development of cognition—thinking processes—is observable and an area for teachers to consider in environment and schedule planning as well as daily lesson planning.

Approaches to learning entwine all the other areas already discussed—attachment and separation, physical development, language, and social and emotional development. In the next few chapters, learning approaches will be the focus of a closer look. Observers need knowledge and clues to examine closely the changes that take place in children's mental processes. Whether the process is called knowledge, imagination, creativity, reasoning, problem solving, classification, logic, symbolizing, or logico-mathematical reasoning, it is relevant to learning.

Born to Learn

Human beings have an innate desire to learn. Those two-year-olds are biologically driven to explore and experience and it often gets them in trouble. Smilkstein in her book *We're Born to Learn* (2003) describes six stages of learning.

Think About It . . .

Think about something difficult that you learned NOT in school such as driving a car, skateboarding, quilting. How did you learn it?

Test out her theory on the task you selected above.

Stage 1: Motivation. Observed and developed an interest, or desire to do it

Stage 2: Beginning practice. Trial and error, making mistakes

Stage 3: Advanced practice: Practice and increased skill, encouragement, feedback

Stage 4: Skillfulness. Positive reinforcement, feeling good about it, confidence

Stage 5: Refinement. Learning new methods, doing it without thinking

Stage 6: Mastery. Teaching it to others, branching into related interests (p. 51)

The innate, inborn drive to learn goes back to the ecological model with genetic traits of temperament, learning styles, multiple intelligence, and sex that set the stage for the rest of the external, socialized influences. The first and greatest of these is the family. The quality of the relationships with family members, types of experiences, and interpersonal exchanges have a profound effect on later learning. The next most influential agent is the school, relationships with teachers and peers, and the quality of educational institutions. Wrapped around these influences are the culture's beliefs about education.

Positive Approaches to Learning. The goal of early childhood education is to help the child develop dispositions for learning by using the language,

refining physical movements, learning to control emotions, negotiating the social environment, and developing abstract thought. Carr (2001) talks about learning dispositions in three parts:

- Being ready—showing interest and enthusiasm for learning
- Being willing—having strategies to respond to new opportunities by becoming actively involved, focusing, and persisting even when it's difficult
- Being able—having the developmental capacities and relevant knowledge to succeed

An approaches-to-learning framework includes two components: enthusiasm, the emotion/motivation; and engagement, action/behavior. Enthusiasm for learning consists of interest or curiosity, pleasure in activities, motivation to learn, and the desire to explore and find new things interesting. Engagement in learning consists of attention or focus, persistence to work through and tolerate frustration, flexibility in finding creative ways to handle frustrations, and self-regulation in governing one's own behavior (Hyson, 2008). These can be used as descriptors for the ways a child interacts with experiences, first getting interested and then staying interested and involved. Obviously both are equally important. If a child does not find pleasure in an activity, his involvement with it will be short-lived. Then that involvement needs to be maintained long enough to make some meaning or find a positive result.

There are many variables and influences on a child's approach to learning. Like the ecological model described in the Introduction, it begins with the genetic temperament, learning styles, and multiple intelligences. The family is the first and foremost influence through secure attachment, encouragement to learn, and positive experiences. Relationships with teachers and the quality of the program or school that provides an active, involved curriculum can have a direct impact on a child's approach to learning. When the child receives positive encouragement for learning and planned experiences that are relevant to the child's everyday life, enthusiasm and engagement follow. When these influences are negative rather than positive—unsupportive relationships between adults and children, an unchallenging and irrelevant curriculum, teaching practices that rely primarily on whole group, teacher-led experiences, and extrinsic rather than intrinsic rewards—children become discouraged and disengaged.

Piaget and Cognitive Development

No discussion of cognition can be complete without a review of the work of Jean Piaget (1896–1980) and his interpreters (Flavell, 2002; Furth, 1969; Ginsburg & Opper,1988). He described the kinds of knowledge and the stages of children's cognitive development.

Piaget was a Swiss scientist, psychologist, and epistemologist (a person who studies the methods and foundations of knowledge). His early work studied the adaptation of mollusks (related to the clam) to different types of water; he was trained in exacting observation skills. He had to look closely to see changes in a mollusk. His life changed dramatically, as most do, when he became a parent. He then transferred his observation skills to a more fascinating subject, his own children, looking and theorizing on the source and meaning of each movement and new skill. Out of those close observations and 60 years of study (talk about a long attention span!) came the foundation for most of what is known about infant and young child maturation cognitive processes.

Kinds of Knowledge. Piaget categorized not only the stages of cognitive development but the types of knowledge developed as well (Figure 7–4).

Social Conventional Knowledge. **Social conventional knowledge** is described as "the rules of the tribe." It is the type of knowledge that parents teach by instruction and example. These are the accepted social and cultural norms for dress, behavior in different settings, greetings, and ways of addressing others. Some might call this

© Cengage Learning 2014

Figure 7–5 In the Sensorimotor Stage, all senses explore the environment.

category manners or customs. Language development is another major cognitive category in conventional knowledge. Interactions with other people affect language directly, but certain cognitive processing must be possible before language can appear.

Physical Knowledge. **Physical knowledge** is the accumulation of facts about how the world works. As the child rolls, scoots, crawls, stands, cruises, and climbs, she is inspecting her environment (Figure 7–5). She finds that pushing a ball makes it roll, but pushing a block does not have the same effect. She soon adapts her hand movements and expectations of results when she pushes round objects and grasps square ones. During the Sensorimotor Stage, the child is gathering data about the properties of all that is around her by manipulating things and watching the results.

Logico-Mathematical Knowledge. **Logico-mathematical knowledge** is the primary area usually associated with cognitive development, the processing of information to draw conclusions, either

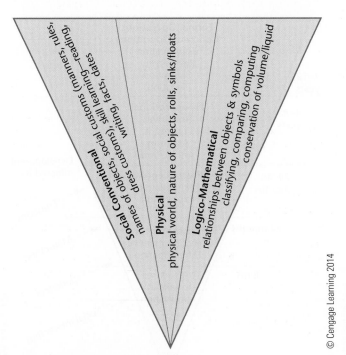

© Cengage Learning 2014

Figure 7–4 Kinds of Knowledge

Source: Adapted from Peterson, R., & Felto-Collins, V. 1986. *The Piaget Handbook for Teachers and Parents.* New York: Teachers College Press.

verbal or mathematical. Seeking relationships is the main task of this type of processing. It is all about the observation of similarities, differences, and commonalities. Variables are manipulated and the results measured. These abstract concepts are clarified when we watch a child play with blocks:

▶ *Similarities and matching*—He places the same size blocks on top of each other.
▶ *Commonalities and classification*—He places all the blocks together and all the toy animals together.
▶ *Cause and effect*—He tries to stand the toy horse on the block that is too small for all four feet. Then he tries to stand it up on the large block, and succeeds.
▶ *Measuring and seriation*—He places the animals in a line according to size (Figure 7–6).
▶ *Rote counting*—He orally counts, perhaps inaccurately or out of order, "1, 2, 3, 6, 8."
▶ *One-to-one correspondence*—He points to each animal as he accurately counts, "1, 2, 3, 4."
▶ *Object permanence*—He knows that if one of the animals falls off the table, out of his sight, it still exists. If he looks for it, he can find it.
▶ *Conservation*—He knows if he sawed one of the two blocks in half, the two halves would weigh the same as the whole block.

These three areas of cognitive development—social conventional knowledge, physical knowledge, and logico-mathematical knowledge—change in a predictable pattern, from simple to complex, over a period of time at individual rates. They have implications for curriculum planning and assessment.

Figure 7–6 Seriation—sorting objects by size or weight.

Piaget's Stages of Cognitive Development

Piaget's Stages of Cognitive Development are easily observable once they are understood (Figure 7–7). The theory strongly relies on the naturally developing brain and body, but also is influenced by social and emotional interactions and daily experiences.

Infancy—Sensorimotor Stage (Birth to 24 Months). What Piaget terms the **Sensorimotor Stage**, birth through 24 months old, gives clues of how the infant is processing information through the senses and acting on information with developing large and small muscles. Vision in a newborn is at the legally blind level (Flavell, 2002) because of the inability to focus or fixate. However, the newborn is able to distinguish between light and dark contrast (figure-ground) about seven to eight inches away, and discern shapes and contours. That is just what is needed to look at a human face at close distance. Visual acuity increases rapidly, and by six months it is at the adult level. Hearing is at a near-adult level at birth. Some research suggests an infant can discriminate the mother's voice from others if it is in "motherese," the up-and-down quality that adults naturally use with babies. The infant has been found able to discriminate between "pa" and "ba" sounds

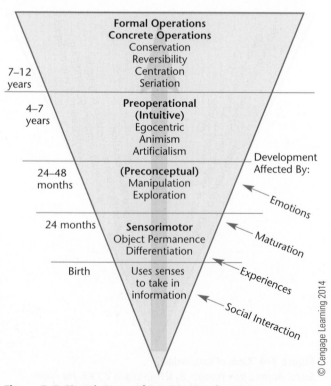

Figure 7–7 Piaget's Stages of Cognitive Development.

at an early age as well. Touch is well developed, especially the sensors for receptive touch, which have caused an interest in baby massage. Those perceptions, along with taste and smell, are present at birth, though at rudimentary levels. Their rapid development necessitates families and teachers to provide sensory-rich environments and experiences for even the youngest infant. In this way, they have a healthy start on the road to cognitive development.

Piaget described intricate substages in which information processing takes circular pathways. Each new piece of information goes through this chain, trying to make a match. Piaget called this constructing knowledge. This basic principle is the foundation for professional practice. The child is involved actively in exploration and experimentation to form his own knowledge. Knowledge is not the transfer of abstract information, but the formation of associations based on information from the senses.

The cognitive tasks of the Sensorimotor Stage is **self-differentiation**. Around six months of age, the infant forms the concept that she is a separate entity from the crib, from the car seat, but most of all from the humans around her. This has implications when adults leave the room and the infant wants them back. Remember the discussion on separation in Chapter 1?

Very closely allied is **object permanence**, the understanding that items and people still exist even when out of sight. Before this understanding is attained, a dropped item over the side of the high chair or visibly hidden under a blanket ceases to exist (Figure 7–8). A few weeks later, if the child drops a spoon over the side of the high chair tray she will look for it. When her teacher leaves the room, she may whine or cry until he comes back. By the end of the second year, infants have both mental representations, which are leading them into the development of language and into the Preoperational Stage.

Of course, stages are not like stair steps but more like escalators, transitions to the next stage in a smooth yet sequential pattern. Piaget's stages of cognitive development are for ease of categorization and description, not to imply that these processes are separate from one another. They are primarily how "people adapt to novel situations because they are internally motivated to learn" (Meier & Henderson, 2007, p. 20).

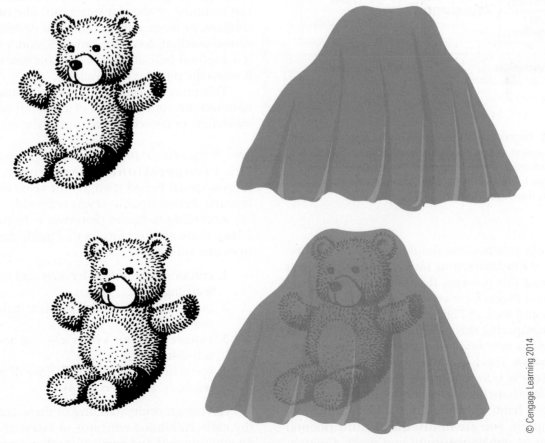

© Cengage Learning 2014

Figure 7–8 Object Permanence. Before a child has reached the stage of object permanence, the bear covered with the blanket out of the child's sight ceases to exist. When the child reaches to pull off the blanket, knowing the bear still exists though out of sight, the child has achieved the cognitive structure of object permanence.

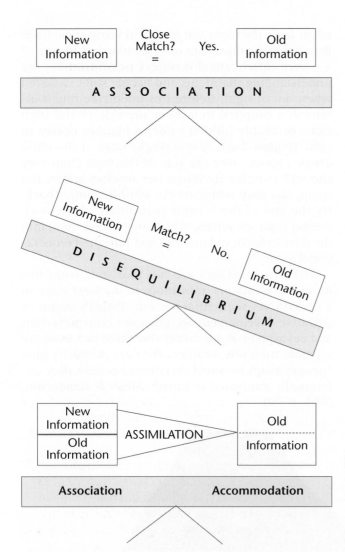

Figure 7–9 Piaget's Construction of Knowledge. New Information is weighed against what is already known (Old Information) for a match—Association. If there is no match, there is Disequilibrium. Once the New Information melds with Old Information there is Assimilation, then Accommodation.

© Cengage Learning 2014

To help you become familiar with this theory, Figure 7–9 illustrates your own cognitive processes as you read this passage. If you already know and understand Piaget's concept of association, as you read this and look at Figure 7–9, your brain is processing, comparing this new information with what you already knew (old information), and you make an association. This is an "aha, I know that" moment.

If it is new information for you, for example, if you realize that this use of the word **association** is different from your previous understanding of the definition, you are in **disequilibrium** (mental confusion or imbalance) until you make a match. Taking in the information and forming a bridge or

relationship to what you already know is called **assimilation**. You have added another building block—or schema—to existing information, or deepened your understanding.

When the new information is associated, assimilated, and added to the old information, you have achieved **accommodation**. You have somewhat changed the structure of what you previously knew, forming new ideas or blocks of knowledge. This is the process of assimilation. Now all of that becomes old information to begin the process all over again the next time a new piece of information is received. You will try to associate it, assimilate it, go into disequilibrium, and then accommodate it.

Here is an example: An infant suckles her mother's breast and receives milk. She builds an association between sucking and milk. As she rolled around in her crib a few months later, the blanket brushed her lips. The reflex motion caused her to suck. "Ugh! I'm not getting milk!" She could not make a match between the milk she received previously and this new substance. She tried to associate the substance to what she already knew, but it was lint instead of milk. She was in disequilibrium. She spit the blanket out and now has another action or reaction to sucking. She can continue or she can spit it out. She can now assimilate, or make a judgment, and decide on a new course of action, accommodation. She may decide that it is a second-best alternative and continue to chew on it when the nipple is not available.

This process occurs thousands of times a day in nanoseconds (one billionth of a second) without any awareness or conscious decision of the thinker.

The Preoperational Stage (Two to Seven Years). The **Preoperational Stage** consists of the Preconceptual Period (two to four years old) and the Intuitive Period (four to seven years old).

According to Piaget (Peterson & Felton-Collins, 1986), there are four factors that guide development from one substage to the next:

1. emotions that create feelings and motivate learning
2. maturation of physical growth, including the nervous system
3. experiences (one's own learning and self-discovery)
4. social interaction and influence of parents, teachers, and peers (p. 4)

Having an understanding of these factors helps the early childhood educator to assess and plan for an environment and curriculum that meets the cognitive needs of this stage.

It Happened to Me

Beginning Geometry

A group of parents and toddlers were gathered to share stories, frustrations, and advice. A less-than-two-year-old toddled over to a swinging door with an automatic closer. When he leaned against it, it opened a little way, then closed with a hissing sound. He seriously looked at the door and tried it again. Push, close, hiss. Push, close, hiss. All this time he was looking up at the top of the door jamb. Mom came running over, "Come away from there." She was probably concerned about pinched fingers and what would happen if he pushed too hard and went on through the doorway. I was fascinated that he was not tempted to do that. He was mesmerized by the action and reaction of the door.

As we took his point of view and looked up as he was doing, we saw that the ceiling produced a bright changing triangle as the door closed. He formed a mental image (schema) of triangles and their changing shapes that day, which will be the foundation of later geometry equations. Someday he will measure the degrees of the angles in a triangle. I like to think about the connection between that task and the day he pushed the door open and watched it close.

In the Preconceptual Period the child is an active participant in learning, intentionally acting on the environment and finding how things work. Problems are attacked mostly through trial and error and by manipulation of materials. Instead of just using a spoon to feed herself, she will use it to feed her dolly. This moves her from the function performed on herself to acting on another. She may even move to symbolic or dramatic use of the play, as when she uses the spoon as a microphone like she saw a singer use on television last night. Throughout this substage, the major task is classification, making connections by physically and mentally placing items in pairs and groups. The vocabulary is rapidly building, and grammar is expanding. Now sentences convey messages and control the environment and other people.

In the Intuitive Period (four to seven years old), as described by Piaget, the reasons the child gives for phenomena are based on appearances or intuition rather than understanding. There are many mental processes the child cannot do until the next stage (the Concrete Operational Stage). Flavell (2002) and others, however, have looked at the Intuitive Period in a more positive light, finding that children in this stage have built large knowledge structures. Although these structures are present, the child may not yet represent them in either language or art. The receptive processes are greater than the expressive. The child understands much more than he can convey either in words, drawings, or writing.

Some classic terminology and experiments demonstrate what a Preoperational child cannot do yet but will attain in the next stage:

Egocentrism—The child believes that everyone thinks and feels as he does. The young child cannot mentally take the perspective of the other person. Researchers are finding that this ability is developing earlier than Piaget and others thought. (A small screen separates the child and a toy from the examiner, who asks, "Can I see the toy?" If the child can see it, she will answer, "Yes," even if a screen blocks the examiner's view.) (See Figure 7–10.)

Conservation—The child does not understand the variables that can make quantity look different while the volume is unchanged. (Pennies are arranged in two rows close together; then one row is spread apart. The child is asked if the rows are still the same. Two glasses of water hold the same level of liquid. The child confirms they have the same amount. Then liquid is poured from one glass into a shallow dish. When asked, "Which has more?" the child will point to the glass because the level appears higher. When shown two balls of clay of the same size and then one is flattened, the child will indicate the round ball is larger. Even when the experiment is reversed and shown to be equal and repeated, the child in the Intuitive stage will give the same "wrong" answer. The Preoperational child, without the understanding of the properties of number, volume, or mass, will say the separated row of pennies, the tall glass of water, or the round ball of clay has more. The child will answer by appearance.) (See Figure 7–11.)

Reversibility—The child is not yet able to mentally reverse an operation. (The examiner asks, "What will happen if I pour this back? Then will it be the same?")

Figure 7–10 Egocentrism. The child sees the face of the doll and thinks that the rabbit does also because she is not yet cognitively developed to see from another's point of view.

© Cengage Learning 2014

Centration—The Preoperational child is only able to focus on one attribute at a time. (If the child is sorting by color but the blocks also have different shapes he will have difficulty centering [concentrating] on sorting by color, ignoring the shape.) (See Figure 7–12.)

Seriation—The Preoperational child is not able to place items in a series according to a rule such as height or weight. (She can probably pick out the largest and smallest but will have difficulty with those in between.)

The Preoperational child makes cognitive errors based on appearance, not reasoning, such as the following:

Animism—The child believes that all objects have the properties of being alive. ("My book will be lonely if I leave it home.")

Artificialism—The child believes that natural phenomena are man-caused. ("Daddy, make it stop raining so we can go on our picnic.")

EXERCISE Try out some of these tasks on some children under five and over eight to see the difference in their thinking.

Concrete Operational Stage (7 to 11 Years). All the processes that the Preoperational child is developing come to bloom in the **Concrete Operational Stage**. Children now can use logical and rational thinking to understand and explain the properties of volume and number, classifying, seriating, centering, and reversing. It does not occur all at once as a child celebrates his seventh birthday; it happens in small, incremental steps as major neurological changes take place. Around seven years old, ways of thinking have changed. The child is now ready physically, socially, emotionally, and cognitively to apply the experiences of the past seven years to the serious business of learning.

The task of sorting and classifying, recognizing similarities and differences, is the recurring curriculum theme. This is not to be interpreted that ways of learning change from those experiential, hands-on explorations. Piaget's theory is complex and full of terminology, but it has practical application for methods, materials, environment, and curricula in any early childhood program. The environment and curriculum allow each child to construct knowledge through exploration, manipulation, and the sensory experiences the adults provide. The role of the adult is still to prepare the environment, facilitate exploration, support and scaffold approximations of development, and record the progress. If the first roles are fulfilled, there will be progress to record.

Number

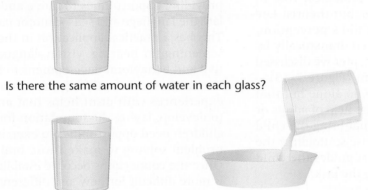

Is there the same number of pennies in each row?

Now is there the same number of pennies in each row, or does one row have more?

Liquid

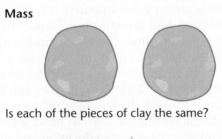

Is there the same amount of water in each glass?

Now does each glass have the same amount of water, or does one have more?

Mass

Is each of the pieces of clay the same?

Now are the pieces the same, or does one have more?

Figure 7–11 Conservation. The child in the Intuitive Stage judges by appearances then attains the cognitive structures to judge by quantity and knowledge that volume stays the same even though the shape may change.

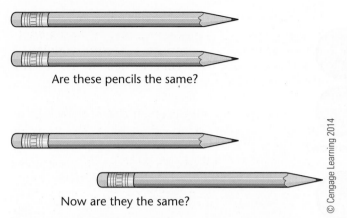

Are these pencils the same?

Now are they the same?

Figure 7–12 Centration. During the Intuitive Stage the child centers, or centrates, on the attribute of the pencil and may say the lower pencil is longer.

© Cengage Learning 2014

Vygotsky's Ideas about Cognitive Development

Piaget's theory emphasizes the biological role in the emergence of cognitive skills, but theorist Lev Vygotsky recognized that the child's perception, attention, and memory are affected dramatically by social interactions. In an earlier chapter we discussed the zone of proximal development (Figure 7–13)— tasks too difficult for the child to do alone but that could approximate success with the help of adults or older children. The interactions that bring the child to that more advance level comprise scaffolding: the intentional verbal instruction that guides the child through the process of completing the task.

Infants and Toddlers and Brain Development

Research on brain development came to the forefront in the late 1990s with the use of new brain imaging technologies coupled with growing concern about the status of children in America.

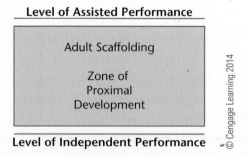

Level of Assisted Performance

Adult Scaffolding

Zone of
Proximal
Development

Level of Independent Performance

© Cengage Learning 2014

Figure 7–13 ZPD and Scaffolding.

What Science Tells Us. The architecture of the brain is formed in the first three years of life, beginning prenatally, influenced by genetics and environmental factors such as the mother's health, both physical and emotional, and the absence of toxins such as drugs and alcohol, certain medications, and environmental hazards. During this time the most significant brain development occurs when neurons are making connections with other neural circuits for the brain to function optimally. Many more connections are developed than it needs, and connections that are not used or useful are pruned away over time. Early environments and experiences during **sensitive periods** (when neurons are exceptionally receptive and requiring certain experiences) form circuitry for sensorimotor development, receptive language, speech production, and reasoning and planning. These sensitive periods occur at different ages for different parts of the brain, calling for age-appropriate experiences during that period. Talking with infants, providing multisensory experiences, and providing opportunities to move and explore stimulate the language and sensorimotor parts of the brain. This has a practical application in the need for early screening for hearing, vision, language, and cognitive and behavioral development to link children to necessary services. Giving preschoolers access and experiences with print helps that area of the brain to develop, laying the foundation for literacy. Older children need opportunities to exercise memory and problem solving to make those brain connections. Once the connections become established (or not), it is more difficult for new and different experiences to alter that architecture. Some recent findings indicate that the window of opportunity or sensitive period does not close at three years old; while negative effects are well-documented, it is not so that "earlier is better." And there is no evidence that videos, DVDs, or specific music have measurable impact (National Scientific Council on the Developing Child, 2008).

In *From Neurons to Neighborhoods* (Shonkoff & Phillips, eds., 2000), scientists looked at child development through the lens of brain development and early childhood relationships to make a case for the policy and practice of early education and intervention. The research reinforced the concept that it is all about making connections between what has been experienced in the past and how this new experience is alike and different from that. As more is known about the lasting neurological effects of positive early experiences at critical times, as well as exposure to negative influences such as poor nutrition and drug and alcohol use by the mother, early education becomes a priority and an investment (Shonkoff & Phillips, 2000). Continued

It Happened to Me

Pay Attention

One of my first-semester college students who worked in an out-of-school program related a story in class one day about a boy with autism in her group. She said she had to speak to the father when he picked up his son. She told the father that the boy was causing a problem because he wouldn't pay attention and follow the rules. She told the father that he should work with his son about that.

What do you think that revealed about the young woman? Did she lack knowledge of a disorder that affected a child in her charge? Did her ignorance lead her to lay a burden on a parent beyond the one he already had? What strategies do you think she had been using to get the boy to pay attention? What would you have said to her if you were the instructor?

research on children's developing brains seeks new answers to learning disabilities, hyperactivity disorders, memory strategy acquisition, suggestibility to misinformation, and the effects of exposure to positive experiences and various traumas (Courage, 2009).

Attention

"Attention is the focusing of the individual's perceptual processes upon a specific aspect of the environment. Learning cannot take place unless the individual is able to focus attention" (Cook, Klein, & Tessier, 2008, p. 294). In a review of long-range studies of children to determine factors of success, after good math and reading skills, came their attention skills (Brooks-Gunn, 2007). To focus attention, a person must concentrate on the object or task at hand while also ignoring other insignificant stimuli. The body is then reoriented to the task and a sequence of actions is performed. Memory is involved in keeping in mind the steps to complete the task (Lewin-Benham, 2010). This is a skill that is being refined from birth and is critical to school performance, social interaction, and even survival. From experiences that come to our attention, the information is coded, and then the sensory and perceptual aspects are consolidated with similar information and knowledge and stored as a memory. The final phase is retrieval or accessing stored information. When new sensory or perceptual experiences occur, they seek out matching or similar ones and the cycle is repeated.

Jensen, in *Teaching with the Brain in Mind* (2005), gives understandable insight into the workings of the brain. He discusses the purpose of attention for survival and to extend pleasurable states. Attention provides sensory information on which to base decisions about our next actions. The pathways of attention consist of alarm, orientation, identification, and decision. A child may see the flicker of fire, but without prior experiences on which to base a decision, the attention and decision to seek it out may prove dangerous. On the other hand, when a child is absorbed in play and the teacher flicks the lights, the decision point is whether to continue the pleasure of play or give attention now to the teacher's agenda. Is it any wonder that children get hurt or in trouble?

The visual system provides 80 percent of the information needed for this process to take place. The brain has to process or sort out irrelevant data and amplify the relevant data. Chemical changes take place during this process, assisting in heightened attention during times of stress and threat. Attention also flows in cycles from high to low throughout the day and night, with periods of inattention of great importance for processing time. When teachers see children gazing out the window or standing and watching, a common response is, "Pay attention." If teachers heeded Jensen's explanation of the processing time, those inactive moments would be seen in a new light. Everyone has experienced profound thoughts that come long after a discussion or experience. The brain just needed that time to process the information and make sense and meaning.

▶❚❚ TEACHSOURCE VIDEO ACTIVITY

Go to the Education CourseMate website, accessed through CengageBrain.com and view the video entitled 2–5 years: Observation Module for Early Childhood.

In the first segment of children dancing in the gym, make a Time Sample for following directions, moving not following directions, and not participating. Observe the girl with ponytail, boy with striped shirt, and boy with yellow shirt. What conclusions can you draw about their attention spans?

As important as attention is to learning, it is just as important that recess breaks contribute to cognitive performance and result in increased attention. By reviewing many studies Pellegrini and Holmes found that inattention of primary children was lower after recess than before (p. 48). Later studies on young children had the same results, and also found increased attention to story reading after playful, unstructured breaks of 10 – 20 minutes where children could interact with peers and materials on their own terms.

Memory

EXERCISE **Take a friend with you to the perfume counter in a department store. Close your eyes and have a friend wave a perfume in front of your nose. You take in the new sensory information and your brain tries to match it with prior information. Have you smelled this before? If so, you have made an association and you can name the perfume. If it is a new smell to you, you are in disequilibrium; however, you have stored that sensory experience with other perfume smells along with the name. Now, here's the test. You are in an elevator or someone walks by and you get a whiff of perfume. Ah, you take in that smell and you can match it with the name because you have assimilated the smell and the name of the perfume along with the others that are stored in your brain.**

Memory consists of three components, encoding information from the environment, storage of the encoded information, and retrieval or accessing the information. Consider the exercise above. Information about the new scent was encoded: its odor, its name, the shape of the container, and the sensory, perceptual and emotional information was stored and then retrieved when you smelled it again, heard the name, and remembered the event. Your information processing memory was at work.

Research has long accepted the concept of infantile amnesia, that before the age of two when language appears, the encoding, storage, and retrieval of memories was nonexistent. Research now is beginning to refute that idea (Rovee-Collier & Cuevas, 2009). During the Sensorimotor and Preoperational stages, the child interacts with real objects and builds memories of the properties of these objects and how they react. This assimilation and accommodation is stored in the memory. John Flavell, whose whole career has been devoted to studying cognitive

development, reinforces the importance of providing young children with experiences that will increase their knowledge of the world in which they live. He says, "What the hand knows has an enormous effect on what the head learns and remembers" (Flavell, 1987, p. 213). Memory is the construction material of cognitive development.

Those who compare memory to an information processing system say there are three components of the hardware: the sensory memory that receives input from the environment; the working memory that is the site of ongoing cognitive activity; and the long-term memory, a permanent storehouse of knowledge that is present but sometimes hard to access. As children get older they acquire more efficient strategies to solve problems and are able to inhibit distractions, and some cognitive processes become virtually automatic, aiding in faster processing of information.

Because the brain functions are integrated, learning can be affected by chronic stress that interferes with the formation and retrieval of memories. Young children are less able to tune out environmental sights and sounds and focus attention on the task at hand, and this ability may be negatively impacted in later years because of early stress. The executive function (discussed in Chapter 5) helps not only to self-regulate behavior but also memory and attention (Thompson, 2008). The stresses experienced by children living in poverty have been shown to impact brain development, reduce memory capacity, and influence the ability to hold items in memory that continue into young adulthood (Evans & Schamberg, 2009).

EXERCISE **Respond to the following statements about yourself:**

I have a (bad/good) memory.
It helps me to remember if I …

There are many different aspects of memory. Recognition is the most basic. Piaget's term for it was association. It is that matching to a past piece of information. Studies of infants and young children show this basic ability is present very early in life. The memory or recall of these objects increases as the child ages and recall was markedly better when an adult narrated exactly what the child was doing. "You put the block in the hole and it rang the bell," rather than "Good job! You rang the bell" (Hanye & Simcock, 2009). This adds evidence to the importance of verbal repetition and presenting children with connected sensory experiences to assist memory. Sensory experiences are usually messy ones that teachers or families are reluctant to allow. However, they are more than fun and mess: they are important to brain development. The sensory object that infants younger than 12 months are most familiar with is their food. Cultural values about playing with food come into conflict with the educational value of sensory experiences. This dilemma must be resolved with sensitivity and an acceptable solution. Other sensory experiences for infants include massage, bathing, rocking, and patting—all done most naturally without thought as to their cognitive development implications.

Visual recognition has high rates of memory: "Ah, yes, I've met you before but don't remember your name." Recall, the next phase after recognition, is more difficult, placing the name with the face recognized. The strategy used to help in that recall or retrieval of information is mnemonics. Figure 7–14 illustrates six keys that might be used to "unlock" memory:

> *Wait time*—One of the most natural keys, used by all ages, involves waiting for a period of time and letting the mind work.
>
> *Rehearsal*—Repeating, either aloud or silently, is a technique that experimenters have taught young children to use. However, it is not long-lasting, nor does it become spontaneous.
>
> *Categories or word associations*—Older children and adults use this technique to put words into categories to aid in retrieval.
>
> *Sensory cues*—Young children use visual and sensory retrieval cues. This reinforces the

emphasis on an active, real approach for teaching young children, using multisensory experiences. For example, reading a story about an apple, accompanied by eating one, will help children remember the story about the apple.

> *Chunking*—Memory is aided by breaking strings of information down into smaller parts, such as Social Security numbers, telephone numbers, or song lyrics. (For example, "two, forty-eight, eleven, seventy-nine, seventy-six" for 248-11-7976, or 1-800-FORKIDS for 1-800-367-5437.) Teachers who use rebus charts to teach children song lyrics use visual cues and teach small portions of the song at a time.
>
> *Writing*—Writing words down helps implant them in the memory and aids in recall. That is the major reason for written observations.

Think back to the perfume exercise. Perhaps if you wait, the smell of the perfume will associate with its name. Or if you had repeated the smell and the name every time you passed the perfume counter, you would remember it better. Or if you made an association of that perfume smell to a person or a flower, you would remember the name easier. Of course if you bought the perfume and used it yourself several times, you could recognize it when someone else wore it. If you organize your perfumes alphabetically and write labels for each on the shelf, you would remember the name easier. That's taking it a bit far, but you get the idea now.

The awareness of the need to remember begins in the Preoperational period. Preschoolers were found to be inaccurate predictors of what they could remember, and ill-equipped to develop or act on strategies. By the time they were seven, however, they could group materials into similarities or categories to help them remember. They used common aids such as making lists or placing items to remember by their coat (Kail, 2007).

The strategies that different people use to learn and remember have been explored from a number of theories. Multiple intelligences and learning styles have caught the interest of researchers. Educators also see the profound differences between children, bringing that recognition to the next step, which is adopting an individualized curriculum and expectations based on each child's learning style and strengths.

Playful Curriculum

Because of what we know about the brain, teachers of young children provide a different kind of learning environment and curriculum than teachers of

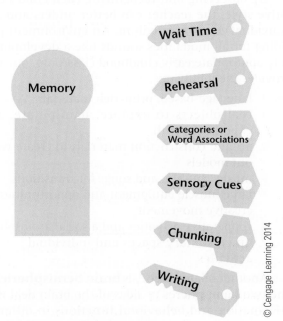

© Cengage Learning 2014

Figure 7–14 Keys to Unlock Memory.

It Happened to Me

Mardi Gras in New York Curriculum

I was observing a student teacher in a child care setting in upstate New York. Several of the staff had just returned from a national conference in New Orleans where they had purchased colorful masks with feathers, bags of beads, and harlequin wall decorations. They excitedly were planning a curriculum unit for the whole center—toddlers through preschoolers—on Mardi Gras.

What do you think? What might have been more appropriate? When and where would this have been more appropriate, if at all?

fourth graders: learning environments and activities that provide active involvement with real objects with sufficient, uninterrupted time to develop ideas and explore possibilities. The process of learning is as important as the outcome. Children learn best when their social and emotional needs are met and where there is flexibility and compromise. Settings that facilitate children's language, attentional skills, problem solving, flexible thinking, and self-regulation will help prepare confident, eager, engaged, and lifelong learners (Hirsh-Pasek, et al., 2009). Young children learn most effectively when learning activities relate to their everyday lives rather than artificially presenting abstract, unfamiliar play contexts.

Multiple Intelligences and Hemisphericity

Howard Gardner (1983) has looked beyond learning styles and identified various different types of intelligence that he calls Frames of Mind. He criticizes schools that only measure and value some while ignoring others. He has identified eight of these **multiple intelligences:**

1. *Linguistic intelligence*—remembering what one hears and reads
2. *Logical-mathematical intelligence*—figuring things out logically using reasoning and problem solving

3. *Spatial intelligence*—recreating what one sees, imagines, visualizes, or creates
4. *Bodily-kinesthetic intelligence*—using one's body to learn, interact, and express oneself
5. *Musical intelligence*—innate musical talent
6. *Interpersonal intelligence*—understanding, cooperative, and communicative with others
7. *Intrapersonal intelligence*—comfortable with self, works best alone, and pursues one's own interests
8. *Naturalist intelligence*—ability to discriminate among living things and a sensitivity to other features of the natural world

In a later book, *Intelligence Reframed* (1999), Gardner goes beyond these, presenting the idea that there may be any number of others. Attempts have been made to assess individuals for various intelligences, but Gardner resists this "assessment mentality" because tests tend to be biased toward some intelligences and thus would not be a true measure. He has worked instead to "observe children at play (or at work) systematically and to arrive at a quantitative description of their intelligences" (p. 138). This work is called Project Spectrum.

EXERCISE **List the people you know who fit into each of the multiple intelligences. Where are your strengths or gifts?**

By observing and recognizing each child's cognitive style, the teacher can better understand and individualize the curriculum. An environment providing for all modalities sounds like a developmentally appropriate early childhood classroom, one that provides the following:

- language-based, print-rich materials
- real objects to explore, manipulate, and experiment with
- art and construction materials to create without models
- music, rhythm, and songs for transitions
- large muscle equipment and opportunities for creative movement
- cooperative activities and a social atmosphere
- quiet, solitary spaces and individual activities

Another related theory is **brain hemisphericity**. The two hemispheres or sides of the brain deal with information and behavioral functions in different ways.

Left—This hemisphere of the brain is where language and speech are produced. It is the site of analytical, logical, sequential, orderly, verbal, computational, linear, concrete thinking.

Right—This hemisphere of the brain is the initial receiver of incoming information and the center of visual, artistic, creative, intuitive, and spontaneous thoughts. (Springer & Deutsch, 1998)

The study of the brain continues as neurological testing techniques advance. Scientists are still sorting out the contributions of nature and nurture to the functioning of the brain and studying the effects when injury or illness affects one hemisphere. Many researchers feel traditional educational teaching and testing methods ignore the sensory, visual, and intuitive functions of the brain. The developmentally appropriate curriculum includes reading, writing, listening, and speaking at the children's level; open-ended building materials; puzzles; music for listening, producing, and moving to; materials and environment for using large and small muscles; attention to receptive and expressive emotions; opportunities for self-reflection; and incorporating plants, animals, and the physical world into the environment, both indoors and outside.

Observing Attention Span in Infants and Toddlers

To infants and toddlers, everything is new, so sights, sounds, and textures demand their attention or ability to focus on an item, task, or event. Observing when the infant is most alert and using that time to advantage by interacting helps to keep the infant in that state longer. Observe the child observing. Watch to see what catches and holds his attention. By careful observation, the child's imitative behavior indicates he has attended and has direct learning. Later or the next day or week when this imitated behavior recurs, the deferred imitation indicates the child has stored that memory and retrieved it now to act it out or repeat the words or phrases he heard. Observe and support the child's imitative behavior and extend it by giving narration such as "Oh, yesterday you saw Henri use the spoon upside down and today you are trying it." The Time Sample is not appropriate for an infant or toddler classroom, but a Time Sample may be kept on an individual child, recording the amount of time the child spends at certain choices.

Helping all Children with Attention Span

Cognitive development, with respect to memory and attention span, is affected by physical, emotional, and cultural influences.

Mental Processing Differences

Different causes such as birth defects, maternal drug use, and poor nutrition may result in difficulties in the basic cognitive processes.

Attention Deficit. Attention is defined as the ability to focus on a specific aspect of the environment and ignore the other stimuli. Some children with extremely short attention spans, difficulty concentrating, and high distractibility have been diagnosed with **Attention Deficit Hyperactivity Disorder (ADHD) or Attention Deficit Disorder (ADD)** without hyperactivity. Children with these disorders have been mislabeled sometimes as emotionally disturbed, mentally retarded, or autistic. It is the nature of young children to be impulsive and easily distracted, especially when the classroom does not provide outlets for their energy or appropriate curriculum. This makes the disorder difficult to diagnose. Is it the environment, the curriculum, or the child? Diagnosis begins with gathering information regarding physical, mental, and social-emotional development from families, medical professionals, and teachers. Federal laws, such as the Individuals with Disabilities Education Act (IDEA) and Section 504 of the Rehabilitation Act of 1973, provide coverage for children with ADD.

Occasionally, children with ADHD have accompanying disorders such as learning disabilities and behavior disorders that challenge teachers who have these children in a group. It is important for the family or school staff not to impose a label or a diagnosis, leaving that to the professionals. Researchers are still looking for the causes. One possible cause may be in genetic transmission found by studies of parents and twins with ADHD (National Institute of Mental Health, 2008). Most children with this disorder respond favorably to a stimulant that paradoxically increases attention and decreases impulsivity and activity, along with child and family counseling. There is a national information support group: CHADD (Children and Adults with Attention-Deficit/Hyperactivity Disorder); information is available at http://www.chadd.org.

The Time Samples of the group will give a quantitative recording of attention behavior. It also will

TOPICS in OBSERVATION

Attention Span and Autism

Autism is characterized as a "pervasive developmental disorder" (Kauffman & Laundrum, 2009) because it affects all areas of functioning, such as impaired communication, abnormal social interaction, peculiar interest and behavior, physical delays or impairment, and inconsistent cognitive development. More children than ever before are being classified with autism spectrum disorders (ASD) perhaps because of greater recognition and diagnosis. It is the second-most-common serious developmental disability after mental retardation. It occurs in 1 in 88 (CDC, 2012) children, and occurs in more boys than girls by a ratio of 5:1. There is no conclusive evidence of the cause of autism, but researchers are looking at genetics, parents' age, environmental factors, and vaccines. While there is no objective measure for diagnosing autism, its effect on the attention span can be an important clue. In contrast to many other cognitive disabilities, such as ADD or ADHD, its onset can be recognized before the age of three. Autism is a spectrum disorder ranging from high-functioning Asperger syndrome to classic autism to mixed autism associated with other conditions such as sensory integration disorder and mental retardation.

Between year one and year two, and certainly by year three, there is a noticeable attention span difference in a child with autism. The child may give little attention to other people, peers, or family. Instead, the child can be preoccupied with an object or a routine to the exclusion of all other interactions and stimuli. The child's behavior can be extreme in response to altered routines or the denial of the obsessive object. Children with autism have been known to attach to vacuum cleaners, ceiling fans, and spinning toys to the exclusion of social interaction, failing even to make eye contact. They can attend to their chosen item to such a degree that all other outside happenings are completely ignored. Many children with autism who have a less severe attachment to specific objects still have difficulty focusing attention on the relevant stimuli in a task. For example, the child with autism who is listening to a story may be so fascinated by a pattern in the rug on which he is sitting that he never gets the context of the story. Language may be affected by echolalia (repeating a phrase over and over) but ignoring the answer, giving attention only to the question, and never noticing or listening to the response.

Asperger syndrome is on the high-functioning end of the autistic spectrum. It is classified with autism because it, too, is a pervasive developmental disorder, one that can range from mild to severe, affecting several domains of development. It often involves the physical domain, particularly balance and coordination. The child may be sensory sensitive (profoundly aware of sensory stimuli such as touch or sound), have irrational fears, and be easily obsessed about things that might happen in his world that would not be stressful to a typical child. This can put children with Asperger syndrome in a terrible state of anxiety. It especially involves their social development because of their inability to understand social cues, their own emotions, or the emotions of others. However, expressive language development for those with Asperger syndrome is often advanced, and the child may display a large vocabulary and savant knowledge about an obscure subject.

You as the observer may recognize symptoms of autism spectrum disorder that otherwise may be described as stubbornness, distractibility, precociousness, or shyness. It is not your role to diagnose but to observe: take specific, accurate information and share the results with the person who needs to know. Remember, students, it is not for you to approach a family member with any of your suspicions. That must be very carefully done by the teacher or special-services personnel. (This was written with the consultation of Liz Smithmeyer and Michael Logalo.)

compare the child in question to his peers. (The word *his* is selected purposefully here because more boys than girls are diagnosed with ADHD.)

Running Records focusing on the child will also aid helping professionals in the diagnosis. Even though a child has a short attention span, high distractibility, high activity, and impulsivity, he may not have ADHD.

Perception. Perception is the ability to interpret the objects and events stimulating the senses. For children with a limited ability in hearing, sight, taste, smell, or touch, the intake of information limits their cognitive processing. The other modalities may compensate for the limited ones but only as much as the cognitive capacity is able to accommodate. Young children especially depend on sight to cue all kinds of behavior with less attention to verbal language. They carefully watch and imitate rather than listen and do.

Perception depends on the ability to discriminate between appearances, sounds, and textures. With impairments of the receptors or the cognitive structures to process the information, these sensory cues go unrecognized and ignored. The teacher of children with such impaired sensory abilities makes adaptations for the other senses to receive a similar message, such as tapping a rhythm that cannot be heard or associating textures with the words *cool, warm, rough,* and *soft.*

Memory is the basic cognitive process received through attention and perception. It is stored in the central nervous system in the various categories of short-term, long-term, visual, rote, recognition, and recall. Children with nervous system difficulties such as muscular dystrophy or multiple sclerosis, as well as children with limited cognitive ability, may experience memory difficulties.

As with all cognitive, physical, or emotional disorders, families, teachers, and those on special education committees seek to place the child in the least restrictive environment where the child can maximize the abilities that are present and make modifications and allowances for areas of lower functioning.

Cultural Differences in Approaches to Learning

Research regarding attention span in various cultures has had mixed results. The assessment of cognitive development must consider the cultural context. When memory tasks used for assessment are unrelated to the child's world, children do poorly (Rogoff, 2003). This is consistent with the principles of fair testing: The test should be culturally relevant to be a valid measurement of ability.

The amount of stimulation in a classroom is affected by culture. Some cultures prefer quiet, peaceful styles of interaction, seeing a busy, noisy environment as over-stimulating and not conducive to thinking. Some cultures value activity and movement as tenets of exploration, problem solving, and developing imagination, while in others children may be less expressive. Even whether the child's gaze at the learning material is direct or sideways may differ by culture (Rogoff, 2003). When children come from cultures of deprivation and predominately outside regulation, the amount of materials available and freedom of choice may be overwhelming. Adults should always consider the child's behavior in the cultural context of the home environment.

Helping Professionals for Attention Concerns

If a difficulty with memory, attention span, or cognitive processing is observed, those concerns are addressed by the teaching team, the supervisor, and then brought to the attention of the child's family with tact and sensitivity. Such difficulties are nebulous and often extremely difficult to diagnose, and even more difficult to treat and strategize. People who may be able to help are described here:

pediatrician—physician specifically trained to treat children

psychologist or psychiatrist—professionals trained in areas of emotional disorders

neurologist—physician specifically trained in sensory or motor responses due to nervous system impairments

special educators—specialists with knowledge of normal and atypical children's development and appropriate education strategies

Other Methods

Other Methods to Record Attention Span:

Anecdotal/Running Records—In recording an incident or sample of behavior, attention span may be observed and noted.

Checklist/Rating Scales—Criteria may be included where an inference about attention span is noted.

Frequency Count—An individual child could be the focus of a Frequency Count, noting every time the child changes activity by choice, inferring a long or short attention span depending on the number of changes over a certain period.

Conversations or Interviews—When talking with a child, the child's ability to sustain the conversation or tendency to wander and not be able to concentrate could give indications of attention span.

Work Samples—The child's work may show a short or long attention span—one swipe with a paint brush, one block placed on end, compared to page-covered paintings or intricate block buildings.

Media—Photographs showing the child concentrating, audio recordings of involved conversations, or video recordings following the child from choice to choice can document attention span.

Key Terms

accommodation
Attention Deficit Disorder (ADD)
Attention Deficit Hyperactivity Disorder (ADHD)
animism
artificialism
assimilation
association
attention deficit
attention span
autism
brain hemisphericity
cause and effect
centration
classification
Concrete Operational Stage
conservation

disequilibrium
egocentrism
logico-mathematical knowledge
matching
multiple intelligences
object permanence
one-to-one correspondence
physical knowledge
Preoperational Stage
reversibility
rote counting
self-differentiation
sensitive periods
Sensorimotor Stage
seriation
social conventional knowledge
Time Sample

Plans

Go to the Education CourseMate website, accessed through CengageBrain.com for the following:

Plan Week 7 Part A, Directions for a Time Sample on Attention Span, including What to Do with It, Portfolio Evidence Sheet Example, Sharing with Child and Family, Actions—Read a Book, In the Environment, In the Curriculum, In the Newsletter

Plan Week 7 Part B, Conversations with Group B for Speech and Language

Plan Week 7 Part C, Reflective Journal

Resources

Armstrong, T. (2000). *In their own way*. New York: Jeremy P. Tarcher/Putman.

Cushner, K. H., McClellan, A., & Safford, P. L. (2008). *Human diversity in education: An integrative approach* (6th ed.). New York: McGraw-Hill.

Grisham-Brown, J., Hemmeter, M. L., & Pretti-Frontczak, K. (2005). *Blended practices for teaching young children in inclusive settings*. Baltimore, MD: Paul Brookes.

Hyson, M. (2008). *Enthusiastic and engaged learners: Approaches to learning in the early childhood classroom*. New York: Teachers College Press.

Jensen, E. (2005). *Teaching with the brain in mind* (2nd ed.). Alexandria, VA: Association for Supervision and Curriculum Development.

CHAPTER 8

Using Standardized Measurements to Look at Cognitive Development

OBSERVATION THOUGHT

"A fair assessment of any child cannot be gathered with any one recording instrument on any one day."

NAEYC Standards naeyc

The following NAEYC Standards for Early Childhood Professional Preparation are addressed in this chapter:

Standard 3: *Observing, Documenting, and Assessing to Support Young Children and Families*

Standard 6: *Becoming a Professional*

IN THIS CHAPTER

▶ Using Tests

▶ Looking at Play and Cognitive Development

▶ Assessing Other Developmental Areas While Observing Math and Science Activities

▶ Topics in Observation: "Real" Curriculum

▶ Helping Professionals for Cognitive Concerns

Using Tests

Every family wants to know how their child is doing. Some want to know how their child is doing compared to the rest of the children in the class. Teachers want to know if the children in their class are learning what the teachers have been teaching. Some people (such as school administrators or policymakers) want to know if the children in a class/school/state/nation are learning what they should be learning at a particular age. Politicians want to know if tax dollars are being used efficiently to produce the desired outcomes from the huge investment in programs for young children through Head Start and state preK programs. These school-readiness programs are supposed to even the playing field between white and nonwhite children, economically more and less advantaged, and to equalize opportunity and benefit society. Results. Outcomes. Accountability. But how will we know?

A World of Tests

We live in a world of tests. Our driving skills are tested before we can obtain a driver's license. Doctors are tested before they can perform surgery or dispense medications. Teachers in most states must take a test before they can be licensed to teach. Manicurists or beauticians must pass a test before they can perform their skills on a person's nails or hair. Tests are administered for specific purposes:

- to gain information on which to take action—such as medical tests
- to certify a certain level of competence in order to issue a license
- to assess knowledge and skills learned in a particular environment

There have always been tests in school to assess knowledge, either developed by the teacher (directly connected to what the teacher taught) or developed for the broader purpose of measuring students against students in other classes, across the state or nation, compared to other nations, or against a sample of similar students. In the twenty-first century, there are movements to test children at younger and younger ages using tests that are developed to compare results on nationwide standards. It is important for the early childhood teacher to understand the use of tests in measuring children's development. It is even more important for teachers to become knowledgeable about when and where tests are appropriate, and to advocate on behalf of children when tests are not appropriate.

Since the first edition of this textbook was written in 1995 there has been an increase in the use of formal assessments and **standardized tests** on young children. These are sometimes "**high stakes tests**" used to make decisions about kindergarten entrance, "readiness" or "placement" in various levels of kindergarten. A milestone in U.S. educational history took place in the fall of 2003. That year the largest administration of a single standardized test—the Head Start National Reporting System, or NRS—was launched. At an estimated total cost in excess of $25 million annually (including direct and indirect costs), approximately 450,000 four-year-olds from every state and nearly every locale in the nation began to be administered the NRS twice yearly. The preliminary results indicated that Head Start participation raised vocabulary and math knowledge and the social-emotional component added later showed increases in cooperation; however these increases were not statistically significant by the end of first grade. Critics say standardized tests have been used

Figure 8–1 Testing has become the accepted measure of child, teacher, and curriculum accountability, but Portfolios show what a child knows and can do.

© Cengage Learning 2012

to unfairly penalize children who are poor, from a racial or ethnic minority, whose first language is not English, or who are divergent and creative thinkers. In testing children in the second grade and younger, Bagnato and Neisworth (2004) call this movement "the mismeasure of young children," using tests designed for older children with no evidence base in early childhood. Young children are unreliable test takers because they are not cognitively mature enough to follow verbal or written directions, make choices from multiple answers, or control behavior long enough to attend to the task. Tests are being used for **screening**, eligibility for special programs, and to determine the effectiveness of teachers and schools, with much riding on the results. An unintended consequence is that often instruction time is focused toward test-taking techniques and test content rather than allowing children to construct knowledge in a way that is relevant to them (Meisels, 2007). This chapter is not designed to teach "how to" use standardized tests, but to familiarize the reader with the uses and misuses of tests (Figure 8–1) and ultimately, of course, to make the case for "authentic assessment" by observation and documentation as a valid and reliable way of finding out what children know and can do.

No Child Left Behind

Here is a brief overview of a very complex and controversial educational law, the No Child Left Behind (NCLB) Act, passed in 2001 and intended to improve the performance of primary and secondary schools. The purpose behind this federal law was to require states, school districts, and schools to focus on the outcomes of teaching, holding schools accountable for improving student achievement in reading and math. According to the law, schools must set measurable milestones to show they are achieving *adequate yearly progress* by the 2013–2014 school year. They must show that they are providing "highly qualified" teachers and funding for low-achieving students in reading. The law mandates annual testing of primary and middle school students (grades 3 through 8) in reading and math. It also requires that schools use "scientifically based research" in establishing curricula, as measured by statistical (quantitative) research methods, primarily standardized tests. There are numerous conditions, penalties, and threats for *schools in need of improvement.*

This sounds like a reasonable plan; however, in reality, critics say the goals are unachievable and unfair. It places a great burden on schools to find, hire, and retain qualified teachers, especially in rural, inner-city, and high-poverty areas. There are few or no provisions or accommodations for children with special needs and non-native English speakers. And for our purposes here, the reliance on standardized test scores, especially for young children (third grade and younger), is inappropriate and not an accurate measure of the child's progress, the teacher's competence, or the school's effectiveness (Neil, 2006; Yell et al., 2006). The mandated tests beginning in grade 3 had a trickle-down effect on grades K–2 to prepare for the tests, even down into the preschool years. There is little doubt that NCLB has had a profound effect on America's educational system, and attempts to reform, modify, or nullify it have resulted in little change.

In 2012, The Race to the Top Early Learning Challenge awarded $500 million in competitive grants to states that demonstrated plans to promote kindergarten readiness, coordinate programs for children from birth through age five, and increase access to high-quality programs for children with high needs. One of the components of the grant application was to develop and support effective uses of comprehensive assessment systems based on the state's early learning standards and consistent with the National Research Council's reports on early childhood. This report, "Early Childhood Assessment: Why, What, and How" (Snow, Van Hemel, 2008) can be accessed online at The National Academies Press website (a direct link is available on the Education CourseMate website).

The Standards Movement

A **standard** is a statement that defines a goal or practice written by authorities in the field. Standards are developed with three principles in mind: to give clarity to the breadth and depth of the subject matter; to set expectations for achievement and performance; and to set **benchmarks** for accountability (Kendall & Marzano, 2004). NCLB mandated that states set high standards in content areas for primary and secondary grades. Early childhood had not historically been included in many of the subject standards. However, since the rise of the school reform movement following the publication of the National Commission on Excellence in Education's *A Nation at Risk: The Imperative for Educational Reform* (1983), which included an imperative for "school readiness," things began to change. Most sets of standards now address the preschool population. There are thousands of educational standards in various disciplines, but most content experts in the field agree that integrating the curriculum among subject areas is necessary. Content standards inform teachers of the what of teaching while weaving them into the who, recognizing the developmental level and community and cultural context of the children in the group. Teaching with standards in mind does not mean a standardized curriculum, *one size fits all*, but it means using knowledge of multiple disciplines and the children in your group to create learning environments and opportunities that advance what children know and can do.

Most people in the early childhood field are familiar with *Developmentally Appropriate Practice in Early Childhood Programs* (Copple & Bredekamp, 2009), setting standards for quality early childhood education practices. But many may be less familiar with other organizations or content monitoring associations that delineate standards for specific content areas. Many have included or are adding early childhood standards as well. Some of the content organizations setting standards are:

Art: *National Visual Arts Standards*—National Art Education Association (http://www.naea-reston.org)

Inclusive Education: *Division for Early Childhood—DEC Recommended Practices: A Comprehensive Guide* (http://www.dec-sped.org)

English: *Standards for the English Language Arts*—National Council of Teachers of English and International Reading Association (http://www.ncte.org)

English as a Second Language: *ESL Standards for PreK–12 Students*—Teachers of English to Speakers of Other Languages (http://www.tesol.org)

Head Start: *Head Start Child Outcomes Framework*—Department of Health and Human Services (http://eclkc.ohs.acf.hhs.gov/hslc)

Health and Safety Standards for Child Care: *Caring for Our Children: National Health and Safety Performance Standards: Guidelines for Out-of-Home Child Care Programs*—American Academy of Pediatrics (http://nrckids.org—Go to Caring for Our Children, Third Edition.

Health Education: *National Health Education Standards*—American Association for Health Education (http://www.aahperd.org)

High/Scope: *Key Experiences*—High/Scope (http://www.highscope.org)

Mathematics: *Principles and Standards for School Mathematics*—National Council of Teachers of Mathematics (http://www.nctm.org)

Compendium of K–12 Standards—McRel Mid Continent Research for Education and Learning. A compendium of standards and benchmarks from many different arenas arranged by content area. (http://www.mcrel.org)

Music: *Benchmarks in Action: A Guide to Standards-Based Assessment in Music*—The National Association for Music Education (http://www.menc.org)

Physical Education: *Active Start: A Statement of Physical Activity Guidelines for Children Birth to Five Years*—National Association for Sport & Physical Education (http://www.aahperd.org)—Go to National Association for Sport and Physical Education.

Science: *Benchmarks for Science Literacy*—American Association for the Advancement of Science (http://www.project2061.org)

Social Studies: *Expectations of Excellence*—National Council for the Social Studies (http://www.ncss.org)

Technology: *National Educational Technology Standards*—International Society for Technology in Education (http://www.cnets.iste.org)

Each state is developing its own early childhood development standards so early childhood professionals also need to be familiar with their own state's early learning standards.

There are standards by which programs can be assessed. (See Chapter 13 for a discussion of these.)

There are also standards for early childhood professionals and preparation programs.

DEC Recommended Practices in Early Childhood Intervention/Early Childhood Special Education (www.dec-sped.org)

Head Start Program Performance Standards (www.acf.hss.gov)—Go to performance standards in the search box.

Family Child Care Accreditation Standards—National Association of Family Child Care (http://nafcc.org)

NAEYC Professional Preparation Standards at Associate Degree, Initial Licensure and Advance Degrees—National Association for the Education of Young Children (http://www.naeyc.org)

Program Standards—National Council for Accreditation of Teacher Education (http://www.ncate.org)

National Board Certification Standards—National Board for Professional Teaching Standards (http://www.nbpts.org)

Child Development Associate Competencies—Council for Professional Recognition (http://www.cdacouncil.org)

With so many standards, it can be difficult to evaluate how to apply and integrate them into a particular curriculum or program. Seefeldt (2005) gives these suggestions for negotiating the standards:

▶ From these standards, what is meaningful for the children I teach?

▶ What elements from these standards set the foundation for further learning?

▶ What do children already know, and what do I want them to learn?

▶ How can I develop firsthand experiences in this subject area for children to be active learners?

▶ How can I integrate this with what children already know?

Standards and Home Visiting

Regardless of the age of the child being served through home-based early education, it is important that the visiting educator is mindful of the system of standards and benchmarks that have been adopted by local preschools and the school system that the child is likely to attend. Having that information helps home educators incorporate content standards into meaningful and relevant learning opportunities in the home. While this initially can seem quite challenging, the questions posed by Seefeldt in the preceding paragraph provide a useful framework for designing meaningful learning opportunities in the home.

Formal Assessment Measures

Fairness is a quality that most people would hold in high esteem. Fairness in assessing children should have even greater appeal.

EXERCISE **Consider the following:**

▶ This bag of potato chips holds 11.2 ounces and is priced at $1.89. Another bag of potato chips holds 8 ounces and is priced at $1.69. Which is a fairer price?

▶ You take a class and the final exam has 100 questions and 10 essays. Your friend takes the same class taught by another teacher and the final is a take-home exam. In evaluating which of you learned more, is one testing approach fairer than the other?

▶ You have been waiting in line to order food. A clerk opens a new line. Another customer walks up and is waited on before you. "It's not fair!"

Trying to determine what is fair necessitates a standard measure. To calculate the best value, you need to convert the price to cost per ounce, a standard comparison. To assess how much you each learned from the class, a common exam would be given. To serve customers in the order in which they came to the counter, the store would need a number system or require clerks to call out, "I'll help the next person in line." Standard measures ensure fairness. The difficulty comes in assessing fairly what one child knows against what another child knows and using a test given on any specific day. To what do we attribute a high or low score? Was it the teacher? Was it the child on that particular day? Was it the family? Fair assessment is always difficult.

Standardized Tests

The word *standardized* means to apply the same measure in the same way to determine an individual result compared to an expected response. It is *conventional* in that all test materials, which may be supplied in a kit or gathered by the tester, are the same and each child is expected to use them in the same way, indicating a level of development. A standardized test is constructed by a content specialist and designed to measure specific aspects of development or behavior. It is usually administered by a trained tester using a specific set of procedures and must be completed in a limited time. It has a **quantitative scoring** system. The results are scored against the **norm**, the group on whom the test was researched, identified by age, gender, race, geographic region, and socioeconomic status. The norm group's average scores then become the scores against which later test-takers are compared.

Norm-referenced tests compare the child on specific characteristics with same-age peers. These are often used to screen for potential developmental delay or disability. They are based on broad abilities that most children will possess, revealing only those children who may need further evaluation (McAfee & Leong, 2002; Pellegrini & Bjorklund, 1998). Criterion-referenced tests compare the child to a predetermined standard or criterion, used to assess current skills or track toward a developmental outcome. These outcomes are determined from a cross section of the population and scored in comparison to that population.

The Checklists discussed in Chapter 3 are standardized, based on common expectations for a child of a certain age, based on maturation (criterion referenced). All children of that age are measured by the same scale because human development has been studied and determined to be fairly "standard."

Standardized Testing as an Assessment Method. Before any standardized test is given, some questions should be answered:

1. What is the purpose of the test? The test should have a clear benefit to the child or the program.
2. What is the design of the test? Is it **valid**? In testing terms, valid refers to whether the test measures what it's supposed to measure. If a test's purpose was to measure the ability to multiply but only asked addition questions, it would not be valid. What is the **reliability** of the test? Would the same score be obtained on subsequent tests of the same nature? Because it is difficult to obtain valid and reliable data, especially on the cognitive abilities of children under six, only trained professionals with a specific need to know should administer that type of test. Standardized tests must fit the developmental level of the child, be administered individually (not in a group) for children under six, be short in duration, and be given in the child's natural setting (home or school), preferably by a person known to the child.
3. How will the results be used? No single test should be the basis for an important decision regarding the child's placement or diagnosis. Other methods of data collection should be considered, such as input from the family, observational data from the school, and direct information from the child.

🏠 Home Visiting and Standardized Tests

Similar to classroom settings, home educators are required to follow the agency's directives around the use/non-use of standardized tests. While developmental screenings are recommended to be used routinely in the home, programs often require additional assessments. Whenever administering screenings or assessments in the home, consideration should be given to the context of the setting and how that might impact the child's participation and resulting outcome. If conditions in the home are not conducive to the child's ability to focus appropriately, home educators should discuss with parents or caregiver possibilities of making adjustments within the environment or moving to a more suitable space.

Appropriate Uses of Early Childhood Assessments. The National Educational Goals Panel (see Shepard, Kagan, & Wurtz, 1998) was formed to "improve methods of assessing the readiness of children for school that would lead to alternatives to currently used early childhood assessments" (Figure 8–2).

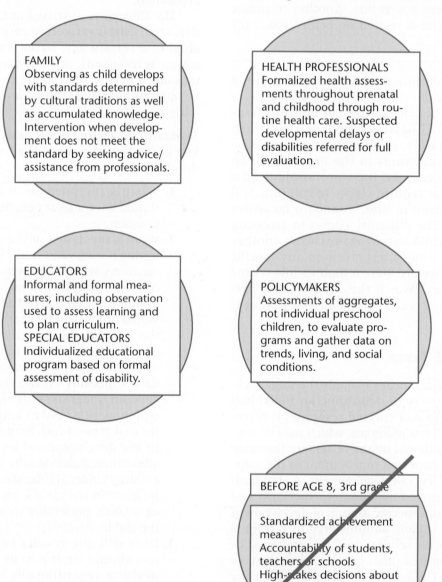

Figure 8–2 Appropriate Assessments of Children. (Adapted from Shepard, L., Kagan, S.L., & Wurtz, E. [1998] *Principles and recommendations for Early Childhood Assessments.* Washington, DC: National Education Goals.)

© Cengage Learning 2014

Purpose 1. Assessing to promote children's learning and development. The classroom teacher, along with the family, knows the child best. Seeing a child day after day, alongside other children the same age, viewed through a lens suffused with the knowledge of child development, an accurate assessment of the child's learning and development can be made without a purchased, standardized test. Observations such as those supported by this book can provide an **authentic assessment** of what the child knows and can do (Meisels, Bickel, Nicholson, Xue, & Atkins-Burnett, 2001; Neisworth & Bagnato, 2004). These are "low-stakes" assessments because significant intervention is not taking place based on these assessments. They are used as benchmarks for development and for curriculum planning purposes.

Purpose 2. Assessing to identify children for health and special services. Federal legislation—the Individuals with Disabilities Education Act (IDEA), passed in 1975—mandated early screening for the identification of children with disabilities. Later amendments required family involvement and earlier screenings of infants and toddlers. Screening involves testing large numbers of individuals in a short amount of time to find those who need to be further evaluated. The IDEA provided the definition of developmental delay, supported by performance on a standardized assessment instrument and specific observations in developmental domains. After a full evaluation indicated by the screenings, the law mandates school districts to provide appropriate services. Some screening instruments commonly used are the Hawaii Early Learning Profile (HELP; VORT Corporation, 1995) and Ages & Stages Questionnaires®, Third Edition (ASQ-3™), Bricker & Squires, 2009. Some full-evaluation instruments commonly used are the Bayley Scales of Infant Development II (Bayley, 1993) and the Brigance Diagnostic Inventory of Early Development II (Brigance, 2004). Most of these require prior training by the person administering the test. These are known as **high-stakes tests** because they may be used to make classification and intervention plans. To fairly represent the abilities of the child, it is important to rely on multiple sources for information, and consensus on an intervention plan must be reached by the family and a range of professionals.

Purpose 3. Assessing to monitor trends and evaluate programs and services. The Goals Panel recommends that preschool programs and services be assessed on a state or national level, focusing only on the conditions of learning, such as the percentage of low-income children who attend quality preschool programs. Early childhood education trends in early learning should be assessed not on individual children's scores but on a matrix or sampling of a nonintrusive standardized test (Shepard, Kagan, & Wurtz, 1998). Individual program assessments are important for quality assurance for the program itself and as an indicator of quality for consumers, families, and funders. See Chapter 13 for a full discussion of program assessment.

Purpose 4. Assessing academic achievement to hold individual students, teachers, and schools accountable. This too is considered high-stakes testing, because these test scores are used to make decisions about the retention of individual students, teachers' tenure, and schools' allocation of funding. The Goals Panel recommends that there be "no high-stakes accountability testing of individual children before the end of third grade" (Shepard, Kagan, & Wrutz, 1998, p. 21). The panel recommends that instructionally relevant assessments be part of the educational program in kindergarten through second grade. Prior to third grade, only the teachers and programs should keep records of individual student achievement.

Meisels and Atkins-Burnett (2000) proposed principles of appropriate assessment for young children. Assessments should be used

▶ for assessing all areas of development through multiple sources of information.
▶ with repeated opportunities to demonstrate developmental competence.
▶ with the involvement of the most trusted caregiver.
▶ as a framework of developmental timetables, but recognizing differences among children.
▶ emphasizing real abilities, not artificial situations.
▶ for identifying strengths and abilities.
▶ collaboratively between families and professionals.
▶ as a first step in potential intervention.
▶ for group and individual planning. (pp. 231–257)

Difficulty in Assessing Young Children with Standardized Tests

There are three major reasons why standardized testing may not be an adequate measure of what a young child knows and can do: the nature of a young child, the test itself, and the uses or misuses of the results.

It Happened to Me

The "Wrong" Answer

This didn't happen to me but to a colleague. She was required to give a standardized test to her class of inner-city kindergartners. One of the questions the tester had to read was the following: "Here are several dogs. What is this one called?" as she pointed to a collie. The child answered "Lassie," and the teacher had to mark it wrong. In that same test, the child had to correctly identify a doily. In many homes, children have never seen a doily. In another assessment the child was asked, "What color is a banana?" The child answered "white"—wrong—a banana is yellow. Mine are more likely black! Do you see how arbitrary some standardized tests can be?

EXERCISE   Imagine that you took a test and found out you failed. Jot down how each of the possible reasons that might have been the cause of your failure:

The room.
The person giving the test.
The subject matter of the test.
The importance of the test to you.
The new format of the test.
The way the test was scored.
Your health.
You are physically challenged.
You are in big trouble that has nothing to do with the test.
Your native language is Russian. The test is in English.
Your mother left you here in this strange building to take the test, but you do not know how you will find her later.

These same influences affect the outcomes of a young child taking a test, only more so because they are not able to understand, rationalize, or adjust.

The Child. A major concern in using standardized tests on young children is the nature of the child. Because young children are just that—young—taking tests may be a new experience for them. The way that children confront new experiences varies from child to child. Some just observe, watch, and wait, paralyzed by the novelty. Others will manipulate it and play with it, not recognizing the purpose. They may not understand or follow directions, but rather explore and adapt it to their own style. If the child takes another form of the same test again in a short time, the score may be drastically different. Now they have experience, or have thought of other ways to try it out.

Preliterate (birth to age 8) children cannot be accurately assessed through written answers on a sheet of paper. The purpose of this book is to provide other methods of gathering information about each child's development in order to assess and plan. The change in children's physical, social, linguistic, cognitive, creative, and emotional development is rapid. Because they do not understand the goals of formal testing ("Do your best," "Do it by yourself without help," or "Keep at it until it's finished"), results of pencil-and-paper tests are not accurate assessments.

The Test. A standardized test is an evaluation instrument written for a definite purpose and application. When it indeed does measure what it proposes to measure, it is described as valid. Early forms of the test are tried out on a segment of the population that will be taking the test eventually. This early test group is the norm group against which the rest of the scores are measured. If the norm group is significantly different from the subjects taking the test, the comparison scores will be inaccurate. For example, suppose the norm group in the tryout of a new test consists of 10 children. There are eight boys and two girls, ranging in age from five to eight years old, living in south Florida and attending the same school. Two children are African American, three are Puerto Rican, and one has been sexually abused. Their scores on the test will set the standard against which children in Idaho, Connecticut, and Minnesota will be measured. This is an extreme example to demonstrate the point, but, unfortunately, it is not far from reality. It is difficult to select a norm group that represents all the variables in exact proportions to the subjects taking the test. Standardized tests have a high risk of being discriminatory because of the comparison to the norm group. The results may be skewed by factors such as geographic region, level of development (urban, suburban, or rural), and different socialization experiences due to culture, economic situation, family dynamics, and native language.

The expectation of standardized tests is that the same subject taking the same type of test in a reasonable period will obtain a similar score. This is known as test reliability. Many standardized tests for young children are not reliable. Children are easily influenced by the test setting, which may be new to them. The examiner may be a stranger to them. They are separated from their family and may not know how to take a test. They lack the ability to screen out noises, hunger, or fear that may divert their attention.

Binet and Simon (1905) developed the original intelligence test in France for a noble purpose, to provide adequate education for children who needed specialized assistance. They never believed that the quantitative score on the test was the inherent and unchangeable measure of intelligence potential, though many have misconstrued their work with that meaning (Feuerstein, 2010). Many tests administered to children today are for a similar purpose, to identify handicapping conditions for which early intervention would be provided.

Uses of the Test. Many federal and state laws mandate such testing. P.L. 94-142 (1975) provides a free and appropriate public education for children with disabilities between the ages of 3 and 21. P.L. 99-457 (1986) includes infants and toddlers and their families in comprehensive early intervention services. To implement these mandates, it was necessary to identify children who needed services. This was accomplished through a screening, an initial step in identifying those children who had a high probability of developmental delay. Once a screening indicates there might be a delay or problem, a full evaluation or follow-up provides the diagnosis. The diagnosis will determine the type of intervention needed to provide services for the child in the least restrictive environment. These laws have been effective in helping many children and families receive the services they need.

The problem arises when the screenings and tests developed for one purpose are used for other, possibly less helpful ones. Meisels (2007) has criticized the Gesell Preschool Readiness Test as an invalid predictor of success in kindergarten. Many schools use this as a developmental screening tool. Based on its results, a recommendation may be made to delay school entrance or for the child to spend a year in a transitional grade between kindergarten and first grade. Meisels contends this is a misuse of a test that lacks reliability and validity. Tests are misused when they are the sole factor in decisions to place a child in special education or to label them as an individual with a handicapping condition. NAEYC's *Developmentally Appropriate Practice in Early Childhood Programs, Revised Edition* (1997) emphasizes the role of observation: "Decisions that have a major impact on children, such as enrollment or placement, are never made on the basis of a single developmental assessment or screening device but are based on multiple sources of relevant information, particularly observations by teachers and parents" (p. 21).

The NAEYC position and constructivist writings, such as Kamii and Kamii (1990) *in Achievement Testing in the Early Grades: The Games Grown-Ups Play,* enumerate the abuses of testing:

- Results of standardized tests might be inappropriately used as readiness screening tests for placement decisions.
- Standardized testing increases the academic emphasis of the curriculum, which should be localized, not centralized.
- Achievement tests frequently do not reflect current theory or research about how children learn.
- Many schools "teach to the test" to raise school scores.
- Standardized tests cannot predict how well students will do in the future.
- Below third grade, development is uneven and still emergent.
- Racial, cultural, and social biases are evident.
- Numerical results are not useful in curriculum planning for individual students.

Considering the standards movement and reliance on standardized testing from a cautionary perspective, the National Association for the Education of Young Children (NAEYC) and the National Association of Early Childhood Specialists in State Departments of Education (NAECS/SDE) have developed a position statement that includes curriculum, assessment, and program evaluation. It recognizes that learning standards can be valuable in young children's educational experiences, but only "if early learning standards (1) emphasize significant, developmentally appropriate content and outcomes; (2) are developed and reviewed through informed, inclusive processes; (3) use implementation and assessment strategies that are ethical and appropriate for young children; and (4) are accompanied by strong supports for early childhood programs, professionals and families" (NAEYC & NAECS/SDE, 2004).

Naturalistic measures such as the ones presented in this text are more accurate methods for describing each child's development, but they do not make it easy to compare children across classrooms, schools, states, or the nation. There are several reasons put forth for making such comparisons:

- identification of children who need more help in school to succeed
- holding teachers and administrators accountable to carry out the responsibility of helping children to learn
- determining the best practices so they can be applied by others to get better results
- conserving or investing public funding wisely in efficient methods

Those are logical reasons for using formal assessment, and there may be times when formal measuring instruments need to be used. This section is designed to be a guide.

The Case Against Standardized Tests. There are many strong voices against standardized testing for young children from birth through second grade. Bagnato (2004) says the mantra should be "No table-top testing," meaning that assessment based on observation and not standardized tests should be the standard in early childhood. Shepard and Kagan (1998) say that "what works for older children or adults will simply not work for younger children." Sam Meisels (2001), author of the Work Sampling System, a method of performance assessment using Portfolios, says that parents must be convinced that performance assessments, using observations and the children's work, are as trustworthy as standardized tests. Alfie Kohn (2001) is another vocal opponent of standardized tests as an extension of his work on rewards and punishments. He describes several problems with testing young children, including the following:

▶ Standardized testing sets the unrealistic expectation that everyone at the same age acquires the same set of capabilities.
▶ Standardized assessments cannot produce an accurate picture of what a child can do.
▶ The stress on young children to perform on the tests interferes with accurate results.

Kohn (2001) encourages teachers to take an organized stand against testing through advocacy with families and administration. Groups such as the National PTA, the National Association of Early Childhood Specialists in State Departments of Education, the Southern Early Childhood Association, and the American Educational Research Association have issued policy statements of caution regarding group standardized, high-stakes tests for young children.

"Accountability shovedown" is the term Hatch (2002) uses to describe the standards movement, stating it is "so pervasive across educational settings today [it] is threatening children in early childhood in the same ways as the curriculum shovedown movement did in the 1980s" (p. 457). He sees child observation changing from a strategy for shaping curriculum to a device for monitoring student progress. Among the troubling results of this trend, Hatch includes the following:

increasing pressure on children
increasing pressure on teachers
narrowing of experiences
accountability as punishment rather than motivation for improvement

teacher deprofessionalization
an emphasis on performance over learning
individual devaluation
an emphasis on sameness versus diversity
questionable benefits to school improvement
increasing corporate mentality

He challenges teachers with this statement: "Our accountability comes from an ethical commitment to do what is right for every child, not from measuring productivity according to an arbitrary set of narrowly defined outcomes" (p. 460).

Stress indicators such as wiggling, chewing on pencils, twisting hair, playing with clothes, complaining of feeling tired, and crying were observed in kindergartners during standardized tests (Fleege, Charlesworth, Burts, & Hart, 1996). These behaviors had not been present in observations done weeks before the California Achievement Test was administered to groups of 10 children. In addition to the stress, other behaviors such as copying, refusing to continue, calling out answers, and asking for reassurance of correct answers indicated that children did not understand, nor could they comply with test-taking rules. Increased stress and inaccurate results due to the developmental level of children are two of the main arguments against group-administered standardized tests for young children. Neuman and Roskos (2000) state, "Because children's knowledge and skills are in constant motion, these tests tend not to be reliable or valid measures of what children can do in typical situations" (p. 24). By watching what a child can do, listening to what a child says, and documenting the changes in those things over time in the developmental domains, an authentic assessment of the child's progress can be made during the regular activities throughout the course of the school day. (Figure 8–3).

Authentic assessment assumes that children in a supportive setting will initiate and direct their own learning, constructing knowledge at their own rate physically, emotionally, socially, and intellectually. It also assumes that learning proceeds from concrete to abstract. Children learn by interacting with an enriched environment that recognizes and values different intelligences and is facilitated by an adult who has specialized training and skills. Teaching is individualized and in small groups. Individual learning needs are acknowledged based on objective evaluation of each child's strengths, moving the child forward in the continuum of learning through relevant curriculum. Assessment is rooted in principles of child growth and development and involves a collaboration of child, teacher, family, and other professionals as needed.

The form of that assessment is in question. Teachers ask, "How can a test manufactured in New Jersey

Figure 8–3 Objective and systematic observation and documentation during play can assess all developmental areas.

measure what the children have learned about magnets in my class in Nevada? How can the test maker in New Jersey even know if my class in Nevada has worked with magnets?" The test can only measure it if the teachers know what is on the test and make sure that it is taught in the classroom. In this way, it is the test determining the curriculum, instead of measuring achievement. Methods of authentic assessment, then, must be locally based to measure the progress of a distinct group of children. This is done by "keeping track" (Kamii & Kamii, 1990, pp. 120, 121) of their work on three levels:

1. Descriptive data about each child that can be analyzed by the teacher as well as outside evaluators.
2. Summaries and interpretations of that data by the teacher to evaluate the effectiveness of teaching methods and the individual progress of the child.
3. Quantitative information that gives statistical analysis of the whole group, against which individual children may be compared to adjust the curriculum.

These principles of performance assessment are consistent with the knowledge of child growth and development, as well as with developmentally appropriate practice. Assessment by observation and recording using multiple techniques is repeated in a systematic way. The Portfolio documents the child's progress and is shared with the parents and the child. That describes what can be achieved by *Week by Week* assessment planning.

What's a Teacher to Do?

The TRACE Center for Excellence in Early Childhood Assessment, funded by the U.S. Department of Education, conducts research on evidence-based early

childhood assessments and the validity and reliability of authentic assessment (Bagnato & Neisworth, 2010). Their guidelines coincide closely with the *Week by Week* system—using multiple observers, over time, in real settings, for the purpose of discovering progress and individualizing the curriculum.

If You Have to Administer a Standardized Test. Because tests are becoming a fact of life for early educators, here is some advice for teachers and families with young children (Benner, 2003; Epstein et al., 2004; Kohn, 2001; S. Martin, 2007; Puckett & Black, 2008; Shepard & Kagan, 1998):

1. No testing of young children should occur unless it can be shown to lead to beneficial results.
2. Know child development ages, stages, and milestones, understanding the range of individual rates and styles for those stages. This will give you a basis against which to measure each child's progress. A red flag should go up when a child does not appear to be progressing in development. Then an evaluation with a standardized instrument may be necessary.
3. If a formal assessment is used, the content, form, validity, and standards for interpretation should match the purpose of the assessment.
4. If a diagnostic test is called for to determine the cause or extent of a developmental lag, the following considerations should be made:
    - The test should be administered by a qualified professional using carefully selected tests (preferably more than one).
    - The child should not be forced to separate from the parents, causing undue stress that could negatively affect the results of the test.
    - Tests that consist of isolated tasks resulting in a score do not give a complete picture of how the child uses those skills in the context of everyday interactions, so the assessment should consist of a wider range of criteria.
    - The tests should not carry more weight for decisions about the child than testimony from families and teachers and direct observations of the child in familiar environments.
5. The test's purpose should be to improve performance, not just to monitor it for measuring the effectiveness of a program, teacher, or school.
6. The test should be individually administered. Young children are still developing the skill of following directions, so a group-administered test is not appropriate.
7. Formal tests should be skill-based rather than verbal or written, allowing the child as much

© Cengage Learning 2014

time as needed to complete the tasks and feel supported by the person administering the test.

8. Do no more preparation than necessary. Time spent in preparation for tests is time not spent on the subjects children want to know about. Families and teachers prepping children on items to be tested may also skew test results.

The National Association for the Education of Young Children (2003) has developed a set of guidelines regarding appropriate curriculum content and assessment in programs serving children ages three through eight. In Chapter 14, these guidelines are applied to the *Week by Week* observation and recording plan.

Advantages

Standardized tests, *used appropriately*, may be

▶ fair, objective assessments of a child's capabilities.

▶ recognized tests and scores used by intervention professionals.

▶ used with other forms of information about the child to contribute to an overall picture of the child.

Disadvantages

Standardized tests are used inappropriately when

▶ children feel pressure during testing.

▶ norms may not match the child's cultural and socioeconomic circumstances.

▶ young children's performance assessment is affected by the child's lack of experience with testing protocol.

▶ they are used to make decisions about the child based on a false reading.

▶ test results punish economically disadvantaged children and children whose first language is not English.

Pitfalls to Avoid

Advice for the use of standardized tests:

▶ Do not allow testing that places children under stress.

▶ Be sure the test is administered by a trained professional.

▶ Advocate for multiple sources of information about the child to be used in any decision about placement, readiness, or intervention.

Go to the Education CourseMate website, accessed through CengageBrain.com for plans and resources.

Using Technology

Several child development rating systems have technology components that collect data and analyze and provide reports and individualized curriculum plans based on the scoring.

How to Find the Time

The whole purpose of using technology is to save time. The benefits of electronic data collection and storage is that retrieval of stored information is much faster than wading through paper files. There is always the cost of time invested to learn a new system, and of course the cost involved in purchasing and maintaining the products. Each program must weigh the cost to determine if the technology really does save time.

What to Do With It

As mentioned above, certain data collection systems store information electronically. It is important, as with all records—hard copies or electronic—that the records be kept confidential, easily accessible for those who need the information, and safe for future use. Electronic files must be backed up by an off-site system and protected by passwords with limited need-to-know access. The Portfolio Evidence Sheet provides a listing of all data collected (See Example in Figure 8–4)

Looking at Play and Cognitive Development

In the last few decades, more and more emphasis has been placed on the "school readiness" of preschool children and meeting standards in the early grades. In this quest for measurable outcomes, the challenge of inputs has swung away from play toward the teaching of literacy and other academic skills. Children engaged in play use large and small muscles in moving and manipulating objects, language skills in describing and directing their play, creativity in using curiosity and imagination in representing mental images, social skills in negotiating with others, emotional skills in exhibiting self-control, and mathematical skills in solving problems of space and quantity. All of these are brain-related experiences, using and expanding cognition. Researchers have found evidence that play contributes to advances in "verbalization, vocabulary, language comprehension, attention span, imagination, concentration, impulse control, curiosity, problem-solving strategies,

PORTFOLIO EVIDENCE OF CHILD'S DEVELOPMENT			
Evidence Type	Date	Recorder	Notes
COGNITIVE – the child's cognitive development including science, math, technology, attention span			
TS	10/24/	BAN	Works in several areas – mostly large blocks
CK	10/29/	BAN	Math checklist – counts to 10, accuracy counting objects to 5
AR	11/19/	MLS	Sorts & classified nature materials
CL	12/13/	MLS	Completed 8 piece puzzle
TS	12/18/	MLS	Worked at computer with 2 other children for 18 min

Figure 8–4 Portfolio Evidence Sheet Example.

REVIEW

STANDARDIZED TESTS

A standardized test is one in which the administration, scoring, and interpretation procedures are prescribed in the test manual and must be strictly followed. The test is usually norm referenced.

Types of Information Gathered by Standardized Tests
- Literacy level
  - Vocabulary
  - Comprehension
  - Communication of ideas
- Mathematics concepts and computation
- Science concepts
- Analytical thinking

cooperation, empathy and group participation" (Bodrova & Leong, 2003). However, more and more classroom practice is depending on "scripted" curriculum that dictates the exact processes, even the words to say, toward achieving the expected outcomes and direct instruction techniques where the teacher leads the whole group in simultaneous paper and pencil exercises.

The Alliance for Childhood (Miller & Almon, 2009) reports on three studies of time spent daily in kindergartens in New York City and Los Angeles (Figure 8–5). Choice time (play) accounted for less than half an hour, but literacy and math instruction amounted to almost twice as much time or more. Testing and test preparation take almost as much time as play time. Teachers in these same classrooms who were asked about the barriers that accounted for the small amount of play and playful learning cited three main reasons: the curriculum does not incorporate it, there was not enough time, and the administration does not value it. While most teachers expressed a desire to incorporate more play, the extrinsic political reasons overrode their beliefs.

The kinds of play that yield the most benefits are not the chaotic, run from one thing to another types, but an environment designed to be child-initiated rather than teacher-directed, that engages and holds children's attention. The teacher sets the stage and then observes and supports the playful learning with additional props or materials, by asking thought-provoking questions to spark more in-depth thinking, and by developing strong relationships with the students. "Children taught in a more playful manner almost always achieve more than children who are subjected to more direct teaching methods . . . (that create) students who are less likely to get along with their peers and feel comfortable in school and more likely to show evidence of stress-induced hyperactivity, to be hostile, and to engage in antisocial acts" (Hirsh-Pasek et al., 2009). Feuerstein (2010) describes a technique he calls mediated learning

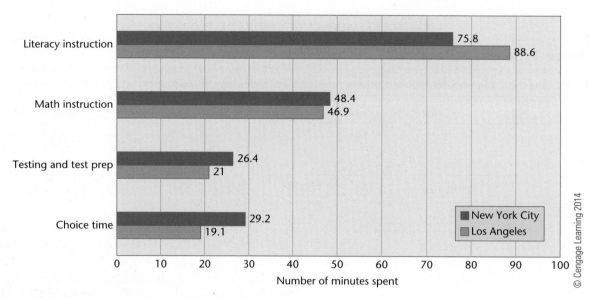

Figure 8–5 Daily Kindergarten Schedule in Two Cities. Two Kindergartens.

Source: Reprinted with permission from Miller, E. & Almon, J., *Crisis in the Kindergarten: Why Children Need to Play in School*. College Park MD: Alliance for Childhood, 2009, p. 28.

experience to change cognitive structures so that even very low functioning children can learn to adapt the way they approach learning with amazing results. It is not direct verbal instruction, but builds on the interest of the child, interacting, guiding, demonstrating, and repeating with intentionality. It sounds very much like the research of Vygotsky.

Play and Vygotsky

In the Vygotskian approach play is constructed with another child or an adult. The younger the child, the larger role the adult has in play by describing what the child is doing and initiating and keeping the play going. In this approach play is defined as an imaginary situation that has roles with expectations, and it includes language by dictating the role, "You be . . . and I'll be . . ." and language creates and maintains the play. The play has specific roles and rules in which the child self-regulates her behavior and negotiates with others. Symbolic thinking, the foundation for literacy, is displayed by the substitution of present objects for imagined objects, and later verbalizing the symbolism, "This block is my phone."

Vygotsky (1966/1977) saw development on two levels: what the child can do independently and what the child can do with assistance from another. The distance between these two levels is the zone of proximal development (ZPD). Vygotskians do not see infant/adult interactions as play, since it is performed at the Sensorimotor Stage of cognitive development, but the attachment to the adult sets the stage for the unorganized elements of play in toddlerhood where the adult is still taking the primary lead. It is during

the preschool years that children's play takes on more complex play themes with multiple players and roles. At this stage the adult's mediation takes simpler play schemes and introduces a way that the actions can become organized. Planning for the next day's play is an important part of Vygotsky's play approach by stimulating memory, gathering materials, or making notes as a reminder of where to take up the play scheme. As children move into the elementary years, games with rules become more important in which the child learns self-regulation, again with the adult taking a minor role in clarifying the rules rather than dictating and enforcing them. Vygotsky's view of play is one of active involvement by the child and the adult, learning in the social context (Bodrova & Leong, 2007).

Cognitive Development: Math, Science, and Technology

By now you should understand that cognitive development and every other developmental domain are interdependent on each other executive function. Galinsky (2010, p. 4) says they are "like a boss managing our attention, our emotions and our behavior in order to reach our goals, not just intellectual skills, they involve weaving together our social, emotional and intellectual capacities." Also, I am sure you realize that even though the rest of this chapter focuses on math, science, and technology, those subjects are but a few of the areas that are affected by cognitive development. Math, science, and technology have been selected for this chapter because of their growing importance, and, sorry to say, their neglected emphasis in many early childhood classrooms (Early et al., 2007; Stipek, 2008; Tu, 2006). The U.S. Department of Education and the National Science Foundation have many initiatives to broaden and deepen the workforce preparation skills in science, technology, engineering, and mathematics (STEM). Many of these are addressing the beginnings of knowledge acquired in the preschool years, placing the burden on the preschool teacher to have foundational competence in these fields as well.

Young children begin learning about these areas by matching, balancing blocks, seeing and making patterns, knowing about animals and rocks, logical reasoning, and using computers. Young children are curious, inventive, and persistent. Math and science concepts are concretely connected to vocabulary in using words to describe the attributes of things and explore "What would happen if . . .?"

Think About It . . .

How do you feel when you read these words?
Mathematics
Physics
Geometry
Hypothesis

In looking further at **cognitive** development, it is important to consider not just the knowledge of the subject matter but the other dimensions of development. Lillian Katz (1988), a great stimulator of thought in the field of early childhood education, reminds educators that learning is not just knowledge as an accumulation of facts, skills, or the ability to function in a certain way. Knowledge also involves **dispositions**, habits of the mind. Those are the ways that each individual responds to experiences. Some people have the disposition to quit after a defeat or embarrassment. The same situation may cause someone else with a different disposition to try harder, while still another casts blame or reflects on the situation and seeks advice.

The dispositions, feelings, or emotional responses to the fields of mathematics and science affect many early childhood educators. Perhaps it is the nonacademic track through which some have entered the field. Perhaps it is the manifestation of learning-style theory: People with strong logical thinking skills become engineers, while those with interpersonal learning styles and skills become educators. Or it may be the sex role socialization that girls unconsciously absorb from school as the "hidden curriculum," and from the media, family, and peers. Whatever the cause, aversion to math and science has kept many early childhood classrooms from having interesting and challenging math and science learning areas. Consequently, the

foundations have not been adequately laid upon which children can build knowledge. Teachers need to have a knowledge base of mathematical and science thinking and learning not only to plan meaningful experiences, but also to recognize when math and science learning is taking place and engage in content-related talk (Baroody, 2004; Isenberg, 2008; Klibanoff et al., 2006). Talking with and involving families in early math and science learning is also an area in which researchers have seen a need for more professional development of early childhood teachers (Cannon & Ginsburg, 2008; Copley, 2004). The math and science experiences begin with the teacher's own learning.

In *Last Child in the Woods*, Louv (2008) raises our consciousness, saying we are raising a generation of children with a "nature-deficit disorder." Possible reasons could be our busy lives, concern for safety, shrinking natural areas near urban centers, and just plain negligence. Rivkin (Harlan & Rivkin, 2000), an early childhood educator, addresses the emotions of science, urging us to cultivate and nurture a joy in the beauty of nature, a childlike curiosity, and the quest to make sense of things. She urges teachers to examine sexist messages that science is a man's field and to work against the perpetuation of that idea.

Using rocks and sand, Ogu and Schmidt (2009) suggest ways to address multiple learning styles through the inquiry-based approach, beginning with asking good questions, investigating new theories outside children's prior knowledge to seek answers, and reflecting and organizing the new knowledge.

Such "science process" skills (Charlesworth & Lind, 2013) sound like authentic assessment of a child's development from Figure 8–6.

If teachers have feelings of inadequacy and avoidance around math, science, and technology, there will be little to observe. The teacher must become conscious of this lack of confidence and competence. The infusion and requirements for math, science, and technology coursework for early childhood teachers will better prepare them to teach young children, planning learning environments and activities that explore foundational concepts.

▶❚❚ TEACHSOURCE VIDEO ACTIVITY

Go to the Education CourseMate website, accessed through CengageBrain.com and view the video entitled School-Age Children – Emergent Curriculum

How did the children in this episode use their creativity to launch into learning, using the Basic Process Skills?

BASIC PROCESS SKILLS

1. *Observing.* Using the senses to gather information about objects or events.
2. *Comparing.* Looking at similarities and differences in real objects. In the primary grades, students begin to compare and contrast ideas, concepts, and objects.
3. *Classifying.* Grouping and sorting according to properties such as size, shape, color, use, and so on.
4. *Measuring.* Quantitative descriptions made by an observer either directly through observation or indirectly with a unit of measure.
5. *Communicating.* Communicating ideas, directions, and descriptions orally or in written form such as pictures, maps, graphs, or journals so others can understand what you mean.

INTERMEDIATE PROCESS SKILLS

6. *Inferring.* Based on observations but suggests more meaning about a situation than can be directly observed. When children infer, they recognize patterns and expect these patterns to recur under similar circumstances.
7. *Predicting.* Making reasonable guesses or estimations based on observations and prior knowledge and experiences.

ADVANCED PROCESS SKILLS

8. *Hypothesizing.* Devising a statement, based on observations, that can be tested by experiment. A typical form for a hypothesis is, "*If* water is put in the freezer overnight, *then* it freezes."
9. *Defining and controlling variables.* Determining which variables in an investigation should be studied or should be controlled to conduct a controlled experiment. For example, when we find out if a plant grows in the dark, we must also grow a plant in the light.

Figure 8-6 Science Process Skills and Authentic Assessment.
Source: Adapted from Charlesworth/Lind, *Math & Science for Young Children*, 6th ed. © 2010 Cengage Learning.

The sections that follow can be used to heighten awareness of what children are doing as they manipulate their environment. They are actively engaging in math and science, even though it may not be on the daily curriculum plan. This will serve also as a curriculum guide of the concepts that can be incorporated into the early childhood program, enriching children's experiences in math and science. Reflective thinking and concept building encourage the teacher's explorations.

Observing Developing Mathematical Concepts

EXERCISE   Which of the following children are learning math?

_____ **(a)** The class is looking at the teacher holding the calendar and counting up to today's date, the 23rd.

_____ **(b)** Two children are setting the table for lunch.

_____ **(c)** Two children are shoving each other at the door to go outside.

_____ **(d)** A child is eating orange sections.

_____ **(e)** Two children are playing with clay.

_____ **(f)** Three children and the teacher are making instant pudding.

_____ **(g)** A child is painting at the easel.

_____ **(h)** The group is sitting on a rug singing "This Old Man."

_____ **(i)** Four children are picking up the blocks and placing them on the shelves.

_____ **(j)** A child in the housekeeping area is squeezed into a doll high chair.

_____ **(k)** A child is passing out birthday party invitations and has one left over.

_____ **(l)** A child is lining up all the shoes in the dress-up corner.

Answers:

If you checked all of the items except the first one, you are correct.

It is through direct interaction with real objects that children construct meaning and make those associations that lead to cognitive development (Figure 8–7). Kamii (1982) has studied Piagetian principles and applied them to mathematics in the early years. She says, "It is good for children to learn to count and to read and write numerals, but a more important objective is for the child to construct the mental structure of number" (p. 25). She advocates teaching numbers through indirect ways in the environment. "Indirect teaching can vary from encouraging the child to put all kinds of things into all kinds of relationships, to asking him to get just enough plates for everybody at his table" (p. 27). While children are working, the observer records and assesses their mathematical and physical knowledge.

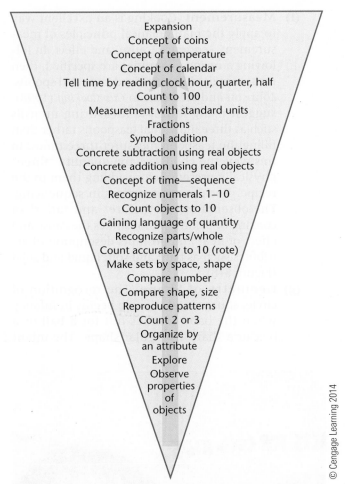

Expansion
Concept of coins
Concept of temperature
Concept of calendar
Tell time by reading clock hour, quarter, half
Count to 100
Measurement with standard units
Fractions
Symbol addition
Concrete subtraction using real objects
Concrete addition using real objects
Concept of time—sequence
Recognize numerals 1–10
Count objects to 10
Gaining language of quantity
Recognize parts/whole
Count accurately to 10 (rote)
Make sets by space, shape
Compare number
Compare shape, size
Reproduce patterns
Count 2 or 3
Organize by
an attribute
Explore
Observe
properties
of
objects

© Cengage Learning 2014

Figure 8–7 Developing Math Concepts through exploration of real objects.

Block Play as the Foundation for Learning

Spatial literacy—the ability to mentally visualize and rotate objects, representing one object for another such as mapping—is critical for the disciplines of science, mathematics, engineering, and technology. Pollman (2010) presents the case that blocks are not only critical to the foundations of mathematics, but also aid in the development of cognitive skills in art and literature, social studies, science and technology. Several research studies have shown a connection between block building and later mathematics achievement, problem solving, drawing and writing, and geometric thinking (Wolfgang, Stannard, & Jones, 2001; Golbeck, 2005; Seo & Ginsburg, 2004). Working with LEGOS and block-building computer programs also is useful in constructing mathematical knowledge (Bers, 2008). Block play can and should be an integral part of every early childhood classroom to promote spatial literacy. (See Chapter 10 for more on block building skills.)

Mathematical Concepts in the Curriculum. By observing with a purpose, the teacher can assess children's learning and development. That is especially true in the area of math and science. As the preceding exercise pointed out, mathematical concepts are all around, posing problems of how many pretzels children can have at snack, which is the heaviest block, or what is another way to accomplish a task. The activities that follow illustrate children learning math concepts in indirect ways from the environment. Calendar math, while an almost universal part of early childhood daily routine, should be reexamined for its usefulness as a learning strategy in light of children's cognitive developmental level. Its reliance on teacher-directed, whole-group learning of an abstract principle, especially the concepts of *yesterday, today, and tomorrow,* is not developmentally appropriate (Ethridge & King, 2005). The mathematical concepts that follow are observable and important ones to note in Anecdotal Recordings and on cognitive domain Checklists, but you have to be able to recognize what is observed:

(a) **Rote**. Saying the numbers does not mean that the child has an idea of quantity. Many programs spend time each day counting the calendar, which may have little relevance to the child's life. (Why should the child care if it is the 23rd or the 89th?) This is not how children learn mathematical concepts. The calendar can be used to plan for anticipated events, counting how many days until the picnic and what must be done each day to prepare for it. In this way, calendars are relevant and perform concrete purposes rather than merely representing the recital of numbers and words that have little meaning.

(b) **One-to-One Correspondence.** Knowing that each number is assigned to a quantity. When children are setting the table, placing one cup or one napkin at each place, they are demonstrating the concept of oneness, the most basic concept of number. This is practiced and can be observed in any number of ways. A child puts on a boot and knows she has two feet, so there must be another boot somewhere. She does not try to put the second boot on the same foot. Materials in the classroom with pieces that fit, match, or can be counted all add to the acquisition of one-to-one correspondence, if the child is at that level.

(c) **Ordinal Numbers.** The idea of **ordinal numbers** (first/second) is learned quickly by children in group settings or in families with siblings. The two-year-old wants his "first." The boys at the door want to be the "first" out. Not that it makes any difference once they get out, but it is the competitive drive for "first" and the disappointment of "last." Would they then tussle to be the "first" in or the "last" in? That would be an indication of their understanding of the terminology of ordinal numbers. In the classroom, familiarity with the schedule becomes rigidly defined in the lives of two-year-olds. Song time must come before the story, and then outside time. If the teacher thinks it might rain that day and decides they must go outside before song and story, many will protest. Having older preschoolers decide which activity to do first, or who will have a first turn, and why, is an excellent way to observe children's understanding of ordinal numbers.

(d) Whole/Part Terminology. As children interact with the environment, the role of the adult is to observe and provide descriptions for their actions, such as, "You've eaten half your orange." By inquiring, the adult can encourage further exploration: "How many sections were in the orange?" "Did each section have a seed, or only some of them?" This type of description can go on incidentally throughout the day. It shows children individual attention by describing ordinary actions. It adds to their vocabulary, raises self-esteem, and promotes thinking.

(e) Conservation. Conservation is the concept that volume or quantity does not change when arranged differently. Clay manipulated into balls and snakes and scrutinized for the concepts of "more" and "less" is an excellent math medium (see Figure 7–10). The conservation of volume is the Piagetian concept that the Preoperational child (two to six years old) has not yet attained. The child uses intuition or appearances by centering attention on one attribute and judging volume by that. Two children have clay balls of equal size. One breaks the ball into several little ones and declares, "I have more." The other one shouts, "Not fair!" There have been efforts to teach conservation with limited results, but the viewpoint now is that it should develop naturally and not taught. However, clay and the water experiments with tall containers and a short squatty one are excellent ways to question children's reasoning to test this hypothesis.

(f) Measurement. Cooking is an excellent way to apply the mathematical principles of measurement, sequence, cause, and effect. In following a recipe, quantities are specified, then measured by different-sized cups and spoons. Johnson and Plemons, in *Cup Cooking* (1998), suggest using multiple measuring utensils such as three individual teaspoons rather than filling the teaspoon measurer three times. In this way, the child sees the quantity "three" physically present before adding them to the recipe. Recipes are practices in sequencing. The observation of "before" and "after" of cooking or baking demonstrates the cause and effect of heat and prompts description of attributes such as hard and soft, liquid and solid (Figure 8–8).

(g) Geometry of Shape. The recognition of circle, square, and triangle begins in infancy when the baby reaches out for a ball or a box or a sharp triangular shape. The infant

Figure 8–8 Measuring is a skill that has many uses both scientific and mathematical. Also important for cooking.

uses all the senses: touching, chewing, seeing, and hearing. Someone says "Ball," or "Box." The words are stored, and each experience associated with the prior one. "Is this shape like that one? Yes? Then it must be a ball, too." The baby is handed an orange. She says "Ball." She is overgeneralizing in calling all round objects balls. As she absorbs more information, those shapes will be differentiated from one another. They will take on more and more meaning based on their various differences. They eventually will be the symbols that are represented in drawing and later writing. Attention to the details and differences are really training for writing skills.

(h) Geometry of Pattern. A pattern can be the visual image of the regular bars of the crib and the figures printed in a row on the sheets. The repetitions of sounds in language and singing also form a pattern. Patterns are expressed in lines painted on the paper at the easel and in the rhythmic clapping of name syllables as children go to wash for lunch. Materials to form patterns are supplied with a card to guide the sequence of shapes, colors, or beads. They begin with simple two-element patterns and gradually increase in complexity. Scientific observation skills are built as the child notices similarities and differences. The teacher watches and notes how the child uses blocks, buttons, and sound to make patterns.

(i) Classifying. Sorting is such an important skill to cognitive development that it is taken for granted or overlooked as a cognitive activity. The toddler fills and dumps, then puts some items in this bucket and some in that one. Finally, by some criteria, he purposefully sorts and selects which ones will go into each bucket. He is on the road to classification skills, which are the basis for scientific discovery. In the block area, the shelves are labeled with the shape of the block that belongs there. All the manipulatives have boxes or trays with picture and word labels. Replacing represents more than just keeping the room tidy; it is a cognitive exercise. In the dramatic play area, tools are outlined above the woodworking bench for their replacement. In the art area, supplies are on labeled shelves. Spontaneous classifying occurs at snack time when children eat the round pretzels before the straight ones, or separate the peas from

It Happened to Me

Toads

I was observing in a first-grade classroom where the teacher told the children to turn to page 45 in their workbook. She asked, "What is that animal?" One of the children said, "Frog." "No, it's not a frog. It's a toad, /t/, /t/, /t/. The letter of the day is *T*, so this has to be a toad. Now copy the word *toad* at the bottom of the page and you can color it in."

It looked like a frog to me. What is the difference? More importantly, what a learning opportunity was missed for the children and me to learn the difference. Instead, a negative message was sent to the one who answered the question. Do any of those children now know about toads because they wrote the letter or colored it? What if the class had gone out and gathered toads, watched them squirm down into the dirt, felt them wiggle, and measured their jumps? What if they compared them to a frog someone had captured in a pond and to tadpoles (another T word to add to their vocabulary)? Then they could have written, drawn, and dictated a story about a toad and a frog. The teacher would have really met her objective to familiarize them with toads and the letter T in a way that they would be more likely to remember. Authentic assessment is a real, not contrived, measurement of a real, not contrived, curriculum.

the carrots. All these are building cognitive schema against which future associations will be made. Children will sort in ways that are not always predictable. Both this ability to sort the "correct" way as well as the ability to sort the "wrong" way can be observed, noted, and questioned to investigate the child's thinking.

(j) Visual-Spatial Skills. Fitting into small spaces is a challenge to young children who are still learning the fine art of spatial awareness. They are prone to putting fingers into tiny holes, heads through spaces, and bodies into containers. Withdrawing from those spaces sometimes is difficult. This spatial awareness is seen on the playground when a child playing "Duck, Duck, Goose" has difficulty finding the spot to join the circle. It can be observed when a child is doing a puzzle, trying to pound the piece in by force rather than turn it to get it to fit. The sand player fills the container, yet continues to shovel and shovel and shovel. The container overflows with each scoop. Still the child does not indicate a recognition that the space is full and can hold no more. Then comes the day when he lines the containers up and fills each one to the top. Aha! A new phase of cognitive development appears.

(k) Problem Solving. It is James's turn to pass out napkins. Maxine had counted them out because she knows how many children are in the class. "Why do you have one left?" This question invites the child to apply the math skills of how many he started with, how many are in the class, how many children are absent, and then use the observation and memory task of deciding who did not receive one. Offering opportunities for problem solving that use mathematics can show children the usefulness of their newfound knowledge. "There are eight crackers left and four children at the table. How can we decide who can have more? How many can they have?" At the computer there are two chairs, and the rule is two workers, but three people want to use it. Problem solving does not have to have a mathematical solution to be helpful in cognitive development. It is also the logical process of mentally creating the situation and the dilemma, generating possible solutions, and deciding on one solution by some criteria. Problem-solving strategies are universal.

(l) Seriation. Placing objects in order according to some rule, such as size, texture, or color, helps the child to look for similarities, but also to distinguish differences. The vocabulary of seriation begins with comparisons (big/little, short/long, heavy/light, empty/full) and expands to middle points and closer variations. This shows the ability to center attention on the one critical variable by which the items are being placed in a series. It is a complex skill that can be observed in its progression. Stories such as "Goldilocks and the Three Bears" can lead to concrete activities for manipulating props from the hand to the mind. Concepts

of small, medium, and large; first and last; and in and out are introduced. Observing what strategies the child uses to come to conclusions about an item's placement also gives clues about the child's thinking processes

Mathematics and Literacy. Mathematics and literacy can be combined by incorporating books into the curriculum that have a mathematical theme. There are many math-related children's books that can help children develop an understanding of concepts and can be a springboard for integrated curriculum. McDonald (2007) suggests looking for books with quantities beyond 10, opportunities to conserve, illustrations of sets of unlike numbers, the introduction of skip counting, exploring number and quantity in other languages, introducing place value or grouping with numbers larger than 10, mathematical problem solving, comparative language such as more or less, and using zero properly. Some of the standards for grades preK–2 from the National Council of Teachers of Mathematics (2000) include the following:

- *number and operations*—accuracy in counting, number words and numerals, beginning addition and subtraction, strategies for whole-number computations
- *algebra*—sort, classify, and order objects by size, number, and other properties; sequencing; patterns; representations of symbolic notations; symbols for qualitative and quantitative change
- *geometry*—recognize, name, draw, and compare two- and three-dimensional shapes; represent shape from different perspectives; recognize geometric shapes in the environment
- *measurement*—attributes of length, volume, weight, area, and time; compare objects by these attributes; select appropriate unit and tool for measuring attributes; compare estimates
- *data analysis and probability*—sort and classify objects in sets, represent data using pictures and graphs, discuss experiences as likely or unlikely
- *problem solving*—recognize, analyze, and strategize how to solve problems that occur in experiences that can be solved through mathematical knowledge
- *reasoning and proof*—use pattern recognition and classifying skills to justify answers

- *communication*—use oral and pictorial language to convey mathematical thinking, listen to others, and evaluate ideas
- *connections*—use experiences to make linkages between two mathematical concepts and between mathematics and real life
- *representation*—represent understanding through oral and written language, gestures, drawing, and symbols

Observing Developing Scientific Concepts

Worth (2005) gives these characteristics of an effective science program:

- Builds on children's prior experiences, backgrounds and early theories.
- Draws on children's curiosity, while encouraging children to pursue their own questions and develop their own ideas.
- Engages children in in-depth exploration of a topic over time in a carefully prepared environment.
- Encourages children to reflect on, present and document their experiences, and to share and discuss their ideas with others.
- Is embedded in children's work and play.
- Is integrated with other domains.
- Provides access to science experiences for all children.

EXERCISE Check the following science activities that would be appropriate for young children.

_____ (a) Caves
_____ (b) Bird's-eye view
_____ (c) Dolphins
_____ (d) Making a sandwich
_____ (e) Let's grow a pumpkin
_____ (f) The Earth—under, over, on
_____ (g) Dirty hands
_____ (h) The food chain
_____ (i) Shadows
_____ (j) When will it snow?

Learning activities are appropriate if they are relevant or real to the group of children and if the concept can be tested through investigation. This was a trick question. The answer to each of them is "It depends." These curriculum ideas may be good ones, but it depends on the context of the children in the group, their age, and their interests.

These curriculum ideas may be good ones, but it depends on the context of the children in the group, their age, and their interests. Each of them may be the spark for a project for exploration using the project approach. Common interests and experiences are the key to curriculum that is meaningful and a springboard for the project approach. If a project comes from the teacher rather than the children, there is a risk that it will become a teacher-telling or teacher-directed experience.

Answers:

(a) Learning about caves would be relevant for children in many states since 38 out of 52 have caves.

(b) All children have knowledge of birds, but thinking about what a bird sees involves moving beyond the egocentric view of the world to see it from above the Earth. This would stimulate not only a study of birds but of positional vocabulary, as well as a growing understanding of the Earth as an orb.

(c) While children are fascinated with benign animals such as dolphins, unless they live in an area where they can experience them, either in the ocean or in an aquarium, it is a stretch for dolphins to develop into a project where children are constructing knowledge from real, firsthand experiences.

(d) Most children have the experience of at least eating a sandwich, but not necessarily making one. It is a familiar food, but the sequence of making a sandwich and the choices available are rich with curriculum possibilities.

(e) Growing things from seed, especially large rambling plants such as pumpkins, can meet many learning objectives. However, climate, season, and indoor/outdoor environmental factors must be taken into consideration.

(f) Children have had contact with the Earth, but to explore by digging into it, studying things above it and things on it pose interesting questions that can be investigated any number of ways. This will bring in language, science, and imagination.

(g) What child hasn't experienced dirty hands? This idea brings with it all kinds of reasons for and possibilities to explore what can be done about dirty hands. Dirty hands can act as a springboard for a health and hygiene lesson, and more. Sensory experiences that get hands "dirty," different cleaners, and "invisible germs" all would be relevant learning themes.

(h) Eating and eliminating are daily activities with which children have an intimate knowledge. Following the cycle for themselves and then thinking about food sources and the whole life cycle chain can be expanded in many different ways.

(i) Light and dark, sun and shadows, day and night are all concepts that touch every child. Using these as springboards for a project can bring about rich learning.

(j) Obviously, this is not a topic for temperate and warm climates but for those who await the first snowflake. Children can predict when it will occur, and projects can be derived from observation of the first snowflake and measurement of accumulation.

The same cognitive processes the child uses for math are also used for science. Scientific discovery and mathematics awareness come from exploring the physical properties of objects through all the senses and identifying the similarities and differences between objects and events. Meaning is attached to the symbols of the environment, such as day and night, summer and winter. The ability to focus on selected pieces of information while ignoring the irrelevant is developed. Vocabulary is expanded to express the concepts of knowledge in various subject areas. These processes—matching, discrimination, sequencing, describing, and classifying—have been pointed out as perceptual skills necessary for literacy as well. Science, math, and literacy are all connected to cognitive development. The world of science for the young child contains all of these elements. Their learning is enriched by reading and listening to stories about the natural world, discussing, and hypothesizing. They wonder about how the guinea pig had babies in the night and what happened to the snowman. Small muscles are used in carefully picking up a worm, and large ones are used when they run with paper streamers in the wind. They listen and count the heartbeats of Stephanie's unborn sibling with a stethoscope on her mother's abdomen. Let's get ourselves, then children, excited about science!

What are the building blocks of science in the early years? They are the same ones used in chemistry laboratories in real life, from observing to experimenting, to concluding and predicting (Figure 8–9). The problem-solving skills in science are explored every day by young children as they construct their own knowledge (Charlesworth & Lind, 2013).

Documenting Science Learning. We can observe, document, and assess science learning in a variety of authentic ways (Jones & Courtney, 2002):

1. Collect various forms of evidence—drawing, dictation, photographs, recordings of children's language
2. Collect forms of evidence over a period of time
3. Collect evidence on the understanding of groups of children as well as individuals

This coordinates well with the Portfolio of work you are gathering on each child using the *Week by Week* system.

Think About It . . .

Go back and look at the skills and tasks in the chart in Figure 8–7. Think about the following activities that provide these kinds of experiences from the child's interests and familiar world.

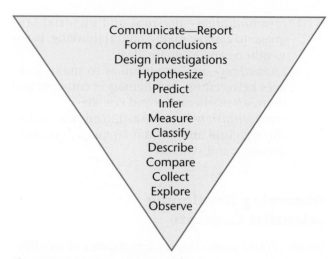

Figure 8–9 Developing Science Concepts.
Source: From Charlesworth/Lind, *Math & Science for Young Children*, 6th ed. © 2010 Cengage Learning.

Observing—"Who can find something green? Hard? Made of wood?"

Comparing—Compare any two objects for likenesses and differences: clothing, shoes, stones, crackers

Classifying—Grouping objects together by a rule; selecting an object that does not belong in the group using a rule

Measuring—Height, weight, growth of a plant, length of a block or the playground

Communicating—Charting, drawing, writing the sequence of events such as planting a bean to eating the bean

Inferring—Brainstorming, wondering, "What makes one toy truck go down the ramp faster than the other?"

Predicting—"What would happen if we place one plant on a windowsill and one in the cubbie?"

Science Curriculum for Young Children. Appropriate science content that would have meaning to the young child is based in their everyday world beginning with their own body, their neighborhood, the world they see, and the way things work (Figure 8–10).

Health and Nutrition. The most relevant lesson to all is health science—the human body, its workings, and healthy practices. This is a vital area for foundation building, illness prevention, and promotion of lifelong wellness. Everyday practices, such as hand washing, are probably the most important

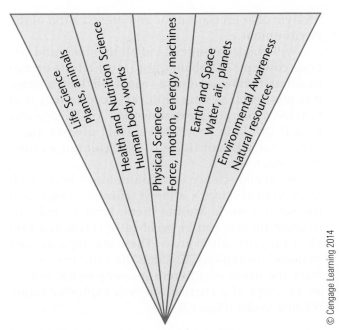

© Cengage Learning 2014

Figure 8–10 Young Children's Science Curriculum.

health lessons that early childhood programs teach. Children are curious about their bodies' appearance and function, both internally and externally. Explorations of healthy eating and exercise habits are relevant, concrete concepts that young children can understand. Measuring, weighing, and charting hair color, eye color, or number of teeth are relevant math and science activities for young children. Having a class baby is a beneficial activity. At the beginning of the year, the class "adopts" a mom having a baby in a month or two. She visits the class, and students ask questions and learn about the baby growing inside her. After its birth (which is a class celebration!), the mother visits the class regularly for the children to observe, measure, and investigate the baby's growth. By the end of the school year, the baby is sitting up, crawling, getting teeth, and becoming social. The children have learned many concepts in math, science, social studies, language, and physical development.

Life Science. Life science is the study of plants, animals, and ecology. Appropriate to every early childhood classroom are growing, living things. There are informal ways of incorporating life science into the environment, and hence the curriculum, such as plants on a windowsill, guinea pigs in a cage, fish in a tank, or a recycling bin next to the garbage can. These can become more formalized with specific activities to observe, identify, describe, and classify.

Physical Science. Physical science is the study of force, motion, energy, and machines. Children themselves are force, motion, and energy in one machine. Their fascination with carrying each other around, moving objects, and what makes things run can be capitalized on in the classroom. Heavy objects (even a teacher sitting on a table) can be moved easily (once they all get moving in the same direction) by a group of 8 or 10 preschoolers. Magnets have always been a part of the classroom, without deep explanation of poles of attraction. Manipulation, exploration, and observation can be augmented with charting what the magnet will pick up or attach to and what it will not. Blocks, a staple area of the classroom, can be augmented with ramps, cardboard tubes, and a facilitator who asks "what-if" questions to expose children to principles of gravity and to give experiences in making predictions. "From which tube will the ball come out first if we start them both at the same time—the long one or the short one? Does it make any difference if it is a big ball or a small ball? Does it make a difference if we tip the short tube up higher? Why?" These concepts cannot be fully understood at this age. Most adults use electricity and television without understanding the principles behind them. The exploration of the effects of the forces of air, water, and machines are suitable activities for the early childhood classroom to explore and pose questions. The physical science area is important as these children grow up in the technological age, where these skills affect their daily life.

Earth and Space Science. All children are in daily contact with weather, water, air, dirt, rocks, sun, moon, and stars. The magic of air's invisibility yet power can spark some interesting investigations for young children, laying foundations for the study of aerodynamics or hot air ballooning. Collecting rocks has been done naturally since the child was a toddler, picking up gravel stones from the driveway. Size, color, weight, geography, and effects of the environment all can be concepts to explore in this area. The sky and its lights have fascinated children and poets. Exploring these from all kinds of curriculum areas begins with familiar stories, such as reading *Goodnight Moon* and singing "Twinkle, Twinkle, Little Star."

Environmental Awareness. The fragility of the balance of environmental resources is an important concept for investigation and understanding from the early years. Charting and measuring temperature and rainfall are concrete activities that can be carried on in an early childhood classroom.

Experiments with water are carried on naturally as children stick their fingers in the faucet to see what happens, or as they plunge a container into the water table and hold it up high to watch the water spill out. This natural resource is a tangible one that even very young children can explore and come to appreciate. The awareness of the finite quantity and quality of natural resources can be taught through recycling and conservation activities, laying the foundation for a lifestyle of appreciation for and preservation of the environment.

Will children understand all the math and science concepts? Probably not. Most adults do not understand how turning a switch will light a lamp, but it is used. Giving children experiences that provide exploration expands their knowledge and logical thinking processes, posing greater questions that will continue to be explored as they grow older.

Math and science curriculum topics begin with ideas from children's interest, current events, and the natural world around them. Projects and curriculum themes can be webbed or integrated into all of the curriculum areas. These are opportunities to make associations, broaden the experiences, and meet the needs of different learning styles. Here is an example of a curriculum web exploring topics relating to dirt (Figure 8–11).

It Happened to Me

Tornados

I was observing a student teacher leading a "science" activity. She had joined two soda bottles at the neck and gave each child in the circle a turn at tipping them over. They watched the vortex of swirling water as it drained from the upper bottle to the lower one. Some waited patiently, others impatiently, as they waited for a turn to make a "tornado." When it finally completed the circle, she asked the question, "And what did we learn about today?" Many were blank and silent, but one dare-to-risk child said "Tomatoes!" There was surprise on the student teacher's face with a "where'd-he get-that?" look.

Afterward we talked about a child's need to manipulate, a child's inability to wait, and the importance of relevancy. We discussed why the child said "Tomatoes." She had no idea other than it sounded like tornados. For children living in Kansas who had seen funnel clouds and knew the word tornado, this lesson might have been more effective. Four-year-olds in New York could make no connection between a tornado and the water in the bottle. Should she not have done it? Possibly. Or perhaps some additional preparations—about wind, funnels, pipes, or even reading *The Wizard of Oz*—would have promoted meaning. This activity that missed reinforces the principle that learning will only occur in context. There has to be some relationship made to what children already know and have experienced.

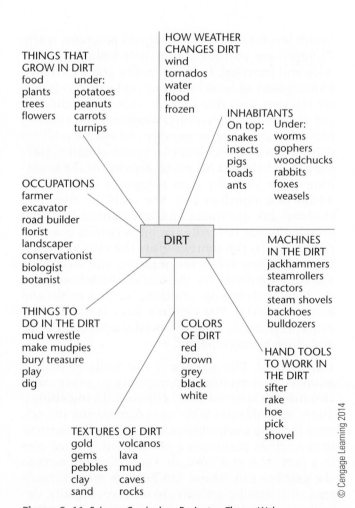

Figure 8–11 Science Curriculum Project or Theme Web.

THINGS THAT GROW IN DIRT
food
plants   under:
trees   potatoes
flowers   peanuts
              carrots
              turnips

HOW WEATHER CHANGES DIRT
wind
tornados
water
flood
frozen

INHABITANTS
On top: Under:
snakes   worms
insects   gophers
pigs   woodchucks
toads   rabbits
ants   foxes
           weasels

OCCUPATIONS
farmer
excavator
road builder
florist
landscaper
conservationist
biologist
botanist

DIRT

MACHINES IN THE DIRT
jackhammers
steamrollers
tractors
steam shovels
backhoes
bulldozers

THINGS TO DO IN THE DIRT
mud wrestle
make mudpies
bury treasure
play
dig

COLORS OF DIRT
red
brown
grey
black
white

HAND TOOLS TO WORK IN THE DIRT
sifter
rake
hoe
pick
shovel

TEXTURES OF DIRT
gold   volcanos
gems   lava
pebbles   mud
clay   caves
sand   rocks

EXERCISE Select one of the topics mentioned in this chapter and make a web to explore possible project activities in each of the learning centers of your classroom or curriculum areas. Use the blank curriculum web in Figure 8–12.

Young Children and Technology

Mathematics, science, and technology are interwoven into daily life; so math, science, and technology concepts should be interwoven into the curriculum in much the same way. They are not discrete subjects, but useful ways to make connections and meaning. Every individual is affected. Everyone uses mathematics, science, and technology in their daily lives. Children today are growing up with electronic technology that some of us only read about in Dick Tracy comic books (if you don't know what that is,

ask your parents or grandparents). A two-year-old child can manipulate a VCR or DVD player, smart phone, iPad, Webkinz, or play games on a computer. Using technology is changing neural pathways in the brain, reacting quicker to visual stimuli, improving some forms of attention (Small & Vorgan, 2009). However, giving partial attention to multiple stimuli may create brain strain that interferes with learning.

Children's programming, screen time that includes children's television shows, videos, and computer games are available 24 hours a day. About 40 percent of U.S. three-month-olds regularly watch an hour or more a day of either TV, videos, or DVDs; and by age two the figure rises to 90 percent, increasing to almost three hours a day for preschoolers and then declining somewhat in elementary age children (Roberts & Foehr, 2008). Children in family child care watch more than in center-based care, and both viewing times were less in programs where teachers had some college education (Christakis et al., 2009).

How Much Screen Time? Nearly three out of four families with children six months to six years of age have a computer at home, and half have a video game player, which has now become the fastest growing segment of the computer industry. The question isn't, "Should they?" but "What is the best way to use technology and also limit the possible harmful aspects." And an even bigger question is about using such technology—computers, videos, and toddler-focused television—in early childhood programs. Access to computers in early childhood programs can help to bridge the digital divide, the third of the families who do not have computers in their homes. Teaching and learning has been, and will always be, a human interaction, but tools, even electronic ones, can expand the learning with opportunities and experiences that can reach beyond the classroom environment. A world of information is now at our fingertips, and having a classroom computer and Internet connection can augment and expand experiences in the classroom. Computer learning programs abound, but the teacher and program must make wise choices for the appropriate use of software. The authors of *Growing up with Technology* (Plowman et al., 2010) state, "While we are not aware of evidence to suggest computers are actively harmful, our research suggests that desktop computers do not appear to promote learning for three- and four-year-old children in situations where they are left to play on their own because preschool staff are busy and need to oversee many children and different activities" (p 16). Using more mobile technologies such as digital still and video

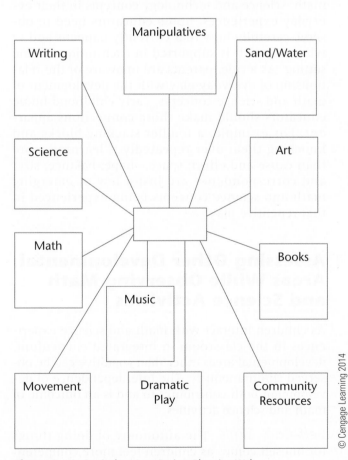

Figure 8–12 Curriculum Area Project Planning Web.

© Cengage Learning 2014

 Go to the Education CourseMate website to download a copy of this form.

cameras, electronic keyboards, and electronic toys promote collaboration and play activities. Communication tools such as email and web pages, cameras, printers and copiers, and audio and video recorders can be a part of the developmental documentation plan.

What Do They Learn? Countless studies have been done since the 1950s on the effect of television—and now videos and television—on children's learning. The adult should always be the first line of defense against inappropriate programming and use of any material, toy, or equipment by children. There is little doubt that children learn from screen time, but what do they learn?

▶ *Consumerism*. Television programming in its infancy was not primarily for entertainment but a vehicle for selling products. Despite regulations to the contrary, advertising is targeted at young consumers. The average school-age child sees about 30,000 TV commercials per year, many of them for foods with high fat, sugar, and salt content (Gantz, 2007). There can be no doubt that these messages influence children to ask adults to purchase specific products. Children do expand memory that includes jingles and song lines, to read product logos, and associate with characters who promote products.

▶ *Social Behavior*. Thousands of studies have concluded that media violence increases children's aggressive verbal and physical behavior. On the other hand, prosocial programs can teach cooperation, helping, and caring (Calvert & Kotler, 2003).

▶ *Stereotypes*. Messages, often not positive ones, appear regarding minorities, women, unattractive bodies, and relationships. Sensitive media choices can broaden viewpoints, teach positively about differences, and reduce biases (Calvert et al., 2003).

▶ *Literacy*. Media can teach various aspects of literacy (see Chapter 9).

Brain research is showing that digital technology is changing neural pathways in the brain, but there are concerns over the drift away from social skills. There is the potential for media to be used as a learning/teaching tool if: regulations for accessible media have necessary protections; screen time is not replacing other worthwhile activities such as physical exercise; adults monitor and filter its use so it is appropriate for the child; and it is used to augment rather than replace everyday learning experiences.

It Happened to Me

"It's a Record"

A friend of mine has a collection of records (those large black disks that play music) that she still uses in her classroom. One day as she was placing one on the record player, one of the children looked up and exclaimed, "Wow, will you look at the size of that CD!"

 Home Visiting and Math, Science, and Technology

While children instinctively call on and integrate math, science and technology concepts in their everyday experiences, home educators need to observe carefully how that currently happens and to what degree it is supported in each unique home setting. As a rule, parents are unaware of the relationship of everyday play with the development of math and science concepts; early childhood home educators should make those connections apparent. For example, a toddler stacking blocks and knocking them over repeatedly is learning more than cause and effect; space, shape, balance, size, and correspondence are just a few of emerging math and science concepts being experienced in that repetitive play.

Assessing Other Developmental Areas While Observing Math and Science Activities

As children interact with math and science experiences in the classroom in integrated curriculum, developmental areas other than cognitive can be observed simultaneously. The interdependence of development both contributes to and is an outcome of math and science activities.

Self-Care Skills. The autonomy of doing things for oneself comes as children feel more competent in their environment. When children can count how many napkins they need to set the table for the group, or when a child sees her name on the chart as the floor sweeper around the table where marigolds were being planted today, the skills interact.

Large Muscle Development. The coordination of the body is observed as the child is running under the parachute to experience the wind or as she follows the game rules to take six steps backward. Both counting to six and walking backward are observed.

Small Muscle Development. The child places one shell in each compartment of the egg carton in one-to-one correspondence. He gently picks up the baby chick that has just been hatched. She squeezes the spray bottle to water plants. Observation of small muscle skills and math and science come together (Figure 8–13).

Literacy. Many teachers have explored the use of manipulatives; journals and situational problem solving have been effective in teaching concepts of mathematics and science. The combination of new skills integrates and maximizes the learning (Jones & Courtney, 2002; Whitin & Whitin, 2003).

Other Areas of Development. Visual perception and knowledge of size-comparison vocabulary can be noted when the child picks up the bowling ball and calls it the "heaviest."

Language can be assessed by listening as the child speaks about solving the dilemma of three friends who want to sit by her at lunch. There are only two chairs left. Where will the third child sit? The logical resolutions considering number of chairs as well as social interactions are observed while listening for clear speech and complexity of sentence structure.

© Cengage Learning 2014

Figure 8–13 Other areas of development may be assessed during math and science activities. What areas of development can you see?

Sharing clay, dividing cookies, and taking turns on two bicycles are opportunities to observe both mathematical concepts and social development. Co-operation in working together to move a heavy object displays not only scientific principles but also an understanding of community.

As children discover math and science concepts in a free environment without fear of "wrong" answers, they do not have to memorize or parrot back "right" answers in reply to closed questions. They can take risks to experiment. That is the basis for all inquiry: the elimination of wrong answers until the right one is arrived at through understanding. Children in the classroom environment dedicated to developmental learning can build and demonstrate that kind of self-concept.

Assessing the Cognitive Development of Infants and Toddlers

The case has already been made throughout this chapter that testing young children is not the most accurate measure of a child's cognitive development. It is even less appropriate for infants and toddlers. While much cognitive development is occurring in the first two years, there are ways to document and assess that development that are nonintrusive and are better suited to the very young child.

The Teaching Strategies GOLD™ (Field Test Edition, July 2009) blends ongoing, authentic, observational assessment for all areas of development for children birth to age six, and is designed to be used as a part of everyday, meaningful experiences in the classroom. Nine areas of development and learning are captured by 36 objectives based on current research. All objectives are organized into levels color-coded by ages with descriptions of expectations by age. Anecdotal recordings and other methods of documentation are then gathered to support the checkmarks on the continuum.

Helping All Children with Cognitive Development

Cognitive development is different for each person, affected by learning styles, strong areas of intelligence, physical characteristics, and experiential factors. Early childhood teachers are faced with the challenge of meeting the learning needs of each child. There are some special populations whose cognitive development presents even more challenges.

TOPICS in OBSERVATION

"Real" Curriculum

"Real" Curriculum Educational advertisements fill teachers' mailboxes, promising easy, fun, ready-to-do activities for every curriculum area, especially math and science. They come with attractive containers, dividers for organization, and free sample plans. Most of these and many idea books for math and science curricula are adaptations of the workbook format. Directions are given such as, "Draw a line to the one that is the same." "Count the red balloons and select the numeral." "Circle the bead that completes the pattern." The purpose of these activities is to teach and assess cognitive concepts. Visual discrimination and classification, counting and reading numbers, and patterning are appropriate learning objectives for activity plans. Using paper-and-pencil tasks, or even teacher-made paper games, is not showing the teacher's knowledge of child development.

We know the attributes of the young, developing child. By knowing child development principles and observing and assessing the individual child's physical, social, emotional, and cognitive development, we can develop curriculum and teaching practices (Figure 8–14). It is not necessary, nor effective, to use workbook pages or folder activities to teach or test concepts. Just watch the child; and help the child do real stuff.

BECAUSE WE KNOW . . .	WE DO
Children learn through their senses.	We provide real, three-dimensional objects for them to manipulate.
Children are making associations with previous knowledge.	We provide materials that are familiar.
Children need time to organize their thoughts.	We provide long periods of uninterrupted time for them to explore.
Children cannot share.	We provide duplicates of popular materials.
Children cannot wait.	We do not expect all of them to do the same thing at the same time.
Children have different attention spans.	We provide a flexible schedule so children can move at their own pace.
Children are egocentric, only seeing things from their own point of view.	We do not force them to internalize someone else's point of view.
Children learn what they want to know.	We listen to them and provide ways for them to learn it.
Children learn from making mistakes.	We allow the mistakes to happen.
Children are frustrated easily.	We provide an environment and materials that are accessible and easy to manage themselves.
Children learn from accomplishing hard tasks.	We let them try without rushing in with solutions.
Children construct their own knowledge.	We provide a way for them to "teach" themselves.

© Cengage Learning 2014

Figure 8–14 Because We Know, We Do.

Minority and Poverty Effects on School Achievement

Equality of educational opportunity has been the theme of Head Start for almost 50 years. The Children's Defense Fund (2011) monitors poverty's effect on school achievement and has found that 80 percent or more of black fourth-grade public school students are performing below grade level in reading and math compared with 68 percent of their white peers (p. H8). Minority children have higher rates of illiteracy, lower reading levels, and, later on, higher drop-out rates, incarceration rates, and unemployment rates. Schools with the highest percentages of minorities, limited English proficiency students, and low-income students had less-experienced teachers, higher class-size ratios, were overcrowded, under-supplied, lacked computer access, and received a smaller per-capita spending budget (Children's Defense Fund, 2011).

One in five children in America lives in poverty; and poverty is a strong predictor of poor school achievement, risk for learning disabilities, and need for special education services (Duncan & Brooks-Gunn, 1997; Hart & Risley, 2004). There are many factors contributing to these depressing statistics. It is even more distressing to know that teaching and assessment methods exacerbated rather than helped minority children and children in poverty to learn. The well-known Rosenthal effect (Rosenthal & Jacobson, 1992) may impact these populations. Teachers' expectations, using IQ scores or labels to categorize people, may contribute to the inequities. Jonathan Kozol's *Savage Inequalities: Children in America's Schools* (1991) captured in several vignettes the differences in schools for the haves and the have-nots. Teachers who gave their all to their students under extremely harsh conditions were portrayed along with teachers who did much harm. The book is a call to self-reflection about attitudes and actions by everyone who works with children.

Children Who Are Cognitively Impaired

A whole group of cognitive impairments is categorized as mental retardation, sub-average intellectual function, and adaptive behavior (Figure 8–15). There are many causes, including the following:

- genetic disorders such as Down syndrome
- prenatal influences (maternal illness, drug abuse, fetal alcohol syndrome [FAS])

Figure 8–15 Cognitive development can be affected by many factors, but inclusive programs accept and adapt.

© Cengage Learning 2012

- birth complications such as anoxia (oxygen deprivation during the birth process)
- postnatal causes such as illnesses with high fevers, head injury, and lead poisoning
- environmental causes such as parental abuse and neglect

The identification and labeling of mild cognitive impairments is difficult in young children because of inaccurate diagnostic methods such as IQ tests and wide cultural definitions of "normal" intelligence. Some symptoms or clues are

- extremely short attention span.
- language delays of more than one year.
- social and emotional difficulties.

Children with undiagnosed cognitive impairments often are detected first by preschool teachers. Approaching families with suspicions or concerns is a sensitive task, done with concrete data and surrounded with care, understanding, and tact. The teacher may refer the family first to the pediatrician or a clinic specializing in full developmental evaluations.

After diagnosis, a placement decision is made for the child in the least restrictive environment. It may be that the child can function in a regular classroom. Cook, Klein, and Tessier (2008, p. 307) give these recommendations for children who need extra time and spaced practice:

1. Provide concrete, multisensory tasks.
2. Find the child's most efficient mode of learning.
3. Monitor pacing; provide shorter work periods with less information.
4. Provide repetition.
5. Plan for modeling and imitation.
6. Task analyze; use short, simple steps in sequence.
7. Give explicit directions.

Inclusion

Public Law (P.L.) 94-142 specifies that every child must be given access to an *appropriate education in the least restrictive environment*. This law and supplementary laws have led to the **inclusion** of children with disabilities in the regular classroom. Children with physical disabilities fare the best in inclusion classrooms. Children with learning disabilities and cognitive disorders require the teacher to implement an individualized program. With a philosophy that every child is unique, individualizing the curriculum for each child is the goal. There are social benefits as well as social risks to inclusion. Children are forming ideas about we and they with basic social skills, so inclusion with peers who may react negatively because they are still learning social skills may result in rejection for the included child. The role of the teacher is expanded here to address social issues and turn inclusion into experiences of greater understanding and caring. Effectiveness in inclusion education depends on the training and support of all people working with the children: teacher, aide, volunteers, and support staff such as bus drivers and lunchroom personnel.

The goal of early childhood programs for all children is enthusiastic engagement and independence. This is true also for children with special needs. The curriculum, the indoor and outdoor physical space, daily schedule, teaching methods, and discipline policies and practices should be examined to eliminate barriers so that the program is universally accessible and appropriate. Watson and MacCathren (2009) have developed a Checklist to rate the inclusiveness of preschool and kindergarten environments for all children: children with physical disabilities, hearing and/or vision impairments, communication and language disorders, intellectual disabilities, sensory integration concerns, and special considerations for outdoor space.

For specific strategies for working with a child with exceptional health, hearing, learning, visual impairments, communication, or physical needs, see *Inclusive Early Childhood Education* (Richey & Wheeler, 2000) and *The Exceptional Child* (Allen & Cowdery, 2009).

Children Who Are Talented and Gifted

This beyond-the-range-of-normal category, **talented and gifted**, is one of the most neglected in working with children with exceptional needs. While high cognitive abilities characterized by early speaking, motor skills, reading, advanced language and reasoning ability, curiosity, and superior memory are the most obvious indicators of cognitive giftedness, other areas also are considered in this category. These children may have fears, emotional sensitivities, and behavioral nonconformity that interfere with social interactions. Gifted children may have difficulty following directions or intense concentration that tunes out classroom activities. Their inquisitiveness may have them labeled as "problem" children (Tomlinson & Imbeau, 2010). The same hindrances to early identification of mental impairments also apply to giftedness. Developmental assessments can indicate advanced attainment of milestones and document behavior that alerts teachers and families to the child's exceptional abilities, finding ways to encourage them by providing enrichment opportunities to support the child's area of strength as well as the areas of normal development.

Helping Professionals for Cognitive Concerns

Families with a child with exceptional cognitive development at either end of the range of normal can first seek help from the following medical personnel:

pediatrician—physician specializing in the health and development of children
neurologist—physician specializing in the nervous system and in brain functioning

Within the educational system, specially trained professionals help the classroom teacher and the family meet the needs of the child, whether cognitively impaired or gifted:

itinerant teacher—visits the classroom or home regularly to see that appropriate methods, materials, and services are provided

special education teacher—a specialist trained to work with children with cognitive disabilities; may have further specialties in reading, speech/language, occupational therapy, physical therapy, behavioral, autism spectrum disorders, or talented and gifted

resource teacher—assesses placement and provides instructional time outside of the regular classroom

Other Methods

Other Methods to Document Cognitive Development:

Anecdotal/Running Records
Checklists/Rating Scales
Discussions/Interviews
Work Samples
Media such as audio/video and still photography

Key Terms

authentic assessment	ordinal numbers
benchmarks	quantitative scoring
cognitive	reliability
dispositions	screening
high-stakes tests	standard
inclusion	standardized tests
norm	talented and gifted
	valid

Plans

Go to the Education CourseMate website, accessed through CengageBrain.com for the following:
Class List Log form

Plan Week 8 Part A, Obtain a copy of a standardized test and review it based on your learning from this chapter. Questions to answer concerning the test.

Plan Week 8 Part B, Directions for a Math and Science Assessment for ALL, including What to Do with It, Portfolio Evidence Sheet Example, Sharing with Child and Family, Actions—Read a Book, In the Environment, In the Curriculum, In the Newsletter

Plan Week 8 Part B, Directions for Work Samples for All

Plan Week 8 Part C, Conversations with Group C for Speech and Language Assessment

Plan Week 8 Part D, Reflective Journal

Resources

Charlesworth, R., & Lind, K. (2013). *Math and science for young children* (7th ed.). Belmont, CA: Wadsworth Cengage Learning.

Copley, J., Jones, C., & Dighe, G. (2007). *Mathematics: The creative curriculum approach*. Washington, DC: Teaching Strategies.

Galinsky, E. (2010). *Mind in the making: The seven essential life skills every child needs*. New York: Harper Studios.

Kostelnik, M., Soderman, A., & Whiren, A. (2011). *Developmentally appropriate curriculum: Best practices in early childhood education*. Boston: Pearson Education.

Plowman, L., Stephen, C., McPake, J. (2010). *Growing up with technology: Young children learning in a digital world*. New York: Routledge.

Schickedanz, J. A. (2008). *Increasing the power of instruction: Integration of language, literacy, and math across the preschool day*. Washington, DC: National Association for the Education of Young Children.

Snow, C. E., Van, H. S. B., & Committee on Developmental Outcomes and Assessments for Young Children. (2008). *Early childhood assessment: Why, what, and how*. Washington, DC: National Academies Press.

Using Rating Scales to Look at Literacy

OBSERVATION THOUGHT

"Children need to see the teacher writing about them every day."

NAEYC Standards **naeyc**

The following NAEYC Standards for Early Childhood Professional Preparation are addressed in this chapter:

Standard 1: *Promoting Child Development and Learning*

Standard 3: *Observing, Documenting, and Assessing to Support Young Children and Families*

Standard 6: *Becoming a Professional*

IN THIS CHAPTER

- Using the Rating Scale
- Looking at Literacy
- Learning to Read and Write
- Topics in Observation: Books in the Sandbox
- Helping All Children with Literacy
- Helping Professionals for Literacy Concerns

Using the Rating Scale

EXERCISE   How hungry are you?
Starved? A little hungry? Fully satisfied?
How is the temperature?
Too cold? Just right? Too hot?
How well do you sing?
Off key? Comfortably with a group? Soloist?

A **Rating Scale** lists specific descriptions of criteria in a horizontal line from the least to the most, early developing to later developing, simple to complex, with

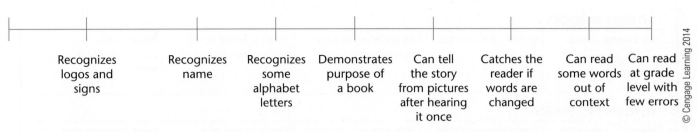

| Recognizes logos and signs | Recognizes name | Recognizes some alphabet letters | Demonstrates purpose of a book | Can tell the story from pictures after hearing it once | Catches the reader if words are changed | Can read some words out of context | Can read at grade level with few errors |

Figure 9–1 Literacy Rating Scale Example.

several choices in between (Figure 9–1). A Rating Scale is similar to a rubric, but a Rating Scale describes criteria over time, whereas a rubric is usually a rating by the criteria at one point in time. The Rating Scale shown here contains seven sequential milestones, or **quality points**, in learning to read. A Checklist such as the one displayed in Figure 9–2 contains the same information but in a vertical formation calling for a "yes" or "no" response from the recorder. The Rating Scale visually portrays the stages of development of a skill and can even include notations at the in-between stages.

Once the rater becomes familiar with the instrument and the child or setting, a rating is chosen that most closely describes what has been observed. It could be used by the teacher, a family member, a volunteer, or an outside observer. When more than one rater uses the same instrument on the same child, the validity increases, thereby reducing rater bias. This is called **interrater reliability**. The scores are compared and, depending on the number of raters, the highest and lowest scores are cast out and the remaining scores averaged. This technique is used in research and in judging Olympic sporting events.

Rating Scales, like Checklists, are self-made or purchased and used to measure certain criteria. The criteria can be a child's development, or a setting or program's adherence to certain aspects of quality. When a measurement is made against these criteria, it is an affirmation of what has been attained and an indicator of what to plan for next. In a child's development, this type of measurement indicates progress or reveals lags that may be cause for concern. This tool, like the Checklist, gives the teacher that zone of proximal development (ZPD) between the acquired and the not-yet-attained

skill that the teacher can scaffold (the adult supports the child to accomplish a new task with help). For example, a child who can print the first letter of his name is encouraged to do so at every opportunity, with the teacher finishing the remaining letters. Eventually, the child will write more of the letters himself. When a setting or program Rating Scale is used, it is an effective self-study tool to measure adherence to guidelines and to indicate areas to be addressed for improvement.

Because the rater is looking for signs of the specific criteria, a Rating Scale is a highly **selective method**. Other observations are irrelevant and not recorded while looking for the specific criteria. A Rating Scale is considered a closed method since no raw data or details are recorded. Exact details of the rater's observation leading to the selection of a rating are not recorded.

A Literacy Rating Scale has been developed to assess the interest, skill, and knowledge of young children's reading and writing. Figure 9–3 is an example of a completed Literacy Rating Scale. Each criterion is rated from observation and dated at its highest level of attainment. When the quality point or milestone is not observed, individualized curriculum or activities are planned for that child to encourage this area of development. It may be that the environment is not conducive for this child's learning style to spawn interest in reading or writing, or the materials are not accessible or meaningful. The tool is a way to accomplish the end result, to stimulate and encourage literacy development and record the progress.

See the Education CourseMate website, accessed through CengageBrain.com for a blank reproducible Literacy Rating Scale.

Rating Scale Examples

The quality points take several forms, depending on the design of the Rating Scale. The scale in Figure 9–1 describes the criteria from which the rater selects the most accurate choice based on observation and the rater's knowledge of the child.

Rating Scales, such as *The Work Sampling System* (Meisels, Dichtelmiller, Jablon, Dorfman, & Marsden, 2001), use quality points of *Seldom/Usually/Always* or *Not Yet/In Process/Proficient*. NAEYC's Center Accreditation Self-Study uses ratings of *Yes/Yes, but . . . /No* adding the requirement for Observable

---

Checklist Example

- ❑ Recognizes logos and signs
- ❑ Recognizes name
- ❑ Recognizes some alphabet letters
- ❑ Demonstrates purpose of a book
- ❑ Can tell the story from pictures after hearing it once
- ❑ Catches the reader if words are changed
- ❑ Can read some words out of context
- ❑ Can read at grade level with few errors

Figure 9–2 Checklist Example.

LITERACY RATING SCALE

Child's Name **Jeremiah Jones**

INTEREST IN BOOKS

No interest, avoids	Only if adult-initiated	Brings books to adult to read	Looks at books as self-initiated activity	Reads books independently @___ level
9/10	10/17			

LISTENING TO BOOKS

Wiggly, no attention	Intermittent attention	Listens in one-on-one situation	Listens as part of a group, tuning out distractions	Long attention span to books with more text than pictures, richer vocabulary, longer sentences, chapters
9/21 10/6	11/17 can't last thru whole story			

INVOLVEMENT WITH BOOKS BEING READ

Little or no response	Emotional response, laugh, frown	Comments, asks questions	Joins in during reading	Participates, predicts, interprets plot, characters
11/11				

HANDLING BOOKS

No voluntary touching	Rough handling	Exploratory manipulation	Books as favorite toys	Handles books with care & places them in their storage spaces
	9/30	10/29 Stacking up in piles by color		

CONCEPT OF BOOK FORMAT

No idea of front/back, up/down	Holds book right side up but skips pages	Demonstrated front/back concept	Looks at pages left to right	Knows and uses book parts—author, illustrator, title page, preface, index
0	0	10/29	2/7 He sat & looked at every page of dinosaur book	

CONCEPT OF STORY BOOK

didn't realize he was listening even though he wasn't sitting

Labels pictures	Retells story in sequence from pictures	Accurately repeats some story lines	Points to print while accurately re-telling from pictures	Retells in sequence
11/21	1/16			

PRINT IN THE ENVIRONMENT

no obs. in this area

Notices signs, labels	Asks, "What's that say?"	Reads signs, labels out of context	"Writes" signs to label constructions	Uses reading and writing for a purpose
0 0	0	0	0	

BEGINNING READING

a start. "J"

Recognizes own name	Recognizes letters in name in other words	Reads simple words	Sounds out letters in unfamiliar words	Can read at grade level competence
11/15 0	3/17			

Figure 9–3 Literacy Rating Scale Completed.

(continued)

Go to the Education CourseMate website to download a copy of this form.

LITERACY RATING SCALE

MANIPULATION OF WRITING TOOLS

Fist hold	High hold on pencil	Adult grip, little control	Adult grip, good control	Uses tools comfortably
9/30	11/6	4/17 Work on this!		

COMMUNICATION THROUGH WRITING   *no interest*

Communicates ideas through drawing	Will describe drawing on request	Initiates description of drawing	Draws and writes words	Can write narrative at grade level competence
2/16 0	4/20 0 0			

BEGINNING WRITING

Scribbles, no reference to writing	Named scribbles "Says my name"	Single letters, random	Writes name	Prints legibly, uses cursive

WRITING IN PLAY

No reference to writing	Asks for signs, words to be written	Asks for adult to spell words	Sounds out words and writes on own	Writes creatively— poems & prose

Figure 9–3

Evidence both written and photographic to support the selection of the rating quality point (NAEYC, 2012 www.naeyc.org/files/academy/file/AllCriteriaDocument.pdf). The *Early Learning Observation & Rating Scale (ELORS)* (Coleman, M.R., West, T., & Gillis, M., 2010) uses the numbers 1 to 4 to indicate *Little or No Concern* to *Great Concern*.

Rating scales such as Teaching Strategies GOLD™ Assessment System (Heroman, 2010) show a continuum with checkpoints for noting skills at four times through the year, with accompanying Work Samples or Anecdotal Records to support the checkmarks for measuring phonological awareness (Figure 9–4).

Rating Scales can translate the written criteria into a number rating that can be added with others to obtain a quantitative score. *The Environment Rating Scale (ECERS-R)* by Harms, Clifford, and Cryer (2005) has seven subscales: Space and Furnishings, Personal Care Routines, Language-Reasoning, Activities, Interaction, Program Structure, and Parents and Staff. These are broken down into 43 separate Rating Scales. Each is arranged on a 7-point scale from *Inadequate* (1) to *Excellent* (7).

Rating scales can also be used to assess the conformity of teacher practices to a protocol. Dialogic Reading employs several types of prompts and reader feedback to increase reading comprehension (Figure 9–5).

 **Advantages**

The Rating Scale is

- fast and convenient. (The rater reads, decides, circles, or checks.)
- efficient for measuring a large number of criteria quickly.
- informative of what "should be" expected.
- useful for tracking progress or a warning of developmental lags.
- an assessment measurement against the ideal and used as a plan for improvement (accreditation).
- revisited to see progress over time.

 **Disadvantages**

The Rating Scale is

- not backed up with raw data.
- not objective. (Judgments are made as observation is taking place with little time for considering the criteria and no place for explanation of circumstances.)
- not free of rater bias, with no way for the reader to know that.
- not useful as a method to record spontaneous actions or conversations.
- not sensitive to a wide range of individual differences.

a. Notices and discriminates rhyme

Not Yet	1	2	3	4	5	6	7	8	9
		Joins in rhyming songs and games • Hums along and joins in random words in rhyme • Sings with a group, "One, two, buckle my shoe…"		**Fills in the missing rhyming word; generates rhyming words spontaneously** • Completes the rhyme in the phrase, "The fat cat sat on the ____ (mat)." • Chants spontaneously, "Me, fee, kee, tee, lee, bee."		**Decides whether two words rhyme** • "Do bear and chair rhyme? What about bear and goat?" • Matches rhyming picture cards		**Generates a group of rhyming words when given a word** • Says, "Bat, sat, lat," when asked, "What words rhyme with cat?"	

b. Notices and discriminates alliteration

Not Yet	1	2	3	4	5	6	7	8	9
		Sings songs and recites rhymes and refrains with repeating initial sounds • Sings, "I'm bringing home a baby bumble bee…"		**Shows awareness that some words begin the same way** • Says, "Max and Maya…our names start the same!"		**Matches beginning sounds of some words** • Groups objects or pictures that begin with the same sound • Picks up a toy bear when asked, "What begins the same way as box, baby, and bike?"		**Isolates and identifies the beginning sound of a word** • Says, "/m-m-m/," when asked "What is the first sound of the word milk?" • Responds, "/t/," after being asked, "What's the beginning sound of toy, toe, teeth?"	

Figure 9–4 Literacy Objectives.
Source: Heroman, C., Burts, D. C., Berke, K., & Bickart, T. (2010) *Teaching Strategies GOLD® Objectives for Development & Learning: Birth through Kindergarten,* Washington, DC: Teaching Strategies, LLC. p83. Reprinted with permission.

⃠ Pitfalls to Avoid

The Rating Scale recorder should

▶ make sure the Rating Scale criteria match the goals and objectives of the program and developmental range of the children.

▶ have more than one person use the same Rating Scale and compare ratings for interrater reliability to limit observer bias.

▶ become familiar with Rating Scale criteria before using it, and be sure that each criterion is observable rather than judgmental: Scribbles/Forms alphabet letters/Writes cursive, *not* Still scribbling/Poor spelling/Good writing.

▶ be sure the quality points describe behaviors rather than attitudes: Leaves when story reading begins/Stays, plays with toys during story reading/Sits, watching pages displayed during story reading, *not* Not interested/Some interest/Very interested.

↗ Using Technology

Rating Scales that have numerical scoring lend themselves to electronic storage and computation of the results. Personal computers and hand-held computers can store the form in an electronic file, and the observer can enter the numerical rating. Using computer programs that perform computation and graphical reporting, the scores can be saved in

individual children's electronic files and also used as aggregate data on the whole group.

🕐 How to Find the Time

Completing Rating Scales on individual children's development does take concentrated observation and recording to obtain objective results. Much of this observation can be done during free-play time. Remember that it requires a person who is not fully responsible for classroom management. Program Rating Scales such as the ECERS-R can be done as a self-assessment by the teaching team or by an

REVIEW

RATING SCALE
Criteria are arranged according to developmental stages or range of quality with the recorder making a judgment based on observation.

Types of Information to Record Using a Rating Scale (depends on focus of Rating Scale)

child development stages
environment appropriateness
teacher performance

DIALOGIC READING RATING SCALE
To assess a teacher's use of an effective way to read to preschoolers

	1 Inadequate	3 Minimal	5 Good	7 Excellent
Prompts the child to say something about the book	Uses no prompts while reading a book to the children	Uses 1 or 2 prompts	Uses 3 or more of the 5 types of prompts	1. Complete – Leaves a blank at the end of a sentence for the child to fill in 2. Recall – Asks questions about what happened 3. Open-ended – Shows illustration for child to describe 4. Wh-prompts-uses wh-questions 5. Distancing – asks for recall outside of book experience
Evaluates the child's response	Gives no attention to child's response	Nods or looks at child with no verbal response	Gives child positive affirmation for the response	Gives child attention and positive verbal response
Expands the child's response by rephrasing and adding information to it	Makes no verbal response to the child's comments about the book	Repeats child's comments verbatim	Rephrases the child's comments	Rephrases the child's comments and adds information to it
Repeats the prompt and the child's comments	Reads the book with no further prompts or expansion	Repeats the prompt	Repeats the prompt and the child's comment	Repeats the prompt, changing slightly, and the child's comment to make sure the child has learned from the expansion

Figure 9–5 Dialogic Reading Rating Scale.
Source: Adapted from Whitehurst, G. J (Russ) Whitehurst (1992) retrieved from www.readingrockets.org/article 400.

objective evaluator. See Chapter 13 for a detailed discussion of program assessment.

Go to the Education CourseMate website, accessed through CengageBrain.com, for Literacy Rating Scales, plans, and resources.

❓ What to Do With It

The Rating Scale on each child should be repeated periodically to measure progress and noted on the Portfolio Evidence Sheet. See the example in Figure 9–6. It needs to be accessible in each child's Portfolio storage so that it can be used as the basis for individualized curriculum planning and for sharing with the family to show the child's areas of strengths and areas still developing. As with all records, it must be kept safe from loss and unauthorized viewing.

Looking at Literacy

EXERCISE What did you read today? What did you write today?

Once you know how, reading and writing are so natural that they are done automatically. When reading the preceding exercise, thoughts might have gone to formally picking up a book or writing a letter. Do not forget about these:

> the numbers on the clock
> the name of the toothpaste you used this
>   morning
> the on/off light switch
> signing a check
> jotting down a phone number
> reading and writing the answers to this exercise

Americans are reading less, and less well, than ever before. The National Endowment for the Arts study (Iyengar, Ball, NEA, 2007) found that if adults are not reading, will children learn to love reading? Reading is critical to success in school and in later life. Despite billions of dollars spent on reading materials, curriculum, studies of various approaches, vast research, and national initiatives, a large number of children in America never learn to read well. This has huge implications because of the connection between poverty and illiteracy.

Literacy Development

Literacy is not an isolated skill from other developmental domains, for it involves motor skills, visual perception, hearing, small muscle development, cognitive development, social interactions, and emotional control. It is simultaneously developing along with language.

Receptive language skills are greater and come earlier than expressive skills. This is true in literacy as well. Hearing and understanding words precede speaking them. Reading words usually occurs before writing them. And writing phonetically (as the word sounds) will precede writing using conventional spelling. Reading and comprehension ability is greater than the ability to write as an expressive form (though some writing seems to be done without thinking).

Learning to Read

The formal instruction of reading and writing formerly began in the first grade. As the field of **emergent literacy** expands, it is now recognized that literacy begins much earlier, with seeing and using print materials. Children come to school knowing much about reading and writing already, but they need more opportunities to read, write, draw, and use symbolic representation. When

PORTFOLIO EVIDENCE OF CHILD'S DEVELOPMENT			
Evidence Type	Date	Recorder	Notes
LITERACY – the child's interest and interaction with reading and writing including work samples			
TS	10/24/	BAN	No literacy choices
CL	10/30/	BAN	Recognizes name on helper chart
RS	11/6/	MLS	Listens to books one on one
WS	12/7	MLS	Prints name – all caps
RS	2/6/	BAN	Pretend reading – retells plot accurately

Figure 9–6 Portfolio Evidence Sheet Example.

Figure 9–7 Children learn while playing.

a child zooms a block along the rug making car noises, this pretend play shows an understanding that an object can stand for something else, which is exactly what reading is—a written word that stands for a spoken word—and that letters alone and arranged in a certain way can represent sounds. As children play, they are developing symbolic processes (Figure 9–7).

The National Early Literacy Panel (NELP) research sought to answer questions on what skills, abilities, and child characteristics predict later reading, writing, and spelling outcomes, and what programs, interventions, and environments contribute to or inhibit gains in skills. More than 500 research studies were reviewed and six variables were found that had clear and consistently strong relationships with later conventional literacy skills. These include the following:

- *Alphabet knowledge*: knowledge of the names and sounds associated with printed letters
- *Phonological awareness*: the ability to detect, manipulate, or analyze the auditory aspects of spoken language (including the ability to distinguish or segment words, syllables, or phonemes), independent of meaning
- *Rapid automatic naming of letters or digits*: the ability to rapidly name a sequence of random letters or digits
- *Rapid automatic naming of objects or colors*: the ability to rapidly name a sequence of repeating random sets of pictures of objects or colors
- *Writing or writing name*: the ability to write letters in isolation on request or to write one's own name
- *Phonological memory*: the ability to remember spoken information for a short period of time (NELP, 2008)

Environmental Print

Literacy begins with communication, verbally and nonverbally. Even the unborn child hears the muffled mother's voice and the rhythm of her heartbeat. Early in the child's life, long before the child can speak to convey thoughts or express feelings, music and visual arts and crafts can be the symbols of thought. Between two and three years of age, children begin to notice and "read" print all around them: McDonald's signs, stop signs, and a print advertisement for their favorite cereal box or television show. This **environmental print** can be the springboard to literacy when it is recognized and followed up with books and activities that build on that knowledge. This is **contextualized literacy**, words and phrases that can be read because they are defined by their context, shape, color, and position. Children are constantly interacting with literacy (Figure 9–8). Besides an environment full of print, children look to role models. They see family members reading the newspaper, the advertising on television, or directions on how to put together the tricycle. They often imitate those actions by picking up papers and babbling or pretending to read. Almost every child has picked up a pencil, pen, lipstick, or permanent marker and made some scribbles in a place not meant for writing.

EXERCISE **Write the alphabet down the side of a piece of paper. Now, begin to think of all the environmental print using the beginning letter. This idea came from *Chicken Starts with CH*! (Xu & Rutledge, 2003). This will get you started:**

A—Advertisement
B—Bumper stickers
C—Coins
D—D_____

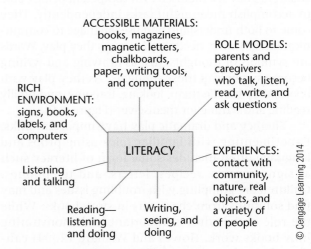

Figure 9–8 Interacting with Literacy.

The Play-Literacy Connection. Both Piaget and Vygotsky placed emphasis on the connection between play and literacy. The connection is present, but in Roskos and Christie's exhaustive analysis of many play-literacy interface studies, it hasn't been proven that there is a cause and effect relationship. The studies supported play's connection with literacy by

» providing settings that promote literacy activity, skills, and strategies;

» serving as a language experience that can build connections between oral and written modes of expression; and

» providing opportunities to teach and learn literacy (Roskos & Christie, 2004, p. 116).

Unlike the genetic predisposition to speaking and drawing, reading and writing must be taught. The symbolic relations of play set the stage for the symbolic representation of letters for sounds that make written words. Oral language is the predictor of the ease with which children will learn to read (Snow et al., 1998), teaching not by drill and practice, but by playful or guided learning that involves the child in pleasurable activities encouraging exploration. This is demonstrated in the Tools of the Mind curriculum based on the scaffolding of Vygotsky's theory (Bodrova & Leong, 2007).

Literacy development is dependent on other domains of development to lay the foundation, the structure, and the expansion; and those fundamentals are interwoven in the child's play. Efficacy, the confidence of achievement, emotional engagement that instills trust and encouragement, language that labels objects and events in the world, and the social supports of the family and the community all contribute to literacy development (Bardige & Segal, 2005). The child achieves these characteristics during social interactions (play) with loving, caring adults and older, more proficient children. They see themselves as competent beings, able to accomplish meaningful tasks independently. They come to both understand and use language to communicate their wants, needs, and ideas as they play. Words are symbols of thoughts, just as drawing and writing become symbols of those thoughts. As they play with books, they handle them, looking, listening, and finally reading and writing for themselves (Figure 9–9).

Literacy and dramatic play have important links. Experimenting with familiar roles using props and language often includes some form of literacy such as signs, menus, recipes, letters, and telephones. Children are grappling with troubling issues and may find solutions from characters in story books. While the role of the adult is important in demonstrating how books work, Howes and Wishard (2004) caution that when young children are constructing

Figure 9–9 Experiences with books precedes learning to read and write.

narratives during social pretend play, the role of the teacher should be more subdued to allow the children to make meaning, and especially to respect the cultural community from which the children come.

Children's play in a classroom may appear spontaneous, but in quality programs much thought and planning goes into the environment, the curriculum, and the teacher's roles as guide, leader, observer, and expander.

Observing similarities and differences is an important skill in beginning to read, discerning the shapes of letters and words to develop letter discrimination. In children's play with blocks, clay, art materials, puzzles, and games, the skill of observation is honed. Taking nature walks with children provides experiences in seeing patterns in flowers, leaves, whole-part relationships, and even seeing shapes and alphabet letters in twigs, cracks in the sidewalk, and building and window shapes. The world of outdoors brings many opportunities to connect with literacy to develop reading and writing fluency.

Learning to Read and Write

Exactly how children learn to read and what is the best curricular approach to take is still a matter of debate and research. There is the ecological view that suggests that every child is a product of biological factors and then is surrounded by relationships of family, friends, peers, and society, all of which affect the child's development, including literacy. The child is exposed to the literacy of the culture from birth. Researchers are studying how these influences form the basis for learning to read.

There are the more formal situations such as child care, preschool, and early elementary classrooms and how the philosophy or approach to literacy in these more formal settings affects the curriculum. A few of the approaches follow:

- *Basal readers*—Books designed for group instruction in teaching whole words that are repeated.
- *Whole language*—Providing a **print-rich environment** through which children have natural interactions with print and literature.
- *Literature-based*—Using children's literature on which to base reading instruction.
- *Phonetic reading*—Children are taught the sounds (phonemes) of the alphabet letters; then they use them to decode words.
- *Thematic centers*—Dramatic play with literacy materials such as those from a library, doctor's office, school, or home.
- *Book reading*—Adult reads, children listen.
- *Dialogic reading*—Adult reads and asks questions about the connection between illustrations, print, and plot.
- *Child narration*—The story comes from the child, either in dictation or a combination of drawing and writing, and the child sits in the "Author's Chair," where the story is explained to other children who may ask questions or make comments.
- *Shared drama enactment*—Children together construct a dramatic episode, play it out, and then the rest of the group ask questions or make comments (Fein et al., 2000).

Most early childhood classrooms use a combination of each of these so that pure research into approach and results has been difficult. In *Breaking the Code*, Gentry (2006) explores what occurs in the brain in relation to reading, writing, and spelling. He points out that spelling is an often neglected and poorly taught skill. Chunking of the sounds of letters is to him the key to breaking the code between

It Happened to Me

B L D Z R

This was demonstrated to me by a group of five-year-old boys who dominated a class I had. As we approached the holiday season, they were interested in making their gift wish lists. Having just been inspired by Schickedanz's book, *More than the ABC's* (1999), instead of dictating their lists to me, I urged them to write or draw their own. To my amazement they worked hard at it for many minutes. Even more amazing was that I could really read what they wrote:
B L D Z R (bulldozer)
G N (gun)
2 W E L R (two-wheeler)
They were struggling to communicate meaning, and they had done so!

a novice reader and a skilled reader. He reviews the phases of learning to read and spell as (1) prealphabetic, where the child uses logos and visual clues to "read" the word on the stop sign, cereal box, or fast food restaurant; (2) partial alphabetic reading, where children begin to pay attention to the first letter of words and match sounds to the letters, where the words *sat, sit, sing* are not recognized as distinct; (3) full alphabetic, where attention is paid to the full spelling with phonemic awareness of all the sounds represented in the word (perhaps not with proper pronunciation yet, but the concept is there); (4) consolidated alphabetic reading, where letter groups are chunked, moving from sounding out the letters of *i-n-t-e-r-e-s-t-i-n-g* to *in-ter-est-ing*. It is in this phase that dyslexia causes problems for the reader.

Phonological awareness. This is a critical part of literacy development where the reader gives attention to the sounds of spoken language such as being able to distinguish between the words *sad, dad, bad,* and *glad*. It is also syllable awareness, the ability to recognize that the word *helicopter* is longer than the word *plane*, concentrating on the sound and not the meaning of the words. It includes matching sounds—words have the same beginning sounds: *plate, cake, pear*; synthesis—blending and adding sounds: *bath, splash, cat/cats*; and analysis—counting syllables, segmenting a word into its parts (sounding it out to write it by its sounds),

TOPICS in OBSERVATION

Books in the Sandbox

EXERCISE   List the literacy materials (reading or writing) in each of the rooms in your home.

Kitchen:

Living room:

Bedroom:

Bathroom:

Most homes have some kinds of literacy materials in every room. From cookbooks to magazines to phone message pads, every room has something to read, something to write on. Why then does the early childhood classroom restrict books to the book area and writing materials to the writing center or art area? It probably is for the protection of the books or the walls from indiscriminate writers. What this does, however, is artificially restrict literacy to certain areas, unlike in real life. If the classroom is to be a microcosm of the world outside, perhaps these restrictions need to be reconsidered. Observe the placement and proliferation of books and writing materials throughout the environment as an assessment tool of the literacy-rich environment and the teacher's own literacy priority.

How about books about the beach or archaeology in or near the sandbox? In the art area, books about colors—even art books with prints of the masters—to stimulate interest in color, form, texture, and art expression. Books about buildings and skyscrapers, and pencils and paper to trace blocks or sketch buildings, will add a literacy component to the block area. Books or magazines on the back of the toilet might capture the interest of a child not ordinarily sitting in one place very long.

In the dramatic play area, books or magazines and writing materials can connect literacy to whatever dramatic play theme that is set up there. A medical office would have an appointment calendar, magazines in the waiting room, and books of anatomy or stories about the hospital. The car repair shop would have auto repair manuals, car magazines, order forms for repairs, and invoices.

Another artificial classroom literacy behavior is reading to the whole group of children at one time. In the outside world, reading and writing are usually individual activities. Individualized reading is enhanced when books and reading materials are integrated throughout the classroom environment. That way, the adult can read to every child in the context of their play or encourage writing as a mode of communication that facilitates the play. Literacy is connected with real objects and real purposes, not just another isolated routine on the daily schedule.

By desegregating literacy from the library or writing centers, children see the practical use of reading and writing. The adult's role is to help fill the span between children's actual ability to read and write and a higher level, providing that scaffold by suggesting researching books for answers to questions or encouraging writing as a way to communicate ideas or preserve details.

Care of the books and writing materials is a valid concern, but there are some principles to follow that can reduce these worries:

▶ Book pockets or racks can be placed near the sandbox, easels, and other play areas. Books and literacy materials can be placed in the block area along with wheeled vehicles and block accessories.

(Continued)

TOPICS in OBSERVATION

▷ When materials are useful and important to children, they will treat them carefully.

▷ Adult role models of caring for books and using writing materials in a constructive way will be attended to by the children.

Think about how the opportunities to observe children's literacy skills will be expanded if the materials are included in every area.

deleting such as in singing the song "B-I-N-G-O, -I-N-G-O, - -N-G-O."

Because of its high relationship to later success in reading and spelling, phonological awareness should be an intentional part of the preschool curriculum. Preschool teachers can support phonological awareness development in the following ways:

▷ Read aloud books that play with sounds, commenting on the book's language play and inviting children to create their own.

▷ Share poetry that plays with sounds with rhymes and chants, reading it several times, drawing attention to the word sounds, and encouraging children to substitute other rhyming words.

▷ Share songs that play with sounds such as "Willoughby Wallaby Woo," substituting initial sounds.

▷ Play games that draw attention to sounds such as "I Spy something that begins with the sound SH." Make sure that the games are fun and do not require participation or correct answers (Yopp & Yopp, 2009).

The connection between language and literacy was discussed in Chapter 6, illustrated so powerfully by the research of Hart and Risley (2004), who studied the gap between the number of words and kind of language used in high- and low-income homes. That gap correlated to the gap in school performance at age nine. It is not early reading skills that matter, but rather the relationships and connections with the spoken word, including vocabulary, open-ended questions, positive feedback, explanations, descriptions, and running dialogue throughout the day that are vital for true early literacy (New, 2001). The implications of this research are clear: It is too late to begin literacy development in preschool programs. Literacy development begins at birth, so the

foundation must be laid by the family and the educators of infants and toddlers.

Jim Trelease (2006) gives this advice about the implications of literacy:

1. The more you read, the more you know.
2. The more you know, the smarter you grow.
3. The smarter you are, the longer you stay in school.
4. The longer you stay in school, the more diplomas you earn and the longer you are employed; thus, the more money you earn in a lifetime.
5. The more diplomas you earn, the higher your children's grades will be in school.
6. The more diplomas you earn, the longer you live. (p. xxv)

Literacy Stages. Literacy begins in infancy through relationships. Four cornerstones that Bardige and Segal (2005) describe are: (1) efficacy, the emotional self-confidence built in a child by mastery of manageable challenges; (2) emotional engagement with trustworthy adults; (3) language environment that provides labels for things and feelings; and (4) social supports such as culture, social and economic ties, and community. Literacy skills develop with age (Figure 9–10).

▶❚❚ TEACHSOURCE VIDEO ACTIVITY

Go to the Education CourseMate website, accessed through CengageBrain.com and view Preschool: Communication Development Through Language and Literacy Activities.

What were some of the activities that engaged the children to promote literacy?

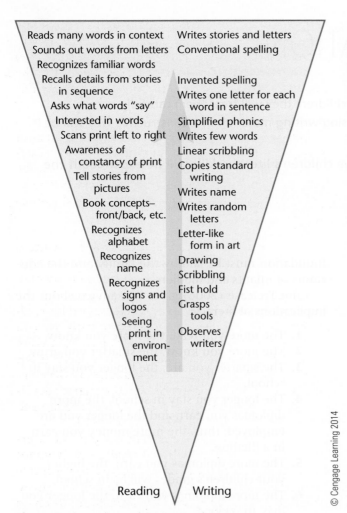

Reading | Writing

Figure 9–10 Reading and Writing Development.

© Cengage Learning 2014

© Cengage Learning 2012

Figure 9–11 Even very young children enjoy hearing stories.

The early childhood teacher can address each of these areas by knowing the ecological context of the children and working to build relationships with the child and the family to share the wonder of literacy development by providing access where books are few, and a classroom that values language and literacy.

Reading to Babies. An important step toward becoming literate is the shared experience of reading a book with bright pictures and simple words about the child's world.

Look at Figure 9–11.

How does this picture make you feel?

What do you think the adult is feeling?

What do you think the child is feeling?

Infants from birth through 18 months are learning through sensory experiences. Hearing the voice reading, seeing not only the colorful page

of the book but the face of the reader expressing emotions, touching the pages, and even tasting them are all a part of babies and books (Zambo, 2007). Even if the reading material is the *New York Times*, building blocks of literacy are being cemented together. The bodies are close. There is a difference in the reading voice from the speaking voice, and a growing awareness that those little marks on the page mean something. Young babies are at the Sensorimotor Stage, so they should have some books that are touchable. The small, cardboard books—ones with texture, cloth, or plastic, ones they can pull on and chew—provide those first experiences. Because infants' language development is at a simple stage, one-word books with repeating sounds soon become their favorites. However, good literature with a simple story line such as *Goodnight Moon* and *Brown Bear, Brown Bear* become favorites of the child and adult, still fun and interesting after many, many readings. The adult and child should be in a comfortable spot and positioned so that the child can point to and even turn the pages. It is best to experience this one-on-one, but if another child is included, that child should have a book to hold.

Reading to Toddlers. As children move into the second year, their memory is lengthening. They are becoming familiar with books and pointing, laughing, and saying words of identification such as "Choo choo" and "Wha's dat?" They become participants by pretending to read. They begin to identify with the characters in the books, empathizing with another's fears and distress, and expressing emotions such as anger, happiness, and sadness for the characters. Words and familiar phrases from favorite books are added to their vocabulary. They ask for their favorites to be

It Happened to Me

Taste of Reading

I loaned a book to a student, and when she returned it she made many apologies for the damage to the book. She explained that she was reading and studying and her toddler climbed up in her lap and chomped down on the side of the book. Sure enough, there was a small crescent of punctures on the edges of several pages. I could just see that little one being envious of this thing that had taken her mother's attention, and so she took an aggressive action against the thing that had wooed her away. I treasure that book and its bitten pages for the story that it tells.

read again, and again, and again. When the adult changes a word in a familiar book, the child notices and protests. This shows that the child knows print and speech are related. Viewing books together should be done in very small groups of not more than two or three children so that each can be close to the book and the reader, and able to actively participate. Read books throughout the day, whenever a child brings one to you or there is a quiet moment, fitting the book to the child's abilities and preferences following the child's cues.

By the end of the third year, the child can accurately tell the story from the pictures in familiar books. They will begin to move eyes and fingers along the row of print while saying the words. They will respond to the book by asking questions and repeating sounds (phonemic awareness) and phrases (memory). This is an indication of the child's awareness that those markings below the pictures are a code to be deciphered. Their developing independence may result in impatience with a page with much text to be read. They should be encouraged to handle the books themselves; yes, they will get them messy, but in handling a book they will learn how to hold it, open it, where to look for their favorite pictures, and eventually have an easier time learning to read (Morrow, 2008).

Children who have been read to begin to recognize the letter names and the sounds of the letters. They know which side is up in a book and the concept of "front to back." In the third year, many recognize familiar logos and signs, their own name, and some short words. They begin to take an interest in the words in books and in the environment, and ask what specific words say. They understand the purpose of a book and begin to turn pages from front to back and scan the pictures from left to right pages. The story sequence of beginning, middle, and end is recognized and can be retold from the pictures. An awareness of rhyming words and an association of letters and sounds appear.

Reading and Preschoolers. Most children learn to listen and speak effortlessly without direct instruction. Traditionally, reading and writing have been taught in formal education. In separate, isolated exercises, the vision, mind, and small muscles were trained for reading with worksheets or activities. The term *emergent literacy* is a broader term, differing from isolated skills, coming out of the whole-language movement (Clay, 1975). It fits very well into the paradigm of developmentally appropriate practice—child-centered, developmentally based, using a curriculum of themes and projects.

Preschoolers who have had early home literacy experiences that included family involvement in reading and writing, and exposure to receptive language (hearing many words, complex sentences, descriptions, and explanations) are more likely to have high test scores. These are directly related to levels of vocabulary, listening comprehension skills, and reading skills in grade 3 (Senechal & LeFevre, 2002). The common characteristics of these children have much to do with their home environment. They

- were read to on a regular basis.
- had a wide variety of print materials available in the home, such as books, magazines, and newspapers.
- had paper and pencil available to scribble and draw and copy objects and letters.
- had people in the home who stimulated their interest by supporting reading and writing as a worthwhile activity (Trelease, 2006).

This is not an endorsement for the "superbaby syndrome." Early reading to babies and young children brings many benefits (Figure 9–12). Forced acceleration of reading training has been shown to have no positive effect on school performance by the third grade. While those two concepts seem in opposition, the difference is in the approach. Young

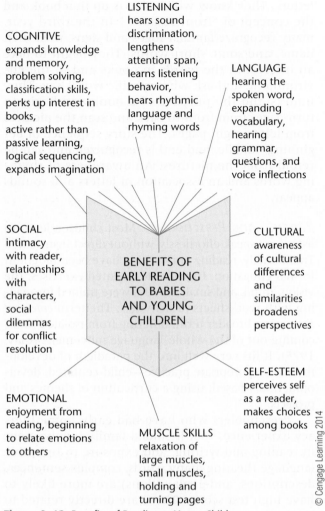

COGNITIVE expands knowledge and memory, problem solving, classification skills, perks up interest in books, active rather than passive learning, logical sequencing, expands imagination

LISTENING hears sound discrimination, lengthens attention span, learns listening behavior, hears rhythmic language and rhyming words

LANGUAGE hearing the spoken word, expanding vocabulary, hearing grammar, questions, and voice inflections

SOCIAL intimacy with reader, relationships with characters, social dilemmas for conflict resolution

BENEFITS OF EARLY READING TO BABIES AND YOUNG CHILDREN

CULTURAL awareness of cultural differences and similarities broadens perspectives

EMOTIONAL enjoyment from reading, beginning to relate emotions to others

MUSCLE SKILLS relaxation of large muscles, small muscles, holding and turning pages

SELF-ESTEEM perceives self as a reader, makes choices among books

© Cengage Learning 2014

Figure 9–12 Benefits of Reading to Young Children.

It Happened to Me

Office

Walking down the hall, a child in my preschool class asked, "Where's the ice?" "What do you mean, where's the ice?" I asked incredulously. He pointed to a door with the sign OFFICE. "It says, 'off- ice.' I wonder where the ice is."

He had learned one aspect of print, the decoding of letters into meaningful words, but had not yet mastered the importance of spacing.

children (as early as two years old) have been taught to read and do mathematics through drill and practice. David Elkind, a noted child psychologist, has sent out the warning against such "superkid" practices in his book *Miseducation: Preschoolers at Risk* (1987). These techniques are based on behaviorist philosophies rather than on the work of developmentalists such as Piaget and Erikson, on which most early childhood principles and practices are founded.

Four- and five-year-old children recognize books as sources of information and entertainment, and recognize the difference between story books and "pictionary" or dictionary format. They can fill in story lines from rebus picture books and sometimes read simple stories word by word. They can retell a story from memory or reconstructed from the pictures. Predictions are made about what might happen next or why a certain event happened, relating

the concept of cause and effect. Many words are recognized by sight; and the children are also sounding out other words by alphabet letters. This **phonemic awareness** of the sounds of speech in syllables and the relationship of alphabet letters to sounds is a critical stage in the process of learning to read.

They are gaining **alphabetic awareness**, more than just memorizing the alphabet, but identifying the sounds of each letter. This is a difficult task in English since there are 26 letters but about 44 sounds from those letters. This is what is known as "breaking the code." They also begin to blend sounds; seeing that letters in sequence blend together to make the word is known as "sounding it out." Children are beginning to notice the spaces between words and the punctuation marks at the end of a sentence and changing their inflection depending on the mark. They act out story characters in their play. Their conversations relate to situations and dilemmas the characters faced and how they solved them. They take an interest in creating and illustrating their own books, either in pretend writing, phonetic spelling, or dictation. Some of them have become readers, either through their families' direct instruction or by natural association of letters and sounds.

Reading in the Early Grades. In kindergarten, children are usually able to tell a story from memorization, write some alphabet letters, read and write their name and many other familiar words, and begin to identify and make rhymes. They recognize that letters and their sounds are combined to form words and there are spaces between words, though they often indicate the spaces with periods. They begin to ask questions about words, asking for their thoughts to be written out. They frequently ask, "How do you spell xxx?" in an attempt to print it out.

From six to eight years old, usually first through third grade, children are gaining competence in being conventional readers and writers. They can read the high-frequency words such as *is, were, she, to, and, of, from* and *with* by sight; and can decode unknown words by letter-sound correspondence. They recognize many familiar blends of letters, such as –tion, -ed,-s, -es, -ing that bring greater fluency to their reading. Their spelling is moving away from phonetic and towards conventional spelling. They are gaining skill at reading aloud with meaning and expression, and many have become successful independent readers.

Governors Association has set Core Standards for the English Language Arts in Reading: Foundation Skills for Grade 1 (Accessed at http://www.corestandards.org. Reprinted by permission of the National Governors Association) are as follows:

Reading Standards: Foundational Skills (K5) Grade 1 Students

Phonics and Word Recognition
- Know and apply grade-level phonics and word analysis skills in decoding words.
- Distinguish long and short vowels when reading regularly spelled one-syllable words.
- Know spelling-sound correspondences for additional common vowel teams.
- Decode regularly spelled two-syllable words with long vowels.
- Decode words with common prefixes and suffixes.
- Identify words with inconsistent but common spelling-sound correspondences.
- Recognize and read grade-appropriate irregularly spelled words.

Fluency
- Read with sufficient accuracy and fluency to support comprehension.
- Read grade-level text with purpose and understanding.
- Read grade-level text orally with accuracy, appropriate rate, and expression.
- Use context to confirm or self-correct word recognition and understanding, rereading as necessary.

Strategies that teachers use in kindergarten and first and second grade are:

- Shared reading with big books—group activity where the teacher reads from a big book while each child follows along in her own copy; later reading it to each other, and then reading it individually to the teacher.
- Shared writing—group activity where the teacher guides and writes a collective piece such as a story, invitation, thank-you letter, or description of an event, with the children providing the wording and some spelling.
- Journal Writing—frequent entries at extemporary writing that can be interactive between the student and teacher; science journals, daily events logs provide practice in writing mechanics.
- Book Clubs or Literature Circles—small group of students read a common text, participate in literature discussions and activities, and meet with the teacher to model, guide, and assess.
- Readers Theater—children select literature to present orally, sometimes turning it into a drama.
- Authors Studies—examine several works by the same author to discuss style, format, and content.

Types of Books

Children enjoy and learn different things from different types of books, and they should be exposed to many types. Machado (2013) lists the types of books, the learning possibilities, and why children like them (Figure 9–13).

Young Children Write

Young children's writing emerges along with language and reading, as well as art. The myth that oral language must be mastered before written language can develop is attacked by Schickedanz in *Writing in Preschool: Learning to Orchestrate Meaning*

It Happened to Me

Permanent Name Writing

A mother came to school one morning and said, "I'm really glad you've been working with name writing and journal writing, but last night Jason wrote his name on the side of the car with permanent marker!" Oops, no guarantees.

TYPES	FEATURES TEACHERS LIKE	FEATURES CHILDREN LIKE
Storybooks (picture books)	sharing moments	imagination and fantasy
• family and home	seeing children enthusiastic and attentive	identification with character's humanness
• folktales and fables	making character's voices	wish and need fulfillment
• fanciful stories	introducing human truths and imaginative adventures	adventure
• fairy tales	sharing favorites	excitement
• animal stories	easy for child to identify with small creatures	action
• others		self-realization
		visual variety
		word pleasure
Nonfiction books (informational) also referred to as content books	expand individual and group interests	provide facts; allow for discovery of information and ideas
	develop "reading-to-know" attitudes	discuss reality and how things work and function
	encourage finding out together	answer "why" and "how"
	provide accurate facts	supply new words and new meanings
	contain scientific content	
Wordless books	promote child speech, creativity, and imagination	provide opportunity to supply their own words to tell the story
		promote discovery of meanings
		include color, action, and visual variety
Interaction books (books with active child participation built in)	keep children involved and attentive	provide for movement and group feeling
	build listening for directions skills	promote individual creativity and expression
		appeal to senses
		have manipulatable features
Concept books (books with central concepts or themes that include specific and reinforcing examples)	promote categorization	add to knowledge
	present opportunities to know about and develop concepts	visually present abstractions
	many examples	
Predictable books (books with repetitions and reinforcement)	permit successful guessing	provide opportunity to read along are repetitive
	build child's confidence	build feelings of competence
	promote ideas that books make sense	
Reference books (picture dictionaries, encyclopedias, special subject books)	provide opportunity to look up questions with the child	provide answers
	promote individualized learning	are used with teacher (shared time)
		are resources that answer their questions
Alphabet and word books (word books have name of object printed near or on top of object)	supply letters and word models	discover meanings and alphabet letters and words
	Pair words and objects	see names of what is illustrated
	are useful for child with avid interest in alphabet letters and words	
	can include letter and word play	

(*continued*)

Figure 9–13 Types of Books for Young Children.
Source: From Machado, *Early Childhood Experiences in Language Arts*, 9th ed. © 2010 Cengage Learning.

TYPES	FEATURES TEACHERS LIKE	FEATURES CHILDREN LIKE
Novelty books (pop-ups, fold-outs, electronic books, stamp and pasting books, activity books, puzzle books, scratch-and-sniff books, hidden objects in illustrations, talking books)	and sense-exploring variety stimulate creativity come in many different sizes and shapes motor involvement for child many include humor	encourage exploring, touching, moving, feeling, smelling, painting, drawing, coloring, cutting, gluing, acting upon, listening to a mechanical voice, and getting instant feedback
Paperback books and magazines (Golden Books, *Humpty Dumpty Magazine*)	are inexpensive come in a wide variety many classics available	include activity pages
Teacher- and child-made books	reinforce class learnings build understanding of authorship allow creative expression record individual, group projects, field trips, parties promote child expression of concerns and ideas build child's self-esteem	allow child to see own name in print provide opportunity to share ideas with others are self-rewarding
Therapeutic books (books helping children cope with and understand things such as divorce, death, jealousy)	present life realistically offer positive solutions and insights present diverse family groups deal with life's hard-to-deal-with subjects	help children discuss real feelings
Seasonal and holiday books	accompany child interest may help child understand underlying reasons for celebration	build pleasant expectations add details
Books and audiovisual combinations (read-alongs)	add variety offer group and individual experiencing opportunities stimulate interest in books	project large illustrations can be enjoyed individually
Toddler books and board books (durable pages)	resist wear and tear	are easy to use (ease in page-turning)
Multicultural and cross-cultural books (culturally conscious books)	Increase positive attitudes concerning diversity and similarity	introduce a variety of people
Oversized books (big books)	emphasize the realities in our society have extra large text and illustrations	are easy-to-see in groups have giant book characters

Figure 9–13

and Marks (2009). This is a helpful resource for the early childhood educator and families. The first step in writing begins with the small muscle control of the writing tool—a pencil, marker, or crayon. This is influenced greatly by the environment that makes these accessible. The adult is a role model by writing lists to remember. Labels are written on items to signify possession. Writing is demonstrated by the adult who says, "This is how you write your name."

Writing is more than mastery of the tools or symbols of reading. In fact, researchers have found that many children actually write before they read, driven by the urge to communicate, although they are limited in the knowledge of writing conventions. When children have something to say, they are motivated to communicate first by drawing, and then by writing (Stonier, 2009).

All children, including those from economically disadvantaged settings, can benefit from effective content- and language-rich instruction that includes:

- time, materials, and resources that actively build language and conceptual knowledge
- a supportive learning environment in which children have access to a wide variety of reading and writing resources
- different group sizes (large, small, individual) and different levels of guidance to meet the needs of individual children
- opportunities for sustained and in-depth learning, including play
- a masterful orchestration of activity that supports learning and social-emotional development (Neuman & Roskos, 2005)

Stages of Writing. Writing develops in predictable stages.

Scribbling. The child makes marks as soon as she can hold a writing tool. She begins by stabbing at the paper, the dragging action making lines. She progresses to unclosed circular motions, then to closed circles, vertical and horizontal lines, and eventually boxlike or square shapes. This phase is the preparation for both drawing and writing. Many children extend scribbling into wavy lines that they call writing after observing adults writing cursive (Figure 9–14).

Drawing. Written communication in the form of pictures has its historical roots in the Egyptian pictorials inside the pyramids. Children (and societies) without writing convey meaningful messages by drawing. Young children are hindered by their lack of small muscle coordination and the inability to represent on paper the ideas they have in their head (Figure 9–15). They have a mental image of a mouse, but what they draw may not be recognizable as a mouse to the viewer. Again, the receptive is greater than the expressive.

© Cengage Learning 2014

Figure 9–14 Linear scribbles approximate writing.

Figure 9–15 Children's drawings often are the expression of inner thoughts and words before writing has developed.

Children can express their thoughts by using drawing. This expressive language, known metaphorically as the "100 languages of children" (Edwards, Gandini, & Forman, 1998), has captivated the world through the work of the children of Reggio Emilia, Italy. Carolyn Pope Edwards, who has studied the Reggio approach in detail, calls the various media such as photography, clay, or drama, "literacies," extending the child's visual expression beyond writing (Edwards & Willis, 2000). Drawing is a precursor to writing, expressing inner thoughts for which the child has no written language yet. Often drawing and alphabet letters are mixed (Figure 9–16).

Making Letters. Between the ages of three and four, children begin to realize there is a difference between drawing and writing, although it may not be evident to the viewer. The first letter they write is usually the first letter of their name. As their knowledge of the sounds and shapes of more letters expands, they will begin to write sentences. The first letter of each word is sounded out and written down, with the expectation that the reader will be able to decipher the message. It is an approximation that brings them closer to the symbols that combine to make words in a sentence. They will often ask for words to be written so they can copy them. They try their hand at **invented spelling**, as the boys did on their gift list, by sounding

it out and writing the letter sounds that they hear (see "It Happened to Me: BLDZR").

Organizing Print. Writing is more than knowledge of letters and their sounds; the proper sequence, organization on the page, and the spaces between form written language. Random letters will appear in children's paintings and artwork whether they have meaning or the children are just practicing the style.

A person's name is important, and it is no different for children. Because they are self-centered at this age, preschoolers are highly motivated to write their names (Tolchinsky, 2003). Name writing can be encouraged with daily sign-in. Through this early literacy experience, name writing was a transition routine into the classroom that formalized the children's presence, developed their fine muscle control, and documented their writing progress. Studies such as those done by Hanye (2002) are seeing a strong correlation between name writing and cognition and language, suggesting that name writing skills could be used as a part of screening for reading difficulties. Awareness of rhyming and beginning sounds, uppercase letters, and the concepts and functions of print is higher in children who

Figure 9–16 Drawing and writing are beginning to separate from one another.

It Happened to Me

Make Love

Another writing incident is an anecdote I will always remember. A dear, sweet little four-year-old girl came over to me in class one day and said, "Mrs. Nilsen, I know how to make love. Want me to show you?" Gulp! "Sure." She got a sheet of paper and proudly wrote L U V. We rejoiced together!

have mastered name writing (Welsch, Sullivan, & Justice, 2003; Foulin, 2005).

Dictation. While a child draws, an adult talking with the child may elicit the thinking that is not revealed in the drawing because of the child's lack of physical ability and representational skills. As the child relates meaning, the adult may ask if the child wants the story written in words that others can read. If so, in the act of dictation the child sees oral language translated into written language. It may even help the child add detail to the drawing by having to

think about it more concretely in order to express the meaning to another person. This is an example of *scaffolding*.

Backward Letters. Preschoolers, in their experimentation with letters, and perhaps due to their still-developing visual perception, often reverse letters to their family's alarm. Sulzby (1993), who has studied children's writing for over 15 years, says it is common for preschoolers to write backward and to switch from backward to forward. These children are also beginning to use the conventions of print, such as using the period between every word and phonetically spelling the sounds (Figure 9–17). In first and second grades, depending on the school district, handwriting receives more emphasis. By the end of second grade, letter reversals have all but stopped. If they persist, there may be other influences, so further evaluations should be done.

Writing to Read. Many kindergarten classes are encouraging children to write their thoughts and tell about experiences using invented spelling and illustration preceding formal reading instruction. Children demonstrate a level of phonemic awareness by sounding out the words and writing down the sounds they hear. Look at Figure 9–18, and you can almost hear my grandson carefully writing the letters

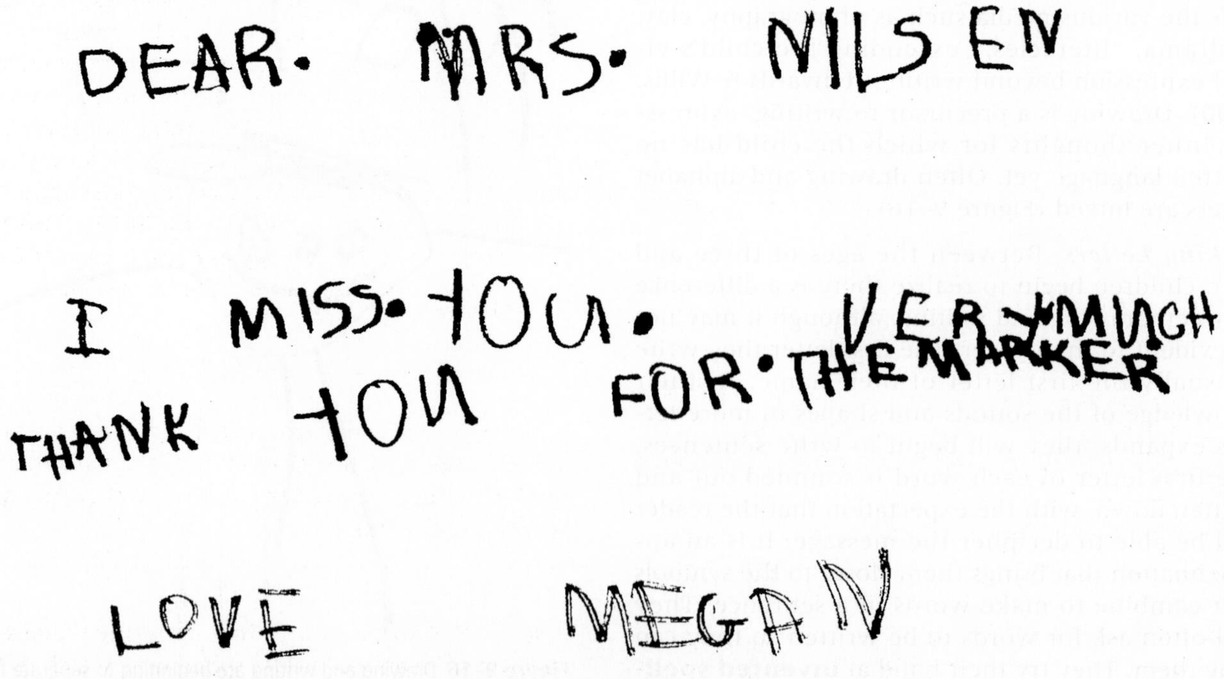

Figure 9–17 Early writing experiments with writing conventions but is precious for its effort and meaning.

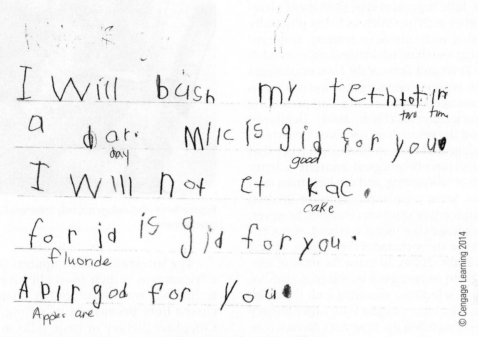

I will básh mŕ tēthtot ĺñ
two tim.
a dat· M⁄ıc ⁄s gıd for youᵥ
day   *good*
I wⁱll nᵒt et kqc⸱
cake
foɾ ıd ıs gıd foɾyoᵤ·
fluoride
Apır gᵒd foɾ youᵥ
Apples are

Figure 9–18 This child's early writing testifies to extensive knowledge of good dental hygiene.

© Cengage Learning 2014

that he hears to convey the meaning of the story about teeth. You can see he has learned about full sentences with a subject and verb and a period at the end of each sentence. The teacher has interpreted his words and written the conventional spelling beneath. The illustration of his family all brushing their teeth completes his story. It is a precious artifact of his pathway to literacy.

Incorporate Writing into Play. By ages five and six, children realize that writing serves the function of conveying information. They will make signs to designate territory or "Do not disturb," print their name on their artwork so they can take it home, and use writing to tell stories or write letters. In the dramatic-play area, writing materials are provided as they would appear in context. In the Home Play area, put a note pad by the telephone; include grocery advertisements, list paper, and a pencil nearby. A shoe store would include sales slip books. A restaurant would need menus with pictures and words, server pads, and checkbooks. A grocery store would need flyers, "Open" and "Closed" signs, "Help Wanted" signs, and worker sign-in sheets.

Journal Writing. Many early childhood classrooms have begun daily journal writing for children to make an entry about the day. The daily entries may begin as pictures, but they will move to include or become exclusively print. If the child dictates, or the

teachers read and interpret the pictures and print, it is a form of personal communication, but it also provides a way of ongoing assessment. Collecting or copying and filing journal entries is a tangible way to watch writing progress over time. Classrooms that promote literacy set aside time for daily writing, include writing tools in activity centers, encourage children to make choices about their writing, and have multiple ways for children to share their writing. Teachers can scaffold young children's writing through daily journals (Kissel, 2008). Journals allow children to control the topics about which they write, use their abilities at any level without risk, and communicate original thoughts (Block, 2001). This journal entry about dental hygiene contains thoughts, plans, as well as illustrations (Figure 9–17).

Literacy and Technology

EXERCISE How much time do you spend in an average day looking at a screen (computer networking, computer games, text messaging, watching DVDs)?

Television and Literacy. More than three quarters of children six years and under spend time watching television, videos, or using a computer (Rideout & Hamel,

2006). Does this inhibit or enhance literacy development? There is little argument that time spent viewing displaces other activities such as being physically active, interacting with others, or reading. Some research shows that watching educational programming such as *Sesame Street* and *Between the Lions* encourages literacy through positive messages showing reading as enjoyable, encouraging book reading, and presenting emergent literacy concepts (Fisch, 2004). Uchikoshi (2009) examined the research on television's effects on children's language and literacy, finding evidence that children can develop phonological awareness, letter naming, decoding, storytelling, and retelling from television programs. Some popular programs for children that are entertainment or situation comedies, however, often portray reading as not useful, too hard, or not enjoyable, and do not show characters reading or writing at all (Moses & Duke, 2009). To make the most of television Moses (2009) recommends establishing goals for the programming selections, watching with the child, supplementing television viewing with other literacy experiences, and extending the program's literacy content and messages with real experiences.

Literacy and Computers. Young children have a great interest in computers, using them to imitate adults. With a myriad of software programs available, children are actively involved in the manipulation of symbols, pictures, and letters. The explosion of software for young children has addressed this market, but not without controversy. In this age of technology, all advances must be carefully considered for their appropriateness and value to the development of the child.

Computers can serve the same purposes as any other learning area. They can be explored by manipulation; be vehicles of social interaction with peers; and provide a time of interaction with an adult (Figure 9–19). These all add to the child's general development as well as literacy competency. With the computer, children produce their own pictures, text, and even their own books. Holdaway (1979) prophetically stated, "The difficulty of handwriting and spelling tend to delay any genuine desire to produce written language for a purpose" (p. 36). The computer removes that obstacle with software that accepts phonetic spelling, spell checks as words are written, and provides picture and word combinations. Preschools inspired by Reggio Emilia have found the computer to be another "language" with which children can organize ideas and represent what they know through documentation of the construction of learning (Hong & Trepanier-Street, 2004).

Figure 9–19 Technology not only enhances literacy but also social development.

The integration of computers into the learning environment is their most effective use. The use of technology was introduced in Chapter 8 and is discussed here because of its strong link to literacy. Computer literacy or basic skills in technology operations and concepts are advocated by the International Society for Technology in Education (ISTE, 2007). This does not mean a computer lab down the hall where children spend a period of time. True integration of technology in the classroom uses it as a tool for exploration, creating, observing, and learning. Used appropriately and intentionally, it can enhance children's learning as effectively and harmlessly as any other piece of learning equipment. There is a great concern over the growing digital divide with children in families and schools with fewer resources having little or no access to the latest technologies (Burdette & Whitaker, 2005). Children from low income, less well-educated families, and Hispanic children often do not have a computer at home (Common Sense Media, 2011).

The computer can enhance language, mathematics, and science, as well as social interactions. Children as young as age 3 enjoy computer activities, and gathering around the computer is often a collaborative activity. The teacher's role in using technology as an early learning experience is no different than any other experience. First, prepare the environment by safely setting up the computer or technology equipment in a place that is inviting and with programs and applications that support the curriculum goals and allow children to learn at their own individual pace (Vernadakis et al., 2005). The adult models safe and appropriate use and turn taking, and guides the children to explore on their own. Facilitating problem solving by pairing children will encourage peer assistance; and observing children as they use the computer will inform the teacher about the child's communication, collaboration, and problem-solving skills.

Children with learning disabilities and different learning styles have been found to use technology as a way of finding success in learning. Assistive technology devices were included in the Education of the Handicapped Act Amendments of 1986 (P.L. 99-457) and the Individuals with Disabilities Act (IDEA: P.L. 101-476). Technology promises new ways for the disabled to access not only learning and knowledge but also focused behaviors. The use of electronic story books can support both developmental and struggling readers by providing pop-ups for definitions, pronunciations, listening versions, and other advanced features (McKenna & Zucker, 2009). However, a research study found that almost half of the parents' talk is about managing the book rather than the story itself; whereas in reading traditional books, almost all the parents' talk is about the story (Parish-Morris et al., 2008). This proves that learning begins with relationships and depends on the adult's understanding of the appropriate and most effective ways to use the technology.

The teacher, according to Beaty (2008), observes the child move from manipulation level to mastery to meaning, and suggests the Computer Area can reveal development in the following areas:

social—turn taking and sharing
physical—eye–hand coordination, visual discrimination
large motor activities—exercise activities
cognitive—shapes, sizes, colors, opposites, matching, classifying, counting, measuring, sequencing, memory skills
language—giving information and directions, asking and answering questions, discussing operations with a partner, making exclamations
creative—drawing, problem solving, music
emotional—autonomy

An issue of concern is the inequity of technology access, creating what has been called the *digital divide*. In the Kaiser Family Foundation Report (2006), 95 percent of high-income homes with a child under six had computer access, compared to 54 percent of low-income homes. Blacks and Hispanics had less access at home than whites. Girls were found to use computers and play video games less often than boys, widening the gap in perceived abilities in the math and science areas. Inequality of access is a valid concern that observant teachers

need to keep in mind. There is still the caution about the amount of time a young child spends at a computer and the type of programs the child is using.

Literacy Assessment

Literacy assessment is used to screen children for school readiness; identify handicapping conditions; whether to retain or promote children in a grade; and hold teachers and schools accountable for children's learning. These purposes have been criticized because the formal assessment tools have not been shown to be accurate enough to make these "high stakes" decisions (Johnston, Rogers, 2001). Informal assessment with the teacher as the primary agent—using observation, Checklists, Running Records, and Work Samples—can be used to assess abilities in order to measure progress and to inform instructional supports. It is this kind of literacy assessment that is addressed in *Week by Week*.

Literacy involvement can be observed across all learning areas. A multitude of methods, then, can be used to observe the various forms that literacy takes.

Class List Logs can survey the group for reading and writing interest, behavior, skill, or participation. Taped on the wall in the book area, the log is used to record each time a child selects a book as a choice activity, acting as a Frequency Count. A Class List Log could be used to record a child's listening behavior during story reading time. Time Samples indicate how long a child chooses to spend in the book area or writing center. Interviews or asking questions about a story can document the child's understanding of what was read. Anecdotal and Running Records might contain information about the child's use of literacy in structured and unstructured situations. Photographs and videos capture children's reading and writing graphically while their computer-generated stories provide technological evidence (Figure 9–20). Tape recordings of a child reading or pretending to read give clues not only of reading ability, but also of speech production.

More formalized assessments, such as Checklists of specific reading and writing skills, can be purchased or self-made. Samples of the child's writing, dictation, and bookmaking provide information about the level the child has attained. Reading records, sometimes called Running Records, are notations made on scripts of book texts during oral reading. This system requires the individual, concentrated attention of the teacher.

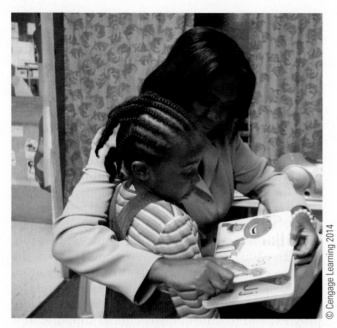

Figure 9–20 Tape recording while a child reads preserves details of the observation.

Whatever method is selected, a systematic gathering of documentation shows the progress of literacy.

Observing Literacy Development in Infants, Toddlers and Preschoolers. The Teaching Strategies GOLD™ Assessment System gives these criteria to watch for and note as emerging in Level 1 (orange) 12–24 months, and observable in Level 2 (yellow) 24–36 months. (See Figure 9–4).

Literacy
Objective 15—Demonstrates phonological awareness

(a) Notices and discriminates rhyme—joins in rhyming songs and games
(b) Notices and discriminates alliteration—Sings songs and recites rhymes and refrains with repeating initial sounds

Objective 16—Demonstrates knowledge of the alphabet

(a) Identifies names and letters—Recognizes and names a few letters, especially those in own name

Objective 17—Demonstrates knowledge of print and its uses

(a) Uses and appreciates books—Shows interest in books
(b) Uses print concepts—Shows understanding that text is meaningful and can be read

Objective 18—Comprehends and responds to books and other texts

(a) Interacts during read-alouds and book conversations—Contributes particular language from the book at the appropriate time
(b) Uses emergent story book-reading skills—Pretends to read a familiar book, treating each page as a separate unit; names and describes what is on each page using pictures as cues
(c) Retells stories—Retells some events from a familiar story with close adult prompting

Observing and Assessing School-age Children's Reading

Assessment of children's reading ability takes two viewpoints, the child's independent reading level and the instructional level (reading with support from the teacher). Many first grades are using Ready Recovery Instruction® based on the work of Clay (1985) as a short-term, one-on-one reading intervention. The child reads books on one of the Reading Recovery Levels and the teacher codes the number and types of errors to determine the accuracy rate, then works with the child in the deficient areas. By going down a level, the teacher can determine the child's independent reading level.

Children's stories can be assessed by noting the child's use of conventional spelling, spacing, punctuation, and capitalization, and by evaluating the story as well plot, theme, and character development.

🏠 Home Visiting Literacy Assessment

By now in this textbook, it should be clear to the reader that early education in the home has both benefits and challenges. One challenge may be the lack of time to work with each child, especially when the development of early literacy is a social process dependent on a "literate other." The importance of a literacy-supportive environment, in this case the home, is well researched. There are tools available to assess literacy supports in the home such as the *Child/Home Early Language and Literacy Observation* (CHELLO, Neuman et al., 2007). The CHELLO measures the physical environment for reading, such as cozy spaces, materials for sustained activity such as blocks and puzzles, and props that encourage literacy play such as envelopes, pencils, and an area specifically for book reading. It measures the social

© Cengage Learning 2014

environment by looking at the emotional security, assistance, and verbal interactions the adults provide.

Another tool widely used by Even Start to assess parents' role with children's literacy development and used by home educators is the Parents Education Profile (PEP) Scale (RMC Research, 2006). This is a tool that uses self-reporting by the parents as well as observation by the home visitor in four areas: Home Environment, Interactive Literacy, Support for Children in Formal Settings, and The Parents' Role. It is a Rating Scale arranged vertically from least to most (Figure 9–21).

Home educators need to be aware of what literacy supports are in the home and in what ways they can involve parents and/or other supportive adults to effectively serve as the "literate others." In addition, while home educators are encouraged to routinely use developmental screenings, home educators should consider the use of additional literacy specific tools such as those outlined in this chapter, using the results to inform content and practice.

Helping all Children with Literacy

With the importance of literacy to life successes, it is little wonder that so much emphasis must be placed on every child in the classroom or group, but some children are at an even greater disadvantage than others.

Physical Disabilities and Literacy

When physical or mental limitations are present, literacy development may be affected. Visual impairments will slow or prevent the progression of reading and writing. By providing high-contrast documents and writing tools, along with tactile materials such as sandpaper letters to trace with the fingers, magnetic letters to move on metal surfaces, and raised alphabet letters, children with limited vision can be included in the world of literacy. Reading to these children is also an important part of their literacy world. Focus the child's attention on the book, giving him time to touch and smell it before reading, talking about the cover and the pictures, and giving additional information that is necessary for the story line (Birckmayer et al., 2009).

Children with hearing impairments may have affected language development, which also affects literacy. For these children, using visual cues for communication may be even more important. Visual cues are a critical component of both receptive and expressive language. Share story books with pictures that tell the story, and that do not require the text to find the meaning. With the help of assistive and adaptive technology, computers can help overcome visual, hearing, and physical limitations. Braille keyboards and voice-activated and audio-output computers open the world of literacy. Helping children with hearing impairments learn to read opens their world.

Learning Disabilities and Literacy

Literacy, the ability to read and write, is the area in which learning disabilities are the most evident. One of the early labels for reading difficulties was **dyslexia**, often characterized by children writing alphabet letters backwards or confusing similarly shaped letters like *b* and *p* (which all children do when learning to write, and continue to six and seven years old). This is just one symptom of a larger range of difficulties. The term **learning disabilities** describes people within the range of normal intelligence, without significant behavioral disorders, who fail to reach their potential—often because of the inability to read and write.

The actual causes of learning disabilities are still under study. Neurological (brain) dysfunction is one explanation. Another is that such disabilities are caused by difficulties with vision and perceptual processing, a theory that has spurred some to seek vision training as a remedy, with mixed results. Psychological and emotional causes have been investigated, but academic difficulties affect a child's psychological and emotional wellbeing, so it has been difficult to determine if this is a cause or an effect. Environmental causes, such as extreme poverty and a lack of cognitive stimulation, have been recognized as connected to learning disabilities; however, there are many middle-class children with learning disabilities, so environmental causes cannot be the total answer either.

A recognized definition, diagnosis, and label are needed to secure services for children with academic underachievement. There are differing and complex definitions of *learning disability*. The National Center for Learning Disability defines it as "a neurological disorder that affects the brain's ability to receive, process, store, and respond to information." Learning disabilities are not limited to, but often include difficulties with literacy (Allen & Cowdery, 2009). Young children with learning disabilities are extremely difficult to diagnose because they are in the pre-reading stage. The two primary behaviors characteristic of learning disabilities are impulsiveness and indiscrimination (the inability to tune out distractions or concentrate on a task in an orderly fashion), as defined by Samuel Kirk, who coined the term *learning*

PARENT'S SUPPORT FOR CHILDREN'S LEARNING IN THE HOME ENVIRONMENT

USE OF LITERACY MATERIALS	USE OF TV/VIDEO	HOME LANGUAGE AND LEARNING	PRIORITY ON LEARNING TOGETHER
1. Home has few books or writing/drawing materials; little or nothing is age appropriate.	1. There is no monitoring of TV; children watch whatever and whenever they choose.	1. Parent does not recognize role of home routines and play in literacy learning. Parent limits child's opportunities for play doesn't join in child's play, doesn't set up opportunities for learning.	1. Family does not have experience of devoting time to family activities and learning together. Family doesn't yet place value on learning together.
2. Home has some books and/or writing/drawing materials but they are not appropriate nor accessible to child. Parent does not yet seek out materials for the child.	2. Parent is aware that it is his/her role to limit television but has not successfully done so.	2. Parent is interested in doing more to build child's literacy learning but parent's choices for child often do not match child's age or ability. Parent and child experience frustration.	2. Family relies on support from outside the immediate family to participate occasionally in family learning opportunities.
3. The home has some examples of appropriate reading, writing, & drawing materials. Parent seeks books and writing materials for child. Parent will read and/or write/draw with child several times a week.	3. Parent encourages some watching of age-appropriate programming.	3. Parent seeks information about age-appropriate learning opportunities and is able to use information to set up appropriate learning activities and/or occasionally join in child's play to extend learning.	3. Parent is aware of the importance of family learning activities and expresses desire to initiate them. Parent occasionally plans family learning opportunities.
4. Home includes books and materials that parent has chosen because parent believes child will like them. Parent uses literacy materials every day with child in engaging ways.	4. Parent tries to set some viewing limits on the type and times for viewing. Parent consistently reinforces viewing rules.	4. Parent often bases his/her choice of activities on observations of child's skills and interests. Parent facilitates learning opportunities for child several times per week and regularly joins play to extend language.	4. Family members routinely make an effort to initiate family opportunities that foster learning, e.g., attending field trip.
5. Home has a variety of materials for reading, writing, & drawing that are accessible to child. Materials are used daily. Parent and child select books based frequently on child's interest and skill levels.	5. Parent uses television as a learning tool; parent watches with child and moderates messages from TV.	5. Parent regularly uses "teachable moments" with child. Parent takes cues from child and allows child to guide choices of learning activities. Parent frequently participates in play and takes proactive role in expanding language.	5. Family members take pleasure in family learning opportunities. Parent is able to make learning opportunities from everyday activities.

Figure 9–21 Parent's support for children's learning in the home environment.

disabled (as cited in Hallahan & Kaufman, 2009). These two characteristics are common in all young children. When they are prolonged or exaggerated, learning disabilities may be suspected. They are also characteristics of hyperactivity and Attention Deficit Hyperactivity Disorder (ADHD).

The role of the early childhood observer is to closely monitor literacy progress, along with other areas of development and behavior, and be aware of indications of difficulties as well as the appropriate referral agents from which to secure help.

Literacy and Children Whose First Language Is Not English

Children enter school with a wide range of prior experiences with language in oral and written forms that provide the foundation for literacy learning. Becoming literate and finding school success, overall wellbeing, and the ability to compete in society is complicated when the child's oral and written language is not English. Language, whether spoken or written, occurs in the context of children's lives. Children who are not native English speakers or Limited English Proficient (**LEP**) may or may not be literacy limited. It depends on the culture and the family circumstances. The family may have limited literacy in their own language. Without literacy materials and role models at home, no matter what the language, children start out at a disadvantage.

Children who are language learners in a language other than English come into the early childhood setting with a wide range of literacy exposure. They may have seen a written form of their own language, either by directly observing adults in their family writing it or by seeing it in books, newspapers, and letters. They may have story books printed in that language. Or they may come from a home environment where none of these things are present. Knowing the home's literacy practices is imperative in respecting the child's home language and culture and in the introduction to English literacy. The children probably already understand English print from logos, signs, television, and billboards. They look at the illustrations in books and can follow the storyline, even though the text is in a different language. Read-alouds showing the pictures will help build vocabulary and the child will hear the cadence of the language. It is helpful if key words in the child's home language can be introduced in the story.

For all children, and especially English language learners, picture books are excellent ways to communicate universal messages and to have

Figure 9–22 Picture books in their home language help children develop literacy.

a shared experience (Figure 9–22). Some strategies for story book reading to young dual language learners are:

- Chose a book with one or a few repetitive phrases
- Use manipulatives, illustrations, and gestures to help children understand vocabulary
- Use the children's home language or a book that depicts familiar people, things or storylines.
- Read the story several times
- Encourage retelling or dramatization of the story
- Expand ideas in the book to other classroom centers (Gillanders, Castro, 2011)

Looking at picture books enhances vocabulary growth. Literacy success in the second language depends on the same factors as oral language for all children—an environment filled with materials and activities. Individual interactions enhance both language and literacy. The environment and curriculum include real opportunities to use literacy, such as name lists, drawing and writing materials, story books to look at, and adults reading and pointing to pictures and words. Samway (2006) says, "The most current research shows that non-native English-speaking children are capable of much more than is generally expected of them" (p. 21–22). All children, even those who have not mastered oral English, can be encouraged to write and draw their stories, using their first language in narratives and sharing with their peers (Shagoury, 2009).

Early writing for these children follows the same stages: scribbling, drawing, and forming letters. The writing may appear in another form if the symbols are not alphabetic, with scribbles appearing vertically rather than horizontally for Asian children, for example. Teachers should pay attention to the home language, provide reading material in that language, and encourage families to engage their children in enriching dialogue and language play (Ordonez-Jasis & Ortiz, 2006). Children will continue to acquire native language literacy from home and an expanded language and literacy in English from the early childhood setting. Children come to school at a disadvantage if they have little or no early experience with print in any language.

All children need a social atmosphere accepting of language attempts. Adults who allow and encourage native language speaking and writing demonstrate an overall acceptance of the child and the family. Pictorial and word labels in the classroom will help all children associate the object with the written word. Meaningful opportunities to write give older children with limited English a way to communicate. Young children with limited English proficiency can learn vocabulary, customs, and find enjoyment through books and literacy materials. As mentioned previously, the home may already be literacy-rich with books and the family may be writing in their home language. Families should be encouraged to read to their child in the home language and to involve the child in community activities in the first language and in English (Grant & Wong, 2003). Stories recorded on tapes, dictionaries that have familiar items in both languages, and books in the first language of every child are helpful toward literacy development. Literacy materials can be sent home for reinforcement and enjoyment by the whole family.

Cultural differences other than native language also affect the child's literacy development. Cultural differences also have been found in the amount and type of early vocalization with infants and young children. Middle-class families and teachers are more verbally responsive and referential, giving names to items and repeating them, such as "Doggie. Doggie." Some cultures rely more on body language, teasing, and traditional stories using dialects and nonstandard English. Many cultures do not consider literacy an important component of the young child's world, but hold it as a rite of passage into the adult world. This cultural difference will pose challenges to the early childhood program in helping these children reach the level of familiarity with not only the spoken language, but the written language as well.

Helping Professionals for Literacy Concerns

Children who need further help in the area of literacy development, reading, or writing should begin first with a physical examination. Vision, hearing, or neurological problems may interfere with literacy development. Speech and language difficulties could be contributing factors, so evaluations in these areas may be considered. Helping professionals in the area of literacy include the following:

reading specialists—teachers with specialized training in the teaching of reading, and diagnosis and remediation of reading and writing difficulties

special education teachers—teachers with knowledge of literacy disorders and strategies for overcoming learning disabilities

bilingual teachers or interpreters—people who can translate writing materials and communications in the family's first language

Other Methods

Other Methods to Record Literacy:

Anecdotal/Running Records—narrative about a child's interaction with reading or writing, wherever it occurs

Checklist—presence or absence of literacy-related skills

It Happened to Me

Working to Communicate

One of my college students was in a practicum placement in a program in which there was a child from Vietnam who spoke no English. She struggled to communicate. Finally, on her own initiative, my student made a book of common items in the classroom from a mail order catalog. She found a translator to write the words for the items in the child's language, as well as phonetic spelling in English so she could pronounce it. That book went back and forth from home to school, aiding both in communicating. Everyone benefited. She earned an A.

Frequency Count—elements of literacy to measure skills such as recognition of sight words in a passage, hesitations in oral reading, number of misspellings in a passage or list of words

Time Sample—attention span during story time, ability to sustain in self-reading, amount of time spent writing a passage in a journal or working on a literacy computer program

Conversations or Interviews—listening to oral reading, discussions about story themes and characters for understanding, conversations preceding writing in a journal or constructing a story

Work Samples—writing samples, tape recordings of oral reading

Media—photographs or videos of the child engaged in reading and writing behaviors

Key Terms

alphabetic awareness	learning disabilities
contextualized literacy	LEP
	print-rich environment
digital divide	phonemic awareness
dyslexia	
emergent literacy	quality points
environmental print	Rating Scale
interrater reliability	selective method
invented spelling	

Plans

Go to the Education CourseMate website, accessed through CengageBrain.com, for the following:

Rating Scales in Literacy form

Plan Week 9 Part A, Directions for a Class List Log on Separation and School Adjustment, including What to Do with It, Portfolio

Evidence Sheet Example, Sharing with Child and Family, Actions—Read a Book, In the Environment, In the Curriculum, In the Newsletter

Plan Week 9 Part B, Conversations to document speech and language development

Plan Week 9 Part C, Reflective Journal

Resources

Bardige, B.S., & Segal, M. M. (2005). *Building literacy with love: A guide for teachers and caregivers of children birth through age 5.* Washington DC: ZERO TO THREE.

Beaty, J. J. (2009). *50 Early childhood literacy strategies* (2nd ed.). Upper Saddle River, NJ: Pearson.

Birkmayer, J., Kennedy, A., & Stonehouse, A. (2008). *From lullabies to literature: stories in the lives of infants and toddlers.* Washington, DC: National Association for the Education of Young Children.

Fisher, B., & Medvic, E. F. (2003). *For reading out loud.* Portsmouth, NH: Heinemann.

Machado, J. M. (2013). *Early childhood experiences in language arts* (10th ed.). Belmont, CA: Wadsworth, Cengage Learning.

National Association for the Education of Young Children (2012). Technology and interactive media as tools in early childhood programs serving children from birth through age http://www.naeyc.org/files/naeyc/file/positions/PS_technology_WEB2.pdf.

Schickedanz, J. (1999). *Much more than the ABCS: The early stages of reading And writing.* Washington, DC: National Association for the Education of Young Children.

Schickedanz, J. A., Casbergue, R. M. (2009). *Writing in preschool: Learning to orchestrate meaning and marks.* Newark, DE: International Reading Association.

Trelease, J. (2006). *The Read-aloud handbook.* New York: Penguin Books.

CHAPTER 10

Using Work Samples to Look at Creativity

OBSERVATION THOUGHT

"Writing meaningful observations as they are occurring cannot happen in a teacher-directed classroom. The teacher is too busy."

NAEYC Standards **naeyc**

The following NAEYC Standards for Early Childhood Professional Preparation are addressed in this chapter:

Standard 1: *Promoting Child Development and Learning*

Standard 3: *Observing, Documenting, and Assessing to Support Young Children and Families*

Standard 6: *Becoming a Professional*

© Cengage Learning 2012

IN THIS CHAPTER

▶ Using Work Samples to Observe a Child's Development

▶ Looking at Children's Creative Development

▶ Observing Creativity in Infants and Toddlers

▶ Topics in Observation: Process versus Product

▶ Helping All Children with Creativity

▶ Helping Professionals for Creative Arts

Using Work Samples to Observe a Child's Development

EXERCISE What can you infer about the child who created the drawing in Figure 10–1?

The word *infer* here is italicized because, of course, by just looking at one drawing we cannot make definitive judgments about the child. But you could probably tell this child has observed a dog closely. The drawing is accurately proportioned and detailed, so the age of the artist could be estimated by one who knew the usual progressive stages of children's drawing to be about six years old. Actually, this drawing was done by an active

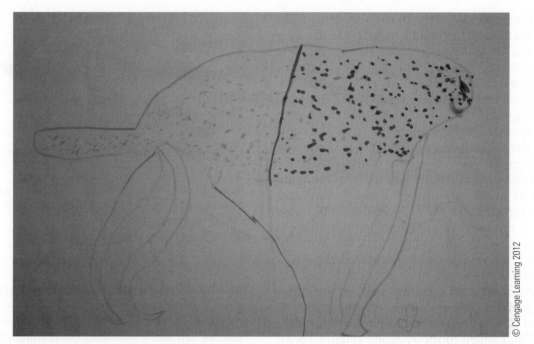

Figure 10–1 Read the story of this drawing in "It Happened to Me."

four-year-old with an avid interest in art. Compared to the stages of creative development, it is advanced for the chronological age of the artist.

Creativity comes from within and reveals the self, whether it is a three-year-old with a crayon drawing on the wall or a great master with oils and canvas. The child's creative products can be used as effective revelations of developmental progress. Almost every developmental area can be assessed by observing a child manipulate creative **media**.

The old saying "A picture is worth a thousand words" is true also of children's creative products. Children's work, done in a home or classroom setting as the child plays and goes through the natural routines of the day, provides information that would take paragraphs to convey. Individual children and groups produce work that can serve as raw data for assessment. These works can be collected over time to show changes in development (McAfee & Leong, 2007). **Work Samples** is the term for any of the child's products, including but not limited to drawing and painting, clay, blocks, or any material the child uses to construct or express meaning. All of which reveal many aspects of the child's development (Figure 10–2).

Materials can be contributed to the Portfolio from various sources—the family, the teacher, or the child—depending on its purpose. In the *Week by Week* Portfolio, information and documents are gathered from all three, with equal access as well. The child's access, of course, depends on the age; but even young children can understand the Portfolio is

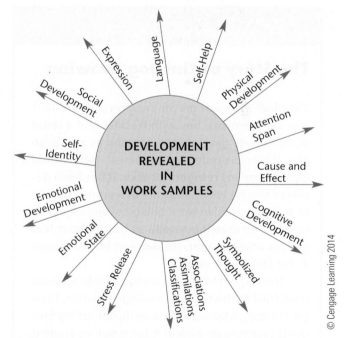

Figure 10–2 Development Revealed in Work Samples.

about them. They often want to see it, just as they love to look at photographs of themselves as babies. By including samples of their work, whether drawing, writing, or photographs, they realize the Portfolio's purpose as a chronicle of their development.

Children should be aware of the Portfolio and its purpose as a receptacle for information about them. They are invited to add to the Portfolio when they have work they feel is important to them. If the Portfolio is a file folder, the child can decorate the four panels of the file folder periodically over the quarters of the school year. This personalizes it but also makes it an episodic documentation of the child's work. The children can comment on their own work as a way of exploring their thinking. The observer listens to the child describe the memory of the work and comments on the progress from the child's viewpoint.

Children are very possessive of their work (as they should be) but usually generous in allowing copies to be made on a copier. Actually having a notebook for each child to draw in over the course of a year is another way of collecting drawings. It is more structured, drawing at the adult's request, and yields less spontaneous or natural art products. It also limits the types of media that can be used.

Three-dimensional creations such as sculpture, collages, mobiles, woodworking, sewing, and even movement can be preserved with photographs, documented, and added to the Portfolio (Figure 10–3). Work can be explained with notes attached to the

© Cengage Learning 2012

Figure 10–3 Compare the Work Sample photo of a mouse to drawing in Figure 9–15. From Koster, *Growing Artists*, 3rd ed. © 2005 Cengage Learning.

back that include the date. The background of the work, how it came to be done, and any dictation or child's words about the work can be written there. The teacher can make notations concerning the child's development that this work especially illustrates.

Portfolios contain samples of the child's work to document progress and illustrate the child's thinking. Because development is seen in children's graphic art products, they are a concrete way to document development. Children's drawings, paintings, scribbles, and photographs or sketches of their block structures are collected periodically to add to the Portfolio. Portfolios can be made from large brown envelopes or brown grocery bags folded flat and filed upright in a cardboard box. Pizza boxes also make excellent Portfolio collection containers. Periodic collection and review of products with the child and family can be a concrete demonstration of the changes in thinking, muscle control, and creativity.

Sharing Work Samples with Families. One of the best ways to communicate change is to compare *then* and *now*. Better than any test score, and understandable by any viewer are samples of a child's work as the child progresses in block building, writing, drawing, or cooperating with other children. It is a comparison not with other children, but with the child's own approach and learning. The Work Sample Portfolio can accompany and amplify developmental Checklists in a visual way. Providing families with an ongoing Work Sample Portfolio that mirrors what educators collect in other ways validates the importance of creative activities; and it provides another way to better engage families in the child's education and in the importance of supporting the "process," while at the same time enjoying the "product."

Other Work Samples for the Portfolio. In thinking about children's creativity, it is easy to concentrate on

It Happened to Me

The Story of the Dog Drawing

The child who made me the drawing in Figure 10–1 was a mischievous boy with freckles and a sense of humor. He gave me the drawing as a surprise gift. It was preceded by a promise that I would display it on my refrigerator door. It has been displayed to a far wider audience as a prime example of a child's creative work going beyond expected stages. The drawing reveals so much about him and his development. His sense of humor is seen in the face of the dog.

The rest of the story: I always wondered what happened to this child. At a college function, I saw his mother, who was there with one of my students receiving an award! It turns out my student was her sister. I asked about her son and explained about the drawing I had saved and used as an example all those years. It turns out he was a student right here at my college, taking—you guessed it— art. I sent him a letter and a copy of this page and asked him to come by my office. He never did! I will always be disappointed that we didn't get to talk about this. Who knows why he didn't come.

the visual arts, such as drawing and painting. Not to be overlooked are a wide variety of physical materials that can be used as Work Samples beyond the traditional kinds already mentioned. Work Samples can also include construction, sculpture, collage, child-produced writing, audio, and video products; language samples of riddles, rhymes, songs, or plays; and movement activities such as dances, acrobatic routines, and pantomimes. These products assist in the assessment of other areas of development. Figure 10–4 is the Work Samples Checklist, which includes areas covered in *Week by Week* and some assessment criteria in the creative realm.

Collaborating with Colleagues About the Significance of Work Samples. Using Jones and Courtney's concept of discussing children's science projects from their book *Documenting Early Science Learning* (2002) as a model, teachers could discuss and collaborate on evaluating children's Work Samples. The authors suggest using language records (see Chapter 6) and Work Samples, with one teacher presenting the factual evidence of Work Samples as well as transcripts of conversations with the child about the work. Others review the materials silently and then summarize the evidence, noting questions for clarification. Then the collaborators can discuss and come to consensus on the meaning and indicators of development based on the evidence provided. In this way, several viewpoints consider the work based on their own frames of reference. The child's work is considered a revelation of thought and feelings. This is in contrast to a parent's comment, tossing the artwork in the trash can, "I'm only going to drive it around in the back of the car for weeks then throw it away anyway." The painful truth.

Advantages

Collecting Work Samples is an effective recording technique because it is done

- in a natural classroom setting, with the child selecting materials and working at her own pace and direction, illustrating many areas of development.
- over a period of time, showing progress of development.
- as an expression of the child's thoughts and feelings more accurately and powerfully than an observer can describe them.

Disadvantages

Work Samples might

- make the child overly conscious of manipulation or practice.

- lead the observer to draw erroneous conclusions from the work.
- reflect the inferences of the selector, as the teacher may only gather scribbling or experimental pieces when actually the child does much more advanced work.

Pitfalls to Avoid

For Work Samples to be part of an authentic assessment plan, they should be

- dated. (The changeable date stamp comes in handy here. Children can learn to date their work themselves.)
- gathered periodically by joint decision of the recorder and the child.
- accompanied by commentary or narrative concerning the work.
- kept in a separate folder from the Portfolio if they become overwhelmingly large or if children want to submit many pieces.

Using Technology

Keeping piles of drawings can get cumbersome and take up valuable storage space. Using technology to file and access Work Samples is becoming easier and easier. Scanners can turn samples such as writings, drawings, and paintings into easily stored electronic documents. Digital photography can capture three-dimensional works such as collages, sculptures, block building, and other constructions. Digital video recordings can capture not only the product but also the process. Electronic storage and access makes it easier to utilize the information for program planning and sharing with the family. It also keeps the whole Portfolio more secure than if it were in a file folder in a drawer or cabinet.

How to Find the Time

Capturing children's Work Samples is relatively time efficient when using a digital camera. A picture tells a thousand words, and the child's work is spoken in a hundred languages or literacies, as mentioned above. Taking photos is less time-consuming than writing descriptions or manipulating Developmental Checklists. It should not be the only method used, but it is very effective.

What to Do with It

Children are possessive of their work, and so they should be. To collect Work Samples, one must either file what the child forgets to take home, make photocopies, or take photographs of the work. There may be

WORK SAMPLES CHECKLIST

Child's Name_____ Dates _____

COMMENTS

Separation
❏ Separates from adult to work alone
❏ Works independently without requiring adult presence or direction

Self-Care
❏ Independently selects materials
❏ Makes preparations to work (Example: Puts on a smock)
❏ Uses materials independently
❏ Cleans up spills, messes
❏ Writes name on work
❏ Places finished product in proper place
❏ Washes and dries hands if necessary
❏ Replaces materials to storage place

Physical Development
❏ Controls whole body movement during work
❏ Controls small muscles to hold tool
❏ Controls tool to form desired product
❏ Draws, prints, paints, pastes
❏ Squeezes glue bottle
❏ Picks up collage materials
❏ Manipulates clay or modeling dough
❏ Cuts with scissors
❏ Controls body to stay within the space (on the paper, building on a rug, clay on table)
❏ Moves body to music
❏ Plays rhythm instrument
❏ Claps to music rhythm

Social Skills
❏ Represents important people in his life in his work
❏ Desires and can work near other children
❏ Shares materials and supplies
❏ Engages in positive commentary on other children's work
❏ Works cooperatively on a joint project
❏ Sings with group

Emotional Development
❏ Uses work to express emotions of happiness, anger, fear
❏ Verbalizes feelings about work
❏ Enjoys manipulation and creation
❏ Controls emotions of frustration when work meets difficulties
❏ Uses the media as a stress release, pounding clay, tearing paper, painting
❏ Uses music to express feelings

Speech and Language Development
❏ Names scribbles, buildings, creations
❏ Talks about work using vocabulary connected with materials and design
❏ Uses language to describe process, intent, and satisfaction with product
❏ Vocabulary reflects knowledge of subject
❏ Sings words to songs

(continued)

Figure 10–4 Work Samples Checklist.

Go to the Education CourseMate website to download a copy of this form.

WORK SAMPLES CHECKLIST

COMMENTS

Memory and Attention Span

❑ Includes details in work from memories of experiences
❑ Focuses attention on project to produce a finished work
❑ Tunes out distractions of simultaneous play, talk, and work
❑ Gives attention and makes connections between environment and own work
❑ Remembers words to songs

Math and Science Knowledge

❑ Includes numerals and quantity in work
❑ Shows one-to-one correspondence in work designs
❑ Shows perceptual awareness of color, space, form
❑ Explores cause and effect and experimentation with variables in media
   (Example: Sees differences in paint when water and sand are added)
❑ Observes similarities and differences, forming theories, and testing them out by manipulating the medium
❑ Working with clay or liquid—displays knowledge of the concept of conservation
   (volume stays the same even though form changes—ball flattened is the same amount)
❑ Can recognize and repeat rhythms

Literacy

❑ Includes literacy in work
❑ Recognizes the difference between drawing and writing
❑ Uses materials to symbolize ideas
❑ Work illustrates or connects with stories
❑ Gives attention to art in story books and knows the difference between text and illustrations

Creativity

❑ Uses materials in a novel way, displaying flexibility in seeing new possibilities in materials
❑ Explores all facets of the medium
❑ Draws from experiences to create representations
❑ Incorporates creativity into other areas of play, constructing with blocks, drawing and constructing in
   dramatic play, forming designs in sand and other media
❑ Demonstrates creativity in sensory awareness (seeing, hearing, touching, smelling, tasting)
❑ Creates own songs with words and/or music

Self-Identity

❑ Displays risk-free attitude in work
❑ Reveals self in content of work
❑ Work shows a sense of identity and individuality
❑ Expresses satisfaction in work, confident self-esteem
❑ Portrays self, family, world in work
❑ Work demonstrates child's sex-role identification
❑ Work shows child moving from egocentric view of self to an awareness of self as part of larger society
❑ Indicates favorite art medium (singular), media (plural)
❑ Sings alone comfortably

Group Time Behaviors

❑ Participates in cooperative and collaborative work and music

Interaction with Adults

❑ Involves adults in work as (facilitator, participant, director)

©Nilsen, B. *Week by Week: Plans for Documenting Children's Development*, 4th ed.. Clifton Park, NY: Thomson Delmar Learning (2005).

Figure 10–4

PORTFOLIO EVIDENCE OF CHILD'S DEVELOPMENT			
Evidence Type	Date	Recorder	Notes
CREATIVITY – the child's creativity and sociodramatic play, including work samples			
WS	9/13/		Self-portrait with markers (copy in portfolio)
WS	10/14/		2nd self-portrait – more details (copy in portfolio)
AR	11/16/	BAN	Worked to make nature collage talking with 2 other children

© Cengage Learning 2014

Figure 10–5 Portfolio Evidence Sheet Example.

a temptation to ask a child to create something for the Portfolio, but that is not what we are seeking here. The purpose is to collect what are called *literacies,* modes of "recording and preserving experiences, reflecting upon, exploring and extending one's thoughts and feelings, and communicating and sharing ideas with others" (Edwards & Willis, 2000). Work Samples are another way of documenting the child's development. They are incorporated into the child's Portfolio, noted on the Portfolio Evidence Sheet (Example in Figure 10–5), with other documents as evidence of development, testimonies from the child that demonstrate physical, social, cognitive, literacy, emotional, and creative development. At the conclusion of the school year, the samples are given to the family. It may be the policy of the school or program to keep copies.

Observing Creativity with Other Recording Methods

Observing a child during the creative process and preserving the finished product as documentation provides valuable developmental information. The products are not only the outcomes of the child's development, but are affected by it as well. **Creativity** is affected by development, yet by observing creativity, development can be observed and assessed (Figure 10–6).

Developmental Checklists with a section on creative development can be used to quickly gather general observed behaviors for the Portfolio. The actual work or replicas of it serve as the documentation or evidence for the decisions made on the Checklist or Rating Scale.

Anecdotal Recordings, detailed narratives of the action and exact words the child uses during and after the creation phase, are like the caption to the illustration. The dictated words or quotations give the

© Cengage Learning 2014

Figure 10–6 Many factors affect creative development.

background or setting of the work. The action of the work is documented along with the exact quotes of the artist. It can inform the viewer and reader of the special circumstances that affected the child and the work.

Interviews while a child is working on a project are another way of gathering information. They reveal the child's understanding of concepts and increase the observer's understanding of the child's work. The child conveys the process and intent. That way, it is not misconstrued by the observer. See the section later in this chapter, "Talking with Children about Their Creative Work."

Plans: Go to Education CourseMate website, accessed through CengageBrain.com, for Creative Work Samples Checklist, plans, and resources.

REVIEW

WORK SAMPLES
Observing and collecting a child's product from which to draw conclusions about development, skills, and behaviors.

Types of Information to Record Using Work Samples

- separation
- self-care
- physical development
- social skills
- emotional development
- speech and language development
- memory and attention span
- math and science knowledge
- literacy
- creativity
- self-identity
- group time behaviors
- interaction with adults

Looking at Children's Creative Development

Analyzing children's creative work is a visual demonstration of developmental principles. All children, all over the world, in whatever age they have lived, progress through the same basic stages in art or graphic representation. Historians who have studied pictorials on caves and rocks and alphabetic systems see the same designs that are seen painted by a child in day care in Chicago. Those combinations of circles, squares, straight lines, and curved lines had meaning for those people long ago, just as they do for today's child. Sylvia Fein, in her fascinating book *First Drawings: Genesis of Visual Thinking* (1993), compares artifacts from all over the world with children's first attempts at art. From handprints of the Anasazi Indians on cave walls in New Mexico (Figure 10–7), to concentric circles from runic stones in Norway (Figure 10–8), to depictions of people from the Caribbean (Figure 10–9), artists in every age use archetypical signs that have universal meaning.

Children's creative work is recognized as a window into their mind. Before children symbolize in writing, and sometimes even verbally, they use drawing as an expressive outlet. Many intelligence and psychological tests analyze a child's art to gain insight

Figure 10–7 Anasazi Indian handprints in New Mexico remind us of fingerpainting handprints that young children make.

on the child's thinking and feeling. The Goodenough-Harris Draw-A-Person Test (Harris, 1963) is a well-known measurement and still used as a prescreener in many schools because it claims to correlate with IQ tests. It can be used as a screening tool to rule out low intelligence for children who cannot perform on traditional intelligence tests; but it is more appropriate as a measure of drawing ability (Jolley, 2010). The use of children's drawings to form a diagnosis in a clinical situation has been discounted. While they may be expressive, drawings should be used to augment other types of diagnostic measures and observations.

There are indications, however, that The Draw-A-Person test is biased to cultural factors. Careful study and classification of children's drawings have found predictable stages common to children worldwide with curiously little variation (Kellogg, 1970; Lowenfeld & Brittain, 1987). This reinforces developmental theory that drawing is the representation of inner thought and connected with stages of development. The same factors that affect all other areas of

Figure 10–8 New Mexico petroglyphs carved in rocks a thousand years ago resemble children's experimentation with form.

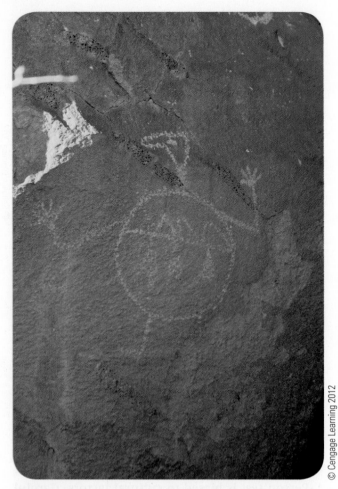

© Cengage Learning 2012

Figure 10–9 Ancient drawings resemble today's children's self-portraits.

development also affect the creative: genetic, environmental, and cultural. To accurately observe and assess a child's development from creative expression, then, knowledge of the stages of creative development is vital.

Creativity and Cognitive Development

It should not be surprising that thinking and all the processes that link thinking and learning are integral to creativity. There are parallels between the stages of Piaget's cognitive theory (Flavell, 1963), the art stages of Kellogg (1970) and Lowenfeld and Brittain (1987), and the social-emotional stages of Erikson (1963). They correspond to stages of development of language, reading, and writing. The ages of these stages are merely guideposts, not firm transition points (Figure 10–10).

When involved in creative activities, the brain and body can be so focused that it has been called the flow by researcher Mihaly Csikszenthmihalyi

(1997). This euphoric feeling is often expressed by athletes when they are pushing themselves to the limit. It stimulates the brain's pleasure centers in such a way that transcends time and space. Creativity is dependent on symbolic thought. It is necessary to have existing structures and beliefs in reality against which to measure new data. It coordinates on cognitive ability, past experiences, and the present environment. Sternberg (1997) calls this Creative Intelligence, the ability to solve novel problems by applying information-processing skills so the working memory is freed for more complex aspects of the situation. The other two interacting intelligences are Analytical Intelligence, that is task-oriented, and Practical Intelligence, adapting thinking to shape environments to meet the demands of the everyday world.

Observing children's creative efforts can indicate the following:

▸ *Long attention span*—When the activity captures their interest, they attend longer.

▸ *Capacity for organization*—The organization of their creative work indicates their classification skills.

▸ *Seeing things in a different perspective*—This does not go against the egocentric idea but refers to the child's ability to see things without preconceived notions.

▸ *Exploring before formal instruction*—They have the need to manipulate first, and later organize into more conventional uses of tools and materials.

▸ *Using solitary time*—Every parent knows that a quiet child is often one that needs to be investigated, for there may be some trouble brewing. Children get into trouble because they try things they do not know are dangerous or forbidden. This is an aspect of creativity, such as drawing on the sheets with lipstick or painting on the recreation room wall with tar.

▸ *Taking a "closer look" at things*—Creative thinking involves manipulation and being close. It could be apples in a plastic bag at the supermarket or a climb to the top cupboard in the kitchen to investigate.

▸ *Using fantasy to solve developmental problems*—Normal aspects of children's thinking are considered frivolous and even deceitful by adults.

▸ *Creativity*—Children use creative ideas to explain, defend, and problem solve, such as "The dog must have ridden my bike to the corner and left it there."

Piaget's Stages of Cognitive Development	Stages of Art Kellogg; Lowenfeld and Brittain; Schirrmacher	Language Development	Writing/ Reading	Erikson's Psycho-social Stages
Sensorimotor (b–24 months) Moving from reflexes to object permanence	Scribbling and mark-making (b–2 years) Random exploration Nonintentional	Pre/Language (b–2 years) Sounds, telegraphic sentences	Book Handling Skills (b–2 years) Right side up, front/back, turn pages	Basic Trust vs. Mistrust (b–2 years) Consistent experiences
Preoperational 2–7 years Egocentric Represen-tation of objects and events by appearances	Personal Symbol and Design (2–4 years) Controlled scribbling, named scribbling	Beginning Language (2–4 years) Acquiring vocabulary, grammar, social speech	Function of print (2–4 years) Reads symbols in context Read pictures Beginning writing	Autonomy vs. Shame/Doubt (2–4 years) Independence, sensory exploration
	Preschematic (4–7 years) Generalized symbols recognizable to others Nonrepresentational	Language (4–7 years) Symbolic language Humor	Readers and Writers (5–8 years) Decode print Invented spelling Word identity	Initiative vs. Guilt (4–7 years) Constructive activities, own decisions
Concrete Operational (7–11 years) Logical, concrete thinkers. Can conserve, classify, seriate	Schematic/Realism (7–9 years) Representation of what he knows, not necessarily what he sees			Industry vs. Inferiority (7 years to puberty) Sense of duty, academic social competence

Figure 10–10 Stage Comparison of Cognitive and Creative Theorists.

▶ *Storytelling and song making*—Playing with words and music combines mental and creative abilities. Children need opportunities and encouragement to express themselves in the arts.

The child's creativity gives information about her cognitive development. The child does not go to bed one night in one stage and wake up tomorrow in another. It is a spiral moving slightly upward that keeps returning to previous stages to find reassurance, success, and comfort when new stages become too stressful. Disequilibrium sometimes invokes a

return to a previous stage or strategy. This is seen in the child who has had a traumatic event in her life return to thumb sucking, which brought so much comfort in a previous stage. In creative work, there is the return to the manipulation stage with the introduction of each new medium. The child uses sensory exploration of the materials, play without any purpose other than to get in touch with reality without pressure, before going on to actually represent thought through creativity.

Stages of Children's Art

Figure 10–11 illustrates the four stages of creative development.

Stage I: Mark-Making Stage (Birth to Two Years). The marks are random, done for pleasure and exploration, involving visual and physical movement. The child uses large muscles and whole arm movement. Over time, the marks become more organized and are repeated. The tool is held in a tight fist grip, with a rigid wrist. The purpose is to experience different materials, not to make some *thing*, but to repeat and repeat, integrating the brain's attention system and eye-hand coordination, while the adult intentionally uses language to describe the appearance,

It Happened to Me

Teaching to Draw

A professor in the art department at a university was asked by his preschool daughter what he did at work. He replied with, "I teach adults how to draw and paint." She came back with, "You mean, they forget?"

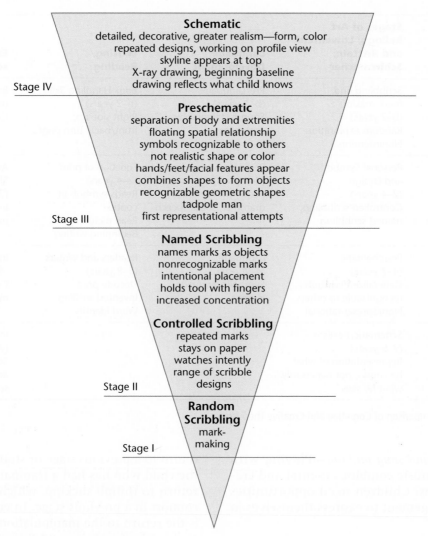

Figure 10–11 The Four Stages of Creative Development.
Source: Adapted from Kellogg, 1970; Lowenfeld & Brittain, 1987; Schirrmacher, 2002.

sounds, textures, tastes, and responds by imitating the infant's emotions (Lewin-Benham, 2010).

Stage II: Scribbling Stage (Two to Four Years). Kellogg (1970) analyzed the scribbles of thousands of young children and cataloged them into separate substages. **Scribbling** becomes more controlled with the development of the small muscles, eye–hand coordination, and cognitive abilities. The child uses a finger grip, with small, more controlled movements. The marks usually are constrained to the confines of the paper. During this stage, the child is still experimenting with line and practicing muscle control. The child intently works and develops designs in variations of the circle. Once language is developed, the child attaches names to the scribbles. There may have been a mental image when the scribble was drawn, but

the mind and muscles are not coordinated enough so the drawings are usually not recognizable to others. Drawings may be named, and as the stage progresses they become more representative of the child's mental image, to the point. The first representation of humans begins to appear in this stage.

A definite progression of geometric shapes and representations occurs in this order:

1. *Circles.* As small muscle coordination develops, the circle becomes rounded. Finally, the line connects to close the circle completely.
2. *Vertical and horizontal lines.* These become more deliberate and crosses and Xs become part of the experimentation with the art medium.
3. *Mandalas.* A **mandala** (Figure 10–11A) is a combination of a cross inside a circle. The

word means *magical circle* in Sanskrit. In Oriental religion, it is regarded as the symbol of the cosmos. In Jungian psychology, the mandala is representative of the psyche with the collective unconscious (Gardner, 1980; Kellogg, 1970, p. 68). These extended meanings raise the mandala's significance. All children universally pass through this stage.

4. *Suns.* The circle with radiating lines (Figure 10–11B) becomes one of the first symbols children draw.

5. *Radials.* Straight lines radiate from a central point to form a circle-like shape (Figure 10–11C). Radials also occur in the controlled scribbling stage.

6. *Tadpole man.* During the third and fourth years, children begin to represent humans in a curious symbol that resembles a **tadpole man** (Figure 10–12D). They combine the circles and lines into a head with features. This is understandable when the earliest images are considered. For months, the infant concentrates closely on the human face. The arms and legs are added later, just as their awareness of them came later. The circle represents the whole body as they know it, so a circle with dots for eyes and a line for a mouth is the early person drawing. Arms, then legs, then fingers and toes, and more features appear in an orderly progression. This should remind the student of child development of the principle of cephalocaudal and proximodistal development.

Stage III: Preschematic Stage (Four to Seven Years). Lowenfeld and Brittain (1987, p. 258) call the symbol a child draws for familiar objects a **schema**. The child experiments with drawing through the scribbling and the **preschematic** stages to develop these symbols. They are unique to each child yet similar because they follow the physical and mental developmental stages through which each child moves. These attempts are **nonrepresentational**. It is difficult, if not impossible, for children in this stage to follow instructions such as "think of your favorite _____ and draw it." Children at this stage are able to think of a favorite, but they lack the fine muscle skills and cognitive ability to physically represent their thoughts. They are more likely to draw what they can, even a scribble, and say, "This is a butterfly." To the viewer, as well as the artist, it is a blob.

Older preschoolers are trying to represent their mental images to others, yet much of what they create is still nonrepresentational and without realism to the viewer. They draw what they *know*, not what they *see*. They surely see more than they are able to

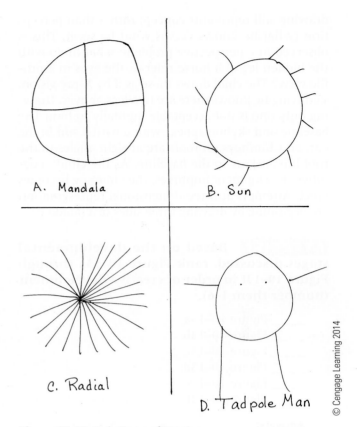

A. Mandala   B. Sun

C. Radial   D. Tadpole Man

© Cengage Learning 2014

Figure 10–12 Early Stages of Drawing.

draw. They experiment with the medium and often play with the tools. No message or intent for representation may be present.

At the beginning of this stage, there is little regard for realism in color, size proportion, or exact details. These aspects continue to be more evident as the stage progresses. By the end of this stage, the child can copy a square by bringing a single line back to the beginning with defined corners.

Details on the human figure increase, with the body becoming more like a snowman. The neck separates the head and body circle, and ovals appear, representing the arms and legs. Hands move from single lines to multiple lines, then accurately drawn five digits, and eventually more of a glove-like hand. Anatomical representations appear as the child strives for realism and gains knowledge of gender differences.

By the end of this period, the child draws an accurate triangle and often uses a repeated pattern or design of symbols. The child begins to use drawings to express feelings, as well as visual images.

Stage IV: Schematic Stage (Seven to Nine Years). In the **schematic** stage, the child now has a well-developed schema repeated in all drawings to represent humans, homes, trees, clouds—all the relevant, important objects in the child's life. The child's drawing still represents concept rather than perception (what he knows versus what he sees). This is observed in a perspective problem: what to do with the hidden leg of a horse rider or the eyes in a profile view? The child draws these as if by X-ray vision, signifying he knows there are two legs or eyes. Drawing only one is not acceptable mentally to him. The baseline and skyline appear with a partial sun in the corner. Chimneys on roofs are at right angles to the roof line, askew to the baseline. As the child's cognitive development improves, the chimney becomes erect. Attempts at three-dimensional representation are beginning by drawing three sides of a building.

EXERCISE **Based on the developmental stages discussed, rank Figure 10–13a through Figure 10–13f in order of creative development (number them 1–6).**

_____ Figure 10–13a
_____ Figure 10–13b
_____ Figure 10–13c
_____ Figure 10–13d
_____ Figure 10–13e
_____ Figure 10–13f

Answers:

Your sequence of stages should have been (1) Figure 10–13c; (2) Figure 10–13b; (3) Figure 10–13a; (4) Figure 10–13f; (5) Figure 10–13c; and (6) Figure 10–13d.

Figure 10–13b

© Cengage Learning 2014

Figure 10–13a

© Cengage Learning 2014

Figure 10–13c

© Cengage Learning 2014

Figure 10–13d

I saw my giney pig.

Figure 10–13e

Figure 10–13f

Figure 10–13a is an example of a tadpole man with the beginning of some features. The circles and firm, straight lines show small muscle control. The artist is four years, one month old.

Figure 10–13b is definitely a scribble, but a controlled scribble. The child left a margin around the page and confined marks to a located area. The artist is three years, two months old.

Figure 10–13c has separate, distinct body parts, characters on a baseline, and shows representation of thought by drawing the basketball team and the important parts such as the basket, the basketball, and the scoreboard. Note that the child has numbers on the team uniforms, not for counting but for realism. There are many signs this child is moving beyond the preschematic stage. The artist is five years, eleven months old.

Figure 10–13d is very realistic. This was by the oldest artist in the group. The drawing fills the page with the sky, sun, and clouds overhead and rain coming down. There is a definite baseline on which the person is walking and the cage and "Giney pig" are sitting. The artist is attempting a profile—note one eye and no arms drawn—but he just cannot resist the smile, though misplaced. The artist is six years, two months old.

Figure 10–13e was done by the youngest artist at two years, three months. The dots are stabs with the markers, and lines run off the paper as the child is attempting to gain control.

Figure 10–13f is the artist's practice, drawing the same form over and over, changing it slightly by altering the features. Alphabet letters are mixed in with the drawings. The artist is four years, five months.

Comparing creative work from different children and sorting them into developmental stages is not dependable, but these are representative of the stages, and their ages happened to correspond. It is not always so. The principles of development prevail. The stages are sequential, but children do not pass through them at the same age. Collecting the drawings of each child and comparing them to ones drawn previously by that child is dependable documentation of progress.

Observing Creativity in Infants and Toddlers

EXERCISE **Think about a very young child that you know. What does the child do that is creative?**

This is a trick question because everything a very young child does is creative. They have never done it before; they use objects in novel ways; and they are not afraid of trying or looking silly. They explore without inhibitions (Figure 10–14).

Infants and toddlers can create in the same ways as older children, producing, building, generating new ideas, and constructing. This is *making something happen* rather than *making something* (Wittmer & Petersen, 2006). They can construct visual arts using any safe materials. In the visual arts, they can draw using knobby crayons and markers. They can paint with non-toxic paint and even (depending on the guidelines of the program) fingerpaint with colorful pureed food such as spinach, beets, peaches, or applesauce. Older infants and toddlers can tear and crinkle paper and glue it to other papers. In construction, they can pile blocks, pound and pinch clay, and glue objects together in freeform sculptures. In the area of music and movement they naturally move to music creating their own dances, and hum and sing along. Their creative products are not mass-produced pumpkin faces or egg carton caterpillars (and should not be), but are experimentation with the medium. This is what young children gain through interacting with art materials and participating in art activities:

- Learning how to create something from "raw" materials
- Exploring materials with their senses
- Learning different ways to express thoughts and ideas
- Learning to make decisions
- Developing the ability to share materials and appreciate others' work

Figure 10–14 It is the sensory experience not the end product that is important. Photo courtesy of BC Center, Binghamton, NY.

- Developing a positive self-concept
- Developing and refining fine motor and cognitive activities

Source: From Deiner, Infants and Toddlers, 2nd ed. © 2009 Cengage Learning.

By observing infants and toddlers as they work with materials and interact with the environment—whether it is visual, auditory, or sensory—you can see that they demonstrate creativity that can be captured in descriptions, photographs, and video, and by preserving objects. It is not the objects themselves that are the important things here; it is the *doing* of them.

Blocks as a Creative Medium

Construction materials are open-ended, used in different ways by each child. This type of material, like any creative medium, gives the observer knowledge about many developmental areas. Blocks are varied in type but provide this kind of experience. Types of blocks include the following:

plastic interlocking blocks—LEGOs® or DUPLOs®
unit blocks—standard units are multiples of each other
hollow blocks—standard units are multiples of each other but are large; constructed of many pieces nailed and glued together
cardboard blocks—lightweight, often homemade from milk cartons
foam blocks—geometric shapes and units; lightweight
special building sets—Lincoln Logs®, Erector sets, TinkerToys®, A-B-C blocks, PVC pipes
cube blocks—one-unit blocks either of wood or plastic, sometimes with locking features

The Educational Research Foundation has conducted years of research on children's visual-spatial work. Miller (2004) trained teachers to closely observe and sketch children's block work. The block sketches were analyzed to identify the skills children gained. Children acquire many skills through visual-spatial work done with blocks. The first is construction where children practice using variously shaped blocks and placing them in patterns. Children gain knowledge of structures and systems, communicating their knowledge of inside and outside an enclosure, entrances and pathways. During their visual-spatial work they convey emotions, working out themes of danger and safety. They practice abstract thinking by recreating visual memories of familiar buildings and making visual analogies by selecting a block to represent another item. They develop science process skills as they collect information by observation, classify, measure, experiment, and draw conclusions. They develop math concepts of height, width, length, size, whole and parts, fractions, geometric shapes, and symmetry. For kinesthetic learners, blocks provide not just physical objects to manipulate, but also to build muscle memory. While working with blocks children interact socially, sharing ideas and negotiating to problem solve, engaging in dramatic play and using rich language.

Block play can accomplish those outcomes more effectively if the teacher helps the children to be more intentional about their work, encouraging them to describe their plan before beginning to build, even if they are too young to actually carry it out. They have formed a mental image of their construction. As children mature they can regulate themselves enough to collaborate with others in a shared activity (Bodrova & Leong, 2007).

The placement of shaped blocks on shelves, labeled with exact tracings of the block, builds one-to-one correspondence skills. The association of the shapes—square, rectangle, triangle, cylinder—is made not only with the shape but also the word, making the literacy connection. Much of what goes on in the block building area is more than construction. It involves dramatic play, social skills, and language practice. The towers with resultant crashes bring excitement and danger themes to the block area. Accompanying props, such as farm and zoo animals, transportation vehicles, and miniature people, expand the play from functional to symbolic. By including textures, such as rug and fabric pieces, small pieces of turf-like carpeting, and soft pillows, the area becomes a stress reducer as well (Figure 10–15).

There are often physical barriers between the dramatic play area (housekeeping or family area) and the block area. This contributes to gender segregation, which is so common in these areas. Physically removing the barrier and encouraging the crossover of materials can help break down the stereotypes of play materials that are already present in preschoolers. Blocks can be taken to the oven to bake as bread. Block structures become homes where dishes and dolls can be added. By carefully planning the environment, the block area becomes another microcosm of development, affording the observer an excellent view of all areas of development.

Stages in Block Play. There are progressive stages in the way children interact with blocks, dependent on cognitive, social, emotional, and physical development (Figure 10–16).

Stage I: Carrying, Filling, and Dumping (Under Two Years). Children are in the Sensorimotor Stage, so

Figure 10–15 Block play areas with accessories, literacy materials, and cross-over play from the dramatic area promote creativity.

© Cengage Learning 2012

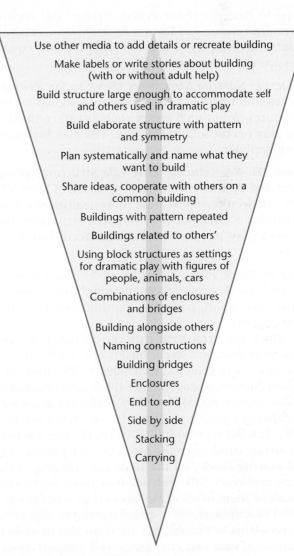

Use other media to add details or recreate building

Make labels or write stories about building (with or without adult help)

Build structure large enough to accommodate self and others used in dramatic play

Build elaborate structure with pattern and symmetry

Plan systematically and name what they want to build

Share ideas, cooperate with others on a common building

Buildings with pattern repeated

Buildings related to others'

Using block structures as settings for dramatic play with figures of people, animals, cars

Combinations of enclosures and bridges

Building alongside others

Naming constructions

Building bridges

Enclosures

End to end

Side by side

Stacking

Carrying

Figure 10–16 Block Play Development.

© Cengage Learning 2014

they are exploring the attributes of blocks by feeling, lifting, and moving them from place to place.

Stage II: Beginning Block Building (Two to Three Years). Children make horizontal rows, laying blocks end to end or stacking. They repeat stacking and knocking down. They are beginning to observe the unstable effect of a small base with large blocks piled on.

Stage III: Bridging (Three Years). Two blocks are placed vertically as pillars with a third block placed across the top. This takes visual acuity, small muscle coordination, and balance.

Stage IV: Enclosures (Three and Four Years). Four blocks are placed at right angles to enclose a space. This corresponds to the child's ability to draw a square, recognizing the connectedness of the angles and associating inside and outside concepts.

Stage V: Patterns (Four Years). Bridges and enclosures are repeated to form a horizontal or vertical pattern. Symmetry, a sense of balance and equal proportions, is demonstrated.

Stage VI: Naming Structures (Four to Six Years). Names and functions of buildings are assigned to the structures. Additional pieces such as cars, animals, and play people add to the play. The play becomes more symbolic.

Stage VII: Reproducing True-Life Structures (Five Years and Up). This stage is an expansion of Stage VI, with children trying to build more realistically and incorporate dramatic play into the structures by moving play people and animals according to a script.

Uses of Block Play. These block-building stages parallel the drawing stages: manipulation, simple experimentation, patterns, naming, and realistic reproduction.

Block play can help children in many developmental domains. Wellhousen and Kieff (2001) provide a list of goals to be included in IEPs (individualized education programs) or IFSPs (individualized family service plans), but they really are goals for all children and also give cues for observing specific skills. This list is given in Figure 10–17. The teacher can attract children to the block area by pulling out and placing blocks on the floor (not playing with them, however). Talk with children about the blocks and allow them to select the blocks they want to use. Verbal descriptions, open-ended questions, and posing problems or possibilities are strategies in verbal scaffolding that can encourage and support more complex block building (Gregory et al., 2003).

Other Creative Media

Other materials or media such as clay, woodworking, or collage illustrate the child's development through stages similar to drawing. Small muscles interact with creativity to produce three-dimensional products. These often are not preserved (but with a digital camera could be!), since the materials—especially in the case of clay or wood—are often returned to be manipulated in another way. The stages correspond to drawing (Figure 10–18).

Interaction with a tangible, movable medium is sensory, involving seeing, feeling, and often smelling. It helps the development of Logico-Mathematical thinking through manipulation. Physical properties of volume, weight, and length are transformed through play.

Music and Movement Development. While most of this chapter has emphasized the visual arts, music and movement as a creative process should not be ignored. A consortium to investigate learning, arts, and the brain found that there is growing evidence of the positive impact on cognitive development through learning of the arts including music, dance, drama, and painting (Gazzaniga, 2008). Music and language are so intertwined that an awareness of music is critical to a baby's language development (Deutsch, 2010). Music and language have basic rules, elements, and melody.

Experiences with music are closely aligned with all areas of development:

▶ Intellectual: differentiation of sounds, rhythms, memory of tune repetition and lyrics, critical thinking, and problem solving by moving
▶ Physical: moving to music as physical control increases in more complex motions, creating and exploring new ways to move, using movement to express emotions or tell a story
▶ Social: interacting with others in responding to music, singing and moving together
▶ Emotional: sensing the mood of music and expressing feelings through it

▶❚❚ TEACHSOURCE VIDEO ACTIVITY

Visit the Education CourseMate website at CengageBrain.com and watch the video entitled *Infants and Toddlers: Creative Activities*

Listen for the verbs "action words" used to describe the children's actions in this video. Though they are working with clay, how many of them relate to the Goals for Block Play Figure 10–16?

Awareness:

❏ Increase body awareness
❏ Improve self-concept
❏ Increase awareness of individual differences

Creativity:

❏ Encourage creativity
❏ Encourage creative problem solving
❏ Stimulate curiosity

Feelings:

❏ Increase awareness of own and others' feelings
❏ Provide outlet for expressing feelings
❏ Increase feelings of group belonging

Language Skills:

❏ Improve expressive language
❏ Increase vocabulary
❏ Follow directions
❏ Increase understanding (receptive language)

Math Skills:

❏ Improve measurement concepts
❏ Improve number concepts
❏ Improve shape concepts
❏ Improve size concepts

Motor Skills:

❏ Improve large motor coordination
❏ Improve small motor coordination
❏ Improve eye–hand coordination
❏ Improve balancing skills
❏ Develop the ability to relax at will

Sensory Skills:

❏ Improve auditory association, closure, comprehension, discrimination, identification, memory
❏ Improve tactile association, closure, comprehension, discrimination, identification, memory
❏ Improve visual association, closure, comprehension, discrimination, identification, memory
❏ Localize sound
❏ Improve sensory integration

Social Skills:

❏ Cooperate with peers/adults
❏ Improve ability to take turns
❏ Improve ability to share
❏ Improve interaction skills

Thinking and Reasoning Skills:

❏ Improve color concepts
❏ Increase attention span
❏ Improve cause-and-effect reasoning
❏ Improve classification skills
❏ Improve decision-making skills
❏ Improve logical reasoning
❏ Improve problem-solving skills
❏ Make predictions

Figure 10–17 Goals for Block Play.
Source: From Wellhousen & Kieff, *A Constructivist Approach to Block Play in Early Childhood,* 1st ed. © 2001 Cengage Learning.

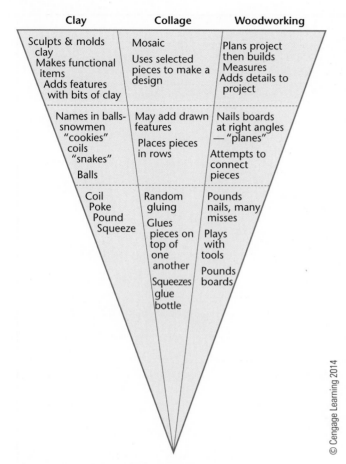

Clay	Collage	Woodworking
Sculpts & molds clay Makes functional items Adds features with bits of clay	Mosaic Uses selected pieces to make a design	Plans project then builds Measures Adds details to project
Names in balls-snowmen "cookies" coils "snakes" Balls	May add drawn features Places pieces in rows	Nails boards at right angles — "planes" Attempts to connect pieces
Coil Poke Pound Squeeze	Random gluing Glues pieces on top of one another Squeezes glue bottle	Pounds nails, many misses Plays with tools Pounds boards

© Cengage Learning 2014

Figure 10–18 Stages of Other Creative Activities.

- Language: recalling words to songs and expanding the vocabulary of music and movement terms such as body parts, ways of moving, relationship words
- Literacy: reading words and musical notes

Music, too, follows a developmental progression that can be observed and documented (Figure 10–19). It begins before birth when the rhythm of the mother's heartbeat starts the child's ear for music. Before birth, fetuses can differentiate between a familiar song and a novel one. In the first 12 months of life, the infant responds to sounds in the environment by listening and moving. As the infant increases in the ability to make sounds, they are musical and more and more rhythmic. With developing physical control comes movement to music as the child waves arms and bounces to music, and moves to play out a familiar story or mimic an animal. Toddlers use the greater control of their bodies to begin dancing, doing finger plays, and singing familiar phrases. Preschoolers can repeat and sing familiar songs, using them to soothe themselves when upset, remind themselves of rules,

and entertain others. They love to make music, loud if not rhythmic, enjoying the marching and moving in group experiences. Children in kindergarten and primary grades are connecting music with literacy by beginning to read words and music and learning to play musical instruments, as well as learning and repeating simple dance steps. All aspects of development influence and produce music and movement development, intertwining with each other.

Sensory Experiences. One of the most common early childhood opportunities for creativity is the sensory experiences—messy play in other words—where children feel, manipulate, pour, fill, scrunch, stretch, squeeze, flatten, roll, splat, or smooth all manner of materials with no expected end product. Often this is set up at a low table with sides to contain the media, along with containers of various sizes that hold materials that can be moved, poured, and even spilled. Most sensory tables or tubs are capable of holding liquid as well as all types of mass quantities of small objects such as sand, flour, seeds, rice, wood chips, dog food, pebbles, marbles, nature materials, and potting soil. The list is endless and reveals the creativity of teachers in finding materials that will intrigue the players. Observing how children manipulate and explore at the sensory table can give information about their sensory integration (Hunter, 2008). The sensory material is transformed by children's imagination, demonstrating their skills in every domain of development: physical development as they manipulate the material; social-emotional development as they share and handle disagreements; approaches to learning as they use prior knowledge and attend and extend the play; creative expression as they play out dramatic themes; language development as they speak freely describing their actions; health and safety as they navigate the risks of sand in the eyes, or slippery water on the floor; executive function as they demonstrate self-control to keep most of the material in the containers; and cognitive development as they develop an understanding of size, shape, conservation, and the properties of solids and liquids.

Sensory Play during Home Visits

Regardless of the context for learning, all infants, toddlers, and preschoolers need ample opportunities to explore and create with a variety of materials. Classroom educators can easily design enticing spaces that invite all kinds of explorations, messy and not so messy. Home educators do not have that same autonomy as they are "guests" in each home;

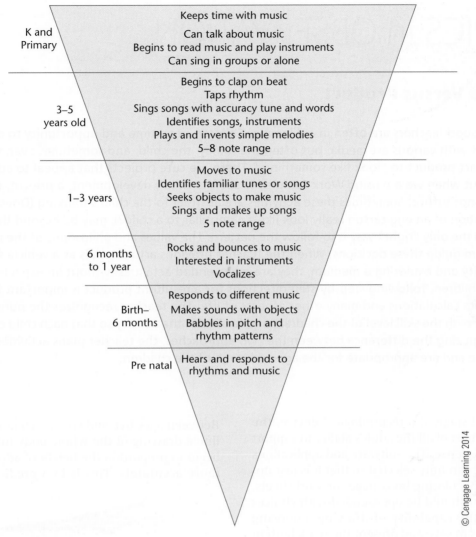

K and Primary	Keeps time with music Can talk about music Begins to read music and play instruments Can sing in groups or alone
3–5 years old	Begins to clap on beat Taps rhythm Sings songs with accuracy tune and words Identifies songs, instruments Plays and invents simple melodies 5–8 note range
1–3 years	Moves to music Identifies familiar tunes or songs Seeks objects to make music Sings and makes up songs 5 note range
6 months to 1 year	Rocks and bounces to music Interested in instruments Vocalizes
Birth–6 months	Responds to different music Makes sounds with objects Babbles in pitch and rhythm patterns
Pre natal	Hears and responds to rhythms and music

© Cengage Learning 2014

Figure 10–19 Stages of Music Development.

the degree to which exploration is permitted is determined by the family. Given that, it is important to gain family perspective (values, beliefs and practices) around experimentation with tools and materials that may be different than what is typically allowed within the home environment. It is important to have parental approval for activities that may temporarily disrupt family's expectations and practices. Engaging families in advance is a purposeful and important task of the home educator.

Using Technology

All kinds of technology—computers, DVD and CD players, digital cameras and all kinds of handheld devices—can be used for creative activities in addition to the math and science learning as discussed

in Chapter 8. The preschool years are years of experimentation as well as laying foundations for later learning, and using technology is commonplace in today's homes and children's programs where children are *Growing up Digital* (Tapscott, 2000) as the title of a best-selling book reminds us. In many schools, children begin in kindergarten to regularly use iPads®, laptops and PCs for both academic and creative work.

There is much debate over how much creativity is involved in using many technological devices. To read more about this see *The Plug-In Drug* (Winn, 2002), *Failure to Connect: How Computers Affect Our Children's Minds* (Healy, 1998), *Tech Tonic: Towards a New Literacy of Technology* (Alliance for Childhood, 2004). Plowman (2010) suggests the common-sense approach of thinking first of the child's

TOPICS in OBSERVATION

Process Versus Product

Early childhood teachers are often in a dilemma. Children need time and opportunity to explore and experiment with various art media, but often the family, the child, and sometimes even the teacher wants the art product to "look like something." There are cute projects that appeal to adults and to children, but when we are using Work Samples to see the child's development, a pre-cut, directed activity does not suffice. Sometimes these activities are abstract to the child's thinking (Does the adult's transformation of an egg carton really look like a caterpillar to a child?), may be beyond their physical ability, and the only "right" way is to follow the pattern. The values and philosophy of the teacher and the program guide these decisions. When the teacher provides art materials as a vehicle for expressing creativity and exploring a medium, they are open-ended activities without an expected product. For older children, following step-by-step directions for a resultant product is important training for mathematics calculations and many other aspects of life. The teacher recognizes the purpose, aligns the project with the skill level of the children, and facilitates the activity so that each child can feel success. Recognizing the difference between the two approaches, the teacher plans activities that meet the purpose and are appropriate for the age and stage of the children.

developmental stage, the technological device, the program, and most of all the adult's ability to support the child's experience. The software and applications used should be carefully selected so that it is just not a digital form of coloring book pages or worksheets. The application should be open-ended with choices that provide the capability of drawing, choosing color, and ways to save and present the work both in digital and printed form.

Using Self-Portraits to Know the Child

EXERCISE Look at the self-portraits by children four to five years old (Figure 10–20a through Figure 10–20d). Describe how different they are in control, detail, and the mood they present.

The child's drawings of humans evolve from the beginning circle with dots for eyes. The child is drawing what is known. The human face, with eyes the predominant feature, represents family and self, drawn by hands that are still developing control. Arms and legs later protrude from this head, and eventually more and more details appear as more "humanoid" drawings in the fourth year. As the child is closer to age five, the neck separates the head and body, and limbs begin to take on more substance than just a line.

Between ages five and six, the child usually can outline a drawing of the whole body in one stroke and begin to proportion the height of adults and children more accurately. This is in a predictable sequence

Figure 10–20a

Figure 10–20b

© Cengage Learning 2014

Figure 10–20c

© Cengage Learning 2014

Figure 10–20d

© Cengage Learning 2014

(Kellogg, 1970). Three-dimensional work follows a similar sequence. In knowing that sequence, just as in knowing all developmental stage milestones, it helps the observer to recognize change and anticipate and recognize the next stage when it appears.

The self-portraits in Figures 10–20a through 10–20d were drawn by four-year-old boys. It would be presumptuous to interpret levels of development from one drawing. However, when the observer periodically collects children's self-portraits, along with the child's commentary about the work, the result is a more valid indication of cognitive and creative development.

Talking with Children About Their Creative Work

The teacher can comment on the work in a way that points out elements:

line—type of line, direction, length, relationship to other lines, straight, curved, wiggly, zigzag, jagged, crisscross, short, long, thick, thin, horizontal, vertical, diagonal

color—primary colors (red, yellow, blue), light colors (magenta, cyan, yellow), secondary colors (mixture of two primary colors), hue (a color), tint (a color lightened by the addition of white), tone or intensity (the relative lightness or darkness of a color), value (range of lightness and darkness of the colors)

texture—soft, hard, bumpy, rough, jagged, smooth, wet, sticky

shape—size, name, solidity, relationship, geometric shapes (square, rectangular, round, triangular, irregular, oval), organic shapes (from nature such as a leaf or butterfly), symbolic shapes (special meaning such as letters or numbers), freeform shapes (follow no rules)

pattern and rhythm, plaid, polka dot, stripe, floral, all over, border, checkered, beats, melody

form—spheres, cubes, pyramids, cylinders, rectangular solids

space—closeness, location, boundaries, empty, open spaces, absence of shape or form

movement—high, low, fast, slow, rhythmic or arrhythmic, fluid, smooth, sharp

(Koster, 2012, pp. 99–103)

While observing children working, whether just enjoyably watching or observing for a purpose, the adult is often called on to comment on a child's work. The child may ask, "How is it?" or "Do you like it?" A ready answer is necessary, one that agrees with personal style, program goals, and theoretical philosophy. The following are presented for consideration and practice so that the teacher's repertoire of comments is consistent with beliefs. Different common responses are listed here, along with commentary and suggestions for improvement.

Complimentary. The child may ask for or expect a reaction from the adult. A natural response is a generalized, polite praise such as "Oh, lovely," "Very nice," or "Beautiful." The problem with this approach is that they are empty words with no specific reaction. The child's may not have meant for it to be "nice" or "lovely." It may be a frightening spider or a bad dream. The adult's comment is a casual remark lacking sincerity; and it becomes a denial of the artist's purpose, which may have been for exploration and practice, not beauty.

> *Instead:* "You worked a really long time at that," "Look how much red you used," or "You really thought about that."

Judgmental. "Great!" "That's wonderful." Again, these are empty words that may not be truthful or reflect what the child is trying to portray. These comments are evaluative from the viewer's opinion. It is more important for the viewer to determine the child's opinion of the work or the inspiration behind it. When we consider that young children are egocentric, they only imagine that the viewer will see it just as they do.

> *Instead:* "What do you like about it?" or "Can you tell me how you did it?" "What part did you do first?"

Valuing. The adult expresses her personal opinion, "I love it." The goal is to help the child find self-satisfaction as the measuring stick of creative work. An outsider's evaluation is not necessary or advisable. What the *adult* sees or thinks is not important. How the *child* feels or thinks about it is the important point.

> *Instead:* "What do you like about it?"

Questioning. When the adult asks, "What is it?" or "What's this supposed to be?" a loud message is conveyed: "You were supposed to make something I could recognize. I can't see it, so you are not doing it right." The adult should know that young children up to age six and seven are nonrepresentational in their art. They may have a mental image of what they want to draw, but their physical abilities for control of the medium and cognitive development concerning perception and reality are still in the formative stages.

> *Instead:* "Would you like to tell me about it?"

Note that with this alternative the child still has the option of saying "No," an option not given by the more commanding "Tell me about it."

Probing. When the questioning approach asks the significance of every piece of work, it may be overused; it is also probing. From what is known about children's art, much of it is for exploration of the medium. The child is getting the feel of the fingerpaint, or practicing rolling snakes and balls of clay, or watching the glue flow out as the bottle is squeezed.

> *Instead:* Just observe. Watch for indications of what the child is getting from the experience. A simple "Hmmmm" suggests interest and invites the child to comment if she chooses.

Correcting. Early childhood educators should know that children's drawings are unrealistic, so it is inappropriate to tell a child, "Grass isn't orange. Here's a green crayon for grass."

> *Instead:* Allow the child to use materials in any way they wish as long as it is safe for themselves and the environment. Give redirection reminders, such as, "We paint on the paper, not on the wall," or "When you walk around with the brush, you are dripping paint all over. If you want to look at Lizzy's side of the easel, place the brush in the container first."

Psychoanalyzing. Much study has been done on the emotional and psychological meaning of children's creative work. It makes fascinating reading, but it is not for amateurs. Deep psychological significance should not be placed on children's art. It is inappropriate for people without training to make diagnoses about the child's emotional state. Some have said, "She uses black all over the page. She must be depressed." The content of children's creative work and their choice of color is not realistic. A teacher mistakenly commented on the red paint the child used and thought, "He told me this was all the blood from the baby. He must wish his new baby brother was dead. Maybe he's planning to stab him." Forming conclusions about the child's inner mind from one drawing is just as unfair and dangerous as evaluating the whole child from one test.

> *Instead:* Note curious, strange, bizarre creations or comments from the child on a notepad for your own use. If they are repeated or accompanied by behavioral indicators, follow it up. If you are alarmed, talk to your supervisor, then possibly the family, to search for further clarification or evaluation. Sometimes children's art *can be* their way of expressing fears or traumatic incidents that cannot be verbalized.

Modeling. This is an acceptable teaching technique in every other area of early childhood practice *except* art. Modeling in the sense of making a pattern for a child to follow is not good professional practice. Planned art "projects" sometimes present materials for the child to construct the adult's idea of a caterpillar, clown face, or dinosaur. These thwart the whole purpose and theory of children's creative development and its benefits. Many teachers say, "Well, I'm just providing the materials for the clown face, they can do it any way they want." The child knows the adult's expectation but may not have the experience with a clown's face or the desire to make one.

> *Instead:* Provide the child with rich experiences in the world around him. Provide creative materials that the child can use himself and allow the child to create whatever he chooses from those experiences.

Whereas modeling a pattern for the art itself is not useful, there are some things that can be modeled: Model an accepting attitude to children's explorations. Model an interest in texture, design, and color, using vocabulary words about them such as *rough, smooth, ridges, pattern, balance, horizontal, vertical, swirls,* and *border* and color names such as *mauve, lavender,* and *chartreuse.* This makes association between the visual image and the word. Young children love big words. Model

processes of using materials by sitting at the clay table and throwing clay to soften it, rolling balls and snakes, and pinching pots. This modeling is not direct instruction but scaffolding manipulation techniques that children will adopt when they are ready.

Describing. This is the best *instead* of the preceding approaches. Every area of development that is seen through creative work can be described (not all at once): physical movement; control of the tools; use of the space; self-help skills in working on the project; social interactions in the art or in the process; control or expression of emotions; vocabulary to describe the product; writing associated with the creations; math and science concepts; self-identity revealed through the art; and interactions with the group and adults through the process.

> "You used a lot of red today." (Making the association between the visual color and the word *red.*)
> "You covered the whole page with paint. That took a lot of concentration." (Commenting on space and attention span.)
> "You made a lot of blue vertical lines and yellow horizontal lines. It made a design that's sometimes called plaid. Look at this. There's the color green where they come together. I don't see any green paint out today. I wonder how that happened?" (Using the vocabulary of design, pointing out colors, helping the child observe cause and effect and wonder. If he does not understand it this time, he might the next time. The association has been made and the disequilibrium has been pointed out. The child will accommodate this new knowledge into color concepts.)

EXERCISE Go back to Figures 10–12a through 10–12d, which you may recall were the drawings in the exercise on the stages of art, and practice your comments to the artist who asks, "How do you like it?"

Reggio Emilia and Children's Art

A discussion of children's creative development would not be complete without mentioning the child-care centers and preschools in Reggio Emilia, Italy. They are the model of community and family collaboration and for the project approach to curriculum; but most of all, they

It Happened to Me

Instinct over Knowledge

I had just discussed the responses to children's art with my college class. The next week, a mother with a newborn came to class to demonstrate the reflexes that were still present. She also brought her preschooler with paper and markers to occupy her while we watched her baby brother. As the demonstration drew to a close, I went over to the big sister and looked at her drawing. Out of my mouth came, "What is it?" The whole class gasped, and then laughed at my embarrassment for doing what I said not to do. It showed how ingrained those old habits are, and how easily the instinctive comments slip out from among the learned behaviors. It takes practice and a concentrated effort!

represent the incredible level of creativity of which children are capable when given such a carefully prepared environment and collaboration between children and adults. Thousands of visitors from all over the world have been enthralled with the visually sensual learning environment that stimulates children to use a vast array of art materials. The image of the child is one of capability and respect. Teachers consider every aspect of the environment as a stimulus for learning and forming mental images that will be called on to organize and construct meaning. The environment of beauty and light is breathtaking as one enters spaces of reception that welcome families with antique pieces of furniture and cozy sitting areas. Light streams through every possible opening and is reflected in mirrors, shiny surfaces, and translucent panels.

Observation is the adult's most important role, and it is conveyed to the children as well. They are guided to closely observe the details of every physical part of the environment—from the smallest seed to the tracks of an animal in the mud to the patterns of clouds in the sky. The adult follows the children's interests and supports the graphic representation of what the child sees and explores. Documentation panels or booklets illustrate not just

the finished product or outcome but the process itself; their only objective is to make the learning public (Figure 10–21). This kind of documentation records not just what the child knows or knows how to do, but what the child can do with various kinds of environmental support—the contexts, opportunities, and materials offered to the child (Krechevsky & Stork, 2000). Documenting processes as well as outcomes is research that has its application in evaluation and curriculum decisions. Those who have visited Reggio Emilia have changed forever their ideas about the teacher's role as curriculum planner, as well as their ideas about the capabilities of young children to represent their world. When teachers change their approach, the result is children's creative efforts surpassing long-held developmental expectations (Dighe, Calomiris, & Van Zutphen, 1998).

The Hundred Languages of Children (Edwards & Gandini, 1998) brings Reggio children's projects to the world both in book and in exhibit form. Reggio advocates point out, however, that their approach is not about art but using art and other Work Samples as products of children's emotional concerns, social relations, and creative and intellectual pursuits as they occur within the context of collaborative problem solving" (New, 1997, p. 224,). The beauty and richness of the colors, the complete absorption of the children in their work, and the planning of each project piques the curiosity of the viewer.

There is much more to the Reggio approach than simply documenting children's work. The approach begins with the image of the child as having legitimate rights, and as an active constructor

Figure 10–21 Documentation Panel.

of knowledge through investigation as a social endeavor. The teacher is not the fount of knowledge, but a collaborator, co-learner, guide, facilitator, and researcher. Curriculum develops from the real interests of the children, who decide how to approach learning and represent what they have learned in a meaningful way (Hewett, 2001). Trust is an important factor in this philosophy, as Linn (2001) points out. First, educators trust children's initiative and intelligence and let them experience things through trial and error, and even allow them to fail. Parents of Reggio children trust the educators without being bound to the necessity of test scores to show that their children are learning. Linn also reminds us that learning is culturally bound and that the lesson from Reggio is not to find ways to duplicate it but to "raise awareness about the connection between culture and educational practice in the United States."

Assessing Creative Program Goals

When work is not linked to standards and formally assessed, it is seen as less valuable to the educational process and becomes endangered when resources are scarce. It is important for schools and programs to include creativity in goals and to assess creativity systematically as a contribution to cognitive development. Here are some of those efforts.

Dance, Music, Theater, Visual Arts: What Every Young American Should Know and Be Able to Do in the Arts: National Standards for Arts Education (Consortium of National Arts Education Associations, 1994) outlines knowledge and skills children must have to fulfill their personal potential, to become productive and competitive workers in a global economy, and to take their place as adult citizens. In the Goals 2000: Educate America Act, the arts are listed as a core academic subject along with English, mathematics, history, science, and foreign language. These are standards for K–12; they are left to individual schools to implement.

Developmentally Appropriate Practice in Early Childhood Programs (Copple & Bredekamp, 2009) recommends that "children have daily opportunities for creative expression and esthetic expression," that they "explore and enjoy various forms of dramatic play, music, and dance and visual arts" (p. 175).

The NAEYC Early Childhood Program Standards and Accreditation Criteria (2006) self-study asks programs to rate their opportunities for creative expression and appreciation for the arts.

Koster, in *Growing Artists* (2012), suggests the following for the space designated for art:

- *Layout*—Art activities should be in an area where the activities of the room are visible and influence the artist.
- *Adequate space*—Children need space to spread out and work comfortably.
- *Traffic patterns*—Flexible areas allow more children to explore, both at tables and on the floor.
- *Water requirements*—Location near the water source or movable pans of water for prewashing minimizes messes.
- *Separate from food areas*—Art and cooking activities must be kept separate using separate tables and trays, or at least covers, for surfaces for one or the other, such as a tablecloth for eating or an old shower curtain for art (pp. 148–149).

EXERCISE **Rate your classroom creative environment according to the preceding criteria.**

Unmet   Partially Met   Fully Met

On a separate sheet of paper, write an action plan to improve aspects of the environment to allow for more creative expression.

Benefits of Creativity

EXERCISE **Which of these children is using creativity?**

- Althea hears a song in the wind.
- Kito writes his name in the frost on the windowpane.
- Nora organizes her books according to the colors of the covers.
- Chianna gathers stones to place in a circle and addresses them with a story
- Ezra stops a fight on the playground and gets his friends to talk it out.

The answer of course is, all of them. None of them has drawn a picture, sculpted clay, written a song, moved to music or acted in a play, which are the usual understandings or expectations of creativity. When asked, many people deny they are creative because they do not paint, draw, play a musical instrument or act yet they are very creative in other ways. It is not just because we need the arts to make the world a more beautiful place but it is vital because every day across the world there are problems that need creative solutions and it takes looking at things in different ways to provide possible solutions; not just one right answer, but many choices. The future of humankind depends on the development of creativity.

Creativity is taking a bit of knowledge and changing it, cognitively and practically transforming it into something else. Picasso is said to have formed the sculpture of the head of a bull after looking at a bicycle's handles and seat and Gutenberg combined the winepress and the coin press (which made images on soft metal) into the printing press. Contrary to the myth that creative people are eccentric, antisocial and even emotionally unhealthy, many researchers have found just the opposite. The difference likes in self-actualization versus special talent. Creativity can be the outlet or expression of the emotional/affective domain. Creative people can use their creativity in ways that help themselves as well as others. Creativity enhances self-esteem and self-worth. A creative person helps create solutions to problems at home or in the workplace; expresses novel ideas in meetings, gaining peer recognition; or produces new process and procedures that save time, energy, materials, or frustration. All of these applications of creative thinking bring a sense of well-being and accomplishment.

The creative person can extend these benefits to others by carefully listening and mentally taking the other person's place or point of view. By thinking of a situation from another's perspective, or by feeling his pain or sorrow, the creative person expresses empathy, bringing comfort and support to others. It may not be an invention that changes the world, or a piece of art that hangs in a gallery for all to see, but the personal benefits of creativity to self and others makes the world a better place. So as we help children develop and learn, encouraging and nurturing creativity has both an education and social benefits.

Helping all Children with Creativity

Creative work is both expressive and receptive. It requires no spoken language to create or enjoy someone else's creation. Even with limitations of language barriers or physical, cognitive, or psychological impairments, creative arts can be a form of two-way communication.

Giftedness: Creative and Cognitive Development beyond Expected Levels

Many parents believe their child is gifted. The definition traditionally referred to an exceptionally high score on an intelligence test, but it has been broadened to include exceptional abilities in other areas as well. In 1969, P.L. 91-230 contained a model program provision for gifted and talented children. Because of the limitations of standardized tests (see Chapter 8), many children were not identified as gifted because of the cultural bias of the tests, resulting in low numbers of minorities participating in gifted programs. Little federal funding has been allocated for gifted programs, but much research has been done in trying to define and identify giftedness. Some have to do with **precocity**, early development in areas such as language, music, or mathematical ability. The Renzulli-Hartman scales (in Torrance, 2000, p. 356) are commonly used for assessing creativity in preschool children:

1. The child has unusually advanced vocabulary for age level.
2. The child possesses a large storehouse of information about a variety of topics.
3. The child has rapid insight into cause-effect relationships.
4. The child is a keen and alert observer; usually "sees more" or "gets more" out of a story, picture, film, sightseeing trip, and so on.
5. The child becomes absorbed and truly involved in certain topics or problems.
6. The child strives toward perfection or excellence, and is self-critical.
7. The child is interested in many "adult" problems such as religion, politics, sex, race, and so on.
8. The child likes to organize and bring structure to things, people, and situations.
9. The child displays a great deal of curiosity about many things and an intense curiosity about something.
10. The child displays a keen sense of humor and sees humor in situations that may not appear humorous to others.

Divergent thinking is the ability to think of a wide range of possibilities. It is associated with giftedness, rather than **convergent thinking**, the ability to arrive at a single answer. Its identification and measurement at an early age is complicated and inaccurate, but close observers of children may see signs of giftedness. Assessment of every child's learning level helps meet the child's needs through curriculum planning. This same reason applies to giftedness.

Cultural Diversity

Art is a universal language. The child may not speak a common language or share a common culture with the rest of the people in the group, but creative work can be a vehicle for becoming absorbed in an activity without pressure to speak or conform. Giving children creative materials with a minimum of direction is appropriate for this population, and can be a comforting and successful activity in which to engage these children. It also gives them a way to express feelings and ideas nonverbally.

Introducing children to the artists and crafts of various cultures brings a global awareness to the environment and the curriculum. Banks (2001) suggests three ways that this can be accomplished:

▶ *contributions*—introduction to music and visual artists from diverse cultures
▶ *additive*—adding projects to the curriculum at the children's developmental level that provide experiences in music and movement and the visual arts using varied materials such as natural clay, coloring agents such as vegetables and plants, and items collected from the natural environment
▶ *transformation*—looking not just at the creations and creators of European artists but also at those from Africa, Native America, and Asia; and connecting with other aspects of the curriculum such as literature, history, and social studies to see the context in which the works were produced

Ability Diversity

Art plans that are open-ended and designed to explore the medium can be adapted to meet the needs of special abilities populations. Children with sight or hearing impairments can find great success in manipulating creative materials. Adaptive devices, such as bicycle grips on paintbrush handles, textured fingerpaint, and modeling dough with scent from powdered nonsweetened drink mixes add multisensory aspects to art media. The manipulation of art materials is also soothing and sustaining for children with attention disorders.

Whatever the cognitive or physical functioning level of the child, art plans can be implemented and adapted to the child's capability to encourage creativity and minimize frustration. Creative media are essential parts of every early childhood program. Art involves every developmental area and easily meets the needs of every child, despite their situation. It is a natural place to focus assessment in a nonintrusive way.

Helping Professionals for Creative Art

Programs or individual teachers who want to enrich the creative environment can enlist the assistance of

art educators—teachers who specialize in the incorporation of the arts into the curriculum

Individual children may be assisted in resolving emotional conflicts or behavior disorders by specialists who use the arts as therapy, such as

art therapist—credentialed professional who helps self-understanding and emotional release through art media
music therapist—certified professional who uses music in treatment goals for people with handicaps for physical and mental health

Other Methods

Other Methods to Record Creativity

Anecdotal/Running Records—narratives about a child's approach to work
Checklists/Rating Scales—Work Samples Checklist or the creative portion of a developmental Checklist
Conversations and Interviews—recording a child's discussions about work produced
Time Sample—measure the amount of time a child spends on a certain task
Media—use photographs, video, or audio recording to document the process or the work produced

Key Terms

convergent thinking	preschematic
creativity	schema
divergent thinking	schematic
mandala	scribbling
media/medium	tadpole man
nonrepresentational	Work Samples
precocity	

Plans

Go to Education CourseMate website, accessed through CengageBrain.com, for the following:

Class List Log form
Plan Week 10 Part A, Directions for collecting Creative Work Samples on all children, including What to Do with It, Portfolio Evidence Sheet Example, Sharing with Child and Family, Actions—Read a Book, In the

Environment, In the Curriculum, In the
Newsletter
Plan Week 10 Part B, Directions for Anecdotal
Recording in Creativity for Group A
Plan Week 10 Part C, Reflective Journal

Resources

Althouse, R., Johnson, M. H., & Mitchell, S. T. (2003). *The colors of learning: Integrating the visual arts into the early childhood curriculum.* New York: Teachers College Press.

Dimensions Foundation, www.Dimensionsfoundation. org

Edwards, C., & Gandini, L. (eds.). (1998). *The Hundred Languages of Children: The Reggio Emilia Approach: Advanced Reflections* (2nd ed.). Greenwich, CT: Ablex Publishing.

Fox, J. E. & Schirrmacher, R., (2012). *Art and creative development for young children* (7th ed). Belmont, CA: Wadsworth Cengage Learning.

Isbell, Rebecca, & Raines, Shirley C. (2012). *Creativity and the Arts With Young Children.* Belmont CA: Wadsworth Cengage Learning.

Kellogg, R. (1970). *Analyzing Children's Art.* Palo Alto, CA: National Press Books.

Koster, J. B. (2011). *Growing Artists: Teaching the Arts to Young Children* (5th ed.). Belmont, CA: Wadsworth Cengage Learning.

Mayesky, M. (2012). *Creative Activities for Young Children,* (10th ed.). Belmont, CA: Wadsworth Cengage Learning.

Pollman, M. J. (2010). *Blocks and Beyond: Strengthening Early Math and Science Skills Through Spatial Learning.* Baltimore: Paul H. Brookes.

CHAPTER **11**

Using Technology for Documentation of Dramatic Play

© Cengage Learning 2012

IN THIS CHAPTER

▶ Using Technology for Documentation

▶ Topics in Observation: Protecting the Rights of the Child

▶ Looking at Dramatic Play

▶ Helping All Children with Dramatic Play

▶ Helping Professionals for Play Concerns

> **OBSERVATION THOUGHT**
> "Observations for assessment cannot be done occasionally because the novelty of being watched may change a child's behavior."

NAEYC Standards **naeyc**

The following NAEYC Standards for Early Childhood Professional Preparation are addressed in this chapter:

Standard 3: Observing, Documenting, and Assessing to Support Young Children and Families

Standard 6: Becoming a Professional

Using Technology for Documentation

Imagine the end of the day. A mother comes to pick up her child at the child-care center. She sits for a few minutes with a cup of coffee and puts on virtual reality glasses. Through them, she views her child in selected videotaped segments of the day's activities. The father sitting next to her is doing the same, watching his own child in a virtual reality recording. Each child has been videotaped simultaneously, cued to their movements by the "school button" they put on each day as they arrive. The teacher has ended the day's taped segment with a reminder for an email response to the family survey. Other family members have watched portions of the day from home or their workplace through a classroom video connected via the Internet. Parenting workshop choices are reviewed for reception on their television monitors through password login to YouTube. A family member who cannot be present in the room for a family conference participates via a web camera. They are invited to pay their tuition bill by electronic bank transfer.

Far out? All of this **technology** exists. Can we afford it? Do we agree with it? Do we want it? These are questions many teachers and administrators will be answering soon.

Using technical or electronic media is not an innovation in classrooms. Tape recorders, cameras, and overhead slide and filmstrip projectors have been used for years. However, electronic and digital technologies have increased the range and quality of products, as well as ease of equipment use. Lower costs have made electronic media a viable option for documentation in the classroom. Electronic media can capture details that not even the most fluent writer can convey. Capturing long sequences of conversation, detail of posture, expression and gestures, complex social interactions, physical skill, and language acquisition are especially effective using technology (Martin, 2007). Tone of voice, nuances of movement, and a visual image all make an incident as alive for the viewer as it was for the original observer. There are legal and ethical considerations regarding the use of technology that are discussed in the Topics in Observation section of this chapter. A sample release form is included in the Plan section.

This recording method section presents the possibilities that are available, although some are out of the question for most programs today. In just the right situation in the future, however, they may be more realistic options. A few years ago, who would have dreamed that computers would replace typewriters? Cell phones for wired phones? Hand-held computers for desktop computers? Now our cell phones take photographs and videos that can be transmitted almost instantly from anywhere and offer text messaging, email, GPS, and even have replaced wrist watches. Who knows what the future holds? Negroponte opens his book *Being Digital* (1995) saying, "Computing is not about computers any more. It is about living." That was a prophetic statement.

Types of Technological Media for Observing and Recording

There are many electronic recording devices. With the arrival of computerization, the options and adaptations are wide. Each has its usefulness, along with

TYPE	USES
Audio tape recording	Language samples Oral reading Singing Conversations
Video recording	Social interactions Dramatic play Challenging behavior Physical/language development
Photography	Children's activities Special occasions Constructions/three-dimensional art products
Computer	Storage of digital recordings Observational recordings Scanned artwork Internet sharing Password-protected videocasts Blogs PowerPoint presentations

© Cengage Learning 2014

Figure 11–1 Technology Media for preserving observations.

disadvantages. The early childhood practitioner's knowledge, skills, experience, and creativity may extend far beyond direct interactions with children into the world of multimedia (Figure 11–1).

Audio Recording. Recording voices is especially useful for conversations to gather speech and language samples (see Chapter 6). "Transcribing and reviewing these conversations at a later date will provide insights regarding children's learning, thinking, and social skills" (Blagojevic & Garthwait, 2001, p. 40). Inexpensive tape recorders are available at any electronics supply store. Children's tape recorders make lower-quality recordings but allow children to record themselves or each other. These can be used as dramatic play props or on project work. Children can record and play back sounds, voices, and music.

Voice-activated **audio recorders** are also available. These can be placed in a selected location where conversations from dramatic play, for example, are taking place. The nonintrusive quality is the advantage of this feature because the teacher does not need to walk over and turn it on. Natural, clear recordings are preserved and may be transcribed and analyzed to assess and evaluate social play level. Problem-solving techniques, learning styles, dramatic play roles, and how the child sustains the role over time can be evaluated.

Parabolic or shotgun microphones (the type sports broadcasters use to catch the coach's instructions and the players' grunts) can be aimed to pick up sound across the room. They can focus on a small, low conversation, screening out all the background noise that is usually going on in an early childhood classroom. They are effective for catching a conversation at the clay table about who has more, who made the long snake, or who made all the little balls. Recordings at the sand table might document Caroline's explanation of how she knows which sand is hers and which belongs to Debbie. The self-talk Nicholas uses as he sets the table for snack is captured. His math skills are assessed as he puts out all the napkins, saying, "Here's one for this chair, one for this chair, one for this chair. Hey, where's the chair for this napkin?"

The advantage of unobtrusiveness can also be a disadvantage. Some regard recording without the subject's approval or knowledge as an invasion of privacy. (See Topics in Observation in this chapter.) Another disadvantage is the cost: approximately $200 to $1,000 and up. It also takes some training to become proficient in operation of these microphones. This method would be ideal for the classroom with a separate observation booth. Often the sound quality in a teaching lab observation booth is so poor that the value of the audible observation is lost. Remote control of the microphone would help overcome this problem.

Computer microphones with speech-to-text programs can turn children's words into print to add dialogue to their artwork. They can also help children in describing their thinking process or in problem solving. Text-to-speech software can turn children's printed words into audio so they can hear their written stories read back to them.

Video. Forman's (1999) use of videotaping the schools of Reggio Emilia as an observation method is widely known. He suggests the use of the video camera as a memory machine recording the details of everyday happenings. Many children are accustomed to being photographed with a **video recorder** today. Cameras are becoming more affordable, and they are smaller, easier to use, and efficient in almost any kind of light and setting. Zoom capabilities allow recording from a distance. Combined with a parabolic microphone, the video and audio can be remotely controlled from across the room. Mounting a camera on the wall, or in a central location in the room, can provide a way to record all the events happening in one area. The block area could be recorded on one day and the dramatic play area on another. Children's actions are more natural when captured by a wall-mounted camera than if a person is manually pointing the camera at them. If a videographer is used, it is important for the children to become familiar with the process and the person taking pictures. With familiarity, their self-consciousness decreases. A camera could be present, or a camera person could take blank pictures days before the actual "shoot," to allow the children to become accustomed to being videotaped. Cameras have point-and-shoot controls, optional date and time, freeze and fast frames, and a bookmark to find the end. The tape can be viewed immediately on a television monitor through the camera. The cameras have a taping capability of 30 minutes to 4 hours.

Digital video cameras record images and sounds in digital format, and the images are stored or downloaded to a computer. Most video cameras have a display screen as well, so the event can be viewed on the small screen immediately after it occurs for a playback discussion. The *Week by Week* plan makes this manageable by breaking down domains and skills to observe for each week. Those plans can be amended to use segments of targeted video to observe a specific area. Digital photography allows computer editing to zoom in or enlarge portions of the photo. Video printers, which can print up to 30 frames per minute, make it possible to capture small changes in action. Still shots selected from video can be used for documentation panels of projects, as discussed in Chapter 10 (Trepanier-Street, Hong, & Bauer, 2001).

Lavalieres (electronic signal devices) can be worn that automatically turn the camera to aim at the subject. These are used in distance learning studios by professors who wander around the room. Extremely small cameras, the size of a pencil, can diminish the awareness of being taped. A teacher could wear one behind his ear or in a pocket. Then he can walk around the room or sit "watching" the children play while he is actually videotaping. Videotaping selected areas could also be done by remote from a control room or an observation room.

Several companies have combined video and email technologies to provide families with a view of their child's day at school. Involved families may want to know more about their child's activities; or concerned families may see this as a protection device. Whatever the motivation, technology is providing the vehicle for electronic observation in the classroom. State-of-the-art child care facilities are outfitted with video cameras in each classroom so that the director has instant access to the day's events, giving some assurance that appropriate actions are taken toward the children there. Surveillance cameras such as baby monitors can enable persons outside the room to view what is happening there. However, a word of caution: *these should NEVER be used in place of direct supervision of children.* Recording capability is useful for the teacher to analyze children's or one's own actions for further study.

Hours and hours of video recordings are unmanageable. There may be segments that are profound, but much of the recording may yield nothing usable for the purpose of evaluation. Editing is time-consuming, and the sample is then adulterated.

The digitizing of video converts the analog video to digital data that computers can read. (Of course, using a digital video camera eliminates the need to convert the video in the first place.) Editing digital video on a computer using basic video editing software is simple, much the same way paragraphs of text are moved with a computer. Videos also can be manipulated visually and enhanced, and parts can be erased. Captions and background music can be added to make a very professional production with a minimum of technical training. Nonlinear editing allows changes in sequence of segments or individual images. Large amounts of tape can be stored on one compact disc (CD-ROM) or on a DVD, which is useful when cataloging large amounts of information in the computer's memory for sorting, filing, and rearranging. This sophisticated and expensive equipment may be available through the school's affiliations in the community. Families are frequently resources for technical work.

Think About It . . .

Is Videotaping an Invasion of the Child's Privacy?
By Patricia Amanna, Ed.D.
Director, The Children's Center at Purchase College, Purchase, NY

I think media and technology can impose an intrusion upon the "private school life" of a child. School is a place where children get the opportunity to see how they fit into the larger world apart from the family. As they develop, they find out about themselves through their interactions with others. Most importantly, they can and should try many different roles in their exploration. In today's world, we often talk about the "rights" of individuals as though we include children in that framework. Many of us would feel horrified and outraged if we were subjected to the invasion of media and technology into our private and professional lives. If our employers decided to videotape us working or look at us doing our jobs using cameras and the Internet, we would be disturbed to say the least. Yet, we are using videotaping in schools without any regard for the

individual child, as long as the parents give permission. Moreover, we often fail to set clear guidelines regarding the usage, access, and storage of these videotapes. Even more alarming is our new use of the Internet to peer into the world of the child in the school setting.

This technological ability brings with it questions regarding its use. Those that come to mind are: Do we have a right to unlimited access to a human being? What good does this information really do anyone or society at large? What damage might it cause in relationships between children and "trusted" adults in their lives? How do we make sure that these data are not used against children?

There are many positive applications of media and technology in the schools, but we must be sure we are not teaching children that the technology ability gives us a right to do it. Otherwise the children of today will be the adults of tomorrow who think they have the right to look in on us electronically because they can. Early childhood professionals should apply the basic principles of the NAEYC Ethical Code of Conduct when using media and technology in their classrooms.

Other valuable uses of video recorders in the classroom follow:

▶ *Historic record*—A videotape can be a memento of a special occasion for the whole class. Later viewing of important events, such as the first day, a special visitor, or a field trip—or just a normal day—serve as enjoyable memories. Events can take on added importance in the

It Happened to Me

The Gloved Hand

The college videography students were using our preschool for a project. During the days of the taping, our hatched chickens were getting bigger and so were allowed some freedom within a circle of children. It made wonderful footage, but one got out. Not being an animal person, I had to put on work gloves to pick up the chickens. In one short clip of the tape, a black gloved hand appears to scoop up a wandering chicken. Only I know (and now you) the story behind the glove.

future. Looking at the tape, children can see how much they have grown.

- *Replay for discussion with the children*—A play segment could be taped, shown to the children involved, and discussed: "What happened here? When Audrey did this, see what happened? What could she have done instead?" The tape is then used for problem solving and instruction, more real than any puppet play or discussion with no visual connection.

- *Video field trip*—A teacher was going on a trip, so she taped it from the child's viewpoint, as if the child were along with her. She pointed out, "Watch out for that" and "Look over there, see that." It was very effective when accompanied by her artifacts and books. Video can be a teaching tool.

- *Teacher observation practice*—Teachers can watch a selected segment and practice recording methods such as Anecdotal and Running Recordings, Frequency Counts, Checklists, and Rating Scales. Then the teachers can compare ratings (interrater reliability) to see if they are interpreting the behavior in relatively the same way. This helps them see deficiencies in the system of recording or finding biases that were not realized before. This would make an excellent staff training for improving teachers' professional practice and reviewing child development principles.

- *Reevaluation and referral*—A video recording, authorized with a written release by the family, can be shown to helping professionals for their interpretation or a resource person for an evaluation. It shows the child in a natural setting, capturing usual behavior.

- *Research*—Analyzing videotape can compare small bits of data for research. Ethical principles of voluntary, informed consent are necessary. Family signatures are required after they have been informed of the nature of the research and the techniques to be used. This must be in language they can understand. It is the investigator's responsibility to carefully evaluate the ethical acceptability of the study regarding the "subject at risk" (*American Psychological Association*, 1990, pp. 390–394).

- *Teacher self-evaluation and reflection*—The tape can be used by the teacher to monitor and receive reactions to teaching practices or for personal reflection. The teacher may be unaware of habits revealed on videotapes. The tape may be used to self-evaluate intervention strategies, play involvement, or language usage.

It Happened to Me

Hands in Pants

During a time of extensive videotaping by professional videographers in my preschool classroom, every time one boy was seen on tape his hand was in his pants. We were accustomed to it, taking into consideration his shyness and hesitancy in social circumstances, especially with unfamiliar people in the room. When his mother viewed the tape for permission to release it for publication, however, she was not pleased. She knew that he did that when he was uncomfortable but did not want the tape, a permanent record, to portray him this way. We discussed his emotional insecurity and, of course, edited him out of the tape at her request. We did some taping of our own later in the school year. We did not see this behavior repeated, so we were able to provide her with some footage of his days at school about which she (and he, someday) could feel more comfortable.

Recording for Evaluation versus Surveillance. School is a transitional place from home and the outside world. It is a place where children and adults alike should feel comfortable. Surveillance cameras do not contribute to that atmosphere; they detract from the trust of staff and the privacy or separation of the child's school life from their home life. There may be a place for such technology, but its purpose should be carefully scrutinized and the rights of all protected.

Confidentiality Guidelines. The APA Ethical Principles of Psychologists and Code of Conduct (American Psychological Association, 2002) offers some good advice.

- *Obtain* **informed consent**—This must be given (and understood) by the individual, or family consent must be given for minors.
- *Maintain confidentiality*—Take reasonable precautions to protect information storage.
- *Obtain prior permission*—Explicit permission is required for voice or image recording, unless the recordings are naturalistic observations in public places and it is not anticipated that the recording will be used in a manner that could cause personal identification or harm.

Record a segment of your classroom if you work with children, or normal routines of your day. Listen and analyze what the recording reveals about yourself.

Photography. Ah, at last something more familiar. Point and shoot. This has become easier and less expensive with digital photography and has gained popularity in the field of teacher inquiry, especially from the influence of Reggio Emilia and documentation panels. Moments in time are captured to reflect on later. Curtis (2008) encourages teachers to "suspend adult agendas" when witnessing a child purposefully engaged in exploration such as the changes in the water stream when a finger is inserted into the faucet or the elusiveness of a shadow on the floor that changes as the curtain blows in the breeze. Capturing moments can be closely examined later to see even more than is seen through the lens as the camera is clicked. It gives a new lens to our observations. Photography is another visual language that conveys meanings. It is encoded by the photographer capturing a moment in time that has meaning in that situation, then is decoded by the viewer, who interprets and inserts inferences without knowing what transpired before or after the photograph was shot (Moran & Tegano, 2005).

Quality photographs have become much easier to take with automatic focusing, built-in flash, and zoom capabilities. The quality of pictures is *almost* foolproof. Most children are accustomed to being photographed, so photos become a natural documentation of play. That is only true if it is done often throughout the year. This can be expensive, but there are ways to reduce the cost. Buying film in bulk makes it the least expensive part of the operation. Developing has become much less expensive, with many places offering discounts for nonprofit organizations.

Digital photography is even less expensive than using and developing film. There are few expenses other than the cost of the camera. Photos can be stored on CD-ROMs that are very inexpensive and can hold up to 43,500 still images and transferred electronically. Photos can be printed out on the printer, copied, and distributed. The photos can be made into individual or class photo albums, or into slide presentations for a family night. They can be made into documentation panels by arranging them in sequence to show the step-by-step progression of a project. They can be used to make a book for the children to keep and revisit the memory. These images can be incorporated into the curriculum for a sequencing activity, showing the steps or stages from beginning to end. Printing photos on regular paper is much less expensive than making photo prints, and the size of the print can be varied for the purpose, from postage stamp–size to poster size. Most digital cameras even have the capability of taking small segments of video as well.

The documentation for meeting the standards for NAEYC Center Accreditation calls for written and photographic evidence as reliable and authentic representations of child developmental progress and program quality.

Many teachers use a photo album in the classroom as a prereading experience, inspiring children to recall details of past events. It helps children get better acquainted with class members. The teacher sends home a school album with a different child each week. In this way, the family can see the other children in the class and some events that have taken place. Conversations about school now have a focus, and the family feels more of a connection to the school. Family pictures on a special bulletin board and photos of family celebrations are a way of learning about similarities and differences (Herr & Larson, 2009).

Hosington (2002) suggests using photographs to support children's science inquiry by helping children analyze and synthesize data, revisit and extend their investigations, reflect on previous experiences, and articulate their strategies for problem solving.

Planning where and when to take the photos makes it manageable, such as a writing center for small muscle development; an outside or inside playground for large muscle development; cubbies for self-help skills; the block area, math area, science area, or puzzle place for cognitive development; and social skills in dramatic play (Good, 2009). For example, what area of development might the photograph in Figure 11–2 document?

Photographs can be used during the year as vehicles to help the child remember and talk about specific incidents. The visual image is a springboard for a description of the event and the feelings surrounding it. The child's narrative could also be taped or dictated, adding a literacy dimension to the experience.

Photographs of each child taken the first week of school can be used in an activity for matching or a concentration game (double prints). This is a personal and unique way for children to get to know each other. Children can dictate captions for photographs taken in the classroom or during special events, adding them to the class album or making a book of their own. Photographs are self-esteem boosters.

Photographs taken throughout the school year are excellent mementos to give the children at the end of the year. They are a lasting reminder of that school year. Photographs taken of the children could be used in an album, on a bulletin board, or

© Cengage Learning 2014

Figure 11–2 What do you see in this photograph?

placed in the Portfolio. At the end of the year, they should be distributed to the children. If the teacher or school is retaining any photographs, a special release form should be signed so the family is aware of that fact and acknowledges consent.

Photos of children and either photos or scans of their work can be stored electronically in a master file of the class and year with folders for each child. These can be inserted into the Progress Report document that can be shared by printing a copy, sending an electronic copy or saving it onto a CD for the family, or incorporating it into a slide show to be used in a family conference (Good, 2009).

Computers and Scanners. As mentioned before, computers can store vast amounts of documentation data, both textual and visual, without taking up closet or file cabinet storage space. Data are easily manipulated into various formats for both individual Portfolios and whole-group documentation. Hand-held computers can easily capture data on-the-spot, with some of the forms and Checklists mentioned in earlier chapters

programmed into the hand-held computer. Information is later downloaded into the regular computer and stored there or on a CD. Scanners can take photographs and drawings and transform them into digital files, easily stored and shared. The child's work can be shared with families via email or CD.

Media as Documentation for Other Areas of Development

Audio recording and videotaping or photography can be used to record and document any area of development. Arrivals and separations can give poignant images of hellos and good-byes. Self-care photos can illustrate the accomplishment of milestone tasks, such as dressing for outside or tying a shoe. A video of outside play could be a delightful reminder of the physical, emotional, language, and social actions of the child. It could show children running down a hill, climbing a slide, or wading in a creek. Social interactions can be preserved with photographs or recorded conversations. Emotionally troubled moments are usually best kept private, but there may be circumstances when these might need to be preserved visually or audibly. Language segments on audio or video preserve not only the words, but also the facial and body expressions that make them even more illuminating. Visual and auditory reminders of past events help expand memory and attention span. They are good teaching tools and document important events. Creative moments, whether art media manipulation or **dramatic play**, are meaningfully captured on video or audio. Incidents illustrating self-identity, group interactions, or relationships with adults in the classroom are more vividly documented with pictures or audio as well. Any observation can be augmented or recorded using these methods. Further commentary will enhance or add the observer's conclusions to the photograph or recording.

Using Technology During Home Visits

While it seems like every person in the world is tech-savvy and quite well-equipped with the latest technology, the educator's use of technology during a home visit with a child can be problematic if educators fail to take some important preliminary steps first. An important first step is to discuss with the family the *potential* use of any technology by sensitively describing the media such as audio or video recording, photography, or written observation using hand-held computer devices. Along

It Happened to Me

Do You Want to Be Pink?

One of the highlights of my days in the classroom was an intergenerational project in my class when four-year-olds made weekly visits to a nearby nursing home. There are a million stories connected with this project (most of which got away because I didn't write them down), but a favorite I will always remember is about Ethel. She was blind and had David for a little friend. He showed empathy that is supposed to be beyond his Preoperational Stage.

One spring day we were making drip-dot paintings, so he helped her by placing the paintbrush in her hand and shaking it to make the drips. She got paint on her hand so he asked me for a tissue to wipe it off. As he was wiping, she asked, "What color is it, David?" He answered, "Blue, the color of robin's eggs." (Perceptive, eh?) She sighed, "Oh!" He looked at her and at me and said, "Do you want to be pink?" "I'd love to be pink," she replied. He painted each finger a pastel color, and I snapped the most rapturous photograph of her face glowing, her hand outstretched with pastel fingers. The significance of the incident and photograph was even more poignant when I learned later from the activities director that the love of Ethel's life was painting. That photo is precious but, alas, I have no permission to print it, so it will have to glow in your own imagination.

with the devices, the family should be informed about what kind of information may be recorded, for what purpose, and who will have access to the recording. The family should have the opportunity to share their perspective and raise any concerns. Once that is done, the home visitor must acquire the expressed permission of the family members who are well-informed of the exact purpose and future potential use of the information collected through the use of technology; a signed approval is recommended. (See Figure 11–3 for an example.)

Whenever possible, the family should have the opportunity to view and/or hear what has been recorded, providing that serves both as a way of information and collaborating, as well as a "golden opportunity" to engage parents in their role as the child's first teacher. Recording a full home visit or

a series of interactions can provide valuable information for the educator, both about the child's development and the educator's own professional development. It can be a valuable tool (but not a substitute) for use in supervisory sessions.

 Advantages

Photographs and recording audio and video are effective observational recording tools because

- ▶ they capture visual or real sound images of the episode, more detailed than is possible through writing.
- ▶ they are less subject to the recorder's bias or inferences.
- ▶ they allow the viewer to form judgments independent from the recorder's.
- ▶ they can be analyzed in a number of ways, for different purposes, at different times.
- ▶ they can be stored efficiently, especially if they are digital.

 Disadvantages

Photographs, videotaping, and audio recording can be all of the following:

- ▶ expensive
- ▶ complicated and time-consuming
- ▶ intrusive to children and teachers
- ▶ a factor causing unnatural behavior
- ▶ against families' values

 Pitfalls to Avoid

Confidentiality is an issue with any documentation technique. But using audio, video, or photography as a documentation technique carries with it some additional concerns. Children other than the target child may be included in a photo, audio recording, or videotape, thus possibly revealing information about that child's behavior to those who have no need or right to know. This is almost impossible to avoid, especially with video photography. Ethical use of video footage is the teacher's responsibility.

Just as equity is important in all other recording methods, it is with audio and video techniques as well. Some children are much more photogenic, do more interesting things, or speak more humorously or in a more interesting way than others. When using audio and video, including photography, all children who are allowed should be recorded in a fair way, both in number and in content of recording.

View the recording from the family's eyes. Is it embarrassing? Does it show the child in an

TOPICS in OBSERVATION

Protecting the Rights of the Child

It is essential to receive the permission of each child's family to record their child using audio, video, or photographic recording methods (Figure 11–3). There are instances when this permission may be denied.

- Some religious groups do not allow photographs.
- The child may be under protective services in a protected, confidential placement. An innocent newspaper photograph of an activity that included the child may jeopardize the child's safety.
- There may be personal reasons for which the family may deny permission.

It is important that staff members are aware of the denied photo release. Just as a life threatening allergy must be made known to all staff, this is important information to be conveyed. Alternative documentation methods must be used if permission is denied. For example, the staff might write down detailed, extensive notes as an alternative to using an audio recording of the child's language sample. If video or still photography is used in the group setting, either for formal or informal uses, the staff is responsible for making the photographer aware of any prohibition. In such cases, sensitivity to the child's feelings is a high priority. The age of the child and reason for prohibition will govern how this exclusion is made. The exclusion from photography or recording should not be obvious to the other children or their families, or even the child, unless it is by the child's request. Techniques of photography could be used to take casual group pictures from the back of the child. All diligence should be given to this serious ethical and legal issue.

Occasionally, photo contests or photos for commercial purposes may arise. If the recordings are used for other than educational or publicity use, the individual child's family should be consulted. A special release form for that specific purpose must be obtained. It is better to be cautious and guard against any possible recriminations.

Any child who does not want to be recorded, videotaped, or photographed has the right to refuse. The staff has the responsibility to respect the child's wishes, even if the family has given permission. No child should be forced to participate in this kind of an activity. This should be a policy in the school, staff, and family handbook.

AUDIO/VIDEO/PHOTO RELEASE

I give permission for my child to be tape recorded, video recorded, or photographed for educational or publicity purposes while participating in the regular activities of this program.

Date _____

❑ YES   ❑ NO

Signature _____

© Cengage Learning 2014

Figure 11–3 Sample Release Form.

---

uncomfortable situation or looking less competent than peers? Reconsider using that recording.

How to Find the Time

It does take time to learn to use new equipment. Just as a child needs to manipulate a new item, you will need to use it and experiment with the equipment before expecting it to perform perfectly. The more you use the technology, the more familiar you will become. After some practice, it will become second nature to use that camera or tape recorder. Once you get to that level, you will see how much time it saves in writing.

Go to Education CourseMate website, accessed through CengageBrain.com, for plans and resources.

❓ What to Do with It

Audio recordings of an individual child are kept in the child's Portfolio. They can be analyzed for speech and language development. Dictated stories or reading abilities, or informal or structured interviews can be filed there. These preserve an audible record of the child's thinking revealed through language.

A videotape is a replay of live action. The episode can be viewed repeatedly, hearing and seeing what took place. Segments can be closely examined for relevance to developmental assessment. An audio commentary can be added for families, other teachers, or referral agents. The accompanying narrative can point out important details: "Watch the way he is picking up that napkin. Watch the movement of the thumb. Let's go back and slow it down. We can stop it right here."

Photographs can be added to the child's Portfolio to illustrate comments about areas of development. They add visual information to Anecdotal Records. They can also be used themselves as the main observation method, with notes explaining the photograph. A photographic Portfolio of three to four photos of each child in each developmental domain gathered over the course of several months can demonstrate growth and development. See Figure 11–4 for the Portfolio Evidence Sheet Example.

Looking at Dramatic Play

In the introduction to his book *The Power of Play*, David Elkind decries the lost hours of free, unstructured playtime: television shows and movies

REVIEW

MEDIA

Action preserved in photographs, audio or video recording

Types of Information to Record Using Technology

- any moment or sequence of a child's day, usual or unusual
- separation and adjustment
- self-care skills
- physical development
- social development
- emotional development
- language and speech (audio or video)
- attention span and interests
- cognitive development
- literacy
- creativity
- sociodramatic play
- self-esteem

that portray children preoccupied with serious issues such as divorce, substance abuse, or job loss; and even cartoons such as Bob the Builder and SpongeBob SquarePants, centered around jobs, not play (Elkind, 2007). The early childhood classroom might be one of the last bastions of planned environments for play, where play is recognized as necessary to development in all domains: cognitive,

PORTFOLIO EVIDENCE OF CHILD'S DEVELOPMENT			
Evidence Type	**Date**	**Recorder**	**Notes**
CREATIVITY – the child's creativity and sociodramatic play, including work samples			
WS	9/13/		Self-portrait with markers (copy in portfolio)
WS	10/14/		2nd self-portrait – more details (copy in portfolio)
AR	11/16/	BAN	Worked to make nature collage talking with 2 other children
Photos	11/20	MLS	Engaged in hospital play for 15 min.
WS	12/13/		Painting of family (photo in portfolio)

Figure 11–4 Portfolio Evidence Sheet Example.

social, physical, and emotional. Unfortunately, even in early childhood classrooms the increasing emphasis on accountability and academic preparation transcends the research on the importance of the role of play, and especially high-quality pretend play.

The Value of Dramatic Play

"Learning is the product of play-generated experiences limited only by the child's level of intellectual development" (Elkind, 2007, p. 103). Play can be categorized into four major types:

Mastery play—repetitive actions in which the child explores the physical properties of an object using all senses. This is repeated, refining physical skills while the brain stores the information gleaned from the exploration.

Innovative play—taking what the child has learned through exploration, the child then experiments on what can be done with the object or movement. Walking is followed by running, climbing, and skipping. Playing with sounds leads to forming words and refining the pronunciation and use of words to convey meaning.

Kinship play—sharing an experience, with or without verbal communication, that creates a bond. We see this especially in young children drawn to each other in public places. They need no introduction and are aware of no cultural or status differences; they just begin to play.

Therapeutic play—using play as a way of dealing with stress. All children the world over play a version of peek-a-boo as a way of replaying the anxiety of the mother's going away and rejoicing at her coming back. After 9/11, children across the world reenacted planes hitting buildings and people running to escape.

All of these kinds of play can be seen as children play, either through their own improvisation or in areas prepared with props that initiate and support dramatic play. In dramatic play, children transform objects and actions symbolically, engage in interactive social dialogue and negotiation, role taking, script knowledge, joint planning, and problem solving (Bergen, 2002). It is easy to see how dramatic play enhances learning.

Watching Dramatic Play

Watching children play grown-up, acting out scenes they have witnessed or imagined, is fascinating. It is more than entertainment or "just make believe." It involves every domain of development and offers a glimpse of the child within. During dramatic play, observers see scenarios unfold. A child puts on a hat, picks up a briefcase, and says, "See ya, honey, I'm goin' to work now." And off she goes. A toddler holds his sweater coiled up in a ball and strokes it saying, "Nice kitty." A four-year-old at the art bench says to himself, "I need a big piece of paper 'cause I'm gonna make a big truck with a trailer. No, I'll use another piece of paper for the trailer and hitch 'em togedder with a piece of tape." Each of these children is displaying imaginative play through his or her thoughts and actions. They are cute to the untrained observer, but meaningful to those who know what each incident reveals about the child's development.

Dramatic play areas are common to the early childhood classroom and enhanced with props that encourage a variety of themes. Most common is the Housekeeping Area (sometimes called Home Area or Family Area) containing furnishings, clothing, and eating and cleaning utensils. Other common dramatic play settings are rotated with correlating props such as office with computers and telephones and dress-up clothes; store with food boxes, aprons, cash registers, and carts; and leisure with camping or beach party props (Figure 11–5). These areas can be infused with literacy materials for writing notes and books associated with the theme. The highest rating on the ECERS-R Rating Scale (Harms et al., 2005) requires props provided to represent diversity and equipment used by people with disabilities.

While *play* is the word used for activities that are not seen as having any worthwhile function, for young children (and for us all), it has many benefits. Research on dramatic play, solitary imaginative play (with or without props), and **sociodramatic play** (a fantasy episode interacting with other children) has important implications for teachers of young children. Studies have found that children who regularly engage in sociodramatic or imaginative play are more friendly, popular, cooperative, verbal, and creative. They are usually less impulsive and aggressive and more likely to take the perspective of others (Lindsey & Colwell, 2003). These are logical outcomes of having sustained interactions with peers. Other benefits are documented as well. Children between two-and-a-half and five years old who participate in make-believe play are more advanced in general

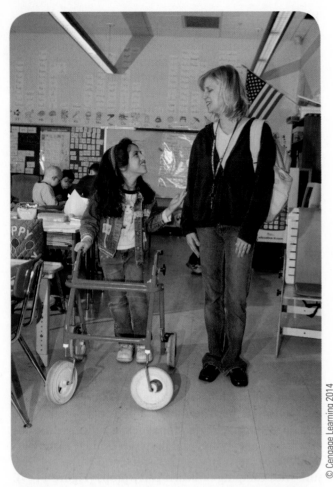

Figure 11–5 Play with equipment for disabilities can reduce fears.

© Cengage Learning 2014

intellectual ability, have better memory, and display higher reasoning ability (Elias & Berk, 2002). A review of pretence (pretend play) literature found that "representational skills, problem-solving abilities, and social-linguistic sophistication" were increased by sociodramatic play (Bergen, 2002). Language development and literacy from play-based instruction with dramatic play scenarios are enhanced (Kavanaugh, 2006). Solitary players among both girls and boys have been associated with difficulties with emergent literacy and more frequent displays of negative affect (Doctoroff et al., 2006). Spontaneous dramatic play is a setting for cognitive, social, affective, and moral development, with conversations that communicate what is real and what is make-believe between the players (Ortega, 2003). Here are some benefits of dramatic play. It helps children

- develop conversational skills and the ability to express ideas in words.
- understand the feelings, roles, or work of others.

- connect actions with words—actions and words go hand-in-hand in dramatic play.
- develop vocabulary.
- develop creativity—children imagine, act, and make things up as play progresses.
- engage in social interaction with other children.
- cope with life, sometimes through acting out troubling situations, thus giving an outlet for emotion (for example, almost every doll in an early childhood center gets a spanking periodically when children play house).
- assume leadership and group participant roles.

With these benefits, can early childhood programs and elementary schools ignore the importance of providing and encouraging this kind of play?

Stages of Dramatic Play

Children play in different ways at different ages and stages (Figure 11–6). The changes in imaginative play are easily observed and do correspond with stages of development by several theorists, including Piaget, Erikson, Smilansky, and Vygotsky. Piaget equated that difference in the way children played with the difference in their thinking, moving beyond exploring with the senses to representational thought where one thing symbolizes another (Piaget, 1951). Vygotsky (1978) emphasized the social role of pretend play from its earliest forms. He saw how culture, customs, and rituals become part of the play. Because of the social aspect of pretend play, especially with a more mature playmate or adult, the child exercises self-regulation and can play in a more complex way beyond the developmental level. Language is fundamentally important to social pretend play.

Infancy. The infant and adult are gazing at each other intently. As the adult opens and closes his mouth and slowly sticks out his tongue, the infant imitates the action. Imaginative play has begun. This has been documented to occur in the early days of the infant's life, setting the stage for responding to another human and turn taking. The game of peekaboo is really the pretend theme of "I'm going away and now I'm back." The repetition of these adult-child interactions is building the foundation for the later plots of sociodramatic play with peers.

Young Toddlers. Between 6 and 18 months, the child is exploring the physical world by playing with

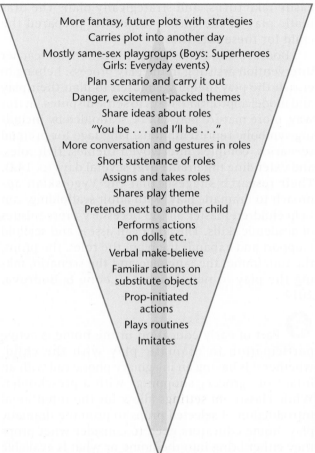

More fantasy, future plots with strategies

Carries plot into another day

Mostly same-sex playgroups (Boys: Superheroes Girls: Everyday events)

Plan scenario and carry it out

Danger, excitement-packed themes

Share ideas about roles

"You be . . . and I'll be . . ."

More conversation and gestures in roles

Short sustenance of roles

Assigns and takes roles

Shares play theme

Pretends next to another child

Performs actions on dolls, etc.

Verbal make-believe

Familiar actions on substitute objects

Prop-initiated actions

Plays routines

Imitates

© Cengage Learning 2014

Figure 11–6 Dramatic Play Development.

objects. Close scrutiny of this play illustrates various patterns.

Repetition with Objects. Manipulations are repeated with the objects in every conceivable way. The young toddler takes her bottle and shakes it, throws it, chews on it, sucks on all parts of it, listens to it, and minutely examines it.

Repetition without Objects. The functions she has learned are played out in her imagination without the object. This is the beginning of imaginary play. She puts her fist to her mouth and makes sucking movements and sounds, pretending to suck the bottle.

Substitution. Other objects become stand-ins for the imaginary one. She picks up anything she can handle and puts it to her mouth and pretend (or actually) sucks it like a bottle. She is mentally substituting this object for the bottle.

Older Toddlers. Dramatic play occurs just at the time when social rules are being enforced by adults.

These rules restrict behavior, such as to avoid dangerous situations and not to tear up books or take toys from others. The child then substitutes imaginary situations to control the rules and work them through to delay immediate gratification. An adult may be offering milk from a cup, so the pretend bottle routine is a symbolic way to cope. Thought is now separated from action and impulsive action is renounced in favor of this situation. The child is making the rules.

The child is the center of imaginative play, with rituals such as eating and sleeping. The actions become more decentered. The child is feeding the teddy bear rather than being fed. More language and muscle skills are used to participate in shared-meaning play with others, but self-control is a problem. Each player must do the acting with the same objects, and none is willing to forgo the selfish desire to possess the toy.

Preschoolers. The three-year-old has an expanded sense of fantasy, using semi-realistic props for adult roles. Each player has a role related to the theme, but acts independently. The players are trying to represent themselves in roles with which they are familiar. There are four types of roles common to dramatic play:

▶ *functional*—performing a common function such as feeding a baby or driving a car

▶ *relational*—representing a family member, friend, or pet

▶ *stereotypic*—highly predictable based on an occupation such as police officer or construction worker

▶ *fictional*—taken from a story or media superhero (Garvey, 1977)

Taking roles helps children understand and feel powerful. To be the parent giving the commands, the superhero with a super power, or the firefighter as a rescuer, the child takes on the characteristics of another person. They are only able to do this because of expanded vocabulary, experiences with models, and objects that they can mentally transform into props.

Toward the end of the preschool age, the ability to have empathetic thoughts and to want social companionship expands the dramatic play into the Sociodramatic Stage. Most children are becoming less egocentric and more empathetic. They understand others' points of view and feelings. They are in Erikson's Initiative Stage, taking control and leadership of their own play, not dependent on specific props or adult leadership. They are likely to play roles such as family, stereotyped television characters, powerful helpers from the community (firefighter or police), cowboys, pirates, or space creatures. However, now roles are assigned and imaginary experiences are shared through explanations outside the role. Children are frequently heard saying things such as, "You be the guy on fire and I'll come with the hose and put the fire out." This often meets with a counterproposal from the victim, "No, *you* be the guy on fire and *I'll* come with the hose." Resolution of the dilemma may indicate language development for negotiation, problem-solving ability, and social status in the group.

Young School-Agers. Dramatic play declines in the early school years. The child has a growing contact with reality, feelings of industry, and pride in motor and intellectual skills. Games with rules are the outlets for these skills and attitudes. Interactions with other children are growing more competitive. Helm and Katz (2001) call this the age of investigations. They are concrete-operational thinkers, ready for group play. Their investigations may be focused on collections of whatever the fad is this week, though Barbie and sports cards have sustained their favor. Games with rules become the play pattern of this age now that the children can accurately keep score,

It Happened to Me

"You're the Wife, You Stay Home!"

In the "Home" dramatic play area, a preschool girl announced, "I'm going to work." She donned a hat, grabbed a briefcase, mounted the rocking horse like a motorcycle, and away she went. A boy in the area went over, grabbed the briefcase, unseated her, and said sternly, "No, you're the wife, you stay home!" One can only imagine a domestic struggle over working wives that this child might have witnessed either at home or in the media. Be careful, though, not to make inferences regarding the child's parents based on dramatic play episodes. What would you have done if you witnessed this drama?

easily take turns, and strategically plan. The dramatic play of the earlier stages has prepared the child for these activities.

Bodrova and Leong (2007) recommend teacher intervention assisting in the play process, helping to enrich the play, helping children to plan their play and model appropriate ways to settle disputes. In this way, more mature play can be scaffolded by including symbolic representations, language for pretend scenarios, complex interwoven themes, rich roles, and extending timeframe over several days (p. 142). Their research suggests that the Vygotskian approach to dramatic play, with adult scaffolding, can help children master all the necessary prerequisites of academic skills. The adult can assess and scaffold (support and expand) the plan, the roles, the props, the timeframe, the language and the scenario, taking the play to new heights. (Leong & Bodrova, 2012).

Part of early education in the home is active participation in dramatic play with the child, whether it is having an imaginary phone call with an infant or "grocery shopping" with a preschooler. While classroom settings allow for the intentional introduction of selected props to promote dramatic play, home educators need to consider what props they either bring into the home or what is available in the home to encourage that play. The second choice is the better one, as children should always have opportunities to repeat and expand play beyond the home visit. As a child moves through the stages of play, home educators also want to consider who is routinely available to the child—whether another adult or another child—who could be a partner in that play and elicit their participation as appropriate.

Using Play Stages to Assess Dramatic Play

The social play stages can be used again when assessing and describing dramatic play (see Chapter 4). A variety of methods can record the play for later analysis, such as Class List Log, Checklist, Anecdotal or Running Record, and Rating Scales.

Onlooker Stage. The child watches the dramatic play of others. The child may lack the entry skills and self-confidence to join the organized play of other children. It may be the child's learning style to watch others before attempting to play, or it may be a shy personality. The adult can give assistance in play entry techniques if it is warranted.

Solitary Dramatic Play. A child of any age may choose to play out dramatic or fantasy play alone. The child selects the props for play and may internally or audibly carry on a dialogue. The observer, just as in the Onlooker Stage, can assess the play and decide if intervention is needed to help the child move to social interaction in the play. The scaffolding of an adult as a parallel player may help the child move to the next stage.

Parallel Dramatic Play. Two-, three-, and four-year-olds are social beings and often play out their dramatic roles alongside other children without interactions. The observer, as in the Solitary Stage, assesses the child's social level and choice of parallel play partners. If it is indicated, the adult can act as an intermediary, with statements such as, "Suzie, you are a Mommy and Joe is a cook. Maybe you could go to his restaurant and order a Kids Meal."

Associative Dramatic Play. In the Associative Stage, children are still each playing parallel but share play theme and conversation. Children are talking, smiling, and offering objects—all corresponding to associative play. It is the stage of social play in which children are playing near each other, in the same play theme, but not together. They do not share props or final results.

Cooperative Dramatic Play. In the Cooperative Stage, children are working together toward a common goal, contributing parts to the whole. Children engage in social exchanges. They plan and act out make-believe stories.

Smilansky (1990) further defines this level of dramatic play as including the following:

- *role playing*—adopting roles
- *make-believe transformations*—symbols stand for objects, actions, and situations
- *social interactions*—directly relating to each other in roles
- *verbal communications*—exclamations and descriptions are used to organize the play by assigning roles, planning story lines, and rebuking players who fail to carry out the role in the expected manner

By using these finer distinctions in describing dramatic play, the observer can make decisions about the need or desirability of intervening in the play. The adult can help dramatic play by role modeling, making suggestions, asking open-ended questions, or giving direct instruction in carrying out the role. Each of these may help the child extend the play and become a more acceptable play partner.

EXERCISE Look at photographs of children in the dramatic play area. Using the stages of Smilansky, determine each child's level or role.

Observing Dramatic Play

The term *dramatic play* refers to the spontaneous play in which a child recreates routines he or she has seen in real life (Figure 11–7). As the child matures, the role is sustained, accompanied by a monologue or dialogue with another, and then imaginative new play themes are explored. *Sociodramatic play* is the interaction of two or more children in a play theme with each holding separate roles. This often follows family-life routines such as cooking, child care, and male/female interactions.

Creative dramatics is *story play* (Isenberg & Jalongo, 2006), play inspired by a book or fingerplay. The classic *Three Little Pigs* or *Goldilocks and the Three Bears* are perfect beginning productions. Block (1997) and Edwards (2006) emphasize the added comprehension of the text and the benefits to learning that

Figure 11–7 Dramatic play offers opportunities to play out familiar roles.

result from story play. Such play has been successful in involving children in literature so that they begin exercising cognitive thinking and move out of egocentrism. It helps children work out difficult concepts and their reactions to real-world situations.

Another variation of this kind of creative dramatics, **story dictation**, has been documented by Vivian Paley (1984, 1988, 1990, 1997) through her accounts of this kind of play in kindergarten classrooms. Her work highlights the rich learning outcomes of such an approach, especially in both the cognitive and affective domains. One child or a group of children write the story line and act as producers and directors, selecting actors to carry out the story line. The rest of the class acts as the audience. The teacher is the facilitator, assisting with the production and presentation; but her more important role is leading the follow-up conversation about the meaning of the play, the conflicts raised, and possible solutions. She also uses storytelling and story acting based on observing a child or children in play, and describes what she sees to the children, asking questions about the intentions of the players to deepen the meaning of the play, expanding the players by inviting others to join in. She often combines this with story dictation, writing down the story scrip so that it can be played again. Using this technique she guides children in problem solving and governing their own play (Dombrink-Green, 2011).

When using videotape to record spontaneous dramatic play, a follow-up interview with the players can yield information about the children's thinking and emotions while they played. The tape can be paused and repeated rather than interrupting the play as it is happening. Sawyers and Carrick (2003) suggest questions that can center on themes, roles, object substitutions, and the distinction between fantasy and reality:

> ▶ "Tell me about what you are playing here."
> ▶ "Why did you choose that?" or "Why did you say that?"
> ▶ "You didn't have a . . . so what did you use instead?" (object substitution)
> ▶ "How does it make you feel to be that?"
> ▶ "Are there things you don't like to be or play? Why?"
> ▶ "If you could play that over again, what would you change?" p. 165

Bringing the dramatic arts into the classroom is an opportunity to express a story, music, or cultural event creatively. That is not to be confused with the spontaneous play episodes created by the children, for the children—not products that are choreographed and presented as special performances for an audience of adults. It takes great skill to keep drama child-centered like Vivian Paley did or to lead children to act out a familiar story such as *Three Billy Goats Gruff*. The reluctant child should be excused from participating, parts should be rotated, and no pressure should be applied for perfection in learning lines and dances to perfection (Copple, 2009).

Techniques for Observing Dramatic Play

Dramatic play can be captured through the use of Anecdotal Recording. Some delightful and insightful Anecdotal Recordings of dramatic play comprise the writings of Vivian Gussin Paley. Her book *Boys and Girls: Superheroes in the Doll Corner* (1984) is a wonderful accompaniment to the discussions of this chapter. (See Resources for others.)

A Class List Log can be used for a quick check on who does and does not participate in fantasy play. This may be expanded into a Frequency Count over the course of a week or so, as children present a dramatic rendition of "Three Billy Goats Gruff" or some other story. Repeating the Class List Log or Frequency Count will indicate if more children are engaged in dramatic play as the year progresses.

Time Samples will indicate if play is occurring in the dramatic play area. The observer may want to develop a code for the Time Sample, perhaps a *D* to designate dramatic play occurring in other areas. Under the climber or outdoors an exciting cops-and-robbers theme may be acted out. In the block area, a city may be constructed in anticipation of an earthquake or a bombing. Children do play out the traumatic events of the news that are even more frightening than the cartoons they watch. If an event that is interesting or important occurs while taking the Time Sample, the observer could turn the paper over and jot down some notes. Later these could be amplified into a more formal Anecdotal Recording for the Class File or child's Portfolio.

Developmental Checklists and Rating Scales often have one or more criteria for recording the presence, absence, or level of involvement of the child in dramatic play.

Beaty's (2010) Dramatic Play Checklist includes the following items in a developmental progression:

> ___Does pretend play by him/herself
> ___Assigns roles or takes assigned roles
> ___Needs particular props to do pretend play
> ___Takes on characteristics and actions related to role

Reflective Journal

It bothered me today when the boys kept shouting "No Girls Allowed!" but I just couldn't think of a way to let them exercise control of their play but still intervene. I wanted to stop the sexism and exclusion of other children from their play. What would I have done if they said "No Blacks Allowed" or "No Chinese Allowed"? I would have done something! Next time I hear the children voicing bias or discrimination against any group, I will act. I better talk with Betty about it. She always seems to know just what to say.

© Cengage Learning 2014

Figure 11–8 A Reflective Journal can be a place to think about what has been observed and make plans for future actions.

___Can pretend with imaginary objects
___Uses language in creating and sustaining the plot
___Enacts exciting, danger-packed themes
___Uses elaborate themes, ideas, details. (p. 379)

The Reflective Journal is a place to ponder the meaning of what is seen and heard during fantasy play, to wonder about its roots, and to explore possible actions in the future (Figure 11–8). Thought given to possible scenarios and responses may be considered *before* they occur, to be ready with comfortable, considered answers.

Observing Dramatic Play for Assessing Other Developmental Areas

While children are engaging in dramatic play, they are using other skills and behaviors that can be observed and assessed simultaneously (Figure 11–9).

Cognitive. Dramatic play is a progressive step toward abstract thinking. The movement from the real toy to the symbolic leads the preschooler to abstract thinking. This is the link with Piaget's

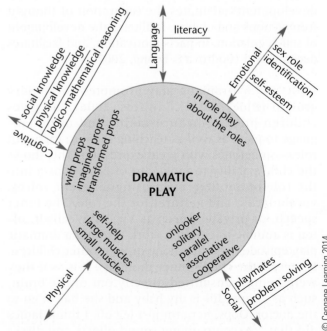

Figure 11–9 Developmental Skills Used and Revealed in Dramatic Play.

Concrete Operations Stage. Children who enjoy pretending score higher on imagination and creativity (Berk & Winsler, 2002). During dramatic play, children shift away from self and take the role of another, which helps them see situations from a different viewpoint, moving them out of egocentrism. The reversibility of the role, knowing they can leave it any time, helps develop the cognitive structures for understanding the reversibility of operations such as equal amounts of water in different-sized containers (Johnson et al., 2005). The planning and carrying out of a thematic role through story and fantasy play have been shown to help children's memory for story lines and serve as a foundation for later memory strategies (Kim, 1999). The ways that teachers interact with children in dramatic play has been found to affect the play in various ways. If teachers acted as a stage manager, coplayer, or play leader, the play lasted longer and children did not leave the scene. (Enz & Christie, 1997). A reciprocal, responsive role between children and adult seems to be the most effective.

Theorists such as Piaget, Vygotsky, Freud, and Erikson view make-believe play as the leading activity of the preschool and kindergarten period. It involves and promotes development in every domain, integrating them to become more complex and refined. Vygotsky saw three components of play: Children create an imaginary situation, take on and act out roles, and follow a set of rules determined by specific roles. Make-believe play creates a zone of proximal development, facilitates the separation of thought from actions and objects, facilitates the development of self-regulation, impacts motivation, and facilitates decentration (Bodrova & Leong, 2007).

Language. Dramatic play promotes vocabulary growth (Block, 2001; Edwards, 2006) and gives children practice in turn-taking and using language to plan, as well as teaching them to carry out roles—sometimes with great expression. This shows the child's ability to move out of egocentrism into the role of another, even using different voices, vocabularies, and gestures for the role. The inner speech, or private speech as Vygotsky calls it, often is audible as children work through a dramatic play episode, whether alone or with other children. It reveals the child's inner thoughts. It is as if they were being transmitted directly out of the brain, such as, "Now this is my baby and she has to go to the doctor. Oops, her arm just fell off. I think James did that." Accompanying sound effects and directions to inanimate objects, such as "Get outta here, chair," are often heard in fantasy play. When the teacher engages the children in conversation about their play, describing their play, introducing novel vocabulary, and repeating their ideas, the frequency and complexity of the language interactions can be increased (Dickinson, 2001).

Literacy. Dramatic play is a natural way to integrate literacy into the child's environment, incorporating it as a natural and important part of the play theme. The use of literacy materials in different learning centers can be observed, such as sign making in the block area, letter writing, and list making in the dramatic play area. Often children will suggest, either spontaneously or at the gentle suggestion of the teacher, that a sign or a list could fill a need in the play. A sign may direct players, such as an "Open" or "Closed" sign for a grocery store or labels for buildings with the name of the builder. Watching the use of literacy materials, including books during play, can give the observer clues about the child's understanding of the usefulness of print. In several research studies by Neuman and Roskos, when literacy materials were added to dramatic play centers, literacy behaviors such as book handling, reading, and writing increased as much as 10 times over a control group (Neuman & Roskos, 1990, 1992, 1997).

Social. Dramatic play is encouraged by families who engage in fantasy with their children, provide props, and comment on the play as real. These children tend to be more securely attached and more imaginative. Children's involvement and success with dramatic play depends also on their level of social development (see Chapter 4). A child in the Parallel Play Stage wants to be near other children, but does not have the language, emotional, or cognitive development to engage in interactive play. The adult can recognize the child's level of social development to help find a role and support success in that role. Experience in groups greatly affects the child's ability to participate in dramatic play. Solving problems in play situations helps children learn the art of negotiation while they divide roles, take turns, and share props. Interacting with an older peer or one more socially experienced will enhance imaginative play. Children seek out familiar same-sex, same-age playmates.

Some children do not participate in dramatic play. There are many possible reasons for this, with many implications for the teacher. Some children are more object-oriented than people-oriented, which may simply be their cognitive style (see Chapter 8). They learn through manipulating the physical environment and are convergent rather than divergent thinkers. Children who are withdrawn and do not participate in dramatic play may later experience peer rejection, social anxiety, loneliness, depression, negative self-esteem, and even negative school success (Rubin & Coplan, 1998). This emphasizes the importance of facilitating dramatic play in the early childhood classroom.

It is well documented that children who are less aggressive are more readily accepted as playmates. The children who introduce wild animal themes and superheroes into dramatic play raise the level of aggressiveness of the play. Research has shown strong relationships between high television and video viewing (particularly shows depicting violence) and aggressiveness (Bushman & Huesmann, 2001; Comstock & Scharrer, 2007; Johnson et al., 2002). High levels of television viewing also result in low imagination, more anxiety, and lower reading levels and school performance (Singer & Singer, 1990). These effects can be reduced if adults are mediators of the child's viewing. Talking about the difference between reality and fantasy and the possible results in real life of aggressiveness and violence can help children understand cause and effect, and hopefully practice self-control. Play themes from television are highly aggressive and antisocial, but television can teach prosocial behaviors with careful adult

intervention. The National Television Violence Study (2002) says that children below the age of seven are most vulnerable to television violence because of their limited abilities to differentiate between fantasy and reality.

Should superhero play be banned? There is much discussion and disagreement over this topic (see Slaby et al., 1995; and Levin & Carlsson-Paige, 2006, in Resources). The observer can conduct ethnographic research about the effect of television superheroes on dramatic play through Anecdotal Recordings and Frequency Counts. There is no doubt that children use dramatic play to feel powerful (when they know they are not), feel grown up (when they know they are little), and do dangerous things (when they know they are not allowed). Dramatic play can provide a way for a child to behave "beyond his average age, above his daily behavior; in play it is as though he were a head taller than himself" (Sutton-Smith, quoted in Berk & Winsler, 2002, p. 68).

Children more frequently play with same-sex playmates, with girls choosing family themes on everyday experiences using props for domestic play such as dishes, groceries, baby-doll clothes, dressing up as mommy; whereas boys act out daddy roles, wearing ties and baseball caps, and using tools and machinery. Boys are more likely to play physically active, superhero roles (Miller, 2007). Studies have been conducted to detect the roots of these differences, biological or cultural. It is the old nature versus nurture question, with the ambiguous answer, "Both." There is no doubt that stereotypical play roles have been reinforced by families, peers, television, story books, toy advertising, and even by teachers. This happens overtly in comments such as, "You girls might want to play with the new dolls we got for the housekeeping area." Such reinforcement of stereotypes also may be less obvious, for example, by providing only action-hero-type dress-up props for boys in the dramatic play area. Observations of dramatic play roles, routines, and partners will give clues about the child's sex role identity. The role of the adult is also to broaden the child's exploration of play things and themes by providing a variety of opportunities.

Emotional. Children's emotions are displayed in dramatic play. Observers of young children have heard and seen the pretend crying of the "baby," or the shrill voice of fear as villains chase the good guys. Obvious enjoyment is seen when children are dressing up to go to the dance. Beyond the enjoyment factor are the emotional skills that are

It Happened to Me

Fan Fascination

A colleague conferred with me about a child who was preoccupied with fans. He watched the ceiling fan at home for long periods of time, his mother reported. At preschool he searched magazines and catalogs looking for pictures of fans. He carried pictures of them around in his pocket and talked about how things reminded him of fans. He was immature socially but linguistically advanced. Curry and Arnaud's (1995) warning signals regarding autism reminded me of this child with the fascination and aberration with fans. He was referred to a psychologist and worked with a play therapist. (See Chapter 7, "Topics in Observation: Autism.")

important for school success, such as the ability to delay gratification, consider the perspectives and needs of others, regulate their behavior, and act in a deliberate and intentional way (Bodrova & Leong, 2007). Play therapy has been used extensively in the treatment of children's emotional disorders, so the connection between dramatic play as a vehicle for expressing inward emotions is well recognized. Important events to the child, such as a new sibling, mommy going to work, a move, or major changes in the family often are seen played out in the dramatic play themes. Exact conversations and gestures accompany the actions that help the child physically and mentally reenact what is troubling them inside. Recurring themes of going to the doctor, the house on fire, or spanking the baby all point to the emotional involvement of young children in dramatic play.

Emotional disturbances can also be observed in children's dramatic play. Curry and Arnaud (1995, pp. 4–9) present three areas of children's play that may suggest an emotional need for intervention:

1. Thematic content: (a) a preoccupation with a single play theme, unchanging and rigid; (b) highly unusual play themes that may be traumatic events the child has witnessed; (c) play with explicit sexual content; or (d) excessive preoccupation with ordinary objects.
2. Style of play: (a) excessively rigid; (b) play in a style of a younger developmental stage; (c) inability to remove himself from the pretend role; or (d) unusual aggressiveness.
3. Social interactions in play: (a) isolated at a stage in the preschool years when dramatic play is at its peak; (b) cannot sustain play because of aggressiveness, disruptiveness, or social ineptness; (c) excessively imitative play; or (d) causes rejections.

Even very young children can exhibit complicated and strange behavior. This kind of behavior can be a clue to deeper difficulties or just a unique characteristic of that particular child. Closer observation of the whole child can help make that determination.

Dramatic play, with its rules of varying complexity, calls for self-control of emotions and impulses. This does have the developmental effect of practicing in play what is required in real life. The private speech in fantasy play has a major role in the development of self-control. Children use it to regulate their own activity, as in, "I gotta be careful here. I'll pour carefully so I don't spill it" (Berk & Winsler, 2002).

▶ ❚❚ TEACHSOURCE VIDEO ACTIVITY

Preschool: Physical Development

View this segment on the Education CourseMate website at CengageBrain.com and note the physical skills developed through dramatic play.

How could you enhance this dramatic play area with REAL props?

Physical. The whole body—both the large and small muscles—is involved in dramatic play. Large muscles are put into action when running away from robbers and lifting heavy boards to construct a fort. Placing tiny horses in a row on a wobbly block wall or buttoning up opera gloves requires small muscle coordination, attention span, and patience.

An environment enriched with interesting props and possibilities expands dramatic play. When children are engaged in imaginative play, they do adapt their own props from whatever is available. Before that stage, however, children first go through the stages of manipulation and exploration. They explore all the physical properties of objects first. Two- and three-year-olds require more realistic props to complete their play theme. Children need to physically manage real things in their lives as a significant part of the project approach (Helm, 2003).

It Happened to Me

Thirty Buttons

I watched in amazement as one of the youngest children in the 3-year-old class sat for about 20 minutes in the dramatic play area. She had put on a dress with fabric loops for buttonholes all the way down the front. There must have been 30 of them. She sat and buttoned every one. That was patience, long attention span, small muscle coordination, and one-to-one correspondence. A planned small-muscle activity would never have taught her the lessons she learned that day. It was an observation full of details about her development.

Dramatic play incorporates the curriculum areas of art, language, science, math, and social studies. It helps develop interpersonal negotiations, physical coordination, language, and cognitive skills. Children ask their own questions, seek their own answers, and enhance all skill areas with the assistance of the teacher as a support.

Helping All Children with Dramatic Play

It is not surprising that differences exist in the ways children approach dramatic play when they come from diverse backgrounds, cultures, and experiences, as well as varying levels of language, cognitive, and emotional development. Some factors influence the play to such an extent that generalizations can be made that help the teacher reflect on appropriate teaching practices.

Cultural Differences in Dramatic Play

While developmental capacities have individual differences, it is widely held that most are universal. For example, children all over the world begin to talk between the ages of one and two. The social and cultural influences on development, attitudes, and dispositions are evident; however, they are even more obvious in dramatic play, especially in the social-emotional realm. Certain cultures do not value fantasy. Those children enter group situations without the desire or skills to interact in this way. Older Mexican American siblings, however, make expert dramatic play partners. In some societies, fantasy and imaginative play appear to be absent (Johnson et al., 2005). It is difficult to draw conclusions from limited evidence. The observer should cultivate awareness so expectations are tempered by consideration of the many possible factors affecting the development.

Socioeconomic Differences in Dramatic Play

Smilansky and Shefatya's (1990) observations give insight into the play of economically deprived children. Their play was more object-centered, with the object determining the theme rather than the theme suggesting the object. The objects were used in a more rigid way and possessed with determination. Verbal interactions were more functional, for management and announcement of roles. They rarely took on the "voice" of the role they were playing. The language was more authoritative than democratic. These children used less humor, more criticism, aggressiveness, and control in dealing with problems.

Differing Abilities and Dramatic Play

Children with physical challenges participate in all kinds of play in the classroom, including dramatic play. The teacher's role supports a higher level of activity by modifications to the environment. The adult interprets for the hearing impaired, gives sensory experiences to the visually impaired, and mediates for children with serious learning and behavior problems. The teacher looks for ways that the child with disabilities can participate.

The child with limited vision or a child who is blind may need explanations about the nature of the play and suggestions on roles or actions she could contribute. They need to know where the props are and how they can be used. Their play may be imaginative and more concrete than sighted children, and they are more likely to play alone. The teacher needs to orient the child to choices, offer specific suggestions for symbolic play, and provide props that are sensory-rich.

Children who are hearing impaired will use realistic props to join in the play, but may need assistance when the play turns to transformational or representational props. The significance of a rope for a fire hose may not be understood. Children with

It Happened to Me

Empty Eyeglasses

One day in my optometrist's office, I offhandedly asked if they ever had any eyeglass frames they could donate to the preschool. They called me in a few weeks with a wonderful collection! These were added to the dramatic play area and at once became favorite props for play. Most of all, they helped all the children relate to a child in the class who wore glasses. It prepared them for that possibility themselves in the future. Sometimes a serendipitous action becomes an important one.

physical disabilities can use their abilities to join in the play, but may need an adult's help with play that is dependent on language. Giving other children ideas about how to involve the child, creating roles for the child, and giving a prop to add to the play are ways that the adult can help. The application of private speech for children with self-regulatory problems such as ADHD is being explored (Berk & Winsler, 2002).

Since play comes naturally to all children and is a central framework for all development, it serves as a context for intervention strategy. Dramatic play invites social interaction and communication, does not need to be limited by physical disabilities when there are environmental accommodations, and provides a vehicle for success. Play behaviors can be taught by:

> arranging for the child to be near other children in a given activity, enabling the teacher to describe what other children are doing to promote imitation, physically guiding the child to a play activity and helping him or her to settle in. Walk with Jenny to the housekeeping area and say, "Everybody's trying on hats. Let's go find one for you to wear". . . and moving the child slowly but steadily toward group play by building small groups of two, then three, nonthreatening children who participate with the child in simple play activities. (Allen & Cowdery, 2012, p. 401)

Helping Professionals for Play Concerns

There may be children who exhibit no desire or attention to dramatic play experiences. This does not mean that these children are not creative; this is just not an area that interests them. Young children are working out the differences between real and imaginary, and they become very arbitrary sometimes in only wanting to be involved in the real rather than the pretend, rejecting the make-believe as younger behavior. This is usually not a problem, just an observation that one can make from the child's play and interactions with the environment.

On the other hand, there occasionally are some children so caught up in dramatic play and the imaginary world that they lose touch with reality. The causes may be varied, from giftedness in the area of creativity to escape from a traumatic

real-world experience. The observer assesses the range of normal expected behavior, alert to excessive or compulsive behavior that may be a clue to a deeper problem. After observation, documentation, and discussion with the teaching team, the family is consulted for advice and insight. If a referral is made, it may be to one of the following psychological professionals:

> *psychologist*—professional trained in human behavior
>
> *psychiatrist*—physician specializing in social or emotional disorders

Other Methods

Other Methods to Record Dramatic Play:

> Anecdotal/Running Records
>
> Checklist or Rating Scale that has dramatic play criteria
>
> Time Sample—length of time in dramatic play area
>
> Work Samples—play written by children, costumes/sets produced

Key Terms

audio recorders	sociodramatic
digital video	play
cameras	story dictation
dramatic play	technology
informed consent	video recorder

Plans

Go to Education CourseMate website, accessed through CengageBrain.com, for the following:

> Class List Log form
>
> Plan Week 11 Part A, Directions for using technology to document dramatic play on all children, including What to Do with It, Portfolio Evidence Sheet Example, Sharing with Child and Family, Actions—Read a Book, In the Environment, In the Curriculum, In the Newsletter
>
> Plan Week 11 Part B, Directions for Running Record in dramatic play or blocks or free play for Group B
>
> Plan Week 11 Part C, Reflective Journal

Resources

Good, L. (2009). *Teaching and learning with digital photography*. Thousand Oaks, CA: Corwin.

Levin, D., & Carlsson-Paige, N. (2006). *The war play dilemma: What every parent and teacher needs to know* (2nd ed.). New York: Teachers College Press.

Paley, V. G. (1984). *Boys and girls: Superheroes in the doll corner*. Chicago: University of Chicago Press.

Paley, V. G. (1988). *Bad guys don't have birthdays*. Chicago: University of Chicago Press.

Paley, V. G. (1997). *The girl with the brown crayon*. Cambridge, MA: Harvard University Press.

Singer, D. G., & Singer, J. L. (2001). *Make-believe: Games and activities for imaginative play: A book for parents, teachers, and the young children in their lives*. Washington, DC: Magination Press.

CHAPTER 12

Using Documentation for Child Abuse Suspicions and Looking at Self-Concept

OBSERVATION THOUGHT

"How we view ourselves is reflected in how we view and treat others."

NAEYC Standards **naeyc**

The following NAEYC Standards for Early Child-hood Professional Preparation are addressed in this chapter:

Standard 3: *Observing, Documenting, and Assessing to Support Young Children and Families*

Standard 6: *Becoming a Professional*

IN THIS CHAPTER

▶ Using Documentation for Child Abuse Suspicions

▶ Diversity and Child Abuse

▶ Looking at Self-Concept and Self-Esteem

▶ Topics in Observation: Dealing with Families Suspected of Child Maltreatment

▶ Helping All Children with Self-Esteem

▶ Helping Professionals for Child Abuse and Self-Esteem Concerns

Using Documentation for Child Abuse Suspicions

Observing children in group settings is not always a pleasant experience. The observer has a grave responsibility to fulfill in recognizing and reporting signs of abuse or neglect. This section is one that everyone wishes were not necessary, but child abuse is a reality. There are people who hurt children physically, psychologically, or use children for sexual purposes. Young children are more likely than older children to be abused or neglected; one-third of the child maltreatment victims in 2009 were between birth and age three (Figure 12–1), with 12 percent

© Cengage Learning 2012

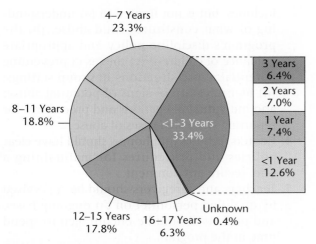

Figure 12–1 Child Abuse Victims by Age.
Source: US Dept of Health and Human Services www.acf.hhs.gov.

less than one year old. Infants and toddlers dispro-portionately account for over three-quarters of child maltreatment fatalities (USDHHS, 2009). Because these early years set the stage for all that follows, they hold the greatest danger for long-term damage and the greatest potential for successful intervention.

Neglect is characterized by failure to provide for the child's basic needs, which include physical, medical, educational, and emotional requirements. A form of neglect in infants and young children is organic "failure to thrive," caused by physiologi-cal problems (in which case the failure is termed "organic") or lack of proper nourishment (termed "nonorganic"). **Physical abuse** includes any non-accidental injury caused by the child's caregiver, in-tentional or unintentional. **Sexual abuse** includes a wide range of behavior, including exploitation through prostitution or pornography. **Emotional maltreatment** is psychological or emotional abuse through blaming, belittling, or rejecting a child that impairs a child's emotional development or sense of self-worth (Child Welfare Information Gateway). Child-care staff are **mandated reporters**—those individuals who by law must report suspicions of child-abuse and maltreatment to specified agencies. Be aware, however, that there is no one nationwide mandated reporter law. Mandated reporting legisla-tion is at the discretion of each state, and laws do change in definition over time. It is very important that all educators, in classrooms and homes, are knowledgeable of the law and what agency policies for reporting abuse and/or neglect are in place. Early childhood or home visiting programs and schools have established policies and protocols that must be followed. Each member of the staff needs to know what to do if abuse or neglect is suspected.

The Abusers

The greatest proportion—more than 75 percent—of child maltreatment leading to fatalities is perpetrated by parents, with 15 percent perpertrated by guard-ians, acquaintances, or other relatives, and less than 10 percent by others (Figure 12–2). This increases the likelihood that the teacher knows and has contact with the person(s) causing the abuse, and thereby has the opportunity to intervene and get help for the child and the perpetrator. Research shows that child maltreatment can result in future mental health problems, such as behavior problems as a child or adult, post-traumatic stress disorder, depression, at-tempted suicide, and alcohol-related difficulties. There is also a strong association with future criminal behavior, doubling the child's risk of being arrested for a violent crime (Gilbert et al., 2009).

For those who have dedicated their lives to the care and teaching of children, the idea that any adult would knowingly harm a child is unthinkable. Child abusers fit no particular mold, cutting across social class, gender, race, and occupations. They are people just like the rest of us. They could be people with-out knowledge of the fragility of the forming body or mind. They could be people with such life stresses that their life is out of control; and perhaps they are addicted to substances that lower inhibitions and self-control. They may be victims themselves who resort to inflicting pain according to a pattern established in their own childhood. While this does not excuse

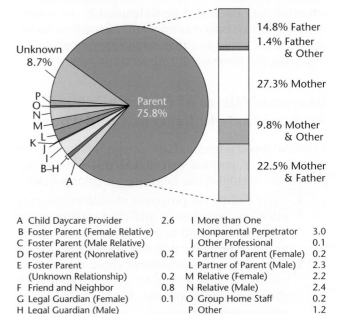

A	Child Daycare Provider	2.6	I More than One	
B	Foster Parent (Female Relative)		Nonparental Perpetrator	3.0
C	Foster Parent (Male Relative)		J Other Professional	0.1
D	Foster Parent (Nonrelative)	0.2	K Partner of Parent (Female)	0.2
E	Foster Parent		L Partner of Parent (Male)	2.3
	(Unknown Relationship)	0.2	M Relative (Female)	2.2
F	Friend and Neighbor	0.8	N Relative (Male)	2.4
G	Legal Guardian (Female)	0.1	O Group Home Staff	0.2
H	Legal Guardian (Male)		P Other	1.2

Figure 12–2 Child Fatalities by Perpetrator Relationship.
Source: US Dept of Health and Human Services www.acf.hhs.gov.

anyone from harming a child, we approach the documentation of child abuse and maltreatment not as law enforcement officers, nor to seek punishment, but to protect the child and get help for the family. While it may be one of the most difficult things an early childhood professional must do, it may be one of the most important ones, even resulting in saving a life.

As teachers interact with children, they win the child's trust. They have the opportunity to see and hear what children do and talk about the experiences they have had. A teacher may be the one who prevents neglect or abuse from happening again. People who abuse children need help; and the child needs help and protection. Not reporting suspected abuse allows it to continue.

🏠 Home Visiting and Child Abuse Reporting

While classroom teachers as mandated reporters generally learn about suspected abuse and/or neglect through observation or dialogue with children, an early educator in the home may directly observe incidences or conditions of abuse or neglect. The close relationship with the family cannot become more important than the child's welfare. It is not the educator's role to excuse, evaluate or investigate the situation based on what an educator may know is happening in the home. While the child's wellbeing is always the first and foremost priority, reporting can potentially put the relationship between the educator and family in a precarious position, and the educator may no longer be welcomed in the home. A good practice is to carefully and factually describe the educator's role as a mandated reporter while introducing the program during recruitment.

Responsibilities of Early Childhood Professionals to Prevent Child Abuse

Early childhood programs have a responsibility to keep children safe. A position state of NAEYC (1996) on the prevention of child abuse lists these program policies:

1. Early childhood programs should employ an adequate number of qualified staff to work with children and to provide adequate supervision of program staff and volunteers.
2. The program environment (both indoor and outdoor areas) should be designed to reduce the possibility of private, hidden locations in which abuse may occur.
3. All program staff, substitutes, and volunteers should receive preservice orientation and refresher training at regular intervals that includes, but is not limited to (a) understanding of what constitutes child abuse; (b) the program's discipline policy and appropriate guidance of children; (c) means of preventing potential abuse situations in group settings; (d) identification of signs of potential abuse; and individual obligations and procedures for reporting suspected cases of abuse.
4. Centers, schools and homes should have clear policies and procedures for maintaining a safe, secure environment.
5. Teachers and caregivers should be supervised by qualified personnel on an ongoing basis, and parents should be encouraged to spend time in the program.
6. Programs should *not* institute "no-touch policies' to reduce the risk of abuse.

Source: Excerpted from the National Association for the Education of Young Children (NAEYC), "Prevention of Child Abuse in Early Childhood Programs and the Responsibilities of Early Childhood Professionals to Prevent Child Abuse." Position statement, (Washington, DC: NAEYC; 1996). Copyright © 1996 NAEYC. Used with permission. Full text of this position statement is available at www.naeyc.org/files/naeyc/file/positions/PSCHAB98.PDF.

Physical and Behavioral Indicators of Abuse

Teachers and child-care workers must be familiar with the physical and behavioral indicators of abuse. Indicators may give clear evidence of maltreatment, but they also may have other explanations. Some may result from the personality of the child, a new setting with new adults, poverty, different cultural values, accidents, or illnesses. Judgment must be used. For the protection of the child, however, it is better to report those suspicions.

Reasonable Cause to Suspect. The suspicion of child abuse or neglect grows from visual observations, verbal disclosures, or an accumulation of circumstances that build to a reasonable cause to suspect. This does not place the reporter in the position of investigator, interrogator, or prosecutor; it simply means the reporter must give an initial alert based on factual observations (Figure 12–3).

The Child's Appearance. For infants and preverbal children, abuse and maltreatment can be observed in the normal routines of being with the child. Concerns are raised by the location and formation of bruises, cuts, and inflammations. Obvious wounds are usually met by a teacher's empathetic comments—"Ooo, that bruise looks sore"—or interested observations of verbal children—"I notice

INDICATORS OF POSSIBLE CHILD ABUSE, MALTREATMENT OR NEGLECT

INDICATORS	PHYSICAL SIGNS	CHILD BEHAVIOR	FAMILY BEHAVIOR
Physical abuse	Unexplained wounds in various stages of healing	Suspicious of adults	Unconcerned about child
	Wounds with recognizable patterns such as belt buckle, electric plug, stove burner	Extreme behavior from withdrawal to aggression	Delays medical care
	Unexplained broken bones, cuts, bruises, welts	Frightened of parents	Harshly disciplines child
	Swollen areas, sensitive to touch	Fear at dismissal time	Conceals child's injuries or gives inconsistent reasons
	Burns, especially cigarette burns or immersion burns to buttocks	Unseasonable long sleeved-shirts or long pants	Sees the child as bad or evil
	Human bite marks	Seeks affection from any adult, stranger	Provides the child with alcohol or other drugs
Maltreatment/ Neglect	Frequent, insatiable hunger,	Steals or hoards food	Consistent lack of supervision
	Poor hygiene	Frequent absences	Emotional disorders
	Unattended medical needs	Unusual fatigue	Exposes the child to dangerous living conditions
	Frequent absences	Reports no caretaker at home	Expects the child to take on adult caretaker role of younger children
Emotional Maltreatment	Speech disorders	Anti-social	Very obvious unequal treatment of children in family
	Delayed development	Regressive behavior	Excessive shaming of child
	Difficulty sleeping, eating	Prefers adults to child companions	Withholds attention and concern for child
	Habituating (rocking, biting, sucking, head banging)	Self-mutilation	Unconcerned with child's problems
Sexual Abuse	Torn, bloody, stained underwear	Withdrawal, infantile behavior	Overly protective or jealous of child
	Pain, swelling, itching in genital area	Acts out sexual behavior or knowledge	Treats child like a grown-up sex object
	Difficulty walking or sitting	Threatened by close physical contact by adults	Engages in sexual behavior in the presence of the child
	Bruises on genitals or anal area	Poor peer interactions	Lacks social contacts outside the family
	Sexually transmitted disease in pre-adolescents	Reports sexual activity	Leaves child with inappropriate caretakers

NOTE: Some behavioral indicators may be common to all children at some time. When indicators are noticeable in a sufficient number and strength to characterize a child's overall manner, they may indicate abuse or maltreatment.

Figure 12–3 Child Abuse and Maltreatment Indicators.
Source: Courtesy of Broome County Family Violence Prevention Council.

you holding your arm. Does something hurt?" The child's response may be a first-hand account of what happened—a **disclosure** statement.

The Child's Description or Disclosure. The child may say, "My mommy twisted my arm" or "Uncle John hurt me in my goo goo." Comments like these always catch teachers by surprise, but it is important to maintain composure so that facial or verbal expressions not reveal the shock, revulsion, or disapproval of what has happened to this child. An appropriate response is, "Would you like to tell me more?" This expresses concern, being open to listening but not probing for more details. These disclosures call for immediate action and documentation. Once a mandated reporter has "reasonable cause to suspect," probing for all the details is not necessary. In fact, detailed probing and leading questions may actually place the child in greater jeopardy. Defense attorneys for the abuser may interpret this as interfering with the witness. The questions should be asked only to answer the question in the reporter's mind: "Do I know enough to *suspect* that this injury or behavior could have been caused by abuse or neglect?" To probe further will inevitably compromise later interviews of the child by child protective authorities. When children must repeat their story to different adults, they may leave out information to protect a loved one. They may recant their story for fear of the consequences or add untrue details to be more believed. This detailed interviewing must be left to the authorities.

If the child willingly offers and needs to talk about it, by all means be a ready listener; then accurately document both the child's comments and anything you say as well (see Figure 12–4). It is important not to act shocked or disgusted; be willing to listen, and do not deny the child's statements. The less you say in these situations, the better. Leave interrogations to the law enforcement and child protective services professionals.

Circumstantial Evidence. Suspicious injuries may suggest child abuse or maltreatment (Figure 12–5). Children's explanations are often protective statements. Behavioral indications by themselves are not sufficient basis for a report, but they should be documented and discussed with a supervisor.

Teachers as Reporters. In a review of the research, some of the findings about early childhood teachers reporting child abuse are surprising (Walsh, Farrell, Bridgestock, & Schweitzer, 2006):

- Teachers are more likely to report physical abuse than emotional abuse or neglect.
- Teachers tend to delay reporting until they feel they have sufficient evidence.

When Talking with the Child
Do:
- Make sure the ECE professional is someone the child knows and trusts.
- Conduct the discussion in a place that allows for privacy but is familiar to the child.
- Use only one or two ECE professionals.
- Sit next to the child at his/her level.
- Engage the child in a conversation but do not press the child to talk about the injuries if he/she does not want to.
- Ask the child to clarify words or terms that are not understood.
- Assure the child that he/she has done nothing wrong.
- _____
- _____

DO NOT:
- Suggest answers to the child.
- Probe or press for answers the child does not willingly offer.
- Force the child to remove clothing.
- Display horror, shock, or disapproval of the parent(s), child, or situation.
- Leave the child alone with a stranger.
- Ask "why" questions.
- _____
- _____

When Talking with the Parent(s)
DO:
- Select the person most appropriate to the situation.
- Conduct the discussion in private.
- Tell the parent(s) why the discussion is taking place.
- Be direct, honest, and professional.
- Reassure parent(s) of the program's support to them and to their child.
- Tell the parent(s) if a report was made or will be made.
- Advise the parent(s) of the program's legal and ethical responsibilities to report.
- _____
- _____

DO NOT:
- Try to prove the abuse or neglect; that is not an ECE professional's role.
- Display horror, anger, or disapproval of the parent(s), child, or situation.
- Pry into family matters unrelated to the specific situation.
- Place blame or make judgments about the parent(s) or child.
- _____
- _____

Figure 12–4 Tips for Talking with a Child or Parent.
Source: Reprinted from *Caregivers of Young Children: Preventing and Responding to Child Maltreatment*, 1992, p. 24. U.S. Department of Health and Human Services.

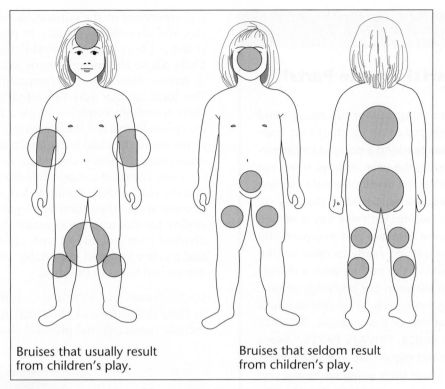

Bruises that usually result
from children's play.

Bruises that seldom result
from children's play.

Figure 12–5 Comparison of the Location of Typical and Suspicious Bruising Areas.
Source: From Kostelnik//Whiren/Soderman/Gregory, *Guiding Children's Social Development and Learning*,
7th ed., 2012 Cengage Learning.

- Boys are more frequently the subject of substantiated abuse.
- Lower socioeconomic groups are more likely to be reported.
- The quality of the relationship with the child and family influenced the willingness to report.
- Male teachers are less tolerant of abuse and neglect, and report more frequently.
- Experienced teachers are more likely to report.
- Teachers' knowledge of indicators and reporting procedures were often inadequate.
- Fear of the negative consequences may prevent or delay reporting.
- The role of the school principal is influential in reporting or not.

Teacher Support. The disclosure, recording, and reporting of child abuse all take an emotional toll on teachers, people who have committed their career to the care and education of children. The first area of support should come from the administration through clear policies, responsive follow-through, and empathy. The local child abuse agency can answer specific questions and clear up any misgivings or doubts about suspected abuse. It may be that the adult will need to spend time with a counselor to sort out feelings of loyalty, betrayal, anger, disappointment, or fear. This is a sensitive area for all the people involved.

Recording Any Indicators of Maltreatment

The most appropriate method for recording episodes that document suspected abuse or maltreatment is the Anecdotal Record. It is effective for this information because the accounts

- are written shortly after the episode or event occurs, based on notes jotted at the time.
- contain a detailed account, including date and time, people involved in the episode, actions, and exact conversations. This is especially important in situations in which a child reveals to a teacher that someone is hurting him or her. The questions and comments that the adult says must be accurately recorded also. This indicates that the child was not led or influenced in the description of the event.
- contain separate comments by the recorder, such as opinions or questions, from the body of the recording.

In addition to the narrative, diagrams and specific descriptions of the size and nature of wounds should be made. Explanations or conjecture about their cause should be separate from the diagram.

Some states allow mandated reporters to take photographs, but this should be confirmed in the recorder's

It Happened to Me

"Private Parts! Private Parts!"

While there is nothing humorous about child abuse, I am reminded of an incident that happened to me. I was teaching a delayed kindergarten entry class, mostly five-year-old boys, smart but not "school ready" as the developmental screening used in that school district declared. One day we were doing body tracings with one boy stretched out on a large piece of paper and everyone else around the edge getting ready to color on the tracing. I was making the outline with a marker and as I traced up between one boy's legs he said, "Don't draw my private parts." Five-year-olds love to chant, and that was all they needed. "PRIVATE PARTS, PRIVATE PARTS, PRIVATE PARTS." Every positive guidance technique I had in my bag didn't work. I could just hear them going home and saying that Mrs. Nilsen traced private parts today! So, the only thing I could think of was to declare, "Outside time! Get your coats on!" It stopped the chanting, and I never heard more about it. And I never again did body tracings and discourage teachers from doing so. Think carefully about it.

state. In most cases, however, photographs taken by those other than the authorities are unnecessary and may be inappropriate. Photographs by authorized persons are considered evidence and can be used as such only under controlled conditions. This is best left to child protection agencies, law enforcement, or medical authorities. Further trauma may be added to the child by photographing the injuries. For many sexually abused children, being photographed may be a part of their history of abuse. In any event, photographs, should they be taken, must be turned over to the authorities immediately. *The accurate recording and prompt reporting of suspected child abuse and maltreatment cannot be stressed enough.*

Next Steps

Immediate notification of the supervisor is the first step. Short, accurate notes made as soon as possible preserve vital details. The Child Abuse Hotline, required in every state, should be called immediately either by the supervisor or the witness, depending on the policies and procedures already in place in the program (Figure 12–6). The national listing for your state's Child Abuse Hotline telephone number can be found at www.childwelfare.gov/responding/reporting.cfm. The local agency may be called to confer if indeed there is enough suspicion to file a Hotline report. The exception to this is if there is suspicion of sexual abuse or the life of the child is in danger. In that case, the law enforcement agency should be called *immediately*. If for some reason the supervisor does not make the call and the teacher has "reason to suspect" there has been possible abuse, then there is a legal and moral responsibility for the teacher to make the call. It is the individual responsibility of each child-care professional and teacher to report reasonable suspicion of harm or threatened harm to the child.

Legal Process of Reporting. Individual states vary in their definitions of child maltreatment, but most include nonaccidental physical abuse, neglect, sexual

© Cengage Learning 2014

Figure 12–6 Hotline reports need to be made promptly once "reasonable cause to suspect" is determined.

abuse, and emotional (or mental) maltreatment by a person responsible for the child's welfare.

EXERCISE **According to the laws in your state, reportable child abuse is defined as what?**

Every state has laws for reporting child abuse and a reporting number, many of which are toll-free telephone calls. School personnel and child-care workers are mandated reporters by law in every state. A mandated reporter must report any "reasonable cause to suspect" a child has been maltreated. Not reporting suspected neglect or abuse could result in legal action. Reporters of suspected abuse are not responsible for proving the abuse, just for presenting the observable facts that led to the suspicions. If the report is **unfounded**—not enough evidence exists to prove it—the reporter is protected from civil action.

EXERCISE **Locate the Hotline or reporting number for child-care workers in your state. Find the state and local agency and telephone number to which you could ask questions. Write them on a separate sheet of paper.**

Reporting telephone number:
Agency and telephone number:

When the Hotline or Law Enforcement Agency Is Called. The reporter will be asked to supply as much of the following information as possible. The lack of complete information *does not* prohibit a report from being made. Requested information includes the following:

▶ the name and address of the child and his or her parents or legally responsible guardian
▶ the child's age, sex, and race
▶ the nature and extent of the child's injuries, abuse, or maltreatment (including any evidence of prior injuries, abuse, or maltreatment to the child or his or her siblings)
▶ the child's present location
▶ the name of the person or persons responsible for causing the injury, abuse, or maltreatment
▶ family composition; others residing in or at the home in regular intervals
▶ person making the report, where that person can be reached, and where the information was obtained; names of other relevant school personnel who may provide critical information
▶ any action taken by the reporting source
▶ any additional information that may be helpful

It Happened to Me

"She Made Me Sit in the Puke"

One day toward the end of the school year, a parent came in and said, "I am considering calling the Hotline on you." My heart stopped, my face got red, I got a lump in my throat. She laughed then and said, "My son said you made him sit in the puke." It turns out that we had been practicing for preschool graduation (we did it back then, but I wouldn't do it now) and we were in the church sanctuary where they sat on the front pew while we assembled to sing on the stage. Pew/puke—I could now understand. I did have him sit in the pew, not the puke.

Though suspicions of abuse or neglect seem obvious by the very act of calling the Hotline, the reporter's concerns must be heard in these terms: "I believe this child to be abused or neglected because. . ." The report is strengthened if the reporter can (1) detail a pattern (not that a mother was overheard screaming at her child once, but this is how she interacts with her child routinely), *and* (2) state the impact on the child (e.g., behavioral signs, the child is doing poorly in school, and so on).

Needless to say, one should not wait for a pattern of injuries before alerting the authorities. If troublesome behavior by a family member and/or the child, though not reportable, has been observed, that information may be helpful to set a framework for the report to the Hotline. Documentation of these earlier concerns should be recorded in the style of an Anecdotal Recording and kept in a confidential file.

Once the call is made, the written Report of Suspected Child Abuse or Maltreatment should be completed and filed according to the directions in the state. Figure 12–7, which is the written mandated reporter form used in New York, is an example of such a form. A copy is kept in a confidential file, separate from the child's Portfolio and separate from the Class File, along with any written records referring to these suspicions. For the reporter's own use, a log should be kept of the time of the incident and the witness's exact response (writing an Anecdotal Recording, reporting the incident to supervisor, action taken, etc.). Additions to the log should be made as each step in the process occurs ("Made out written report, date," "Answered questions by. . .," etc.). This should be kept in a confidential file according to the program's policy.

LDSS-2221A (Rev. 10/2008) FRONT
NEW YORK STATE
OFFICE OF CHILDREN AND FAMILY SERVICES
**REPORT OF SUSPECTED
CHILD ABUSE OR MALTREATMENT**

Report Date	Case ID	Call ID
Time : ☐ AM ☐ PM	Local Case #	Local Dist/Agency

SUBJECTS OF REPORT

List all children in household, adults responsible and alleged subjects.

Line #	Last Name	First Name	Aliases	Sex (M, F, Unk)	Birthday or Age Mo/Day/ Yr	Race Code	Ethnicity (Ck Only If Hispanic/Latino)	Relation Code	Role Code	Lang. Code
1.							☐			
2.							☐			
3.							☐			
4.							☐			
5.							☐			
6.							☐			
7.							☐			

☐ MORE

List Addresses and Telephone Numbers (Using Line Numbers From Above)	(Area Code) Telephone No.

BASIS OF SUSPICIONS

Alleged suspicions of abuse or maltreatment. Give child(ren)'s line number(s). If all children, write "**ALL**".

____ DOA/Fatality
____ Fractures
____ Internal Injuries (e.g., Subdural Hematoma)
____ Lacerations/Bruises/Welts
____ Burns/Scalding
____ Excessive Corporal Punishment
____ Inappropriate Isolation/Restraint (Institutional Abuse Only)
____ Inappropriate Custodial Conduct (Institutional Abuse Only)

____ Child's Drug/Alcohol Use
____ Poisoning/Noxious Substances
____ Choking/Twisting/Shaking
____ Lack of Medical Care
____ Malnutrition/Failure to Thrive
____ Sexual Abuse
____ Inadequate Guardianship
____ Other (specify) ____

____ Swelling/Dislocation/Sprains
____ Educational Neglect
____ Emotional Neglect
____ Inadequate Food/Clothing/Shelter
____ Lack of Supervision
____ Abandonment
____ Parent's Drug/Alcohol Misuse

State reasons for suspicion, including the nature and extent of each child's injuries, abuse or maltreatment, past and present, and any evidence or suspicions of "Parental" behavior contributing to the problem.

(If known, give time/date of alleged incident)
MO
DAY
YR
Time : ☐ AM ☐ PM

☐ Additional sheet attached with more explanation.
The Mandated Reporter Requests Finding of Investigation ☐ YES ☐ NO

CONFIDENTIAL **SOURCE(S) OF REPORT** *CONFIDENTIAL*

NAME	(Area Code) TELEPHONE	NAME	(Area Code) TELEPHONE
ADDRESS		ADDRESS	
AGENCY/INSTITUTION		AGENCY/INSTITUTION	

RELATIONSHIP

___ Med. Exam/Coroner ___ Physician ___ Hosp. Staff ___ Law Enforcement ___ Neighbor ___ Relative ___ Instit. Staff
___ Social Services ___ Public Health ___ Mental Health ___ School Staff ___ Other (Specify)

For Use By Physicians Only	Medical Diagnosis on Child	Signature of Physician who examined/treated child X	(Area Code) Telephone No.
	Hospitalization Required: ☐ None ☐ Under 1 week ☐ 1–2 weeks ☐ Over 2 weeks		

| Actions Taken Or About To Be Taken | ☐ Medical Exam ☐ X-Ray ☐ Removal/Keeping ☐ Not. Med Exam/Coroner |
| | ☐ Photographs ☐ Hospitalization ☐ Returning Home ☐ Notified DA |

Signature of Person Making This Report:
X
Title
Date Submitted Mo. Day Yr.

Figure 12–7 New York State Child Abuse Reporting Form.
Source: Report of Suspected Child Abuse or Maltreatment Form. Reprinted by permission of the New York State Office of Children and Family Services.

Do Not Discuss Suspicions with the Family or the Child. This is the one time when what was observed should not be discussed with family or the child after the initial disclosure. The authorities should be allowed to take further action.

If the family member comes to school and asks who made the report, he or she should be referred to the supervisor. Families should always be treated respectfully and tactfully. When they know a report has been made, they can be referred to the family handbook where it states the policy of the program and the legal responsibility of mandated reporters. They are offered assistance to seek help and given referrals to agencies and support groups in their area. The family member may be angry and abusive, but the child's safety is of the utmost consideration. Arguing with and relating details to the family are inappropriate actions. Supervisors may make a statement such as, "We have observed something that made us suspect the child may have been abused, and we have a legal obligation to report that suspicion. We have done what we think is best for the child. We stand ready to help in whatever way we can." That is all one needs to say, and all one should say—perhaps even *more* than one should say. It all depends on the circumstances.

Another caution here about confidentiality: Please do not discuss this suspicion or report with anyone other than the supervisor of the program and the authorities. This is an extremely upsetting situation, but it is inflammatory to discuss it with persons outside of those just mentioned. This is a good use for your Reflective Journal. Ask the supervisor if there is a counselor available if you feel you need to discuss this with someone else. They are bound by confidentiality ethics as well.

As a reminder the NAEYC Code of Professional Ethics regarding this issue is included here:
NAEYC Code of Ethical Conduct and Statement of Commitment (NAEYC, 2005)
Principles

P-1.8—We shall be familiar with risk factors for and symptoms of child abuse and neglect, including physical, sexual, verbal and emotional abuse and physical, emotional, educational and medical neglect. We shall know and follow state laws and community procedures that protect children against abuse and neglect.

P-1.9—When we have reasonable cause to suspect child abuse or neglect, we shall report it to the appropriate community agency and follow up to ensure that appropriate action has been taken. When appropriate, parents or guardians will be informed that the referral will be or has been made.

P-1.10—When another person tells us of his or her suspicion that a child is being abused or neglected, we shall assist that person in taking appropriate action in order to protect the child.

P-1.11—When we become aware of a practice or situation that endangers the health, safety, or wellbeing of children, we have an ethical responsibility to protect children or inform parents and/or others who can.

Diversity and Child Abuse

Child-rearing customs and practices are not standard between any two families, but they are often even more varied because of racial, cultural, economic, and religious differences. Sometimes these come into conflict with the value of who has the right to interfere in the family's life. In the case of child abuse, it is important that all families understand the law's mandate and the program's responsibility to report all cases of suspected maltreatment. This issue faces all people who work with children and families. It is shocking to read child abuse statistics and think about the hurt each statistic represents, but the professional staff are the children's protectors.

Cultural Differences

Children of families of many cultures are participating in educational experiences. Sensitivity to cultures whose values and customs are different from one's own is an important trait in early childhood professionals. Child-rearing has distinctive differences among various cultures concerning obedience, punishment, dependency, and eye contact. "*Cultural reciprocity* is the process of learning about our own culture, learning about other cultures, explaining our recommendations and collaborating with families" (Seibel et al., 2006, p. 5–6). This emphasizes listening to and learning from one another. For example, understanding cultural practices regarding female clothing may overrule the clothing indicators suggesting a "covering up" of signs of physical abuse. Other practices such as coining—placing hot coins as an alternative medicine procedure—could be seen as abuse. Research linking child abuse to broad ethnic categories is impossible and unfair since there is so much diversity within groups described as non-Latino white, African-American, Latino, and Asian-American. It is more likely that the elements of the ecological culture—such as beliefs about parenting, family and gender role expectations, socioeconomic status, availability of drugs and alcohol, unemployment, education level, and experiences of discrimination and social capital—are more likely to be areas of determination (Elliott & Urquiza, 2006).

Many traditional cultures use an authoritarian style of parenting demanding total obedience and respect from their children, and disciplining by using corporal punishment. Whether this is physical abuse depends on its frequency and severity (Fontes, 2005). The responsibility of the teacher, however, is still to report child abuse and neglect as defined by the state regulations. There is an ethical dilemma of protecting the child while preserving and understanding the cultural practices of the home. Strong lines of communication, especially having translators of the home language, are vital to establishing trust with the family from the beginning of the relationship. Then, if abuse suspicions arise, there is common ground while still protecting the child, always responding in a supportive and respectful way. If the program has immigrant populations, efforts should be made to provide support services to assure that the family has sufficient subsistence assets, legal assistance, and social and emotional resources.

Immigrants to the United States come from a wide variety of backgrounds within their home countries, ranging from agricultural or abject poverty backgrounds to highly-trained professionals. Just as we seek to individualize the curriculum for each child, interactions with the family on all topics, but especially these sensitive ones, should consider the cultural backgrounds and stressors of newly immigrated families. There could be extreme culture shock in trying to adjust to differences in every aspect of daily living. Immigrants could have feelings of isolation, being separated from extended families and others who speak and understand their language, as well as facing discrimination. There may be poverty issues that impact health, nutrition, transportation, and communication. Poverty issues may lead to their neglecting nutrition, adequate seasonal clothing, or medical care. All of these variables make it imperative to get to know the families, their cultural attitudes and practices, and build respect and trust.

Different Abilities

Children with developmental disabilities are also victims of abuse, with some indications that abuse occurs at higher rates among these children than in the regular population. Children with special needs present challenges for parents, teachers, and caregivers who can feel isolated, frustrated, unsupported, and with no control of the situation (Gore & Janssen, 2007). Children with special needs are often perceived as an "easy target" with limited defenses or protection. Subgroups of children with disabilities are at special risk. Boys and young children with disabilities between three and six years of age are at increased risk for severe physical disability resulting in bodily injury. Girls and older children with disabilities are more likely to be victims of forceful sexual attacks. Children with disabilities are less likely to

disclose abuse (Hershkowitz et al., 2007). Observation of abuse is even more critical for children with disabilities because they may lack the verbal, physical, or mental skills to protect themselves or disclose what has been happening. The same criteria for signs of abuse are used for children with different abilities. Any questions that need to be asked should be simple and concrete—who, what, when, but *not* why. Drawings, dolls, or a sign interpreter may help the child express the details he or she wants to disclose. Remember, the observer need not gather all the evidence. All that is needed for a report to try to protect the child is "reason to suspect." Child Protective Services personnel will take the next steps.

⊕ Advantages

Reporting suspicions of child abuse or maltreatment

- protects the child from possible further harm if the suspicions are founded.
- knowledgeable officials investigate and make determinations as to whether the suspicions are founded.
- connects the family with assistance if the suspicions are founded.

⊖ Disadvantages

Reporting suspicions of child abuse or maltreatment

- is a traumatic situation in the life of a teacher/ caregiver.
- possibility that suspicions are circumstantial and incorrect inferences have been made.
- raises fear of reprisal by the family.

⊘ Pitfalls to Avoid

In such an important situation, it is vital to make sure you avoid doing the following:

- doing nothing when you have strong suspicions
- talking about your suspicions to people who do not have a right to know
- asking the child too many questions or leading questions
- not writing down all the exact details of the disclosure or your observations

Go to the Education CourseMate website, accessed through CengageBrain.com, for Class List Log on Self-Esteem forms, plans, and resources.

❓ What to Do with The Information

Keep your immediate notes, a copy of the report, and a log of the follow-up in a secure place. This is important, but extremely confidential, information. Know the policy of your program or school regarding the storage of this information.

Observation documentation gathered about the child's self-concept is stored in the Portfolio and recorded on the Portfolio Evidence Sheet. See Figure 12–8 for an example.

 Using Technology

Do not use photographs of the child's body or record interviews with the child. Leave that to the child protective services. By interrogating the child or gathering this kind of evidence, you may be jeopardizing the veracity of the reporting and investigation process. Remember, you need not *prove* abuse or neglect, but you must have reasonable cause for concern. The teacher's role is not to prosecute but to protect.

Looking at Self-Concept and Self-Esteem

Linking the documentation of child maltreatment and the topic of self-esteem is not circumstantial. Child maltreatment results in harmful effects on all areas of development but especially the emotional domain. When parents abuse children with ridicule, rejection, and physical pain, it results in low self-esteem, high anxiety, self-blame, depression, and academic failure in the children (Wolfe, 2005). The trauma of abuse leaves physiological and psychological scars that can last a lifetime.

Perhaps no other area of development is more nebulous and difficult to document than self-concept, yet it is at the root of social, academic, and personal success. Where does the development of **self-concept** (sometimes called self-identity) begin? This book began the review of child development with attachment and separation. The circle is now

complete, coming back to that same important connection between a child's relationships and the development of self-concept and self-esteem. Whether it is family and child, family and program, or new concepts and established schemata, relationships and connections are what it is all about. The development of healthy **self-esteem** (the evaluation of the self-concept, whether the attribute is positive or negative) is dependent on certain kinds of relationships. This chapter explores the contributing factors to the development of self-esteem, the stages of the development of a sense of self, and how it can be observed in the classroom. Families and teachers are major influences on self-concept, with the goal of helping the child have high self-esteem based on a truthful vision of the self.

Self-concept resides in the cognitive, what one knows about oneself in many different areas. Self-esteem resides in the emotional realm of how one evaluates and feels about oneself. Physical appearance and ability are very important in American culture, with millions spent on products, clothing, exercise

PORTFOLIO EVIDENCE OF CHILD'S DEVELOPMENT			
Evidence Type	**Date**	**Recorder**	**Notes**
SOCIAL/ EMOTIONAL – the child's social and emotional development, self-concept			
RR	10/1/	BAN	Freeplay – blocks, painting books
CL	10/3/	MLS	Solitary
FC	10/11/	MLS	Mostly positive interactions
AR	10/13/	BAN	Waiting turns
CL	11/27/	MLS	Strong confidence, parallel play, sometimes cooperative

Figure 12–8 Portfolio Evidence Sheet Example.

TOPICS in OBSERVATION

Dealing with Families Suspected of Child Maltreatment

It needs to be said here that discussions with families about their relationship with and treatment of their child are ongoing dialogues between teachers and families. That basic partnership relationship, which has been emphasized throughout this text, is never more important than in this section. Whether we feel the family just does not know about good hygiene, appropriate discipline techniques, or are deliberately hurting or neglecting their child to the point of placing them in danger, our position is the same. It is one of advocacy for the child and support and assistance to the family. When viewing the child in the cold with no socks or boots, or with a nasty bruise the shape of an adult hand, think again of the surrounding factors. This is not to make excuses but to try to understand the context in which the family lives.

The difference between sympathy—feeling sorry for the child and family—and empathy is doing something about it. In cases where it seems that the child does not have the necessities for health and comfort, such as adequate clothing or food, the teacher's first response is not to report the family to the Hotline but to try to supply the need, if there truly is one. It takes all the tact and caring one can muster to determine if the child does not have a coat or just will not wear one. Then, the next step may be some work with the family on parenting skills to help the family take the responsibility for enforcing basic needs (Figure 12–9).

Even in cases in which reports must be made for the health and protection of the child, an attitude of empathy for the family still must prevail. The teacher tries not to see the family as ogres or monsters, but as people who themselves are so needy or uninformed that these actions are really reactions to their own condition. The reporting then is not "tattling," but providing assistance to the family to get the help they all need— as well as protecting the child from harm. This can be communicated again and again to the family, but it is made even more evident by actions that support the family with physical acts of kindness, such as rides to appointments, a home-baked loaf of bread, or a phone call just to see how they are doing.

The teacher is an instrument of change in lives not only of the children in the group but their families. That is an awesome responsibility.

This section was prepared with the help of Jean Rose-Klein, Coordinator of the Broome County Child Abuse Council, Binghamton, N.Y.

Figure 12–9 The partnership attitude of teacher and families is never more important than when maltreatment is suspected.

© Cengage Learning 2014

machines, and clubs to improve that appearance. Sports figures are idols because they can jump, throw, catch, or move with outstanding coordination and skill. People measure themselves against others in appearance and physical ability.

Humans are social beings and crave approval, so interactions with other people profoundly affect how people perceive themselves. Connected to that social dimension is the emotional (or affective) side, where feelings sometimes overrule what one knows to be

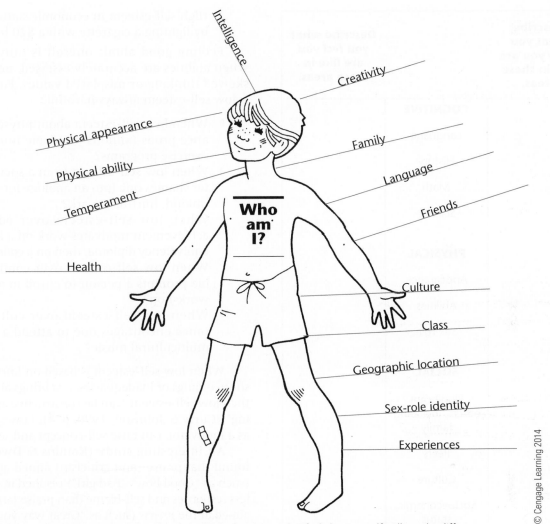

Figure 12–10 Who am I? What do others think of me? How do I feel about myself? All may be different.

© Cengage Learning 2014

true. One's ability to function mentally affects not only educational achievements but also life's decision making, possibly affecting economic status, which also has an affect on the perception of self. All of these components contribute to one's self-perception (Figure 12–10).

Assessing these areas objectively is the self-concept, what one knows about oneself. It is not, however, simply a matter of assessing those areas. Another dimension enters in, the affective domain: the emotions. For example, a person may know her weight is in the range of normal on the charts (self-concept) but feel she is too heavy. She feels fat and not very good about herself (self-esteem). It may not be a true measurement, but it is how the person perceives herself. It may be reflected from the appraisal of other people or distorted, as in anorexia nervosa.

EXERCISE Think about yourself in each of the areas listed in Figure 12–11. In the left column, write three words or phrases that you *know* about yourself in this category. In the right column, write three words or phrases about how you *feel* about yourself in this area.

Here is the tricky part: the dichotomy as Curry and Johnson (1990) call it, the division or two sides to the issue. They say, "Dichotomous thinking is also evident in the idea that good feelings about the self are always healthy, whereas bad self-feelings are to be avoided. But good feelings about the self can be self-deceptive and narcissistic (excessive pride)" (p. 4). For example, is it always desirable to have high self-esteem?

Describe what you *know* you are like in these areas.		Describe what you *feel* you are like in these areas.
	COGNITIVE	
	Language	
	History	
	Math	
	Science	
	PHYSICAL	
	Appearance	
	Abilities	
	Sex role	
	SOCIAL	
	Significant others, including family	
	Peers	
	Culture	
	Socioeconomic status	
	EMOTIONAL	
	Temperament	
	Emotional state	

© Cengage Learning 2014

Figure 12–11 Self-Concept and Self-Esteem Worksheet.

▶ High self-esteem about physical appearance is attained when a person finally diets down to 86 pounds?

▶ High self-esteem in sexual prowess is gained when a man brags he has fathered 12 children by 12 different women?

▶ High self-esteem in cognitive ability is demonstrated because a person has memorized the phone book?

▶ High self-esteem in peer acceptance is attained when a high school student gets a 20 on a math quiz because "Dumb is cool"?

▶ High self-esteem in economic status is proven by lighting a cigarette with a $20 bill?

Feeling good about oneself is only desirable when abilities are accurately assessed, not based on skewed thinking or misplaced values. For example, is low self-esteem always harmful?

▶ When low self-esteem about physical appearance prods millions of people into diets and exercise programs?

▶ When low self-esteem from a social encounter shames one into an apology for saying that unkind, hurtful remark?

▶ When low self-esteem over educational achievement motivates work on a high school equivalency diploma, then on a college degree?

▶ When low self-esteem over computer phobia prompts a person to enroll in a computer workshop?

▶ When low self-esteem over cultural ignorance encourages one to attend a concert of multicultural music?

When low self-esteem is based on knowing one's shortcomings or inadequacies, *and* brings about action, then low self-esteem "can be constructive and energizing" (Curry & Johnson, 1990, p. 4). Low self-esteem, as a motivator, can raise self-concept and self-esteem.

An interesting study (Kamins & Dweck, 1999) found that praise (and criticism) aimed at the *person* (such as "Good boy," "Bad girl") resulted in more helpless responses and self-blame than praise (and criticism) aimed at the *process* (such as "Great way you picked up your room," "You haven't picked up your room yet"). It makes sense. Excessive praise (such as, "You're so beautiful," "You're so smart" actually may lower self-esteem, because internally the child knows they are not always beautiful or smart. This may make children reliant on external rather than internal controls, constantly needing other's approval and discounting that little voice inside that gives a more realistic evaluation (Leary & McDonald, 2003). Selective praise is genuinely deserved for an action, such as "Wearing that color brings out the blue in your eyes," "you kicked that goal with power." Specific praise provides explicit information about what is being positively recognized without comparisons (Kostelnik et al., 2012).

Well-meaning people giving indiscriminate praise for the purpose of raising self-esteem can actually have the opposite effect. Insincerity, whether expressed to a child or an adult, is not believed and tends to be dismissed. When one knows or feels the praise is undeserved, it does not raise self-esteem. If the perception, or self-esteem, is higher than the actual ability, a false pride is present that may prevent future work on this area. This image of self is important to everyone, for it directly affects the motivation to change and learn.

EXERCISE Now look back at those words you wrote in the previous exercise. Where you see low self-esteem, let it be the motivator for a plan. Work to raise the competency, then the self-concept, then the self-esteem: self improvement plan!

Development of Self-Concept

Development, the progression from simple to complex over a period of time in sequential stages but at individual times, applies to both self-concept and self-esteem (Figure 12–12). The self-awareness of being separate and different from the environment and other people, a person in one's own right, is self-concept. It resides in the cognitive development realm, but connects with self-esteem in the emotional valuing of characteristics in the self-concept as positive or negative.

The First Year. The newborn infant is not aware of separateness from the environment. Actions are merely reflexes to stimuli. There is no recognition of self in the mirror, no recognition of people in his life. Between two and four months, the infant still has no concept of being separate. Now, however, needs are expressed in signals the family comes to understand. Coos and smiles appear as responses to those people who are cooing and smiling. The child begins to reach toward that image seen in the mirror because it may be something to touch and handle. No, it is just something cold and flat that cannot be put in the mouth to be explored.

The knowledge of separateness is attained by the end of the first year. The infant now knows he is separate from the people around him and the physical environment. Important people still magically appear and disappear (object permanence). Attempts to keep them present with smiles and sounds work only temporarily. They go away, perhaps never to return. The new mobility of the one-year-old allows the child to go look for those disappearing objects. The knowledge is there that they exist somewhere. If the legs could only support the body, those objects could be found. The baby reaches for the baby in the mirror. When a toy is seen in the mirror, the baby reaches to the mirror to grab it. The long journey of individuation is complete when the self or personal identity is developed.

During infancy and toddlerhood, the child's self-concept is primarily influenced by the family and those closest to the child. Information is received about being "good," "cute," "lovable," "capable," "smart," and "accepted." This forms the child's ideas about identity and capability (Figure 12–13).

Figure 12–12 Self-Concept Development.

Self-Esteem

Same-sex play partners reinforce gender identity
Gains identity in group membership
Comparing with peers: self-evaluation is reflected in what others think
Can describe attributes of self— boy/girl, tall, smart, physical
Measures self-esteem by physical accomplishments
Realizes inner thoughts are private
Tries other roles in play
Acts proud and ashamed
Talks about self
Self-assertion
Recognizes self
Attachment
Object permanence
Becoming separate

Wondering what others think

Looking at others and comparing to self

SE influenced most by family

Looking up at older children to see what is ahead

© Cengage Learning 2014

Figure 12–13 Self-identity begins in the mirror.

© Cengage Learning 2014

It Happened to Me

"My gamma"

My grandson lives a distance away from me, so visits were infrequent. In his second year, he acquired names for things that belonged to him. He proudly took me on a tour on one of my visits, holding my hand and pointing out "My chair," "My truck," My tebby-dare (teddybear)." Then he looked up at me and said "My gamma!" That's when the teardrops started.

The Second Year. After mastering walking, the toddler practices becoming more separate physically. She now takes journeys away and comes back, farther away, and back again. The toddler is checking each time that a return is possible if necessary. Trust is building that the person will be there when she needs her. Toward the second birthday, if a dot is placed on the child's nose and shown in the mirror, the toddler reaches not to the mirror but to the nose to take it off. Ah, the emergence of self!

Words are multiplying, and some important ones that show an increasing sense of self are "me," "mine," "me do it," and "NO." The child displays great pride when she attempts to do a task and it ends in success. If efforts fail, the child expresses disappointment. If scolded, the child shows shame. Sometimes a tantrum erupts when the emotions are so strong they cannot be controlled. This may bring embarrassment or a feeling of unworthiness from those the child knows best. Everyone has witnessed or felt helpless when a child throws a tantrum if his wants are not fulfilled. The child is really helpless also, unable to control his strong emotions.

Older Preschoolers. In the preschool years, children talk about being a boy or a girl, how old they are, how big they are, and what toys they have. Toward kindergarten age, they begin to remember the dreams they had last night and can talk about their thinking. They are beginning to realize their thoughts are part of a private self. No one else can see or know their thoughts unless they are revealed. They used to play with brooms to sweep and trucks to dump; then those brooms became horses and trucks were spaceships. Now they play with their friends in elaborate scenarios in which they leave themselves behind and become other people, talking with other people's words and voices and gestures, doing what grownups do. They constantly read their playmates' faces to look for acceptance. The teacher's words are carefully weighed against what they know they really can do. They are beginning to worry about what others will think of them.

Confronted with many new tasks to try, encouragement and approval of the attempts bring pleasant feelings of competence. This gives motivation to try the next new challenge, expending effort with the confidence of past successes. Success brings more success and even risks at failure. The overall feeling of well-earned, high self-esteem will emerge.

Another child may try as well at all those new things, drawing a circle, tying his shoe, naming his colors. But he is reminded his circle is not round. His shoe does not stay tied. This color is red, not green. Attempts at other tasks he is working on may not even be noticed. When he tries again, he feels anxiety because he does not really think he can do it. He could not do it before. Maybe he will not even try, or perhaps he will try but not very hard; then he will not be disappointed when he cannot do it. He looks to see who is watching, but no one is, so he does not even try. Someone comes along and says he did it perfectly and wonderfully, but he knows they are wrong. Even when he tries and it works, he believes it was just an accident. He really did not cause it to work. The child's feeling of incompetence is reinforced by powerful adults, such as family members and teachers, which causes a decline in motivation, unwillingness to try or risk, and results in lowered self-esteem. This is the beginning of the cycle of failure many children experience in school.

The social comparisons of this age are limited to the child's estimation of performance, mainly physical. They have come so far and can now do so many tasks that they could not do in toddlerhood, still a strong memory. They compare themselves to those big seven-year-olds who can ride a two-wheeler. Because of the successes of the past, they have no doubt they will be able to do it. Social comparisons to older, more developed children only bring hope and confidence of coming accomplishments.

Just as the preschooler is beginning to differentiate and classify colors, shapes and sizes, the he begins to classify people by race, social class (rich/poor), abilities and disabilities. It is a cognitive task to notice differences and form stereotypes based on children's limited knowledge and experience. Attitudes and then behaviors from these stereotypes are strongly influenced by those around them, families, peers, media (Epstein, 2009).

School-Agers. Feedback from formal schooling will be about peer acceptance, academic and athletic competence, and moral worth (Curry & Johnson, 1990). New abilities may be heightened by new challenges

It Happened to Me

"Listen to What He Did Now!"

Every day when Jason's mother would come to school, she had a horror story to relate about Jason's latest episode. He had deliberately poured grape juice on the white rug, painted the basement paneling with tar, and pulled up the neighbor's pumpkin patch. I tried to get her not to talk about these things in front of Jason and all the other families and children, but each day she came with a new story of his escapades. One day as the children arrived, I suggested they go check the incubator. "Oh no, you hatched chicks. Don't let Jason go near them. He'll kill them," she exclaimed. Well, you guessed it. Sometime during the free play time, Jason opened the incubator and squeezed a baby chick. Was this Jason's fault? He was just living up to expectations. It is sad that those expectations were not for kind acts, gentle touches, and controlled behavior. I often wonder about what happened to Jason. I wonder what I could have done to try to change his mother's attitude.

There is a sad follow-up to this story. Years later this child's grandfather was arrested for pedophilia. I wonder now if Jason was giving us signals that there was something awful happening in his life. For years I've wondered about Jason and now I have even more worrisome concerns.

competitiveness bring more reality to self-estimations than in the preschool years. The self-esteem is fragile with inside doubts of abilities and acceptance. Clubs, exclusive friendships, and put-downs of others stem from this quest to feel good about oneself.

Families and Schools That Build Self-Esteem

What makes the difference in children's self-esteem? Basic intellect? Innate ability? The family had more money? The family lived in the ghetto? It is all about acceptance. When efforts and independence are praised, they produce internal rewards (Harter, 1999). This gives the feeling of competence and confidence that motivates greater efforts, more independence, and higher self-esteem. The opposite is also true. Dependence is increased when efforts are criticized, and it is accompanied by feelings of incompetence and a lack of control. Anxiety and doubt fail to motivate. Future efforts are then approached tentatively, with expectations of failure. External rewards and the approval of others, which is rarely forthcoming, increase dependency. Competency and self-esteem are lowered.

The socialization of the family toward competency sets the course of the path. Children with high self-esteem have parents who are warm and accepting, provide reasonable expectations for mature behavior, and engage in positive problem solving (Rudy & Grusek, 2006). Children with low self-esteem, on the other hand, have families who are coercive, disapproving, insulting, rejecting, and controlling by strict restrictions (Kernis, 2002). The family has a primary influence over the child's self-esteem.

Schools also have a major part to play in the building of a child's self-esteem. Children need to build a sense of competency, to have an environment with experiences that develop real skills in the cognitive, physical, social, and emotional realms. They need to feel they have the power to make things happen. Involvement in decision making and understanding clear and realistic expectations helps children feel powerful. They thrive in a predictable environment where there are plenty of opportunities to make choices. Their opinions and ideas are accepted as worthy, and the curriculum capitalizes on their strengths. Teachers give informative praise that gives specific reactions and focuses on what children know and do. Negative labels are avoided. Questions about differences are answered directly and factually, discussing differences while calling attention to similarities. The classroom has non-stereotypic

or squashed by criticism and labeling. In this stage of Industry versus Inferiority, as Erikson (1963) called it, much of the self-esteem is dependent on school success. The child is moving into a new stage of cognitive development, Concrete Operations (Piaget, 1968). She is now in new social settings and more interested in the acceptance of friends than family. Most of the abilities in the physical realm will now be used more competitively in sports and in the writing tasks of school. All of these new opportunities can negatively or positively affect self-concept and self-esteem.

This is the age when comparisons to others and the internalization of what other people think is very important. Constant comparisons and materials such as books, dramatic play clothes and props, activities and role models. Children are seen as individuals.

That sounds like the teachers *know* each child and her accomplishments. The teachers have watched closely to determine the level of development of each child and have provided an environment where the child can have success. That is a place where a child can go to a Portfolio with his name on it and look at a history of his work. He can even add to it or take something out. He knows it was about all the things he could do.

🏠 Home Visitors and Developing Self Concept

Educators in the home truly get to see how the seeds of self-concept are planted in the everyday interactions of families and children in the natural environment of the home. Observing where the child fits in that home environment and what kinds of nurturing attention is paid to the child beginning in infancy gives the educator important information into how that child's sense of self will evolve. Home educators need to consider how to help families design the kinds of environments that support a child's sense of self. In some homes that can be very challenging, given the family's circumstances and the educator's own beliefs. It is important to feel comfortable having discussions with families about a child's sense of self. Connecting self-concept to school readiness and later success in school and life is often a motivating reason for parents to engage in the practices that support their child.

Self-Concept and Acceptance, Power, Morality, and Competence

Curry and Johnson (1990) present four themes, revisited throughout life as each person seeks to define the self (Figure 12–14).

Acceptance. From the attachment of the infant to the desire for friendship, **acceptance** is the human quest. Young children desire to please adults and other children. They want to feel they are worthy of being heard. From the crawler tugging on dad's pant leg to the tattler reporting other children's misdeeds, self-concept and self-esteem involve acceptance.

Power. The infant is exercising **power** when he struggles away from the shirt being pulled over his head. The toddler is exercising power when she says, "No." The preschooler exercises power when he

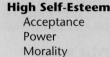

High Self-Esteem
Acceptance
Power
Morality
Competence

Low Self-Esteem
Isolation
Vulnerability
"Bad" Label
Dependent

© Cengage Learning 2014

Figure 12–14 Self-Esteem Factors.

chews his bread into a gun shape to escape the "No guns in school" rule. The teenager exercises power by sporting radical hairstyles or fashions. Adults exercise power through the vote, purchasing power, or in any number of ways. It is all a way of saying, "I can make things happen." That is part of self-concept, the knowledge that one has the ability to influence events rather than passively receive or observe them, resigned to accept their consequences.

Empowerment, Wald (2000) believes, is helping children toward self-awareness, encouraging willingness to take reasonable risks and explore their natural curiosity. To shift from teaching to empowering, she suggests the following:

▶ designing the environment to include child-directed activities
▶ implementing child-initiated curriculum
▶ recognizing individual talents
▶ encouraging peer help
▶ asking open-ended questions (pp. 14–15)

Morality. **Morality** is the innate desire to be considered "good" rather than "bad": the distinction between right and wrong by society. Self-esteem is affected by knowing the expectations or the rules and following them. The rules may be social, such as manners or certain behavior codes (such as being quiet in the movies or exhibiting a controlled rowdiness at a sports event). They may be legal (such as the observing the speed limit or not stealing), or they may be religious in nature. Self-esteem is increased by following the rules or meeting expectations. Rules and expectations can differ according to their context. Rules may even be contrary to the code of the majority of society, such as the Code of Thieves, or in the case of a cult or terrorist group. No matter what the group's expectations, following them gains acceptance, illustrates self-control, and represents a feeling of competence.

Kohlberg built upon Piaget's cognitive stages to consider stages of morality. Young children are in the Preconventional stage:

Obedience and punishment—there are fixed rules and when they are broken just punishment results.

Individualism and exchange—judging actions on how they serve individual needs. Beginning to see rules through their own lens.

Later stages of Interpersonal (living up to social expectations), and maintaining social order to consider society as a whole, considering different values, and universal principles that may conflict with laws are based on the foundations laid in early childhood, impacted by cognitive, social and emotional development (Kohlberg, 1973).

Robert Coles adds his advice to the area of morality in *The Moral Intelligence of Children* (1997), combining his stories of children he has interviewed with his thoughts about building character. He explores and wonders about children who are facing insurmountable odds and yet have a basic morality or strong character, and who are concerned about others above themselves. He does not call it self-esteem, and in fact eschews self-absorption and self-satisfaction in favor of self-denial and delayed gratification. He says therein lies the power and moral integrity that families and teachers should seek to impart.

Competence. Satisfaction is the result of accomplishing a task by applying knowledge, skill, and energy and seeing the expected result. This **competence** raises the self-concept and self-esteem. Self-evaluation of positive results brings positive feelings, the feeling of competence, gaining acceptance, demonstrating power, and adding to moral worth.

Acceptance, power, morality, and competence are threads that weave through all developmental areas as we observe children's behavior. Their influence affects self-concept and self-esteem.

Sex-Role Identity and Self-Esteem

Once the baby's **sex** (biological identification as male or female) is announced, the **sex-role** and **gender identity** begins to form, influenced by the people around the infant (Figure 12–15). In the first few days of life, the infant receives a name. This distinguishes her sexual identity to the rest of the world. Girls are held more gently, sometimes covered with a blanket of a certain color, and congratulations to her parents are sometimes tempered with resignation. She receives gifts that are soft

Figure 12–15 Sex-role identity is affected by society.

and pastel-colored, or toys that inspire nurturing actions instead of construction. She watches her mother to see what women are like and watches her father to see what men are like. Even at two years old, when she pretends to be grown up, she plays the role of mommy, not daddy. By three she tells people she is a girl because she has long hair. She knows that someday she will be a woman, though until she is almost six, she may think she can still change her mind. When she looks at toy advertising, she sees that the girls are playing dolls or the boys are building with blocks. When she watches television, she sees that most of the powerful roles are male. When she has boy playmates, they say, "You can't do this. You're a girl." Her grandma frowns when she climbs a tree and smiles when she pours the tea. She goes to preschool and the teacher says, "The girls can line up first because they're the quietest."

The child's understanding of human sexuality develops in stages. The infant begins to build a sense of being male or female and explores and gains pleasure from touching genitals. Toddlers learning vocabulary learn the terms (and possibly their positive or negative connotations) for body parts. They begin to view themselves as a boy or girl and classify others as one or the other by attributes such as length of hair or wearing certain colors. Preschoolers are keen observers, and sexual behavior and attitudes they see at home and on television play out in the classroom. They are more curious about the body parts of others and may want to touch and explore them. Early school-agers are learning the limits of privacy and are gaining knowledge of sexual behavior and pregnancy by asking questions. They have formed strong stereotypic roles, attitudes, and activities by generalizing what they have experienced (Sciaraffa, Randolph, 2011).

Children are **socialized**, taught the ways to behave in both overt and covert ways. Sexual identity begins with the physiology, the biological indicators of male or female. The view of one's own sexuality is gender identity—the socialized behaviors by parents, siblings, peers, significant other people, culture, and media—communicated by imitation, direct instruction, and reinforcement. **Gender** (the social and cultural construction of what it means to be male or female) enters the subject of self-concept and self-esteem when it is examined according to those four factors that Harter (1999) builds on—the same four issues as Curry and Johnson (1990) speak of as lifelong issues:

▶ *Acceptance*—Does she feel accepted as a girl, valued for her worth, not just because of her sex, or does she feel like she is valued less because of it?
▶ *Power and control*—Has she been given autonomy—power over herself—in making decisions, allowed to take risks?
▶ *Moral virtue*—Has she had opportunities to feel useful and "good," not guilty?
▶ *Competence*—Does she know about all the things she can do well, given opportunities to show her physical strength, logical mind, and self-reliant behaviors?

These are much more at issue for girls than boys, so the choice of using "she" in this section was deliberate. Stereotyping female gender behavior, such as dependency and weakness, has prevented girls from feeling powerful and competent, sometimes in subtle ways. Dr. Leonard Sax in *Why Gender Matters* (2005) suggests that parents and teachers recognize how boys and girls develop differently, and supports gender separate education and sports. He contends that coed schools reinforce stereotypes, limiting girls

from excelling in math and science, and boys from excelling in reading and writing by providing self-esteem building through academic excellence rather than appearance (for girls) and risk taking (for boys).

Perceptions about the body, even those acquired in infancy and toddlerhood during diapering, can affect self-esteem. When adults use words such as *dirty* or *nasty*, genital areas become associated with negative feelings. Children often engage in masturbation for a variety of reasons, most often because it is pleasurable. If the child perceives adults' reactions as negative, they can have an effect on how the child feels about his body, his sexuality, and total self-esteem. Children will also commonly engage in sex play, just as they play out other adult roles. In a similar way, the breadth of experiences will determine how much reality is incorporated into the play. Children often play out explicit television scenes in the preschool classroom or home playroom. Adult reactions to these simulations will also bring value judgments and affect self-concept and self-esteem about their play, and ultimately their sexual identity.

Observing Self-Concept and Self-Esteem

All areas of human development contribute to self-concept and self-esteem. Observable behavior demonstrates what a person knows and can do, and the feeling about that knowledge or ability. Self-esteem has defied researchers' attempts to devise measurements for it, especially for young children and those socialized in other cultures. The formation of the concept of self is highly variable in different cultures. Studying Euro-American children, Harter (1990) found two main categories early childhood educators used to define the high self-esteem child:

1. active displays of confidence, curiosity, initiative, and independence
2. adaptive reaction to change or stress

Inferring high or low self-esteem from observing behavior can be highly biased. Indicators of self-esteem in the Euro-American culture are the following:

▶ independent and takes initiative
▶ eager to try new things
▶ smiles and talks freely
▶ makes eye contact
▶ comfortable with peers
▶ takes pride in work and accomplishments
▶ uses imagination and takes initiative
▶ tolerates frustration, perseveres after mistakes (adapted from Fuchs-Beauchamp, 1996; Samuels, 1977)

The child's self-concept is observed while assessing each child's developmental areas. It is revealed in each of the domains of development detailed in the preceding chapters of this book. The Self-Esteem Class List Log will be used in Observation Plans: Week 12 Part A to note these characteristics or behaviors.

Separation. How the child separates from the family member at the beginning of the school year or day depends on the child's self-concept. The child has the sense of belonging and trust in the adult. He feels so worthy of love and care that he is sure his family member would not think of not returning to reclaim this treasure.

Self-Care. The child who is secure in her self-concept will feel capable and competent and will want to do things independently. She will want to take care of physical needs and not depend on adults. This is observed in the self-care area of toileting, eating, and dressing. The children whose families have given them instructions, let them try, and rewarded their attempts are more likely to be independent and do things for themselves.

Physical. Physical competence or ability instills pride (Figure 12–16). Climbing to the top of the climber and sliding down, riding the two-wheeler without training wheels, or printing one's name can raise a child's self-esteem. The child may have the physical ability but lack confidence in the ability. The resulting behavior is avoidance of the activity, need for assistance, or unsteadiness, resulting in a fall. All these behaviors only end in lowering self-esteem. The observer infers self-esteem while watching the physical skills and recording what the child accomplishes. The child's reactions when attempts are successful or unsuccessful give clues of self-esteem.

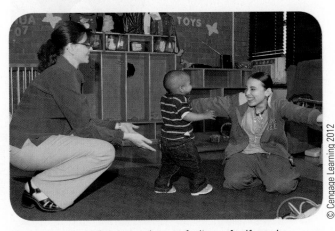

Figure 12–16 Abilities contribute to feelings of self-worth.

© Cengage Learning 2012

Social. Excessive withdrawal from social encounters show that the child may not feel worthy to be a friend. There may be other reasons, but self-concept is a strong determining factor in a child's social development. By observing children's interactions, the self-concept can be assessed. Self-esteem can be heightened when classroom activities promote prosocial behaviors.

Emotional. Self-esteem resides in the emotional realm. It is the feeling about the various competencies, the feeling about how capable one is compared to other people, the feeling about how acceptable one is as a playmate. This is observable in the demeanor of the child, the facial and verbal expressions that indicate the emotions inside. Children with good feelings about themselves will appear happy, while those who are uncertain of their competencies and worthiness will appear unhappy, sober, or expressionless. The inborn personality or temperament of the child enters into play here. Care must be taken not to misinterpret a more quiet, introspective person as one with low self-esteem.

Speech and Language. When people are in stressful situations or new encounters where they feel uncertain, it is normal to be more quiet and reserved. They may not risk revealing the self by speaking. As one becomes more accustomed to a situation, one feels more free to speak and less concerned about the hearer's reactions or judgments. The child who freely talks to teachers, other children, the janitor, the bus driver, or the UPS delivery person is usually displaying a strong self-concept. "I am important enough for you to listen to what I have to say." Hearing a child constantly say "I can't" will give clues that the child is feeling incompetent and unwilling to risk, indicating low self-esteem.

This is an area in which children who are unsure of their language (especially nonnative language speakers) are observed and often misjudged as having low self-esteem. Because they cannot speak or are unsure about their competencies in communication, they do not speak, even after they have learned many words. These children need to find other areas in the classroom in which to feel competent. Then language attempts will not be so much of a risk to self-esteem.

Memory and Attention Span. Just as emotions govern self-esteem, cognitive abilities govern self-concept. The child is using her cognitive and memory abilities to observe other children's capabilities. She remembers past attempts and failures. Because so many adult-child conversations rely on closed questions like a constant quiz—"What color is your shirt?" "How many crackers are on your napkin?" "What shape is this puzzle piece?"—children form an image very quickly of what they know and do not know in comparison to the adult's expectations. In creating an environment to build cognitive structures and positive self-esteem, opportunities should be presented for divergent thinking and exploring, not reciting.

Cognitive. Success breeds success. When a child feels successful and smart, she is more likely to approach challenges with confidence, extend herself to try new experiences, and tolerate a certain amount of less than perfection until the skill or concept is mastered. The success when a difficult task is accomplished raises confidence and self-esteem, so the cycle is on an upward motion. This is the spiral that families, teachers, and schools want for every child. Unfortunately, when a child feels unsuccessful, he is sometimes less willing to try harder, gives in to frustration, and perceives that his self-identity is totally affected by being less competent in one area. This downward spiral is difficult to reverse. The levels and expectations of academic content may not fit every child, so the risk exists for lowering self-esteem. Relative age to other children in the group also has an effect on self-esteem (Thompson et al., 2004). When children are relatively younger than classmates, they may experience lowered self-confidence and self-esteem, and older, age-advantaged children will feel greater confidence when they compare themselves to younger classmates. Older children in a group or grade cohort have been found to be placed in gifted and advanced programs more often. Younger classmates are more likely to be held back, be referred for psychological assessment, and labeled in need of remedial instruction. They may experience depression and hopelessness.

The skillful and aware parent and teacher know the child, recognize accomplishments, and scaffold areas where competence is close but not yet present. Learning is closely entwined with the emotions, so *feeling* smart is the first step in successful learning.

Literacy. School is a place of literacy. Watching the child's contact with the written word, whether in signs, books, or attempts at writing, can reveal self-concept. The child who has had the advantage of many opportunities with literacy will feel very comfortable in the literacy classroom. The child who has not will exhibit discomfort there, unable to listen and uninterested in stories. No connections are made between the sign in the block area and the sounds the alphabet letters make. It is difficult for the child to find his name on the helper chart. Behavior observations will inform the watcher. What the child is

not choosing is as revealing as what is chosen. Those areas and activities about which the child feels the least competent will not be chosen.

Creativity. Whether it is wondering about what a magnet will pick up, using a variety of materials to glue a design on a piece of tile, or acting as the pilot on an airplane bound for Disney World, children can be observed exhibiting creativity. There may be a child who is unwilling to try the magnet, depends on a pattern for art projects or avoids dramatic play. This gives the observer clues about not just creativity, but also self-esteem. It takes comfort and confidence in oneself to venture away from the tray of metal pieces the teacher has put out and into the room to test out other materials. It takes boldness to try to glue a nail on end to a collage. It inspires others to announce to the passengers on the pretend plane that she is about to have a baby. Creativity is being observed here, as well as self-concept and self-esteem (Figure 12–17).

Figure 12–17 Children should feel proud of their work.

© Cengage Learning 2014

Adjustment to a New Setting. Because of that secure attachment with the family, the child has the self-esteem to feel lovable. This makes the child feel capable enough to be comfortable in any setting after a nominal settling-in period. The child who learns self-control and follows the routines of the classroom shows confidence. Trust is exhibited that the teacher is a supporter, not an enemy. The child will feel secure enough to want to participate with the group. This gives the observer information, not just about the child's adjustment, but also about self-concept. Acceptable behavior is assumed and success is expected. This is observable behavior.

Are self-concept and self-esteem observable? Not in themselves, but by watching the child interact with the environment, peers, and adults, some substantial assumptions about self-concept and self-esteem can be made.

Independence or Interdependence?

Gonzalez-Mena (2008) asks this question and guides the teacher's thinking toward what the family wants for and expects of their child. In homes and cultures that value becoming an independent, autonomous individual, children are encouraged

and praised for separation without a fuss, early self-care, and high self-esteem. In homes and cultures where **interdependence** is valued and encouraged, children are expected to depend on adults to feed, clothe, and bathe them, are expected to center on serving the needs of others above self, and are encouraged to exhibit humility and a reticence to put the self forward.

Why Not Ask?

If a person wants the answer to a question, the most logical thing to do is ask someone who is most likely to know. Marshall (2001) suggests some questions an observer might ask a child, probably above four years old, that would get first-person information concerning self-esteem:

"What can you tell me about yourself? Why is that important?"
"What can you tell me that is best about you?"
"What are you good at doing?" (p. 46)

This is consistent with the principle of the child as the informant. When the adult asks the child, the child verbalizes what they may have never thought of before. "What am I good at?"

Helping All Children with Self-Esteem

It cannot be ignored that different ethnic, racial, cultural, and gender factors affect self-esteem. By two years old, when children have achieved a sense of self, they are capable of being shamed and feeling ashamed (York, 2003) and perceiving negative social status resulting in lowered self-esteem. Girls receive messages from parents and teachers that they do not have the ability to do math, and so reduce their efforts Bleeker & Jacobs, 2004). Low socioeconomic, ethnic minority children more often receive negative feedback from teachers resulting in low

It Happened to Me

"Bambino"

When I visited the city of Reggio Emilia, I took great pleasure in observing families on the street, in cafes, and in shops. In the city piazza, when a two-year-old refused to get on the back of his mother's bicycle and threw a tantrum on the sidewalk, I watched the old people for their reaction. No one looked critical or "tsked, tsked" the mother for not being in control. They were sympathetic with the child and said something that sounded like, "Poor bambino." When families were in cafes and restaurants, children of four and five were being fed every mouthful. I was fascinated. It was apparently the mark of good, loving parents to feed their children. In the Reggio Emilia schools, however, these same children were competent in feeding themselves, even using glasses, china, and sharp knives.

▶ ❚❚ TEACHSOURCE VIDEO CASE

Visit the Education CourseMate website at CengageBrain.com and watch the video entitled 5–11 Years: Self Concept in Middle Childhood.

Observe the children in each of these interviews asking "What can you tell me about yourself? How are they different by age?

academic self-esteem and achievement (Harris & Graham, 2007).

Culture, Race, and Self-Esteem

While the toddler's autonomy and the preschooler's independence may be a Western value, other cultures may hold those same accomplishments with contempt for children in their families. Expectations of competence and styles of interpersonal relations vary between cultures. For example, praising a Middle Eastern boy's ability to clear his dishes and wash the table may not raise his self-esteem in his own culture, where there is a strong division of male/female labor. The child who refuses to participate in a holiday event may not be antisocial but acting according to a religious tradition. Cultural differences affect behavior. They may be misinterpreted as a self-esteem issue. Conversely, expectations in the classroom may conflict with the positive self-concept and self-esteem of a child of a minority group.

Marshall (2001) cautions that behaviors that are valued and interpreted as indicators of high or low self-concept are strongly culture based. The value placed on independence, individuality, and self-assertion in Western society may not be shared by Eastern, African, or Latino cultures that value harmonious, interdependent relationships. Marshall makes the following suggestions:

1. Be aware of the ways your own culture influences your expectations of children.
2. Consider the cultural backgrounds of the children in your setting and their community.
3. Learn about the cultures from which the children in your program or school may come.
4. Use your basic knowledge of the culture to talk with each family about its values and practices.
5. Build what you have learned from each family. (p. 22)

Even awareness of ethnicity follows a developmental progression. At about three years old, a racial awareness begins, and by six years old it is well ingrained (Derman-Sparks & Edwards, 2010). Young children are in the throes of classification tasks. They are sorting by color and shape, looking for similarities and differences, and making matches of everything in their environment. It is only natural for them to look at each other and compare and contrast. They will notice racial cues, mainly the color of skin and texture of hair. While they are classifying, they are also labeling objects. Family and societal labels often have values attached, which the child also absorbs. Experiences and attitudes about groups that bear high or low self-esteem are transmitted. The young child absorbs all this as well.

Observation of racial awareness, especially when it is in the form of children's questions or negative comments, should be addressed right away. Derman-Sparks in *Anti-Bias Curriculums* (1989) recommends the following:

- Do not ignore.
- Do not change the subject.
- Do not answer indirectly.
- If you are uncomfortable, identify what gets in the way of your responding directly, matter-of-factly, and simply. (p. 33)

Disabilities and Self-Esteem

When disabilities interfere with a child's functioning while included in a regular classroom, self-concept and self-esteem issues arise (Figure 12–18). Peer relations are especially affected when hearing impairment impedes communication. Visual impairment depends on manual contact and results in less smiling. Physical impairments prevent active participation with other children. Autism spectrum disorder or mental retardation may reduce responsiveness or limit play options.

For these children, the self-concept and self-esteem issues are acceptance and the power to be independent and feel competent. Children with disabilities who have difficulty developing peer relationships suffer from loneliness, which results in poor self-esteem and increased anxiety

Figure 12–18 Peer relations contribute to self-concept and self-esteem.

and depression. This, in turn, prevents satisfactory friendships, and may result in even more serious emotional consequences (Pavri, 2001).

Children with normal abilities in an inclusive classroom become very aware of differences when they compare themselves to other children. Observers may see children playing at being visually, hearing, or physically challenged, making up explanations for the disability, and exhibiting fear (Kostelnik et al., 2012). All children should be recognized for their abilities rather than their disabilities, the labels applied to them, or the things they cannot do. This attitude or viewpoint will help all gain an understanding of differences, not disabilities, and give the acceptance that they all want. By recognizing the child's abilities and giving clear explanations of limitations, other children will be made aware of opportunities to help; but the disabled child must have plenty of opportunity to do what he can for himself. It is that old "never do for *any* child what he can do for himself" philosophy. It increases independence, raises competency levels, and ultimately results in positive self-esteem.

Child Maltreatment and Self-Esteem

Not every child lives in a positive environment that results in a healthy self-concept and self-esteem. Some may have unresponsive parents who are struggling with issues of their own, or they may be separated from parents and placed in a sequence of foster care placements. Unfortunately, children from birth to age three are the group most likely to be maltreated resulting in long-lasting developmental and mental health needs. These needs are often unrecognized and unmet by child agencies (Mulvihill, 2005). Children who have been abused have been found to give more focused attention to angry faces and voices, displaying anxiety symptoms and less attention to other relevant information (Shackman, Shackman, & Pollak, 2007).

Children who have had insensitive care feel themselves less worthy and less self-reliant. They tend to have difficulty interacting with peers, displaying hostility, aggression and lack of empathy. They expect rejection so they elicit rejection from others (Ferber, 2007). Again, the caution is not to infer child abuse in children who are reluctant to participate or take a risk (or always risking). The purpose of close, frequent observations with accompanying documentation is to build bodies of evidence to support

conclusions, and of course to use them to benefit the child and the family.

These are sensitive, yet vitally important, issues to young children's self-concept and self-esteem. They are challenging.

Helping Professionals for Child Abuse and Self-Esteem Concerns

There are many agencies and professionals in most communities to prevent, investigate, advise, protect, and even punish child abuse. Researchers, psychologists, and sociologists are seeking causes and solutions.

Child Protective Services—This is a governmental agency that receives, investigates, and takes action on reports of child abuse or maltreatment. The agency is a resource for education for mandated reporters, available to answer individual questions and work to advocate for the protection of the child. It protects the confidentiality of all records dealing with the family.

Psychologists and psychiatrists—With specialized training in social and emotional disorders, these professionals work with children and families on issues concerning the causes and results of abuse and maltreatment, but also issues dealing with self-esteem. Either abuse or self-esteem issues may interfere with the child's functioning in the social realm. These professionals may serve as resources for parenting education for the prevention of child abuse or the development of healthy self-concepts and self-esteem.

Other Methods

Other Methods to Record Self-Esteem:

(Be cautious about making judgments about a child's self-esteem. All that can be observed is the outward behavior, which may be interpreted inaccurately.)

Anecdotal/Running Records
Checklist/Rating Scale
Interviews/Conversations
Work Samples—Be careful about interpreting a
   child's art.
Media

Key Terms

acceptance	neglect
competence	physical abuse
disclosure	power
emotional	self-concept
maltreatment	self-esteem
gender	sex
gender identity	sex-role
interdependence	sexual abuse
mandated reporters	socialized
morality	unfounded

Plans

Go to the Education CourseMate website, accessed through CengageBrain.com, for the following:

Class List Log on Self-Esteem for all
Plan Week 12 Part A, Directions for a Class List Log on Self-Esteem, including What to Do with It, Portfolio Evidence Sheet Example, Sharing with Child and Family, Actions—Read a Book, In the Environment, In the Curriculum, In the Newsletter
Plan Week 12 Part B, Directions for Anecdotal Recording to observe self-identity for Group C
Plan Week 12 Part C, Reflective Journal

Resources

Crosson-Tower, C. (2010). *Understanding child abuse and neglect.* Boston: Allyn & Bacon.
Derman-Sparks, L. (1989). *Anti-bias curriculum: Tools for empowering young children.* Washington, DC: National Association for the Education of Young Children.
Derman-Sparks, L., Edwards, J. O. (2010). *Anti-bias education for young children and ourselves.* Washington, DC: NAEYC.
Ensher, G. L., Clark, D. A., & Songer, N. S. (2009). *Families, infants, and young children at risk: Pathways to best practice.* Baltimore, MD: Brookes.
Epstein, A. S. (2009) *You, me, us: Social-emotional learning in preschool.* Ypsilanti, MI: HighScope.
Ferber, J. (2007) "A look in the mirror: Self-concept in preschool children." In Koplow, L. *Unsmiling faces: How preschools can heal.* New York: Teachers College Press.
Fontes, L. A. (2005). *Child abuse and culture: Working with diverse families.* New York: Guilford Press.
Karageorge, D., & Kendall, R. (2008). *The role of professional child care providers in preventing and responding to child abuse and neglect.* Washington, DC: DHHS. Available: www.childwelfare.gov/pubs/usermanuls/childcare.
Kostelnik, M., Gregory, K. Soderman, A., & Whiren, A. (2012). *Guiding children's social development and learning* (7th ed.). Belmont, CA: Wadsworth Cengage Learning.
NAEYC. (1996). Position statement on the prevention of child abuse in early childhood programs and the responsibilities of early childhood professionals to prevent child abuse. Washington, DC: Author.
Prevent Child Abuse America, www.preventchildabuse.org
Seibel, N. L., Britt, D., Gillespie, L. G., & Parlakian, R. (2006). *Preventing child abuse and neglect: Parent-provider partnerships in child care. A Zero to Three training curriculum.* Washington, DC: Zero to Three.
Young-Eisendrath, P. (2008). *The self-esteem trap: Raising confident and compassionate kids in an age of self-importance.* New York: Little, Brown.

CHAPTER 13

Using Program Assessments to Look at Children in Groups

OBSERVATION THOUGHT

"Pointing the finger of blame at others—the child, the family or the program—leaves three fingers pointing back at us. We must reflect on what we can do to make things better for the child, the family, and the program."

NAEYC Standards **naeyc**

The following NAEYC Standards for Early Childhood Professional Preparation are addressed in this chapter:

Standard 3: Observing, Documenting, and Assessing to Support Young Children and Families

Standard 6: Becoming a Professional

IN THIS CHAPTER

▶ Assessing Early Childhood Programs

▶ Topics in Observation: Assessing the Environment—Pointing Back at You

▶ Looking at the Adjustment of the Child to the Program

▶ Observing How Infants and Toddlers Adjust to Group Settings

▶ Helping All Children in Group Settings

▶ Helping Professionals for Program Evaluation and Support

Assessing Early Childhood Programs

The child is enrolled in an early childhood group setting. It could be in a child-care center of many types: for-profit, nonprofit, employer-supported family day-care home, or a religiously affiliated program. It may be a part day program called a preschool, nursery, nursery school, play group, or parent cooperative. Head Start programs serve thousands of three- to five-year-olds across the country, and in some places Early Head Start serves infants and toddlers. Public and private schools provide educational experiences for children from kindergarten up. Some schools also have programs for prekindergarten and some for infants and toddlers as well. Many school districts and outside agencies provide programs for children before and after school and on school holidays. There are many programs for children with special needs to receive early intervention in separate settings or included in regular classrooms. Some programs draw specific audiences, such as music, gymnastics, and dance schools. No matter what kind of program a child is enrolled in, the primary responsibility of that program is to keep the child safe and to deliver the services the family expects. But how does one know if it is a quality program?

With the role of the family as the primary educator and socializing agent of children, it becomes increasingly important for all of society to support those roles. When the family is strengthened, society is strengthened. Children's programs providing child care while family members work or are in school also provide respite from the stresses of parenting, strengthen child development, and strengthen the family with positive outcomes for all. When looking at the total environment enveloping a child, relationships between young children and adults that are emotionally secure and characterized by high-quality instruction are key factors in children acquiring academic and social and emotional competence (Mashburn & Pianta, 2006).

Accountability of a program's ability to meet outcomes and expectations has been discussed earlier in this book, but this section presents some vehicles for doing so. Meisels (2006) suggests, "The way to measure program quality is to gather data on low child-staff ratios; training of staff in early childhood development; provision of continuing professional development; use of practices that are developmentally appropriate; levels of positive interaction between children and staff; continuity and competitive salaries and working conditions for staff; and the creation of a safe, caring environment and one that encourages strong parental involvement" (pp. 16–17). Notice that many of these quality benchmarks focus on the teacher. This section will not review the implications of teacher qualifications, training, working conditions, and salaries, but recognize the readers of this text as those pursuing excellence and valuing professional preparation as advocates not only for themselves but also for the programs and children with whom they will work. The assumption is made that you recognize, advocate for, and seek employment in such programs.

Whenever young children are in group settings outside their home, the program should be evaluated by some regulating body or agency, for its safety and appropriateness for children. Each state has its own criteria and process for licensing or regulating the care and education of children in groups.

There are various labels for the terms under which programs operate:

- **Standard**—defines a goal of practice with an incentive for compliance, not a legal term but agreed upon by evidence-based research to be best practice.
- **Recommendation**—a statement of practice issued by an organization that provides a health benefit to the population it serves.
- **Guideline**—advice issued by a professional organization or instruction on practices focused on a specific area.
- **Policies**—individual set of practices adhered to by an organization.
- **Regulation**—legal rules usually based on standards, guidelines or recommendations.

EXERCISE **Identify the regulatory agency for the program in which you work or are doing observations.**

child care—state licensing agency
school—state agency

Obtain a copy of the regulations and look for the method of program evaluation: yearly review or report, on-site visit, or accreditation.

Program evaluations collect information to make informed judgments and decisions about the program. It could be to

- evaluate the program against a standard.
- assess the program's adherence to its stated mission and philosophy.
- receive feedback from various constituencies, such as children, families, program administrators, teachers, funders, and community agency personnel.
- assess the program's suitability for an individual child.
- provide measures of accountability (LaMontagne & Russell, 1998).

Families are the most important evaluators, as well as those with the greatest risk, of their own child. Families have the right and responsibility to freely access the building in which their child is enrolled. They should ask questions and observe that the program meets their expectations and their child's needs. Families should have a voice in evaluating the program, no matter what type it is. There are many family surveys available that can be adapted to ask specific questions about the program. These surveys typically include questions concerning families' satisfaction with the facilities, program, and staff; communication; interactions between the child and staff; comfort with the policies and procedures; and suggestions or recommendations.

Administrators, staff, and families should regularly evaluate all aspects of the program. There are many organizations that offer an accreditation component to their members (listed in a later section). The common standards against which the accreditation process evaluates the program are the following:

environment
health and safety
administration
curriculum
staffing
relationships: child to adult and families
    to program
evaluation

Some sample questions for program evaluation are included in Figure 13–1.

The observation-and-recording method of this section is not focused on the child, but on the program. Several program evaluation tools are presented to familiarize the reader with options available to assess the quality of the early childhood program. The Program Evaluation Questions in Figure 13–1 can be applied to all settings where children spend time outside of the home, regardless of age of child or type of program.

A Setting Observation

EXERCISE **Let's take a trip to a child-care center or school. You can think about one you have visited or make up one in your mind. No children need to be present. You will observe the setting to see what it tells you. Drive into the parking lot.**

What do you see? What could it mean? (Record your answers on a separate sheet of paper.)

From the parking lot:
Sign for the program:
Playground:
Entrance way:
Inside a classroom:
Children's spaces:
Learning materials:
Displays:
Adult spaces:

Reactions to a Setting Observation

Without ever observing a program in action, much information is gathered, impressions formed, and judgments made. A program's purpose and practices are readily observed and interpreted from the

environment. It is healthy to inspect one's own environment with a visitor's eye. It is also an exercise in professionalism to visit other programs. These bits of information are taken in by the senses and associated with information already stored. Reflection on possible meanings of what is observed may give insight or allow the viewer to make inferences about the values, philosophies, economic sponsorship, and even the housekeeping habits of the teacher. Some decisions for action can result, such as the following:

"Oh, I can't wait to get back to my classroom and use that idea."
"I could really tell they emphasize. . . ."
"I wonder what they did with that. I'll have to ask."
"I wonder how they provide for. . . ."
"If that were my room, I would. . . ."
"I certainly don't agree with . . . but they must have a different philosophy."
"I will not comment on . . . but I can talk about. . . ."

As a professional courtesy, write a note of appreciation for allowing the visit and a specific aspect that you liked. Remember the evaluation principles: Look for the accomplishments, not the deficits; specific praise raises self-esteem.

Program Assessments

EXERCISE **What do these things tell you?**

checkbook balance
bathroom scale
speedometer
wristwatch
windsock
mirror
bookmark
diploma
roadmap
report card

▶❚❚ TEACHSOURCE VIDEO ACTIVITY

Visit the Education CourseMate website at CengageBrain.com and watch the video entitled Preschool Children: Appropriate Learning Environments and room Environments.

View this before and after segment of arranging the learning environment. Compare the components to the Program Evaluation Questions in Figure 13–1.

PROGRAM EVALUATION QUESTIONS

Evaluation instruments vary with the purpose of the program evaluation. Moreover, a survey of various program evaluations shows that many are designed to be program-specific; that is, the evaluation itself is devised to examine one program only. Individualized assessments are difficult to generalize. However, it appears that most program evaluations assess several, if not all, of the following areas:

The Physical Environment

Are the facilities clean, comfortable, safe?

Are room arrangements orderly and attractive?

Are materials and equipment in good repair and maintained?

Is there a variety of materials, appropriate to age levels?

Are activity areas well defined?

Is cleanup and room restoration a part of the daily schedule?

Are samples of children's work on display?

Is play space adequate, both inside and out?

Is personal space (e.g., cubby) provided for each child?

The Staff

Are there enough teachers for the number of children? How is this determined?

Are the teachers qualified? What criteria are used?

Is the staff evaluated periodically? By whom and how?

Does the school provide/encourage in-service training and continuing education?

Do the teachers encourage the children to be independent and self-sufficient?

Are the teachers genuinely interested in children?

Are teachers aware of individual abilities and limitations?

What guidance and disciplinary techniques are used?

Do teachers observe, record, and write reports on children's progress?

Are teachers skilled in working with individual children, small groups, and large groups?

Does the teaching staff give the children a feeling of stability and belonging?

Do teachers provide curriculum that is age-appropriate and challenging?

How would you describe the teachers' relationships with other adults in the setting? Who does this include, and how?

Can the teaching staff articulate good early education principles and relate them to their teaching?

Family Relationships

How does the classroom include families?

Are family members welcome to observe, discuss policies, make suggestions, help in the class?

Are different needs of families taken into account?

Where and how do families have a voice in the school?

Are family–teacher conferences scheduled?

Does the school attempt to use community resources and social service agencies in meeting families' needs?

The Organization and Administration

Does the school maintain and keep records?

Are there scholarships or subsidies available?

What socioeconomic, cultural, religious groups does the school serve?

What is the funding agency, and what role does it play?

Is there a school board and how is it chosen?

Does the school serve children with special needs or handicaps?

Are the classroom groups homo- or heterogeneous?

What hours is the school open?

What age range is served?

Are there both full- and part-day options?

Is after-school care available?

Does the school conduct research or train teachers?

What is the teacher–child ratio?

The Overall Program

Does the school have a written, stated education philosophy?

Are there developmental goals for the children's physical, social, intellectual, and emotional growth?

Are the children evaluated periodically?

Is the program capable of being individualized to fit the needs of all the children?

Does the program include time for a variety of free, spontaneous activities?

Is the curriculum varied to include music, art, science, nature, math, language, social studies, motor skills, etc.?

Are there ample opportunities to learn through a variety of media and types of equipment and materials?

Is there ample outdoor activity?

Is there a daily provision for routines: eating, sleeping, toileting, play?

Is the major emphasis in activities on concrete experiences?

Are the materials and equipment capable of stimulating and sustaining interest?

Are field trips offered?

Do children have a chance to be alone? In small groups? In large groups?

Figure 13–1 Program Evaluation Questions.

It Happened to Me

Where Is Everyone?

I was attending a meeting at the office of a child-care director. I arrived on time and walked through the center without hearing a sound, an eerie feeling. What could that mean?

As I walked down the hall, I smelled, then saw, vomit puddles ahead of me. I called out, "Anybody here?" A weak voice from the other end of the hall replied, "In here." It was from the bathroom where two staff people and one child were huddled over sinks. A volatile virus had struck, and all other children and staff had been sent home, some sick, and the rest as a precaution. This little person and two staff were the last ones left but were sick as well. What a pitiful sight! I donned gloves and helped them clean up. The meeting had been cancelled since the director had gone home, too sick to think of calling me. Illness can strike quickly and powerfully when people are in group settings.

Child Observation Method	Program Observation
Developmental Checklists	Checklists: Safety Appropriate programming
Anecdotal Records	Teacher's stories
Frequency Counts	Teacher behaviors Use of slang Negative discipline
Time Samples	Assess learning center use Measure effect of adult presence in learning area
Interviews	Family/child surveys Family/teacher conferences
Work Samples	Examples of teacher projects Bulletin boards Newsletters
Observation	Outside reviewers Licensing agents Accreditation validators

© Cengage Learning 2014

Figure 13–2 Observation Techniques for Program Evaluations.

Yes, you guessed it. You are so clever. These are all measurements or visual indicators of important facts. Money, weight, speed, time, wind direction, hair check, last chapter read, course completed, roads traveled, evaluation—constant vigilance is part of life.

In *Week by Week*, many areas of child development have been examined for indicators of progress and possible delays. Programs need evaluation as well for indicators of progress and warning signs of poor quality situations. **Program evaluation** can be informal, such as a staff discussion at the end of the year to recap the successes, the difficulties, and forecasts based on the past. Aspects of program quality can be measured with some of the same methods used to observe children's development (Figure 13–2).

An important measuring stick of a program's effectiveness is the growth and development of the children enrolled. Attendance figures give indicators of the health and safety procedures of the program: Young children in close surroundings do not share toys, but they do share germs, and staff must give constant consideration to infection control. High absence rates could be a sign of lax infection control standards and procedures.

Children require nourishment to grow. If they are nourished developmentally, they will show progress. Portfolios measuring children's progress are one indication of an effective program. Another indicator is children's active involvement with the learning environment. Peeks into classrooms should show children busy working on a variety of activities with the adults facilitating the learning. The rooms should be filled with children's voices—talking and laughing—with a minimum of adult voices. Children can be surveyed to hear what they have to say about the school, the program, and the learning activities. Even very young children can tell what they like about their school or child-care center and what they do not like. Adults should listen.

Periodic evaluations of early childhood programs are necessary to measure the effectiveness of the program and for accountability. Some indicators stated in the NAEYC, NAECS/SDE position statement (2003) include the following:

Evaluation is used for continuous improvement.
Goals become guides for evaluation.
Comprehensive goals are used.
Multiple sources of data are available.
Sampling is used when assessing individual children as a part of large-scale program evaluation.
Safeguards are in place if standardized tests are used as part of evaluations.
Children's gains over time are emphasized.
Well-trained individuals conduct evaluations.
Evaluation results are publicly shared.

Total Program Evaluations

There are many evaluation instruments available; some are mandated by the type of the program, others are voluntarily chosen. All have evaluation for program improvement as their basic premise: the assessment or measurement of aspects of the program, comparison with an accepted standard of quality, and action implemented to bring the program into compliance or increased effectiveness.

Quality Rating and Improvement Systems (QRIS). Many states have launched initiatives to raise the quality of early childhood programs in their state through a system of rating systems, with participation either voluntary or linked to state and private funding for improvement. The ratings are aligned with state early learning standards and regulatory requirements, and can assist consumers in educating and communicating about early childhood education quality.

Accreditation. **Accreditation** is a program evaluation completed on-site by an outside body, usually a professional organization, for the purpose of recognizing programs that meet pre-established criteria. The accreditation process usually begins with an extensive self-study that leads to improvements in the program before the validation visit. Fees are charged for accreditation, and usually some kind of periodic reports are required to describe the maintenance of the level of quality. Families can use accreditation as a measuring tool when selecting a program. See Figure 13–3 for a comparison chart of some of the systems.

High/Scope—PQA High/Scope Program Quality Assessment. High/Scope has developed a program evaluation tool for all early childhood settings, especially those implementing the High/Scope Curriculum, the *High/Scope Program Quality Assessment,* second edition (2003). It has expanded sections for evaluating the following:

- learning environment
- daily routine
- adult–child interaction
- curriculum planning and assessment
- family involvement and family services
- staff qualifications and staff development
- program management

Potential uses of the PQA include staff training, program assessment and monitoring, observation and feedback, research and evaluation, and information and dissemination.

NAEYC Center Accreditation. The National Association for the Education of Young Children (NAEYC) has an accreditation system for early childhood programs, the *NAEYC Early Childhood Program Standards and Accreditation Criteria* (2005), which is the National Commission on Accreditation Reinvention's plan to improve the quality of care and education for young children in early childhood programs. To be eligible for accreditation, programs must serve a minimum of 10 children from birth through age five in part- or full-day group programs, have been in operation at least one year, and meet state **license requirements** (or be exempt from state requirements). The criteria measure interactions between staff and children and staff and families. They also look at the administration of the program, curriculum, physical environment, health, safety, and nutrition. Staff needs are assessed by criteria for staff qualifications and development, staffing patterns, and program evaluation through a three-step process in which program personnel and families conduct a self-study, rating various standards as unmet, partially met, or fully met. This self-study is designed to indicate areas that need improvements; an improvement plan is implemented and ratings are changed. Classroom staff, administrators, and families have their own components to assess. Once the self-study and ensuing improvements are complete, the administrator submits the program description to the NAEYC Academy and applies for a validation visit. The NAEYC Academy assigns a "validator" to observe in the classrooms and spot check the documentation of the administrator's report to validate or confirm that the ratings are accurate. That validation

Crosswalk of Early Childhood Program Standards

	NAEYC Program Accreditation	Head Start Program Standards	National Health & Safety Standards	High/Scope PQA	National Association for Family Child Care Accreditation	Middle States Association of Colleges & Schools
Child Development and Education	1. Relationships 2. Curriculum 3. Teaching 4. Assessment	1304.21 Education & Early Childhood Development	2. Program: Activities for Healthy Development 3. 7 IDA Eligible Children	Adult/Child Interaction Curriculum Planning & Assessment Daily Routine	1. Relationships with Children 3. Developmental Learning Activities	Indicators for Schools with early age programs 8.18-8.20 Integrated Curriculum
Child Health & Safety	5. Health	1304.22 Child Health and Safety	3. Health Promotion & Protection 6. Infectious Diseases	Learning Environment	4. Safety and Health	Standard 7. Health & Safety
Nutrition	5. Health	1304.23 Child Nutrition	4.Nutrition & Food Service		4. 73 Nutrition and Food Preparation	
Mental Health	1. Relationships	1304.24 Child Mental Health				
Parent Involvement	7. Families	1304.4 Family Partnership		Parent Involvement & Family Services	1. Relationships with Parents and Family	3.17 Family input
Management Systems	10. Leadership and Management	1304.51 Management Systems and Procedures	8. Administration	Program Management	5. Professional and Business Practices	2. Governance & leadership 6. School Climate & organization
Staff Management	6. Teachers	1304.52 Human Resources Management	1. Staffing	Staff Qualifications & Staff Development	5. Assistants and Substitutes	
Facilities and Equipment	9. Physical Environment	1304.53 Facilities, Materials, & Equipment	5. Facilities, Supplies		2. The environment—Home	5. Facilities
	www.naeyc.org/ accreditation	www.eclkc.ohs.acf. gov/hs/c/standards/ HeadStartrequirements	http://nrckids.org	www.highscope.org	Http://nafcc.org	www.msche.org

Figure 13–3 Program Evaluation Comparison.

report is submitted to a three-person commission for the accreditation decision. Programs are not required to demonstrate 100 percent compliance. The accreditation is valid for 3 years; then the self-study and validation are repeated.

NACCP Program Accreditation. The National Association of Child Care Professionals (NACCP) serves child-care center owners, directors, and administrators, regardless of tax status or corporate sponsorship. Their National Accrediting Commission makes the decision to award accreditation to programs following the self-study phase, where improvements can be made, and validation of the self-study report by an on-site observation. The standards' key components are curriculum, interaction, parents, health and safety, and administration.

NECPA Program Accreditation. National Early Childhood Program Accreditation (NECPA) calls for the owner or director to assemble demographic information and lead a self-paced, self-study evaluation. Surveys are completed by staff and families, along with classroom observations. Improvements are made to the program based on the evaluations, and the program participates in an on-site verification visit by an assigned validator. The scored indicators and program profile are presented to the NECPA's National Accreditation Council for the accreditation decision. The accreditation is valid for three years.

The NECPA's accreditation system is entering the technological age with a new automated process, dubbed *Automated Accreditation Indicator Systems (AAIS)*.

Family Child Care Accreditation. The National Association for Family Child Care (NAFCC) also has an accreditation system for family child-care workers: the *National Association for Family Child Care Accreditation*. These are teachers who provide licensed or regulated care for other people's children in the provider's home for more than 18 months. The standards include relationships, environment, developmental learning activities, safety and health, and professional and business practices. It requires a provider self-evaluation with the assessment profile for family child care, family questionnaires, a family observation, and validator observation. This also is valid for three years.

School-Age Program Accreditation. The National AfterSchool Association has a program improvement and accreditation process to promote quality in programs serving children 5–14 years old in afterschool programs. Following a self-study, endorsers conduct an on-site visit to verify the self-study report.

Home-visiting Program Accreditation. Because there are so many models of home visiting, there is no one accrediting body or tool that is used nationwide. Each program uses its own tool that gathers data to measure the outcomes of the specific program. A fairly new tool that shows promise is the Home Visit Rating Scales-Adapted (HOVRS-A) which measures the quality of the home visitor's interactions, responsiveness, relationships, and nonintrusiveness with the family; the parent's interaction and engagement; and the child's engagement during the home visit (Roggman et al., 2008).

Special Focus Instruments

There are some formal program assessment tools that can be used to evaluate one aspect of a program. This can be accomplished as a self-study, by the administration, or by a consultant. The advantage of a self-study is that the staff considers quality criterion items, standards set by an outside source. These are less threatening and not taken as criticism or a pet peeve, but as objective benchmarks against which to compare and consider their appropriateness for the particular situation.

When evaluations are done by the director or administrator, it gives them first-hand information about the program, recognizing its strengths. It also may indicate areas that need attention, from which they can implement change. Often the staff have been aware of the situation and desiring change, but were not in a position to make the change themselves. Now that can happen. This type of evaluation, however, can stress the staff and alienate them from administrators if they feel they are under scrutiny. Evaluation is only helpful if it focuses on strengths and if plans build on those strengths, and not the deficits. They can be addressed in a cooperative way with group decision making more effectively than from edicts or top-down proclamations.

Outside consultants may be enlisted to perform the assessment. This objective outside person can observe, evaluate, and make recommendations without fear of recriminations from administrators or alienation from the staff. Issues that staff or administrators have been aware of can surface from an outside consultant, and can be addressed easier than from within. Whatever the source of evaluation, the outcome should be to discover and proclaim the strengths of the program and recommend changes or next steps that are reasonable, attainable, and measurable. This is the same principle that is used in the child's developmental evaluation.

Here are a few program evaluations that may be used and a short description of each evaluation's use.

Early Childhood Environment Rating Scale—Revised (ECERS-R).
The ECERS-R (Harms, Clifford, & Cryer, 2005) is a comprehensive rating scale to assess personal-care routines, furnishings and displays, language-reasoning experiences, fine and gross motor activities, creative activities, social development activities, and adult needs. Each is rated on a scale of one to seven, with quality points of one, three, five, and seven described in detail. ECERS-R's format gives clear criteria and a goal for improvement if a score of less than seven is determined (see example in Chapter 9, Figure 9–5).

Family Child Care Environmental Rating Scale (FCCERS-R).
The FCCERS-R (Harms, Cryer & Clifford, 2007) is very similar to the ECERS-R described above, but designed to be used in family child-care homes.

Assessing Quality in The Early Years: Early Childhood Environment Rating Scale (ECERS-E), 4e.
ECERS-E, 4e (Sylva & Siraj-Blatchford, 2011) is an adaptation of the ECERS-R with ratings specific to curriculum areas. One of the criteria of quality in this rating scale is planning for individual learning needs based on records kept on individual children. (See Figure 13–4.)

Assessment of Practices in Early Elementary Classrooms (APEEC).
The APEEC (Hemmeter et al., 2001) is also modeled after the ECERS-R with the rating scale format, designed to measure developmentally appropriate practices in the primary grades, helping practitioners and researchers understand elementary school practices in grades K–3 serving children with and without disabilities.

Rating Observation Scale for Inspiring Environments (ROSIE).
ROSIE (Deviney et al., 2010) is a companion observation guide for the book *Inspiring Places for Young Children* (Deviney et al., 2010). It is a rating scale to measure the aesthetic design elements of color, focal points, texture, lighting, displays, and the use of space and nature. It uses quality points of "1—sprouting," "2—budding," and "3—blooming" to measure the indicators.

Infants and Toddlers.
The *Infant/Toddler Environment Rating Scale, Revised Edition*—ITERS (Harms, Cryer, & Clifford, 2006) follows the same format as the ECERS-R, but is specific to younger age groups.

Neither one of these rating scales specifically looks at curriculum. The *Family Day Care Rating Scale* (Harms & Clifford, 2007) and the *School-Age Care Environment Rating Scale* (Harms, Jacobs, & White, 1996) are two additional rating scales measuring environments for special settings.

Quick Quality Check for Infant and Toddler Programs by Knoll and O'Brien (2001) is just that: a quick, easy-to-use checklist that rates classrooms for standards of quality care not typically covered in licensing guidelines.

National Health and Safety Performance Standards (2112).
The American Academy of Pediatrics, Public Health Association, and National Resource Center for Health and Safety in Child Care have developed an extensive set of **performance standards** that include educational as well as health and safety guidelines. The standards are based on 18 guiding principles that include program policies and procedures.

Staff Performance.
There are many instruments created to measure staff performance. *Measuring Performance: The Early Childhood Educator in Practice* (Elliott, 2002) is a comprehensive guide that can be used for both program performance and spot checks on teacher-demonstrated cognitive, creative, affective, language/literacy, social, and physical behaviors. It also contains separate checklists for measuring child development, diversity, and safety forms for developing staff and program action plans.

Classroom Assessment Scoring System (CLASS) by Pianta and associates (2008) is an observation tool to assess classroom quality in prekindergarten through grade 3 based on teacher-student interactions in the classroom rather than the environment or curriculum.

Quality of Early Childhood Care Settings: Caregiver Rating Scale (QUEST) by Goodson and associates (2005) is a Caregiver Rating Scale that focuses on caregiver warmth/responsiveness and caregiver support for the child's development in cognitive, language, early literacy, emotional, social, and physical areas.

Administration.
The *Program Administration Scale* (Talan & Bloom, 2004) uses the same rating scale format as the ECERS (Harms, Clifford, & Cryer, 2005) with criteria to assess the administration of a child-care center.

Anti-Bias Curriculum.
Derman-Sparks (1989) lists questions to be answered from videotaped classroom observations. Peers examine interactions between

	INADEQUATE		MINIMAL		GOOD		EXCELLENT
	1	2	3	4	5	6	7

DIVERSITY

13. Planning for Individual Learning Needs

Ask to see the records kept on individual children.

INADEQUATE (1–2)	MINIMAL (3–4)	GOOD (5–6)	EXCELLENT (7)
1.1 Activities and resources are not matched to different ages, developmental stages, or interests.* P,Q	3.1 Some adaptation is made to address specific needs of individuals or groups (Ex. additional learning or English language support).*P, Q	5.1 The range of activities provided draws on children's interests and includes all developmental stages and backgrounds, enabling all children in the group to participate to promote their success and learning.* P, Q	7.1 The planning and organization for social interaction enables children of all developmental stages and backgrounds to participate at an appropriate level in both individual and common task (F pairing children of different ages and abilities for certain tasks).* Q, P
1.2 Planning is not written down.* P	3.2 Some of the written planning shows differentiation for particular individuals or groups.* P	5.2 Daily plans are written with the specific aim of developing activities that will satisfy the interests and needs of each child, either individually or as groups.* P	7.2 Planning sheets identify the role of the adult when working with individuals/pairs/groups of children. Planning also shows a range of ability levels at which a task activity may be experienced.* P
1.3 Written planning takes no account of specific individuals or groups. P	3.3 Written records indicate some awareness of how individuals have responded to activities, or of the appropriateness of activities, (Ex. needs bilingual support, able to count to 2).* R	5.3 Children are observed frequently and individual records are kept on their progress in areas of development.* R	7.3 Observations and records of progress are used to inform planning.* P, R, Q
1.4 No records kept, or if records are kept, they describe activities rather than the child's response or success in that activity (Ex. completed check-lists or samples of children's work). R	3.4 Staff shows some awareness of children as individuals (Ex. recognizing work of children of all abilities by encouragement or praise).	5.4 Staff consistently draw children's attention to diversity in a positive way.* (D)	7.4 Staff specifically plan activities that draw the attention of the whole group to difference and abilities in a positive way (Ex. showing children who are disabled in a positive light, celebrating bilingualism).* P, D, R

*Notes for clarification

Activities and planning

1.1/3.1/5.1/1.2/3.2/5.2. There should be evidence that differentiated activities and/or resources are offered to children with particular needs (e.g., those who do not speak English as their first language) and according to age and developmental stage.

—1.1/3.1/5.1 relate to the provision/adaptation of activities and resources offered to children (whether these are planned or informal) and the extent to which these cater to differing needs.

—1.2/3.2/5.2 specifically assess the extent to which differentiation is *planned for*.

Examples of appropriate differentiation can be found in All *About the ECERS-E* (Mathers & Linskey, forthcoming).

5.1/5.2. The range of activities should provide for all children (e.g. children of different ages/stages, children with English as a second language) and not simply those with identified special needs.

7.1. It may be necessary to ask about this as it will not always be apparent why children have been encouraged to work together on a task. For example: "Why have you encouraged those children to work together?" "Do you ever encourage particular children to work together? Why? Can you give some examples?"

7.2 The adult guidance should be more detailed than simply listing which adult works with which activity/group. Both elements of the indicator (i.e., the adult guidance and the range of capability levels) must be met in order to give credit.

Observations and record-keeping

3.3. At this level credit can be given for records/observations that show fairly minimal awareness of how individuals have coped with activities (or of the appropriateness of activities).

5.3. To give credit, children should be observed weekly (or almost weekly) in some form. This may take the form of post-it notes recording specific incidents or achievements, rather than formal observations. Records of progress do not need to be updated weekly.

7.3. It may be necessary to ask a question to establish whether this happens (for example, ask staff to provide or show specific examples of observations being used to inform planning).

Celebrating difference

3.4. Give credit if it is clearly part of usual practice to praise all children in the group regularly.

5.4. This indicator relates to celebration of differences among children in the group. To give credit, the discussion must be more specific than is required for 3.4 (e.g., drawing specific attention to a new skill a child has mastered; a sensitive discussion with the group at lunchtime about why a particular child doesn't eat meat; explaining in an appropriate way why a child with a disability needs to sit on a special chair). At least one example must be observed, and supporting evidence may also be found in display (e.g., children's work displayed with specific comments about their achievements).

7.4. This indicator goes beyond the children in the group to consider the celebration of difference more generally. Observers should check planning for evidence that celebration of difference and capability are specifically planned for (e.g., discussing blindness and deafness as part of a topic on senses). Evidence may also be found in display or in children's records. To give credit, at least one example of explicit planning for celebration of difference should be found in the materials reviewed.

Figure 13–4 Planning for individual learning needs.

TOPICS in OBSERVATION

Assessing the Environment—Pointing Back at You

When I tattled, my mother always said, "When you point your finger at someone else, three fingers are pointing back at yourself." That axiom has applications in observing children's development or lack of it. When we are careful observers, the attention is focused on the child, pointing at characteristics, skills, and behaviors. We tend to lay the source of the problem with the child. "Why is the child like that?" "Why can't she . . .?" "What's the matter with that child?"

The finger pointing up can be interpreted as, "That's just the way those people are." Substantial elements of a child's development are genetically programmed. The adults in the child's life act as the observers of how that script is played out. However, the three fingers pointing backward are a reminder of the important role the adult plays (Figure 13–5). Rather than blaming the child or the genetic program, some reflection may help. The influence of the adults in the child's life cannot be overlooked.

© Cengage Learning 2014

Figure 13–5 When you point a finger at someone else, three fingers are pointing back at you.

teachers and children that may subtly teach gender, racial, or disability biases. The whole book, *Anti-Bias Curriculum: Tools for Empowering Young Children* (1989), is a self-evaluative, consciousness-raising experience for the reader to promote reflection about diversity attitudes and practices.

Playground Safety. Evaluation is more than assessment. It is making a change because of the assessment. Programs periodically should perform safety checks inside and outside using checklists such as the ones in Chapter 3. Deteriorating equipment, overlooked hazards, and bad habits can be detected in these checklist formats for the protection of children's health and safety.

Environment and Development

Repeatedly, the influence of the environment, in particular the early childhood setting, has been emphasized as a powerful force in each area of development. The role of the teacher is to provide, modify, enrich, support, supervise, and adapt that environment for each child. It begins with knowledge of the child's physical development. How large are they?

What do they need to be kept safe? What kind of equipment is needed for the routines and activities of the child while in this environment? These decisions are based on the purpose and philosophies of the program. If it is a library story hour, then certain kinds of equipment and materials are appropriate, whereas a gymnastics program may select different criteria.

The cognitive environment in a developmentally based program will provide materials that prompt children to ask questions. Answers are sought by following the child's level of thinking. Engaging or participating in the actual manipulation of real objects replaces one-dimensional worksheets, watching an adult, or a video explanation of a principle. The adults in the environment support the exploration by asking open-ended questions, such as, "How do you think that happened?" or "Is there another way . . .?" "What would happen if . . .?"

The emotional environment of the early childhood setting provides for realistic expectations. Because young children are spillers, mops, paper towels, brooms, and dustpans are handy for clean-up. Group experiences can be noisy and stressful for some children. A quiet, alone space is provided from which to watch the action or withdraw to rest and reduce the adrenaline flow. Because children are learners, approximations for a task are recognized and efforts are rewarded before full accomplishments are attained. Children are made to feel competent by being trusted with responsibility that matches their ability.

The social atmosphere of the environment is monitored constantly to promote cooperation rather than competition, sociability rather than sarcasm, and friendship rather than isolation. Small groups are encouraged to work and play together by the physical arrangement of the furnishings into small areas. Planned and spontaneous activities bring children physically close to one another. This helps them understand the rights and space needs of each person as well as the principle of cooperation. Whenever observing the child, give attention to the environment and note its possible influence on the child. If it is influential in a negative way, changes need to be made. That is the response of a responsible adult.

Go to Education CourseMate website, accessed through CengageBrain.com for suggested assignments to assess the environment. The second assignment helps to assess the suitability to the needs of the child by observing the child's interactions with the group. A program may have a wonderful facility, the nicest equipment, materials, and supplies, but for some reason the child is not comfortable or learning there.

Assessing the Home Learning Environment

While this chapter is dedicated to assessing classroom environments, the "home classroom" should also be thought of as a subject of study. However, for the early educator in the home, the control of the classroom (home environment) is really limited to how effectively the educator can work within a variety of settings, some much more challenging than others. Home educators should consider either modifying or condensing an accepted child care environmental rating tool such as the Family Child Care Environment Rating Scale (FCCERS-R) (Harms & Clifford, 2007) or develop a an informal tool that addresses how the home environment supports the child's physical, language, cognitive, social, and emotional development, approaches to learning, health nutrition, and safety. Information collected can then be used in developing content and thinking about ways to design the learning environment to better support

the child's development. In any discussions about modifying the environment, sensitivity to the family's circumstances and perspective is critical.

Advantages of Formal Program Assessment

By using internal and external evaluation methods, programs measure and maintain the quality necessary for the safety, health, growth, and development of the children they serve. Other advantages include the following:

- It ensures that the professionalism of the staff is monitored.
- Objective criteria are used to measure this program against others of the same type.
- Staff, administrators, and consultants have an objective instrument with which to measure.
- Evaluation has program improvement as its goal, not revocation of licensing or censure.

Disadvantages of Formal Program Assessment

The disadvantages of formal program assessments include the following:

- There is usually a cost involved.
- They are time consuming.
- Occasionally, when the instrument does not fit the program, erroneous messages are given that are not really helpful.
- Follow-up is necessary so that the assessment is like seeing a smudge on your face and not washing it off.
- Circumstances, such as economic or leadership, pose barriers to the implementation of evaluation findings.

Pitfalls to Avoid

When considering a program evaluation, the following will help overcome these disadvantages:

- Careful consideration of a good match of instrument to program ensures that the results will be helpful.
- Planning for the added cost not only of the evaluation process, but also the implementation helps it not be an exercise in futility.
- Using knowledgeable, objective evaluators—they are key components to the success of the evaluation.

Using Technology

Any of the rating systems for program assessments mentioned in this chapter can be tabulated electronically. Using Excel, each of the classroom ratings can be entered and the data can be reported in text or a variety of charts. If you store and use electronic databases for program assessments, strong and weak areas are easily recognized, a quality improvement plan can be made and implemented, and the ratings revisited to see indicators of improvement. Selecting a program assessment instrument that fits the program's goals and objectives can be a very useful tool for use in long-range planning, reporting to administrators and decision-making bodies, as well as providing justification for grants.

How to Find the Time

The director or administrator has many day-to-day responsibilities, but quality assurance should be at the top of the list. Make a plan for program assessment and do more than go through the motions. This should be one of the most important tasks each year (and it *should* be yearly).

Self-assessments are valuable planning tools, but to ensure the validity of that evaluation, an outside evaluator is usually used. This should be someone who is familiar with the world of early childhood education but not a colleague, client, or board member. Those individuals may have a conflict of interest, and the evaluation would not be credible for some of the purposes listed above. Some evaluation systems include an on-site validator to verify self-study reports. Evaluation from an outside evaluator not only takes time, but also involves financial costs, so that is a consideration. It is a worthwhile endeavor, however.

An excellent way to look at environments is through staff exchanges where staff members visit each other's workplaces. This is affirming, and it can be inspiring to see how others utilize their environments.

What to Do with It?

Program assessments should not be done just to fill a notebook and place it on a shelf. The time, effort, and cost involved should bring more benefit than simply completing a necessary task. The report itself should be a dynamic document, used for program improvement so its components are the baseline for an ongoing program improvement plan. The report results should be communicated to those who have a need to know and those who should know. A report to families about the findings can include favorable ratings—"Our program received excellent ratings in. . . ."—as well as not-so-favorable ratings—"Our program is less effective in . . . and this is how we are working to improve it." This is not only ethical, but can also help enlist family support in making those improvements, especially those that directly affect them—such as record keeping or safety.

Program assessments, especially when they result in an accreditation or certification, should be communicated to the community at large. Many states are now undertaking Quality Rating Scale projects as a way for families as consumers to make choices about child care. Some program assessment awards bring financial gains as well in the form of increased child-care subsidies, staff bonuses, and center quality-enhancement stipends. Press releases, press conferences, letters to government officials, and notices to board members and local community agencies all bring positive recognition to the program. Program assessments are used for affirmation, improvement, and recognition.

Go to the Education CourseMate website, accessed through CengageBrain.com. for directions for a Setting Observation, plans, and resources.

Looking at the Adjustment of the Child to the Program

While we recognize that evaluating the program is an important way to measure quality, it is considered an input. The output of that quality answers the question of the African Masai greeting, "How are the children?" If the children are good, then life is good and the society is good. Making judgments on quality is subjective, for a program may be a good fit for one child but not for another, be consistent with one family's values and beliefs but not with another's. So this section is not about measuring a child's development directly, but about observing the child's **adjustment** and how the child is benefiting from the program. Changes in adults, peers, environments, schedules, expectations, and values ultimately affect development, and may influence later success in school.

Often children are in more than one program simultaneously or have moved from one to another so they have experiences in making adjustments

REVIEW

PROGRAM ASSESSMENTS

A measurement tool used to evaluate the program environment, curriculum and administration, staff qualifications and interactions with children, and suitability for an individual child.

Use Program Assessments to Look at

- interactions among teachers and children
- curriculum
- relationships among teachers and families
- staff qualifications and professional development
- administration
- staffing
- health and safety
- environment
- nutrition and health service
- anti-bias policies and procedures

Methods for Assessing Programs

- accreditation process
- checklists
- classroom observations—Running Records
- interviews with children, staff, administration, families
- surveys of staff, families
- data collection—attendance records, accident/ incident reports, family participation in center
- related activities, staff turnover rates

PROGRAM

Figure 13–6 Does the program fit the child?

The responsibility lies with programs to give careful attention to transitions, mealtimes, small- and large-group activities, and peer relations (Gable, 2002). Every quality program may not be a good place for every child. Families and program staff evaluate whether the child's needs are being met (Figure 13–6). Many of the characteristics that have been discussed already as indicators of development are also indicators of the appropriateness of a program for a child. These are reviewed along with the impact of group size, adult-child ratio, and program structure on the child's adjustment to the program.

Sometimes a program may not meet the needs of children. There may be a discontinuity between the child's home situation and the philosophy of the school. A child from a very structured home that stresses adult permission, obedience, and neatness may have difficulty adjusting to a program that promotes independence and allows choices and sensory exploration. A child from a small family with little contact with other children may find the large-group setting a hard adjustment. The high energy of a colorful, noisy, busy center may be too much for a highly distractible child. Consideration should be given to the families' values, the program's goals, and the child's personality and experience.

Families and staff watch for signs of that adjustment to judge if the program is meeting the needs of the child. The use of the Portfolio to document the child's participation can give specific information on areas of development. Periodically, it is necessary to step back and view the whole child. Looking at the child's adjustment to the program does that. These

that may assist or pose problems in each new setting. From what we know about children's development and attachment theory, children need to form a strong relationship with the teacher who serves as a substitute for the mother. Adjustment is also influenced by the child's temperament factors (see the discussion of temperament in Chapter 5) and the child's ability to socialize with peers and adults. The policies and practices of the program around the child's relationships to adults affect the child's adjustment. When a child is unable to attach to a primary caregiver, the need for emotional security is ignored and could be detrimental to further development (Dalli, 2000).

indicators are for toddlers through early school age. Some require an advanced level, especially in language, but behavior can be interpreted even beyond language.

Behavioral Indicators of Comfort

Children may not, or possibly cannot say, "I just love going to this program." There are behavioral signs that the child is emotionally, physically, socially, and cognitively comfortable there. Or the opposite may occur. The child may protest attending strongly or indicate a lack of comfort through the regressive behaviors of bed-wetting, thumb-sucking, or other earlier stage behaviors. This is not to put the decision of program choice into the child's domain, but to give families and teachers an indication that the child is not totally comfortable and further investigation is needed. Walsh and Gardner (2005) suggest that a high-quality learning environment contains these keywords: motivation, concentration, independence, confidence, wellbeing, social interaction, respect, multiple skill acquisition, and higher-order thinking skills.

The child gives behavioral indications of the suitability of the program for developmental needs. Some criteria may be answered with a "No" because the child is going through separation anxiety or another emotional upset. It is important for families and staff to give attention to a child's discomfort. It is a form of communication. The program is appropriate when the child

- begins the day at the program without a fuss.
- knows the schedule for the day and can anticipate what is coming next.
- feels an affinity to the school and says things like, "My school," "My cubby," and "My teacher."
- has opportunities to play actively inside and outside every day.
- talks freely at school (at maximum of language level).
- is able to make choices from sufficient equipment and materials.
- is not exhibiting stress, such as crying or regressive behaviors.
- has enough time to work at choice activities.
- is warned of impending change in activities and is given opportunity to finish and clean up.
- moves from one activity to the next comfortably.

- does not have to wait before the next activity can begin.
- does not have to receive step-by-step directions for activities, but can explore materials independently.
- is not forced to continue in an activity.
- is able to watch or choose not to participate in an activity.
- displays pride in the work brought home.
- can relate what occurred at school when prompted specifically. (Children need a reminder to trigger memory association.)
- talks about playing with other children in the group.
- knows the teachers' names.
- interacts with the teacher on a one-to-one basis several times during the day.
- goes to the adult for assistance and comfort.
- sleeps, eats, and toilets at school without difficulty.

Families and staff should work together to determine if the child is in the right placement, where the child is receiving not just physical care but also learning and feeling acceptance and belonging (Figure 13–7). These indicators could be used for Class List Logs from Chapter 1.

Looking at the Program through the Child's Eyes

At times any one or more of the previously listed indicators may be answered with a "No." That does not mean necessarily there is an adjustment problem. It may mean that the child is moving through a developmental phase, struggling with the change in thinking or feeling. It may mean there are personality differences between the child and a staff member. The child may feel threatened by an aggressive child in the group. There may be changes happening at home that are affecting the child at school. When a child appears to have difficulty in adjusting to a program, the teacher's dilemma is whether the child just needs more time or needs immediate or systematic intervention. A child exhibiting such behaviors should be closely observed in an attempt to learn the cause. There are many factors that influence the child's adjustment to the program.

Child–Adult Ratios. Child–adult ratios are one of the most basic indicators of adequate care. When there are too many children or the group is too large, a child's adjustment and even wellbeing are jeopardized.

WELCOMING ENVIRONMENT

When considering the program through the children's eyes, some additional features should be examined:

Entry	Are the doors and entry halls attractively decorated at a child's eye level ?
Personal spaces	Are there places where children can store and freely access their belongings such as outer clothing, toys and objects from home, and supplies?
Names	Does the child's first name (and photograph) appear close to the entry of the classroom so that the child can locate cubby and take responsibility for attendance for older children?
Families	Are there spaces within the classroom where photos of the child's family are present to aid in a feeling of belonging?
Culture	Are there items within the classroom that reflect the culture and traditions and people of the child's culture, such as cooking items in the Home area, photographs, books, and clothing items?
Furniture	Do the chairs fit the size of the children in the group so that their feet can reach the floor or rest on a footrest?
Eating utensils	Are the mealtimes that are served family style with utensils that the child can manage independently such as small bowls of food to pass and pitchers with spill-proof tops?
Consistent adults	Does the program make every effort to provide a consistent staff member at the daily arrival time so the child feels comfortable in separating and adjusting to the classroom environment?
Schedule	Does the schedule allow for sufficient time for routines so the child does not feel rushed or hurried, provide transitions so changes from one activity to another can be anticipated, and some flexibility to allow the child some autonomy over participation in activities?

© Cengage Learning 2014

Figure 13–7 Welcoming Environment Considerations.

The Make-Up of the Peer Group. Different activities depend on a certain number of people to be successful.

EXERCISE **How many people would you like in your group for the following activities?**

Cheering your team at a football game:
Sleeping:
Changing a light bulb:
Taking a shower:
Talking on the phone:
Eating:
Riding in a car:
Birthing a child:
Numbering all the books in a library:
Playing a card game:

Some activities are solitary, or at least intimate. The space and action also determine the number of people who can participate in certain activities. The size of the task at hand and the skill required—or the occasion—are also factors in group size. When thinking of young children in group settings, some of these same factors need to be considered. Two out of three mothers of preschool children are in the workforce. More than 60 percent of children younger than 5 whose mothers are employed are cared for by non-relatives. Of those children, 60 percent are in center-based care, while 29 percent are in family child-care homes (ACF, 2009). Children are grouped together by different criteria in different programs. There are rationales, advantages, and disadvantages to each decision.

Chronological Age Groups. Most center-based child-care centers and public schools group children by chronological age. Grouping children by age assumes that children who are in the same age range have similar needs and interests. This is usually the case, especially when curriculum is open-ended so that a range of developmental abilities can all find success. Individual differences, especially of exceptional children (those with disabilities or giftedness), and arbitrary age cutoffs sometimes make decisions about group placement difficult. At 15 months a child might be advanced physically, walking steadily. She is interested in the wider environment of the young toddler room. Regulations or policies might prevent her advancement into the next group. The wobbly walker may be arbitrarily "promoted" to the young toddler room at 18 months. For a slow-to-walk infant, a room of two-year-olds is a fearsome place. Grouping of children by age has different criteria and functions for the child's interactions in the group setting.

© Cengage Learning 2012

Figure 13–8 Mixed-age groups bring benefits to all.

Continuity of Care. Some early childhood programs have moved away from arbitrarily moving children from one group to another based on birth date or walking ability. Instead, those children who begin a program around the same time as infants move as a cohort, staying together with the same teachers as well, as they advance toward preschool age. In this way, the children, families, and teachers become very well known to each other. Equipment, materials, and even the room may change, but the group and adults stay together.

Mixed-Age or Multi-Age Groups. **Mixed-age groups**, or heterogeneous grouping, most resemble the family group with members of different ages (Figure 13–8). This gives young children the opportunity to observe, imitate, and learn from older ones. It gives older children occasions to practice nurturing skills, reteach learned skills, and feel competent. Most family child-care settings have children of mixed-age groups, since they usually care for siblings. The average family child-care group age was between five and eight (6.7), according to data gathered by the National Child Care Information Center (Clarke-Stewart & Vandall, 2002). Some centers have mixed-age groups or vertical grouping, with the state regulating the size of the group and the adult-child ratio. Prosocial behaviors, such as giving help, sharing, and turn-taking, are elicited in the older children toward the younger ones. Older children exhibit more leadership when they lead younger ones to higher levels of cognitive thinking by assisting in collaborative efforts as "experts." Younger children have seen models of help-giving and nurturing, and hopefully will replicate them when they are the older ones. Research shows that even young children can modify the complexity of their vocabulary based on the ages of the persons they are addressing, so mixed-age groupings sharpen communication skills. Logue (2006) reports that in the teachers' action research findings of multi-age groupings aggressive behaviors were

reduced, children shared more often, and younger children imitated language and conversed more.

The Size of the Group. The size of the group and adult-child ratio, both in family child-care homes and in centers, matter a great deal. "With too many children for one teacher to attend to, children suffer and so do the adults" (Clarke-Stewart & Allhusen, 2005). The class-size-reduction debate has long raged in the public school arena, with teachers and parents advocating lower class sizes so that children will get more individual attention, whereas economists say the added costs are not justified by learning outcome data (Gilman & Kiger, 2003).

In child care, various states have a wide range of children allowed in groups according to age. Look at Figure 13–9 to see group-size state comparisons from the National Child Care Information and Technical Assistance Center (2009).

Infants (Birth to 18 Months). It is common sense that the younger the child, the more care they require, so the size of the group should be smaller. Newborn infants need care and attention from a few of the same people. It is critical that infants receive the required care. The National Institute of Child Health and Human Development (NICHD), in its longitudinal study of children in child care, Infant Child Care & Attachment Security (1996), found that children under two years needed a small group and low staff-infant ratios (Figure 13–10). It also found strong teacher qualifications predicted positive outcomes. Infants should be cared for in groups no larger than six with two adults, or in a group of three with one adult (American Academy of Pediatrics, 2012). The quality and frequency of adult-child interactions are the critical variables in infant care. The interaction with adults provides for each infant's individual physical and emotional needs. This includes feeding, diapering, and holding. Infants younger than eight months interact with the teacher while in close physical proximity to other infants. Space size requirements vary by state regulation, but 35 square feet per child is considered minimum.

Observing the infant in the group setting, one would expect to see her looking at other infants, smiling, and touching them. The adult monitors the physical contact, for the infant has no knowledge that her squeezes and hair pulling hurt. She also lacks the self-control to keep from doing it. Other children are part of the world to be manipulated. Once infants become mobile by crawling, creeping, cruising, or walking, they approach other children with simple chase games and peekaboo. They enjoy little fingerplays and songs together and a book shared with another child on the lap of the adult. They begin to make vocal exchanges with each other, using vocal signals

State Requirements for Child–Staff Ratios and Maximum Group Sizes for Child Care Centers in 2008

Licensing is a process administered by State governments that sets a baseline of requirements below which it is illegal for facilities that provide child care services to operate, unless they are legally exempt from licensing. States have regulations that include the requirements child care facilities must comply with and policies to support enforcement of those regulations. The National Resource Center for Health and Safety in Child Care and Early Education (NRC) has the full text of State child care licensing regulations on its Web site at http://nrckids.org/STATES/states.htm. Additional information about licensing is available on NCCIC's Web site at http://nccic.acf.hhs.gov/topics/licensing. A directory of all State child care licensing agencies is also available on NCCIC's Web site at http://nccic.acf.hhs.gov/statedata/dirs/display.cfm?title=licensing. NCCIC does not endorse any non-Federal organization, publication, or resource.

The following table includes information about States' child-staff ratio and maximum group size requirements for child care centers in 2008. These data are from *The 2008 Child Care Licensing Study* (2010), by NCCIC and the National Association for Regulatory Administration (NARA). The full report, executive summary, and State data tables and profiles from this study are available on NARA's Web site at http://www.naralicensing.org/displaycommon.cfm?an=1&subarticlenbr=2

STATES	AGE OF CHILDREN										
	6 Weeks	9 Months	18 Months	27 Months	3 Years	4 Years	5 Years	6 Years	7 Years	8 & 9 Years	10 Years & older
Alabama	5:1 NR	5:1 NR	7:1 NR	8:1 NR	8:1 NR	18:1 NR	21:1 NR	21:1 NR	21:1 NR	22:1 NR	22:1 NR
Alaska	5:1 10	5:1 10	5:1 10	6:1 12	10:1 20	10:1 20	14:1 28	14:1 28	18:1 36	18:1 36	18:1 36
Arizona	5:1/11:2 NR	5:1/11:2 NR	6:1/13:2 NR	8:1 NR	13:1 NR	15:1 NR	20:1 NR	20:1 NR	20:1 NR	20:1 NR	20:1 NR
Arkansas	6:1 12	6:1 12	9:1 18	9:1 18	12:1 24	15:1 30	18:1 36	20:1 NR	20:1 NR	20:1 NR	20:1 NR
California	4:1 NR	4:1 NR	6:1 12	6:1 12	12:1 NR	12:1 NR	14:1 NR	14:1 NR	14:1 NR	14:1 NR	14:1 NR
Colorado	5:1 10	5:1 10	5:1 10	7:1 14	10:1 20	12:1 24	15:1 30	15:1 30	15:1 30	15:1 30	15:1 30
Connecticut	4:1 8	4:1 8	4:1 8	4:1 8	10:1 20	10:1 20	10:1 20	10:1 20	10:1 20	10:1 20	10:1 20
Delaware	4:1 NR	4:1 NR	6:1 NR	8:1 NR	10:1 NR	12:1 NR	15:1 NR	15:1 NR	15:1 NR	15:1 NR	15:1 NR
District of Columbia	4:1 8	4:1 8	4:1 8	4:1 8	8:1 16	10:1 20	15:1 25	15:1 30	15:1 30	15:1 30	15:1 30
Florida	4:1 NR	4:1 NR	6:1 NR	11:1 NR	15:1 NR	20:1 NR	25:1 NR	25:1 NR	25:1 NR	25:1 NR	25:1 NR
Georgia	6:1 12	6:1 12	8:1 16	10:1 20	15:1 30	18:1 36	20:1 40	25:1 50	25:1 50	25:1 50	25:1 50

Figure 13–9 State Requirements for Child–Staff Ratios and Maximum Group Sizes for Child Care Centers in 2008.
Source: From the National Child Care Information and Technical Assistance Center.

Hawaii	4:1 8	4:1 8	6:1 12	8:1 NR	12:1 NR	16:1 NR	20:1 NR	20:1 NR	20:1 NR	20:1 NR	20:1 NR
Idaho	NL	NL	NL	NL	NL	NL	NL	NL	NL	NL	NL
Illinois	4:1 12	4:1 12	5:1 15	8:1 16	10:1 20	10:1 20	20:1 20	20:1 30	20:1 30	20:1 30	20:1 30
Indiana	4:1 8	4:1 8	5:1 10	5:1 10	10:1 20	12:1 24	15:1 30	15:1 30	15:1 30	15:1 30	15:1 30
Iowa	4:1 NR	4:1 NR	4:1 NR	6:1 NR	8:1 NR	12:1 NR	15:1 NR	15:1 NR	15:1 NR	15:1 NR	20:1 NR
Kansas	3:1 9	3:1 9	5:1 10	7:1 14	12:1 24	12:1 24	14:1 28	16:1 32	16:1 32	16:1 32	16:1 32
Kentucky	5:1 10	5:1 10	6:1 12	10:1 20	12:1 24	14:1 28	15:1 30	15:1 30	20:1 30	20:1 30	20:1 30
Louisiana	6:1 NR	6:1 NR	8:1 NR	12:1 NR	14:1 NR	16:1 NR	20:1 NR	25:1 NR	25:1 NR	25:1 NR	25:1 NR
Maine	4:1 8	4:1 8	4:1/5:1 12/10	4:1/5:1 12/10	8:1/10:1 24/20	8:1/10:1 24/20	13:1 NR	13:1 NR	13:1 NR	13:1 NR	13:1 NR
Maryland	3:1 6	3:1 6	3:1 9	6:1 12	10:1 20	10:1 20	15:1 30	15:1 30	15:1 30	15:1 30	15:1 30
Massachusetts	3:1/7:2 7	3:1/7:2 7	4:1/9:2 9	4:1/9:2 9	10:1 20	10:1 20	15:1 30	15:1 30	15:1 30	15:1 30	15:1 30
Michigan	4:1 12	4:1 12	4:1 12	4:1 12	10:1 NR	12:1 NR	12:1 NR	18:1 NR	18:1 NR	18:1 NR	18:1 NR
Minnesota	4:1 8	4:1 8	7:1 14	7:1 14	10:1 20	10:1 20	10:1 20	15:1 30	15:1 30	15:1 30	15:1 30
Mississippi	5:1 10	5:1 10	9:1 10	12:1 14	14:1 14	16:1 20	20:1 20	20:1 20	20:1 20	20:1 20	25:1 25
Missouri	4:1 8	4:1 8	4:1 8	8:1 16	10:1 NR	10:1 NR	16:1 NR	16:1 NR	16:1 NR	16:1 NR	16:1 NR
Montana	4:1 NR	4:1 NR	4:1 NR	8:1 NR	8:1 NR	10:1 NR	10:1 NR	14:1 NR	14:1 NR	14:1 NR	14:1 NR
Nebraska	4:1 12	4:1 12	6:1 NR	6:1 NR	10:1 NR	12:1 NR	12:1 NR	15:1 NR	15:1 NR	15:1 NR	15:1 NR
Nevada	4:1 NR	6:1 NR	8:1 NR	10:1 NR	13:1 NR	13:1 NR	13:1 NR	13:1 NR	13:1 NR	13:1 NR	13:1 NR
New Hampshire	4:1 12	4:1 12	5:1 15	6:1 18	8:1 24	12:1 24	15:1 30	15:1 30	15:1 30	15:1 30	15:1 30
New Jersey	4:1 12	4:1 12	6:1 20	10:1 20	10:1 20	12:1 20	15:1 20	15:1 30	15:1 30	15:1 30	15:1 30
New Mexico	6:1 NR	6:1 NR	6:1 NR	10:1 NR	12:1 NR	12:1 NR	15:1 NR	15:1 NR	15:1 NR	15:1 NR	15:1 NR

Figure 13–9 (*continued*).

New York	4:1 8	4:1 8	5:1 12	5:1 12	7:1 18	8:1 21	9:1 24	10:1 20	10:1 20	10:1 20	15:1 30
North Carolina	5:1 10	5:1 10	6:1 12	10:1 20	15:1 25	15:1 25	25:1 25	25:1 25	25:1 25	25:1 25	25:1 25
North Dakota	4:1 8	4:1 8	4:1 8	5:1 10	7:1 14	10:1 20	12:1 24	18:1 36	18:1 36	18:1 36	18:1 36
Ohio	5:1/2:12 10	5:1/2:12 10	7:1 14	7:1 14	12:1 24	14:1 28	14:1 28	18:1 36	18:1 36	18:1 36	18:1 36
Oklahoma	4:1 8	4:1 8	6:1 12	8:1 16	12:1 24	15:1 30	15:1 30	20:1 40	20:1 40	20:1 40	20:1 40
Oregon	4:1 8	4:1 8	4:1 8	5:1 10	10:1 20	10:1 20	15:1 30	15:1 30	15:1 30	15:1 30	15:1 30
Pennsylvania	4:1 8	4:1 8	5:1 10	6:1 12	10:1 20	10:1 20	10:1 20	12:1 24	12:1 24	12:1/15:1 24/30	15:1 30
Rhode Island	4:1 8	4:1 8	6:1 12	6:1 12	9:1 18	10:1 20	12:1 24	13:1 NR	13:1 NR	13:1 NR	13:1 NR
South Carolina	5:1 NR	5:1 NR	6:1 NR	9:1 NR	13:1 NR	18:1 NR	21:1 NR	23:1 NR	23:1 NR	23:1 NR	23:1 NR
South Dakota	5:1 20	5:1 20	5:1 20	5:1 20	10:1 20	10:1 20	10:1 20	15:1 20	15:1 20	15:1 20	15:1 20
Tennessee	4:1 8	4:1 8	6:1 12	7:1 14	9:1 18	13:1 20	16:1 20	20:1 NR	20:1 NR	20:1 NR	20:1 NR
Texas	4:1 10	4:1 10	9:1 18	11:1 22	15:1 30	18:1 35	22:1 35	26:1 35	26:1 35	26:1 35	26:1 35
Utah	4:1 8	4:1 8	4:1 8	7:1 14	12:1 24	15:1 30	20:1 40	20:1 40	20:1 40	20:1 40	20:1 40
Vermont	4:1 8	4:1 8	4:1 8	5:1 10	10:1 20	10:1 20	10:1 20	13:1 NR	13:1 NR	13:1 NR	13:1 NR
Virginia	4:1 NR	4:1 NR	5:1 NR	8:1 NR	10:1 NR	10:1 NR	18:1 NR	18:1 NR	18:1 NR	18:1 NR	20:1 NR
Washington	4:1/3:1 8/9	4:1/3:1 8/9	7:1 14	7:1 14	10:1 20	10:1 20	15:1 30	15:1 30	15:1 30	15:1 30	15:1 30
West Virginia	4:1 8	4:1 8	4:1 12	8:1 16	10:1 20	12:1 24	12:1 24	16:1 32	16:1 32	16:1 32	16:1 32
Wisconsin	4:1 8	4:1 8	4:1 8	6:1 12	10:1 20	13:1 24	17:1 32	18:1 32	18:1 32	18:1 32	18:1 32
Wyoming	4:1 10	4:1 10	5:1 12	8:1 18	10:1 24	12:1 30	12:1 30	18:1 40	18:1 40	18:1 40	18:1 40

Key:

NL = Facility not licensed
NR = Group size not regulated

Figure 13–9

Figure 13–10 Infants need small groups.

© Cengage Learning 2014

to invite attention or alert the teacher that they need to be removed from a stressful situation.

The babies' and toddlers' compliance with the adults' requests begin with realistic expectations for children's behavior. Here are some guidelines for behavior from Jennifer Birckmayer (2001):

▶ Have age-appropriate expectations for children's behavior.
▶ Tell children what they can do.
▶ Distraction is a good technique to use with very young children.
▶ Change the environment instead of the behavior.
▶ Offer choices only when you can accept the child's decision.
▶ Use words and actions to guide behavior.
▶ Have a few simple rules consistently enforced.
▶ Recognize children's efforts.
▶ Be a friend.
▶ Be a good role model.

The teacher watches for developmental milestones, which occur almost daily at this age, and marks the developmental checklist the program is using. Daily contact sheets are used to document the amount of time and the type of activities provided for the infant each day. A copy is kept in the child's file. It is desirable to send a copy home at the end of every day (Figure 13–11).

Toddlers (18 Months to 3 Years). The recommended ratio is 5 toddlers to 1 adult and a total group size of 10. This ensures the safety and exchanges with responsive adults needed for this age. Considerations for the toddler in a group setting begin with a safe, healthy environment. The emotional environment provides support, with places to withdraw. The toddler needs consistent teachers and adequate space and materials. He is still developing coordination and has limited social skills. The child is observed as he interacts with the materials, demonstrating his physical

development. He can participate in small groups for very short periods of time. This could include songs, fingerplays, and short story books. His play with other children is at the functional level, using toys in a repetitive manner but advancing to more make-believe play, simulating grown-up activities. He will pretend to drive a car, bake a cake, and sweep the floor, especially when he sees the steering wheel, cake pans, or broom. Interactions with other children will be stormy because of limited language and the inability to take another's viewpoint. He wants the big ball of Play Doh, so he takes it. When the other player protests, there is little self-restraint in the responses.

Toddlers are fast moving and independent, yet they need much adult assistance with self-care skills. Observations include documentation of the child's ability to dress, eat, and the beginning interest in toileting. Socially, the child is taking an interest in other children, but with little emotional control or awareness of the feelings of others. This leads to aggressiveness and the possibility for physical harm. The child is rapidly developing language skills but often uses biting as an expression of frustration or aggression.

Toddlers have learned the sequence of the events of the day and depend very heavily on its stability. Arrivals and departures are handled in a routine way that allows for a relaxed, unrushed atmosphere. They need programming that allows them mostly free-play activities from a wide range of choices, including outside play and soft, quiet areas. Sleep and rest time should be adaptable to individual schedules and needs, with some children needing frequent short naps and others needing long afternoon naps. Eating times are social opportunities, with self-care skills, food exploration, and casual conversation included.

Transitions between periods of play, sleeping, eating, and diapering or toileting should be natural and relaxed. Waiting time should be eliminated and children warned that the end of that phase of the day is coming. When these elements are included in the program, the child is observed as she follows routines, interacts with adults and children, and maximizes the learning environment

Circle times for toddlers include songs, fingerplays, creative movement, and short books or storytelling. Participation should be optional. It can last as long or as short as they remain interested. Guidelines for group behavior, including self-discipline, depend on a knowledge of child development to be realistic (Figure 13–12).

The young child is egocentric, not able to put himself in someone else's place and impulsive, without the ability to control emotional urges. Language is not fully developed yet, with vocabulary centered on things rather than on ideas and symbolic actions, not

**Broome Community College
Child Care Center
607 - 778-5437**

INFANT DAILY CARE SHEET

Child's Name: _____

Today's Date: _____

PARENT INFORMATION

How did your child sleep last night/wake up time? _____

Is there medication today? _____

What's your child's feeding schedule? _____

Is there any other information/last diaper change? _____

CAREGIVER INFORMATION

BATHROOMING

Time	Wet	BM	Dry

NAPPING

From _____ to _____
_____ to _____
_____ to _____

NUTRITION

Breakfast:

Snacks: A.M.   P.M.

Lunch: None   Some   Most   All

SOME THINGS WE HAVE OBSERVED TODAY. . . .

_____ Sensory Table	_____ Babbled/Talked	_____ Soft books
_____ Dolls	_____ Ball Play	_____ Climbed
_____ Rattles/Shakers	_____ Danced	_____ Stacking
_____ Outside	_____ Cried, but comforted when held	_____ Blocks

Special Activity: _____

_____

What I Need:

Signed _____

Figure 13–11 Infant/Toddler Daily Care Sheets.
Source: Reprinted with permission from the BC Center, Broome Community College, Binghamton, NY.

Broome Community College
Child Care Center
607 - 778-5437

TODDLER DAILY CARE SHEET

Child's Name: _____

Today's Date: _____

PARENT INFORMATION

How did your child sleep last night/wake up time? _____

Is there medication today? _____

CAREGIVER INFORMATION

Diaper changes/toilet training

Time	Wet	BM	Dry	Tried on potty

Napping: From _____ to _____

Some of the things I did today....

_____ Books	_____ Markers/Crayons	_____ Legos
_____ Climber	_____ Painted	_____ Playdough
_____ Outside	_____ Water table	_____ Movement
_____ Puzzles	_____ Housekeeping area	_____ Music
_____ Special games		

Special Activity of the day: _____

Meals

Breakfast:

Snacks:

A.M.

P.M.

Lunch: None   Some   Most   All

Signed_____

Figure 13–11

Figure 13–12 Toddler circle times are VERY brief.

developed enough to present a rational point of view or to capably negotiate. Experience in life has been limited, and memory is still developing, so that does not help in self-control. Adults control the environment by placing matches where the child cannot reach them or by placing furniture where a child cannot use it to climb to forbidden objects in cupboards or on shelves. Adults' directions need to be clear and specific, giving warning of an impending change in activities. It is the child's desire to please adults yet develop autonomy, but often the two desires come into conflict. The payoff might be a reward or the absence of punishment. Adults may give direct instruction about expectations of behavior in what is called a "personal message" (Kostelnik et al., 2012):

- *Rules must be reasonable*—within the capability and knowledge necessary to carry out the desired behavior.
- *Rules must be definable*—specifying the *exact* behavior that is acceptable.
- *Rules must be positive*—telling them what to do rather than "don't . . ." or "stop . . ." (pp. 315)

Observing the toddler during play gives information about her concept of right and wrong. She might paint continually on the wall, even after being reminded to paint on paper. It is noted that her inner controls might be missing. She does not understand the directions. The cause may be emotional in nature, an act of attention seeking, or an example of demonstrating an open defiance to rules.

When the child knows clearly what is expected, observing the child adhere to those expectations gives information about memory, cognitive, and emotional development. The child understands and can resist temptation to do whatever he wants to follow the standard. When adults set firm limits about what behavior is not allowed, children learn to comply, first because of outside control, but eventually by internalizing the standards. The adults are role models who make

suggestions about how the child can meet the standards, giving them choices. By providing children with alternative activities, the adult provides a way for the child to focus his own attention and energies in another direction. When the adult indicates what effect the actions have on others, the child is receiving instruction on cause and effect and the consequences of his actions. Giving the child an outside view of how the actions appear to others begins the movement away from egocentrism.

Preschoolers (Three- to Five-Year-Olds). A total group size of 15 to 20 is recommended, with younger children in the lower range. The recommended adult-child ratio is two adults for that size group. Developmentally appropriate practices recommend that the schedule of the day include long periods of uninterrupted involvement in a variety of areas, commonly called learning centers (Copple & Bredekamp, 2009). These usually are set up for independent use to develop physical, cognitive, creative, and social skills. When the integrated curriculum approach or the project approach is used, there is a thematic connection between learning center areas. Woven throughout the schedule are routines for eating, sleeping or resting, toileting, and outside play. Circle time for the whole group, meetings, and small-group gatherings may be included, depending on the curriculum model.

Early School Age. Children attending public school traditionally have been placed in grades by chronological age. The cut-off dates for school entrance may vary by as much as six months. Some are in early summer, and others are not until the end of the calendar year. There are many in between. This makes it difficult when children are moving from one school district or state to another. Attempts to place children in classes by developmental age have met with difficulties (Figure 13–13). There are

Figure 13–13 Children come in all size, ages, and stages—the teacher's dilemma.

different opinions on the criteria and validity of the assessment instruments being used to determine developmental age. Questions have been raised regarding screenings being used inappropriately as placement tests rather than for their intended purpose.

Children of different ages and at different stages present either a dilemma or an opportunity to the school, depending on the philosophy. Some schools have divided each class into smaller groups by ability. This is to teach lessons closer to the levels of development. Many oppose early tracking or separating children by abilities. Whole-group instruction is difficult when children are functioning at a wide range of abilities. This is addressed by the selection of curriculum and teaching practices calling for "developmentally appropriate" rather than "age-appropriate" strategies.

Whole-Group Times. A whole-group time may occur at the beginning of the day as a transition between home and school. It welcomes the group and informs them of the choices of the day. It is sometimes held in the middle of the day, usually right before lunch, at which time it serves as a transition to review the work done in the morning and prepare for lunch, rest time, and afternoon activities. At the end of the day, some programs have a whole-group time to summarize the day, recalling the highlights, looking forward to tomorrow, and transitioning to home. Whole-group times help children feel a common bond, a sense of community. They can include singing, fingerplays, large motor games and musical games, and creative movement. Hohmann and Weikart (2008) say group times should *not* include rigid routines, competitive games, or teacher-led lessons. They recommend that group times be held in a spacious location, with a specific plan. The adult should have the materials prepared and draw children in with a transition activity. They begin right away, not waiting until every child is in place. The activity is then turned over to the children. The adult's role is to watch and listen while the children are leaders, and then to transition the group into the next experience. It is a different vision from the traditional whole-group time.

Unscheduled class meetings may be called to address class announcements, class problems, or mistaken behaviors. Gartrell (2011) refers to Glasser's model (1969) of class meetings that build a sense of togetherness. The general rules: anyone can talk, take turns, be honest, and be kind.

It Happened to Me

"I Don't Do Naps."

During the orientation to the routines at the beginning of the year, I was explaining the half-day sessions' routines to my new class of four-year-olds. "And after you play and then clean up, we wash our hands and have snacks." One boy stood up, stretched out his arms, palms up, and strongly protested, "I don't do naps." He wanted it understood right from the beginning what he would do and would not do. When I said more clearly that it was "snacks," not "naps," he was more agreeable to staying.

Besides the opening, middle, and closing meetings, unscheduled meetings are called out of necessity for spontaneous discussion. Problem solving by the group is underlined by protection of the dignity of the people involved in the problem. The situation is described using "I" messages; solutions are brainstormed, and a course of action is decided by the group. This promotes community responsibility and cooperation.

Questionable Value of Calendar and Show and Tell

Think About It . . .

Imagine you are sitting on the floor. The leader says, "Now let's recite the Dow Jones Averages. What was it yesterday? Which stocks sold the most shares? How much was bid for IBM? How much offered? Now say after me, Alco Standard Corp., American Home Products, Apple Computer, AT&T, Bell Atlantic, Chase Manhattan. Now you know the top-selling stocks. Don't you?"

- Do you *really* know them?
- How would you feel if you couldn't remember?
- What if you heard others around you saying them but you couldn't?
- Think about this in relation to children reciting numbers from the calendar and days of the week that have no meaning to them.

There are many programs that include counting the days on the calendar and reciting the days of the week and months of the year. These are abstract principles, not readily understood by young children. This exercise is rote memorization without much value. The time could be better spent on other topics of relevant interest to the children. If counting is the purpose or objective of the group time, there should be concrete objects for the children to count. This is according to child development principles. The association of the numeral is symbolic of the quantity and beyond the level of this developmental stage.

Think About It...

Now you are sitting on the rug and it is Show-and-Tell time. Mary brings a full-length mink coat out of her backpack. She puts it on and walks around, but you are told not to touch it. You might get it dirty. Then Gabriel brings out a new shotgun his father just gave him. He is so proud of it, but the teacher is horrified. "Put that away. We don't allow guns at school." Next, it is Katharine's turn. She has an hour-long video of her trip to the Mall of America. There are things all around that you want to do, but you have to sit there and watch it.

Would you
- touch Mary's coat anyway?
- feel disappointed and angry that you did not get to talk about your prized gift?
- wiggle, reach for a toy, pinch a neighbor, and not listen to Katharine's trip monologue?

Show-and-Tell has its champions who claim that it raises the self-esteem of children to bring an object from home and talk about it. They point out the value also of speaking before the whole group. Show-and-Tell usually involves long waiting. The children become disinterested in someone else's object because they are egocentric. The pressure builds to show bigger and better toys. These reasons present contrary evidence of its worth. Many have attempted to resolve the difficulties of Show-and-Tell with creative alternatives, some of which may be successful. Again, a careful consideration should be given to the objectives of the program. This is because of the knowledge of what young children are like:

They cannot wait and watch without touching.
They learn best by doing.
They have limited capacity to describe an object.
They have sensitivity already to the "haves" and the "have-nots."

Teaching practices should be based on what is known about how children learn and develop. Reconsideration of practices sometimes causes resistance and defensiveness in teachers. Calendar and Show-and-Tell are topics for reflection and reconsideration.

Small-Group Time. Without espousing any curriculum model, the small-group time of High/Scope gives effective principles for any program's group time (Hohmann & Weikart, 2008). Small-group time is conducted in an intimate place. It is just the right size for a few children and the adult. The same adult and children hold group time every day in that place, where the adult initiates a learning activity with real materials. The children explore the materials, deciding what to do with them. The adult helps the children carry out their plan if they need assistance. At the end, she helps them recall what they did.

Transitions. Even though a daily routine necessitates many changes, most humans are resistant to change.

EXERCISE List on a separate sheet of paper all the changes in activities and places you have been today.

Some people have difficulty getting out of bed, out of pajamas and into clothes, or out of the house and off to work or school. Every change means an adjustment in body position, temperature, and sometimes clothing; a change in social contacts, and perhaps a change in behavior.

This is difficult for adults, but even harder for children. They have no concept of time, minutes, hours, or days. They are stationed in the present. "I am doing this now and I want to continue doing it." They may be forced to change activities. There was not enough time to finish what they were doing. They are led to another activity that they are not so sure they can or want to do. They become stressed. This is the time when children act out, cry, or withdraw.

Transition times need planning, with just as much consideration as the activities themselves. Routine signals such as bells, music, gentle whispers, and simple games all give children a clue rather than a command that it is time to make a change. When the schedule of the day is consistent, children quickly come to anticipate and adjust to the changes, especially when they are pleasantly carried out (Figure 13–14).

When adults consider the child's needs first, plans are made for the program, activities, and

Figure 13–14 Planned transitions give children time to adjust to change.

interactions to fit those needs. When adults then consider each child as an individual and adapt the plans for that particular child, then the program is truly individually appropriate. If the child is exhibiting adjustment problems, it is likely that the program is at fault, not the child.

Observing How Infants and Toddlers Adjust to Group Settings

Because of their internalized view of the world, infants and toddlers are especially vulnerable to the interactions they have with adults in group settings. The teachers, the visitors to the classroom, the cook, the package delivery person all are equal in the child's eyes and have potential for exchanges that the child interprets as accepting or threatening.

The teacher as the observer is the gatekeeper to mediate, if necessary, if a child exhibits stress when certain adults enter the room. How does the child react to familiar and unfamiliar people? Does the child react differently to a man or woman? Are the reactions predictable or do they vary? Does the child attempt to communicate or attract attention? How? These observations are crucial for seeing the world through the child's eyes as he seeks to understand the human environment (Cohen et al., 2008). When caregivers give attention to the infant's attempts at communication, the infant even as young as four months old coordinates attention and gets a sense the other is with him (Markova & Legerstee, 2008). Caregiver's responses can reflect what the infant appears to be feeling, showing understanding and empathy (Gillespie & Parlakian, 2009): "It looks like you are missing Mommy already" or "I know you want to play with LeLe's hair but it hurts when you pull it."

Low staff ratios with consistent primary caregivers, safe attractive and interesting environments, and quality relationships between the program, caregivers, and home are all important to the infant's and toddler's adjustment to group settings (Gallagher & Mayer, 2008). Elliot's (2003) narrative of an infant who went through months of difficulty separating from her mother and adjusting to the caregiver shows how important those low staff ratios and sensitive, knowledgeable caregivers are to the child's adjustment to center care.

The teacher also observes how each child interacts with other children. Does the child have preferences? What qualities in another child instill distrust or rejection? How is the child initiating social exchanges with another child? Do other children gravitate toward this child or ignore or avoid her? What is her reaction? All of these questions give insight into the adjustment of the child to being a part of a group. Recording the details of the child's interactions with adults and other children is important to measuring the level of stress the child is exhibiting from being a part of a group. When the stress level is continually high, interventions should be taken to prevent developmental harm.

Helping All Children in Group Settings

When a child appears to have difficulty adjusting to a program, the teacher's dilemma is whether the child just needs more time or needs immediate or systematic

© Cengage Learning 2014

intervention. The fit of the program to the needs of the child is vitally important to every child, but for a child with special needs, it is even more critical. *Mainstreaming, integration, inclusion,* and *least restrictive environment* are all terms related to the legal-legislative postures as well as to child advocates promoting normalizing educational settings for children with special needs. The benefits of regular early childhood settings for children with special needs are many:

▶ In regular placements, negative views of children with disabilities are reduced because they are not isolated.

▶ When children of all abilities are grouped together, tolerance and understanding increase.

▶ Through interactions with typical children, peers become the behavior and skill role models in a demanding environment.

▶ Early intervention is beneficial for most disabilities.

▶ Younger children accept others more readily than older children, who may have learned to stigmatize those who are different from themselves.

Planning and consideration of many factors ensure a successful placement for children with special needs in regular classrooms:

▶ *Developmental levels rather than age groupings*— Placing children with special needs with younger children decreases the developmental differences.

▶ *Ratio of integrated children in the group*—Some have suggested that when only one or two children with special needs are integrated into a group, they still experience isolation. When more than one and up to one-third of the class are children with special needs, true integration is more likely to be successful. The caveat here is dependent on the nature of the special needs, the training of the teacher, and supplemental classroom assistance available.

▶ *Individualized learning experiences*—The curriculum for all children should be based on their interests and their strengths. Building on what they can do and modifying the environment and activities so that each child finds success is the principle of developmentally appropriate curriculum for all children.

▶ *Partnerships with families*—The families of children with special needs must be advocates for their own child. They are involved in more educational decisions about their child than other families, and must monitor their child's progress closely. This places the relationship and communication between the teacher and these families in a priority position.

The placement decisions for children with special needs must be carefully considered so their abilities are maximized and needs are met.

Observations of the child's adjustment to the program are stored in the Portfolio. See Figure 13–15 for the example of the Portfolio Evidence Sheet.

PORTFOLIO EVIDENCE OF CHILD'S DEVELOPMENT			
Evidence Type	Date	Recorder	Notes
ADJUSTMENT TO GROUP – the child's separation and adjustment to the program and interacting in groups as well as interactions with adults.			
CL	9/12/	BAN	Waved bye, involved in play
RR	10/26/	BAN	Dramatic play with 3 children, 7 min.
CL	11/4/	MLS	Participates in rhythm band
AR	12/10/	MLS	Comforted when hurt
TS	1/14/	BAN	Longer periods of work in centers

© Cengage Learning 2014

Figure 13–15 Portfolio Evidence Sheet Example.

Helping Professionals for Program Evaluation and Support

Help can come from experts or from others with similar concerns and experiences.

Consultants—The humorous definition of a consultant is someone from more than 100 miles away. A consultant is a specialist who is enlisted, and paid, for their advice. Programs that want an impartial, outside evaluation often contract with a consultant to provide that service.

Support groups—Groups with like concerns often informally or formally band together to discuss, seek answers, commiserate, and give advice to one another. They can become a legislative force for change or a united voice to raise the public's awareness regarding an issue. Many support groups have been formed of families with children who have a specific diagnosed disorder. The program should be aware of these in the local community to make them known to families in the program who may benefit from such an alliance.

Other Methods

Other Methods to Record a Child's Adjustment to Group Settings:

Class List Log
Anecdotal/Running Records
Developmental Checklists
Frequency Counts of social interactions
Conversations and Interviews with the child
Time Samples—measuring activity involvement
Rating Scales

Key Terms

accreditation	policies
adjustment	QRIS (quality rating
continuity of care	and improvement
license requirements	systems)
mixed-age groups	Recommendation
performance	Regulation
standards	Standard
program	transitions
evaluation	

Plans

Go to Education CourseMate website, accessed through CengageBrain.com, for the following:

Class List Log form
Plan Week 13 Part A, Directions for Setting Observation, including What to Do with It, Portfolio Evidence Sheet Example, Sharing with Child and Family, Actions—Read a Book, In the Environment, In the Curriculum, In the Newsletter
Plan Week 13 Part B, Directions for Class List Log on Group Participation
Pan Week 13 Part C, Anecdotal Recording of Group Interactions for Group D
Plan Week 13 Part D, Reflective Journal

Resources

National Association for the Education of Young Children. (2005). *NAEYC Early Childhood Program Standards and Accreditation Criteria: The Mark of Quality in Early Childhood Education.* Washington, DC: Author.

National Early Childhood Program Accreditation (NECPA). http://www.necpa.net.

National Health and Safety Performance Standards. (2012). http://nrc.uchsc.edunrckids.org.

Quality Standards for NAFCC. *National Association for Family Child Care Accreditation.* (2005). NAFCC Accreditation Standards. http://www.nafcc.org.

U.S. Department of Health and Human Services, Administration for Children and Families. *Head Start program performance standards.* (2006). http://eclkc.ohs.acf.hhs.gov/hslc.

Using the Portfolio for Communications with Families and Looking at the Child's Interactions with Adults

OBSERVATION THOUGHT

"Families are the authorities on the child. They lend them to us and we pay them back with interest."

NAEYC Standards **naeyc**

The following NAEYC Standards for Early Childhood Professional Preparation are addressed in this chapter:

Standard 3: Observing, Documenting, and Assessing to Support Young Children and Families

Standard 6: Becoming a Professional

IN THIS CHAPTER

▶ Communications with Families

▶ Using Portfolios for Progress Reports and Child Studies

▶ Looking at the Child's Interactions with Adults

▶ Observing Infants and Toddlers

▶ Topics in Observation: Does the *Week by Week* Plan Meet NAEYC Guidelines for Assessment?

▶ Helping All Children through Home and School Communications

▶ Helping Professionals for Home and School Communications

© Cengage Learning 2012

Communications with Families

All through *Week by Week*, sharing observations with the children and their families has been emphasized. This shows that the child is being watched and listened to by a person who knows child development in general and this child in particular. When the family knows the child is not only safe but also is learning and developing while out of their care, they can feel secure and gain respect for the program and the teacher. Families who feel secure about the child's program become better partners in the child's learning.

Family Involvement

Family involvement does not have to be spaghetti suppers, fundraisers, or discipline classes (though all of those are worthwhile). Involvement, in its truest sense, is the knowledge families have about their child while in the program. Involved families are familiar with the goals of the program, its policies and procedures, and how those relate to their child. They also know what the child's day is like and how the child is functioning in the group setting. Their confidence builds that the staff will keep them informed of important facts about their child.

EXERCISE Using a separate sheet of paper, construct a family diagram for a child you know. Draw a triangle with mother, father, and child at each point. Write *M* to stand for Mother, *F* for Father. If there are stepparents, grandparents, or other adults who are responsible for the child, either legally or practically, designate them in the diagram. Let *C* stand for the child. Now draw lines—solid and bold, or dotted and barely visible—for the relationships between these adults and the child. For some children the diagram is easy; for others the diagram is complex. Now place a *T* for yourself (in pencil that can be erased, for you have a temporary part in that family grouping). You are probably not in the center, but closer to the child than you are to the family, yet not in between them. Perhaps you are below them as a support. Now draw lines of communication between yourself and the family members. These may be by telephone, written communication, or even email; but whatever form, the goal is to make it a solid, two-way communication to ultimately benefit the child.

No Child Left Behind legislation Section 1118 mandates parent involvement that includes two-way and meaningful communication between home and school, ensuring

- that parents play an integral role in assisting their child's learning;
- that parents are encouraged to be actively involved in their child's education at school;
- that parents are full partners in their child's education and are included, as appropriate, in decision making and on advisory committees to assist in the education of their child;
- the carrying out of other activities, such as those described in Section 1118 (U.S. Department of Education, 2005).

Section 1118 and the 44-page *The Parent's Guide to No Child Left Behind* are holding schools accountable for implementing written policies that are more than just having a few parent representatives on an advisory council, but explain in detail what the expectations are for parent partnership.

The 2011 states' competition for funds in the Race to the Top initiative also includes criteria to address *engaging and supporting families*, acknowledging that success in school begins in the home.

Sociological research and principles are the foundation for the importance of family involvement, beginning with communication with the school or program. Children's learning and success is recognized as a shared responsibility of the family and the school, including all families in the six types of involvement—parenting, communicating, volunteering, learning at home, decision making, and collaborating with community (Epstein, 2005). Families are the authorities on their own children. In group settings, the responsibility for the education and care of children is shared with other people—teachers—who can provide a different perspective on the child. This is an awesome responsibility.

Daily contact with families is the preferable mode of communicating the observations and assessments between home and school, and such opportunities should be maximized. Sometimes written communication about the child is the vehicle of transferring information. There are advantages and pitfalls to this mode of exchange. More formal written reports, such as progress reports and child studies, are sometimes warranted, so templates and advice for writing reports about the child are included in this chapter. Combining verbal and written reports in a family conference presents a unique time for sharing between home and school. Family conferences are more effective with careful preparation and implementation. This chapter gives guidance for successful family conferences. Occasionally, family conferences of a distinct type are necessary, such as conferences for addressing specific problems, questions, or complaints, or an exit interview. Whenever family and program staff have a discussion, there is great potential to benefit the child. That is this chapter's guiding beacon.

Guide for All Communication with Families

The first step is a well-planned intake process, informing families of the facts they need to know. Through their personal contact with the teacher

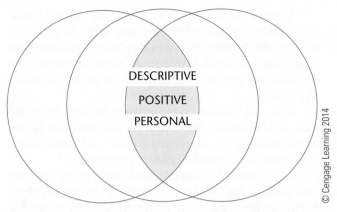

Figure 14–1 Home-School communications must be positive, descriptive, and personal.

© Cengage Learning 2014

and other program staff, families will build trust in the program. Even if they may not understand all that the program is about, they can tell these people on the staff care about them and their child. This trust is extended in various ways during the year, through daily contacts, written communications, progress reports, and conferences. Whatever the mode, these communications should be positive, descriptive, and personal (Figure 14–1).

While the family is the most accurate source of information about their child, it has been found that the public at large has some gaps in their knowledge about children in general. In a national study of 3,000 adults, including more than 1,000 parents of young children, it was found that there are vast over-expectations regarding the behavior of babies and young children (Lally, Lerner, & Lurie-Hurvitz, 2001). These include beliefs about the intentionality of behavior by infants and toddlers: "She knows I just sat down to eat and chooses this time to get fussy." It was also found that adults were misinformed about spoiling and discipline, and had little understanding of the importance of play. The early childhood professional has the opportunity to educate parents and the public about child development, realistic expectations for behavior, and the effects of the environment (including families, media, and health issues) on young children. This can be done through every contact, both formal and informal, not by sermonizing but by constantly pointing out children's actions and what their actions reveal about development. That is exactly what observation, recording, and communicating are all about.

Personal. The best way for home/school interactions to be personal is if the staff and families know

It Happened to Me

Families Raising Children

I recently visited an early childhood program during a holiday gathering where families were invited. My eyes were opened to the fact that more than half the adults there were not either of the child's biological "parents." There were grandparents, aunts and uncles, stepparents, foster parents, and other extended family members, along with some unrelated but caring friends. I was reminded of the statement about every child needing one person who is crazy about him or her.

The world is constantly changing, and so has the configuration of the child's home life. More and more children are living with one parent or with grandparents or other extended family members as their guardians. Throughout *Week by Week*, the involvement of the parent and the program through interaction with the teacher has been stressed. In this book, the term "family" is used which includes parents and others who make decisions about the child. In many cultures, decisions about the child are made by the whole family, not just the parent. In an effort to be inclusive, I have been retraining myself to use "family" more often, and I find that it fits. I am not making a statement that "anyone will do," because I still strongly believe that a child needs a mother and a father to develop, but I recognize that people who fill that role may not necessarily be related genetically.

each other. Through home visits, open houses, visits to the classroom, phone calls, and notes, the staff establishes rapport with each family. This is not to become friends, though that may happen, but to extend friendliness, courtesy, and partnership in a shared interest—the child. The teacher may have to make the effort again and again. It is like the persistent salesperson using different techniques to reach the customer. Many teachers react that it is their job to teach or care for the child, not the family. But they cannot adequately and single-handedly do that job without the family's cooperation, or at least acknowledgment of the role each plays.

Programs that have daily contact with family members who drop off and pick up their children have wonderful opportunities for interaction. Each day, tidbits of information about the child are casually shared. This provides background and breadth to what the teacher knows about the child, helping the teacher to better interpret behavior and help the child develop. Sharing the tidbits of the day with family members at dismissal time gives them insight about the child's day, their accomplishments and near accomplishments. This is an important, crucial part of the teacher's responsibility. The teacher establishes rapport with each family, seeing them day in and day out. Getting to know them and their child should be a priority. Noticing a new hairstyle, employment badge, or hurried look indicates to the family member that they are recognized as human beings. The teacher sees them not just as the client, the tuition check writer, or Amber's daddy. Not all are suited to this task, so the person on the teaching team who is the most adept at personal contacts should be the "doorperson." That person provides a friendly, welcoming face and attitude, a receptive ear, and tactful conversation.

Personal communication also means that confidentiality is maintained in face-to-face conversations wherever they may occur, at the door or at the grocery store, and also in written observations and communications. Remember that in Anecdotal and Running Records, children's identity other than the target child is maintained. In publications such as newsletters, websites, and blogs, care should be taken when using children's full names and photographs. Personal means confidential.

Descriptive. It is a luxury to be able to greet families at the end of the day and complete the circle by relating a bit of the child's day. It gives a springboard for later conversations about the day that may need a little nudge. A flood of talk springs forth when families have a little seed to get the child started. The comments at the door also let the family have an idea of not only what the child did, but how she is doing. They make comparisons with other children: "Gee, all the children in Heather's class can put on their own boots. Maybe I better work with her to learn how," or "The teacher said Tamiche played for a long time with the play dough and she gave me a recipe to make it at home. Maybe that would occupy

her while I fix dinner." Family education occurs in subtle ways.

It is impossible to give daily detailed comments to every family. Using the many communication modes, descriptive little vignettes like those in the examples in Share with the Family should be communicated to families often. Just as it is important to observe every child in the group, it is important to share information with every family. It is easy to share those shining moments, the ones that really stand out. "Chen wrote his name today for the first time!" For some children, however, remembering to turn the water off after they wash their hands is an accomplishment to be shared. It takes tact and practice to describe daily happenings accurately and without sarcasm. With practice it becomes natural. A little tip: The doorperson can keep a Class List Log in a private spot and jot down who received little "gems" at the door. After a few days, a spot check will show that some children have not had any good news shared for a while. The teacher can then make a conscious effort to observe and share a bit of information.

Positive. All comments shared informally, at the door or by other means, should be *positive*. At the end of the day, the family member is tired. The child has long forgotten his mistaken behavior. Other people are present. This is no time to bring out a litany of problems the child had that day. Those conflicts, whether with another child, the staff, or the materials, cannot be solved then and there, so there is no need to talk about them. Staff who relay "bad news" at the end of the day are venting anger. They could be displaying their ineptness at guiding the child's behavior. They seem to be expecting the family to take action on something that happened at school. That is an unfair request. It could even be interpreted as laying blame on the family for raising such a destructive, aggressive, unruly child. Teachers list "tattletale" at the top of the listing of characteristics they do not like in children. Telling families about a child's mistaken behaviors at the end of the day is in the same vein. The doorperson should only pass on good news (Figure 14–2).

Development is always looked at from the positive viewpoint: "What has the child accomplished so far?" No matter the level of development, an accomplishment has been made and can be shared as good news.

"Derek made it to the bathroom once today."
Rather than: "Derek had three toilet accidents today."
"Cecilia used her blanket for comfort today but did let go of it to go down the slide."

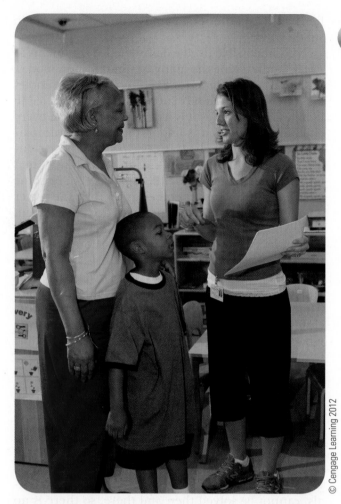

Figure 14–2 Greetings at the door, both at arrivals and departures, should be positive and personal.

Rather than: "Cecilia whined most of the day and hardly played at all."

"Roshann made an R today."

Rather than: "Roshann painted an R on the wall."

It may not be possible to relate "good news" stories to every family member at the end of every day, but all families should receive frequent, descriptive, positive messages. If families pick up their children at the center, *every family* and *every child* should be acknowledged as they leave. (This also relieves those anxious moments when suddenly someone says, "I didn't see Serina leave." The doorperson can say, "I was at the door and Mrs. Bigelow was in a hurry so she scooted in and out. I saw them leave." A sign-out system also safeguards this possibly dangerous time of the day. (Most regulatory agencies require a sign-out at the end of the day.) The personal touch brings closure to the day for the child and reinforces the friendly relationship between the home and program.

▶❙❙ TEACHSOURCE VIDEO ACTIVITY

Go to the Education CourseMate website, accessed through CengageBrain.com, and view Communicating with Families: Best Practices in an Early Education Setting.

What are the several ways that the teacher points out to the parent different ways they can communicate with each other?

In the parent conference, what elements from Chapter 14 do you see illustrated?

High-quality programs make every effort to involve families in a number of ways that fit the families' needs. This emphasizes the partnership, demonstrating the program's recognition of the vital role families play in the child's life, including their education. Supporting the family's culture is the first step toward this partnership. DiNatale (2002) suggests asking each family to print a welcome sign in their home language for the classroom. Of course, written materials for families should be translated into languages spoken at home, home-language literacy materials in the classroom should be present, and all cultural holidays should be respected.

Ethical Responsibilities to Families

Teachers and the family have a common interest in the child's welfare. The family is the primary influence on the child. The teacher's role is to collaborate with the family, offering a specialized knowledge, but always approaching interactions with the family with respect and consideration. The National Association for the Education of Young Children expressed these ideals in the Ethical Code of Conduct (NAEYC, 2005). According to these guidelines, the early childhood educator should

▶ be familiar with the knowledge base related to working effectively with families and stay informed through continuing education and training.

▶ develop relationships of mutual trust and create partnerships with the families we serve.

▶ welcome all family members and encourage them to participate in the program.

▶ listen to families, acknowledge and build on their strengths and competencies, and learn from families as we support them in their task of nurturing children.

▶ respect the dignity and preferences of each family and make an effort to learn about its structure, culture, language, customs, and beliefs.

▶ acknowledge families' childrearing values and their right to make decisions for their children.

▶ share information about each child's education and development with families and help them understand and appreciate the current knowledge base of the early childhood profession.

▶ help family members enhance their understanding of their children and support the continuing development of their skills as parents.

▶ participate in building support networks for families by providing them with opportunities to interact with program staff, other families, community resources, and professional services.

Types of Communication

There are many vehicles for communication with families. The purpose of the communication will determine the method and frequency of that communication (always remembering personal, descriptive, and positive).

Written Communication. Writing things down helps us remember and preserve the information. In all written communication, keep that in mind.

EXERCISE **You've collected the day's mail from your home mailbox. In sorting the items of mail, you decide which ones to open first. Number the following pieces of mail from 1 to 10 in the order you would open them:**

_____ card-sized envelope with no return address

_____ credit card preapproval

_____ offer for a free water test

_____ newsletter from an organization

_____ advertisement for a new early childhood magazine

_____ letter from your grandmother

_____ letter from the IRS, stamped "Refund"

_____ telephone bill

_____ letter from the "love of your life"

_____ registered letter from a collection agency

A letter from a friend or someone highly regarded is opened expectantly. Those unsolicited pieces of mail often are not even read. Some mail brings apprehension and anxiety as it is opened, causing feelings of depression, anger, or uncertainty.

Written communications from the early childhood program should be closer to the beginning of such a list than the end. The same points about daily contacts apply to written communications. They should be personal, descriptive, and positive.

Family Handbook. A thorough but reader-friendly Family Handbook is necessary to fully inform families of the philosophy, policies, and procedures the program follows. Educational institutions, from playgroups to universities, have policies or sets of guidelines under which they operate. The people involved with those institutions need to know what those guidelines are before they can follow them. This is the role of the Family Handbook, a guide with all the necessary information parents need to know. It should include the following information and policies (compiled from American Academy of Pediatrics, 2011; Berger, 2008; Gestwicki, 2013; Talan & Bloom, 2004):

information about the program—mission; philosophy/goals; calendar of operation (days, hours, holidays); groups (ages, adult-child ratios); curriculum, child assessments; staffing (qualifications, background checks); payments, fees, refunds, insurance; decision making (board member information); regular evaluation of program by families; modes of communication with families; confidentiality

enrollment and attendance—forms required (health, immunization, family/child information, emergency contacts, consent, photo release); special needs or circumstances information; inclusion of children with special needs; orientation for new children and families; transition to next group or to kindergarten; sign-in and sign-out procedures; late pick-up policies; attendance policies

parent involvement—open door policy (parents' right to visit any time); types of information to expect daily and at other times; volunteer opportunities; family supports; family conferences; special events; facilities for parent at school (library, suggestion box, bulletin boards)

health and safety—sanitation; hygiene of facility and staff; restricted access of facility; emergency care procedures; illness exclusion policies; medication administration; emergency closings and evacuation procedures; nutrition (meals, snacks, food from home, celebrations); napping procedures and policies; pets and animals on premises; prohibitions (alcohol, tobacco, illegal substances, firearms); mandated reporters of child maltreatment

Families are often too busy to read the guide book, or find it too involved and intimidating. Efforts to make the guide book user-friendly, with indexes, graphics, and a concise format have proven to be effective. Providing in-person orientations where the most important details are presented verbally can help the nonreader, the visual learner, and reinforce important elements. Home visits and individual conversations can clarify those points that families need to know most. All of this is done with respect for the families, with an attitude of partnership and consideration for the ultimate benefit of the child.

Newsletters. A periodic newsletter informing families of current news helps encourage family involvement. Descriptions of past events with short anecdotes from the children give the readers a sense of being there. This should be easy to compile from the Anecdotal Recordings. Names of children and volunteers in a newsletter increase readers' interest. Details families need to know should be bold and concise, not embedded in lines and lines of writing. Short daily or weekly plans in a calendar format will give the families and children a conversation topic. Future events could be anticipated: "It says here that a bunny will visit today. Maybe you want to take a carrot to feed it?" Past events are remembered: "It says here that you had a beehive and beekeeper visit your class. I didn't know that. Can you tell me about it?" Positive encouragement for families should be the theme of all newsletter writing. Parenting is a tough job. Families are not interested in articles telling them they should be doing more, more, and more.

> "Did you know that we have books to borrow so you don't have to make a trip to the library?"
> *Rather than:* "You should read to your child 15 minutes every day. If you don't, they won't be good readers."

There are some well-done commercial newsletters that can be personalized by adding pages or by using only edited portions of them. The newsletter should be friendly in tone and fun to read, with short, informative articles. The print should be clear and readable, with one-half as much white space as there is print. That means that drawings by the

children, poems centered in columns, and graphics should comprise one-third of the space. These will catch the reader's eye and illustrate the text. They will draw the reader's interest to an article a few paragraphs in length (Figure 14–3).

Happy Notes. In situations in which families and teachers do not have daily contact, "happy notes" serve the purpose of comments made at the door. These brief, personal, descriptive, and positive comments about the child on that day can be written and tucked in a knapsack or handed to a family member at the end of the day. Every recording assignment could bring out material from which to draw these comments. Finding the time to do these is a consideration. How about one a day? Does that seem manageable? If so, then use a class list and write one a day, focusing on one positive achievement or skill that child displayed that day. See Chapter 1 for an example.

Documentation Panels. These are more than bulletin boards with posted announcements and seasonal decorations. **Documentation panels** articulate to the family the philosophy of the classroom and give tangible evidence that children are engaged in active learning. Documentation panels can inform the families of the benefits of play and illustrate the learning that is taking place. While the panels are informational, they also should be esthetically pleasing. The display may contain photographs, children's artwork and dictation, transcripts of the teacher's observations, and curriculum webs, all outlining step-by-step processes around a central theme. Document panels convey much more information than a newsletter, and they become interactive when the children are the ones explaining the panel, thus enhancing their thinking and language skills.

The documentation panel can communicate information on a variety of topics:

- learning environments
- projects/emergent curriculum
- themes
- special events
- specific curriculum areas
- child development
- skill acquisition (Brown-DuPaul, Keyes, & Segatti, 2001)

Traveling Journals. Many programs have made traveling journals that go back and forth between school and home. Some are notes written between the family and the teacher. Several programs have a traveling journal in a tote bag with toys or art materials. In one preschool, families were asked to do something with Rags,

CONKLIN PRESCHOOL
MARCH NEWSLETTER

Home is where the heart is, it is as much a state of mind as a physical structure. Children watch construction with fascination, awed by the undertaking of a crew as it creates a structure. At school this month we will be cooperating to build a house, complete with an outside pool! The children will have an opportunity to try some interesting tools and machines, such as pulleys, hammers, and pipes.

This type of hands-on-learning, or play, is a vehicle for the child's mental growth. Play enables children to progress from the sensorimotor intelligence of infancy to pre-operational thought in the preschool years. Play is not only essential to cognitive development but serves important functions in children's physical, emotional, and social development. Come in to PLAY, learn and grow with us at preschool, we love to have a mom, dad, grandparent, aunt or uncle on snack day.

FAMILY CONFERENCES

Throughout the school year I have observed your children involved in regular preschool activities. March 15-19 is conference week. There will be no morning classes on the 15th and 16th and no afternoon classes on the 18th and 19th, giving us the opportunity to meet and discuss your child's progress and readiness for school. A sign up sheet for appointments will be posted. If you are unable to make one of these times, we can make alternate arrangements. Call me 775-0511 to schedule an appointment. You are welcome to come early and stay late; we will provide activities and childcare. It is important to be prompt and keep discussions to a maximum of 15 minutes.

TOTE BAGS

On Wednesday, March 17th at 9:00 we will begin to sew tote bags for next year's classes. We need your HELP! We need those who can sew and have sewing machines, those who can iron and pin, and anyone else who can help. Bring sewing machines, pins, white thread, scissors and yourselves. Our goal is to make over 100 bags. The hospitality committee has made arrangements to serve a delicious lunch. Childcare will be provided giving you the opportunity to experience a good old fashion-sewing bee.

CLEANING A ROOM TEACHES ORDER

Did you know that cleaning up a room is a learning activity? It can teach them order and structure. In their room, everything should have a place where it belongs. Toys, for example, each have their place. Teddy Bear goes here, the doll goes there, the ball goes over there. As a child learns about individual objects and the place it goes, they are learning basic lessons about space and how objects are organized in space. Later on in school, this concept will help learn the difference between "b" and "d" and "p" and "q".

Figure 14–3 Newsletter Example. (Courtesy of and reprinted with permission. Conklin Preschool, Conklin, NY.)

Rags' first day at my house was very pleasant. Rags took a nap with my brother Christopher. My brother helped me take care of Rags. Rags went with me to my Daddy's house and spent the night.

Rags also went with me to the baby sitter's house. I took Rags in my tent with me. I held Rags and hugged him the whole time he was with me. I had a great time with Rags. I even shared Rags with my brother.

Figure 14–4 Journals from home to school are a part of family communication and involvement. (Courtesy of and reprinted with permission. Conklin Preschool, Conklin, NY.)

a cute stuffed puppy, write about it, and then send it back to school for the next child. The responses are delightful, showing families' creativity, and encouraging the child to draw or write as well. While the family has the journal at home, they read the other entries and look at the drawing and writing attempts. Figure 14–4 shows a sample page from the story of Rags.

The teacher can record songs sung in school or a short review of projects in progress that could be sent home with the traveling journal to inform families of school events. Recordings with each child adding a bit to the tape have also been successful.

Technology. Electronic and technical innovations are changing the ways people communicate.

Email. With email, it is possible to send electronic messages, electronic happy notes, digital photographs, and compressed videos to families with Internet access. The day's events or monthly newsletter could be "mailed" to everyone in the class via the computer and a distribution list. However, with the ease of electronic communication, it is important to remember to write

sensitively, respecting confidentiality, and being careful that spur-of-the-moment writing is professional.

Voice Mail. Families with voice mail (answering machines or message systems) can receive short messages of good news from the program. It would be a good welcome home at the end of the day to hear the teacher's voice say: "Mr. and Mrs. Jones, listen to what James learned today. James, want to sing the Snowman song for Mommy and Daddy?" Answering machines at the school could provide reminders for the next day, little parenting tips, or songs by the children. Anyone who wants to call the program in the evening after hours would hear them and be able to leave a message for the teacher "after the beep."

Blogs. Teachers can create a blog on which they write a diary of what is happening in the classroom. Photos, videos, and children's work all can be electronically transmitted either to a closed list of just the families in that group or to the general public. It can be a way of sharing children's discoveries; but the same caution of confidentiality applies. Refrain from posting children's names and photos in social networking sites on the Internet. If you are going to write a blog for families, arrange for it to be password protected so that only the families of the children in the class or group may access it. This always needs prior permission after the family is informed of what kinds of things will be posted and who will have access.

Websites. As discussed in Chapter 11, the program may maintain a website on which children's work is displayed. This is a great tool for family communication posting all the information found in the Family Handbook, newsletters, and up-to-the-moment announcements. Families may have access to secure areas of the website where information about the children's activities is posted, maintaining confidentiality.

Home Visiting and Family Communication

One distinct advantage for providing early education in the home is the continual opportunity to engage family members and other caregivers in their important roles as teachers of the child. Beginning with recruitment, home educators should consider inviting family members to both participate in and to observe home teaching sessions. As a part of each session, educators should provide the family with meaningful and feasible ways to extend the child's learning. To do this successfully and to increase the probability of the family following up with suggestions, educators need to be aware of how that learning can be adapted to fit into the everyday routines of each family's life. While this engagement of parents may fall into the realm of parent education, it is an important outcome of home-based early education.

Using Portfolios for Progress Reports and Child Studies

Why is report card time so dreaded by families, children, and teachers? It is a time of stress. The teacher is placing a value on the child's efforts that may come as a surprise to the families, and sometimes even the child.

Think *About It...*

Imagine going to the doctor for a routine physical examination. You feel fine but they run tests and now you are there for the results. What are you feeling?

There is always some apprehension that tests may reveal some unsuspected problem. If that is the case,

there are various reactions. First of all, the patient wants to see the file and the test results to verify that there is no mistake. If the doctor will not show the actual test results, suspicions are raised. The diagnosis may be rejected because there were no previous indicators. The doctor must be wrong. The patient may want to wait a while or have the tests repeated to see if there is a change. A second opinion may be sought to decide exactly what the extent of the problem is and how to remedy it. These same apprehensions and reactions are common in family–teacher interactions.

When there is an ongoing exchange of descriptive information from school to home, there are no surprises when progress reports or report cards are issued. When families see the Portfolio and know they have access to it, they develop trust that the information about the child is based on credible evidence, not just guesses. How often do families say, "She doesn't like my child so she gave him a failing mark"? The work in the Portfolio documents educational decisions. Even if the families never look at the Portfolio, when they understand what it is about, they have confidence they can look at it if they want. That knowledge brings trust. So-called sunshine laws afford people the right to examine public records, including those of state and local educational agencies and most states' child-care regulations. Such laws are only acted on by a few, but they give everyone confidence in their ability to exercise it if the need or desire arises.

The same advice about sending only positive notes home to families applies to report cards as well. Rather than "telling on" the child, if there is a concern or problem, it is best addressed in person, with both parties prepared for the topic. A "bad news note" is like receiving medical test results in the mail, with no explanation. It leaves a knot of anxiety in the stomach. Most people would rush to the phone for an explanation. That is exactly what families do. They want to know more, usually calling with feelings of anxiety, anger, and frustration at the bad surprise.

Think *About It...*

Read the note in Figure 14–5 that the family of a second grader received. How would it make you feel if you were the family? What elements do you notice?

This is the second page of what is at least a four-page note. The teacher went on and on and on. If there were so many concerns, a conference could explain this so much better. Did you notice every comment is negative? Not a single positive line! The teacher also is giving a strong order—"Please see to

PUPIL _Marcy Johnson_   GRADE _2_

Teacher Comment

Dear Parent:

    She is also behind in the independent reading series in the classroom. She must get caught up in these areas as they are a mandatory part of Reading. She has been allowed to take a few books home to catch up. Please see to it that she works on these. She must learn to use her time wisely!

    I am not pleased with Marcy's math grade this term. She must practice.

                     Mrs. Marshfield

        TEACHER: _____

Figure 14–5 Read this note and see how you would feel as a parent or a family member.

it . . ." Would a family treasure this note? Would the child feel encouraged to work harder? And what about the impersonality of the opening: "Dear Parent"? What if it is not the parent who is responsible for the child? Either the family member would call for an appointment or be so intimidated that no response but anger or resentment would be felt.

EXERCISE **On a separate sheet of paper, write about a report card you remember as a child.**

Many people still have report cards on which teachers wrote negative, sarcastic comments and made dire predictions that this person was doomed to fail. Thankfully, most of those people did not believe the teacher and went on to succeed and prove her wrong. Remember, what is written is permanent and could be misinterpreted. The teacher must exercise caution, even in happy notes, to make sure that words are not misconstrued or the comments questionable in meaning.

EXERCISE **Rewrite the following comments to make them positive, descriptive, and personal.**

"She usually shares with other children."
"Grady only will play with other children if he can have his own way."

"Stephanie can't write her name, zip her own coat, or tie her shoes."
"Lynn is always the mother giving orders when playing in the dramatic area."

The word *usually* is one to avoid when writing progress reports. It leaves so many questions about what happens at other times. That is an example of the care and caution necessary in writing progress reports.

Sharing Portfolio Documentation

Observations have been accumulating in the Portfolio. Their effective use in home and school communication is one of the reasons professionals write down their observations (see Figure I–4 in the Introduction chapter). "Good information is priceless, but if we can't get to it, it's useless," someone said recently concerning the usefulness of becoming computer literate. This could be extended: "And if we don't do something with it, it's foolish." That applies to all the information and documentation accumulated about the child in the Portfolio. Writing Progress Reports periodically through the year and a Child Study—a summary of the child's development at the close of the program year or as the child moves to another group or another school—is aided greatly by having written observations from which to draw conclusions. These are also the points of discussion in Family Conferences. Students may think that writing research papers ends with the graduation diploma, but a Portfolio and subsequent Child Study summary is a form of research paper, writing about what has been learned and referencing the sources from which that information has been gleaned.

Progress Reports. Progress Reports are just what the name implies. They are short reviews of a child's development in written format. They give families a glimpse of the child from another's perspective. They should be positive in tone. They are reporting progress. Unless there is some serious trauma, all children make progress over time. It definitely is not at the same rate in each developmental area. It most likely is different from any other child, but it is still progress (Figure 14–6). This form also appears on the Education CourseMate website, accessed through CengageBrain.com. The narrative of the Progress Report follows closely the outline of the Portfolio Evidence Sheet. Developmental Checklists and documentation in the Portfolio supply the criteria. A short, descriptive sentence or two in each area is all that is required. An outline and "progress at a glance" can be included in the Portfolio to aid in organizing your thoughts for writing. It should be headed with the child's name, the date, the writer's full name, and the name of the program.

A Positive and Negative Example. Compare the tone and wording of the Progress Reports shown in Figure 14–7. These reports were written about the same child, each presenting the same information, but with a different tone. The first portrays the child as active and imaginative in the beginning stages of socialization. The second typifies the child as an airhead, unable to do many things that are expected. The second uses language such as one-to-one correspondence and cooperative play stage that is not understood by most families and should be avoided.

Tips for Progress Reports. The following suggestions will aid in writing progress reports:

> short, concise descriptive statements
> *positive*
> child "can do"
> *positive*
> no technical terms
> *positive*
> Keep a copy in the Portfolio and in the class file.

Child Study. A comprehensive narrative of the child is called a **child study** or **case study**. It can be used as an end-of-the-year report. It can also be sent with the family as the child moves to another program or

as a report to a referral agency, upon the written request of the family. A child study follows much the same format as the **Progress Report** but amplifies the information given in each area and references comments with the documentation. This referencing is much like the way an author references information from another source. In this way, the reader can go to the source for further information, possibly to examine evidence of what the author said or to learn more about the subject. The reader may then draw a different conclusion from that source.

Figure 14–8 is a sample child study of the same child presented in Figure 14–7 at the end of the year.

After reading the child study and reviewing the documentation, the reader should feel acquainted with the child. The child study is extensive because there are so many specific details, gathered week by week, on which to draw conclusions. The summaries of the child study are also *positive*, relating what the child can do. The documentation is there for proof of the inferences about the child's progress and development. An extensive child study may not be necessary for every child, especially if the child is remaining in the program, moving from one classroom to another. A series of progress reports may be sufficient.

Template for a Progress Report and Child Study. The mechanics of preparing the child study are much the same as any term paper. (The Progress Report is shorter, with only one or two main points under each topic and without references to documentation, although documentation evidence is present.)

1. Begin by calculating the child's age. The child's age is calculated in years and months at the time the report is written. In the life of a young child, much change takes place in a year, so the difference between "just three" and "almost four" is very great. This poses a bit of a mathematical problem for report writers.

EXERCISE **Try these for practice:**

a) The date is October 2012. Joseph's birth date is July 2008. How old is he? (Simple)

2012	10th month
– 2008	– 7th month
4 years	3 months

b) The date is October 2012. Martha's birth date is November 2008. How old is she? (Trickier)

2012	10th month
– 2008	– 11th month

PROGRESS AT A GLANCE

Child's Name _____

PERIOD 1: Date _____ Recorder _____

Strengths _____

Areas still developing _____

_____

Educational plan to facilitate development _____

_____

_____

PERIOD 2: Date _____ Recorder _____

Strengths _____

Areas still developing _____

Educational plan to facilitate development _____

_____

_____

PERIOD 3: Date _____ Recorder _____

Strengths _____

Areas still developing _____

Educational plan to facilitate development _____

_____

_____

PERIOD 4: Date _____ Recorder _____

Strengths _____

Areas still developing _____

_____

Educational plan to facilitate development _____

_____

_____

Figure 14–6 Progress at a Glance (form).

XYC CENTER
NICOLE LIND
November 29, year
Age: 4 yrs., 3 mo.
Sandra Richards, Teacher

ADJUSTMENT TO SCHOOL: Nicole had no difficulty from the first day of school. She hangs up her coat and is ready to participate.

SELF-HELP: She can unzip, zip with help. She can pour juice and cut food with ease. She handles the bathroom by herself. She participates in picking up the room.

PHYSICAL DEVELOPMENT: She runs with coordination, balances on one foot. She makes circles and lines with markers and cuts slashes with scissors.

SOCIAL: She plays primarily with two other girls but joins small groups in organized activities.

EMOTIONAL: She smiles a lot and allows herself to be comforted if she is hurt or tired.

SPEECH AND LANGUAGE: She can be understood and speaks freely to adults and other children.

MEMORY AND ATTENTION SPAN: She spends long times in dramatic play and active outdoor play. She knows the words to songs we sing and knows the sequence of the day's activities.

LITERACY: She knows how to look at a book right side up and turn pages. She listens to stories individually read.

MATH AND SCIENCE: She can count out loud to 10. She has a wide knowledge about hamsters, including their birth. She has several at home and has provided little ones for the class.

CREATIVE ARTS: She fills the page with color and notices lines and shapes in her art. She prefers easel painting to table art like collage, watercolors, or clay.

DRAMATIC PLAY: This is the area she chooses most frequently, dressing up, taking on a variety of roles, using her language in an imaginative way.

ADJUSTMENT TO SCHOOL: She seems happy here, comfortably follows the routine, and is making progress mainly in dramatic and physical play.

WORKING ON: Providing her with dramatic play props that require small hand muscle movement. We are beginning small group storybook reading time into the dramatic play area.

XYC CENTER
NICOLE LIND
November 29, year
Age: 4 yrs., 3 mo.
Sandra Richards, Teacher

ADJUSTMENT TO SCHOOL: Nicole is indifferent to parent leaving. Arrives in a whirl.

SELF-HELP: Can't zip her own coat. Serves self more food than she can finish. Licks the spoon. Needs reminding about washing hands after toileting.

PHYSICAL DEVELOPMENT: Runs and climbs. Cannot pedal bicycle yet. Scribbles. Still working on cutting.

SOCIAL: Parallel play stage, not cooperative.

EMOTIONAL: Happy most of the time, sometimes has bouts of silliness.

SPEECH AND LANGUAGE: Talks a lot. Sometimes hard to understand.

MEMORY AND ATTENTION SPAN: Does not participate in whole group activities though she listens to the songs. Reminds teacher what should be happening next.

LITERACY: Not interested in story time yet.

MATH AND SCIENCE: Does not have one-to-one correspondence yet. Often lets hamsters loose in the classroom.

CREATIVE ARTS: Paints whole page one color, then paints on lines and circles, mixing the paint.

DRAMATIC PLAY: Habitual play area in a fantasy world. Makes up words and imaginary language.

ADJUSTMENT TO SCHOOL: She seems happy here as long as she gets to play in the dramatic area or outside. Those are her favorite things to do. Seems uninterested in learning materials or group times.

WORKING ON: Zipping, cutting, small manipulatives, language.

Figure 14–7 Progress Report Examples: Positive and Negative.

XYC CENTER   **NICOLE LIND**   **June 14, year 4 yrs. 9 mo.**

Reporter: Mary McGwinn, 4's Teacher

Nicole is the oldest of three children, all of whom attend the XYC Center. Nicole has been at the XYC Center since September and will be attending kindergarten at Brinker School in the fall. She lives with her family next door to her grandparents with whom she spends much time. She talks about them lovingly. She has many cousins and extended family that make up her social circle. She attends church weekly where she participates in a children's choir. She attends dance lessons on Saturdays and will be dancing in her first recital in a few weeks.

PHYSICAL DEVELOPMENT: She is of average height and weight and in good health as evidenced by her almost perfect attendance record (see attendance record). She was absent for one week with chicken pox and a day occasionally with slight fevers accompanying colds. Her interest in dancing and advanced body coordination skills work together to demonstrate agility and confidence in movement. Her writing and hand muscles for smaller tasks are developing. She can fringe paper with scissors and put together eight-piece puzzles (checklist: physical development). She can write her name in large letters progressing from just the first N to the whole name (samples 10/05/0X, 1/17/0X, 4/4/0X).

SOCIAL DEVELOPMENT: Nicole is comfortable with the staff at XYC seeking help mainly for comfort from falls (which are infrequent) or frustration with small muscle tasks. She has little confidence in her abilities and seeks adults to assist her (anecdotal record 11/1/0X, 3/17/0X). With adults holding the paper or providing her with encouragement, she can perform those tasks she tries. Nicole is called friend by many children in the class (photo of Nicole and friends taken 2/2/0X). She plays mostly with girls in the dramatic play area, dressing in the various theme props provided there. She had an especially long play sequence when the area was set up as an animal hospital (class video, running record 3/13/0X). Through this interest in dramatic play she has gained negotiation skills. Compare anecdotal record of 10/6/0X and 2/27/0X. She has moved from playing alongside other children along the same theme to interacting and problem solving, assigning, and carrying out intricate play-acting roles, even putting on accents. This is demonstrated on the audio tape.

ADJUSTMENT TO SCHOOL: Nicole has adjusted to the routine of this center since she entered in September. She often goes down the hall "to see how the babies are doing," as she refers to her little sisters. She is welcomed by the teachers and allowed to spend time there, playing with the younger children. She has been observed in a protective, nurturing role captured in some photos (10/1/0X and 12/17/0X). She is comfortable with the routine, using free-play time to be involved in the dramatic play themes. She begins the day with painting since she often arrives before her friends. Her paintings have moved from experimentation with paint (9/29/0X) to more intricate designs (1/6/0X) and on to recognizable forms of people and animals (4/26/0X).

SELF-ACCEPTANCE: She acts independently in caring for her own needs in dressing, eating, and toileting (overview sheet). She independently chooses play areas, companions, and activities (time samples 10/21/0X, 2/03/0X). She exhibits a feeling of competence in physical activities, taking leadership roles (4/7/0X). She has a cheerful temperament. She displays no aggressiveness or antisocial behaviors (frequency counts 10/12/0X, 3/11/0X). She appears to be self-assertive in relations with others. She has a firm sense of self (interviews 11/2/0X, 2/17/0X).

COGNITIVE DEVELOPMENT: Nicole recognizes the letters in her name but not by themselves. She can count to 10 accurately and to 20 if assisted with the "teens." She knows the names of the colors, the names of the geometric shapes, and is beginning to add small numbers mentally (see interview 11/19/0X, 5/2/0X).

She has a wide knowledge of animal life, and a special interest in hamsters. She has raised several litters and provided several classmates with pets along with explicit directions on how to care for them (audio recording 3/22/0X). Her interest and ability in writing is at the beginning stages but her concern for the hamster's care prompted her to write a book. It told her friends how to care for hamsters. She dictated the book then illustrated it (sample, 12/12/0X). This was duplicated and given to each hamster owner. She felt this was a significant work. She talked about it on the tape (12/19/0X).

When listening to Nicole speak on the tape, some irregularities are noticed that are not apparent when talking to her casually (tape 9/29/0X). This was reviewed by her parents and pediatrician and a decision was

Figure 14–8 Child Study Example.

made to wait six months for these sounds to develop. Another tape on 04/6/0X showed those sounds were now present. This was reviewed by her parents and the pediatrician and confirmed. No further action was necessary.

CREATIVITY: Nicole's creativity is centered in the dramatic play realm. She can carry out a role imaginatively and encourage others to do so as well, displaying an advanced degree of concentration and social awareness (running record 1/29/0X). Her drawings are more realistic than her daily paintings, almost methodical in nature from one day to the next (samples 10/30/0X, 10/31/0X, 11/1/0X, 11/2/0X). She called it "practicing." She used scissors, collage, and clay in much the same way by experimenting with the same materials day after day then leaving them for months.

Nicole will enter kindergarten with strong social skills, confidence in her physical abilities, and the beginnings of literacy. Her adaptability to the group setting and helping adults should ensure that her school experience is a good one. She talks of school and all the things she will learn there. Once she saw the loft in the kindergarten rooms with extensive dramatic play areas, she was convinced that it was a good place.

I am happy to answer any questions about this review of Nicole's time at XYC Center. She is a joy to know.

Signed _____

Figure 14–8

Oops! We have to borrow 12 months from 2012.

2011	22 months
– 2008	– 11 months
3 years	11 months

Rule: When the child has not yet had a birthday in that year, you have to borrow 12 months from the current year to calculate the year and month age. Try some:

Janice was born in August 2009.
Frederick was born in February 2010.
Natalie was born in October 2009.

The correct answers will depend on the month and year you are reading and calculating this equation. Now calculate your own age in years and months.

2. Next define the topic. Know about whom you are writing and focus on one child at a time.
3. Assemble the raw data, the research, and the reference material. Have the Portfolio and notes either in chronological order or organized by developmental area.
4. Prepare an outline:
   Heading: Child's name, birth date, name of program, name of reporter.
   Family: Birth order, family make-up, contact with extended family, other teachers, community contacts.
   Physical: Appearance, size, build, ways of moving, health, attendance, large and small muscle development.

Social development: With adults—families, other adult helpers, teachers, visitors to the classroom. With children—stage of play, who are the child's friends, how the child interacts with other children, how the child solves problems with other children.
Adjustment to school: Separation behavior, areas of interest, participation and avoidance, adjustment to school routines, ability to follow directions, mistaken behaviors requiring guidance.
Self-acceptance: Self-care skills, independence, level of self-esteem, emotional development, self-control, aggressiveness.
Cognitive development: What the child knows—numbers, alphabet, shapes, interest in books, language vocabulary, clarity of speech, child's attitude toward learning.
Creativity: Child's use of imagination in art, movement, dramatic play, language.
Closing: Final paragraph, personal best wishes, signature of writer, date of report.
5. Write a rough draft from the outline. Think about the child in relation to each of those topics and jot some notes.
6. Document your statements by making references to sources. Look through the Portfolio and find representative pieces to provide data. Note the type of recording and dates.
7. Prepare the final document. This is a document that might be kept by the family for a

long time, maybe for the life of the child. It represents the professionalism of the program and the integrity of the writer. It should be written in complete, grammatically correct sentences. Type it and check for spelling.

8. Proofread. Have a team member who knows the child (for confidentiality, not an outsider) read the document for content, grammar, and tone.

9. Produce the document. Type it as neatly as possible, or, more likely, use a computer and print the final child study document as perfectly as you can make it.

10. Copy the document. The family should receive the original, either alone or with the Portfolio. A copy should be kept in the Class File. If applicable, file the family's written request for a copy to be sent to a referral agent in the Class File, along with the program's copy of the document.

These 10 steps will become more automatic with experience in writing this type of report. If they are written for the whole class, the task can be divided as are the other observation assignments, with one-fourth of them done each week. The *Week by Week* plan gives you assignments to help you make sure that you accomplish this several times a year. It will come easier.

What to Do with the Progress Report or Child Study. Once the child study is printed, two copies are made, one to be kept in the Portfolio and one to go in the Class File.

The child study belongs to the family. It is best presented to them in a conference (discussed later in this chapter). In this way, each section can be discussed using even more personalized anecdotal remembrances. The child study can be mailed if a conference cannot be arranged. There is always the risk that the family may misinterpret the wording or tone. There should always be an opportunity for reply or challenge.

The child study may be included in the Portfolio if it is to be given to the family. With the family's permission, the child study could be sent to the next program, school, or a referral agent such as a therapist or pediatrician. In that case, copies of the referenced documentation should also be included.

Family Conferences

The family conference's main purpose should be to present and discuss a developmental overview of the child. The early childhood program may be the first contact the child has had with people outside the family. It is a serious responsibility to be allowed to get so

intimately acquainted with their child. This conference is not just to allow the teacher to give information to the family; it is also meant as an exchange of information, a discussion, a sharing of points of view. The teacher is seeking feedback from the family for the benefit of the child. By conveying openness toward the family's input and participation in both word and behavior, the conference has a better chance at success.

Special education and Head Start experiences have proven that family involvement and even guidance in interventions with the child have the best chances for success (Benner, 2003). The strengths-based model (Dunst, Trivette, & Mott, 1994) reminds professionals that families have unique strengths and that the professional should work not to "fix" the family but to find ways for the family to take responsibility for any behavior changes.

The progress reports and child study can be the points of reference on which discussion is based. These conferences should be held periodically throughout the year, or any time at the request of the family. Head Start Program Performance Standards 1304.21(2) (2005) state that parents must be

▸ invited to become integrally involved in the development of the program's curriculum and approach to child development and education.

▸ provided opportunities to increase their child's observation skills and to share assessments with staff that will help plan the learning experiences.

▸ encouraged to participate in staff–parent conferences and home visits to discuss their child's development and education.

One of the opportunities for two-way communication is the parent (family) conference. Often the conference is held toward the end of the school year when children, teachers, and families are preparing to separate and move on. Much has been written giving advice about family conferences. Their success is fragile, and dependent on so many variables. Many preparations and precautions should be taken to guarantee an open, informative, positive exchange.

Tips for Family Conferences. Family conferences can be successful exchanges of information, as well as socially satisfying and affirming for family, teacher, and child. Here are some practical suggestions adapted from Seplocha (2004) and Wilford (2004):

1. Make the conference times convenient for the family and provide child care if needed.

2. Prepare the environment by having comfortable chairs at the same height, next to one another or at right angles with no table

between; making sure that the location is private so no one else can hear and there are no interruptions.

3. Be prepared. Have the progress report or child study complete, with accompanying documentation in an organized system. Open the Portfolio and let the family know what it holds.

4. Begin with social exchange, greetings, and small talk, and lead into a summary of the child's strengths, interests, and abilities.

5. Ask open-ended, nonthreatening questions; ask for questions, making eye contact, leaning forward, nodding to their comments; LISTEN and reflect.

6. Speak in understandable language, not using jargon such as *cognitive development, fine motor skills, phonemic awareness.*

7. Respect diverse cultures, using the conference to learn more and appreciate diverse cultures and family structures. Accept differences and avoid stereotyping.

8. Summarize and make plans for further contact.

9. End with looking ahead to the next year, increasing strengths, development, and challenges of the next grade or program.

10. Avoid giving drill and practice advice, but encourage reading, experimenting outdoors, dramatic-play opportunities, and chances to enjoy the summer with lots of family time.

Home Visiting Conferences

Even though a home visitor has many informal interactions with the family that allow for timely communications about the child, there should also be periodic scheduled formal conferences which allow collaborative discussion about the child's growth and development. The home setting may not always be conducive to conferencing, so home educators will need to give some thought to alternative settings.

Conferences with the Child. It is also useful to discuss the Portfolio with the child. Children above four years old love to look at their own work, and even nonreaders can understand the concept of the teacher keeping notes about them. Looking at work from an earlier stage brings a sense of accomplishment to the child, and provides an opening to discuss the meaning of the work and the incidents recorded there. Including the child in the family conference can also be beneficial. Anxiety about what the teacher will say dissolves. The child hears the teacher review the progress. Of course, this should be a "positive only" conference. This gives the family positive feedback

with the child present, hearing what development has occurred this year and indicating the positive effect of the family's relationship with the child. With so many families feeling blame and heavy responsibility, it is an important role of the teacher to give plaudits for a job well done, to both the child and the family.

Family Conferences When a Problem Is Suspected. Positive stories are related at the door. Positive statements are printed in the newsletters. Positive progress reports and positive child studies are written. But questions arise: "When do you ever tell them the bad news?" "When do you tell them the truth?" "When do you tell them what the child is *really* like?" When? Only after a certain process has taken place should the teacher talk to the parent about a concern (Figure 14–9).

Listening is required for effective family conferences, but few teacher preparation programs include active listening strategies in the course of study. McNaughton and colleagues (2007) found that a four-step process could increase mutual understanding and respect between teachers and parents: Listen, empathize, and communicate respect; ask questions and ask permission to take notes; focus on the issues; and find a first step within the teacher's zone of control. These can be applied to the suggested strategies that follow.

Documented Observations. If there is a concern for a child in a specific area or areas, it is critically important to gather data. This should be done with the methods that are the least inferential and the most accurate. The Anecdotal Record meets those criteria. If possible, have another member of the teaching team also gather data.

Review Developmental Guidelines. The observers should read some basic information about

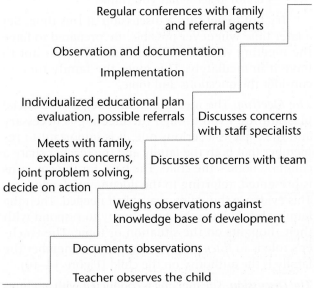

Figure 14–9 Steps in a Problem-Solving Family Conference.

Regular conferences with family and referral agents

Observation and documentation

Implementation

Individualized educational plan evaluation, possible referrals — Discusses concerns with staff specialists

Meets with family, explains concerns, joint problem solving, decide on action — Discusses concerns with team

Weighs observations against knowledge base of development

Documents observations

Teacher observes the child

© Cengage Learning 2014

developmental expectations and have a clear under-standing based on research.

Confer with the Team and Your Supervisor. The group should look at the data, review the research, and look again at the child. Theories should be explored, searching for possible causes or influences. Every attempt should be made to eliminate biases, whatever their origin. When it is the consensus of the group that the family should be consulted, the team should decide on the approach and determine who should be involved. Usually the classroom teacher alone is sufficient for the first step in this process. Discussion topics, possible scenarios, and options can be explored. Resources for referral should be researched and prepared for the family, beginning with the least alarming—usually a full physical evaluation.

Approach the Family. In *private*, the teacher conveys concerns and a request for a conference to discuss those concerns. The teacher may ask the family to think about the areas of concern or give the family some reading material to think about before that meeting.

> "We have been noticing and documenting . . . and wondering if you have noticed this at home? When would it be convenient to get together to discuss it?"
>
> "We've been trying different things to help Robert with . . . but we need some suggestions from you. Can we stop by on our way home tomorrow or could you come by here?"
>
> "The next time you take Lucy to the doctor you may want to ask about . . . Would you have time later on this afternoon to give me a call so we could talk about it? I really don't think it's serious but it has been nagging at me and I'd like to see what you think."

Try not to get into a discussion at this time. Set a later time whenever possible. Be prepared to have the meeting within 24 hours, but it is best not to have it immediately. This gives the family time to consider the questions and topic.

The Meeting. The meeting should begin with social pleasantries. Even though the meeting is necessary and the topic is a serious one, it is important to remember that both the family and the teacher share a common bond—the child. The basis for the concerns is presented, referring to the documented evidence. This evidence should be available if needed. Then the family should have the opportunity to respond with their thoughts on the situation or topic. The teacher's role is to *listen*. The teacher must remember the family is the authority on the child (Figure 14–10).

The Discussion. The meeting is conducted with attempts at clear communication and empathy. Possible solutions

Figure 14–10 The teacher listens to the family because they know the child best.

can be explored, from moderate to drastic. The teacher should be prepared for strong reactions from the family. These reactions may be denial, projection of blame, fear, guilt, mourning or grief, withdrawal, rejection, and finally acceptance (Berger, 2008).

The Decision. The family and teacher come to a decision and an agreement to carry out the next steps. Referral information should be available if the decision is to seek outside help. The progression is usually to begin with medical personnel to investigate or rule out physical causes. Other agencies may be referred to the family, depending on the nature of the concern.

Follow-Up. The program should make every effort to implement the plan the family has made. It is the responsibility of the program to keep the family informed of the actions taken and the results. If the family is taking an action, they should be asked to keep the program informed.

Documentation. A record of the conference's main points, the decisions made and actions planned, as well as the follow-up should be kept in the school's file. Notes of the Family Conference may be filed in the child's Portfolio and noted on the Portfolio Evidence Sheet as in Figure 14–11. It may be warranted to keep it in the confidential file rather than the Class File, depending on the nature of the concerns.

Advantages of Using the Portfolio for Communication with Families

Conferencing with families using the Portfolio

- gives concrete examples of the child's development.
- provides a common point of interest for the conversations about the child's progress.
- shows the family samples of the child's development over the course of time.

PORTFOLIO EVIDENCE OF CHILD'S DEVELOPMENT			
Evidence Type	Date	Recorder	Notes
SPEECH/ LANGUAGE – the child's speech and language development			
CL	10/16/	BAN	Difficult to understand
CK	10/19/	MLS	Many unchecked items. Referral?
Audio tape	11/20/	KBE	Conversation between Teacher and child for use in further evaluation
Notes	12/12/	BAN/MLS	Family conference. Send home list of agencies for full evaluation
AR	1/27/	BAN	Classroom therapy – ideas for reinforcement

Figure 14–11 Portfolio Evidence Sheet Example.

Disadvantages of Using the Portfolio for Communication with Families

Sometimes using the Portfolio in a Family Conference, the Portfolio

- may be misunderstood.
- may be used as a comparison with siblings.
- may overwhelm the family with the amount of information.
- if the family is one whose primarily language is not English, it may be difficult for them to follow and understand the information in the Portfolio.

Pitfalls to Avoid for a Successful Conference of Any Kind

Gestwicki (2013) lists the following pitfalls:

1. Avoid using technical terminology, such as *motor development* or Piagetian terminology.
2. Avoid the role of "expert." Remember the real experts on the child are the family.
3. Avoid negative evaluations. Avoid using words such as *problem, behind, immature, never, can't,* and *hyperactive.*
4. Avoid unprofessional conversation
   - about other children, families, staff.
   - about personal topics: marital status, financial, lifestyle.
   - about taking sides: between family members, between other staff, between this and other programs.
5. Avoid giving advice, either requested or unsolicited. It is the teacher's role to enhance not only parenting skills, but also parental self-esteem.
6. Avoid rushing into solutions; see this as a collaborative effort.

Using Technology

Earlier in the chapter, email and voice mail were mentioned as ways to communicate with families. School websites, blogs, and communication listservs not only send out information and news, but also act as discussion vehicles. Children's electronic Portfolios can be made available to the family by using password-protected areas so that only the family with the password can access the Portfolio. Advances in technology are occurring faster than many of us can adapt; but rather than become slaves to technology, we can use it to make our job easier and better.

How to Find the Time

It does take time to work with families to keep the lines of communication open. It is essential to value the family as the child's first and foremost teacher, and to work in partnership with family members for the benefit of the child. That being the case, we will find the time, make the time, use the time for this important part of the job.

What to Do With It

At the end of a school year, or when a child leaves the program, a question common to the readers of

It Happened to Me

Excuse Me!

I was holding family conferences midway through the year. They were scheduled every half hour, one after another. Between two conferences I had to leave the room. When I came back, the next parent was looking through all the Portfolios I had arranged for the next conferences. I was dumbfounded. What nerve! I got her child's folder and said, "Excuse me! This must be the one you're looking for." My mind raced through what else I could say, but I was so angry that nothing positive came to mind. So I went on with the conference. After all, it was about her child that we came together.

It taught me a lesson that I share with you: Keep all records secure. I did from that day onward.

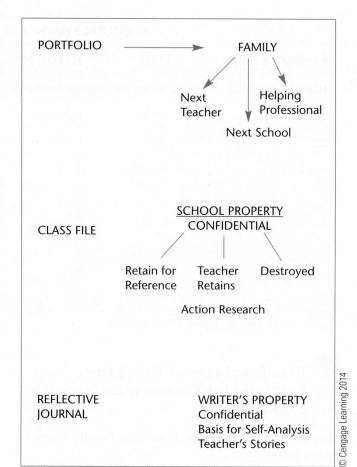

Figure 14–12 What to Do With It.

© Cengage Learning 2014

this book comes to mind: "What to do with it?" Consider the transfer or storage of each child's Portfolio, the Class File, and Reflective Journals (Figure 14–12).

The Portfolio. At the end of the year comes the question, "What to Do with It?" The future possession of the Portfolio, the Class File, and the Reflective Journal conclude this section.

The program or school implementing a Portfolio system should set a policy at that time. The family has the right of access to the Portfolio at all times. It remains the property of the school, however, and it is the right of the school to decide when to give it to the family or retain ownership. Any records retained by the school are kept confidential. Child studies are retained as comprehensive overviews and are the property of the program, not the teacher. They can be transferred to other agencies only with the written permission of the family.

The Portfolio could be transferred to the following:

- *Family*—At the close of the year or on leaving the program, the Portfolio may be given to the child and family. For some these become precious mementos. They contain vast amounts of information about the child, along with samples of the child's work.
- *Next teacher within the school*—If the child remains in the school or program, a Portfolio could be passed on and added to by the next teacher. Because of the large volume of material, it may be sorted and reduced in size. The next teacher can

refer to the Portfolio to come to know the child through it. The teacher may decide not to read the Portfolio, opting instead to form an independent viewpoint. That is the teacher's prerogative.

- *Next school*—The family may designate sending the Portfolio to the child's next school or program. Upon written authorization, that request is carried out.
- *Referral agent or helping professional*—Families may wish to release the Portfolio to medical or psychological personnel. Again, the family's authorization for this must be in writing.
- Observations taken periodically through a multitude of techniques can be valuable for diagnosis of disorders or disabilities.

Class Files. Again, the school policy is set for the retention of this file. It may be considered the property of the school and retained as a record of that class. It could be used for accountability of the teacher and the program. The Class File may be the property of the teacher, kept as a record of the work done that year. The documentation in the Class Files represents the whole class rather than focusing on individual children.

Reflective Journal. This is the property of the writer. It has been used for personal and professional reflection, and represents the thoughts and feelings of the writer. From these thoughts may come insights and deeper understandings of self and the profession. This is what is referred to as action research. This process begins with observation, that kind of "child watching" that comes with the pictures the eyes take and the sounds the ears hear. Those observations register against what is known about child development. Thinking about what matches and what clashes is the reflective process. This is frequently shared in an informal way.

Action research is a collaborative effort between observers, who get together to discuss principles and practices of early childhood, new ideas, questions, and theories. They consider the difference between what is seen and what is known. The environment for this collaboration is of primary importance. It must be among people who trust one another, in an intimate group setting where each person is free to speak. Time is provided for an unhurried discussion. It is possible that an article, a book, a video, or a report from one person's workshop could stimulate the discussion. Teachers relate difficult experiences without revealing a child's or family's identity, and try to make sense of the problem. They may decide to go away and experiment with different approaches and come back to report. The lessons learned from reflection and action research make meaningful reading for others, commonly called **teacher's stories**—interesting glimpses into the classroom and the teacher's reflections on the meaning of the occurrences. The Reflective Journals could be used as a basis for action research and teacher's stories. But the journal itself is a private document, for the writer's use alone, and should be protected for privacy.

Go to the Education CourseMate website, accessed through CengageBrain.com, for plans and resources for this week.

Looking at the Child's Interactions with Adults

Children, entrusted to other adults in other settings, must adjust and adapt to other schedules, expectations, and ways of interacting. Everyone has seen the difference in a child's behavior between when they are with the parents and when they are with the grandparents. How well they know their allies! In this final child development portion of this book, the important topic of the adjustment of the child to other adults is discussed.

When a child enters a child-care program or school, it is the beginning of moving out into the world. The

---

REVIEW

PORTFOLIOS

A comprehensive collection of teachers' observations and children's work to document the child's progress in all developmental areas.

Observation and Recording Methods That May Be Included in the Portfolio

Class List Log notations (dated)
Developmental Checklists and Rating Scales
Anecdotal and Running Records
Time Sample summaries (dated)
Frequency Count summaries (dated)
transcriptions of Interviews or Conversations
descriptions of Cognitive Task Experiments
Work Samples
media documentation such as photographs, audio recordings, or videotape segments
child study
Questionnaires about the child filled out by a family member
Notes inserted by a family member

Portfolios May Include Documentation of

separation and adjustment to the program
physical development
social development
emotional development
speech and language development
attention span
cognitive development
literacy
creativity
sociodramatic play
self-concept
interaction with adults

---

child begins to realize there are differences in people and their views on behavior. As the child gains self-control, adherence to the expectations for behavior is possible. The interactions with adults involve a pro-social model by the adult establishing a secure, trusting relationship with the child. Children have been found to be more socially competent with peers and others when they first feel emotionally secure with their teachers

REVIEW

The adults also model behavioral guidance by first establishing a secure attachment, setting the boundaries, communicating realistic expectations, and helping facilitate the child's behavior to meet them. By looking at the child through this lens, the observer gets a glimpse of the child's development in all the other developmental areas.

The role of the teacher is different from that of the family. To the teacher, the child is technically the client, to be kept at an emotional distance. That definition is foreign to the intensely personal relationship of child and teacher, but the objective detachment must be recognized. The teacher does not love the child as a family member does. This **unconditional positive regard** was first described by Rogers (1961) as "full acceptance of the child as a developing human being and member of the group." This is in accord with the positive view of the child's development. Observation assessment methods are used, not to catch children who are failing or to find their "weaknesses." Assessment methods measure individual levels of accomplishments and facilitate the next step in the progressive stage for each child.

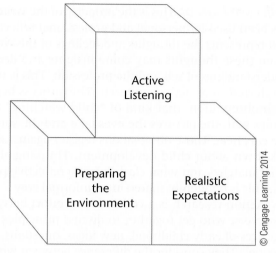

Figure 14–13 Building Blocks of the Teacher's Role in Child Guidance.

(Howes & Ritchie, 2002). When children are from culturally diverse backgrounds, they experience culture shock and can be overwhelmed with the classroom atmosphere. The teacher is an empathetic mediator with the environment, the language, and peers.

How Observation and Recording Aids Child–Adult Interactions

The connection with child–adult interactions should be clear. As observations are made and documented, the adult interacts with the child. The child knows the adult is writing about what he is doing because the teacher tells him. She asks questions about his work and writes about it. Samples of his work are collected for the Portfolio the teacher has shown him. He is interviewed, photographed, and recorded. As a result of observations, the adult knows the child from these interactions. The child knows the teacher's unconditional acceptance. She has not told him he is doing it

wrong, but has just observed and written descriptions of what he is doing without judgment. In classrooms where children are treated and moved as a group, where the whole class does art or science or math or story activities, where the teacher's time is spent giving directions rather than interacting, the teacher does not know the individual child. When the curriculum is appropriate for each child, with the teacher as the facilitator in the learning, then positive interactions between child and adult occur (Figure 14–13).

Various recording techniques can be used to record the child–adult interactions as well:

- Class List Logs allow quick surveys of different aspects of child–adult interactions, often from memory. Some examples of criterion items:

  seeks the adult for comfort
  behavior within state guidelines
  guidance needed in situations of . . .
  still gaining self-control in . . .

- Anecdotal or Running Records are ideal for capturing all the factual information of an incident showing the adult and child interacting.
- A Frequency Count could measure how many times in a day or week the child needed adult intervention.
- Time Sampling could indicate the presence of the adult and the presence of the child, inferring relationships from contacts with the adult.
- Conversations with the child give information about the nature of the relationship. The child's cooperativeness, comfort with the adult, and willingness to speak indicate a good relationship.
- Work Samples may demonstrate the child's feelings for the adult with love notes and

letters, gifts of drawings and work (such as my spotted dog in Chapter 10).

▶ Checklists and Rating Scales may have criteria regarding adult–child interactions to observe and document. These are inferred by the observer with no details recorded.

▶ Media, such as photographs, audio, and video may capture child and adult interactions. It is hoped that if they are to be preserved, they are positive interactions.

The documentation accumulated in the Portfolio presents a view of the child from the staff's eyes, with contributions from the child with Work Samples. Some ways to use the Portfolio to communicate with families and other individuals comprise this section of the chapter.

The Teacher's Role in Child Guidance

The adult takes the initiative to get acquainted with the child, recognizing the stages of stranger anxiety, differences in temperaments, and range of experiences the child has had with strangers outside the family. This was discussed in Chapter 1, which outlined strategies for staff members to begin the relationship with the child and family. It was repeated in the discussions on attachment, social and emotional development, and self-concept and self-esteem. With the foundation knowledge of child development, specific knowledge about the child, and close observation of developing situations, the teacher helps the child develop self-control and independence.

Expulsion rates from preschools have been at a higher rate than high schools due to children with challenging behaviors. Challenging behaviors have been defined as aggressive, out-of-control, disruptive, destructive, and interfering with the child's learning as well as that of the rest of the group. In a Policy Brief, the National Institute for Early Education Research (NIEER) suggests that there should be no expulsion from preschool, but rather interventions and supports for the teachers and the child. The institute proposes that quality preschool education can reduce challenging behavior and address the social and emotional development needs of the child (McCabe, 2007).

Three strategies the teacher uses to help guide children's behavior are the environment, expectations, and active listening.

Preparing the Environment. This has been mentioned many times as the first step in planning a curriculum. It is the active involvement of the child with her environment in which she constructs her own learning. The adult's role is to prepare that environment.

It is also prepared to help children control their own behavior. The equipment and materials are organized, accessible, in good condition, varied, and sufficient for the numbers of children in the group. The space is divided into clearly defined areas from which to choose, with enough floor or table space to adequately use the materials. For example, blocks are organized on labeled shelves next to a carpeted surface, out of the way of people walking through. Thus the builders can be comfortable, undisturbed, and not frustrated by having their constructions tipped or knocked down. Blocks of time are needed so teachers are not interrupting play for their own purposes.

Realistic Expectations. The observer has a knowledge base of child development against which to measure skills and behavior. When adults have inappropriate expectations of children's behavior, it is like expecting an infant to walk and punishing him when he does not. Adults' interactions with children must be based on developmental norms and appropriate practice principles so that children are not expected to behave in a way beyond their years or ability. That phrase "Children can't wait" is so true in many ways. When that principle is understood, the adult modifies his or her own behavior rather than struggling to make children do what they cannot do. For example, the teacher will not make all the children wait until everyone has washed their hands before they begin to eat.

The realistic expectations are stated in terms that children can understand, from the positive—what they can rather than cannot do. Because of what is known about attention span, selective listening skills, and cognitive structures, we know that when young children hear "Don't run," they get the opposite message, "Run." It is the word emphasized, heard last and loudest, without the child's knowledge of the negating feature of the word preceding it.

Active Listening. Another facet of adult–child interactions is **active listening**, a strategy in Gordon's *Teacher Effectiveness Training* (1978), that focuses on what the child is saying, listening carefully for the meaning and the feelings expressed, suspending judgment and waiting to respond to the implied feelings. In the development of emotions, children have strong feelings but lack the vocabulary to express them.

The adult manages the environment, sets realistic stated expectations, and actively listens. Then the adult–child interactions can focus on more important topics, such as where butterflies go when it rains or how this ball can stay on top of the block building.

Adult Intervention of Problem Behavior

The adult role is first to keep children safe. Sometimes in the execution of that role for one child, interactions with another child strain relationships. A child starts throwing chairs, ripping other children's artwork, or yelling obscenities at another child. In the positive guidance model children are not punished, but guided to help control their behavior and seek solutions and remedies for problems. Gartrell (2011) uses the term *mistaken behavior* as "errors in judgment and action made in the process of learning life skills" and suggests a direct approach that employs the strategy of describe-express-direct:

- *Describe without labeling*—The teacher describes the unacceptable situation: "I heard unfriendly words and saw hitting going on. It has to stop and we'll figure out what to do about the anger."
- *Express displeasure without insult*—The teacher expresses personal feelings without condemning persons: "My job is to keep everyone safe and I am worried about these kinds of actions. I want to help figure out what to do about the anger."
- *Correct by direction*—The teacher not only tells what not to do, but what to do instead: "Our classroom rules are to speak to each other with respect and not hurt anyone. I cannot let you hit each other. Let's take a breath and talk about it. Tell each other why you are upset and I'll help you find a solution." (p. 425)

This coincides with Vygotsky's scaffolding philosophy, helping the child to a higher level of competence.

Possible Causes of Problem Behavior. The close observer and interpreter of children's behavior looks beyond misbehavior and considers the consequences in light of the child's individual situation. Again, it is the empathetic, reflective professional looking at behavior indicators to seek reasons, causes, and contributing factors before blaming the child for deliberately breaking rules. Kostelnik et al. (2012) suggest these possible causes for behavior problems:

- Children are not sure of what the rules are.
- Children are not sure how to follow the rule.
- Children don't know appropriate actions to substitute for unacceptable ones.
- Children do not have the ability or instrumental know-how to follow a particular rule.
- Children think the rule is unjustified.
- Children have no investment in the rule.
- Children are gaining positive payoffs from negative actions.
- Children are getting mixed messages about the importance of certain rules.
- Children are testing adults to see how far they will bend regarding rule enforcement. (p. 328)

It Happened to Me

The Bare Room

A student teacher warned me of the room's lack of equipment in the setting where she was working. When I visited her, I saw she was not exaggerating. The children were jumping from the top of a play refrigerator, the only piece of equipment in the room besides a table and chairs and a shelf with partially used coloring book pages and broken crayons. She told me she was having a terrible time "controlling" the children's behavior, trying to keep them from climbing and jumping off the refrigerator. The story was that each time the children "misbehaved," the lead teacher took away a piece of equipment, and now they were down to the last piece. Children must play, so they used the refrigerator in place of the large muscle equipment they were missing. Needless to say, the lead teacher and director were not providing an appropriate environment, nor practicing positive guidance approaches. Behavior problems persist when teachers do not adequately prepare the environment.

Through observation and appropriate professional practice, the child in group settings can be assessed for physical and psychological safety. Nonpunitive, positive guidance techniques are used to help the child gain self-control. In this way, the teacher does not give up on any child and has a career of **liberation teaching** (Ginott, in Gartrell, 2011). The teacher sees the child as an individual, recognizing and respecting cultural differences. Teachers work to help each child be a self-directed, competent, accepted, and moral individual.

Observing Infants and Toddlers

Because infants and toddlers are developing at such a rapid rate, it is necessary to capture details about their behavior and development every day. By using intake forms that the family fills out at the beginning of each day, and noting important care events such as eating, sleeping and diapering, a daily log documents and notes any changes or concerns. Adapting the *Week by Week* plan to more frequent

TOPICS in OBSERVATION

Does the Week by Week *Plan Meet NAEYC Guidelines for Assessment?*

The National Association for the Education of Young Children (NAEYC) and the National Association of Early Childhood Specialists in State Departments of Education (NAECS/SDE) jointly developed guidelines to evaluate assessment practices. The *Week by Week* system should provide affirmative responses to *all* the guidelines (NAEYC, 2003).

1. Ethical principles guide assessment practices.

    The *Week by Week* system organizes observation documentation so that developmental information is gathered on every child and no single assessment is the basis for making decisions about the child.

2. Assessment instruments are used for their intended purposes.

    The documentation using various methods can be used to benefit the child, plan for individual children, improve instruction, identify children's interests and needs, and individualize instruction.

3. Assessments are appropriate for ages and other characteristics of children being assessed.

    The documentation methods preserve raw data or are formalized developmental checklists assessing each child on a continuum, compared only to him or herself. The assessment procedure reflects individual, cultural, and linguistic diversity, and can be used for any age child.

4. Assessment instruments are in compliance with professional criteria for quality.

    The documentation methods are widely used in early childhood programs and are not linked to a specific curriculum or philosophy. The uses and protocol for various methods are reviewed within the *Week by Week* system so that the most appropriate method is used to record specific developmental domains.

5. What is assessed is developmentally and educationally significant.

    Each child's strengths and capabilities are assessed. The word *weakness* does not appear in the *Week by Week* system. It is continually emphasized that assessment of development is looking for progress, measuring accomplishments, and developing competence.

6. Assessment evidence is used to understand and improve learning.

    The *Week by Week* system not only looks at all areas of development through observation plans giving indicators of development and insights into behavior, but also includes suggestions for enhancing the curriculum in various subject areas, including bibliotherapy or related children's books.

7. Assessment evidence is gathered from realistic settings and situations that reflect children's actual performance.

    The observer using the *Week by Week* system is the classroom teacher, familiar to the child, acting during the normal routine of the classroom environment and activities.

8. Assessments use multiple sources of evidence gathered over time.

    The *Week by Week* system guides the observer to use at least seven different methods of recording to control bias and meet the objectives for the observation. Interviews and dialogues with the child are included, and the child is informed of and can review the Portfolio that contains samples of his or her work gathered periodically over time.

(Continued)

TOPICS in OBSERVATION   *(Continued)*

9. Screening is always linked to follow-up.

   When developmental delays or areas of concern are revealed through the *Week by Week* assessments, the teacher has hard data to discuss with the family and referral agents (with the permission of the family).

10. Use of individually administered, norm-referenced tests is limited.

    Norm-referenced developmental checklists are included not only to measure gains, but also to give information to the teachers and families about the next milestone in the developmental domain. The *Week by Week* system cautions teachers regarding the use of standardized tests with young children, advocating instead naturalistic assessment methods.

11. Staff and families are knowledgeable about assessment.

    ***Week by Week* presents various methods of recording children's development, along with each method's advantages and disadvantages. By practicing these, the reader becomes knowledgeable about the methods, their uses, and their practical application. All through the *Week by Week* system, regular communication with families is emphasized. Families are invited to read and contribute to the Portfolio, and reminded in the *Week by Week* system that the Portfolio is a changing collection of documents open for their inspection and comment. Daily contacts, review of the Portfolio, and family conferences are all ways that the child's development is conveyed to the families—not in a score, but in oral and written form that they can understand. It appears that the *Week by Week* system meets the NAEYC and NAECS/SDE guidelines. *Week by Week* assessments of every child's development, using a variety of observation techniques and professional reflection, have been braided together. Together they make the whole strand stronger—the strand of professional practice.**

assessments of developmental milestones is recommended using established checklists such as Marotz and Allen (2013) *Developmental Profiles* that list what the child should be accomplishing on a month-to-month basis.

Helping All Children through Home and School Communications

Children from Diverse Backgrounds

Communication is the key component to working in partnership with families. Whether the family speaks a language unknown to the teacher or lives such a different lifestyle that it is almost impossible to comprehend, it is the teacher's responsibility to find some common ground. That common ground is concern for the child and the desire to

know and assist the child in development. When that is the motivation, interpreters, schedules, and overlooking lifestyles without judgment all can be managed with creativity and conviction.

Children with Special Needs

Families whose children have special needs must be advocates for their child. They want for their child what every other family wants: an opportunity to learn and be treated equally. For some children to receive what they need in the classroom, some interventions or modifications must be made. It takes an intense amount of understanding between families and teachers to come to satisfactory arrangements that do not overburden the teacher or the program, yet provide for the needs of every child in the group. This may mean adding extra adults who specifically help that child. It may mean the teacher modifies the environment and the routines

It Happened to Me

As I Wrote This Book

Week by Week. This book could never have been accomplished had I not set *Week by Week* goals for myself. On a calendar near my computer, I plotted chapters, working back from deadlines, so that if I stayed on course I could meet the deadlines. It worked for me. It can work for you!

It is my sincere goal for everyone using this plan to know the child. Because of what we know, this is what we do. In that knowing, we will do what is right for that child.

for one particular child while meeting the needs of the rest as well. This can only be accomplished through open communication between the family and teachers. By regularly sharing information, expressing frustrations, and problem solving together, it *can* be done.

Helping Professionals for Home and School Communications

Psychologists and social workers can help as intermediaries between schools, programs, and families. They can assess an individual child's emotional state in relation to the adults in the program, determine how the program is meeting the child's particular needs, and help the family deal with agencies with their own policies and procedures.

No matter what the circumstances of the family, the teacher's first responsibility is to provide for the needs of the child within the goals and objectives of the program. Working with families in a cooperative partnership helps accomplish those goals.

Other Methods

Other Methods to Record the Child's Interaction with Adults:

Class List Log
Anecdotal/Running Records
Frequency Count

Time Sampling
Conversations/Interviews
Work Samples
Checklists and Rating Scales

Key Terms

active listening
case study (child study)
documentation panels

liberation teaching
progress report
teacher's stories
unconditional positive regard

Plans

Go to the Education CourseMate website, accessed through CengageBrain.com, for the following:

Plan Week 14 Part A, Directions for a Class List Log on Interaction with Adults, including What to Do with It, Portfolio Evidence Sheet Example, Sharing with Child and Family, Actions—Read a Book, In the Environment, In the Curriculum, In the Newsletter

Plan Week 14 Part B, Directions for Checklist on Physical Development on all children

Plan Week 14 Part C, Reflective Journal

Resources

Burman, L. (2009). *Are You Listening? Fostering Conversations That Help Young Children Learn*. St. Paul, MN: Redleaf Press.

Gartrell, D. (2011). *A Guidance Approach for the Encouraging Classroom* (5th ed.). Belmont, CA: Wadsworth Cengage Learning.

Gestwicki, C. (2013). *Home, School, and Community Relations* (8th ed.). Belmont, CA: Wadsworth, Cengage Learning.

Jalongo, M. R. (2008). *Learning to Listen, Listening to Learn*. Washington, DC: National Association for the Education of Young Children.

Marion, M. (2011). *Guidance of Young Children* (8th ed.). Boston, MA: Pearson-Prentice Hall.

Marotz, L. & Allen, K. E. (2013). *Developmental Profiles: Prebirth Through Adolescence* (7th ed.). Belmont, CA: Wadsworth Cengage Learning.

CHAPTER 15

Using the Yearly Plan to Observe and Record Children's Development

OBSERVATION THOUGHT

"The *Week by Week* plan answers these questions:

Who? Every child in the group equally

What? Behaviors that take place within the normal routines of the day

How? Observation and recording for Portfolio evidence collection

By Whom? Informed teachers, caregivers, family

When? Repeatedly throughout the year, at regular intervals, and spontaneously when important events occur

Why? Measurement, individualizing curriculum, communication, and intervention."

NAEYC Standards **naeyc**

The following NAEYC Standards for Early Childhood Professional Preparation are addressed in this chapter:

Standard 3: Observing, Documenting, and Assessing to Support Young Children and Families

Standard 6: Becoming a Professional

Students

You have used this book as a guide for learning about observing children throughout a semester, but all along you have noticed that this book has a dual purpose. It is used to learn and practice various methods of observing while also reviewing the basics of child development. There are extensive directions in the plans on the Education Course-Mate website, accessed through CengageBrain .com. It is the author's intention that this textbook be used as a reference and guide when you have a classroom of your own, using the *Week by Week* plan for compiling documentation on every child, in every developmental area, every week.

REVIEW

Here is your last Review Box, a summary of all of the methods you have in your toolbox. Use the right tool for the job.

Method	Definition	Useful for Recording
Class List Log	Alphabetical first name list to record small, specific pieces of information on each child in the class	Single elements of adjustments to routines Single elements of self-care Single elements of physical development Social development stage Clear articulation of speech Single elements of basic concepts in math/science Single elements of literacy Frequency of choices of Learning Centers
Reflective Journal	Personal diary kept separate and private from children's records	Thoughts Expressions of emotions Questions Self-examination
Anecdotal Recording	Detailed incident on one child, including the setting, action/reaction exact quotes, and result	Separation and adjustment Self-care skills Physical development Social development Emotional development Language and speech Attention span and interests Cognitive development Literacy Creativity Sociodramatic play Child abuse disclosure Self-esteem
Checklists	Listing of related criteria against which skills, knowledge, or behavior is measured indicating yes or no, present or not present. Can indicate milestones attained and areas yet to be developed	Self-care skills Physical development Stages of social development Stages of emotional development Stages of cognitive development Specific criteria such as "knows colors, shapes, recognizes numbers" Stages of literacy Stages of creative development Stages of sociodramatic play Aspects of self-concept

REVIEW

Method	Definition	Useful for Recording
Frequency Count	A recording of predetermined frequently occurring behaviors to quantify their frequency, and later used for comparison after a strategy is implemented	Frequently occurring separation difficulties Frequent requests for assistance Frequent prosocial and antisocial incidents Frequency of language used in certain functions Frequency of choices of activities
Conversations or Interviews	Recording a child's verbal interactions either in writing or in audio recording	Informal conversations Interviews to obtain: Child's viewpoint on school adjustment Self-responsibility views Self-evaluation of physical skills Self-evaluation of friendships and social interactions Self-evaluation of emotional difficulties Evaluate speech/language Assess cognitive development Assess literacy development Discuss creative work or play
Time Sample	Recording children's play area free choices every five minutes for a half-hour interval and drawing conclusions about interests, abilities, attention span, preferred playmates, level of social play	Presence of child in area Sustained play in that area Interaction with others in that area Presence of adult
Rating Scale	Criteria are arranged according to developmental stages or range of quality with the recorder making a judgment based on observation	Child development stages Environment appropriateness Teacher performance
Work Samples	Collection of child's products from which to draw conclusions about development, skills, and behaviors	Separation Self-care Physical development Social skills Emotional development Speech and language development Memory and attention span Math and science knowledge Literacy Creativity Self-identity Group time behaviors Interaction with adults

(Continued)

REVIEW

Method	Definition	Useful for Recording
Technology	Action preserved in photos, audio/video recording	Any moment or sequence Separation and adjustment Self-care skills Physical development Social development Emotional development Language and speech Attention span and interests Cognitive development Literacy creativity Sociodramatic play Self-esteem
Child Abuse Reporting	Precise, descriptive, immediate note taking, State Reporting Form	Indicators of physical abuse Indicators of neglect Indicators of sexual abuse Indicators of emotional abuse
Program Assessment	Tool to evaluate program environment, curriculum and administration, staff qualifications and interactions with children, suitability of program for individual child	Interactions among teachers and children Curriculum Relationships among teachers and families Staff qualifications and professional development Administration Staffing Health and safety Environment Nutrition and health service Anti-bias policies and procedures

The purpose is to *know* each child in order to fulfill our responsibility to the global village in helping each one develop into a caring, thinking, reliable human being. This plan is only successful if it helps attain that goal by measuring progress, individualizing the environment or curriculum to assist in development, documenting the child's activities, and sharing with families.

Practitioners

To those of you who are already working in a classroom, now you have the tools (the various methods presented in this book). You have the knowledge of how to use the tools (the overview of areas of development). The *Week by Week* plan on the Education CourseMate website contains the plan for building individual child Portfolios that contain documentation of all areas of development, revisited at least three times to measure progress.

The Introduction chapter section of the Education CourseMate website, contains a file to help you get started using the website. Also in this section is the schedule for the *Week by Week* plan. (The file for this schedule is titled "Overview.") You will divide the children into groups of three or four children, depending on the size of the class, in alphabetical order by their first name (remember the Class List Log), calling the group A, B, C, or D. This will give you an arbitrary plan so that certain children are not overlooked during observations while others are frequently observed. The Weekly Plans are posted to the Education CourseMate website and contain plans for weeks 1–40. You may have to adjust for your own program calendar, for vacations, or for necessary suspensions of recording. But like a diet, even if you slip some, just try to get back into the routine in order to meet your goal: a well-developed Portfolio for each child.

The "Forms" section of Education CourseMate website, accessed through CengageBrain.com, includes the forms you can copy and/or modify for your observations.

The Reflective Journal pages for weeks 1 through 40 are also included on the Education CourseMate website. You can fill these out week by week to guide your introspection as well as the plans for observing children. Keep these at home, in a private place, and use them to reflect on your attitudes, practices, and feelings.

The Education CourseMate website also includes access to the TeachSource videos and their associated questions, glossary flashcards, and tutorial quizzes.

It is my hope that as you observe, document, reflect, and use the *Week by Week* plan, you will know each child as the unique creation that he or she is, and use your time with each child to appreciate, celebrate, and communicate that uniqueness.

Glossary

A

acceptance—the feeling of being loved and appreciated, contributes to self-esteem (12)

accommodation—takes in new information, balances with previous knowledge, and adjusts response (7)

accreditation—voluntary submission to a standard through a review process, usually consisting of a self-study and verification (13)

action research—informal collection of information about a child or children, nonstandardized (6)

active listening—technique for clarifying the message and the feelings (14)

adaptive skills—social, self-management and communications skills necessary for functioning in the community or culture in which a child lives (2)

ADD, ADHD—attention deficit disorder with hyperactivity professionally diagnosed impairments that affect attention span and cause impulsivity and distractibility (7)

adjustment—ability of a child to adapt socially and emotionally (13)

aggression—actions that injure people, things, or emotions (5)

alphabetic awareness—understanding that spoken language is comprised of graphic symbols of sounds that can be organized into separate words comprised of syllables and phonemes (9)

Anecdotal Recording—factual narrative of an incident (2)

animism—preoperational child believes natural world is ruled by willful intent like humans (7)

articulation—the sounds of speech (6)

artificialism—preoperational child believes that humans create and influence nature (7)

arts words—words describing attributes of visual works (10)

assessment—process of observing, recording, and documenting a child's actions, skills, and behaviors to measure against a standard (I)

assimilation—information received that adjusts previously related information (7)

association—information received that matches previously related information (7)

associative play—play that is similar, in the same theme but still with each player playing individually (4)

attachment—the emotional bond that infants show to a person (usually the mother) with whom they have had a stable, trusting relationship (1)

attention deficit—inability to focus; medical diagnosis, may or may not be accompanied by hyperactivity (7); see also ADD/ADHD

attention span—focus perceptual processes on a specific aspect of the environment (7)

audio recorders—devices that make taped or digital reproductions of sound (11)

authentic assessment—measurement of knowledge or skill in context, in as realistic a setting as possible (8)

autism—pervasive spectrum disorder with a range of effects on several domains (4, 7)

autonomy—the process of governing oneself (2)

B

benchmark—descriptions of knowledge, skills, development that are measurable outcomes of standards (8)

bias—preconceived attitudes that may affect objectivity, either positively or negatively (3)

brain hemisphericity—two hemispheres, or sides, of the brain deal with information and function in different ways (7)

C

case study (child study)—a comprehensive written overview of the child; it may be documented by written evidence and the child's work (14)

cause and effect—ability to perceive the link between two events with one as a result of the other (7)

centration—focus of attention on one attribute, ignoring other variables (7)

cephalocaudal—sequence of the development of muscle control from head to toe (3)

Checklist—a method of documenting the presence or absence of a skill or behavior in a developmental sequence (3)

classification—matching or grouping similar data (7)

Class List Log—method of gathering a specific piece of information on every child in the group (1)

closed method—the recorder makes a judgment from observation and records it with a check, slash, few words; raw data is not available for the reader (3)

closed question—one expected answer, like a test (6)

cognitive—knowing, thinking, reasoning, and remembering (8)

collectivists—the tradition or political system where the individual is devalued and the focus is on the group and interdependence (2)

competence—the feeling of capability, independence, and autonomy; contributes to self-esteem (12)

Concrete Operational Stage—period of development (7 to 11 years old), using logic and reasoning; mental actions are still related to "concrete" objects (7)

confidentiality—the professional attitude and practice of preserving the privacy of information (I)

conservation—understanding that volume or measurability of objects remains the same if nothing is added or subtracted but the form is changed (7)

constructive play—manipulating objects, such as blocks, to create a physical product (4)

contextualized literacy—ability to read words when other clues are present, such as cereal names, restaurants, and traffic signs (9)

continuity of care—practice of child care advancing children as a cohort, staying together with the same teachers as well (13)

convergent thinking—the ability to arrive at a single answer, more difficult for young children with still-developing classifying, listening, and attending skills (10)

conversations—two-way verbal exchanges (6)

cooperative play—play where players are in the same theme and working toward a common goal (4)

coping mechanisms—strategies for overcoming uncomfortable circumstances (1)

coping skills—strategies to overcome emotional traumas (5)

core emotions—basic emotions present at birth from which other emotions evolve (5)

creativity—novel thinking or product (10)

criterion-referenced—method that provides a predetermined standard or guideline to look for and measure against (e.g., Checklist, Rating Scales) (I)

curriculum—plan for learning experiences and teaching strategies that is used to help children reach goals for development and learning (I, 2, 3, 5, 8)

D

daily log or journal (also called diary)—end of the day account from recall (1)

development—change that takes place in a predictable sequence, from simple to complex, but at a different pace for individual people (2)

diagnostic interview—conversations designed to yield developmental information about a child (6)

digital divide—the gap between those who have access to electronic technology and those who do not (9)

digital video cameras—devices that record images and sound electronically (11)

disclosure—a statement that indicates the speaker has been a victim of abuse or maltreatment (12)

disequilibrium—cognitive conflict when new information does not associate or match previous data (7)

displacement—turning angry feelings away from the source of the anger (5)

dispositions—the feelings or responses to a body of knowledge (8)

divergent thinking—ability to think of a wide range of possibilities, associated with creativity and giftedness (10)

diversity—broad range of differences, individual uniqueness (6)

document (verb)—the action of preserving data for later review; **documentation (noun)**—the product that preserves the data (evidence, artifacts) (I)

documentation panels—displays of children's work that show the process of their thinking and planning and the resulting product (10, 14)

dramatic play—symbolic play, pretend (4, 11)

dysfluent—speech disorder in which the speaker repeats a beginning sound or a word (6)

dyslexia—an impairment of the ability to read (9)

E

ecological view—consideration of all aspects that influence a human being (I)

egocentric—the cognitive stage in which the child is not able to take another's point of view (4)

egocentrism—preoperational child's inability to understand that others do not share his or her perspective (7)

emergent literacy—continuous process of becoming a reader and writer (9)

emotional intelligence—type of intelligence that motivates oneself, persists in frustration, controls impulses, delays gratification, and empathizes with others (5)

emotional maltreatment—psychological damage from blaming, belittling, or rejecting a child (12)

environmental print—the signs and labels that appear on everyday objects in homes, media, and neighborhoods (9)

ethics—the moral principles and practices under which an individual operates (I)

evaluation—comparison of information gathered against a standard or set of criteria (I)

executive function—ability to self-regulate thought, action, and emotion because of the development of cognitive and neural skills (5)

expressive language—messages that are communicated through words and gestures (6)

F

facilitated conversation—planned conversation times to determine knowledge base (6)

failure to thrive—developmental delays caused by physical or emotional factors (3, 5)

family—the group of related or unrelated adults who are legally responsible for a child (I)

file access log—a form in a Portfolio that records the name, purpose, and date of each person who views the file (I)

frame of reference—individual point of view influenced by many factors (3)

Frequency Count—recording method to measure how often a specified event occurs (5)

functional play—manipulation of objects with no particular goal other than to examine and practice repetitive motions (4)

functional skills—sometimes called self-care skills (2)

G

games with rules—play where players take turns and act according to a mutually understood standard (4)

gender—general term for the social and cultural constructions of sexual identity, whereas sex is the term for the biological distinction between male and female (12)

gender identity—*see* sex-role identity (12)

good-bye rituals—established routines to help the child with separation (1)

goodness of fit—adult's recognition and ability to adjust to the child's temperament (3)

growth—quantitative change that can be measured in numbers (3)

guideline—advice issues by a professional organization or instruction on practices focused on a specific area (13)

H

high-stakes tests—on the basis of the tests, decisions are made that affect the child, the teacher, or the school (8)

holographic—one-word sentences that have meaning (6)

I

IEP—individualized education program—a document mandated for every student with a disability ages 3–21, describing child's current level of functioning and short- and long-term goals (2)

IFSP—individualized family service plan—similar to IEP for children ages 0–3 and their families (2)

inclusion—the practice of including children with special needs within the least restrictive environment (8)

individualists—tradition, political cultural system that values independence (2)

inference—conclusion; judgment; explanation (2)

informal conversations—spontaneous conversations between adult and child that yield information (6)

informed consent—ethical practice of obtaining permission before using a person as the subject of a study or in photos, audio, or video recordings (11)

interdependence—serving the needs of others above self, and a humility and reticence to put self forward (12)

interrater reliability—two or more raters use the same instrument on the same child to control bias (9)

invented spelling—phonetic spelling with a letter for each sound (9)

L

language—the meaning of the words and gestures that are communicated (6)

large muscle (gross motor)—muscles used in moving the body from one place to another (3)

learned helplessness—feeling of inadequacy results in lack of motivation and increased dependence on others (2)

learning disabilities—an interference with the ability to process written communication (9)

least restrictive environment—legal term referring to the educational placement of exceptional children in regular settings to the maximum extent possible (3)

LEP—limited English proficiency (9)

liberation teaching—theory that the teacher, by seeking to meet the child's needs, does not give up on any child (14)

license requirements—required standards, usually set by the individual states (13)

logico-mathematical knowledge—understanding principles of the nature of matter by reasoning rather than intuition or appearances (7)

M

mandala—universal symbol combining circle and intersecting lines (10)

mandated reporters—those individuals who by law must report suspicions of child abuse to specified agencies (12)

matching—recognizing the similarities of an attribute of an object (7)

media—art materials (singular: **medium**) (10)

mixed-age groups—also known as heterogeneous, multi-age, vertical, ungraded, nongraded, and family grouping; groups of children not separated by chronological age (13)

morality—characteristic of making choices based on standards set by social group (12)

morphemes—smallest unit of language; words (6)

multiple intelligences—individual ways of processing information (7)

N

narrative—method that tells a story, includes all the details of an incident (e.g., Anecdotal Recording, Running Record) (I, 2)

nature deficit disorder—not a medical condition but a social alienation from spending time outdoors (3)

neglect—the withholding of basic survival needs of food, water, shelter, clothing, medical care; constitutes maltreatment (12)

nonrepresentational—young child's drawing a symbol of mental image; not able to "represent" a recognizable symbol; difficult to draw what they are thinking (10)

norm—standard against which others are measured (8)

O

objective—detached, impersonal, observed, unprejudiced, data-only recordings (I)

object permanence—the cognitive understanding that objects and persons continue to exist even out of sight (4, 7)

observing—watching children to know more about their development (I)

one-to-one correspondence—ability to count objects accurately by assigning one number to each object (7)

onlooker play—watch others play; may talk or ask questions (4)

open method—recording method that preserves the raw data; only records actions and words so separate conclusions can be drawn (2)

open question—no single correct answer, creative answers (6)

ordinal numbers—indicating the order or succession, such as first, second, or third (8)

overgeneralization—early stage in grammar construction where child adds *s* to all words for plural and *ed* to all words for past tense (6)

P

parallel play—play that is near, maybe even doing the same actions or using the same equipment or toys, but not interacting (4)

performance standards—criteria by which individuals or programs are measured (13)

phonemes—basic unit of sound in spoken language (6)

phonemic awareness—child's understanding and conscious awareness that speech is composed of identifiable units, such as spoken words, syllables, and sounds (9)

physical abuse—any nonaccidental physical injury caused by the child's caretaker (12)

physical knowledge—knowledge about the general properties of the physical world: gravity, motion, and nature (7)

policies—individual set of practices adhered to by an organization (13)

Portfolio—a systematic collection of documentation about the child's development (I)

power—the ability to control one's actions and destiny, rather than depending on outside agents (12)

precocity—exceptional early development in cognitive or creative ability (10)

Preoperational Stage—stage of cognitive development with distinct characteristics, according to Piaget's theory, ages 4–7 (7)

preschematic—stage in drawing development before the child has attained the small muscle coordination and cognitive abilities to draw recognizable symbols (10)

print-rich environment—literacy materials available to promote recognition of symbols of alphabet and their sounds, phonemic awareness (9)

program evaluation—the process of examining all the components of a program to measure effectiveness and quality (13)

progress report—a periodic written overview of short-term goals the child has achieved (14)

proximodistal—development of muscle control from center of body to extremities (3)

Q

quality points—milestones or measurement intervals on a rating scale (9)

quality rating and improvement systems (QRIS)—standardized measurements of child care centers and homes on which to base improvement plans (13)

quantitative—method that provides a numerical count of individual or group actions (e.g., Frequency Counts, Time Samples) (I)

quantitative scoring—an assessment tool that reports results with a numeric score (8)

R

Rating Scale—measuring a specific behavior, skill, or attribute by choosing from three or more descriptors (9)

receptive language—that which is heard, taken in (6)

recommendation—a statement of practice issued by an organization that provides a health benefit to the population it serves (13)

record—documentation of an event; may be written, recorded as audio, video, or photography (6)

recording—a system or method of writing down what has been observed (I)

referral—a recommendation made for further evaluation by a helping professional (I)

reflection—thoughtful consideration of past events for analysis (1)

Reflective Journal—a private, written record in which to express feelings; not a part of child's record; property of the writer (1)

reflexes—muscle reactions to stimuli, not controlled by intent (3)

regulation—legal rules usually based on standards, guidelines or recommendations with sanctions for noncompliance (13)

reliability—quality of tests that will produce a similar score by the same individual on the same test (8)

resilient—child who escapes from childhood psychological trauma without harm (5)

responsive care—when adults adjust to the child's temperament (5)

reversibility—the concrete-operational child understands that any change can be mentally reversed, for example, think of an ice cube as water (7)

rote counting—counting by memory, may be inaccurate or out of sequence (7)

RTI—Response to Intervention—a three-tiered framework intended to prevent learning delays from becoming learning disabilities (4)

Running Record—detailed account of a segment of time; recording all behaviors and quotes during that time (4)

S

scaffolding—process of linking what a child knows or can do with new information or skills the child is ready to acquire, assisted by a more knowledgeable or skilled individual (4)

schema—symbol in art that is repeated over and over representing a real object (10)

schematic—stage in which symbolic representations go through modifications as child develops cognitively (10)

screening—a test given to a broad population to indicate possibilities that are evaluated further (8)

scribbling—experiments with drawing media, can be uncontrolled or controlled (doodling) (10)

selective method—the recording instrument dictates what is to be observed (9)

self-care—ability to eat, toilet, dress, keep clean, and keep safe (2)

self-concept—the qualities one attributes to one's self, self-identity (12)

self-differentiation—cognitive ability to recognize self as separate from environment and others (7)

self-esteem—the valuing of that knowledge based on self and social comparisons (12)

self-regulation—control of bodily functions, managing powerful emotions, working to maintain focus and attention (5)

sensitive periods—when neurons are exceptionally receptive and requiring certain experiences, form circuitry for sensorimotor development, receptive language, speech production, and reasoning and planning (7)

Sensorimotor Stage—stage from birth to age two when the child "takes in" information mainly by sensory means and gains differentiation of self from the environment (7)

sensory integregation—takes in information through the senses (vision, hearing, touch, movement, taste, and smell) and organizes or integrates this information with the increasing body control over the actions and reactions (5)

separation anxiety—distress when a parent leaves an infant's presence, beginning at 8 or 9 months and usually disappearing at about 24 months (1)

seriation—the ability to order objects by some standard rule, height, weight, shade, or tone (7)

sex—noun—physical attributes that denote male or female (12)

sex-role (gender identity)—socialized preference of behavior identified with one gender or the other (12)

sexual abuse—sexually explicit conduct with a minor (12)

shyness—hesitance in social situations, self-consciousness (5)

small muscle (fine motor)—muscles that control hands and fingers (3)

social competence—ability to maintain interactions, to have friends (4)

social conventional knowledge—information gathered from influential adults about general rules of conduct acceptable to that group (7)

socialization—process of learning social skills and personal identity (4)

socialized—behavior learned to adapt to the expectations of the social group (12)

sociodramatic play—fantasy play episode with others involved (11)

solitary play—play that is focused on objects or movements, not involved with others (4)

speech—the sounds produced to make words, phonemes (6)

standard—description of knowledge, skills, and development that children should acquire by a certain age/stage/grade (8)

Standard—defines a goal of practice with an incentive for compliance, not a legal term but agreed upon by evidence-based research to be best practice (13)

standardized tests—scores are measured against the norm group that has taken the test (8)

story dictation—children write and produce a story or episode (11)

stranger anxiety—distress when approached by an unfamiliar person, beginning at seven to nine months and ending around one year (1)

stress—physiological reactions to emotional events (5)

structured interview—planned conversations to find out specific information about a child (6)

subjective—influenced by state of mind, point of view, inferential, interpreting the meaning, or cause of an event (1)

summative observation—cumulative evaluation describing progress (1)

syntax—order of words in a sentence that gives them meaning; grammar (6)

T

tadpole man—beginning drawings of humans with lines protruding from circles (10)

talented and gifted—designation for higher than average cognitive, linguistic, social, creative development (8)

teacher's stories—the relating of classroom experiences to child development or professional practice principles; may be related orally or in written form (14) technology—tools used to perform a task (11)

telegraphic speech—few-word sentences that have meaning (6)

temperament—inborn personality traits (5)

Time Sample—method of recording where children are by choice at a certain time, measuring attention span and interests (7)

transitions—period between activities, time periods, or programs; may be problematic without planning (13)

U

unconditional positive regard—feelings a teacher should have for a student (14)

unfounded—child abuse reports that upon investigation lack evidence for criminal or civil charges (12)

Universal Design for Learning (UDL)—the concept that environments, materials, and approaches to learning should be usable by everyone, including those with disabilities, to the greatest extent possible (3)

unoccupied play—not interested in play, wanders around room (4)

V

valid—describes quality of a test that measures what it proposes to measure (8)

video recorder—device that makes a taped reproduction of image and sound (11)

W

Working Portfolio—includes selected but typical Work Samples along with teacher documentation to show the child's progress (I)

Work Samples—method that preserves the child's work as a documentation of development (e.g., drawings, writings, constructions, media-preserved work such as audio or video recordings or photographs) (I, 10)

Z

zone of proximal development—behavioral levels that can be approximated with assistance (4)

References

Adams, E. J. (2011). Teaching children to name their feelings. *Young Children*, 66 (3) 66–67. **5**

Adamson, S. (2005). Making the calendar meaningful. *Young Children*, 60 (5), 42. **8**

Administration for Children and Families ACF. (2009). FFY 2006 CCDF data tables. Retrieved from www.acf.hhs.gov/programs/ccb/data/ccdf_data/06acf800/table13.htm **13**

Ahnert, L., Gunnar, M. R., Lamb, M. E., & Barthel, M. (2004). Transition to child care: Associations with infant-mother attachment, infant negative emotion and cortisol elevations. *Child Development*, 75 (3), 639–650. **1**

Ainsworth, M., Blehar, M., Waters, E., & Wall, S. (1978). *Patterns of Attachment*. Hillsdale, NJ: Lawrence Erlbaum Associates. **1**

Allen, K. E., & Cowdery, G. (2012). *The Exceptional Child: Inclusion in Early Childhood Education* (7th ed.). Belmont, CA: Wadsworth Cengage Learning. **2, 8, 9, 11**

Alliance for Childhood. (2004). *Tech Tonic: Towards a New Literacy of Technology*. College Park, MD: Alliance for Childhood. **10**

American Academy of Pediatrics. (2001). Children, adolescents and television: Policy statement. *Pediatrics*, 10 (2), 423–426. **3**

American Academy of Pediatrics, American Public Health Association, & National Resource Center for Health and Safety in Child Care. (2011). *Caring for Our Children: National Health and Safety Performance Standards: Guidelines for Out-of-Home Child Care Programs* (3rd ed.). Elk Grove Village, IL: American Academy of Pediatrics and Washington, DC: American Public Health Association. Retrieved from http://nrc.uchsc.edunrckids.org **I, 1, 2, 13**

American Academy of Pediatrics, Committee on Public Education. (2001, November). Media violence. *Pediatrics*, 108 (5):1222–1226. Retrieved from http://aappolicy.aappublications.org/cgi/content/full/pediatrics;108/5/1222 **5**

American Speech-Language Hearing Association. (2012). Social language use—Pragmatics. Retrieved from http://www.asha.org/public/speech/development/pragmatics.htm **6**

Anderson, C. A., & Bushman, B. J. (2001). Effects of violent video-games on aggressive behavior, aggressive cognition, aggressive affect, physiological arousal, and prosocial behavior: A meta-analytic review of the scientific literature. *Psychological Science*, 12 (5), 353. **5**

Anderson, C. A., & Huesman, L. R. (2003). Human aggression: A social-cognitive view. In M. A Hogg & J. Cooper (Eds.), *Handbook of Social Psychology* (pp. 296–323). London: Sage. **5**

APA (American Psychological Association). (2002). *Ethical Principles of Psychologists and Code of Conduct*. Washington, DC: Author. Retrieved from www.apa.org/ethics/code2002.pdf **11**

APA (American Psychological Association). (2011). Resilience guide for parents and teachers. Retrieved from www.apa.org/helpcenter/resilience.aspx **3, 5**

Aratani, Y., Wight, V. R., Cooper, J. L. (2011). Racial gaps in early childhood: Socio-emotional health, developmental and educational outcomes among African-American boys. National Center for Children in Poverty. Retrieved from www.nccp.org/publications/pub_1014.html **5**

Archer, J. (2004). Sex differences in aggression in real-world settings: A meta-analytic review. *Review of General Psychology*, 8, 291–322. **5**

Armstrong, T. (2000). *In Their Own Way*. New York: Jeremy P. Tarcher/Putman. **7**

Artman, K. Hemmeter, M. L., & Feeney-Kettler, K. (2011). *Observation Toolkit for Mental Health Consultants*. Georgetown, VA: Center for Early childhood Mental Health Consultation, Georgetown University. Retrieved from www.ecmhc.org/documents/CECMHC_Observation_Toolkit.pdf **5**

Association for Childhood Education International. (2006). Global guidelines for the education and care of young children in the 21st century. Retrieved from www.acei.org/wguides.htm **4**

August, D., & Shananah, T. (2006). *Developing Literacy in Second-Language Learners: Report of the National Literacy Panel on Language, Minority Children and Youth*. Mahwah, NJ: Erlbaum. **6**

Bagnato, S. J. (2006). Quality: Standards, curriculum and assessment. Keynote address at NAEYC National Institute for Early Childhood Professional Development, June 4, 2006. **8**

Bagnato, S. J., Neisworth, J. T., & Pretti-Frontezak, C. (2010). *Linking Authentic Assessment and Early Childhood Intervention: Best Measures for Best Practice* (2nd ed.). Baltimore, MD: Paul H. Brookes. **8**

Baker, B. L., & Brightman, A. J. (2004). *Steps to Independence: Teaching Everyday Skills to Children with Special Needs 4e*. Baltimore, MD: Brookes. **2, 4**

Bakley, S. (2001). Through the lens of sensory integration: A different way of analyzing challenging behavior. *Young Children*, 56 (6), 70–76. **3**

Balaban, N. (2006). *Everyday Goodbyes: Starting School and Early Care: A Guide to the Separation Process*. New York: Teachers College Press. **1**

Bandura, A. (1977). *Social Learning Theory*. Englewood Cliffs, NJ: Prentice Hall. **5, 6**

Banks, J. A. (2001). *Cultural Diversity and Education: Foundations, Curriculum, and Teaching*. Boston, MA: Allyn & Bacon. **10**

Barbarin, O. A. (2010). Halting African American boys' progression from pre-K to prison: What families, schools and communities can do! *American Journal of Orthopsychiatry*, 80 (1), 81–88. **3**

Bardige, B. S., & Segal, M. M. (2005). *Building Literacy with Love: A Guide for Teachers and Caregivers of Children Birth Through Age 5*. Washington, DC: Zero to Three Press. **6, 9**

Baroody, A. J. (2004). The developmental bases for early childhood number and operations standards. In D. Clements, J. Sarama, & A. DiBiase (Eds.), *Engaging Young Children in Mathematics: Standards for Early Childhood Mathematics Education* (pp. 173–219). Mahwah, NJ: Erlbaum. **8**

Bauer, P. J., Wenner, J. A., Dropik, P. L., & Wewerka, S. S. (2000). Parameters of remembering and forgetting in the transition from infancy to early childhood. *Monograph of the Society for Research in Child Development*, 65 (4), 1–204. **7**

Bayley, N. (1993). *Bayley Scales of Infant Development* (2nd ed.). San Antonio, TX: The Psychological Corp. **8**

Beaty, J. (2006). *Observing Development of the Young Child* (6th ed.). Upper Saddle River, NJ: Merrill. **3**

Beaty, J. (2008). *Preschool Appropriate Practices* (2nd ed.). Clifton Park, NY: Delmar Cengage Learning. **9**

Beaty, J. (2010). *Observing Development of the Young Child* (7th ed.). Upper Saddle River, NJ: Merrill. **3, 11**

Belsky, J., Vandell, D., Burchinal, M., Clarke-Stewart, K. A., McCartne, K., Owen, M., et al. (2007). Are there long-term effects of early child care? *Child Development*, 78, 681–701. **5**

Benner, S. (2003). *Assessment of Young Children with Special Need: A Context-Based Approach*. Clifton Park, NY: Thomson Delmar Learning. **2, 6, 8, 14**

Bentzen, W. (2009). *Seeing Young Children: A Guide to Deserving and Rewarding Behavior* (6th ed.). Clifton Park, NY: Thomson Delmar Learning. **2, 3, 5**

Bergen, D. (2002). The role of pretend play in children's cognitive development. *Early Childhood Research and Practice*, 4 (1). Retrieved from http://ecrp.uiuc.edu/v4n1/bergen.html **11**

Bergen, D., Reid, R., & Toprelli, L. (2009). *Educating and Caring for Very Young Children: The Infant/Toddler Curriculum*. New York: Teachers College Press. **I**

Berger, E. (2012). *Parents as Partners in Education: Families and Schools Working Together* (8th ed.). Upper Saddle River, NJ: Merrill. **I, 14**

Berk, L. E., & Winsler, A. (2002). *Scaffolding Children's Learning: Vygotsky and Early Childhood Education*. Washington, DC: NAEYC. **9, 11**

Bers, M. U. (2008). *Blocks to Robots: Learning with Technology in the Early Childhood Classroom*. New York: Teachers College Press. **8**

Bertrand, J., Mars, A., Boyle, C., Bove, F., Yeargin-Allsopp, M., & Decoufle, P. (2001). Prevalence of autism in a United States population: The Brick Township, New Jersey, investigation. *Pediatrics*, 108 (5). Retrieved from www.pediatrics.org **7**

Besharov, D. (1990). *Recognizing Child Abuse: A Guide for the Concerned*. New York: The Free Press. **12**

Bierman, K. L., Torres, M. M., Domitrovich, C. E., Welsh, J. A., & Gest, S. D. (2009). Behavioral and cognitive readiness for school: Cross-domain associations for children attending Head Start. *Social Development*, 18 (20), 305–323. **4**

Birckmayer, J. (2001). *Discipline for Babies and Toddlers* (3rd ed.). Ithaca, NY: Cornell University. **13**

Birckmayer, J., Kennedy, A., & Stonehouse, A. (2009). Using stories effectively with infants and toddlers. *Young Children*, 64 (1), 42–47. **9**

Bjorklund, D. F., & Bjorklund, B. R. (1992). *Looking at Children: An Introduction to Child Development*. Pacific Grove, CA: Brooks/Cole Publishing Co. **1**

Blagojevic, B., & Gathwait, A. (2001). Observing and recording growth and change: Using technology as an assessment tool. *Scholastic Early Childhood Today*, 15 (8), 36–44. **11**

Bleeker, M. M., & Jacobs, J. E. (2004). Achievement in math and science: Do mothers' beliefs matter 12 years later? *Journal of Educational Psychology*, 96, 97–109. **12**

Block, C. C. (2001). *Teaching the Language Arts: Expanding Thinking Through Student-Centered Instruction* (3rd ed.). Boston, MA: Allyn and Bacon. **9, 11**

Bloom, B., & Cohen, R. A. (2007). National Center for Health Statistics Attention Deficit Hyperactivity Disorder. Summary Health Statistics for U.S. Children: National Health Interview Survey, 2006. Retrieved from www.cdc.gov/nchs/data/series/sr_10/sr10_234.pdf **3**

Bodrova, D., & Leong, D. J. (2006). Adult influences on play: The Vygotskian approach. In D. P. Fromberg & D. Bergen (Eds.), *Play from Birth to Twelve: Contexts, Perspectives and Meanings* (pp. 167–172). New York: Routledge. **4, 8**

Bodrova, E., & Leong, D. (2005). Why children need play. *Early Childhood Today*, 20 (1) 6–7. **11**

Bodrova, E., (2007). Make-believe play versus academic skills: A Vygotskian approach to today's dilemma of early childhood education. *European Early Childhood Education Research Journal*, 16. September 2008. **11**

Bodrova, E., & Leong, D. J. (2003). The importance of being playful. *Educational Leadership*, 60 (7), 50–53. **8**

Bodrova, E., & Leong, D. J. (2007). *Tools of the Mind: The Vygotskian Approach to Early Childhood Education* (2nd ed.). Upper Saddle River, NJ: Prentice Hall. **4, 9, 10, 11**

Bornstein, M. H., & Cote, L. R. (2001). Mother-infant interaction and acculturation: Behavioral comparisons in Japanese-American and South-American families. *International Journal of Behavioral Development*, 25, 549–563. **4**

Bowe, F. G. (2007). *Early Childhood Special Education* (4th ed.). Clifton Park, NY: Thomson Delmar Learning. **2**

Bowlby, J. (1969). *Attachment*. New York: Basic Books. **1**

Brendtro, L., Brokenleg, M., & Van Bockern, S. (2002). *Reclaiming Youth at Risk*. Bloomington, IN: National Education Service. **5**

Brendtro, L., & Longhurst, J. E. (2005). The resilient brain. *Reclaiming Children & Youth*, 14 (1), 52–60. **5**

Bricker, D., & Squires, J. (2009). *Ages and Stages Questionnaires (ASQ-3)* (3rd ed.) Baltimore, MD: Brookes. **3, 8**

Brigance, A. H., & Glascoe, F. P. (2010). *Brigance Diagnostic Inventory of Early Development II*. North Billerica, MA: Curriculum Associates. **3, 8**

Brooks-Gunn, J., Duncan, G. J. et al., (2007). School readiness and later achievement. *Developmental Psychology*, 43, (6), 1428–1446. **7**

Brown, E. T. (2005). The influence of teachers' efficacy and beliefs regarding mathematics instruction in the early childhood classroom. *Journal of Early Childhood Teacher Education*, 26, 239–257. **8**

Brown-DuPaul, J., Keyes, T., & Segatti, L. (2001). Using documentation panels to communicate with families. *Childhood Education*, 77 (4), 209–213. **14**

Bruner, J. S. (1983). *Child's Talk: Learning to Use Language*. New York: Norton. **I**

Bryen, D. N., & Gallaher, D. (1983). Assessment of language and communication. In K. D. Paget & B. A. Bracken (Eds.), *The Psychoeducational Assessment of the Preschool Child*. New York: Grune & Stratton. **6**

Burchinal, M., & Forestieri, N. (2011). Development of early literacy: Evidence from major U.S. longitudinal studies. In S. B. Neuman & D. K. Dickinson (Eds.), *Handbook of Early Literacy Research* (Vol. 3, pp. 85–96). New York: Guilford Press. **9**

Burdette, H., & Whitaker, R. C. (2005). A national study of neighborhood safety, outdoor play, television viewing and preschool children. *Pediatrics*, 116 (3) 657–662. **3, 9**

Burman, L. (2009). *Are You Listening? Fostering Conversations That Help Young Children Learn*. St. Paul, MN: Redleaf Press. **6**

Bushman, B. J., & Huesmann, L. R. (2001). Effects of televised violence on aggression. In D. G. Singer & J. L. Singer, (Eds.), *Handbook of Children and the Media* (pp. 223–254). Thousand Oaks, CA: Sage Publications. **11**

Buysse, V., Goleman, B. D., & Skinner, M. L. (2002). Setting effects on friendship formation among young children with and without disabilities. *Exceptional Children*, 68 (4), 503–517. **4**

Caldwell, B. M. (2001). Déjà vu all over again: A researcher explains the NICHD Study. *Young Children*, 56 (4), 58–59. **I**

Calvert, S. L., & Kotler, J. A. (2003). Lessons from children's television: The impact of the Children's Television Act on children's learning. *Applied Developmental Psychology*, 24, 275–335. **8**

Calvert, S. L., Kotler, J. A., Zehnder, S. M., & Shockey, E. M. (2003). Gender stereotyping in children's reports about educational and informational television programs. *Media Psychology*, 5, 139–162. **8**

Campbell, S. B. (1995). Behavior problems in preschool children: A review of recent research. *Journal of Child Psychology and Psychiatry*, 36, 113–149. **5**

Cannon, J., & Ginsburg, H. P. (2008). "Doing the math": Maternal beliefs about early mathematics versus language learning. *Early Education & Development*, 19, 238–260. **8**

Carlson, F. M. (2011). *Big Body Play: Why Boisterous, Vigorous and Very Physical Play is Essential to Children's Development and Learning.* Washington, DC: NAEYC. **3**

Carlsson-Paige, N., & Levin, D. E. (1987). *The War Play Dilemma: Balancing Needs and Values in the Early Childhood Classroom.* New York: Teachers College Press. **4**

Carr, M. (2001). *Assessment in Early Childhood Settings: Learning Stories.* London: Paul Chapman. **2, 7**

Center on the Developing Child at Harvard University. (2011). *Building the Brain's "Air Traffic Control" System: How Early Experiences Shape the Development of Executive Function: Working Paper No. 11.* Retrieved from www.developingchild.harvard.edu **5**

Centers for Disease Control. (2008). Autism Information Center. Retrieved from http://www.cdc.gov/ncbddd/autism/data.html **7**

Centers for Disease Control (2012). Obesity prevalence. Retrieved from www.cdc.gov/nccdphp/dnpa/obesity/childhood/prevalence.htm **3**

Chandler, L. K., Dahlquist, C. M., Repp, A. C., & Feltz, C. (1999). The effects of team-fased functional assessment on the behavior of students in classroom settings. *Exceptional Children*, 66, 101–122. **5**

Charlesworth, R., & Lind, K. (2013). *Math and Science for Young Children* (7th ed.). Belmont, CA: Wadsworth/Cengage Learning. **8**

Child Welfare Information Gateway. (2006, April). *What is child abuse and neglect?* Fact Sheet. Retrieved from www.familycourt.org/documents/whatiscan.pdf **12**

Children's Defense Fund. (2011). *The State of America's Children Yearbook, 2011.* Washington, DC: Author. Retrieved from http://www.childrensdefense.org/child-research-data-publications/data/state-of-americas-2011.pdf **8, 14**

Chomsky, N. (1965). *Aspects of the Theory of Syntax.* Cambridge, MA: MIT Press. **6**

Chomsky, N. (1968). *Language and Mind.* New York: Harcourt, Brace and World. **6**

Chomsky, N. (2000). *New Horizons in the Study of Language and Mind.* New York: Cambridge University Press **6**

Christakis, D. A., & Garrison, M. M. (2009, December 1). Preschool-aged children's television viewing in child care settings. *Pediatrics*, 124, (6), 1627–1632. **8**

Clark, A. (2007). A hundred ways of listening: Gathering children's perspectives of their early childhood environment. *Young Children*, 62 (3), 76–81. **6**

Clarke-Stewart, A., & Allhusen, V. D. (2005). *What We Know About Child Care.* Cambridge, MA: Harvard University Press. **13**

Clarke-Stewart, K. A., & Vandell, D. L. (2002). Do regulable features of child-care homes affect children's development? *Early Childhood Research Quarterly*, 17 (1), 52–86. **13**

Clay, M. (1975). *What Did I Write?* Auckland, New Zealand: Heinemann. **9**

Clay, M. M. (1985). The Early Detection of Reading Difficulties, (3rd ed.). Portsmouth, NH: Heinemann. **9**

Coakley, J. J. (2004). *Sport in Society: Issues and Controversies* (8th ed.). St. Louis: Mosby. **3**

Cohen, D. H., Stern, V., Balaban, N., & Gropper, N. (2008). *Observing and Recording the Behavior of Young Children* (5th ed.). New York: Teachers College Press. **1, 13**

Cohen, J., Onunaku, N., Clothier, S., & Pope, J. (2005, September). *Helping young children succeed: Strategies to Promote Early Childhood Social and Emotional Development.* Early Childhood Research and Policy Report. Denver, CO: National Conference of State Legislatures. **4**

Cohen, J. H., & Wiener, R. B. (2003). *Literacy Portfolios: Improving Assessment Teaching and Learning.* Upper Saddle River, NJ: Prentice Hall.

Cole, A. (2004). *When Reading Begins.* Portsmouth, NH: Heinemann. **9**

Coles, R. (1997). *The Moral Intelligence of Children.* New York: Random. **12**

Common Sense Media. (2011). Zero to eight: Children's media use in America. Retrieved from www.commonsensemedia.org/sites/default/files/research/zerotoeightfinal2011.pdf **9**

Comstock, G., & Scharrer, E. (2006). Media and popular culture. In K. A. Renninger & I. E. Sigel (Eds.), *Handbook of Child Psychology: Vol. 4. Child Psychology in Practice* (6th ed., pp. 817–863). Hoboken, NJ: Wiley. **8**

Comstock, G., & Scharrer, E. (2007). *Media and the American Child.* Burlington, MA: Elsevier. **11**

Consortium of National Arts Education Associations. (2007). *Dance, Music, Theatre, Visual Arts: What Every Young American Should Know and Be able to Do in the Arts: National Standards for Arts Education.* Reston, VA: Music Educators National Conference. **10, 11**

Cook, R. E., Klein, M. D., & Tessier, A. (2008). *Adapting Early Childhood Curricula for Children in Inclusive Setting* (7th ed.). Upper Saddle River, NJ: Pearson Education. **6, 7, 8**

Coplan, R. J., & Hughes, K., & Rowsell, H. C. (2010). Once upon a time there were a blushful hippo and a meek mouse: A content analysis of shy characters in young children's storybooks. In K. H. Rubin & R. J. Coplan (Eds.), *The Development of Shyness and Social Withdrawal.* New York: Guilford Press. **5**

Coplan, R. J., & Weeks, M. (2010). Unsociability and the preference for solitude in childhood. In K. H. Rubin & R. J. Coplan (Eds.), *The Development of Shyness and Social Withdrawal.* New York: Guilford Press. **5**

Copley, J. (2004). The early childhood collaborative: A professional development model to communicate and implement standards. In D. Clements, J. Sarama, & A. diBiase (Eds.), *Engaging Young Children in Mathematics: Standards for Early Childhood Mathematics Education* (pp. 401–415). Mahwah, NJ: Erlbaum. **8**

Copple, C., & Bredekamp, S. (2009). *Developmentally Appropriate Practice in Early Childhood Programs: Serving Children from Birth through Age 8* (3rd ed.). Washington, DC: NAEYC. **I, 7, 8, 10, 11, 13**

Cost, Quality & Outcomes Study Team. (1995). *Cost, Quality & Child Outcomes in Child Care Centers.* Denver: Department of Economics, University of Colorado. **13**

Council for Early Childhood Professional Recognition. (1996). *Preschool Caregivers in Center-Based Programs: The Child Development Associate Assessment System and Competency Standards.* Washington, DC: Author. **I, 1, 4, 10, 14**

Courage, M. L., & Cowan, N. (Eds.). (2009). *The Development of Memory in Infancy and Childhood.* New York: Psychology Press. **7**

Crick, N. R., Ostrov, J. M., Appleyard, K., Jansen, E. A., & Casas, J. F. (2004). Relational aggression in early childhood. In M. Putallaz & K. L. Bierman (Eds.), *Aggression, Antisocial Behavior, and Violence Among Girls: A Developmental Perspective,* (pp. 71–89.) New York: Guilford Press. **5**

Crosson-Tower, C. (2003). *The Role of Educators in Preventing and Responding to Child Abuse and Neglect*. Washington, DC: U.S. Department of Health and Human Services. **12**

CSEFEL (Center on the Social and Emotional Foundations for Early Learning). (2008). Retrieved from www.vanderbilt.edu/csefel/index.html **5**

Csikszentmihalyi, M. (1997). *Creativity: Flow and the Psychology of Discovery and Invention*. New York: Harper Collins. **10**

Cuppens, V., Rosenow, N., & Wike, J. (2007). *Learning with Nature Idea Book: Creating Nurturing Outdoor Spaces for Children*. Lincoln, NE: The National Arbor Day Foundation. **3**

Curry, N., & Arnaud, S. (1995). Personality difficulties in preschool children as revealed through play themes and styles. *Young Children, 50* (4), 4–9. **11**

Curry, N., & Johnson, C. (1990). *Beyond Self-Esteem: Developing a Genuine Sense of Human Value*. Washington, DC: NAEYC. **12**

Curtis, D. (2008, November–December). Seeing children. *Child Care Exchange, 184,* 38–42. **11**

Curtis, D., & Carter, M. (2008). *Learning Together with Young Children: A Curriculum Framework for Reflective Teachers*. St Paul, MN: Redleaf Press. **1, 11**

Dalli, C. (2000). Starting child care: What young children learn about relating to adults in the first weeks of starting child care. *Early Childhood Research and Policy, 2* (2). Retrieved from http://ecrp.uiuc.edu/v2n2/dalli.html **13**

Daniels, M. (2001). *Dancing with Words: Signing for Hearing Children's Literacy*. Westport, CT: Bergin & Garvey. **6**

Danielson, C., & Abrutyn, L. (1997). *An Introduction to Using Portfolios in the Classroom*. Alexandria, VA: Association for Supervision and Curriculum Development. **1**

Davis, B. C., & Shade, D. D. (1994). Integrate, don't isolate!: Computers in the early childhood curriculum. *ERIC Digest*. Urbana, IL: Clearinghouse on Elementary and Early Childhood Education. EDO-PS-94–17. **9**

Day, B. (1994). *Early Childhood Education: Developmental/Experiential Teaching and Learning* (4th ed.). New York: Merrill. **10**

Day, M., & Parlakian, R. (2004). *How Culture Shapes Social-Emotional Development: Implications for Practice in Infant-Family Programs*. Washington, DC: Zero to Three Press. **5**

de Villiers, P. A., & de Villiers, J. G. (1986). *Early Language*. Cambridge, MA: Harvard University Press. **6**

Deiner, P. L. (2009). *Infants & Toddlers: Development and Curriculum Planning* (2nd ed.). Clifton Park, NY: Delmar Cengage Learning. **10**

Derman-Sparks, L. (1989). *Anti-Bias Curriculum: Tools for Empowering Young Children*. Washington, DC: NAEYC. **12, 13**

Derman-Sparks, L., & Edwards, J. O. (2010) *Anti-Bias Education for Young Children and Ourselves*. Washington, DC: NAEYC. **12**

Deutsch, D. (2010, July/August). Speaking in tunes. *Scientific American Mind, 21* (3), 36–43. **6, 10**

Deviney, J., Duncan, S., Harris, S., Rody, M. A., & Rosenberry, L. (2010). *Inspiring Spaces for Young Children*. Silver Spring, MD: Gryphon House. **13**

Deviney, J., Duncan, S., Harris, S., Rody, M. A., & Rosenberry, L. (2010). *Rating Observation Scale for Inspiring Environments*. Silver Spring, MD: Gryphon House. **13**

DeVries, R., & Kohlberg, L. (1987). *Constructivist Early Childhood Education: Overview and Comparison with Other Programs*. Washington, DC: NAEYC. **4**

Diamond, A. (2006). The early development of executive functions. In E. Bialystok & F. Craik (Eds.), *Lifespan Cognition: Mechanisms of Change* (pp. 70–95). New York: Oxford University Press. **4**

Diamond, K. E. (2001). Relationships among young children's ideas, emotional understanding and social contact with classmates with disabilities. *Topics in Early Childhood Special Education, 21* (2), 104–114. **1, 4**

Dickinson, D. K. (2001). Large-group and free-play times: Conversational settings supporting language and literacy development. In D. Dickinson & P. Tabors (Eds.). *Beginning Literacy with Language* (pp. 257–288). Baltimore, MD: Brookes. **11**

Dickinson, D. K., & Tabors, P. O. (Eds.). (2001). *Beginning Literacy with Language: Young Children Learning at Home and School*. Baltimore, MD: Brookes. **6**

Dighe, J., Calomiris, Z., & Van Zutphen, C. (1998). Nurturing the language of art in children. *Young Children, 53* (1), 4–9. **10**

DiNatale, L. (2002). Developing high-quality family involvement programs in early childhood settings. *Young Children, 57* (5), 90–95. **14**

Division of Early Childhood—Council for Exceptional Children. (2005). *DEC Recommended Practices in Early Intervention/Early Childhood Special Education*. Missoula, MT: Author. **2**

Doctoroff, G. L., Greer, J. A., & Arnold, D. H. (2006). The relationship between social behavior and emergent literacy among preschool boys and girls. *Journal of Applied Developmental Psychology, 27* (1), 1–13. **11**

Dombrink-Green, M. (2011, September). A conversation with Vivian Gussin Paley. *Young Children, 66* (5), 90–93. **11**

Duncan, G., & Brooks-Gunn, J. (1997). *Consequences of Growing Up Poor*. New York: Russell Sage. **8**

Dunlap, G., Fox, L., Smith, B., & Strain, P. (2002). Center for evidence-based practice: Young children with challenging behaviors. University of South Florida, Tampa, FL. Proposal submitted to the office of Special Education Programs, U.S. Department of Education (Grant No. H324Z010001). **5**

Dunlap, G., Strain, P. S., Fox, L., Carta, J. J., Conroy, M., Smith, B. J. et al. (2006). Prevention and intervention with young children's challenging behavior: Perspectives regarding current knowledge. *Behavioral Disorders, 32* (1), 29–45. **5**

Dunn, J. (2004). *Children's Friendships: The Beginnings of Intimacy*. Malden, MA: Blackwell Publishing. **4**

Dunst, C. J., Trivette, C. M., & Mott, D. W. (1994). Strengths-based family-centered intervention practices. In C. J. Dunst, C. M. Trivette & A. G. Deal (Eds.), *Supporting and Strengthening Families: Methods, Strategies and Practices, Vol. I* (pp. 115–131). Cambridge, MA: Brookline. **14**

Early, D. M., Maxwell, K. L., Burchinal, M., Alva, S., Bender, R., Bryant, D., et al. (2007). Teachers' education, classroom quality and young children's academic skills: Results from seven studies of preschool programs. *Child Development, 78,* 558–580. **8**

Eastman, P. D. (1988). *Are You My Mother?* New York: Random House. **1**

Edwards, C. P., & Willis, L. M. (2000). Integrating visual and verbal literacies in the early childhood classroom. *Early Childhood Education Journal, 27* (4), 259–265. **9, 10**

Edwards, C., & Gandini, L. (Eds.). (1998). *The Hundred Languages of Children: The Reggio Emilia Approach: Advanced Reflections* (2nd ed.). Greenwich, CT: Ablex Publishing. **5, 9, 10**

Edwards, L. C. (2006). *The Creative Arts: A Process Approach for Teachers and Children*. Upper Saddle River, NJ: Pearson Education. **11**

Eisenberger, N., Lieberman, M., & Williams, K. (2003). The pain of social exclusion. *Science, 302,* 290–292. **5**

Elias, C. I., & Berk, L. E. (2002). Self-regulation in young children: Is there a role for sociodramatic play? *Early Childhood Research Quarterly, 17,* 1–17. **11**

Eliassen, E. K. (2011, March). The impact of teachers and families on young children's eating behaviors. *Young Children*, 66 (2), 84–89. **2**

Elkind, D. (1987/2000). *Miseducation: Preschoolers at Risk.* New York: Alfred A. Knopf. **2, 9**

Elkind, D. (2007). *The Power of Play: How Spontaneous, Imaginative Activities Lead to Happier, Healthier Children.* Cambridge, MA: Da Capo Lifelong. **11**

Elliot, E. (2003). Challenging our assumptions: Helping a baby adjust to center care. *Young Children*, 58 (4), 22–28. **13**

Elliott, B. (2002). *Measuring Performance: The Early Childhood Educator in Practice.* Clifton Park, NY: Thomson Delmar Learning. **13**

Elliott, K., & Urquiza, A. (2006). Ethnicity, culture and child maltreatment. *Journal of Social Issues*, 62 (40), 787–809. **12**

Elliott, S. N., & Gresham, F. M. (1990). *Social Skills Rating System.* Circle Pines, MN: American Guidance System. **4**

Elliott, S. N., McKevitt, B. C., & DiPerna, J. C. (2002). Best practices in preschool social skills training. In A. Thomas & J. Grimes (Eds.), *Best Practices in School Psychology IV* (pp. 1041–1056). Bethesda, MD: National Association of School Psychologists. **4**

Emma, L., & Jarrett, M. (2010). How we play: Cultural determinants of physical activity in young children. Retrieved from http://aahperd.org/headstartbodystart/toolbox/upload/HowWePlay_litReview.pdf **3**

Enz, B., & Christie, J. (1997). Teacher play interaction styles: Effects on play behavior and relationships with teacher training and experience. *International Journal of Early Childhood Education*, 2, 55–69. **11**

Epstein, A. S., Schweinhart, L. J., Debruin-Parecki, A., & Robin, K. B. (2004). Preschool assessment: A guide to developing a balanced approach. *Preschool Matters*, 7, 1–12. National Institute for Early Education Research. **8**

Epstein, A. S. (2009a) *Me, You, Us: Social Emotional Learning in Preschool.* Washington DC: NAEYC. **6, 12**

Epstein, A. S. (2009b). *You, Me, Us: Social-Emotional Learning in Preschool.* Washington, DC: NAEYC. **4, 5**

Epstein, J. L. (2005). Attainable goals? The spirit and letter of the No Child Left Behind Act on parental involvement. *Sociology of Education*, 78 (2), 179–182. **14**

Epstein, J. L., & Sheldon, S. B. (2006). Moving forward: Ideas for research on school, family and community partnerships. In C. F. Conrad & R. Serlin (Eds.), *SAGE Handbook for Research in Education: Engaging Ideas and Enriching Inquiry* (pp. 117–138). Thousand Oaks, CA: Sage Publications. **1**

Erickson, D. M., & Ernst, J. A. (2011, July/August). The real benefits of nature play every day. *Exchanged*, 33 (4, No. 200), 97–99. **3**

Erikson, E. (1950/1963). *Childhood and Society* (2nd ed.). New York: Norton. **2, 4, 5, 10, 12**

Espinosa, L. M. (2008). Challenging common myths about young English language learners. Foundation for Child Development. Retrieved from www.fcd-us.org **6**

Ethridge, E. A., & King, J. R. (2005). Calendar math in preschool and primary classrooms: Questioning the curriculum. *Early Childhood Education Journal*, 32 (5), 291–296. **8**

Evans, G. W., & Schamberg, M. A. (2009). Childhood poverty, chronic stress and adult working memory. Retrieved from www.pnas.org/content/early/2009/03/27/0811910106.full.pdf.html **7**

Evans, R. I. (1973). *Jean Piaget: The Man and His Ideas.* New York: E. P. Dutton. **6**

Fein, G. G., Ardila-Rey, A. E., & Groth, L. A. (2000). The narrative connection: Stories and literacy. In K. Roskos & J. F. Christie (Eds.), *Play and Literacy in Early Childhood.* Mahwah, NJ: Erlbaum. **9**

Fein, S. (1993). *First Drawings: Genesis of Visual Thinking.* Pleasant Hill, CA: Exelrod Press. **10**

Ferber, J. (1996). A look in the mirror: Self-concept in preschool children. In L. Kaplow (Ed.), *Unsmiling Faces: How Preschools Can Heal* (pp. 29–46). New York; Teachers College Press. **12**

Feuerstein, R., Feuerstein R. S., & Falik, L. H. (2010). *Beyond Smarter: Mediated Learning and the Brain's Capacity for Change.* New York: Teachers College Press. **8**

Finzi, R., Ram, A., Har-Even, D., Shnit, D., & Weizman, A. (2001). Attachment styles and aggression in physically abused and neglected children. *Journal of Youth and Adolescence*, 30 (6), 769. **5**

Fisch, S. M. (2004). *Children's Learning from Educational Television: "Sesame Street" and Beyond.* Mahwah, NJ: Erlbaum. **9**

Flavell, J. (1977). *Cognitive Development.* Englewood Cliffs, NJ: Prentice Hall. **4**

Flavell, J. H. (1963). *The Developmental Psychology of Jean Piaget.* New York: Van Nostrand. **10**

Flavell, J. H. (1987). *Cognitive Development* (2nd ed.). Englewood Cliffs, NJ: Prentice Hall. **7**

Flavell, J. H., Miller, P. H., & Miller, S. A. (2002). *Cognitive Development.* Upper Saddle River, NJ: Prentice Hall. **7**

Fleege, P. O., Charlesworth, R., Burts, D. C., & Hart, C. H. (1996). Stress begins in kindergarten: A look at behavior during standardized testing. *Journal of Research in Childhood Education*, 7 (10), 20–26. **8**

Florez, I. (2011, July). Developing Young children's self-reguation through everyday experiences. *Young Children* (66) 4, 46–51. **5**

Folio, M. R., & Fewell, R. R. (2000). *Peabody Developmental Motor Scales* (2nd ed.). Allen, TX: Developmental Learning Materials Teaching Resources. **3**

Fontes, L. A. (2005). *Child Abuse and Culture: Working with Diverse Families.* New York: Guilford Press. **12**

Forman, G. (1999). Instant video revisiting: The video camera as a "tool of the mind" for young children. *Early Childhood Research and Practice*, 1 (2). Retrieved from http://ecrp.uiuc.edu/v1n2/forman.html **11**

Forrest, R., & McCrea, N. (2002, January). How do I relate and share professionally? *Child Care Information Exchange*, 143, 49. **1**

Foulin, J. N. (2005). Why is letter-name knowledge such a good predictor of learning to read? *Reading and Writing*, 18 (2), 129–155. **9**

Fox, J. E., & Schirrmacher, R. (2012). *Art and creative development for young children* (7th ed.). Clifton Park, NY: Thomson Delmar Learning. **10**

Frankenburg, W. K., Dodds, J. B., & Fandal, A. W. (1990). *Denver Developmental Screening II (DDST-II).* Denver, CO: Denver Developmental Materials, Inc. **3**

Freud, S. (1953). *The Standard Edition of the Complete Psychological Works of Sigmund Freud* (J. Strachey, Ed. and Trans.). London: Hogarth and the Institute of Psychoanalysis. **4**

Fuchs-Beauchamp, K. D. (1996). Preschoolers' inferred self-esteem: The behavioral rating scale of presented self-esteem in young children. *Journal of Genetic Psychology*, 157 (2), 204–210. **12**

Furth, H. G. (1969). *Piaget and Knowledge.* Englewood Cliffs, NJ: Prentice Hall. **7**

Gable, S. (2002). Teacher–child relationships throughout the day. *Young Children*, 57 (4), 42–44. **13**

Galinsky, E. (2010). *Mind in the Making: The Seven Essential Life Skills Every Child Needs.* New York: Harper Studios. **5, 8**

Gallagher, K. C., & Mayer, K. (2008). Enhancing development and learning through teacher-child relationships. *Young Children*, 63 (6), 80–87. **13**

Gallahue, D. L. (2003). *Developmental Physical Education for Children*. Champaign, IL: Human Kinetics. **3**

Gantz, W., Schwartz, N., Angelini, J., & Rideout, V. (2007). Food for thought: Television food advertising to children in the United States. Kaiser Family Foundation. Retrieved from www.kff.org/entmedia/7618.cfm **8**

Garbarino, J. (1999). *Lost Boys: Why Our Sons Turn Violent and How We Can Save Them*. New York Free Press. **5**

Garcia, E. E., & Frede, E. C. (2010). *Young English Language Learners: Current Research and Emerging Directions for Practice and Policy*. New York: Teachers College Press. **6**

Gardner, H. (1980). *Artful Scribbles: The Significance of Children's Drawings*. New York: Basic Books. **10**

Gardner, H. (1983). *Frames of Mind: Theory of Multiple Intelligences*. New York: Basic Books. **7**

Gardner, H. (1999). *Intelligence Reframed: Multiple Intelligences for the 21st Century*. New York: Basic Books. **7**

Gartrell, D. (2004). *The Power of Guidance: Teaching Social-Emotional Skills in Early Childhood Classrooms*. Clifton Park, NY: Thomson Delmar Learning. **3**

Gartrell, D. (2011). *A Guidance Approach for the Encouraging Classroom* (5th ed.). Belmont, CA: Wadsworth Cengage Learning. **5, 13, 14**

Garvey, C. (1977). *Play*. Cambridge, MA: Harvard University Press. **11**

Gazzaniga, M. (2008). *Learning, Arts and the Brain: The Dana Consortium Report on Arts and Cognition*. (Asbury, C., & Rich, B., Eds.). Washington, DC: Dana Press. **10**

Genesee, F., Paradis, J., & Crago, M. B. (2004). *Dual Language Development and Disorders: A Handbook on Bilingualism and Second Language Learning*. Baltimore, MD: Brookes. **6**

Gentry, J. (2000). In Chamberlin, J. Working to create a violence-free future for young children. *Monitor on Psychology*, 31 (8), 54–55. **5**

Gentry, J. R. (2006). *Breaking the Code: The New Science of Beginning Reading and Writing*. Portsmouth, NH: Heinemann. **9**

Gerecke, K., & Weatherby, P. (2001). High/Scope strategies for specific disabilities. In N. A. Brickman (Ed.), *Supporting Young Learners 3: Ideas for Child Care Providers and Teachers* (pp. 255–266). Ypsilanti, MI: High/Scope Press. **3**

Gestwicki, C. (2013). *Home, School, and Community Relations* (8th ed.). Belmont, CA: Wadsworth, Cengage Learning. **14**

Gilbert, M., Widom, C. S., Browne, K., Fergusson, D., Webb, E., & Janson, S. (2009). Burden and consequences of child maltreatment in high income countries. *The Lancet*, 373 (9657), 68–81. Retrieved from www.thelancet.com **12**

Gillanders, C., & Castro, D. C. (2011, January). Storybook reading for young dual language learners. *Young Children*, 66 (1), 91–95. **9**

Gillespie L. G., & Parlakian, R. (2009). Rich responses help babies learn and thrive. *Young Children*, 64 (2), 58–59. **13**

Gilliam, W. (2005). Prekindergarteners left behind: Expulsion rates in state prekindergarten systems. Yale University Child Study Center, May 4, 2005. Retrieved from http://198.134.159.51/issues/wsd/education/NationalPreKExpulsionPaper.pdf Feb 13, 2009. **4, 5**

Gilliam, W. S. (2004). Prekindergarteners left behind: Expulsion rates in state prekindergarten systems. Retrieved from www.fcd-us.org/usr_doc/ExpulsionCompleteReport.pdf **5**

Gilman, D. A., & Kiger, S. (2003). Should we try to keep class sizes small? *Educational Leadership*, 60 (7), 80–86. **13**

Ginsburg, H., & Opper, S. (1988). *Piaget's Theory of Intellectual Development* (3rd ed). Englewood Cliffs, NJ: Prentice Hall. **7**

Glasser, W. (1969). *Schools Without Failure*. New York: Harper & Row. **13**

Golbeck, S. L. (2005). Building foundations for spatial literacy. *Young Children*, 60 (6), 72–83. **8**

Goldman, B., & Buysse, V. (2007). Friendships in very young children. In O. Saracho & B. Spodek (Eds.), *Contemporary Perspectives on Research in Socialization and Social Development* (pp. 165–192). Greenwich, CT: Information Age Publishing. **4**

Goldstein, N. E., Arnold, D. H., Rosenberg, J. L., Stowe, R. M., & Ortiz, C. (2001). Contagion of aggression in day care classrooms as a function of peer and teacher responses. *Journal of Educational Psychology*, 93 (4), 708. **5**

Goleman, D. (2006). *Emotional Intelligence: Why It Can Matter More Than IQ*. New York: Bantam Books. **5**

Gonzalez-Mena, J. (2008). *Diversity in Early Care and Education: Honoring Differences* (5th ed.). New York: McGraw Hill. **2, 4, 12**

Good, L. (2009). *Teaching and Learning with Digital Photography*. Thousand Oaks, CA: Corwin Press. **11**

Goodenough, F. (1926). *Children's Drawings as Measures of Intellectual Maturity*. New York: Harcourt Brace Jovanovich. **10**

Goodman, Y. M., & Owocki, H. (2002). *Kidwatching: Documenting Children's Literacy Development*. Portsmouth, NH: Heinemann. **I, 4**

Goodson, B. D., Layzer, J. I., & Layzer, C. J. (2005). *Quality of Early Childhood Care Settings: Caregiver Rating Scale (QUEST)*. Cambridge, MA: Abt Associates Inc. **13**

Goodway, J. D., & Smith, D. W. (2005). Keeping all children healthy: Challenges to leading an active lifestyle for children qualifying for at-risk programs. *Family and Community Health*, 28 (2), 142–145. **3**

Gordon, T., & Burch, N. (1978) *T.E.T. Teacher Effectiveness Training*. New York: David MCcay Co. **14**

Gore, M. T., & Janssen, K. G. (2007). What educators need to know about abused children with disabilities. *Preventing School Failure*, 52 (1), 49–55. **12**

Grant, R. A., & Wong, S. D. (2003). Barriers to literacy for language-minority learners: An argument for change in the literacy education profession. *Journal of Adolescent & Adult Literacy*, 46 (5), 386–394. **9**

Green, C. F. (1998). This is my name. *Childhood Education*, 74 (4), 226–231. **9**

Greenspan, S. (2002). *The secure child: Helping Children Feel Safe and Confident in a Changing World*. Cambridge, MA: Perseus Publishing. **5**

Greenspan, S., & Wieder, S. (2006). *Engaging Autism: Using the Floortime Approach to Help Children Relate, Communicate and Think*. Cambridge, MA: DaCapo Lifelong Books. **4**

Gregory, K. M., Kim, A. S., & Whiren, A. (2003). The effect of verbal scaffolding in the complexity of preschool children's block construction. In D. E. Lytle, (Ed.), *Play and Educational Theory and Practice* (pp. 117–134). Westport, CT: Praeger Publishers. **10**

Gronlund, G., & Engel, B. (2009). *Focused Portfolios: A Complete Assessment for the Young Child*. St Paul, MN: Redleaf Press. **I**

Gronlund, N. E. (2003). *Assessment of Student Achievement* (7th ed.). Boston, MA: Allyn and Bacon. **I**

Gunner, M. R. (2007). Stress effects on the developing brain. In D. Romer & E. F. Walker (Eds.), *Adolescent Psychopathology and the Developing Brain: Integrating Brain and Prevention Science* (pp. 127–147). New York: Oxford University Press. **5**

Hallahan, D. P., & Kaufman, J. M. (2009). *Exceptional Children* (11th ed.). Boston, MA: Allyn & Bacon. **9**

Hampton, V. R., & Fantuzzi, J. W. (2003). The validity of the Penn Interaction Peer Play Scale with urban low income kindergarten children. *School Psychology Review*, 32 (1), 77–91. **4**

Haney, M. R. (2002, Winter). Name writing: A window into the emergent literacy skills of young children. *Early Childhood Education Journal*, 30 (2), 101–105. **9**

Hannaford, C. (2005). *Smart Moves: Why Learning Is Not All in Your Head* (2nd ed.). Salt Lake City, UT: Great River Books. **3**

Hanye, H., & Simcock, G. (2009). Memory development in toddlers. In M. L. Courage & N. Cowan (Eds.), *The Development of Memory in Infancy and Childhood* (pp. 43–68). New York: Psychology Press. **7**

Harlan, J. D., & Rivkin, M. (2000). *Science Experiences for the Early Childhood Years: An Integrated Approach* (7th ed.). Upper Saddle River, NJ: Merrill. **8**

Harms, T., Clifford, R. M., & Cryer, D. (2005). *Early Childhood Environment Rating Scale ECERS-R*. New York: Teachers College Press. **9, 11, 13**

Harms, T., Cryer, D., & Clifford, R. M. (2006). *Infant/Toddler Environment Rating Scale (ITERS-4)* (rev. ed.). New York: Teachers College Press. **13**

Harms, T., Cryer, D., & Clifford, R. M. (2007). *Family Day Care Rating Scale (FCCERS-R)*. New York: Teachers College Press. **13**

Harms, T., Jacobs, E. V., & White, D. R. (1996). *School-Age Care Environment Rating Scale (SACERS)*. New York: Teachers College Press. **13**

Harris, D. B. (1963). *Children's Drawings as Measures of Intellectual Maturity: A Revision and Extension of the Goodenough Draw-a-Man Test*. New York: Harcourt, Brace & World. **10**

Harris, Y. R., & Graham, J. A. (2007). *The African American Child: Development and Challenges*. New York: Springer. **12**

Harrison, P. L., & Oakland, T. (2003). *Adaptive Behavior Assessment System (ABASII)* (2nd ed.). San Antonio, TX: Harcourt Assessment.

Harste, J., Woodward, V., & Burke, C. (1984). *Language Stories & Literacy Lessons*. Portsmouth, NH: Heinemann. **6**

Hart, B., & Risley, T. (2004). *Meaningful Differences in the Everyday Experiences of Young American Children*. Baltimore, MD: Brookes. **6, 8, 9**

Harter, S. (1990). The self-perceptions of uncommonly bright youngsters. In R. J. Sternberg & J. Kolligan Jr. (Eds.), *Competence Considered* (pp. 67–97). New Haven, CT: Yale University Press. **12**

Harter, S. (1999). *The Construction of the Self: A Developmental Perspective*. New York: Guilford Press. **12**

Hatch, J. A. (2002). Accountability shovedown: Resisting the standards movement in early childhood education. *Phi Delta Kappan, 83* (6), 457–463. **8**

Healy, J. (1998). *Failure to Connect: How Computers Affect Our Children's Minds*. New York: Simon & Schuster. **10**

Helm, J. H. (2003). Contemporary challenges in early childhood education. In J. H. Helm & S. Beneke (Eds.), *The Power of Projects: Meeting Contemporary Challenges in Early Childhood Classrooms*. New York: Teachers College Press. **11**

Helm, J. H., Beneke, S., & Steinheimer, K. (2007). *Windows on Learning: Documenting Young Children's Work*. New York: Teachers College Press. **I**

Helm, J. H., & Katz, L. (2001). *Young Investigators: The Project Approach in the Early Years*. New York: Teachers College Press. **11**

Hemmeter, M. L., Maxwell, K. L., Ault, M. J., & Schuster, J. W. (2001). *Assessment of Practices in Early Elementary Classrooms*. New York: Teachers College Press. **13**

Hendrick, J. (2004). *Next Steps Toward Teaching the Reggio Way*. Upper Saddle River, NJ: Pearson Education. **1**

Heroman, C. (2010). *Teaching Strategies GOLD: Objectives for Development & Learning : Birth through Kindergarten*. Washington, DC: Teaching Strategies. **8**

Herr, J., & Larson, L. Y. (2009). *Creative Resources for the Early Childhood Classroom*. Clifton Park, NY: Thomson Delmar Learning. **11**

Hershkowitz, I., Lamb, M. E., & Horowitz, D. (2007). Victimization of children with disabilities. *American Journal of Orthopsychiatry, 77* (4), 629–635. **12**

Hewett, V. M. (2001). Examining the Reggio Emilia approach to early childhood education. *Early Childhood Education Journal, 29* (2), 95–100. **10**

High/Scope Educational Research Foundation. (2003). *Child Observation Record (COR) and Child Assessment Record (CAR)* (2nd ed.). Ypsilanti, MI: Author. **3**

High/Scope Press. (2003). *Program Quality Assessment* (2nd ed.). Ypsilanti, MI: High/Scope Educational Research Foundation. **13**

Hirsch, E. S. (1996). *The Block Book* (3rd ed.). Washington, DC: NAEYC. **10**

Hirsh-Pasek, K., Golinkoff, R. M., Berk, L., & Singer, D. (2009). *A Mandate for Playful Learning in Preschool: Presenting the Evidence*. Oxford: Oxford University Press. **7, 8**

Hohmann, M., & Weikart, D. P. (2008). *Educating Young Children: Active Learning Practices for Preschool and Child Care Programs* (3rd ed.). Ypsilanti, MI: High/Scope Press. **5, 13**

Holdaway, D. (1979). *The Foundations of Literacy*. Sydney, Australia: Ashton Scholastic. **9**

Hong, S. B., & Trepanier-Street, M. (2004). Technology: A tool for knowledge construction in a Reggio Emilia inspired teacher education program. *Early Childhood Education Journal, 33* (2), 87–94. **9**

Honig, A. S. (2002). Soothing separations. *Scholastic Early Childhood Today, 17* (1), 20–22. **1**

Hosington, C. (2002). Using photographs to support children's science inquiry. *Young Children, 57* (5), 26–31. **11**

Howes, C., & James, J. (2002). Children's social development within the socialization context of childcare and early childhood education. In P. K. Smith & C. H. Hart (Eds.), *Blackwell handbook of Childhood Social Development*. Malden, MA: Blackwell Publishers. **4**

Howes, C., & Ritchie, S. (2002). *A Matter of Trust: Connecting Teachers and Learners in the Early Childhood Classroom*. New York: Teachers College Press. **14**

Howes, C., & Wishard, A. G. (2004). Revisiting shared meaning: Looking through the lens of culture and linking shared pretend play through proto-narrative development to emergent literacy. In E. F. Zigler, D. G. Singer, & S. J. Bishop-Josef (Eds.), *Children's Play: The Roots of Reading* (pp. 143–158). Washington DC: Zero to Three. **9**

Huffman, J. M., & Fortenberry, C. (2011). Helping preschoolers prepare for writing Developing Fine Motor Skills. *Young Children, 66* (5) 100–103. **3, 9**

Hunter, D. (2008). What happens when a child plays at the sensory table? *Young Children, 63* (6), 77–79. **10**

Hut, V., Dennis, B., Koplow, L., & Ferber, J. (2007). Lesson plans for emotional life. In L. Koplow (Ed.) *Unsmiling Faces: How Preschools Can Heal*. New York: Teachers College Press. **5**

Hyson, M. (2003). *Preparing Early Childhood Professionals: NAEYC's Standards for Initial Licensure, Advanced, and Associate Degree Programs*. Washington, DC: NAEYC. **I, 7**

Hyson, M. (2008). *Enthusiastic and Engaged Learners: Approaches to Learning in the Early Childhood Classroom*. Washington, DC: NAEYC. **4, 7**

International Association for the Child's Right to Play (IPA). (1992 Revised). *IPA declaration*. Retrieved from http://ipaworld.org/category/about-us/declaration/ **4**

International Reading Association. (2003). *Standards for Reading Professionals*. Newark, DE: Author. **9**

Isbell, C., & Isbell, R. (2007). *Sensory Integration: A Guide for Preschool Teachers*. Beltsville, MD: Gryphon House. **3**

Isenberg, J., & Jalongo, M. (2006). *Creative Thinking and Arts-Based Learning: Preschool Through Fourth Grade* (4th ed.). New York: Merrill. **11**

Isenberg, J. P. (2008). The state of the art in early childhood professional preparation. In D. Hom-Wingerd & M. Hyson (Eds.), *New Teachers for a New Century: The Future of Early Childhood Professional Preparation* (pp. 17–58). Washington, DC: U.S. Department of Education. **8**

Iyengar, S., Ball, D., & National Endowment for the Arts. (2007). *To Read or Not to Read: A Question of National Consequence.* Washington, DC: National Endowment for the Arts. **9**

Jalongo, M. R. (2007). *Learning to Listen, Listening to Learn: Building Essential Skills in Young Children.* Washington, DC: NAEYC. **6**

Jensen, E. (2005). *Teaching with the Brain in Mind* (2nd ed.). Alexandria, VA: Association for Supervision and Curriculum. **7**

Jervis, K., & Polland, B. K. (2007). *Separation: Supporting Children in Their Preschool Transitions.* Washington, DC: NAEYC. **1**

Jewett, J., & Peterson, K. (2002). *Stress and Young Children.* Urbana, IL: ERIC Clearinghouse on Elementary and Early Childhood Education, ED471911-2002-12-00. **5**

Jeynes, W. H., & Littell, S. W. (2000). A meta-analysis of studies examining the effect of whole language instruction on the literacy of low-SES students. *The Elementary School Journal,* 101 (1), 21–34.

Johnson, B., & Plemons, B. (1998). *Cup Cooking: Individual Child-Portion Picture Recipes.* Ithaca, NY: Early Educators Press. **8**

Johnson, J. G., Cohen, P., Smailes, E. M., Kasen, S., & Brook, J. S. (2002). Television viewing and aggressive behavior during adolescence and adulthood. *Science,* 295 (5564), 2468–2471. **11**

Johnson, M. E., Christie, J. F., & Wardle, F. (2005). *Play, Development, and Early Education.* Boston, MA: Pearson/Allyn & Bacon. **11**

Johnston, P. H., & Rogers, R. (2001). Early literacy development: The case for "informed assessment." In S. B. Neuman & D. K. Dickinson (Eds.), *Handbook of Early Literacy Research.* New York: Guilford Press. **9**

Jolley, R. P. (2010). *Children and Pictures: Drawing and Understanding.* Malden, MA: John Wiley & Son **10**

Jones, E., & Cooper, R. (2006). *Playing to Get Smart.* New York: Teachers College Press. **4**

Jones, J., & Courtney, R. (2002). Documenting early science learning. *Young Children,* 57 (5), 34–41. **8, 10**

Juster, F. T., Ono, H., & Stafford, F. P. (2004). *Changing Times of American Youth: 1981–2003.* Ann Arbor, Michigan: University of Michigan, Institute for Social Research. Child Development Supplement **3**

Kail, R. V. (2007). *Children and Their Development* (4th ed.). Upper Saddle River, NJ: Prentice Hall. **7**

Kamii, C. (1982). *Number in Preschool and Kindergarten: Educational Implications of Piaget's Theory.* Washington, DC: NAEYC. **8, 10**

Kamii, C., & Kamii, M. (1990). Why achievement testing should stop. In C. Kamii (Ed.), *Achievement Testing in the Early Grades: The Games Grown-Ups Play.* Washington, DC: NAEYC. **8**

Kamins, M. L., & Dweck, C. S. (1999). Person versus process praise and criticism: Implications for contingent self-worth and coping. *Developmental Psychology,* 35 (3), 835–847. **12**

Katz, J. R. (2001). Playing at home: The talk of pretend play. In D. K. Dickinson & P. O. Tabors (Eds.), *Beginning Literacy with Language.* Baltimore: Paul H. Brookes Publishing 53–74. **11**

Katz, L. G. (1988). *Early Childhood Education: What Research Tells Us.* Bloomington, IN: Phi Delta Kappa. **8**

Katz, L. G., & Chard, S. C. (2000). *Engaging Children's Minds: The Project Approach* (2nd ed.). Stamford, CT: Ablex Publishing Corp. **I, 8**

Kauffman, J. M., & Landrum, T. J. (2009). *Characteristics of Emotional and Behavioral Disorders of Children and Youth* (9th ed.). Upper Saddle River, NJ: Merrill. **7**

Kavanaugh, R. D. (2006). Pretend play and theory of mind. In L. Balter & C. S. Tamis-LeMonda (Eds.), *Child psychology: A Handbook of Contemporary Issues* (2nd ed., pp. 153–166). New York: Psychology Press. **11**

Kellam, S. G., Ling, X., Merisca, R., Brown, C. H., & Ialongo, N. (1998). The effect of the level of aggression in the first grade classroom on the course and malleability of aggressive behavior in middle school. *Development and Psychopathology,* 10, 165–185. **5**

Kellert, S. R. (2002). Experiencing nature: Affective, cognitive, and evaluative development in children. In P. H. Kahn and S. Kellert (Eds.), *Children and Nature: Psychological, Sociocultural, and Evolutionary Investigations.* (pp. 117–152). Cambridge, MA: The MIT Press. **3**

Kellogg, R. (1970). *Analyzing Children's Art.* Palo Alto, CA: National Press Books. **10**

Kelly, K. (2000). False promise. *U.S. News & World Report,* 129 (12), 48–55. **9**

Kemple, K. (2004). *Let's Be Friends: Peer Competence and Social Inclusion in Early Childhood Programs.* New York: Teachers College Press. **4**

Kendall, J. S., & Marzano, R. J. (2004). *Content Knowledge: A Compendium of Standards and Benchmarks for K–12 Education.* Aurora, CO: Mid-continent Research for Education and Learning (McREL). Retrieved from www.mcrel.org/standards-benchmarks/ **8, 11**

Kern, L., Vorndran, C. M., Hilt, A., Ringdahl, J. E., Adelman, B. E., & Dunlap, G. (1998). Choice as an intervention to improve behavior: A review of the literature. *Journal of Behavioral Education,* 8, 151–170. **5**

Kernis, M. H. (2002). Self-esteem as a multi-faceted construct. In T. M. Brinthaupt & R. P. Lipka (Eds.), *Understanding Early Adolescent Self and Identity* (pp. 57–88). Albany, NY: State University of New York Press. **12**

Kim, S. (1999). The effects of storytelling and pretend play on cognitive processes, short-term and long-term narrative recall. *Child Study Journal,* 29 (3), 176–191. **11**

Kinnell, G. (2002). *No Biting: Policy and Practice for Toddler Programs.* St. Paul, MN: Redleaf Press. **6**

Kinnell, G. (2004). *Good Going!* St. Paul, MN: Redleaf Press. **2**

Kissel, B. T. (2008, March). Apples on train tracks: Observing young children reenvision their writing. *Young Children,* 63 (2), 26–32. **9**

Klibanoff, R., Levine, S. C., Huttenlocher, J., Vasilyeva, M., & Hedges, L. (2006). Preschool children's mathematical knowledge: The effect of teacher "math talk." *Developmental Psychology,* 42, 59–69. **8**

Knoll, M., & O'Brien, M. (2001). *Quick Quality Check for Infant and Toddler Programs.* St. Paul, MN: Redleaf Press. **13**

Knutson, J. F., DeGarmo, D., Koeppl, G., & Reid, J. B. (2005). Care neglect, supervisory neglect and harsh parenting in the development of children's aggression: A replication and extension. *Child Maltreatment,* 10 (2), 92–107. **5**

Kohlberg, L. (1973). The claim to moral adequacy of a highest stage of moral judgment. *Journal of Philosophy,* 70 (18), 630–646. **12**

Kohlberg, L. (1981) *Essays on Moral Development, Vol I: The Philosophy of Moral Development.* New York: Harper and Row. **4**

Kohn, A. (2001). Fighting the tests: Turning frustration into action. *Young Children,* 56 (2), 19–24. **8**

Koplow, L., (2007). *Unsmiling Faces: How Preschools Can Heal.* New York: Teachers College Press. **5**

Kostelnik, M. J., Gregory, K., Soderman, A. K., Whiren, A. P., Soderman, A. K., & Gregory, K. (2012). *Guiding Young Children's Social Development & Learning* (76th ed.). Belmont, CA: Wadsworth Cengage Learning. **4, 5, 12, 13, 14**

Koster, J. B. (2012). *Growing Artists: Teaching Arts to Young Children* (5th ed.). Belmont, CA: Wadsworth Cengage Learning. **10**

Kozol, J. (1991). *Savage Inequalities: Children in America's Schools.* New York: Harper Perennial. **8**

Kratcoski, A. M., & Katz, K. B. (1998). Conversing with young language learners in the classroom. *Young Children, 53* (3), 30–33. **6**

Krechevsky, M., & Stork, J. (2000). Challenging educational assumptions: Lessons from an Italian-American collaboration. *Cambridge Journal of Education, 30* (1), 57–75. **10**

Kristal, J. (2005). *The Temperament Perspective: Working with Children's Behavioral Styles.* Baltimore, MD: Brookes. **5**

Kuhl, P. K. (2004). Early language acquisition: Cracking the speech code. *Nature Reviews Neuroscience, 5,* 831–843. **6**

La Paro, K. M., Pianta, R. C., & Stuhlman, M. (2004). Classroom Assessment Scoring System (CLASS): Findings from the pre-k year. *Elementary School Journal, 104* (5), 409–426. **4, 13**

Ladd, G. W. (2005). *Children's Peer Relations and Social Competence: A Century of Progress.* New Haven, CT: Yale University Press. **4**

Lally, J. R., Lerner, C., & Lurie-Hurvitz, E. (2001). National survey reveals gaps in the public's and parents' knowledge about early childhood development. *Young Children, 56* (2), 49–53. **14**

LaMontagne, M. J., & Russell, G. W. (1998). Informal and formal assessment. In L. J. Johnson (Ed.), *Early Childhood Education: Blending Theory, Blending Practice* (pp. 201–232.) Baltimore, MD: P. H. Brookes. **13**

Landsmann, L. Tolchinsky. (2003). *The Cradle of Culture and What Children Know about Writing and Numbers before Being Taught.* Mahwah, NJ: Erlbaum. **9**

Leary, M. R., & McDonald, G. (2003). Individual differences in self-esteem: A review and theoretical integration. In M. Leary & J. P. Tangney (Eds.), *Handbook of Self and Identity* (pp. 402–418). New York: Guilford. **12**

Leonard, A. M. (1997). *I Spy Something: A Practical Guide to Classroom Observations of Young Children.* Little Rock, AR: Southern Early Childhood Association. **6**

Leong, D. J., & Bbodrova, E. (2012). Assessing and scaffolding make-believe play. *Young Children, 67* (1), 28–34. **11**

Levin, D., & Carlsson-Paige, N. (2006). *The War Play Dilemma: What Every Parent and Teacher Needs To Know* (2nd ed.). New York: Teachers College Press. **11**

Lewin, K. (1948). *Resolving Social Conflicts, Selected Papers on Group Dynamics (1935–1946).* New York: Harper. **6**

Lewin-Benham, A. (2010). *Infants & Toddlers at Work: Using Reggio-Inspired Materials to Support Brain Development.* New York: Teachers College Press. **7, 10**

Lickona, T. (1983). *Raising Good Children.* New York: Bantam Books. **5**

Lindfors, J. W. (1987). *Children's Language and Learning* (2nd ed.) Englewood Cliffs, NJ: Prentice Hall. **5, 6**

Lindsey, E. W., & Colwell, M. J. (2003). Preschoolers' emotional competence: Links to pretend and physical play. *Child Study Journal, 33,* 39–52. **11**

Linn, M. I. (2001). An American educator reflects on the meaning of the Reggio experience. *Phi Delta Kappan, 83* (4), 332–335. **10**

Lively, V. E., & Lively, E. (1991). *Sexual Development of Young Children.* Clifton Park, NY: Thomson Delmar Learning. **12**

Loeber, R., Lacourse, E., & Homish, D. L. (2005). In R. E. Tremblay, W. W. Hartup, Archer (Eds.), *Developmental Origins of Aggression,* New York: Guilford Press. **5**

Loerber, R., & Farrington, D. P. (1998). *Serious and Violent Juvenile Offenders: Risk Factors and Successful Interventions.* Thousand Oaks, CA: Sage. **5**

Logue, M. E. (2006). Teachers observe to learn: Differences in social behavior of toddlers and preschoolers in same-age and multiage groupings. *Young Children, 61* (30), 70–76. **13**

Louv, R. (2005). *Last Child in the Woods: Saving Our Children from Nature-Deficit Disorder.* Chapel Hill, NC: Algonquin Books. **3, 8**

Lowenfeld, V., & Brittain, W. L. (1987). *Creative and Mental Growth* (8th ed.). New York: Macmillan Publishing Co., Inc. **10**

Lynch, E. W., & Hanson, M. J. (2011). *Developing Cross-Cultural Competence: A Guide for Working with Young Children and Their Families* (4th ed.). Baltimore, MD: Brookes. **2**

Machado, J. M. (2013). *Early Childhood Experiences in Language Arts* (10th ed.). Belmont, CA: Wadsworth, Cengage Learning. **6, 9**

Marion, M. (2011). *Guidance of Young Children* (8th ed.). Boston, MA: Pearson-Prentice Hall. **14**

Markova, G., & Legerstee, M. (2008). How infants come to learn about the minds of others. *Zero to Three, 28* (5), 26–31. **13**

Marotz, L. R. (2012). *Health, Safety and Nutrition for the Young Child* (8th ed.). Belmont, CA: Wadsworth Cengage Learning. **I, 3**

Marotz, L., & Allen, K. E. (2013). *Developmental Profiles: Prebirth Through Adolescence* (7th ed.). Belmont, CA: Wadsworth Cengage Learning. **3**

Marshall, H. H. (2001). Cultural influences on the development of self-concept: Updating our thinking. *Young Children, 56* (6), 19–25. **12**

Martin, S. (2009). *Take a Look: Observation and Portfolio Assessment in Early Childhood* (5th ed.). Toronto, ON: Person Addison Wesley. **I, 2, 5, 8, 11**

Maschinot, B. (2008). *The Changing Face of the United States: The Influence of Culture on Early Child Development.* Washington, DC Zero to Three. **I**

Mashburn, A. J., & Pianta, R. C. (2006). Social relationships and school readiness. *Early Education and Development, 17* (1), 151–176. **13**

Maslow, A. H. (1970). *Motivation and Personality.* New York: Harper & Row. **4**

McAfee, O., & Leong, D. (2002). *Assessing and Guiding Young Children's Development and Learning* (4th ed.). Boston, MA: Pearson Allyn and Bacon. **I, 8, 10**

McCabe, L. A., & Frede, E. C. (2007, December). Challenging behaviors and the role of preschool education. National Institute for Early Childhood Research (NIEER). *Preschool Policy Brief 16.* Retrieved from www.nieer.org **5, 14**

McDonald, J. (2007, May). Selecting counting books: Mathematical perspectives. *Young Children, 62* (3), 38–42. **8**

McIver, K. L., Brown, W. H., Pfeiffer, K. A., Dowda, M., & Pate, R.R. (2009, Spring). Assessing children's physical activity in their homes: The observational system for recording physical activity in children's homes. *Journal of Applied Behavior Analysis. 42,* 1–16. **3**

McKenna, M. C., & Zucker, T. A. (2009). Use of electronic storybooks in reading instruction: From theory to practice. In A. G. Bus & S. B. Neuman (Eds.), *Multimedia and Literacy Development: Improving Achievement for Young Learners* (pp. 47–87). New York: Routledge. **9**

McNaughton, D., Hamlin, J. D., McCarthy, J., Head-Reeves, D., & Schreiner, M. (2007). Learning to listen: Teaching an active listening strategy to preservice education professionals. *Topics in Early Childhood Special Education, 27* (4), 223–231. **14**

Meier, D. R., & Henderson, B. (2007). *Learning from Young Children in the Classroom: The Art and Science of Teacher Research.* New York: Teachers College Press. **1, 7**

Meisels, S. (1987). Uses and abuses of developmental screening and school readiness testing. *Young Children, 42* (2), 4. **8**

Meisels, S. J. (2006). *Accountability in Early Childhood: No Easy Answers.* Herr Research Center for Children and Social Policy, Occasional Paper, Number 6. Erikson Institute. **13**

Meisels, S. J. (2007). Accountability in early childhood: No easy answers. In R. C. Pianta & M. J. Cox (Eds.), *School Readiness, Early Learning and the Transition to Kindergarten in the Era of Accountability* (pp. 31–47). Baltimore, MD: Paul H. Brookes. **8**

Meisels, S. J., & Atkins-Burnett, S. (2000). The elements of early childhood assessment. In J. Shonkoff & S. Meisels (Eds.), *Handbook of Early Childhood Intervention* (pp. 231–257). New York: Cambridge University Press. **8**

Meisels, S. J., Bickel, D. D., Nicholson, J., Xue, Y., & Atkins-Burnett, S. (2001). Trusting teachers' judgments: A validity study of a curriculum-embedded performance assessment in kindergarten–grade 3. *American Educational Research Journal, 38* (1), 73. **8**

Meisels, S. J., Dichtelmiller, M. L., Jablon, J. R., Dorfman, A. B., & Marsden, D. B. (2003). *The Work Sampling System* (4th ed.). New York: Pearson Education Early Learning. **3, 9**

Meisels, S. J., Mardsden, D. B., Dombro, A. L., & Weston, D. R. (2003). *The Ounce Scale.* Redford, MI: Pearson Early Learning. **2**

Meisels, S. J., Xue, Y., Bickel, D. P., Nicholson, J., & Atkins-Burnett, S. (2001). Parental reactions to authentic performance assessment. *Educational Assessment, 7* (1), 61–85. **8**

Merrell, K. W. (2002). *Preschool and Kindergarten Behavior Scales* (2nd ed.). Austin, TX: PRO-ED. **4**

Miles, S. B., & Stipek, D. (2006). Contemporaneous and longitudinal associations between social behavior and literacy achievement in a sample of low-income elementary school children. *Child Development, 77,* 103–117. **4**

Miller, D. L. (2004, February 26). More than play: Children learn important skills through visual-spatial work! *Special Supplement to Dimensions Early Education Program Newsletter* **10**

Miller, E., & Almon, J. (2009). *Crisis in the Kindergarten: Why Children Need to Play in School.* College Park, MD: Alliance for Childhood. **8**

Miller, S., & Britt, D. R. (2008). Helping babies make transitions. *Young Children, 63* (3), 60–62. **1**

Miller, S. A. (2002). Easing the transition from home to school. *Scholastic Early Childhood Today, 17* (1), 33–34. **1**

Miller, S. A. (2007). Delightful discoveries. *Scholastic Parent & Child, 15* (3), 76. **11**

Montessori, M., & Holmes, H. W. (1912). *The Montessori Method: Scientific Pedagogy as Applied to Child Education in The Children's House with Additions and Revision by the Author* (2nd ed.). New York: Frederick A. Stokes, Co. **2**

Moran, M. J., & Tegano, D. W. (2005). Moving toward visual literacy: Photography as a language of teacher inquiry. *Early Childhood Research Policy and Practice, 7* (1). Retrieved from http://ecrp.uiuc.edu/v7n1/moran.html **11**

Morrow, L. (2008). *Literacy Development in the Early Years: Helping Children Read and Write* (6th ed.). Boston, MA: Allyn & Bacon. **9**

Moses, A. M. (2009). What television can (and can't) do to promote early literacy development. *Young Children, 64* (2), 80–89. **9**

Moses, A. M., & Duke, N. K. (2009). Portrayals of print literacy in children's television programming. *Journal of Literacy Research, 40* (3), 251–289. **9**

Mulvihill, D. (2005). The health impact of childhood trauma: An interdisciplinary review, 1997–2003. *Issues in Comprehensive Pediatric Nursing, 28,* 115–136. **12**

Murray, C. G. (2008, December). Co-creating scripts with young children to help them feel better. *Teaching Young Children, 2* (2). **5**

NAEYC. (2002). *Early Learning Standards: Creating the Conditions for Success. Executive Summary.* Washington, DC: Author. **I**

NAEYC. (2003). *Position Statement. Early Childhood Curriculum, Assessment and Program Evaluation: Building an Effective, Accountable System in Programs for Children Birth through Age 8.* Joint position statement of the National Association for the Education of Young Children (NAEYC) and the National Association of Early Childhood Specialists in State Departments of Education (NAECS/SDE). Washington, DC: Author. **I, 13, 14**

NAEYC. (2005). *NAEYC Early Childhood Program Standards and Accreditation Criteria.* Washington, DC: Author. **1, 2, 10**

National Association for Family Child Care. (2005). *Quality standards for NAFCC Accreditation.* Salt Lake City, UT: Author. **5, 14**

National Association for Sport and Physical Education. (1995). *Moving into the Future: National Standards for Physical Education.* Reston, VA: Author. **3**

National Association for Sport and Physical Education. (2001). *Active Start: A Statement of Physical Guidelines for Children Birth to Five Years.* Reston, VA: Author. **3**

National Association for the Education of Young Children and the National Association of Early Childhood Specialists in State Departments of Education (NAEYC and NAECS/SDE). (2003). *Early Childhood Curriculum, Assessment, and Program Evaluation, Position Statement.* Washington, DC: Author. **14**

National Association for the Education of Young Children. (2003). NAEYC and NAECS/SDE position statement: Early childhood curriculum, assessment and program evaluation—building an effective, accountable system in programs for children birth through age 8. Retrieved from www.naeyc.org/resources/position_statements/pscape.pdf **I, 13**

National Association for the Education of Young Children. (2005a). *Code of Ethical Conduct & Statement of Commitment.* Washington, DC: Author. **I, 12, 14**

National Association for the Education of Young Children. (2005b). *NAEYC Early Childhood Program Standards and Accreditation Criteria.* Washington, DC: Author. **8, 13**

National Association for the Education of Young Children. (2005c). *NAEYC Self-Study Classroom Observation Tool for Preschool Groups.* Washington, DC: Author. **9**

National Association for the Education of Young Children. (2007). *NAEYC Early Childhood Program Standards and Accreditation Criteria, Revised.* Washington, DC: Author. **7**

National Association of Early Childhood Specialists in State Departments of Education. (2002). Recess and the importance of play: A position statement on young children and recess. Retrieved from http://naecs.crc.uiuc.edu/position/recessplay.html **3**

National Association of Family Child Care. (2005). *Quality Standards for NAFCC Accreditation.* Salt Lake City, UT: Author. **13**

National Center for Learning Disabilities. Retrieved from www.ncld.org **9**

National Clearinghouses for English Language Acquisition and Language Instruction Educational Programs. Retrieved from www.ncela.gwu.edu **6**

National Commission on Excellence in Education. (1983). *A Nation at Risk: The Imperative for Educational Reform; A Report to the Nation and the Secretary of Education, United States Department of Education.* Washington, DC: Author. **8**

National Council for the Social Studies. (1994). *Expectations of Excellence: Curriculum Standards for Social Studies.* Waldorf, MD: Author. **4**

National Council of Teachers of Mathematics (NCTM). (2000). *Principles and Standards for School Mathematics.* Reston, VA: Author. **8**

National Early Literacy Panel. (2008). *Developing Early Literacy: Report of the National Early Literacy Panel*. Washington, DC: Author. Retrieved from www.nifl.gov.nifl/NELPreport.htm **9**

National Endowment for the Arts. (2004). *Reading at Risk: A Survey of Literary Reading in America*. Research Division Report No. 46, June 2004. **9**

National Governors Association Center for Best Practices (NGA Center). (2011). Common core state standards. Retrieved from http://www.corestandards.org/the-standards

National Institute of Child Health and Human Development (NICHD). (1996). *Infant Child Care & Attachment Security: Results of the NICHD Study of Early Child Care*. Providence, RI: NICHD. **13**

National Institute of Child Health and Human Development Early Child Care Research Network. (2002). Early child care and children's development prior to school entry: Results from the NICHD study of early child care. *American Educational Research Journal*, 39, 133–164. **4**

National Institute of Child Health and Human Development. (2005). Autism and genes. Retrieved from www.nichd.nih.gov/publications/pubs/upload/autism_genes_2005.pdf **13**

National Institute of Mental Health—NIMH. (2008). *Attention Deficit Hyperactivity Disorder (ADHD)*. Retrieved from http://www.nimh.nih.gov/health/publications/attention-deficit-hyperactivity-disorder/complete-index.shtml **7**

National Scientific Council on the Developing Child. (2008a). *Mental health problems in early childhood can impair learning and behavior for life*. Working paper 6. Retrieved from www.developingchild/net/pubs/wp/Mental_Health_Problems_EarlyChildhood.pdf **5**

National Scientific Council on the Developing Children. (2008b). *The timing and quality of early experiences combine to shape brain architecture*. Working paper 5. Cambridge, MA: National Scientific Council on the Developing Children. Retrieved from www.developingchild.net/pubs/wp/Timing_Quality_Early_Experiences.pdf **7**

National Television Violence Study. (2002). *Executive Summary*. Santa Barbara, CA: Center for Communication and Social Policy. **11**

Negroponte, N. (1995). *Being Digital*. New York: Alfred A. Knopf, Inc. **11**

Neill, M. (2006). The case against high-stakes testing, *Principal*, 85 (4), 28–33. **8**

Neisworth, J. T., & Bagnato, S. J. (2004). The mismeasure of young children: The authentic assessment alternative. *Infants and Young Children*, (17) 3, 198. **I, 8**

Nelson, D. A., Robinson, C. C., & Hart, C. H. (2005). Relational and physical aggression of preschool-age children: Peer status linkages across informants. *Early Education and Development*, 16, 114–139. **5**

Nemeth, K. N. (2009). *Many Languages, One Classroom: Teaching Dual and English Language Learners*. Silver Spring MD: Gryphon House. **6**

Neuman, S. B., Copple, C., & Bredekamp, S. (2000). *Learning to Read and Write: Developmentally Appropriate Practices for Young Children*. Washington, DC: NAEYC. **9**

Neuman, S. B., Dwyer, J., Koh, S. (2007). *Child/Home Early Language & Literacy Observation (CHELLO) Tool*. Baltimore, MD: Paul H. Brookes Publishing Co.

Neuman, S. B., & Koh, S., & Dwyer, J. (2008). CHELLO: The child/home environmenttal language and literacy observarion. *Early Childhood Research Quarterly*, 23 (2), 159–172. **9**

Neuman, S. B., & Roskos, K. (1990). The influence of literacy-enriched play settings on preschoolers' engagement with written language. *National Reading Conference Yearbook*, 39, 179–187. **11**

Neuman, S. B., & Roskos, K. (1992). Literacy objects as cultural tools: Effects on children's literacy behaviors in play. *Reading Research Quarterly*, 27 (3), 202–225. **11**

Neuman, S. B., & Roskos, K. (1997). Literacy knowledge in practice: Contexts of participation for young writers and readers. *Reading Research Quarterly*, 32 (1), 10–32. **11**

Neuman, S. B., & Roskos, K. A. (2000). How can we enable all children to achieve? *Early Childhood Today*, 15 (2), 21–24. **8**

Neuman, S. B., & Roskos, K. (2005). Whatever happened to developmentally appropriate practice in early literacy? *Young Children*, 60 (4), 22–27. **9**

New, R. (1997). New steps in teaching "The Reggio way." In J. Hendrick (Ed.), *First Steps Toward Teaching the Reggio Way* (pp. 224–233). Upper Saddle River, NJ: Prentice Hall. **10**

New, R. S. (2001). Early literacy and developmentally appropriate practice: Rethinking the paradigm. In S. B. Neuman & K. K. Dickinson (Eds.), *Handbook of Early Literacy Research* (pp. 245–262). New York: Guilford Press. **9**

Novak, D. E. (2000). *Help! It's an Indoor Recess Day*. Thousand Oaks, CA: Corwin Press. **3**

Novick, R. (2002). Learning to read the heart: Nurturing emotional literacy. *Young Children*, 57 (3), 84–89. **5**

O'Brien, L. M. (2003). The rewards and restrictions of recess: Reflections on being a playground volunteer. *Childhood Education*, 79 (3), 161. **3**

Ogden, C., & Carrol, M. (2010). *Prevalence of Obesity among Children and Adolescents: Untied States, Trends 1963–1965 through 2007–2008*. National Center for Health Statistics. Retrieved from http://www.cdc.gov/nchs/data/hestat/obesity_child_07_08/obesity_child_07_08.pdf **3**

Ogu, U., & Schmidt, S. R. (2009). Investigating rocks and sand: Addressing multiple learning styles through an inquiry-based approach. *Young Children*, 64 (2), 12–18. **8**

Olds, A. R. (2001). *Child Care Design Guide*. New York: McGraw-Hill. **3**

Ordonez-Jasis, R., & Ortiz, R. (2006). Reading their worlds: Working with diverse families to enhance children's early literacy development. *Young Children*, 61 (1), 42–48. **9**

Ortega, R. (2003). Play, activity, and thought: Reflections on Piaget's and Vygotsky's theories. In D. E. Lytle (Ed.), *Play and Educational Theory and Practice* (pp. 99–116). Westport, CT: Praeger. **11**

Ouseg, H. L. (Ed.). (1995). *International Dictionary: The Words You Need in 21 Languages*. New York: Philosophical Library. **6**

Owocki, G., & Goodman, Y. (2002). *Kidwatching: Documenting Children's Literacy Development*. Portsmouth, NH: Heinemann. **9**

Pack, J. A., & Knight, M. E. (2000). Developing a school portfolio: A tool for staff development. *Young Children*, 55 (5), 42–46. **I**

Paley, V. G. (1984). *Boys & Girls: Superheroes in the Doll Corner*. Chicago, IL: The University of Chicago Press. **4, 11**

Paley, V. G. (1988). *Bad Guys Don't Have Birthdays*. Chicago, IL: University of Chicago Press. **11**

Paley, V. G. (1990). *The Boy Who Would Be a Helicopter*. Cambridge, MA: Harvard University Press. **11**

Paley, V. G. (1997). *The Girl with the Brown Crayon*. Cambridge, MA: Harvard University Press. **4, 11**

Panico, J., Daniels, D. E., & Claflin, M. S. (2011). Working in the classroom with young children who stutter. *Young Children*, 66 (3), 91–95. **6**

Pantley, E. (2010). *The No-Cry Separation Anxiety Solution: Gentle Ways to Make Good-Bye Easy from Six Months to Six Years*. New York: McGraw-Hill. **1**

Papalia, D., Olds, S., & Feldman, R. (2008). *A Child's World* (11th ed.). Boston, MA: McGraw Hill. **5**

Parish-Morris, J., Hirsh-Pasek, K., Golinkoff, R. M., & Collins, M. (2008). Smarter books = smarter children?: Electronic console books and emergent literacy. Manuscript submitted for publication. In Hirsh-Pasek, K., Golinkoff, R. M., Berk, L, E., & Singer, D. G. (2009). *A Mandate for Playful Learning in Preschool: Presenting the Evidence.* New York: Oxford University Press. **9**

Parten, M. B. (1932). Social participation among pre-school children. *Journal of Abnormal and Social Psychology, 27,* 213–269. **4**

Pate, R. R., Pfeiffer, K. A., Trost, S. G., Ziegler, P., & Dowda, M. (2004). Physical activity among children attending preschools. *Pediatrics,* 114 (5), 1258–1263. **3**

Pavri, S. (2001, July/August). Loneliness in children with disabilities: How teachers can help. *Teaching Exceptional Children,* 52–57. **12**

Pellegrini, A. D. (1991). *Applied Child Study: A Developmental Approach.* Hillsdale, NJ: Lawrence Erlbaum Associates. **6**

Pellegrini, A. D. (2006). Rough-and-tumble play from childhood through adolescence. In D. P. Fromberg & D. Bergen (Eds.), *Play from Birth to Twelve: Contexts, Perspectives and Meanings* (pp. 111–118). New York: Routledge. **3**

Pellegrini, A. D., & Bjorklund, D. F. (1998). *Applied Child Study: A Developmental Approach.* Mahwah, NJ: Erlbaum. **I, 8**

Pellegrini, A. D., & Holmes, R. M. (2006). The role of recess in primary school. In D. G. Singer, R. M. Golinkoff, K. Hirsh-Pasek (Eds.), *Play = Learning: How Play Motivates and Enhances Children's Cognitive and Social-Emotional Growth* (p. 36–53). **3, 7**

Penn, A., Harper, R. E., & Leak, N. M. (2008). *The Kissing Hand.* Perfection Learning Prebound. **1**

Peterson, R., & Felton-Collins, V. (1986). *The Piaget Handbook for Teachers and Parents: Children in the Age of Discovery, Preschool–Third Grade.* New York: Teachers College Press. **7**

Peth-Pierce, R. (2000). A good beginning: Sending America's children to school with the social and emotional competence they need to succeed. *Monograph from the Children's Mental Health Foundations and Agencies Network, 9.* Bethesda, MD: National Institute of Mental Health. Retrieved from www.nimh.nih. gov/childhp/fdnconsb.htm **5**

Piaget, J. (1951). *Play, Dreams and Imitation in Childhood.* New York: Norton. **11**

Piaget, J. (1968). *On the Development of Memory and Identity.* Worcester, MA: Clark University Press. **12**

Piaget, J., & Inhelder, B. (1969). *The Psychology of the Child.* New York: Basic Books. **I**

Pianta, R. C., LaParo, K. M., & Hamre, B. K. (2008). *Classroom Assessment Scoring System (CLASS).* Baltimore, MD: Brookes Publishing. **13**

Pica, R. (2006). Physical fitness and the early childhood curriculum. *Young Children,* 61 (3), 12–19. **3**

Pica, R. (2008). Learning by leaps and bounds: Why motor skills matter. *Young Children,* 63 (4), 48–49. **3**

Pica, R. (2010). *Moving and Learning Series. Preschoolers & Kindergartners.* Belmont, CA: Wadsworth Cengage Learning. **3**

Plowman, L., Stephen, C., & McPake, J. (2010). *Growing Up with Technology: Young Children Learning in a Digital World.* New York: Routledge. **8, 10**

Pollack, S. D. (2008). Mechanisms linking early experience and the emergence of emotions: Illustrations from the study of maltreated children. *Current Directions in Psychological Science,* 17 (6), 370–375. **5**

Pollak, S. D., Cicchetti, D., Hornung, K, & Reed, A. (2000). Recognizing emotion in faces: Developmental effects of child abuse and neglect. *Developmental Psychology,* 36 (5), 679–688. **3**

Pollman, M. J. (2010). *Blocks and Beyond: Strengthening Early Math and Science Skills through Spatial Learning.* Baltimore, MD: Brookes Publishing. **8**

Power, T. (2000). *Play and Exploration in Children and Animals.* Mahwah, NJ: Erlbaum. **3**

Puckett, M. B., & Black, J. K. (2008). *Authentic Assessments of the Young Child: Celebrating Development and Learning* (3rd ed.). Upper Saddle River, NJ: Pearson Education. **8**

Qi, C. H., & Kaiser, A. P. (2003). Behavior problems of preschool children from low-income families. Review of the literature. *Topics in Early Childhood Special Education, 23,* 188–216. **5**

Raikes, H. H., & Edwards, C. P. (2009). *Extending the Dance in Infant and Toddler Caregiving: Enhancing Attachment and Relationships.* Baltimore, MD: Brookes Publishing Co. **5**

Ramstetter, C. L, Murray, M., & Garner, A. S. (2010). The crucial role of recess in schools. *Journal of School Health,* 80 (11), 517–526. **3**

Raver, C. C., & Knitzer, J. (2002). *Ready to Enter: What Research Tells Policymakers about Strategies to Promote Social and Emotional School Readiness among Three and Four Year Olds.* New York: National Center for Children in Poverty. **4**

Reid, J. (1993). Prevention of conduct disorder before and after school entry: Relating interventions to developmental findings. *Development and Psychopathology,* 5, 243–262. **5**

Reisman, M. (2011). Learning stories: Assessment through play. *Exchange,* 33 (2), 198, 90–94. **2**

Richey, D. D., & Wheeler, J. J. (2000). *Inclusive Early Childhood Education.* Clifton Park, NY: Thomson Delmar Learning. **8**

Rideout, V., & Hamel, E. (2006). *The Media Family: Electronic Media in the Lives of Infants, Toddlers, Preschoolers and Their Parents.* Menlo Park, CA: Henry J. Kaiser Family Foundation. Retrieved from http://kff.org/entmedia/upload/7500.pdf **3, 9**

Riley, D., San Juan, R. R., Klinkner, J., & Ramminger, A. (2008). *Social & Emotional Development: Connecting Science and Practice in Early Childhood Settings.* Washington, DC: NAEYC. **1, 4, 5**

Rimm-Kaufman, S. E., & Pianta, R. C. (1999). Patterns of family–school contact in preschool and kindergarten. *School Psychology Review,* 28 (3), 426. **1**

Rivkin, M. S. (1995). *The Great Outdoors: Restoring Children's Right to Play Outside.* Washington, DC: NAEYC. **3**

RMC Research. (2006). *Parent Education Profile (PEP) Scale.* Portsmouth, NH: RMC Research. **9**

Roberts, D. F., & Foehr, U. G. (2008). Trends in media use. *The Future of Children,* 18 (2). Retrieved from www.futureofchildren. org/usr_doc/18_02_Roberts.pdf **8**

Rogers, C. R. (1961). *On Becoming a Person.* Boston, MA: Houghton Mifflin Co. **14**

Roggman, L. A., Cook, G. A., Norman, V. K. J., Cristiansen, K., Boyce, L. K., & Innocenti, M. S. (2008). Home visit rating scales HOVRS). In L. A. Roggman, L. K. Boyce, M. S. Innocenti (Eds.), *Developmental Parenting: A Guide for Early Childhood Practitioners.* Baltimore, MD: Brookes Publishing. **13**

Rogoff, B. (2003). *The Cultural Nature of Human Development.* New York: Oxford University Press. **7**

Rosen, H. M. (2002). Name writing: A window into the emergent literacy skills of young children. *Early Childhood Education Journal,* 30 (2), 101–105. **9**

Rosenthal, R., & Jacobson, L. (1992). *Pygmalion in the Classroom: Teacher Expectation and Pupils' Intellectual Development.* New York: Holt, Rinehart, and Winston. **8**

Roskos, K., & Christie, J. (2004). Examining the play-literacy interface: A critical review and future directions. In E. F. Zigler, D. G. Singer, & S. J. Bishop-Josef (Eds.), *Children's Play: The Roots of Reading* (pp. 95–123). Washington, DC: Zero to Three Press. **9**

Rovee-Collier, C., & Cuevas, K. (2009). The development of infant memory. In M. L. Courage & N. Cowan (Eds.), *The Development of Memory in Infancy and Childhood* (pp. 11–42). New York: Psychology Press. **7**

Rubin, K., & Thompson, A. (2002). *The Friendship Factor: Helping Our Children Navigate Their Social World—And Why It Matters for their Success and Happiness.* New York: Penguin. **4**

Rubin, K. H. (2001). *The Play Observation Scale* (POS). Center for Chidlren, Relationships & Culture, University of Maryland. Retrieved from www.rubin-lab.umd.edu/Coding Schemes/POS Coding Scheme 2001.pdf **4**

Rubin, K. H., & Coplan, R. J. (Eds.). (2010). *The Development of Shyness and Social Withdrawal.* New York: Guilford Press. **5**

Rubin, K. H., & Coplan, R. K. (1998). Social and nonsocial play in childhood: An individual differences perspective. In O. N. Saracho & B. Spodek (Eds.), *Multiple Perspectives on Play in Early Childhood* (pp. 144–170). Albany: State University of New York Press. **11**

Rubin, K. H., Fein, G., & Vandenberg, B. (1983). Play. In E. M. Hetherington (Ed.), *Handbook of Child Psychology: Vol 4. Socialization, Personality, and Social Development.* New York: Wiley. **4**

Rubin, K. H., Maioni, T., & Hornung, M. (1976). Free play behaviors in lower-class and middle-class preschoolers: Parten and Piaget revisited. *Child Development, 47,* 414–419. **4**

Rubin, Z. (1980). *Children's Friendships.* Cambridge, MA: Harvard University Press. **4**

Rudy, D., & Grusek, J. E. (2006). Authoritarian parenting in individualist and collectivists groups: Associations with maternal emotion and cognition and children's self-esteem. *Journal of Family Psychology, 20,* 68–78. **12**

Rutter, M. (2006). Implications of resilience concepts for scientific understanding. In B. M Lester, A. S. Masten, & B. McEwent (Eds.), *Resilience in Children* (pp. 1–12). Boston, MA: Blackwell Publishing for the New York Academy of Sciences. **5**

Ruud, L. C., Lambert, M. C., Satterwhite, M., & Zaier, A. (2008). Mathematical language in early childhood settings: What really counts? *Early Childhood Education Journal, 36,* 75–78. **8**

Samuels, S. C. (1977). *Enhancing Self-Concept in Early Childhood: Theory and Practice.* New York: Human Science Press. **12**

Samway, K. (2006). *When English Language Learners Write.* Portsmouth, NH: Heinemann. **9**

Sandall, S. R., Hemmeter, M. L., Smith, B. J., & McLean, M. E. (2005). *DEC Recommended Practices: A Comprehensive Guide.* Denver, CO: Sopris West. **7, 11**

Savage, J., Fisher, O. & Birch, L. (2007). Parental influence on eating behavior: Conception to adolescence. *Journal of Law, Medicine & Ethics, 35* (1), 22–34. **2**

Sawyers, J. K., & Carrick, N. (2003). Symbolic play through the eyes and words of children. In D. E. Lytle (Ed.), *Play and Educational Theory and Practice* (pp. 159–182). Westport, CT: Praeger. **11**

Sax, L. (2005). *Why Gender Matters.* New York: Doubleday. **5, 12**

Schaffer, H. R., & Emerson, P. E. (1964). *The Development of Social Attachments in Infancy.* Lafayette, IN: Child Development Publications of the Society for Research in Child Development. (1)

Schickedanz, J. (1999). *Much More Than the ABCs: The Early Stages of Reading and Writing.* Washington, DC: NAEYC. **9**

Schickedanz, J. A., & Casbergue, R. M. (2009). *Writing in Preschool: Learning to Orchestrate Meaning and Marks.* Newark, DE: International Reading Association. **9**

Schiller, P. (2009). *Seven Skills for School Success: Activities to Develop Social & Emotional Intelligence in Young Children.* Beltsville, MD: Gryphon House. **5**

Schirrmacher, R. (2009). *Art and Creative Development for Young Children* (5th ed.). Clifton Park, NY: Thomson Delmar Learning. **10**

Sciaraffa, M., & Randolph, T. (2011). "You want me to talk to children about what?": Responding to the subject of sexuality development in young children. *Young Children, 66* (4), 32–38. **12**

Scott, E., & Panksepp, J. (2003). Rough-and-tumble play in human children. *Aggressive Behavior, 29,* 539–551. **3**

Seefeldt, C. (2005). *How to Work with Standards in the Early Childhood Classroom.* New York: Teachers College Press. **4, 8**

Seguin, J. R., & Zelazo, P. D. (2005). Executive function in early physical aggression. In R. E. Tremblay, W. W. Hartup, & J. Archer, *Developmental Origins of Aggression* (pp. 307–329). New York: Guilford Press. **5**

Seibel, N. L., Britt, D., Gillespie, L. G., & Parlakian, R. (2006). *Preventing Child Abuse and Neglect: Parent-Provider Partnerships in Child Care. A Zero to Three Training Curriculum.* Washington, DC: Zero to Three. **12**

Senechal, M., & LeFevre, J. (2002). Parental involvement in the development of children's reading skill: A five-year longitudinal study. *Child Development, 73* (2), 445–461. **9**

Seo, K. H., & Ginsburg, H. P. (2004). What is developmentally appropriate in early childhood mathematics education? IN D. H. Clements, J. Sarama, & A. M. DiBiase (Eds.), *Engaging Children in Mathematics: Standards for Early Childhood Mathematics Education* (pp. 91–104). Mahway, NJ: Lawrence Erlbaum Associates. **8**

Seplocha, H. (2004). Partnerships for learning: Conferencing with families. *Young Children, 59* (5), 96–98. **14**

Shackman, J. E., Shackman, A. J., & Pollak, S. D. (2007). Physical abuse amplifies attention to threat and increases anxiety in children. *Emotion, 7,* 838–852. **12**

Shagoury, R. (2009). Language to language: Nurturing writing development in multilingual classrooms. *Young Children, 64,* (2), 52–57. **9**

Shepard, L., Kagan, S. L., & Wurtz, E. (Eds.). (1998). *Principles and Recommendations for Early Childhood Assessments.* Washington, DC: National Education Goals Panel, U.S. Department of Education. **8**

Shonkoff, J. P., & Phillips, D. A. (Eds.). (2000). *From Neurons to Neighborhoods: The Science of Early Childhood Development.* Washington, DC: National Academy Press. **5, 7**

Shores, E. F., & Grace, C. (2005). *The Portfolio Book: A Step-by-Step Guide for Teachers.* Upper Saddle River, NJ: Pearson Education. **I**

Simmons, D. A. (1994). Urban children's preferences for nature: Lessons from environmental education. *Children's Environments Quarterly, 11* (3), 194–203. **3**

Singer, D. G., Golinkoff, R. M., & Hirsh-Pasek, K. (2007). *Play = Learning: How Play Motivates and Enhances Children's Cognitive and Social Emotional Growth.* New York: Oxford. **4**

Singer, D. G., & Singer, J. L. (1990). *The House of Make-Believe: Children's Play and the Developing Imagination.* Cambridge, MA: Harvard University Press. **11**

Skinner, B. F. (1953). *Science and Human Behavior.* New York: Macmillan. **4**

Skinner, B. F. (1957). *Verbal Behavior.* New York: Appleton-Century-Crofts. **6**

Slaby, R., Roedell, W., Arezzo, D., & Hendrix, K. (1995). *Early Violence Prevention: Tools for Teachers of Young Children.* Washington, DC: NAEYC. **11.**

Small, G., & Vorgan, G. (2009). *iBrain: Surviving the Technological Alteration Of The Modern Mind.* New York: Collins Living. **8**

Small, M. (2005). Dare to bare. *New York Times,* 11. Oct. 2005: 23. **2**

Smilansky, S. (1990). *Sociodramatic Play: Its Relevance to Behavior and Achievement in School, in Children's Play and Learning*. New York: Teachers College Press. **11**

Smilansky, S., & Shefatya, L. (1990). *Facilitating Play: A Medium for Promoting Cognitive, Socio-Emotional and Academic Development in Young Children*. Gaithersburg, MD: Psychosocial & Educational Publications. **11**

Smilkstein, R. (2003). *We're Born to Learn: Using the Brain's Natural Learning Process to Create Today's Curriculum*. Thousand Oaks, CA: Corwin Press. **7**

Smith, B., & Smith, A. (2006). *101 Learning and Transition Activities*. Clifton Park, NY: Thomson Delmar Learning. **2**

Smith, B. J., & Fox, L. (2003). Systems of Service Delivery: A Synthesis of Evidence Relevant to Young Children at Risk of or Who Have Challenging Behavior. Center for Evidence-Based practice: Young Children with Challenging Behavior. Retrieved from www.challengingbehavior.org **3, 5**

Snow, C., Burns, M. S., & Griffin, P. (Eds.). (1998). *Preventing Reading Difficulties in Young Children*. Washington, DC: National Academy Press. **6, 9**

Snow, C. E., Van, H. S. B., & Committee on Developmental Outcomes and Assessments for Young Children. (2008). *Early Childhood Assessment: Why, What, and How*. Washington, DC: National Academies Press. **7, 8, 9**

Springer, S. P., & Deutsch, G. (2001). *Left Brain, Right Brain: Perspectives from Cognitive Neuroscience* (5th ed.). New York: W. H. Freeman and Company. **7**

Sprung, B., Froschl, M., & Hinitz, B. (2005). *The Anti-Bullying and Teaching Book for Preschool Classrooms*. Beltsville, MD: Gryphon House. **5**

Squires, J., & Bricker, D. (2009). *Ages and Stages Questionnaire* (3rd ed.). ASQ-3. Baltimore, MD: Brookes. **1**

Stephens, M. (2002). Children, physical activity, and public health: Another call to action. *American Family Physician*, 65 (6), 1033. **3**

Sternberg, R. J. (1997). The triarchic theory of successful intelligence. In D. P. Flanagan & P. L. Harrison (Eds.), *Contemporary Intellectual Assessment: Theories, Tests and Issues* (pp. 103–119). New York: Guilford. **10**

Stipek, D. (2008). The price of inattention to mathematics in early childhood education is too great. *Society for Research in Child Development Social Policy Report*, 22, 13. **8**

Stonier, F. W., & Dickerson, D. L. (2009). When children have something to say, writers are born. *Young Children*, 64 (1), 32–36. **9**

Sulzby, E. (1993). Encouraging emergent writers. *Scholastic Pre-K Today*, 7 (4), 30. **9**

Swallow, W. K. (2000). *The Shy Child: Helping Children Triumph over Shyness*. New York: Warner Books. **5**

Sylva, K., Siraj-Blatchford, I., & Taggart, B. (2011). *Assessing Quality in the Early Years: Early Childhood Environment Rating Scale Extension (ECERS-E)*, 4^e. New York: Teachers College Press. **13**

Szamreta, J. M. (2003). Peekaboo power: To ease separation and build secure relationships. *Young Children*, 58 (1), 88. **1**

Tabors, P. O. (2006). *One Child, Two Languages*. Baltimore, MD: Brookes. **6**

Takeuchi, L. M. (2011). *Families matter: Designing media*

Talan, T. N., & Bloom, P. J. (2004). *Program Administration Scale: Measuring Early Childhood Leadership and Management*. New York: Teachers College Press. **13, 14**

Tannock, M. T. (2008). Rough and tumble play: An investigation of the perceptions of educators and young children. *Early Childhood Education Journal*, 35, 357–361. **3**

Tapscott, D. (2000). *Growing Up Digital*. New York: McGraw Hill. **10**

Taylor, A. F., & Kuo F. M. (2011) Could exposure to everyday green spaces help treat ADHD? Evidence from children's play settings. *Applied Psychology: Health and Well-Being*, 3 (3), 281–303. **3**

Teachers of English to Speakers of Other Languages. (2006). *PreK–12 English Language Proficiency Standards in the Core Content Areas*. Alexandria, VA: Author.

Teaching Strategies. (2006). *The Creative Curriculum for Infants, Toddlers & Twos Developmental Continuum Assessment System*. Washington, DC: Teaching Strategies, Inc. **9**

Thomas, A., & Chess, S. (1977). *Temperament and Development*. New York: Brunner/Mazel. **2, 5**

Thomas, A., & Chess, S. (1980). *The Dynamics of Psychological Development*. New York: Brunner/Mazel. **2**

Thomas, A., Chess, S., & Birch, C. (1968). *Temperament and Behavior Disorders in Children*. New York: New York University Press. **7**

Thompson, A. H., Barnsley, R. H., & Battle, J. (2004). The relative age effect and the development of self-esteem. *Educational Research*, 46 (3), 313–320. **12**

Thompson, R. A. (2008, December). Connecting neurons, concepts and people: Brain development and its implications. *Preschool Policy Brief Issue 17*. New Brunswick, NJ: National Institute for Early Education Research. **7**

Thompson, R. A. (2009) Doing what doesn't come naturally: The development of self-regulation. *Zero to Three*, 30 (20), 33. **5**

Tomlinson, C. A., & Imbeau, M. B. (2010). *Leading and Managing a Differentiated Classroom*. Alexandria, VA: ASCD. **8**

Torrance, E. P. (2000). Preschool creativity. In B. A. Bracken (Ed.), *The Psychoeducational Assessment of Preschool Children* (3rd ed.). Boston, MA: Allyn and Bacon. **10**

Tortora, S. (2006). *The Dancing Dialogue: Using the Communicative Power of Movement with Young Children*. Baltimore, MD: Paul H. Brookes Publishing Company. **3**

Trelease, J. (2006). *The Read-Aloud Handbook* (6th ed.). New York: Penguin Books. **9**

Tremblay, R. E., Nagin, D.S., Seguin, J. R., Zoccolillo, M., Zelazo, P., Bolvin, M., et al. (2004). Physical aggression during early childhood: Trajectories and predictors. *Pediatrics*, 114 (1), 43–50. **5**

Trepanier-Street, M. L., Hong, S. B., & Bauer, J. C. (2001). Using technology in Reggio-inspired long-term projects. *Early Childhood Education Journal*, 28 (3), 181–88. **11**

Trister-Dodge, D. (2002). *The Creative Curriculum for Early Childhood* (4th ed.). Washington, DC: Creative Associates International, Inc. **5**

Tu, T. (2006). Preschool science environment: What is available in a preschool classroom? *Early Childhood Education Journal*, 33 (4), 245–251. **8**

Tyler, K. M., Boykin, A. W., Boelter, C. M., & Dillihunt, M. L. (2005). Examining mainstream and Afro-cultural value socialization in African-American households. *Journal of Black Psychology*, 31 (3), 291–310. **4**

U.S. Clearinghouse for English Language Acquisition. (2006). FAQ: How many school-aged English language learners (ELLs) are there in the U.S.? Retrieved from www.ncela.gwu.edu/expert/faq/01leps.html **6**

U.S. Department of Education. (2005). Elementary & Secondary Education Part A—Improving Basic Programs Operated by Local Educational Agencies. Retrieved from www.ed.gov/policy/elsec/leg/esea02/pg2.html **14**

U.S. Department of Health and Human Services. (2003). Trends in the well-being of America's children and youth 2003. Retrieved from http://aspe.hhs.gov/ **1**

U.S. Department of Health and Human Services. (2005). Head start program performance standards. Retrieved from www.acf.hhs.gov **5, 13, 14**

U.S. Department of Health and Human Services. (2009). Child maltreatment. Retrieved from http://www.acf.hhs.gov/programs/cb/stats_research/index.htm#can **12**

U.S. Department of Health and Human Services, Administration for Children and Families. (2003). *The Head Start Child Outcomes Framework*. Washington, DC: Author. **6, 9, 10**

U.S. Department of Health and Human Services, Administration for Children and Families. (2010) Head start impact study final report. Retrieved from http://www.acf.hhs.gov/programs/opre/hs/impact_study/reports/impact_study/executive_summary_final.pdf

Uchikoshi, Y. (2009). Effects of television on language and literacy development. In A. G. Bus & S. B. Neuman (Eds.), *Multimedia and Literacy Development: Improving Achievement for Young Learners* (pp. 182–195). New York: Routledge. **9**

Vernadakis, N., Avgerinos, A., Tsitskari, E., & Zachupoulou, E. (2005). The use of computer assisted instruction in preschool education: Making teaching meaningful. *Early Childhood Education Journal*, 33 (2), 99–104. **9**

Villareale, C. (2009). *Learning from the Children: Reflecting on Teaching*. St. Paul, MN: Redleaf Press. **1**

VORT Corporation. (1995). *HELP for Preschoolers: Assessment and Curriculum Guide*. Palo Alto, CA: Author. **8**

Vygotsky, L. S. (1962). *Thought and Language*. New York: John Wiley. **6**

Vygotsky, L. S. (1966/1977). Play and its role in the mental development of the child. In M. Cole (Ed.), *Soviet Developmental Psychology* (pp. 76–99). White Plains, NY: M. E. Sharpe. (Original work published 1966) **8**

Vygotsky, L. S. (1978). *Mind and Society: The Development of Higher Mental Processes*. Cambridge, MA: Harvard University Press. (Original work published 1930) **3, 4, 11**

Wald, G. S. (2000). Moving from "I think I can" to "I know I can." *Young Children*, 55 (4), 14–15. **12**

Wallace, M. (2006). *Social Studies: All Day, Every Day in the Early Childhood Classroom*. Clifton Park, NY: Thomson Delmar Learning. **4**

Walsh, G., & Gardner, J. (2005). Assessing the quality of early years learning environments. *Early Childhood Research and Policy*, 7 (1). Retrieved from http://ecrp.uiuc.edu/v7n1/walsh.html **13**

Walsh, K., Farrell, A., Bridgestock, R., & Schweitzer, R. (2006). The contested terrain of teachers detecting and reporting child abuse and neglect. *Journal of Early Childhood Research*, 4 (1), 65–76. **12**

Watson, A., & McCathren, R. (2009). Including children with special needs: Are you and your early childhood program ready? *Young Children*, 64 (2), 20–26. Retrieved from www.journal.naeyc.org/btj/200903 **8**

Watson, J. B. (1914). *Behavior: An Introduction to Comparative Psychology*. New York: Holt, Rinehart, & Winston. **5**

Watson, J. B. (1950). *Behaviorism*. New York: Norton. **4**

Weikart, P. S. (2000). *Round the Circle* (2nd ed.). Ypsilanti, MI: High/Scope Press. **3**

Wellhousen, K., & Kieff, J. (2001). *A Constructivist Approach to Block Play in Early Childhood*. Clifton Park, NY: Delmar Thomson Learning. **10**

Welsch, J. G., Sullivan, A., & Justice, L. M. (2003). That's my letter!: What preschoolers' name writing representations tell us about emergent literacy knowledge. *Journal of Literacy Research*, 35 (2), 757–776. **9**

Wetherby, A. M., & Prizant, B. M. (2003). *CSBS Manual: Communication and Symbolic Behavior Scales*. Baltimore, MD: Paul H. Brookes. **4**

Wesson, K. A. (2001). The "Volvo" effect: Questioning standardized tests. *Young Children*, 56 (2), 16–18. **8**

West, J., Denton, K., & Germin-Hausken, E. (2000). *America's Kindergartners*. Washington, DC: National Center for Educational Statistics. **3**

White, R. (2001) *Moving from Biophobia to Biophilia: Developmentally Appropriate Environmental Education for Children*. White Hutchinson Leisure & Learning Group. Retrieved from www.whitehutchinson.com/children/articls/biophilia.shtml **3**

Whitin, P., & Whitin, D. J. (2003). Developing mathematical understanding along the yellow brick road. *Young Children*, 58 (1), 36–40. **8**

Widen, S. C., & Russell, J. A. (2003). A closer look at preschoolers' freely produced labels for facial expressions. *Developmental Psychology*, 39 (1), 114–128. **5**

Wiener, R, B., & Cohen, J. (2002). New paradigms for familiar concepts: Portfolios and conferencing as performance based assessment tools. *Journal of Early Education and Family Review*, 9 (3), 8–16. **1**

Wilford, S. (2004). Making evaluations meaningful. *Early Childhood Today*, 18 (7), 9–10. **14**

Williamson, G. G., & Anzalone, M. E. (2001). *Sensory Integration and Self-Regulation in Infants And Toddlers: Helping Very Young Children Interact with their Environment*. Washington, DC: Zero to Three Press. **5, 7**

Willis, C. A., & Schiller, P. (2011). Preschoolers' social skills steer life success. *Young Children*, 66 (1), 42–49. **4, 6**

Wilson, R. (1997). The wonders of nature: Honoring children's ways of knowing. *Early Childhood News*, 6 (10), 16–19. **3**

Wilson, R. (2011). Becoming whole: Developing an ecological identity. *Exchange*, 33 (3–199), 103–105.

Winn, M. (2002). *The Plug-In Drug: Television, Computers and Family Life* (25th ed.). New York: Penguin Putnam. **10**

Wittmer, D. S., & Petersen, S. H. (2006). *Infant and Toddler Development and Responsive Program Planning: A Relationship-Based Approach*. Upper Saddle River, NJ: Pearson Merrill Prentice Hall. **10**

Wolfe, D. (2005). *Child Abuse* (2nd ed.). Thousand Oaks, CA: Sage. **12**

Wolfgang, C. H., Stannard, L. L., & Jones, I. (2001). Block play performance among preschoolers as a predictor of later school achievement in mathematics. *Journal of Research in Childood Education*, 15 (2), 173–180. **8**

Wolvin, A. D., & Coakley, C. G. (2000). Listening education in the 21st century. *International Journal of Listening*, 12, 143–152. **6**

Worth, K. (2005). *Going from Knowledge to Practice. Mathematical and Scientific Development in Early Childhood: A Workshop Summary*. Washington, DC: The National Academies Press. **8**

Wortham, S. C. (2008). *Assessment in Early Childhood Education* (5th ed). Upper Saddle River, NJ: Merrill Prentice Hall. **6**

Xu, S. H., & Rutledge, A. L. (2003). Chicken starts with ch!: Kindergartners learn through environmental print. *Young Children*, 58 (2), 44–51. **9**

Yairi, E., & Ambrose, N. G. (2005). *Early Childhood Stuttering*. Austin, TX: Pro-Ed. **6**

Yarrow, L. J. (1964). Separation from parents during early childhood. In M. L. Hoffman & L. W. Hoffman (Eds.), *Review of Child Development Research, Vol. I* (pp. 89–136). New York: Russell Sage Foundation. **1**

Yell, M. L., Katsiyanna, A., & Shiner, J. G. (2006, March/April). The No Child Left Behind Act, adequate yearly progress and students with disabilities. *Council for Exceptional Children*, Mar./Apr. 2006, 32–39. **8**

Yopp, H. K., & Yopp, R. H. (2009). Phonological awareness is child's play. *Young Children*, 64 (1), 12–18. **9**

York, S. (2003). *Roots and Wings*. St. Paul, MN: Redleaf Press. **12**

Zambo, D., & Hansen, C. C. (2007). Love, language and emergent literacy. *Young Children*, 62 (3), 32–37. **9**

Zavitkovsky, D. About Docia Zavitkovsky. Retrieved from www.playmatters.net **4**

Zero to Three. (2009). Child abuse and neglect. Retrieved from www.zerotothree.org **12**

Zins, J. E. (2004). *Building academic success on social and emotional learning: What does the research say?* New York: Teachers College Press.

Index

A

Ability diversity and creativity, 295
Acceptance, 338
Accidental Aggression, 143–144
Accommodation, 194
Accountability, 5
Áccountablility, 216
Accreditation, 352
Achievement Testing in the Early Grades: The Games Grown-Ups Play (Kamii and Kamii), 215
Acting out and anxiety, 47–48
Action research, 33, 158
Actions, 24–25
Active Listening, 399
ACTIVE START: A Statement of Physical Activity Guidelines for Children Birth to Five and Physical Activity for Children: A Statement of Guidelines for Children 5-12 2nd Ed., 95, 96, 210
Adaptive skills, 75
The Adaptive Behavior Assessment System (Harrison & Oakland, 2003), 88
ADD. *See* Attention Deficit Disorder (ADD)
ADHD. *See* Attention Deficit Hyperactivity Disorder (ADHD)
Adjectives, 56
Adjustment
    behavioral indicators of comfort, 361
    child to program, 359–361
Administration performance evaluation, 355
Adult-child interactions. *See* Child-adult interactions
Adult-child ratio. *See* Child-Adult Ratios; Staff Requirements for Child-Staff Ratios and Maximum Group Sizes for Child Care Centers
Adverbs, 56
African American/Black English (AAE/BE), 176
Ages and Stages Questionnaire, 3rd Ed., 41, 83, 88, 159
Aggression
    accidental aggression, 143–144
    in boys and girls, 145–146
    causes of aggression, 145
    challenging behavior, 146–147
    changing to assertion, 146
    definition of, 143
    developmental stages of, 143
    expressive aggression, 144–145
    hostile aggression, 145
    reducing, 146
    and social play, 315
Alliance for Childhood, 219
Alphabet knowledge, 245
Alphabetic awareness, 252
Americans with Disabilities Act of 1990, 50
Anecdotal Recording
    and adjusting to group, 375
    and attention span, 205
    and child abuse, 325–326, 328, 345
    and child-adult interactions, 398
    and the child's portfolio, 59–60
    and cognitive development, 237
    and creativity, 295
    and curriculum planning, 60
    definition and use of, 53–55
    disadvantages of, 58
    and dramatic play, 312, 318
    and emotional development, 156
    evidence to protective services, 61
    example of, 54–55
    and family communication, 75, 379, 403
    finding the time, 59
    and group settings, 375
    and handwriting, 103
    and home visits, 58
    and infants and toddlers, 187
    language of, 55–56
    learning stories, 56–57
    and literacy, 267
    and physical development, 106
    pitfalls to avoid, 58–59
    and portfolio access, 10
    review of, 405
    and Running Records, 107–108
    and self-esteem, 345
    and separation anxiety, 51
    and sharing with families, 60, 101
    and sharing with helping professionals, 60–61
    and sharing with team teachers, 60
    and social development, 126, 129
    and speech and language development, 181
    and superhero play, 315
    talking with the child, 61
    and technology, 306
    technology for, 59
    uses for, 58
    what to write, 57–58
Anger, 142–143
Animism, 196
Anti-bias Curriculum, 355–357
Antisocial behavior, 134–135, 143
Approaches, Learning
    born to learn, 190
    postive approaches, 190
    types of, 189–190
Appropriate Assessments of Children, 212
Arbor Day Foundation, 100
Arrivals and Departures
    early childhood programs, 43–45
    primary school, 45
Articulation, 169
Artificialism, 196
ASD. *See* Autistic Spectrum Disorders (ASD)
Asperger's Syndrome, 204
Assertion, 119, 146
Assessing EC Programs
    advantages of, 358
    disadvantages of, 358
    home learning programs, 358
    need for, 347–349
    pitfalls to avoid, 358
    program assessments, 349–351
    special focus instruments. *see* Special focus instruments (program evaluations)
    time management for, 359
    total program evaluations. *see* Program Evaluations, total
    uses for assessment, 359
Assessing EC Programs, through child's eyes
    child-adult ratios, 361
    size of group, 363–371
Assessing home learning, 358
Assessing Quality in The Early Years: Early Childhood Environment Rating Scale (ECERS-E) 4e, 355
Assessment
    appropriate usage in early childhood. *see* Early Childhood, appropriate assessment
    and checklists, 78–79
    and child development stages, 84–88
    and child protective services, 61
    creative work as development assessment tool, 275–276
    and the curriculum braid, 152–153
    of dramatic play, 313–314
    informal program assessment, 359
    of literacy, 261

Assessment (*continued*)
  and minority children, 235
  observation of, 2
  and parents, 41
  process of, 4–5
  and professional standards, 18
  of program, 213, 361–362
  and Rating Scales, 241
  of self by the child, 10
  and self-care skills, 75
  and standarized tests, 211–215, 217
  and time management for, 36
  and *week by week* recording, 8
Assesssing EC Programs, through
    child's eyes, 361–362
Assimilation, 194
Assistance, and observation, 2
Assisting children, when to, 64–65
Assistive technology, 261
Association, word, 194, 201
Associative dramatic play, 312
Associative play, 120, 124
Attachment
  and children with disabilities, 50
  and coping mechanisms, 47
  noting in class list log, 31
  promoting healthy attachment, 42
  and separation, 37–39
Attention, 199–200. *See also* Attention
    Deficit Hyperactivity Disorder
    (ADHD); Attention span
Attention Deficit Disorder (ADD),
    203–205
Attention Deficit Hyperactivity Disorder
    (ADHD), 265
  and attention span, 203–205
  and autism, 205
  and gender differences, 101–102
  and literacy, 263–265
  and outdoor play, 100
Attention Span. *See also* Attention Deficit
    Hyperactivity Disorder (ADHD)
  and ADHD, 203–205
  and autism, 204
  and creativity, 276
  factors affecting, 183–184
  infants and toddlers, 203
  other methods for recording, 205
  and self-concept, 341–342
  and time samples, 184–185
  and Time Samples, 203–205
Audio recorders, 298–299
Authentic assessment, 213, 221
Autism
  and attention span, 204
  description and occurrence of, 128
  and emotional development, 155
  and play, 114
Autistic Spectrum Disorders (ASD)
  and attention span, 204
  description and occurrence of, 128
  and emotional development, 155
  and play, 114
Autonomy, 62–64
Autonomy vs. Shame and Doubt, 62

B

Backward letters, 258
Basal readers, 247
Behaviorist social learning theory, 117
Behaviors, concerning
    infants and toddlers, 154–155
    preschoolers, 155
    young school agers, 155
Benchmarks for Science Literacy, 210
*Benchmarks in Action: A Guide to Standards-
    Based Assessment in Music*, 210
Benefits of Reading to Young Children, 252
Between the Lions, 260
Biases, 86–87
Bilingualism in the classroom, 177–178
Block play
    as foundation for learning, 282–283
    goals for, 285
    as learning foundation, 223
    Stage I: Carrying, Filling, and Dumping,
      283
    Stage II: Beginning Block Building, 284
    Stage III: Bridging, 284
    Stage IV: Enclosures, 284
    Stage V: Patterns, 284
    Stage VII: Reproducing True-Life
      Structures, 284
    StageVI: Naming Structures, 284
    uses for, 284
Block Play Development, 282
Blogs, 385
Body composition, 94
Books, types of for Young Children,
    253–256
Boys and aggression, 145–146
Boys and Girls: Superheroes in the Doll Corner,
    312
Brain development, 198–199
Brain hemisphericity, 202–203
"Breaking the code", 252
*The Brigance Diagnostic Inventory of Early
    Developmental II (Brigance, 2010)*, 87
Bruising, 325
Bullying, 147–148
Bully-Victim Syndrome, 147–148

C

Calendar, questionable value of, 371–372
California Achievement Test, 216
Cardiovascular efficiency, 94
CARES, 119
*Caring for Our Children: National Health and
    Safety Performance Standards: Guidelines
    for Out-of-Home Child Care*, 68, 72, 210
Case Study, 387
Categories or word associations, 201
Cause and effect, 192
CDA. *See* Child Development Associate
    (CDA)
Centration, 196
Cephalocaudal, 90
CHADD. *See* Children and Adults with
    Attention-Deficit/Hyperactivity
    Disorder (CHADD)

Challenging behavior, 146–147
Checklists, 399. *See also* Development
    Checklists
  advantages of, 83
  and anecdotal recording, 57
  and attention span, 205
  and child abuse, 345
  and child interacting with adults, 403
  and cognitive development, 237
  and creativity, 295
  description and examples of, 78–83
  developmental, 14, 20, 31
  disadvantages of, 83–84
  and dramatic play, 312, 318
  environment and physical
    development, 98
  and family communication, 79, 403
  and group settings, 375
  and handwriting, 103
  and home visits, 83
  limitations of, 79–83
  and literacy, 267
  and literacy assessment, 261
  Outdoor Area Checklist, 96–97
  Physical Developmental Milestones,
    80–83
  pitfalls to avoid, 84
  review of, 405
  and self-care skills, 75, 76
  and self-esteem, 345
  and separation anxiety, 51
  and sharing with family, 101
  and social development, 126–127, 129
  and speech and language
    development, 181
  as standardized tools, 211
  time management for, 84
  uses for, 83, 84–85
  using technology, 84
Child Abuse
  abusers, 321–322
  advantages of reporting, 330
  and children with disabilities, 330
  and child's appearance, 322–323, 325
  child's disclosure, 324
  circumstancial evidence, 324
  and cultural differences, 329–330
  disadvantages of reporting, 330
  discussing suspicions (or not), 329
  emotional maltreatement, 321
  handling information, 330–331
  and home visits, 322
  legal process of reporting, 326–327
  neglect, 321
  next steps after disclosure, 326
  physical abuse, 321
  pitfalls to avoid, 330
  reasonable cause to suspect, 322
  recording indicators, 325–326
  responsibilty for preventing, 322
  review of, 407
  and self-esteem, 345
  sexual abuse, 321
  suspicion of, 320–321
  teacher support, 325

teachers as reporters, 324–325
tips for talking to child or parent, 324
unfounded reporting, 327
using technology, 331
when law enforcement is called, 328
Child Abuse and Maltreatment Indicators, 322–324
Child Abuse Hotline, 326
Child Abuse Reporting Form, 10, 328
Child Abusers, 321–322
Child Development Associate (CDA), 13
Child Development Associate Competencies, 210
Child Study, 387–392, 390–391
Child-Adult interactions, 397–399, 403
Child-Adult Ratios
    early school age, 370–371
    infants, 363–367
    preschoolers, 370
    and program assessment, 361
    toddlers, 367–370
    whole group times, 371
Child Fatalities by Perpetrator Relationship, 321
Child/Home Early Language and Literacy Observation (CHELLO, Neuman et al., 2007), 262
Childhood, 86
Children
    and adjusting to programs, 359–361
    behavioral indicators of comfort, 361
    and cognitive impairment, 235–236
    communication with, 3
    with disabilities and literacy, 263
    helping with cognitive development, 233–234
    helping with emotional development, 154
    helping with group settings, 373–374
    helping with physical development, 104–105
    helping with self-care skills, 75
    and the home visitor, 17
    and inclusion, 236
    and narration, 247
    observation of development, 15–16
    and portfolio access, 11
    portfolio evidence of development, 22
    the program through child's eyes, 361–362
    sharing observations with, 24
    talking to about creativity, 289–291
    and technology, 231–232
    when to help, 64–65
Children, talking about art
    complimentary, 290
    correcting, 290
    describing, 291
    elements of work, 289–290
    judgmental, 290
    modeling, 291
    probing, 290
    psychoanalyzing, 290–291
    questioning, 290
    valuing, 290
Children and Adults with Attention-Deficit/Hyperactivity Disorder (CHADD), 203

Children with exceptionalities
    and child abuse, 330
    and language development, 178
    and least restrictive environment, 105
    observation of, 16–17
    and play, 317–318
    and self-care skills, 75
    separation and adjustment of, 50
    and technology, 261
Children's art and Reggio Emilia, 291–293
The Child Observation Record (COR), 87
Chomsky, Noam, 167
Chunking, 201
Circle of Courage, 141
Class File, 31, 42, 60, 136, 188
Class Files, 396
Class List Log
    and adjusting to group, 375
    advantages of, 30
    and child interacting with adults, 403
    departures and goodbyes, 49
    description of, 27–29
    disadvantages of, 30
    and dramatic play, 312
    example of, 28
    and family communication, 31, 403
    and group settings, 375
    and literacy assessment, 261
    and physical development, 106
    pitfalls to avoid, 30
    and portfolio evidence sheet, 31
    review of, 37, 405
    and self-care skills, 76
    and social development, 129
    and speech and language development, 181
    use of, 8, 20–21
    uses for, 29
    using technology, 30
Classification, 192
Classifying, 225
Classroom Assessment Scoring System (CLASS), 355
Closed method, 78, 133, 187, 239
Closed question, 160
Code of Ethical Conduct (NAEYC, 2005), 10
Cognitive development
    and Anecdotal Recording, 60–61
    assessing in infants and toddlers, 233
    and attention, 198
    and attention span, 189, 203–207
    and cognitive impairment, 235–236
    and concrete operational stage, 195–198
    Concrete Operational Stage, 196–198
    and conversations or interviews, 206
    and creativity, 276–277
    and emotional development, 139
    and the environment, 122–123
    and fear, 148
    and gifted and talented children, 236
    and hearing, 63
    helping children with, 233–234
    and helping professionals, 205
    as indicator of development, 221
    and language development, 90

language development, 161–162, 165
logico-mathematical knowledge, 191–192
math, science and technology, 220–222
media, 206
and memory, 200–201
multiple intelligences and hemisphericity, 202–203
other methods for recording, 237
and physical development, 92, 94
physical knowledge, 191–192
and play, 218–220
and playful curriculum, 201–202
and Portfolio Evidence, 22
preoperational stage, 194–196, 201
problem solving, 124
and referrals, 4
and self-concept, 342
and self-initiator, 124
Sensorimotor Stage, 177, 192–194
social conventional knowledge, 191
stages of, 88
and Vygotsky, 198
work samples, 206
Collaborative play, 120
Collectivism, 129
Collectivists, 62
Communication
    beginning, 170–171
    and child from diverse backgrounds, 402
    with children, 3
    and children with special needs, 402–403
    with families, 376–377
    with family, 4–5
    guide for family communication, 377–378
    and observation, 153
    personal communication, 378–379
    when a problem is suspected, 393–394
Community agencies, 11
Comparisons, and recording, 6
Compendium of K-12 Standards, 210
Competence, 339
Computers and literacy, 260–261
Computers and scanners, 303
Concrete Operational Stage, 195–198, 313–314
Confidentiality, 23, 24, 379
Confidentiality Guidelines
    informed consent, 301
    obtain prior permission, 301
    and the rights of the child, 305
Conservation, 192–194, 195, 197, 198, 224
Constructive play, 121
Constructivist Theory, 114
Consumerism, 232
Contextualized literacy, 245
Continuity of care, 363
Convergent thinking, 294
Conversational environments, 158
Conversations
    and adjusting to group, 375
    advantages of, 163–164

Conversations (*continued*)
and child abuse, 345
and child interacting with adults, 403
and child-adult interactions, 398
and cognitive development, 206, 237
and creativity, 295
facilitated conversations, 161
and family communication, 403
and group settings, 375
and home visits, 159–160
informal, 158
and literacy, 267
and memories, 174
pitfalls to avoid, 164
review of, 406
and self-care skills, 76
and self-esteem, 345
and separation anxiety, 51
Cooperation, 119
Cooperative dramatic play, 120, 312
Cooperative play, 120
Coping mechanisms, 45, 47
Core emotions, 136
Corporal punishment, 330
Creative Development, 275–276
Creative media
music and music development, 284–286
Creative Program Goals, Assessing, 293
Creativity
and ability diversity, 295
and block play, 282–284
blocks as creative medium, 282–283
and cognitive development, 276–277
and cognitive development, examples of,
280–281
cultural diversity and art, 294–295
and Developmental Checklists, 274–275
giftedness, 294
and helping professionals, 295
methods for recording, 295
observing in infants and toddlers,
281–282, 293–294
other methods for recording, 295
and self-concept, 342
and self-portraits, 288–289
sensory experiences, 286
stages of children's art, 277–281
and talking with children, 289–290
and technology, 287–288
using Work Samples, 268–274
Criterion-referenced, 8, 211
CSBS-DP, 128
Cultural Reciprocity, 330
Culture
and child abuse, 329
definition of, 17
diversity and art, 294–295
and dramatic play, 317
and eating skills, 65–68
and facial expressions, 138
and learning and teaching styles, 205
and separation, 50
and social development, 128–129
and toilet training, 70
Cup Cooking (Johnson and Plemons), 224

Curriculum
anti-bias curriculum, 355–357
"Real", 234
Curriculum planning
and bullying, 147–148
and emotional development, 142, 153
and gender differences, 102–103
and physical development, 100–101
playful and cognitive development,
201–202
science for young children, 228–231
and self-care skills, 65
and social development, 116
and toileting, 69

D

Daily log or jounal diary, 35
*DEC Recommended Practices in Early Childhood
Intervention/Early Childhood Special
Education*, 210
Departures, permanant, 49
Detail, preservation of, 6
Development. *See also* Physical
development
dressing, 70–71
eating skills, 65–68
environmental interactions, 72–73
and growth, 88–90
and media documentation, 303
observation of, 15–16
personal hygiene, 71
and self-care skills, 61
toileting, 68–69
Development, physical. *See* Physical
development
Development, Social. *See* Social
Development
Development Checklists
and adjusting to group, 375
advantages of, 83
and anecdotal recording, 57
and creativity, 274–275
description and examples of, 78–83
disadvantages of, 83–84
and emotional development, 156
and home visits, 83
limitations of, 79–83
Physical Developmental Milestones,
80–83
pitfalls to avoid, 84
self-care skills, 75
time management for, 84
uses for, 83, 84–85
using, 14, 20, 31
using technology, 84
Development Revealed in Work Samples,
269
Developmental assessment and dramatic
play, 313–314
Developmental profiles, 402
*Developmental Profiles: Pre-Birth through
Adolescence* 7th Ed., 87
*Developmentally Appropriate Practice in Early
Childhood Programs, Revised Edition*
(NAEYC, 1997), 215

Diagnostic interviews, 161
Dialogic reading, 247–248
Dialogic Reading Rating Scale, 248
Diary, 32, 35
Dictation, 258
Digital divide, 261
Digital video cameras
reevaluation and referrals, 301
replay for discussion, 301
teacher observation practice, 301
and teacher self-reflection, 301
video field trips, 301
Dimensions Educational Research
Foundation, 100
Dimensions Foundation, 100
Direct Instruction, 138
Disabilities and self-esteem, 344–345
Disclosure statement, 322–323
child's disclosure, 324
Disequilibrium, 194
Displacement, 142
Display Portfolios, 9
Dispositions, 221
Divergent thinking, 294
Diverse cultures, 17
Diversity, 179–180
*Division for Early Childhood-DEC
Recommended Practices: A Comprehensive
Guide*, 209
D'Nealian script, 103
Documentation. *See also* Technology
Anecdotal Recording. *see* Anecdotal
Recording
Class List Log. *see* Class List Log
daily log or journal, 35
diary, 32, 35
ethics of, 23
and media, 303
Observation. *see* Observation
Portfolios. *see* Portfolios
and recording, 7
Reflective Journal. *see* Reflective
Journal
using technology. *see also* Technology
Documentation panels, 382
Documenting Early Science Learning (Jones
and Courtney, 2002), 271
Dramatic enactment, 247
Dramatic play
and children with exceptionalities, 317–318
cultural differences in, 317
differing abilities and play, 317
documenting, 303
and helping professionals, 318
infants, 308
necessity of, 306–307
observing for development assessment,
313–314
older toddlers, 309
other methods for recording, 318
pretend play, 308
sociodramatic play, 307–308
socioeconomic differences in, 317
techniques for observing, 312
Types of Play, 120

value of, 307
young toddlers, 308–309
Dramatic play, developmental assessment
cognitive development, 313–314
emotional development, 315–316
and language development, 314
and literacy, 314
and physical development, 316–317
and social development, 314–315
Dramatic play, preschoolers
functional play, 309–310
relational play, 309–310
stereotypic play, 309–310
Dramatic play, young toddlers
repetition with objects, 309
repetition without objects, 309
substitution, 309
Drawing, 256
Dressing, 70–71
Dual Language Learners (DLL), 177–178
Dysfluent, 169–170
Dyslexia, 263

E

Early Childhood, appropriate assessment
difficulty of using standardized tests,
213–214
purpose 1: promote learning, 213
purpose 2: identify children for services,
213
purpose 3: evaluate programs and
services, 213
purpose 4: assess academic achievement,
213
"Early Childhood Assessment: Why, What
and How" (Coleman, West & Gillis,
2010), 209
Early Childhood Environmental Rating
Scale - Revised, 355
Early Head Start, 42
Early Learning Observation & Rating Scale, 88
Earth and Space science, 229
Eating
and anxiety, 46
infants and toddlers, 75
and self-care skills, 65–68
Ecological view, 12, 190
Education and Training, 86
Education of the Handicapped Act
Amendments of 1968, 261
Egocentric (egocentrism), 117, 119, 195
Egocentrism, 195
"Eight stages of man", 116
Electronic media and obesity, 93
Email, 384
Emergent literacy, 244–245
Emotional development, 92
Emotional Development
absence of joy, 140
aggression, 143–147
anger, 142–143
behaviors that warrant concern, 154–155
and bullying, 147–148
and challenging behavior, 146–147

and children under stress, 141
and children with disabilities, 155
and dramatic play, 315–316
and fear, 148–149
helping children with, 154
and helping professionals, 155–156
and home visits, 152
and joy, love and happiness, 139–140
and language development, 162
other methods for recording, 156
and the secure environment, 150–151
and shame, 149
and shyness, 149–150
and socialization, 138–139
stages of emotional development,
136–137
and young English learners, 155
"Emotional Illiteracy", 145
Emotional intelligence, 138
Emotional maltreatment, 321
Emotional regulation, 138
Emotionally Secure Environment,
150–152
Empathy, 119
Empowerment, 338
*Engaging Children's Minds: The Project
Approach* (Katz & Chard, 2000), 25
English as Second Language (ESL),
176–178
English Language Learners, 176–178
Entering school, preparations for
formal family orientation, 43
home visits, 41–42
infant transition, 43
information gathering, 39–41
personal meetings, 41
transitions, 43–44
visit to school, 42–43
Environment
literary-rich, 7
Environment and development, 92, 358
Environmental awareness (science
curriculum), 229–230
Environmental print, 245
Erickson, Deanna
and Nature Play, 100
Erikson, Erik
autonomy versus Shame and Doubt, 62
and behavior philosophies, 252
and developmental childhood
principals, 252
and dramatic play, 314
and infant's trust, 139
Initiative and Industry stage, 62
Social Learning Theory, 116–117
stages of play, 308
ESL Standards for PreK-12 Students, 209
Ethical responsibilities, 380–381
Ethics, 18, 19, 23
Ethnograpic eyes, 54
Evaluation
and assessment, 152, 153
formal evaluation instruments, 9
and language development, 160
objective, 216

and observation, 4
observe-decide-act sequence, 2
Evaluation vs. Surveillance, 301
Everyday Goodbyes (Balaban, 2006), 38
The Exceptional Child (Allen & Cowdery,
2009), 236
Executive function, 138
Expectations of Excellence, 210
Experiences and development, 92
Experssive Aggression, 144–145
Expressive language, 166–167, 168

F

Facilitated conversations, 161
*Failure to Connect: How Computers Affect Our
Children's Minds* (Healy, 1998), 287
Failure to Thrive Syndrome, 90, 140
Family
and communication, 4–5
and portfolio access, 11
sharing observations with, 24
sharing physical development
observations, 101
sharing work samples, 270–271
Family Child Care Accreditation, 354
Family Child Care Accreditation Standards,
210
Family Child Care Environmental Rating
Scale (FCCER-S), 355, 358
Family communication
and anecdotal recording, 75
and blogs, 384–385
and checklists, 79
child study or case study, 387
and class list logs, 31
documentation panels, 382
and email, 384
and ethical responsibilities to family,
380–381
Family Handbook, 381–382
guide for family communication,
377–378
happy notes, 382
keeping things positive, 379–380
need for, 376–377
newsletters, 382
personal communication, 378–379
the portfolio and progress reports,
385–386
positive and negative examples,
387, 389
and progress reports, 387
template for progress reports and child
study, 387–391
traveling journals, 382–384
and voice mail, 384
websites, 385
written communication, 381
Family conferences
advantages of portfolio, 394
description of, 392
disadvantages of using portfolio, 395
finding the time, 395

Family conferences (*continued*)
 and home visits, 393
 pitfalls to avoid, 395
 and technology, 395
 tips for talking to child or parent, 392–393
 uses for, 395–396
Family conferences, when a problem is suspected
 when a problem is suspected, steps for, 393–394
Family Handbook, 381–382
Family Information Form, 40
Family structure and obesity, 93
The Family Day Care Rating Scale, 355
Fear, 148–149
Fictional play, 309–310
First Day preparations
 formal family orientation, 43
 home visits, 41–42
 infant transition, 43
 information gathering, 39–41
 personal meetings, 41
 transitions, 43–44
 visit to school, 42–43
First Drawing: Genesis of Visual Thinking (Fein, 1993), 275
Flexibility, 93
Fluency, reading, 253
Formal assessment measures, 210–211
Four A's of sensory integration, 187
Four Levels of Language Development, 177
Four Stages of Creative Development, 278
Frame of reference, 86–87
Frequency counts
 and adjusting to group, 375
 advantages of, 135
 and attention span, 205
 and child interacting with adults, 403
 and child-adult interactions, 398
 disadvantages of, 135
 example of, 135
 and family communication, 403
 and group settings, 375
 and home visits, 135
 and literacy, 267
 to measure prosocial and antisocial behavior, 134–135
 as measurement, 131–133
 pitfalls to avoid, 135
 and repeated behaviors, 132
 review of, 406
 and self-care skills, 76
 and social development, 129
 time management for, 135
 uses for, 135–136
 using, 8
 using technology, 135
Freud, Sigmund, 314
From Neurons to Neighborhoods (Shonkoff & Phillips, eds. 2000), 198
Functional play, 120–121, 309–310
Functional skills, 75

G

Games with rules, 121
Gender, 340
Gender differences in play, 101–103, 145–146, 315
Gender Identity, 339
Genetics, 89, 92
Geometry of pattern, 225
Geometry of shape, 224–225
Gesell Preschool Readiness Test, 215
Gifted and Talented Children
 and creativity, 294
 description of, 236
 and self-concept, 342
 and standarized tests, 294
Girls and aggression, 145–146
Goals for Block Play, 285
Goals Panel, 213
Goldilocks and the Three Bears, 312
Good Going, 69
Good-bye rituals, 38–39, 44, 45
Goodenough-Harris Draw-A-Person Test, 275
Goodness of fit, 153
Grammar, 162, 169, 171
Group settings, adjustment
 calender and show and tell, 372–373
 groups sizes. *see* child-adult ratios
 helping all children with, 373–374
 make-up of peer group, 362–363
 observing in infants and toddlers, 363
 other methods for recording, 375
 small group times, 372
 whole group times, 371
Growing up Digital, 287
Growth, physical, 88–90
Guidance, 3–4
Guideline, 348

H

Habitual behavior, 131–132
Handwriting, 103
Happiness, 139–140
Happy notes, 382
Hawaiian Early Learning Profile (HELP), 213
Head Start, 209
Head Start Child Outcomes Framework, 209
Health, 92–94
 and observing child, 2–3
Health and nutrition (science curriculum), 228–229
Healthy People 2020, 92
Hearing, 63
Height, 96
Height and Weight Charts, 89
"Heirarchy of Human Needs", 117–118
Helper attitude, 54
Helping Children, when to, 64–65
Helping Professionals
 and anxiety, 50
 and autism, 236–237
 and child abuse and self-esteem, 345
 and cognitive development, 205, 236–237
 and creativity, 295
 and dramatic play, 318
 and emotional development, 155–156
 and group settings, 375
 and language development, 178–179
 and literacy, 266
 and physical development, 105–106
 as referral agents, 17
 self-care skills, 75
 and social development, 129
 and teacher's role, 403
Hemisphericity, brain, 202–203
Heterogeneous grouping, 363
"High stakes tests", 208, 213
High/Scope-PQA High/Scope Program Quality Assessment, 352
HIPPY. *See* Home Instruction for Parents of Preschool Youngsters (HIPPY)
Holographic phrases, 170
Home Instruction for Parents of Preschool Youngsters (HIPPY), 42
Home Visitation Programs, 42
Home visits, 358
 and ancedotal recording, 58
 and the daily log or journal, 35–36
 to discover child's interests, 3
 and dramatic play, 310
 and emotional development, 152
 and family communication, 385
 and family conferences, 393
 and Frequency Counts, 135
 getting ready for first day, 41–42
 and home visits, 322
 and kids with special needs, 50
 and literacy assessment, 262–263
 and math, science and technology, 232
 observing social development, 121–122
 and physical development, 97–98
 and the portfolio, 17
 and Running Records, 111
 and self-care skills, 74
 and self-concept, 338
 and sensory play, 286–287
 and standards, 210, 212
 and technology, 303–304
 and time samples, 187
 using the Portfolio, 17
Hostile Aggression, 145
"Hot zones", emotional, 151
The Hundred Languages of Children (Edwwards & Gandini, 1998), 292

I

IEP. *See* Individualized Education Program (IEP)
"If You're Sad and You Know It" (Koplow 2007), 140
IFSP. *See* Individualized Family Service Plan (IFSP)
Inclusion, 236
Inclusive Early Childhood Education (Richey & Wheeler 2000), 236

Independence, development of, 38, 343
Individualists, 62
Individualized Education Program (IEP), 75
Individualized Family Service Plan (IFSP), 75
Individuals with Disabilities Act (IDEA), 203, 213, 261
The Indviduation Process and Appropriate Adult Responses, 125
Indoor Play, 97
Industry vs. Inferiority, 337
Infant Daily Care Sheet, 368
Infants and toddlers
  and aggression, 143
  assessing cognitive development, 233
  and attention span, 203
  behaviors that warrant concern, 154–155
  and block play, 283–284
  and brain development, 198–199
  development and attachment, 37–38
  and dramatic play, 308–309
  and emotional development, 137
  and fear, 148–149
  feeding and development, 65–68
  group size, infants, 363–367
  group size, toddlers, 367–370
  observation and week by week plan, 400–402
  observation of, 16
  observing creativity in, 281–282, 293–294
  observing emotional development, 153
  observing in group settings, 373
  observing language development, 176
  observing literacy in, 262
  observing physical development, 103–104
  observing routines, 75
  observing social development, 127
  Physical Developmental Milestones, 80–83
  program assessments, 355
  reading to babies, 250
  reading to toddlers, 250–251
  Self, 122–123
  self-gratification, 123
  sensorimotor stage, 187, 192–194
  separation anxiety warning signs, 46–47
  and shyness, 150
  and social development, 116–117
  stages of art, 277–278
  and Time Samples, 187
  transition to school, 43
Infant/Toddler Environmental Rating Scale, Revised Ed. (ITERS), 355
Inference, 53
Informal conversations
  listening to language play, 158
Information gathering, 39–41
Informed consent, 301
Initiative and Industry stage, 64
Innovative play, 307
Intelligences, multiple, 202–203
Interacting with Literacy, 245

Interdependence, 343
Interests, discovery of, 2, 3, 5, 13, 25
International Association for the Child's Right to Play (IPA), 114
International Society for Technology in Education (ISTE), 260
Interrater reliability, 239
Intervention, of problem behavior
  and mistaken behavior, 399–400
  possible causes for, 400
Interviews, 159–160
  and adjusting to group, 375
  advantages of, 163–164
  and child abuse, 345
  and child interacting with adults, 403
  and cognitive development, 206, 237
  and creativity, 274, 295
  diagnostic interviews, 161
  disadvantages of, 164
  and family communication, 403
  and group settings, 375
  and literacy, 267
  pitfalls to avoid, 164
  review of, 406
  and self-care skills, 76
  and self-esteem, 345
  and separation anxiety, 51
  and social development, 129
  structured interviews, 160
  uses for, 165–166
Intuitive Period, 195–197
Invented spelling, 257

J

Job charts, 72–73
Journal diary or daily log, 35
Joy, 139–140

K

Kaiser Family Foundation Report (2006), 261
Key Experiences, 210
Kinesthetic sense, 122
Kinship play, 307
Knowledge, types of (Piaget)
  logico-mathematical knowledge, 191–192
  physical knowledge, 191
  social conventional knowledge, 191
Kohlberg, Lawrence, 339
  and Constructive Theory, 114
  Social Learning Theory, 118

L

Language
  acquisition of, 167–168
  and the art of listening, 173
  beginning communication, 170–171
  development of, 170
  and diversity, 179–180
  documenting child's usage, 162
  and dramatic play, 314
  and eating skills, 65–68

English Language Learners, 176–178
  expressive, 166–167
  facilitating, 173
  functions of, 171–172
  and growth, 88
  and home visits, 159–160
  listening and development, 162, 166
  and literacy, 171
  and music, 169
  observing infants and toddlers, 176
  observing informal conversation, 158
  oral, as reading predictor, 246
  other methods for recording, 181
  and physical development, 92
  and the quiet child, 173–174
  receptive, 166–167
  role models, 175–176
  and self-concept, 341
  social and nonverbal, 172
  and speech acquisition, 168–169
  taping language development, 162–163
  and teacher volume, 175
  when to seek help, 180–181
Language, of observation, 55–56
Large muscle development, 91
Last Child in the Woods (Louv, 2008), 99, 221
Lavalieres, 299
Learned helplessness, 65
Learning
  extending through observation, 3
Learning Approaches
  born to learn, 190
  and culture, 205
  and helping professionals, 205
  postive approaches, 190
  types of, 189–190
Learning Disability, 263–265
Learning disabled, 263–265
Learning from the Children: Reflecting on Teaching (Villareale, 2009), 33
Learning from Young Children in the Classroom: The Art and Science of Teacher Research (Meier & Henderson, 2007), 33
Learning stories, 56–57
Learning styles, 3
Learning Together with Young Children: A Curriculum Framework for Reflective Teachers (Curtis & Carter, 2008), 33
Least restrictive environment, 105
"Lesson Plans on Emotional Life", 151
Letters, making, 257
Liberation teaching, 400
License requirements, 352–354
Life science, 229
Limited English Proficient (LEP), 176–178, 265–266
Listening
  advantages of conversations and interviews, 163–164
  art of, 173
  and begining communication, 170–171
  and confidentiality, 163
  and diagnostic interviews, 161

Listening (*continued*)
   disadvantages of conversations and interviews, 164
   and diversity, 179–180
   and documenting language, 162
   environments for conversation, 158
   and expressive language, 168
   and facilitated conversations, 161
   and facilitating language, 173–174
   and functions of language, 171–172
   and home visits, 159–160
   informal observations in language, 158
   and language acquisition, 167–168
   language and literacy connection, 171
   language development, 162, 170
   and language role models, 175–176
   and learning about child, 161–162
   learning to, 167
   and memories, 174
   as an observation method, 157–158
   observing infants and toddlers, 176
   pitfalls to avoid, 164
   and receptive language, 166–167
   and Show and Tell, 174
   to speech and language development, 166
   and speech development, 168–169
   and structured interviews, 160
   taping language development, 162–163
   and teacher volume, 175
   and time management for, 164–165
   uses for, 165–166
   using technology, 164
   when to seek language help, 180–181
Literacy. *See also* Reading
   alphabetic awareness, 252
   and American children, 244
   assessment, 261–262
   assessment and home visits, 262–263
   and children with disabilities, 263
   and computers, 260–261
   development of, 244
   and dramatic play, 314
   emergent literacy, 251–252
   and English as second language, 265–266
   and environmental print, 245
   and functions of language, 171
   and helping professionals, 266
   in the home, observing, 248–249
   and learning disabilities, 263–265
   and learning to read, 244–245
   and math, science and technology, 233
   observing in infants and toddlers, 262
   other methods for recording, 267
   and parent's support in the home, 264
   phonemic awareness, 252
   and phonological awareness, 247–249
   Play-Literacy connections, 246
   reading in the early grades, 252–253
   Reading Standards: Foundational Skills, 253
   reading to babies, 250
   reading to toddlers, 250–251
   and self-concept, 342
   stages of, 249–250
   stages of writing, 256
   and technology, 232
   and television, 259–260
   and writing in young children, 253–256
Literacy and Mathematics, 226–227
Literacy Objectives, 242
Literacy Rating Scale Example, 239, 240–241
Literature-based, 247
Love, 139–140

M

Magic Bracelet, 44
Make-up of peer group, 362–363
Maltreatment. *See* Child Abuse
Mandala, 278–279
Mandated reporters, 321, 326
Mapping, 223
Mark-making, 277–278
Maslow, Abraham
   Social Learning Theory, 117–118
Mastery play, 307
Matching, 192
Math, Science and Technology, 220–222
   and children, 231–232
   home visits, 232
   and large muscle development, 233
   and literacy, 233
   and other developmental areas, 233
   and self-care skills, 232–233
   and small muscle development, 233
Math concepts
   and block play, 223
   classifying, 225
   conservation, 224
   and the curriculum, 223–226
   geometry of pattern, 225
   geometry of shape, 224–225
   measurement, 224
   observation of, 222–223
   one-to-one correspondence, 223
   ordinal numbers, 223–224
   problem solving, 226
   rote, 223
   seriation, 226
   visual-spatial skills, 225–226
   whole/part terminology, 224
Mathematics and Literacy, 226–227
Maturation, 92
Measurement, 224
Measuring Performance: The Early Childhood Educator in Practice, 355
Media
   audio recording, 298–299
   and child abuse, 345
   and child-adult interactions, 399
   and cognitive development, 237
   and creativity, 269, 295
   digital video recorders, 301
   as documentation, 303
   and emotional development, 156
   and literacy, 267
   photography, 302
   and physical development, 106
   and self-care skills, 76
   and self-esteem, 345
   and separation anxiety, 51
   and social development, 129
   television and obesity, 93
   Television Turn Off Day, 184–185
   video recording, 299
Memories, 174
Memory
   aspects of, 200–201
   chunking, 201
   rehearsal, 201
   and self-concept, 341–342
   wait time, 201
   word association, 201
   writing, 201
Mental processing differences, 203–205
Methods for observation, 16–17
Microphones, in the classroom, 299
Minorities and school achievement, 235
Mirror, Reflective Journal as, 33–34
Miseducation: Preschoolers at Risk (Elkind, 1987), 65, 252
Mixed-Age Groups, 363
Modeling, 138
Moral development, 124
Morality, 338–339
The Moral Intelligence of Children (Coles, 1997), 339
Morphemes, 168
Multiple intelligences, 202–203
Muscle Control and Skill Development, 91
Muscle development, large, 91, 233
Muscle development, small, 91, 233
Muscular strength and endurance, 93
   and Running Records, 108
Music and language, 169
Music and music development, 284–286

N

NACCP Program Accreditation, 354
NAECS/SDE. *See* National Association of Early Childhood Specialists in State Departments of Education (NAECS/SDE)
NAEYC. *See* National Association for the Education of Young Children (NAEYC)
NAEYC Center Accreditation, 352
NAEYC Professional Preparation Standards at Associate Degree, Initial Licensure and Advanced Degrees, 210
Narrative
   as anecdotal recording, 53, 126, 266
   from the child, 247
   order of, 56–59
   recordings of, 8, 14
National Association for the Education of Young Children (NAEYC), 302
   and child abuse, 329
   and confidentiality of portfolios, 10
   and ethics in communication, 380–381
   and portfolio assessment, 12
   and program assessment, 352
   and standardized tests, 218

National Association of Early Childhood Specialists in State Departments of Education (NAECS/SDE), 12, 94, 215
National Board Certification Standards, 210
National Center for learning Disability, 263
National Clearinghouse for English Language Acquisition, 176
National Council for the Social Studies, 116
National Early Literacy Panel (NELP), 245
National Education Goals Panel, 212–213
National Health and Safety Performance Standards (2112), 355
National Health Education Standards, 210
National Institute of Child Health and Human Development (NICHD), 363
National Institute of Mental Health (NIMH), 203
National Television Violence Study, 315
National Visual Arts Standards, 209
Nature deficit disorder, 99
Nature Explore Classrooms, 100
NECPA Program Accreditation, 354
Neglect, 321
Newsletters, 382, 383
Next Steps Toward Teaching the Reggio Way: Accepting the Challenge to Change (Hendrick, 2004), 33
NICHD Early Child Care Research, 116
No Child Left Behind (NCLB) Act, 42, 208–209, 377
"No table-top testing", 216
The No-cry Separation Anxiety Solution (Pantley, 2010), 44
Non-English speaking children, 50, 105, 129, 155, 176–178, 265–266
Nonrepresentational, 277, 279, 290
Nonverbal language, 172
Norm, 211
Norm-referenced tests, 211

O
Oberver, roles of, 7–8
Obesity, childhood, 92–93
Object permanence, 117, 192, 193
Objective, *23*, 35
Observable Evidence, 239–240
Observation
  and accountability, 5
  and actions, 24–25
  and assessment, 4
  assessment and curriculum braid, 152–153
  assessment and dramatic play, 313–314
  and assistance of child, 3
  and attention span, 183–184
  and checklists, 86–87
  and child development, 15–16
  and child maltreatment, 332
  and communication, 3, 4–5
  and confidentiality, 24
  of creativity, 281–282
  and creativity, 288
  and the daily log or journal, 35

definition of, 1–2
and developing scientific concepts, 227–228
and diverse cultures, 17
and diversity, 179–180
of dramatic play, 312–313
eating, 65–68
and ecological view, 12
and evaluation, 4
and exceptionalities, 16–17
and guidance, 3–4
and helping children, 16–17
of infants and toddlers, 16, 75
and interest discovery, 3
and learning and teaching styles, 3
and listening. *see* Listening
of literacy in the home, 248–249
of math concepts, 222–223
as means to extended learning, 3
and measuring progress, 4
observe-decide-act sequence, 2
and other professionals, 17
and physical development, 95–97
and physical health, 2
and privacy, 299, 300
and progress measurement, 4
and referrals, 4
and the Reflective Journal, 10–11, 21–33, 32
and Running Records, 107–109
and safety, 2
self-care skills, 65–72
and self-reflection of teaching methods, 5
separation and adjustment of infants and toddlers, 49
of settings, 349
sharing with the child and family, 24
of social development, 124–127
Time Samples. *see* Time Samples
of toileting skills, 68–69
using senses, 63–64
week by week and NAEYC guidelines, 401–402
when to observe, 12
Observation, Language of, 55–56
Observation and Recording Method
  advantages and disadvantages of, 14
  finding the time, 14–15
  pitfalls to avoid, 14
  review box, 15
  usage, 14
  using technology, 14
Observation techniques for Program Evaluators, 351
Observation Toolkit for Mental Health Consultants, 135
The Observational System for Recording Physical Activity in Children-Preschool (OSRAC-P), 105
Observe, Ask and Respond (OAR), 39
Observe-decide-act sequence, 2
Observer bias, 56
Observer effect, 109
Observing Development of the Young Child 7th Ed., 88

Observing Development of the Young Child 7th Ed. (Beaty, 2010), 79
Olfactory observing, 64
"100 Languages of Children", 257
One-to-one correspondence, 192, 223
Onlooker play, 119–120
Onlooker stage, 311
Open method, 53
Open question, 160
Oral language, 246
Oral teaching, 56–57
Ordinal numbers, 223–224
Orientation, school entrance, 43
Ounce Scale, 57
Outdoor Area Checklist, 96–97
Outdoor Play
  benefits of, 99
  checklist for, 96–97
  nature play, 99–100
  and physical development, 96, 97
Overgeneralization, 171

P
Parallel play, 120
Parents
  and anecdotal recording, 58
  as assessors of their child, 41, 187, 263
  and developmental checklists, 83
  of dual language learners, 176–178
  and literacy, 264
  and portfolio access, 10, 25, 50
  and self-care skills, 72–73
Parents as Teachers Born, 42
"Partnering in children's separations", 48
Peer group
  chronological age groups, 362
  continuity of care, 363
  mixed-age or multi-age groups, 363
Penn Interactive Peer Play Scale, 126–127
Performance standards, 355
Personal hygiene, 71
Personal meetings, 41
Phonemes, 168
Phonemic awareness, 252
Phonetic reading, 247
Phonics, 253
Phonological awareness, 245, 247–249
Phonological memory, 245
Photo albums, 302
Photography, 302
Physical abuse, 321
Physical development
  and children with disabilities, 105
  cognitive development, 94
  and curriculum planning, 100–101
  and dramatic play, 316–317
  and health, 92–94
  helping children with, 104–105
  and the home visitor, 97–98
  importance of, 92
  individual timetables for, 90
  other methods for recording, 106
  and play, 95
  predictable sequence for, 90

Physical development (*continued*)
readiness, 90
and self-concept, 341
social-emotional development, 94
Physical development, observing
Anecdotal Recording, 101
for assessment, 96–97
Checklists for, 101
in the environment, 97
gender differences, 101–102
infants and toddlers, 103–104
for safety maintenance, 95–96
sharing with families, 101
small muscle, 102–103
Physical Developmental Milestones, 80–83
Physical environment and development, 150–152
Physical health, and observation, 2, 13
Physical science, 229
Physical skills. *See* Physical development
Piaget, Jean
and behavior philosophies, 252
Cognitive questioning method, 3
Cognitive Theory, 117
Concrete Operational Stage, 195–198
and developmental childhood principals, 252
and dramatic play, 314
early works of, 190–191
and egocentrism, 119
and interviews, 159
logico-mathematical knowledge, 191–192
memory association (recognition), 200
physical knowledge, 191
play catagories, 121
and Play-Literacy connections, 246
preoperational stage, 194–196, 201
sensorimotor stage, 192–194
Social conventional knowledge, 191
stages of play, 308
Pick up songs, 74
Pitfalls
Anecdotal Recording, 58–59
Class List Log, 30
Development Checklists, 84
and family conferences, 395
of formal program assessment, 358
of Frequency Counts, 135
of interviews and conversations, 164
Observation and Recording Method, 14
of Rating Scales, 242
Reflective Journal, 36
of reporting child abuse, 330
Running Record, 111
of standardized tests, 218
of technology, 304–305
of Time Samples, 188
of Work Samples, 271
Planning for Individual Learning Needs, 356
Play
associative, 120
and autism, 114
block play. *see* Block play

and cognitive development, 218–220
collorative play, 120
concept map, 115
constructive, 121
cooperative, 120
and culture, 317
and development, 95
dramatic play, 121. *see also* Dramatic play
fictional play, 309–310
functional play, 120–121, 309–310
and gender, 315
gender differences, 101–102
indoor, 97
innovative play, 307
kinship play, 307
listening to language, 158
mastery play, 307
negative play or nonplay (unoccupied play), 119
and observing child, 12
and observing social development, 124–127
onlooker play, 119–120
outdoor, 96–97, 99–100
parallel play, 120
play stages. *see* Play, Stages of
playful curriculum, 201–202
Play-Literacy connections, 246
pretend play, 308
and the Running Record, 110–113
social attention play, 120
and social development, 95, 114–115
sociodramatic play, 307–308
and socioeconomic differences, 317
solitary play, 115, 120
stereotypic play, 309–310
therapeutic play, 307
and Vygotsky, 219–220, 246
and writing in young children, 259
young school agers, 310
Play, Stages of
associative dramatic play, 312
cooperative dramatic play, 312
onlooker stage, 311
solitary dramatic play, 312
Play catagories
Piaget, Jean and Smilansky, Sara, 121
"Play is the child's work", 114
Play Skills Checklist, 127
Play-based assessment, 12, 13
Playground safety, 357
Play-Literacy connections, 246
The Plug-In Drug (Winn, 2002), 287
Policies, 348
Portfolio assessment
definition of, 8
principals for, 12
reasons for usage, 11–12
Portfolio Evidence Sheet
and child abuse, 330–331
and class list logs, 31
example of, 219, 331–335
and Frequency Counts, 135–136
and group settings, 374

and Running Records, 112
samples of, 22, 59, 76, 112, 136, 165, 189, 219, 244, 274, 306, 374
uses for, 10, 21–22
and the *week by week* plan, 25
and work samples, 274
Portfolios
advantages of using for conferences, 394
and anecdotal recording, 56–60
and checklists, 84–85
child's contributions, 9
and communication with families, 376–377
and creativity, 269–270
disadvantage of using for conferences, 395
Display Portfolios, 9
evidence of child's development, 22
family contributions, 9
and handwriting, 103
and the home visitor, 17
and information about family, 39–40
and interviews, 165–166
and observation, 4–5
and photography, 302–303
previous teacher's contributions, 9
and program assessment, 351
and progress reports, 385–386
referrals agent's contributions, 9
and Running Records, 112–113
Showcase Portfolios, 9
staff contributions, 9
teacher's contributions, 9
and technology, 306
using progress reports, 385
and Week by Week systematic plan, 13
what is in one, 188
what not to document in portfolio, 10
what to do at end of year, 396
Working Portfolios, 9
Portfolios, access to
and children, 11
and community agencies, 11
and ethics, 10–11
and families, 11
and practitioners, 11
Positive Emission Tomography (PET) scans, 94
Positive or Negative Reinforcement, 138
Poverty and school achievement, 235
Power, 338
The Power of Play (Elkland, 2007), 306
Practitioners
and portfolio access, 11
and the *Week by Week plan*, 407–408
Precocity, 294
Preconceptional Period, 195
Prenatal care, 89
Preoperation stage, 194–195, 201
Preschematic art, 279
Preschoolers
and backward letters, 258
and block play, 284
and child-adult ratio, 370
fictional play, 309

functional play, 309
observing literacy in, 262
preoperational stage, 194–196
reading to, 251–252
relational play, 309
and self-concept, 336
and stages of art, 278–279
stereotypic play, 309
Pretend play, 308
"Preventing Reading Difficulties in Young Children" (Snow, Burns, & Griffin, 1998), 171
Principals and Standards for School Mathematics, 210
Print, organizing, 257–258
Print-rich environment, 247
Printscript, 103
Privacy and observation, 299, 300. *See also* Confidentiality Guidelines
Problem behavior
possible causes for, 400
recognizing reasons for, 399–400
Problem solving, 226
Professional Preparation Standards, 18
Professionals, Helping
and anxiety, 50
and autism, 236–237
and child abusse and self-esteem, 345
and cognitive development, 205, 236–237
and creativity, 295
and dramatic play, 318
and group settings, 375
and language development, 178–179
and literacy, 266
and physical development, 105–106
as referral agents, 17
self-care skills, 75
and social development, 129, 155–156
and teacher's role, 403
Program Assessment, 349–351, 407
Program evaluation, 351
Program Evaluation Comparison, 353
Program Evaluation Questions, 350
Program Evaluations, total
accreditation, 352
Family Child Care Accreditation, 354
High/Scope-PQA High/Scope Program Quality Assessment, 352
Home-visiting Program Accreditation, 354
NACCP Program Accreditation, 354
NAEYC Center Accreditation, 352–354
NECPA Program Accreditation, 354
Quality Rating and Improvement Systems, 352
School-Age Program Accreditation, 354
Program Standards, 210
The Program Administration Scale, 355
Progress, measurement of, 4
Progress at a Glance Form, 388
Progress Reports
description of, 387–389
and helping professionals, 403
and portfolio access, 385

uses for, 392–393
using photographs for, 302–303
Prosocial behavior, 134–135
Proximodistal, 90
Pyramid Model for Promoting Infants and Young Children's Social Development, 147

Q

Quality of Early Childhood Care Settings: Caregiver Rating Scale (QUEST), 355
Quality points
definition of, 239
Not Yet/In Process/Proficient, 239
Seldom/Usually/Always, 239
Yes/Yes, but.../No (NAEYC), 239
Quality Rating and Improvement Systems, 352
Quanitative scoring, 211
Quantitative, 8
Quick Quality Check for Infant and Toddler programs, 355
Quiet children, 173–174

R

Race to the Top Early Learning Challenge, 209
Rapid naming of letters, 245
Rating Observation Scale for Inspiring Environments (ROSIE), 355
Rating Scales, 8
and adjusting to group, 375
advantages of, 241
and attention span, 205
and child abuse, 345
and child interacting with adults, 403
and child-adult interactions, 399
and cognitive development, 237
and creativity, 295
disadvantages of, 241
and dramatic play, 312, 318
and emotional development, 156
Dialogic Reading Rating Scale, 243
example of, 239–240, 240–241
and family communication, 403
and group settings, 375
pitfalls to avoid, 242
review of, 406
and self-care skills, 76
and self-esteem, 345
and separation anxiety, 51
and sequential milestones or quality points, 238–239
and speech and language development, 181
and time management for, 242–244
uses for, 244
Read a Book, 25
Reading. *See also* Literacy
to babies, 250
in the early grades, 252–253
to preschoolers, 251
Standards: Foundational Skills, 253
to toddlers, 250–251

types of books, 253–255
and writing in young children, 253–256
Reading and Writing Development, 250
Ready Recovery Instruction, 262
"Real" curriculum, 234
Receptive language, 166–167, 173
Recommendation, 348
Recording, 129
for comparisons, 6
criterion-referenced, 8
and details, 6
and documentation, 7
infants and toddlers, 75
for later amplification, 6
as literary role model, 6–7
and the narrative, 8
quantitative, 8
for remembrance, 6
Running Record. *see* Running Record
and time, 13
and Work Samples, 8
as written account, 5
Recording, Anecdotal. *See* Anecdotal Recordings
Recording, of interviews, 161
Reducing Aggression, 146
Referrals
and challenging behavior, 147
and child abuse, 329
and conferences, 393
and digital video recording, 301
for emotional concerns, 156
recording for, 2, 4, 9, 11, 17
for separation anxiety, 50
and speech and language development, 180–181
Reflections, 33, 36
Reflective Journal
advantages of, 36
and child abuse, 329
description of, 32–33
disadvantages of, 36
and dramatic play, 312–313
examples of, 32, 34
for a home visitor, 35
as a mirror, 33–34
pitfalls to avoid, 36
as private diary, 25
review of, 37, 405
and technology, 36
time management for, 36
uses for, 34–35, 36
what to do at end of year, 397
and Working Portfolio, 10–11
Reflex actions, 88–89
Reggio Emilia, 291–293
Regression, emotional development, 140
Regulation, 348
Regulatory agencies, 348
Rehabilitation Act of 1973, 203
Rehearsal, 201
Relational play, 309–310
Reliability, 211, 214
Remembrance, 6

Reporting child abuse suspicions
    advantages of, 330
    disadvantages of, 330
Resilient, 141
Response to Intervention Model (RTI),
    127–128
Responsibility, 119
Responsive care, 153
Reversibility, 195
Rights of the Child, 305
Role models, 6–7
Role models and language, 175–176
Rote counting, 192, 223
Rough-and-tumble play, 102
Running Record
    and adjusting to group, 375
    advantages of, 109–110
    and attention span, 205
    and child abuse, 345
    and child interacting with adults, 403
    and child-adult interactions, 398
    and cognitive development, 237
    and creativity, 295
    description of, 107–109
    disadvantages of, 110
    and dramatic play, 318
    and emotional development, 156
    example of, 110
    and family communication, 379
    and group settings, 375
    and home visits, 111
    and infants and toddlers, 187
    and literacy, 267
    and literacy assessment, 261
    and physical development, 106
    pitfalls to avoid, 111
    practice writing, 111
    rating, 111
    review of, 112
    and self-care skills, 76
    and self-esteem, 345
    and separation anxiety, 51
    and social development, 126, 129
    and speech and language development, 181
    and superhero play, 315
    time management for, 111–112
    uses for, 109, 112–113
    using technology, 111

S

Safety, and observation, 2, 13, 95–96
Sax, Leonard, 145–164, 340
Scaffold, 118
Schematic art, 279–280
School achievement, 235
School adjustment, 49–50
School agers
    adult-child ratios, 370–371
    and self-concept, 336–337
School readiness, 219
School readiness and social conciousness,
    115–116
School-Age Care Evnironment Rating
    Scale, 355

School-Age Program Accreditation, 354
Science, Technology, Engineering and
    Mathematics, (STEM) National
    Science Foundation, 221
Science curriculum
    earth and space science, 229
    environmental awareness, 229–231
    health and nutrition, 228–229
    life science, 229
    physical science, 229
Science Curriculum Project or
    Theme Web, 230
Science learning
    curriculum for young children, 228–231
    documenting, 228
    observing, 227–228
Science Process Skills and Authentic
    Assessment, 222
Screen time
    how much, 231–232
    what is learned?, 232
Screening, 208
Scribbling, 256, 278–279
Selective method, 239
Self and social development, 122–123
Self conciousness and observation, 109
Self-Assertion, 124
Self-assessment, 11
Self-care, 61
Self-care skills
    and automony, 62–64
    caring for the classroom, 72–73
    and the curriculum, 65
    development of, 61–62
    by developmental age, 66
    dressing, 70–71
    eating, 65–68
    and helping children, 64–65
    helping children with, 75
    and home visitors, 74
    importance of, 74
    looking at, 61
    and math, science and technology,
        232–233
    other methods for recording, 76
    personal hygiene, 71
    and self-concept, 341
    sleeping, 71–72
    toileting, 68–71
Self-concept
    in 2 yr olds, 336
    and acceptance, 338
    and adjustment to new setting, 343
    asking the child, 343
    and attention span, 341–342
    and cognitive development, 342
    and competence, 339
    and creativity, 342
    and culture, race and self-esteem, 344
    description of, 331
    development of, 332
    disabilities and self-esteem, 344–345
    and home visits, 338
    in infants, 335–336
    and literacy, 342

and memory, 341–342
and morality, 338–339
observation of, 340–341
older preschoolers, 326
and physical competence, 341
and power, 338
and school agers, 336–337
and self-care skills, 341
and self-esteem, 341
and separation, 341
and speech and language development,
    341
Self-concept Development, 335
Self-control, 119
Self-differentiation, 193
Self-esteem
    building, 337–338
    description of, 331–335
    and helping professionals, 345
    and maltreatment, 345
    observation of, 240–341
    other methods for recording, 345
    and self-concept, 341
    and sex-role identity, 339–340
Self-Esteem Class List Log, 341
Self-esteem Factors, 338
Self-gratification, 123
Self-initiator, 124
Selfless society, need for, 122
Self-portraits, 288–289
Self-reflection, of teaching methods, 5
Self-regulation, 154
Senses, using for observation, 63–64
Sensitive periods, 198
Sensorimotor Stage
    accommodation, 194
    assimilation, 194
    description of, 192–193
    disequilibrium, 194
    infants and toddlers, 187
    object permanence, 193
    self-differentiation, 193
    word association, 194
Sensory integration, 94, 154, 184
Sensory play, 286–287
Separation
    children with special needs, 50
    cultural diversities, 50
    other professionals, 50
    preparing for, 49
    and self-concept, 341
Separation anxiety
    and acting out, 47–48
    arrivals and departures, 43–44
    behavior, 45
    and children with special needs, 50
    development of, 38–39
    infant transition, 43
    in infants, 123
    other methods for recording, 51
Separation anxiety attack, 45
Separation anxiety, warning signs
    acting out, 47–48
    description of, 45–46
    eating, 46

in infants, 46
participation in classroom, 47
sleeping, 46–47
social interactions, 47
toileting, 47
Sequence, 56
Seriation, 192, 196, 226
Sesame Street, 260
Setting Observations, 349
Sex (biological identification), 339
Sex-role Identity, 339–340
Shame, 148–149
Show and Tell, 174, 371–372
Showcase Portfolios, 9
Shyness, 148–149, 149–150
Sight, 63
"Sixth Sense", 64
Sleeping
    and anxiety, 46–47
    infants and toddlers, 75
    and self-care skills, 71–72
Small group times, 372
Small muscle development, 91, 102–103
Smart Moves: Why Learning Is Not All in Your Head, 94
Smell, 64
Smilansky, Sara
    play catagories, 121. *see also* Piaget, Jean
    stages of play, 308
Social attention play, 120
Social Behavior, 232
Social competence, 119
Social conciousness and school readiness, 115–116
Social conventional knowledge, 191
Social Development
    checklist for, 92
    and children with autism, 128
    and children with disabilities, 127–128
    and cognitive development, 90
    and culture, 128–129
    and dramatic play, 314–315
    and helping professionals, 129
    other methods for recording, 129
    and physical development, 92, 94
    and play, 95, 114–115
    Pyramid Model for Promoting Infants and Young Children's Social Development, 147
    and relationship establishment, 113–114
    self-assertion, 124
    self-gratification, 123
    self-initiator, 124
    young children and social studies, 116
Social Development, observing
    anecdotal and running records, 126
    checklists, 126–127
    Individuation Process and Appropriate Adult Responses, 125
    in infants and toddlers, 127
Social Development, stages of
    associative play, 120
    collaborative play, 120
    constructive play, 121
    cooperative play, 120

dramatic play, 121
functional play, 120–121
games with rules, 121
negative play or nonplay (unoccupied play), 119
observing in the home, 121–122
onlooker play, 119–120
parallel play, 120
Rubin play matrix, 120
Self, 122–123
social attention play, 120
solitary play, 120
Social Development, theories of
    Behaviorist social learning theory, 117
    Erickson, 116–117
    Kohlberg, 118–119
    Maslow, Abraham, 117–118
    Piaget, Jean, 117
    Vgotsky, Lev, 118
Social interactions and anxiety, 47
Social language, 172
Social Learning Theory
    Behaviorist social learning theory, 117
    Erickson, 116–117
    implications of, 119
    Kohlberg, 118
    Maslow, Abraham, 117–118
    Piaget, Jean, 117
    Vgotsky, Lev, 118
Social Studies, 116
Social-emotional development, 94
Socialization, 114, 119
Socialized, 340
Sociodramatic play, 307–308
Socioeconomic differences and play, 317
Solitary dramatic play, 312
Solitary play, 115, 120
Solitary time, 276
Spatial literacy, 223
Special focus instruments (program evaluations)
    anti-bias curriculum, 355–357
    Assessing Quality in The Early Years: Early Childhood Environment Rating Scale (ECERS-E) 4e, 355
    Classroom Assessment Scoring System (CLASS), 355
    description of, 354–355
    Early Childhood Environmental Rating Scale - Revised, 355
    Family Child Care Environmental Rating Scale (FCCERS-R), 355
    The Family Day Care Rating Scale, 355
    Infant and Toddler Environmental Rating Scale, 355
    Measuring Performance: The Early Childhood Educator in Practice, 355
    National Health and Safety Performance Standards (2112), 355
    playground safety, 357
    The Program Administration Scale, 355
    Quality of Early Childhood Care Settings: Caregiver Rating Scale (QUEST), 355
    Quick Quality Check for Infant and Toddler programs, 355

Rating Observation Scale for Inspiring Environments (ROSIE), 355
School-Age Program Environment Rating Scale, 355
Speech. *See also* Language; Listening
    assessing, 161
    development of, 168–169
    and expressive language, 168
    listening and development, 166
    other methods for recording, 181
    Speech and Language Development, 163
    stuttering and, 169–170
    tests for, 159–160
Staff performance evaluation, 355
Staff Requirements for Child-Staff Ratios and Maximum Group Sizes for Child Care Centers, 364–366
Stage Comparison of Cognitive and Creative Thoughts, 277
Stages of Children's Art
    Stage I: Mark making, 277–278
    Stage II: Scribbling, 278–279
    Stage III: Preschematic, 279
    Stage IV: Schematic Stage, 279–280
Stages of Music Development, 287
Stages of Other Creative Activities, 286
Standard, 348
Standardized tests. *See also* Early Childhood, appropriate assessment
    administration of, 217–218
    advantages of, 218
    as assessment method, 211
    case against, 216–217
    and the child, 214
    description of, 208
    difficulties with, 214–215
    difficulty of using with young children, 213–214
    disadvantages of, 218
    and home visits, 212
    pitfalls to avoid, 218
    and the teacher, 217–218
    technology for, 218
    time management for, 218
    uses for, 218
    uses of, 215–216
Standards, 17–18
Standards, Reading: Foundational Skills, 253
Standards for English Language Arts, 209
Standards Movement
    Active Start: A Statement of Physical Guidelines for Children Birth to Five Years 2e, 210
    Benchmarks for Science Literacy, 210
    Benchmarks in Action: A Guide to Standards-Based Assessment in Music, 210
    Caring for Our Children: National Health and Safety Performance Standards: Guidelines for Out-of-Home Child Care, 210
    Child Development Associate Competencies, 210
    Compendium of K-12 Standards, 210

Standards Movement (*continued*)
  DEC Recommended Practices in Early Childhood Intervention/Early Childhood Special Education, 210
  Division for Early Childhood-DEC Recommended Practices: A Comprehensive Guide, 209
  ESL Standards for PreK-12 Students, 209
  Expectations of Excellence, 210
  Family Child Care Accreditation Standards, 210
  Head Start Child Outcomes Framework, 209
  Head Start Program Performance Standards, 210
  and home visits, 210, 212
  Key Experiences, 210
  NAEYC Professional Preparation Standards at Associate Degree, Initial Licensure and Advanced Degrees, 210
  National Board Certification Standards, 210
  National Educational Technology Standards, 210
  National Health Education Standards, 210
  National Visual Arts Standards, 209
  Principles and Standards for School Mathematics, 210
  Program Standards, 210
  Standards for English Language Arts, 209
Stereotypes, 232
Stereotypical play, 309–310
The Stew, 113
Story Dictation, 313
Stranger anxiety, 37–38
Stress, 141, 216
Structured interviews, 160
  uses for, 165–166
Stuttering, 169–170
Subjective, 31, 35
Summative observation, 29
"Superbaby Syndrome", 251
Superhero play, 315
Surveillance vs. evaluation, 301
Syntax, 170

T

Tadpole Man, 279
Talented and Gifted Children, 236
Taste, 64
Teacher
  as role model, 6–7
Teachers as Reporters, 324–325
Teacher's Role
  active listening, 399
  preparing the environment, 399
  realistic expectations, 399
Teacher's Safety Checklist: Indoor Spaces, Outdoor Spaces 84–85
Teacher's stories, 397
Teaching Strategies GOLD Assessment System (Field Test Ed. July 2009), 233, 262
Teaching styles, 3
Teaching with the Brain in Mind (Jensen, 2005), 199–200
Tech Tonic: Towards a New Literacy of Technology (Plowman, 2010), 287

Technology
  advantages of, 304
  anecdotal and running records, 59
  audio recording, 59, 298–299
  blogs, 384–385
  and Class List Log, 30
  clipboards, 30
  computers and scanners, 303
  considerations in school room usage, 297–298
  and creativity, 287–288
  date stamp, 30
  and Developmental Checklists, 84
  for developmental documentation, 303
  and digital video recording, 299–301
  disadvantages of, 304
  and dramatic play, 303
  email, 384
  evaluation vs. surveillance, 301
  and family conferences, 395
  and formal program assessment, 359
  and Frequency Counts, 135
  hand-held computer, 30
  and home visits, 303–304
  index cards and sticky notes, 30
  and Listening, 164
  mailing labels, 30
  media for observation, 298
  and Observation and Recording Method, 14
  and photography, 302
  pitfalls to avoid, 304
  and privacy, 300
  and Rating Scales, 242
  and Reflective Journals, 36
  review of, 407
  Running Record, 111
  and Running Records, 111
  smart phones and texting, 59
  for standardized tests, 218
  and time management for, 305–306
  and Time Samples, 188
  uses for documentation, 306
  using for interviews, 164
  video recording, 59, 299–301
  voice mail, 384
  websites, 385
  and work samples, 271
Technology and Young Children
  screen time, 231–232
Telegraphic phrases, 170
Television
  and obesity, 93
Televison
  and aggressive play, 315
  and literacy, 259–260
Televison Turn Off Day, 184–185
Temper Trantrum Book, 151
Temperament, 137
Tense, 56
Tests
  appropriate usage in early childhood. *see* Early Childhood, appropriate assessment
  case against standardized testing, 216–217

  formal assessment measures, 210–211
  No Child Left Behind, 208–209
  purpose of, 207
  standardized testing, 208
  standardized tests and the teacher, 217–218
  and Standards Movement, 209–210
  the standards movement, 209–210
The Center for Evidence Based Practice: Young Children with Challenging Behavior, 147
The Play Observation Scale, 127
Therapeutic play, 307
Three Little Pigs, 312
Time and recording, 13, 14–15
Time management
  and anecdotal recording, 59
  and assessing EC programs, 359
  and class list logs, 30
  and family conferences, 395
  and frequency counts, 135
  and Rating Scales, 242–244
  and recording, 6
  and the reflective journal, 36
  Running Record, 111–112
  and standardized tests, 218
  and technology, 305–306
  and Time Samples, 188
  using checklists, 84
  and *Week by Week Plan*, 13
  and Work Samples, 271
Time Samples, 8, 406
  and adjusting to group, 375
  advantages of, 187–188
  analysis of, 185–187
  and attention span, 203–205
  and child interacting with adults, 403
  and child-adult interactions, 398
  and creativity, 295
  disadvantages of, 187–188
  and dramatic play, 312, 318
  example of, 185
  factors affecting attention span, 183–184
  and family communication, 403
  and group settings, 375
  and home visits, 187
  and literacy, 267
  measuring attention span, 184–185
  pitfalls to avoid, 188
  and social development, 129
  time management for, 188
  uses for, 188–189
Toddler Daily Care Sheet, 369
Toddlers. *See also* infants and toddlers
  and child-adult ratio, 367–370
  and play, 309–310
  and self-concept, 336
Toileting
  and anxiety, 47
  and culture, 70
  direct instruction, 70
  environmental considerations, 69–70
  infants and toddlers, 75
  role models, 70
  as self-care skill, 69

Touch, 64
TRACE Center for Excellence in Early Childhood Assessment, 217
Transitions, 43–44, 367, 372–373
Traveling journals, 382–384
Trends in Obesity, 93
Types of Books for Young Children, 253–255

U

Unconditional positve regard, 398
Unfounded reporting, child abuse, 327
United States Department of Health and Human Services, 92
Universal Design for Learning (UDL), 105
Unoccupied play, 119

V

Valid (validity of), 211
Verbs, 55
Vertical grouping, 363
Video recorders, 299
Visual clues, 63
Visual-spatial skills, 225–226
Vocabulary, 159–160, 169, 170. *See also* Language; Listening
Vocabulary Explosion, 170
Voice mail, 384
Vygotsky, Lev
  and cognitive development, 198
  and dramatic play, 314
  and language development, 167
  and play, 219–220
  play and development, 118
  and Play-Literacy connections, 246
  stages of play, 308
  zone of proximal development, 100

W

Wait time, 201
Warning signs, separation anxiety
  acting out, 47–48
  description of, 45–46
  eating, 46

in infants, 46
participation in classroom, 47
sleeping, 46–47
toileting, 47
Websites, 385
Week by Week systematic plan. *See also* Observation; Portfolio assessment; Portfolios
  and aggression, 148
  and ancedotal recording, 58
  described, 13
  and digital recording, 299
  ethics of, 23
  example of, 20–22
  information for using, 19–23, 25
  and NAEYC, 218
  and NAEYC guidelines, 401–402
  and Professional Preparation Standards, 18
  and program assessment, 351
  and progress reports, 20–21
  and TRACE, 217
  and work samples, 269
Weight, 96. *See also* Obesity, childhood
Welcoming Environment, 362
We're Born to Learn, 190
Whole group times, 371
Whole/part terminology, 224
Wh-questions, 160
Why Gender Matters (Sax, 2005), 145–146, 340
"Women's Work", 74
Word association, 194, 201
Work Samples
  advantages of, 271
  checklist for, 272–273
  and child abuse, 345
  and child interacting with adults, 403
  and child-adult interactions, 398–399
  child's satisfaction in, 11
  and cognitive development, 206, 237
  and collaborating with colleagues, 271
  definition of, 269
  disadvantages of, 271
  and dramatic play, 318
  and family communication, 403
  and literacy, 267
  media, 237

and observing child, 8
pitfalls to avoid, 271
and the portfolio, 9, 20–21, 22, 269–270, 274
review of, 406
and self-care skills, 76
and self-esteem, 345
and separation anxiety, 51
sharing work with families, 270–271
and social development, 129
and time management for, 271
uses for, 271–274
using technology, 271
Working Portfolios, 9, 10, 25, 188
The Work Sampling System 4th Ed. (Meisels et al., 2003), 88
The Work Sampling System (Meisels, Dichtelmiller, Jablon (et al., 2001), 239
Writing
  and literacy, 245
  reading and writing development, 250
  and young children, 253–256
Writing, stages of
  backward letters, 258
  dictation, 258
  drawing, 256–257
  incorporate writing into play, 259
  journal writing, 259
  making letters, 257
  organizing print, 257–258
  scribbling, 256
  writing to read, 258–259
Writing and memory, 201
Writing in Preschool: Learning to Orchestrate Meaning and Marks, 253–255
Written communication, 381

Y

Young Children's Science Curriculum, 229

Z

Zone proximal development, 100–101, 118, 218